Beiträge zum
ausländischen öffentlichen Recht und Völkerrecht

Edited by

the Max Planck Society
for the Advancement of Science
represented by Prof. Dr. Armin von Bogdandy
and Prof. Dr. Anne Peters

Volume 346

Michael Rodi | Johannes Saurer [Eds.]

Comparative Perspectives on the Law of Energy Transition in Europe

Nomos

The Deutsche Nationalbibliothek lists this publication in the Deutsche Nationalbibliografie; detailed bibliographic data are available on the Internet at http://dnb.d-nb.de

1st Edition 2025

Published by
Nomos Verlagsgesellschaft mbH & Co. KG
Waldseestraße 3–5 | 76530 Baden-Baden
www.nomos.de

Production of the printed version:
Nomos Verlagsgesellschaft mbH & Co. KG

Waldseestraße 3–5 | 76530 Baden-Baden

ISBN (Print): 978-3-7560-3326-3
ISBN (ePDF): 978-3-7489-6260-1

DOI: https://doi.org/10.5771/9783748962601

Online Version
Nomos eLibrary

Table of Contents

Contributors

Anker, Helle Tegner: Professor of Law at the University of Copenhagen. *Contact: hta@ifro.ku.dk*

Ason, Agnieszka: Senior Visiting Research Fellow, Oxford Institute for Energy Studies; Expert and Strategic Advisor, Ason Energy. *Contact: a.ason@asonenergy.com*

De Fontenelle, Louis: Associate Professor in Public Law, TREE, CNRS, Université de Pau et des Pays de l'Adour and Director of the European Research Platform for Energy and Climate Law. *Contact: louis.defontenelle@univ-pau.fr*

Fehling, Michael: Professor of Public and Comparative Law and Academic Director of the Center for Interdisciplinary Research on Energy, Climate and Sustainability at the Bucerius Law School, Hamburg. *Contact: michael.fehling@law-school.de*

Fracchia, Fabrizio: Full Professor in Administrative Law at the Bocconi University and Director of Observatory on Public Procurement and Sustainability-Green-Bocconi University. *Contact: fabrizio.fracchia@unibocconi.it*

Gram Mortensen, Bent Ole: Professor in Public Law including Environmental and Energy Law at the University of Southern Denmark, Odense. *Contact: bom@sam.sdu.dk*

Knap, Aleksandra: Lecturer at the Department of Civil Law and Junior Specialist for sustainability cooperation at the Kozminski University. *Contact: aknap@kozminski.edu.pl*

Lamoureux, Marie: Professor at the Faculty of Law and Political Sciences of Université d'Aix-Marseille. *Contact: marie.lamoureux@univ-amu.fr*

Malafry, Melina: Associate Professor and Senior lecturer in Environmental Law at the Uppsala University. *Contact: melina.malafry@jur.uu.se*

Mari, Chiara: Assistant Professor in Administrative Law at the Sapienza University of Rome, Department of Political Science. *Contact: chiara.mari@uniroma1.it*

Markus, Till: Deputy Head of the Department of Environmental and Planning Law at the Helmholtz-Centre for Environmental Research, Leipzig, and Senior Lecturer at the University of Bremen. *Contact: till.markus@ufz.de*

McKenzie, Kate: Director and Chief Executive Officer of the Climate Change Legal Initiative (C2LI) and Managing Editor of the Carbon & Climate Law Review (CCLR). *Contact: kate.mckenzie@c2li.org*

Mehling, Michael: Deputy Director of the Center for Energy and Environmental Policy Research, Massachusetts Institute of Technology, Cambridge; Professor at the University of Strathclyde School of Law, Glasgow. *Contact: mmehling@mit.edu*

Nowak, Bartłomiej: Vice-Rector for Cooperation with the Environment, Kozminski University Dean, Law Department, Kozminski University. *Contact: bnowak@kozminski.edu.pl*

Ogbumgbada, Chitzi: Lecturer in Law at the University of Exeter and Member of the Exeter Centre for Environmental Law. *Contact: c.ogbumgbada@exeter.ac.uk*

Penttinen, Sirja-Leena: Associate Professor in Law and Sustainability Transitions, University of Lapland. *Contact: sirja-leena.penttinen@ulapland.fi*

Pielow, Johann-Christian: Professor of Public and Comparative Economic Law and Managing Director of the Institute for Mining and Energy Law at the Ruhr-University Bochum. *Contact: christian.pielow@ruhr-uni-bochum.de*

Rodi, Michael: Director of the Institute for Climate Protection, Energy, and Mobility (IKEM) in Berlin and Brussels, Professor emeritus at the University of Greifswald. *Contact: michael.rodi@ikem.de*

Saurer, Johannes: Professor of Public Law, Environmental Law, Law of Infrastructure and Comparative Law at the University of Tuebingen. *Contact: johannes.saurer@uni-tuebingen.de*

Talus, Kim: Professor of European Economic and Energy Law at the University of Eastern Finland Law School and the Director of the Center for Climate Change, Energy and Environmental Law. *Contact: ktalus@uef.fi*

Introduction

Johannes Saurer and Michael Rodi

The transition of fossil fuel-bound systems of energy generation and supply towards carbon neutrality is a common task of legal orders across Europe. All European Countries and the European Union are members of the Paris Agreement that aims to limit global warming to 2 degree better 1,5 degree Celsius.[1] As parties of the Paris Agreement they have committed to the goal of global carbon neutrality in the second half of the 20th century which requires – inter alia – the world wide decarbonization of energy systems to meet the obligations under international climate change law. The EU has launched a series of ambitious policy proposals including "Clean energy for all Europeans",[2] the European Green Deal[3] and Fit for 55.[4] The European Green Deal established the goal of Europe as the "first climate neutral continent" by 2050.[5] The European Climate Law of 2021 sets legally binding climate targets of greenhouse gas emission reduction in the EU of 55 % compared to 1990 by 2030 and to net zero by 2050.[6] Greenhouse gas emissions in the EU energy sector have already decreased

1 Paris (France), 12 Dec. 2015, in force 4 November 2016, available at: UNFCCC, 'The Paris Agreement' <http://unfccc.int/paris_agreement/items/ 9485.php> accessed 11 September 2024.

2 European Commission, Communication, 'Clean Energy For All Europeans' (2016) COM 860 final.

3 European Commission, Communication 'The European Green Deal' (2019) COM 640 final.

4 European Commission, Communication '"Fit for 55": delivering the EU's 2030 Climate Target on the way to climate neutrality' (2021) COM 550 final.

5 See Edoardo Chiti, 'Managing the ecological transition of the EU: The European Green Deal as a regulatory process' (2022) 59 Common Market Law Review 19 (25 ff.); Josephine van Zeben, 'The European Green Deal: The future of a polycentric Europe?' (2020) 26 European Law Journal 300 (300 ff.).

6 Regulation (EU) 2021/1119 of the European Parliament and of the Council of 30 June 2021 establishing the framework for achieving climate neutrality and amending Regulations (EC) No 401/2009 and (EU) 2018/1999 [2021] OJ L 243/1 (EU Climate Law), Art. 4 Sec. 1, Art. 2 sec 1.

significantly.[7] However, the production and use of energy is still responsible for more than 75 % of the EU's greenhouse gas emissions.[8] Thus, significant additional decarbonization efforts are necessary in the EU energy sector to reach climate neutrality in 2050.

The climate-based rationale for energy transition is complemented by rationales of energy autonomy and energy security.[9] The autonomy and security dimension of energy transition was reenforced in the RePower EU Plan of 2022[10] that reacted to the Russian invasion in Ukraine in 2022 and the interrelated natural gas-supply crisis.[11] The reduction of fossil fuel imports and the expansion of carbon-neutral energy in Europe are intertwined key elements of EU strategies for autonomy and security in energy supply.[12] A further goal is a fair and just energy transition[13] that is committed to procedural justice,[14] aims for equitable distribution of both benefits

---

7 According to the State of the Energy Union Report 2024, greenhouse gas emissions that are covered by the EU Emissions Trading System (EU ETS) have decreased by 47 % compared to 2005 levels, see European Commission, Communication 'State of the Energy Union Report 2024' (2024) COM 404 final 2.

8 European Parliament, 'Renewable Energy' (March 2024) <https://www.europarl.europa.eu/factsheets/en/sheet/70/renewable-energy> accessed 27 October 2024.

9 Severin Fischer, 'Global energy security and EU energy policy' in Rafael Leal-Arcas (ed), *EU Energy Law and Policy* (2nd ed. Edward Elgar 2024) 223 (232).

10 European Commission, Communication 'REPower EU Plan' COM (2022) 230 final.

11 See Ingmar von Homeyer/Sebastian Oberthür/Claire Dupont, 'Implementing the European Green Deal during the Evolving Energy Crisis' (2022) 60 Journal of Common Market Studies 125 (125 ff.); Penelope Crossley, 'From the climate change to war: the evolving role of renewable energy law and policy in meeting the EU's energy security challenges' in Rafael Leal-Arcas (ed), *EU Energy Law and Policy* (2nd ed. Edward Elgar 2024) 617 (619 ff.); see also International Energy Agency, 'World Energy Outlook 2024' (2024) 15, 257 f.

12 European Parliament, 'Four challenges of the energy crisis for the EU's strategic autonomy' (*European Parliament*, 2023) <https://www.europarl.europa.eu/RegData/etudes/BRIE/2023/747099/EPRS_BRI(2023)747099_EN.pdf> accessed 11 September 2024.

13 Raphael J. Heffron/Darren McCauley, 'The Concept of Energy Justice Across the Disciplines' (2017) 105 Energy Policy 658 (658 f.); Raphael J. Heffron/Louis de Fontenelle (eds), *The Power of Energy Justice & the Social Contract* (Palgrave Macmillan 2024); Kai Menzel/Jan Schmitz, 'Energy justice: microeconomics, political obstacles and remedies for a carbon neutral future', in Rafael Leal-Arcas (ed), *EU Energy Law and Policy* (2nd ed. Edward Elgar 2024) 402 (402 ff.).

14 Chiara Armeni, 'What justice? The scope for public participation in the European Union Just Transition' (2023) 60 Common Market Law Review 1027 (1038 ff.).

and burdens of energy services,[15] attenuates social and economic costs of energy transition in most affected regions[16] and assures the affordability of energy prices for consumer households and enterprises. Moreover, energy transition is linked to industrial policy goals. The EU aims to perpetuate and expand the role of European companies in world markets for energy transition technologies.[17]

Over the last decades, the most significant effect of energy transition in the European energy mix was the rise of renewable energies. The quantity of electricity generation from renewable sources increased tremendously with an ever growing share of "new" renewable energy technologies (wind, solar, biomass) compared to the "traditional" renewable energy technology hydropower. The rise of renewable energies was catalyzed by falling generation costs for renewable energies.[18] In recent years, EU-wide electricity production from renewable sources surpassed electricity production from fossil fuels.[19] In 2022 the EU produced 38,2 % of electricity from renewable energy sources, 20,1 % from gas fired plants and 15,9 % from coal fired power plants.[20] In the broader perspective of gross final energy consumption – that includes electricity, but also liquid fuels with particular importance for transport and heating – the share of renewable energies in the EU increased from under 10 % in the early 2000s to 23 % in 2022.[21] However, the significance of renewable energies in individual European countries

15 Marzena Czarnecka/Marcin Krazniewski, 'Solving Energy Justice in the European Union' in Raphael J. Heffron/Louis de Fontenelle (eds), *The Power of Energy Justice & the Social Contract* (Palgrave Macmillan 2024) 193 (194 f.).

16 Regulation 2021/1056/EU of the European Parliament and of the Council of 24 June 2021 establishing the Just Transition Fund [2021] OJ L 231/1.

17 European Commission, Communication 'A Green Deal Industrial Plan for the Net-Zero Age', COM (2023) 62.

18 See International Renewable Energy Agency, 'Renewable Power Generation Costs in 2023' (2024) 14 ff.

19 Eurostat, 'Electricity and Heat Statistics, Table 1: Gross electricity production by Fuel, EU, 2000–2022 (GWh)' (*European Commission*, August 2024) <https://ec.europa.eu/eurostat/statistics-explained/index.php?title=Electricity_and_heat_statistics> accessed 26 October 2024.

20 Eurostat, (*European Commission*, August 2024) 'Electricity and Heat Statistics' <https://ec.europa.eu/eurostat/statistics-explained/index.php?title=Electricity_and_heat_statistics> accessed 26 October 2024.

21 Eurostat, 'Electricity and Heat Statistics, Table 1: Gross electricity production by Fuel, EU, 2000–2022 (GWh)' (*European Commission*, August 2024) <https://ec.europa.eu/eurostat/statistics-explained/index.php?title=Electricity_and_heat_statistics> accessed 26 October 2024.

is very different. While Sweden (66,0 %) and Denmark (41,6 %) are far above the EU average in the share of renewables in energy consumption, Germany (20,8 %), France (20,3 %), Italy (19,0 %) and Poland (16,9 %) are close to average or below.[22] Recent statistics for the former EU member state United Kingdom report a share of 42 % for renewable energies in electricity production (in 2022) and a share of 14 % for renewable energies in total energy supply (in 2021).[23]

Moreover, renewable energies became an increasingly relevant geographical factor. In many European regions renewable energy installations developed into integral elements of the landscape, of coastlines and of building infrastructure, e.g., onshore and offshore wind energy sites, photovoltaic sites, biomass facilities and roof top solar panels. However, the growing spatial significance of renewable energy installations also led to an increase of land-use conflicts including conflicts with agriculture, nature conservation and habitat protection policies. Accordingly, renewable energy expansion has become a focal point of public deliberation on energy transition concepts and strategies.[24]

Against this backdrop, this volume explores the legal framework for energy transition at the European level and legal dimensions of energy transition experiences at the national level. The chapters assess convergences between national transition processes, particularly the integration into international and supranational climate and energy policies with harmonizing effects for national goals and instruments of energy transition. The authors analyze streamlining effects resulting from obligations of the EU and individual countries under the Paris Agreement and its characteristic bottom-up-approach that requires them to report specific decarbonization goals and implementation measures including in the energy sector.[25] However, the chapters also explore divergences resulting from specific national

22 Eurostat, 'Electricity and Heat Statistics, Table 1: Gross electricity production by Fuel, EU, 2000–2022 (GWh)' (*European Commission*, August 2024) <https://ec.europa.eu/eurostat/statistics-explained/index.php?title=Electricity_and_heat_statistics> accessed 26 October 2024.

23 International Renewable Energy Agency (IRENA), 'Energy Profile United Kingdom' (*IRENA*, 31 July 2024) <https://www.irena.org/-/media/Files/IRENA/Agency/Statistics/Statistical_Profiles/Europe/United-Kingdom_Europe_RE_SP.pdf> accessed 26 October 2024.

24 See Jerzy Jendrośka/Alina Anapyanova, 'Towards a Green Energy Transition: REPowerEU Directive vs Environmental Acquis?' (2023) 23 elni Review 1 (1 ff.).

25 See Sabine Schlacke/Helen Wentzien/Eva-Maria Thierjung/Miriam Köster, 'Implementing the EU Climate Law via the 'Fit for 55' package' (2022) 1, oiab002, Oxford

choices between energy sources, e.g., concerning the role of coal, natural gas or nuclear power[26] in electricity generation, traditional structures of national economies and specific technological or resource-bound path dependencies.[27]

The book contributes to a growing body of literature on comparative aspects of the law of energy transition. Comparative research on transitory dimensions of energy law can build upon a range of scholarly works on comparative energy law in general perspective, in a regional perspective[28] or comparing national legal orders.[29] Recent focal points of the comparative discourse concerned energy transition as a dimension of comparative cli-

Open Energy 2 ff. <https://doi.org/10.1093/ooenergy/oiab002> accessed 10 November 2024.

26 In March 2024, the DG Energy of the European Commission reported that 12 EU countries include nuclear energy in their energy mix, see Directorate-General for Energy of the EC, 'In Focus: EU nuclear energy policy – why it matters to us all' (*European Commission*, 13 March 2024) <https://energy.ec.europa.eu/news/focus-eu-nuclear-energy-policy-why-it-matters-us-all-2024-03-13_en?pk_campaign=ENER%20Newsletter%20March%202024> accessed 26 October 2024.

27 Johannes Saurer/Jonas Monast, 'Renewable Energy Federalism in Germany and the United States' (2021) 10 Transnational Environmental Law 293 (316 f.)

28 Kim Talus, 'Energy Law' in: Jan M. Smits/Jaakko Husa/Catherine Valcke/Madalena Narciso (eds), *Elgar Encyclopedia of Comparative Law*, Vol. 2 (Edward Elgar 2023) 10 (10 ff.); the contributions in Adrian J. Bradbrook/Rosemary Lyster/Richard L. Ottinger/Wang Xi (eds), *The Law of Energy for Sustainable Development* (Cambridge University Press 2005) 291–404; for a comparison of energy law of regional organization see Jorge E. Viñuales, *The International Law of Energy* (Cambridge University Press 2022) 375 ff.

29 See, e.g., Helle Tegner Anker/Brigitte Egelund Olsen/Anita Rønne, 'Wind energy and the law: a comparative analysis (2009) 27 Journal of Energy & Natural Resources Law 145 (145 ff.); the contributions in Michèle Knodt/Jörg Kemmerzell (eds), *Handbook of Energy Governance in Europe* (Springer International Publishing 2022) Vol. 2.

mate change law,[30] the law of energy transition in federal systems,[31] energy transition in the Baltic Sea area[32] and comparative issues of energy justice.[33]

This volume adds to the comparative discourse a legal comparison of general perspectives on energy transition experiences in a plurality of European jurisdictions and specific aspects of renewable energy expansion. The research focus on renewable energies acknowledges the rise of renewable energies as the most significant effect of energy transition in the European energy mix over the last decades (see above), but that massive further expansion is necessary to reach climate neutrality until 2050. The comparative perspective is particularly helpful to put into contrast the different national renewable energy expansion pathways that led to significantly different results in the current national shares of renewables in energy consumption in individual European states (see above).

The volume assembles contributions on legal orders across Europe. The individual chapters focus on the supranational legal order of the European Union and a plurality of national jurisdictions including France, United Kingdom, Germany, Poland, Sweden, Denmark and Italy. The choice of legal orders represents energy transition experiences in a broad geographic spectrum including Western Europe, Mid-Europe and Eastern European, Northern Europe and Southern Europe. It enables the analysis of the significance of different geographic conditions for aspects of energy generation and supply. Moreover, the choice of legal orders enables the analysis of similarities and differences in terms of size of population and economic structures. The book analyzes France, United Kingdom, Germany, Poland and Italy as industrial states with comparable size of population. It assesses Denmark and Sweden are frontrunners in the share of energy of renewable energies in energy consumption (see above).

---

30 Michael Mehling, 'The Comparative Law of Climate Change: A research agenda' (2015) 24 RECIEL 341, 344 ff.; Jacqueline Peel/Hari M. Osofsky, *Climate Change Litigation* (Cambridge University Press 2015) 54 ff., 108 ff., 221 ff.; Daniel Farber, 'Climate Change Law', in: Jan M. Smits/Jaakko Husa/Catherine Valcke/Madalena Narciso (eds), *Elgar Encyclopedia of Comparative Law* (Vol. 1 (Edward Elgar 2023) 262 (262 ff.).

31 See the contributions in (2021) 10 Transnational Environmental Law 211–263 and Johannes Saurer/Jonas Monast, 'Symposium Foreword: The Law of Energy Transition in Federal Systems' (2021) 10 Transnational Environmental Law 205 (205 ff.).

32 Farid Karimi/Michael Rodi (eds), *Energy Transition in the Baltic Sea Area. Understanding Stakeholder Engagement and Community Acceptance* (Routledge 2022).

33 Raphael J. Heffron/Louis de Fontenelle (eds), *The Power of Energy Justice & the Social Contract* (Palgrave Macmillan 2024).

The coverage of jurisdictions extends beyond the spectrum of EU Member States to the United Kingdom as a former EU Member State that has pursued ambitious climate and energy transition policies over several decades and is still very much influenced by the European Union legal framework.[34]

Section A: EU Law Framework for Energy Transition

Section A addresses the legal framework for energy transition in EU law. The EU is an original party of the Paris Agreement and committed to reach climate neutrality in 2050 (see above). In the EU strategy towards climate neutrality the energy sector plays a central role (see above). As a supranational compound of nation states the EU relies on the member states to fulfil its decarbonization commitments. The core legal qualities of primacy and direct effect of EU law[35] and a broad spectrum of supranational implementation mechanisms[36] give significant legal power to EU legal acts addressed at the EU Member States. Thus, the EU's goals and instruments on energy transition are highly influential upon energy policies and legal concepts in the EU Member States.

In his contribution "European Climate and Energy Transformation Law", Michael Rodi presents international energy and climate law, the legislative competences of the Union, and EU climate and energy transition policies. Against the backdrop of increasingly ambitious climate targets, Rodi examines the system of energy and climate governance, with a particular focus on Regulation 2018/1999/EU on the Governance of the Energy Union and Climate Action. He further analyzes regulations in the areas of GHG emission mitigation, renewable energy law, energy efficiency law, and recent

34 See the analysis of Ana Stanič/Julian Bowden, 'Brexit and UK´s Renewable Energy and Climate Change Policies. Implications and Opportunities' in Ana Stanič/Silke Goldberg (eds), *Brexit and Energy Law: Implications and Opportunities* (Routledge 2023) 92 ff.

35 See Bruno de Witte, 'Direct Effect, Primacy, and the Nature of the Legal Order' in Paul Craig/Gráinne De Búrca (eds), *The Evolution of EU Law* (3rd ed. Oxford University Press 2021) 187 (187 ff.) Martin Hedemann-Robinson, *Enforcement of European Union Environmental Law* (3rd ed. Routledge 2015) 30 ff.

36 Miroslava Scholten, 'Mind the trend! Enforcement of EU law has been moving to 'Brussels´', Journal of European Public Policy 24 (2017), 1348 (1350 ff.); the contributions in András Jakab/Dimitry Kochenov (eds), *The Enforcement of EU Law and Values* (Oxford University Press 2017).

legislation promoting net-zero technologies. Within the regulatory framework outlined by Rodi, national energy transition law is closely intertwined with EU law.

Johannes Saurer analyzes the "EU Law Framework for Expansion of Renewable Energies". He discusses the relevant competence norms for environment and energy (esp. Art. 191, 192 and 194 TFEU) and shows the most recent increase in EU goals on renewable energy expansion that came along with the amendment of the EU's Renewable Energy Directive 2018/2001/EU by Directive (EU) 2023/2413 of the European Parliament and of the Council of 18 October 2023 (RED III) and the significance of Regulation 2018/1999/EU on the Governance of the Energy Union and Climate Action for renewable energy expansion in the Member States. Moreover, Saurer illustrates that EU renewable energy law increasingly addresses national planning and permit granting procedures for renewable installations.

The contribution "Tomorrow's EU Framework for Sustainable Fuels: The emerging regulatory framework for hydrogen and related fuels" by Kim Talus and Sirja-Leena Penttinen explores the law of renewable fuels as a dimension of the European energy transition. The authors observe a "hydrogen boom" in the EU. They examine the relevant strategies of the EU (e.g., the Hydrogen Strategy of 2020) and objectives established in the Renewable Energy Directive for the deployment of renewable fuels. Talus and Penttinen distinguish different types of renewable fuels and the respective legal regime. The chapter places particular emphasis on the regulatory framework for hydrogen including the classification of "green hydrogen" under EU law.

Michael Mehling takes a transatlantic perspective on the energy transition law in Europe. In his contribution "Advancing the Energy Transition through Industrial Policy: Lessons from a Transatlantic Comparison" he analyzes the efforts of the U.S. and the EU to harness green industrial policies as a means of reaching climate targets alongside further social and economic objectives. According to Mehling, the U.S. relies on extensive fiscal incentives, centered around the Inflation Reduction Act, while the EU has established a detailed regulatory framework building up on the European Green Deal, including the Carbon Border Adjustment Mechanism, and the Critical Raw Materials Act. Mehling explores the merits and possible risks of the distinct approaches, providing guidance for other jurisdictions seeking to transform their industries.

Section B: General Perspectives on the Law of Energy Transition

Section B covers national approaches to energy transition in a general perspective. Countries analyzed are France, United Kingdom, Germany, Poland, Sweden, Denmark and Italy. Section B gives room to address national paradigms of energy transitions, choices on energy sources including on nuclear energy, phase-out concepts for coal and gas, frameworks for carbon capture storage and/or use (CCS/CCU) and green hydrogen, consequences of energy transition for infrastructure, e.g., grid line expansion, questions of energy storage facilities, issues of sector coupling concerning, e.g., mobility sector and heating sector and potential trade-offs between phase-out of fossil fuels, security of energy supply and affordability of energy prices.

Till Markus analyzes the distinctive features of the German energy transition. He gives an account of relevant provisions of the German federal constitution, e.g., on federal competence allocation in the energy sector and on ecological obligations of the state. Markus emphasizes that the trajectory the German energy transition encompasses phase-outs of nuclear and coal power. He highlights the significance of sector coupling for the decarbonization of the mobility and the heating sector and and describes hydrogen as an emerging element of energy transition.

Marie Lamoureux examines the development of France's legislation on energy transition, beginning with the "Energy Transition for Green Growth Act" of 2015 and the codification of the main objectives of energy transition in Article L. 100–4 of the French Energy Code. According to Lamoureux, the French energy transition is substantially based on a compromise between the use of nuclear energy and the promotion of renewable energy. She discusses the Nuclear Acceleration Act, adopted in June 2023, and the Renewable Energy Acceleration Act, adopted in March 2023, as measures aimed at facilitating energy transition in France.

Fabrizio Fracchia provides an overview of Italy's energy transition, outlining the key elements of Italian energy policy and its transition objectives. Fracchia identifies the National Recovery and Resilience Plan (NRRP) as central legislative framework for the Italian energy transition. Through the NRRP, Italy provides funding for energy transition projects, such as expanding electric recharging infrastructure and developing a hydrogen supply chain. He describes a multifaceted set of legal measures intended to support Italy's energy transition. Fracchia outlines the energy transition as a theoretical concept aimed at fulfilling intergenerational responsibilities.

Kate McKenzie and Chitzi Ogbumgbada provide an overview of the United Kingdom's energy transition law. They emphasize the country's distinctive legacy in establishing zero-emission strategies and codifying them into binding legislation. Their contribution underscores the significance of the Energy Act 2023, a legislative framework that builds upon various policies, including the Net Zero Strategy, the Hydrogen Strategy, and the Heat and Buildings Strategy. Key provisions of the Energy Act 2023 are highlighted, including energy security, the advancement of emerging technologies, carbon capture and storage, and the development of interconnectors. Additionally, McKenzie and Ogbumgbada address the problem of trade-offs in the process of energy transition.

Bent Ole Gram Mortensen examines the overarching aspects of energy transition law in Denmark, grounding his analysis in historical patterns of Denmark's energy production and consumption. Mortensen outlines the current legal framework for energy generation and supply in Denmark and provides a sector-by-sector analysis that highlights special features such as the high distribution of district heating (combined with an early and strict ban of other technologies), of biomass (with a high share of imports) and of offshore wind energy. He also addresses conflicts between the expansion of renewable energies and competing ecological goals such as nature conservation. Moreover, Mortensen explores options to enhance public acceptance of energy transition infrastructure.

Melina Malafry presents an overview on the law of energy transition in Sweden in general and the law of renewable energies in particular. She shows the country as a pioneer in decarbonization combining nuclear and renewable sources (with a strong contribution of hydropower and biomass). Malafry emphasizes contextual factors that have shaped Swedish energy transition including geography, natural resources and population density. In contrast to the comparatively high overall share of renewable energies, she notes the continued dominance on fossil fuels in sectors like transportation and specific industries including steel production. Malafry emphasizes the municipal planning monopoly and the Swedish Environmental Code as decisive factors in the realization of renewable energy projects.

Bartłomiej Nowak and Aleksandra Knap provide an analysis of Poland's energy law. They highlight the current predominance of fossil fuels, especially coal, in the national energy mix, while also discussing the transformative goals of Polish politics and legislation. Nowak and Knap describe the influence of obligations under EU law on the Polish energy transition with the National Energy and Climate Plan (NECP) in the center. They emphasize the expansion of renewable energies, the plans to include nuclear power in the future national energy mix, the importance of hydrogen, the decarbonization efforts made in the mobility and heating sectors and the relevance of energy security concerns.

Section C: Special Focus: Law of renewable energy expansion in comparative perspective

Section C addresses legal dimensions of renewable energy expansion which is a common goal of energy policies of all countries analyzed in the book. The specific focus of section C. on the law of renewable energy expansion enables a particularly detailed analysis of goals, instruments and challenges in this dimension of energy transition. Section C. analyzes and discusses national commonalities and differences in the share of specific renewable energy technologies (esp. onshore and offshore wind energy; solar energy), land-use allocation for installations, conflicts with biodiversity protection and mechanisms to enhance participation and social acceptance. Moreover, section C. identifies legal techniques intended to accelerate the expansion of renewable energy on the national scale. Countries covered are Germany, France, Italy, the United Kingdom and Denmark. The law of renewable energy expansion in Sweden and Poland is covered as part of the chapters on these countries in Section B in general perspective.

Michael Fehling analyzes the development of Germany's regulatory framework for the promotion of renewable energy expansion and situates it in the country's multi-level governance structure. He emphasizes recent changes in promotion schemes and refinancing mechanisms for renewable energy expansion. Fehling describes and discusses the continuing efforts of the federal legislature in Germany to provide for additional land for renewable energy installations (e.g. Wind Areas Requirements Act), to accelerate permit procedures and to prioritize renewable energies over specific competing interests.

Louis de Fontenelle analyzes the renewable energy law in France on the background of a strong nuclear energy tradition. He gives an account on legal developments since 2005 and puts specific emphasis on the most recent legislation designed to accelerate renewable energy deployment. De Fontenelle highlights legal mechanisms of funding and planning for renewable energies including the designation of renewable energy acceleration zones. He explores a range of measures intended to boost public acceptance of renewable energies such as landscape integration and financial participation for local municipalities.

Chiara Mari analyzes Italy's legal framework for renewable energy expansion. She explains that Italy's goals are primarily set out in the National Recovery and Resilience Plan (NRRP) and the Plan for the Ecological Transition (PET). Mari highlights recent procedural reforms aimed at accelerating renewable deployment, such as simplifying procedures (e.g., with single authorization and unified permits). She explores public-private cooperations as an essential strategy for encouraging private investment in renewable projects. Mari argues that reducing informational asymmetries between government bodies and private entities is key to fostering mutual understanding and speeding up the expansion of renewable energy projects.

Agnieszka Ason addresses the expansion of renewable energies in the United Kingdom, emphasizing the crucial role of contracts for difference (CfD). Ason explains that during the past decade CfD have become the main instrument in supporting renewable energy generation. The CfD-system guarantees operators a "strike price" per unit of renewable energy that is determined in auctions. The government-owned Low carbon Contracts Company (LCCC) compensates the operator for the difference to market price. Ason highlights the UK's plans to extend the CfD-system to other clean energy projects, such as low-caron hydrogen.

Helle Tegner Anker and Bent Ole Gram Mortensen examine Denmark's legal framework for renewable energy expansion, emphasizing its primary focus on wind power onshore and offshore. In addition, the authors describe a growing importance of energy generated from solar and biomass. They analyze the influence of EU law and of national policy initiatives on Denmark's laws that support renewable energies in national electricity production including rules on funding, planning and permission procedures. Moreover, Anker and Gram Mortensen address issues of social acceptance of renewable energy installations including Denmark's local compensation schemes that were explicitly designed to with the purpose to boost public acceptance of wind energy.

The concluding essay "Comparing the Law of Energy Transition in Europe" by Christian Pielow and Kate McKenzie delivers a synthesis of key issues of the book and draws comparative conclusions.

Bibliography

Anker H T/ Olsen B E/ Rønne A, 'Wind energy and the law: a comparative analysis' (2009) 27 Journal of Energy & Natural Resources Law 145–178.

Armeni C, 'What justice? The scope for public participation in the European Union Just Transition' (2023) 60 Common Market Law Review 1027–1054

Bradbrook A J/Lyster R/Ottinger R L/Xi W (eds), *The Law of Energy for Sustainable Development* (Cambridge University Press 2005)

Crossley P, From the climate change to war: the evolving role of renewable energy law and policy in meeting the EU's energy security challenges, in: **Leal-Arcas R** (ed), *EU Energy Law and Policy* (2nd ed. Edward Elgar 2024) 617–641

Czarnecka M/Krazniewski M, 'Solving Energy Justice in the European Union' in **Heffron R J/de Fontenelle L** (eds), *The Power of Energy Justice & the Social Contract* (Palgrave Macmillan 2024) 193–197

de Witte B, 'Direct Effect, Primacy, and the Nature of the Legal Order' in **Craig P/De Búrca G** (eds), *The Evolution of EU Law* (3rd ed. Oxford University Press 2021) 187–227.

European Commission, Communication 'The European Green Deal' COM (2019) 640 final

European Commission, Communication 'REPower EU Plan' COM (2022) 230 final

European Commission, Communication 'A Green Deal Industrial Plan for the Net-Zero Age' COM (2023) 62

European Commission, Communication 'State of the Energy Union Report 2024' COM (2024) 404 final 2

European Commission, Communication 'Clean Energy For All Europeans' COM (2016) 860 final

European Commission, Communication 'Fit for 55': delivering the EU's 2030 Climate Target on the way to climate neutrality' COM (2021) 550 final

European Parliament, 'Four challenges of the energy crisis for the EU's strategic autonomy' <https://www.europarl.europa.eu/RegData/etudes/BRIE/2023/747099/EPRS_BRI(2023)747099_EN.pdf> accessed 11 September 2024

Farber D, 'Climate Change Law' in **Smits J M/Husa J/Valcke C/Narciso M** (eds), *Elgar Encyclopedia of Comparative Law* (Vol. 1 Edward Elgar 2023) 262–270

Fischer S, 'Global energy security and EU energy policy' in **Leal-Arcas R** (ed), *EU Energy Law and Policy* (2nd ed. Edward Elgar 2024) 223–236

Hedemann-Robinson M, *Enforcement of European Union Environmental Law* (3rd ed. Routledge 2015)

Heffron R J/de Fontenelle L (eds), *The Power of Energy Justice & the Social Contract* (Springer Nature 2024)

Heffron R J/McCauley D, '*The Concept of Energy Justice Across the Disciplines*' (2017) 105 Energy Policy 658–667.

Huhta K/Romppanen S, 'Comparing Legal Disciplines as an Approach to Understanding the Role of Law in Decarbonizing Societies' (2023) 12 Transnational Environmental Law 649–670

International Energy Agency, 'World Energy Outlook 2024' (2024) <https://www.iea.org/reports/world-energy-outlook-2024> accessed 10 November 2024

International Renewable Energy Agency, 'Renewable Power Generation Costs in 2023' (2024) <https://www.irena.org/-/media/Files/IRENA/Agency/Publication/2024/Sep/IRENA_Renewable_power_generation_costs_in_2023.pdf> accessed 10 November 2024

Jendrośka J/Anapyanova A, 'Towards a Green Energy Transition: REPowerEU Directive vs Environmental Acquis?' (2023) elni Review 1–5

Karimi F/Rodi M (eds), *Energy Transition in the Baltic Sea Area. Understanding Stakeholder Engagement and Community Acceptance* (Routledge 2022)

Knodt M/Kemmerzell J (eds), *Handbook of Energy Governance in Europe* (Vol. 2 Springer International Publishing 2022)

Mehling M, 'The Comparative Law of Climate Change: A research agenda' (2015) 24 RECIEL 341–352

Peel J/Osofsky H M, 'Climate Change Litigation' (Cambridge University Press 2015)

Romppanen S/Huhta K, 'The Interface between EU Climate and Energy Law' (2023) 30 Maastricht Journal of European and Comparative Law 45–62

Saurer J/Monast J, 'Renewable Energy Federalism in Germany and the United States' (2021) 10 Transnational Environmental Law 293–320

Saurer J/Monast J, 'Symposium Foreword: The Law of Energy Transition in Federal Systems' (2021) 10 Transnational Environmental Law 205–210

Schlacke, S/ Wentzien H/ Thierjung E/ Köster M, 'Implementing the EU Climate Law via the 'Fit for 55' package' Oxford Open Energy (Vol. 1 2022), oiab002, https://doi.org/10.1093/ooenergy/oiab002 accessed 10 November 2024

Scholten, M 'Mind the trend! Enforcement of EU law has been moving to 'Brussels′′ (2017) 24 Journal of European Public Policy 1348 ff.

Stanič A/Bowden J, 'Brexit and UK′s Renewable Energy and Climate Change Policies. Implications and Opportunities' in **Stanič A/Goldberg S** (eds), *Brexit and Energy Law: Implications and Opportunities* (Routledge 2023) 92 ff.

Talus K, 'Energy Law' in **Smits J M/Husa J/Valcke C/Narciso M** (eds), *Elgar Encyclopedia of Comparative Law* (Vol. 2 Edward Elgar 2023) 10–16

UNFCCC, 'The Paris Agreement' <http://unfccc.int/paris_agreement/items/9485.php> accessed 11 September 2024

Van Zeben J, *'The European Green Deal: The future of a polycentric Europe?'* (2020) 26 European Law Journal 300–318

Viñuales J E, *The International Law of Energy* (Cambridge University Press 2022)

Von Homeyer I/Oberthür S/Dupont C, 'Implementing the European Green Deal during the Evolving Energy Crisis' (2022) 60 Journal of Common Market Studies 125–136–136

Part A –
EU Law Framework

European Climate and Energy Transformation Law

Michael Rodi

In this volume, the energy transition laws of selected EU Member States are analyzed in a comparative approach. It also covers the United Kingdom, which has been part of the European Union until recently, so its legislation is still influenced by it to a huge degree. Legal comparison within the European Union is special, as it happens within one legal sphere[1] or one common legal system.[2] European Union law and the laws of its Member States are closely intertwined, and in this context legal comparison is more useful and necessary (to better understand national laws as well as European Union law) than usual.[3] Due to the interconnections, comparison in this area is only possible if European Union law is taken into consideration, as Member States can only legislate within the leeway framed by it.

This contribution deals with those features of European energy transformation law that seem to be especially relevant to the comparison of national energy transformation laws addressing the following aspects: The object of the comparison, climate and energy transformation law, will be outlined in more detail (Chapter A). As the European Union itself is bound by international law, the respective international legal framework will be taken into account (Chapter B). The competences of the European Union in the field of climate policy and energy transformation (Chapter C) and the respective policies have to be addressed (Chapter D). Regarding European climate and energy transformation we will give an overview on the climate and energy transformation objectives (Chapter E), the overall climate and energy governance (Chapter F), and the European climate and energy transformation law *stricto sensu* (Chapter G).

1 Armin von Bogdandy, 'European Law Beyond "Ever Closer Union" Repositioning the Concept, its Thrust and the EJC's Comparative Methodology' (2016) 22 European Law Journal 519–538.

2 Allan Rosas, 'European Law and National Law: A common legal system?' in K. Karjalainen et al. (eds), *International Actors and the Formation of Laws* (Luxembourg 2022) 11–26, under chapter 4.

3 Sabrina Raggone, 'European Comparative Law: Reasons for "enhanced comparison" and the role of the CJZU' (2021) 112 Revista de Derecho Politico 297–325, under chapter 2.

A. Climate and Energy Transformation Law as Objects of Comparison within the European Union

The topic of this volume is comparative energy transition law. If this contribution refers to climate and energy transformation in relation to the European legal framework, this different terminology requires a brief explanation.

On the one hand, this concerns the concept of transformation. Climate protection policy essentially refers to complete decarbonization, which some countries are aiming for by the middle of the century (or even earlier, such as Germany with the date 2045). This implies a complete transformation of the energy system and consequently of society as such, as it is based on the energy system.[4] In sociology, social transformation refers to a "deep and lasting, non-linear systemic change"[5] in a society. The term "transition" is not the opposite of the term "transformation".[6] Rather, transition refers to the process of "passing through" and implies a movement from one state or condition to another.[7] In contrast, the term transformation describes changes that profoundly influence the characteristics of the "things being transformed".[8] It emphasizes more strongly the normative aspect, the dimension of challenge and the political task. Against this background, it becomes clear why it is better to speak of energy transformation and not just energy transition.

For the analysis of the respective laws (be it at the international, EU or national levels), it is important to consider that energy transformation law is an area of law at the intersection of climate law and traditional energy

4 See regarding transformative law Laura Mai, 'Navigating transformations: Climate change and the international law' Leiden Journal of International Law 2024.

5 Björn-Ola Linnér/Victoria Wibeck, 'Conceptualising variations in societal transformations towards sustainability' Environmental Science & Policy (2020), 106:222.

6 Katharina Hölscher/Julia M. Wittmayer/Derk Loorbach, Transition versus transformation: What`s the difference, Environmental Innovation and Societal Transitions 27 (2018), 1 – 3; James Patterson/Karsten Schulz/Joost Vervoort/Sandra van der Hel/ Oscar Widerberg/Carolina Adler/Margot Hurlbert/Karen Anderton/Mahendra Sethi/ Aliyu Barau, 'Exploring the governance and politics of transformations towards sustainability' Environmental Innovation and Societal Transitions 24 (2017) 1, 3: Laura Mai, 'Navigating transformations: Climate change and the international law' Leiden Journal of International Law 2024 4 f.

7 Laura Mai, 'Navigating transformations: Climate change and the international law' Leiden Journal of International Law 2024 4 f.

8 ibid, with reference to the Oxford Dictionary.

law.[9] On one side, energy law comprises all legal norms that regulate the extraction, production, transportation and use of energy products. It is governed by specific principles like energy security, energy justice, and national sovereignty regarding energy resources; sustainability and resilience are increasingly seen as independent energy law principles. Climate law, on the other side, consists of climate protection (mitigation) law and climate adaptation law (with climate finance law cross-cutting). It is climate protection law that overlaps with energy law: all legal norms that are directed to setting or implementing climate goals thus affect the mitigation of greenhouse gas emissions (GHG). Key principles like common but differentiated responsibility and the precautionary principle are vested in the international climate law framework (UNFCCC), indicating the close relationship to environmental law.

Considering different options to reach decarbonization clarifies the importance of energy transformation law: (1) reducing energy consumption (energy efficiency) or/and transforming a fossil-based energy system into a decarbonized one, by installing renewable energy (or other non-fossil sources like nuclear); (2) implementing carbon management (Carbon Capture and Storage (CCS) or Carbon Capture and Utilization (CCU)) and negative emission technologies (Direct Air Capture and Carbon Storage (DACCS), peatland restoration etc.); and (3) reducing GHG emissions by a change in transport or land use. Overall, the change in production and use of energy towards decarbonization in service of an energy transition forms the main pathway to decarbonization; the law regulating this, the energy transformationlaw, thus forms the main legal field regarding decarbonization.

At the heart of climate law is the goal of decarbonization, which serves as a central point of orientation for energy transformation law and policy. In turn, energy transformation law and policy are (an extremely important) part of climate (mitigation) policy. Alongside energy efficiency, decarbonization requires a shift towards carbon free energy sources or technologies to capture, store or use greenhouse gases produced by burning fossil fuels (other areas of climate protection policy comprise e.g. land use changes or a mobility transformation beyond avoiding fossil fuels).

9 For the relationship between these fields of law see Kaisa Huhta/Seita Romppanen, 'Comparing Legal Disciplines as an Approach to Understanding the Role of Law in Decarbonizing Societies' (2023) 12 Transnational Environmental Law 649–670; Seita Romppanen/Kaisa Huhta, 'The Interface between EU Climate and Energy Law' (2023) 30 Maastricht Journal of European and Comparative Law 45–62.

Thus, energy transformation and climate protection law are extremely intertwined, which becomes apparent for example, when analyzing the scope of competences which the EU treaties provide for the European legislator (see Chapter C).

B. European Climate and Energy Transformation Under the International Umbrella

Thus, as in European Union law and national law, two areas of international law are relevant: international energy law and international climate law.

1. International Energy Law

International energy law comprises all norms dealing with energy as a real phenomenon and important part of economies and societies. Energy can be seen as an object of law from three perspectives: as a resource (stocks like fossil fuels), as a product (like electricity) or as an activity (like production or trade)[10].[11] Energy law is not aligned with one overarching objective, but plays a role within manifold regulatory objectives (like energy security and sustainability) relevant to different legal areas like trade law, investment law or environmental law.[12]

Apparently, states are reluctant to give up sovereign rights regarding energy as a crucial national economic factor. Thus, a real international energy law with specific goals, principles and instruments never came into existence. Rather, states followed other (common) interests like liberalizing trade or securing energy supply, applying these to energy topics and in some cases concretizing them. The Energy Charter Treaty (ECT) of 1994 (in force since 1998), dealing mainly with specific trade and investment protection issues, is the most relevant example of this. Apparently, investment protection, with a historic focus on fossil fuels, appeared to be in conflict with necessary climate action. Reforms of the ECT could not really

10 See e.g. the "Energy Cycle" described in Article 19(3)(a) ECT.

11 Jorge E. Viñuales, *The International Law of Energy* (Cambridge University Press 2022) 14 ff., who sees "energy technologies" as a fourth important aspect (e.g. regarding the law of intellectual property rights).

12 Viñuales (n 11) 21 ff.

solve them[13], and thus the European Union – like other countries with committed climate policy – quit the treaty.[14]

Climate protection has appeared as an independent objective which is more and more relevant for regulating the objectives of energy policies, leading to an international law of energy transformation as a new area of law.[15]

2. International Climate Law

Accordingly, international energy transformation law as a shared legal area of (traditional) international energy law and (general) international climate law can also be analyzed from the climate policy perspective.

In 1992, international climate law gained a solid foundation with the United Nation Framework Convention on Climate Change (UNFCCC).[16] This established a general objective (Article 2) and guiding principles (like the principle of common but differentiated responsibilities); these were formulated quite abstractly and vaguely but had the potential to strive for concretization through subsequent treaties and protocols. As a "regional economic integration organization", the European Union is a member of the UNFCCC (Article 22 UNFCCC), the Kyoto Protocol[17] (Article 24 Kyoto Protocol), and the Paris Agreement[18] (Article 20 (1) 1). Thus, as Article 20 (2) 1 of the Paris Agreement expressly states, it is "bound by all the obligations under the Agreement".

The Paris Agreement drew the conclusion that the policy of binding top-down targets has failed. Instead, it set up a procedural governance mechanism with Nationally Determined Contributions (NDCs) as its central pillar. The EU started with the first NDC, with the objective, among

13 See e.g. Mattia Colli Vignarelli, 'Making the Energy Charter Treaty Climate-Friendly: An (Almost) Impossible Leap' (2022) European Yearbook of International Economic Law, 267–293.

14 Notification by the Council and the Commission of 28 June 2024 based on Council Decisions of 30 May 2024, entry into force on 28 June 2025. Please note that according to Article 47(3) of the ECT, all investments covered by the treaty at the time of the withdrawal takes effect will continue enjoying protection for 20 years from such date.

15 Viñuales (n 11) 395 ff.

16 Adopted 9 May 1992, entry into force on 21 March 1994, S. Treaty Doc No. 102–38, 1771 U.N.T.S. 107.

17 Adopted 11 December 1997, entry into force 16 February 2005, 2303 U.N.T.S. 162.

18 Adopted 12 December 2015, entry into force 4 November 2016, T.I.A.S. No. 16–1104.

others, of reducing greenhouse gas emissions by at least 40 % below 1990 levels by 2030.[19] On the 11 December 2020 the European Council endorsed a new and more ambitious EU climate target for 2030, applicable to the EU and its 27 Member States, of "a net domestic reduction of at least 55 % in greenhouse gas emissions by 2030 compared to 1990", and submitted it to the UNFCCC Secretariat as an updated and enhanced NDC on 18 December 2020. On 5 March 2021 the goal of greenhouse gas neutrality in 2050 was submitted, as had been decided by the European Council in December 2020. An updated NDC of the European Union and its Member States followed on 16 Oct. 2023.[20] Next to components of the Fit for 55 Package it included a more ambitious 55 % reduction target for 2030 (compared to 40 % before). In September 2025 a post-2030 NDC has been due presenting a 2040 target and outlining an emissions reduction plan up to 2035.

The EU has a long tradition of leading international climate policy by example. Against this background, the EU has always submitted its newest set of climate regulations to the UNFCCC as NDCs. As the focus of this chapter lies on the EU legal framework for national climate and energy transformation laws, it is important to consider the legal and political consequences of these NDCs (for the European Union, but also for the Member States). There are good reasons to qualify them as legally non-binding; in any case, they are non-enforceable.[21] But they clearly have political functions, like providing transparency and trust, or acting as a yardstick for assessing progress towards climate neutrality.[22] Especially for the EU, which still tries to provide an international example, they are, if not legally so, at least de facto binding. To a certain extent this can be seen as an internal measure against withdrawal: the EU is willing to provide strong NDCs to bind itself (present and future institutions) and Member States.

---

19 Estelle Brosset/Sandrine Maljean-Dubois, 'The Paris Agreement, EU Climate Law and the Energy Union' in Eliantonio/Peeters (eds), *Research Handbook on EU Environmental Law* (Edward Elgar 2020) for the history of EU international climate politics 412–427.

20 European Commission, 'Update of the NDC of the European Union and its Member States' <https://unfccc.int/sites/default/files/NDC/2023-10/ES-2023-10-17%20EU%20submission%20NDC%20update.pdf> accessed 20 August 2024.

21 For details see Sharaban Tahura Zaman, 'Exploring the Legal Nature of Nationally Determined Contributions (NDCs) under International Law' (2015) 26 Yearbook of International Environmental Law 98.

22 Maria Järnnäs, 'Governing through the Nationally Determined Contribution (NDC): Five functions to steer states' climate conduct' (2024) 33 Environmental Politics 530–551.

This international climate law framework obliges the European Union as well as its Member States. Comparative (climate and) energy transformation law will definitely have to take notice of it.

C. Competences of the European Union

As shown above, climate law and policy are closely intertwined with energy law and policy, as the transformation of the energy system is a vital part of it (renewables, energy efficiency etc.). Thus, this policy field centrally relies on two competences, which are shared ones according to Article 4 (2) lit. e (environment) and i (energy) TFEU: environment (Article 192 TFEU)[23] and energy (Article 194 TFEU). Beyond this *lex specialis*, general competences with relevance for energy policies remain applicable, especially the market harmonization competences (as the wording "without prejudice to the application of other provisions of the Treaties" in Article 194 TFEU makes clear; Article 192 (2) explicitly mentions Article 114 TFEU).[24] Some regulations, for example the RED III Directive, have been based on several competences.[25] As the EU doesn't have exclusive competences in these areas, the policies necessarily lead to a multi-level governance.[26]

Moreover, the EU legislator is restricted by significant unanimity requirements regarding environmental measures significantly affecting a Member State's choice between different energy sources and the general structure of its energy supply (Article 192 (2) lit. c TFEU). Correspondingly, without prejudice to this, energy measures shall not affect a Member State's right to determine the conditions for exploiting its energy resources, its choice between different energy sources and the general structure of its energy supply (Article 194 (2) TFEU). The fact that the EU has refrained from

23 It is not disputed that climate is part of environment in that sense.

24 See Saurer, in this volume, 51 (54) and Michael Fehling, 'Energy Transition in the European Union and its Member States: Interpreting Federal Competence Allocation in the Light of the Paris Agreement' (2021) 10 Transnational Environmental Law 339–363, for state aid control.

25 See Saurer, in this volume, 51 (55 f.)

26 See e.g. Michèle Knodt, 'Instruments and modes of governance in EU climate and energy policy: from energy union to the European Green Deal', in Knodt (ed), *Handbook on European Union Climate Change Policy and Politics* (2023) 202–215.

setting RES targets beyond 2030 for Member States could be seen in this light.[27]

D. EU Climate and Energy Transformation Policy

Climate and energy transformation policies began in the 1990s, the first decade of clear-cut policy measures in this regard.[28] At the international level, this has been triggered by the UNFCCC in 1992, a turning point in international climate policy. Since the insertion of the Environmental Chapter into the European Treaties in 1987, the European Union has had quite a strong legal base for climate competences; the Energy Chapter following in 1992 did not change this situation fundamentally.

But the 1990s saw limited progress, marked by the failed carbon/energy tax proposal of the Commission.[29] The 2000s (2nd decade) were marked by an expanding climate policy toolbox making the Emission Trading Scheme (ETS) a key policy measure. The first half of the 2010s (as 3rd decade) was a period of a slowed-down climate policy development. The second half showed new policy efforts, especially regarding target setting, with the European Green Deal (EGD) as a crowning highlight. Overall, in 2021 a 29 % reduction of GHG compared to 1990 levels has been reached (2023: 37 %[30]).[31]

Three decades of development in climate and energy transformation policy have led to several main patterns of climate governance:

- increasingly adequate decade-wise target setting;
- comprehensive policy packages that integrate more policy fields and multi-level governance;

---

27 See Saurer, in this volume, 51 (56 ff.).

28 For an empiric analysis of EU (and Member States) climate policies regarding policy density, sectoral coverage, and policy mix thickness see Margherita Bellanca, `What, how and where: an assessment of multi-level European climate mitigation policies´, npj climate action 3 (2024) 119 <https://doi.org/10.1038/s441168-024-00200-7> accessed 18 July 2025.

29 For a historic overview reflected in the following see Claire Dupont et al., 'Three Decades of EU Climate Policy: Racing towards climate neutrality?' (2024) WIREs Climate Change 2024:15:e863.

30 European Commission, 'Communication 'EU-wide assessment of the final updated national energy and climate plans: Delivering the Union's 2030 energy and climate objectives' COM (2025) 274 final 2.

31 European Environmental Agency (EEA), 'Trends and projections in Europe 2022' (2022) 10 EEA Report, 15.

- setting pillar instruments (like ETS) and revising them in several rounds; this allows entry in a "soft" way (regarding Member States and citizens) and a predictable, path-dependent pattern of development.

The EGD, as the starting point of the 4th decade from 2020 on, can be seen as a highlight of this development: It sets extremely ambitious targets (climate neutrality in 2050 and a 55 % reduction in 2030). It comprises more policies than ever (including e.g. agriculture, social policy, finance and food). It strengthens the procedural multi-level governance approach. It establishes new pillar instruments, such as the Carbon Border Adjustment Mechanism (CBAM) or the Social Climate Fund.

Following the election of a new Commission, the mid-2020s could mark a turning point in the development of European climate law. Recognizable trends lie in the areas of de-bureaucratization or deregulation, climate-oriented competition and industrial policy as well as climate adaptation.[32] It is currently unclear whether this will jeopardize the climate law acquis.

32 See for that e.g. European Commission, 'A Competitiveness Compass for the EU' COM 2025) 30 final; European Commission, 'The Clean Industrial Deal' COM (2025) 85 final; a Climate Adaptation Plan has been announced for 2026, see European Commission, `Joint Communication on the European Preparedness Union Strategy´ JOIN (2025) 130 final 7 f.

Figure: The Long Journey of EU Energy and Climate Policy

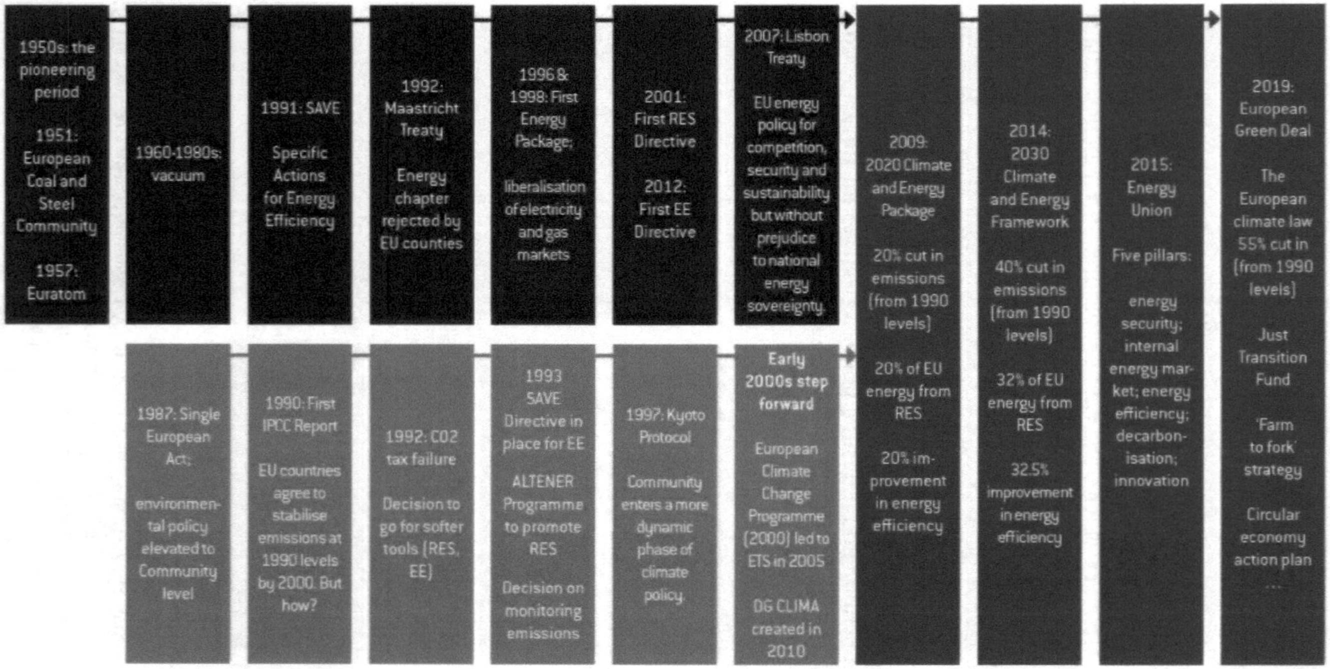

Source: Bruegel[33]

E. Climate Objectives of the European Union and Burden Sharing

1. General Climate Targets

As described above, the EU climate targets started modestly (a stabilization target for 2000, a 8 % reduction target for 2008–2012 and a 20 % reduction target for 2020). Ambition grew only in the 3rd decade of climate policies. Now, starting with the 4th decade, the European Climate Law of 30 June 2021 (ECL)[34] sets a binding climate neutrality objective in Article 2 (1): "Union-wide greenhouse gas emissions and removals regulated in Union law shall be balanced within the Union at the latest by 2050, thus reducing emissions to net zero by that date, and the Union shall achieve negative emissions thereafter". Intermediate Union climate targets are, according to Article 4 (1), a domestic reduction of net greenhouse gas emissions by 2030 of at least 55 % compared to 1990 levels. The contribution of net removals shall be limited to 225 million tons of CO2 equivalent. Regarding a 2040 goal in the framework of the European Climate Law, the Commission proposed in February 2024 a 90 % net greenhouse gas reduction (compared to 1990 levels) but left the legislative initiative to the newly elected Commission.[35]

Regarding national climate targets, the Effort Sharing Regulation was amended in 2023.[36] The 2030 targets range from 10 % to 50 % reductions in 2030 (compared to 2005 levels), based mainly on Gross Domestic Product (GDP) per capita. An obligation for Member States to achieve climate neutrality in 2050, as proposed by the European Parliament, has not been

33 Bruegel, 'The Long Journey of EU Energy and Climate Policy'<https://www.bruegel.org/policy-brief/new-governance-framework-safeguard-european-green-deal> accessed 21 August 2024.

34 Regulation (EU) 2021/1119 of the European Parliament and of the Council of 30 June 2021 establishing the framework for achieving climate neutrality and amending Regulations (EC) No 401/2009 and (EU) 2018/1999 (European Climate Law) [2021] OJ L 243/1:.

35 European Commission, 'Communication from the Commission to the European Parliament, the Council, the European Economic and Social Committee of the Regions, 'Securing our future. Europe's 2040 climate target and path to climate neutrality by 2050 building a sustainable, just and prosperous society' COM (2024) 63 final.

36 Regulation (EU) 2023/857 of the European Parliament and of the Council of 19 April 2023 amending Regulation (EU) 2018/842 on binding annual greenhouse gas emission reductions by Member States from 2021 to 2030 contributing to climate action to meet commitments under the Paris Agreement, and Regulation (EU) 2018/1999 [2023] *OJ L 111/1.*

accepted.[37] Thus, at the moment, only about 50 % of the Member States have set national net-zero targets.[38]

2. Targets for Renewables

The EU has set binding targets for renewable energy from the beginning (e.g. a 12 % objective for 2010 set in 1997).[39] The 20 % target for 2020 set by RED I has been reached.[40] With RED III the ambition for 2030 was raised from 32 % (RED II) to 42.5 % (with an "endeavor" to reach 45 %); in 2023 24 % have been reached.[41] As mentioned above, there are now no more binding national targets for Member States with regard to 2030.

RED III instead specifies various sub-targets. These include a 49 % share of the energy taken from the grid for consumption in the building sector in 2030 (Article 15a (1) RED III); a 29 % share of renewable fuels or renewable electricity in the transport sector in 2030, and 60 % in 2035; and a 5.5 % share of advanced biofuels and biogas in 2030 (Article 25 (1) RED III). Regarding renewable fuels of non-biological origin, the target is 42 % of the hydrogen used in industry in 2030, and 60 % in 2035 (Article 22a (1) RED III).[42]

37 Kati Kulovesi et al., 'The European Climate Law: Strenghening EU Procedural Climate Governance?' (2024) 20 Journal of Environmental Law 1, 7.
38 As of spring 2022, see Marjan Peeters et al., 'Towards an EU Climate Governance Framework to Deliver on the European Green Deal' (2023) 7 ff.
39 See Saurer, in this volume, 51 (56 ff.).
40 European Commission, 'Report to the European Parliament and Council, '2022 report on the achievement of the 2020 renewable energy targets' COM (2022) 639 final, under 2.
41 European Commission, 'Report to the European Parliament and Council, '2022 report on the achievement of the 2020 renewable energy targets' COM (2022) 639 final, under 2.
42 For details see Talus/Penttinen, in this volume, 71 ff.

3. Energy Efficiency Targets

As part of the energy and climate package, the EU has set in Article 3 of the Energy Efficiency Directive 2012/27/EU (EED)[43] a 20 % reduction target in the EU's primary and final energy consumption by 2020; although influenced by the COVID-19 pandemic, both targets were exceeded.

Article 4 (1) of the revised Energy Efficiency Directive[44] sets a target of reducing final energy consumption by at least 11.7 % compared to projections of the expected energy use for 2030 according to the 2020 reference scenario.

F. Overall Energy and Climate Governance

According to Article 2 (2) ECL, it is a common responsibility of relevant Union institutions and the Member States to take the relevant measures (at Union and national level) to enable the collective achievement of the climate neutrality objective. At the EU level, the ECL contains the main topics of procedural climate governance (target setting, monitoring, evaluation, scientific expert advice, access to justice, inclusiveness and public participation). In parallel, the Governance Regulation[45] sets up a governance process to assure adequate contributions of the Member States.[46]

---

43 Directive (EU) 2023/1791 of the European Parliament and of the Council of 13 September 2023 on energy efficiency and amending Regulation (EU) 2023/955 [2023] OJ L 231/1 (Energy Efficiency Directive).

44 Energy Efficiency Directive: "Member States shall collectively ensure a reduction of energy consumption of at least 11,7 % in 2030 compared to the projections of the 2020 EU Reference Scenario.".

45 Regulation (EU) 2018/1999 of the European Parliament and of the Council of 11 December 2018 on the Governance of the Energy Union and Climate Action, amending Regulations (EC) No 663/2009 and (EC) No 715/2009 of the European Parliament and of the Council, Directives 94/22/EC, 98/70/EC, 2009/31/EC, 2009/73/EC, 2010/31/EU, 2012/27/EU and 2013/30/EU of the European Parliament and of the Council, Council Directives 2009/119/EC and (EU) 2015/652 and repealing Regulation (EU) No 525/2013 of the European Parliament and of the Council [2018] OJ L 328/1 (Governance Regulation).

46 For a (positive) evaluation of the Governance Regulation see European Commission, 'Report of the Commission to the European Parliament and the Council on the Review of the Regulation on the Governance of the Energy Union and Climate Action' COM (2024) 550 final.

This legislative technique shall ensure coordination of Member States' policies to align them with a common European goal. It stems back to the "Open Method of Coordination" (OMC), which originates from policy areas where the Union had no or only few competences (e.g. employment policy, general economic policy etc.). It is mainly built on formal reporting obligations of the Member States, an assessment by the Commission, recommendations to the Member States and, once again, reporting obligations of Member States on how to cope with them. This "iterative process"[47] is very appropriate for climate policies as it sets up a similar process as framed by the Paris Agreement. In its "soft" variant it is solely built on a "blaming and shaming" mechanism. But in reality, it always has "harder" (enforceable) elements, especially in the area of climate and energy policies where the Union possesses quite some competences. Ultimately, to enforce binding Member State obligations under EU law, the infringement procedure (Articles 258, 259 and 260 TFEU) can be used.[48] Here, especially, there is an ongoing debate on further "hardening" soft governance.[49]

The Governance Regulation is an integrated climate and energy instrument and addresses five Energy Union dimensions: (1) decarbonization of the economy, (2) energy efficiency, (3) energy security, (4) the internal energy market, and (5) research, innovation and competitiveness. Article 3 requires EU Member States to prepare medium-term National Energy and Climate Plans (NECPs) every 10 years and to update them every 5 years. Importantly, NECPs must specify the national contributions not only to the EU's overall decarbonization target, but also to its renewables and energy efficiency targets. Every 10 years Member States must submit Long-Term Strategies (LTS) covering at least the next 30 years, which are demanded in Article 4.19 of the Paris Agreement ("should strive for"). LTSs comprise national objectives and targets, alongside policies or instruments to reach them; thus, they serve as important guidance.[50] The procedural character of the Governance Regulation is underlined by transparency (report and

47 See Saurer, in this volume 51 (56 ff.).

48 For further details see European Parliamentary Research Service (EPRS), `Briefing: Roadmap to EU climate neutrality – Scrutiny of Member States´ May 2025, 2 f. <https://www.europarl.europa.eu/RegData/etudes/BRIE/2025/772887/EPRS_BRI(2025)772887_EN.pdf> accessed 28 July 2025.

49 Michèle Knodt/Marc Ringel/Rainer Müller, '"Harder" soft governance in the European Energy Union' (2020) 22 Journal of Environmental Policy & Planning 787–800.

50 See Marjan Peeters/Sebastian Oberthür/Brendan Moore/Ólöf Söebech, 'Towards an EU Climate Governance Framework to Deliver on the European Green Deal' (2023)14 ff.

review) features, participation requirements (regarding experts and civil society) and access to justice.

For national legislatures this means that, at first glance, they have quite a lot of leeway in defining pathways to decarbonization. Additionally, they are not strictly bound to the contents of their NECPs. But there is something of path-dependency: in the course of the decarbonization process, it will get increasingly difficult to change the path taken. Additionally, implementation can be fostered by national courts ("access to justice"), infringement proceedings of the Commission according to Articles 258 and 260 TFEU and increasingly by funding instruments (including conditionality criteria).[51]

G. European Climate and Energy Transition Law

Apart from the governance process regarding national climate and energy policies, there is material European legislation. This may be directly applicable (regulations) or at least contain obligations to implement (directives).

As mentioned above, climate is a cross-cutting field of law affecting various other fields of law. Thus, today we are confronted with a huge number of different EU acts. For legal comparison at the national level, it is important to describe and define the scope of regulatory leeway of the EU Member States. In the case of directly applicable regulations, this can only concern supplementing and administering them .

1. Emission Mitigation

The European Emissions Trading Scheme (ETS)[52] is the most powerful greenhouse gas reduction instrument at the European level.[53] It covers

51 ibid 27 ff.

52 For the regulatory design of the EU ETS see e.g. Edwin Woerdman, 'Emissions Trading: Design, diffusion, and drawbacks' in: Kenneth R. Richards/Josephine van Zerben (eds), *Policy Instruments in Envrironmental Law* (2020) 261–278.

53 According to recent studies it is responsible for a 10 % reduction of greenhouse gases, while having a positive effect on the economic record of the regulated companies, see e.g. Antoine Dechezleprêtre et al., 'The Joint Impact of the European Union Emissions Trading System on Carbon Emissions and Economic Performance' (2023) 118 Journal of Environmental Economics and Management 102758.

around 45 % of greenhouse gases (mainly industrial plants, as well as aviation since 2012). According to EU NDC of 16 October 2023, no. 12, these emissions shall be reduced by 62 % by 2030, compared to 2005 levels (nearly 50 % have been achieved in 2024). While Member States had great leeway in designing the scheme at the beginning (2005), it is now nearly fully harmonized. A central problem of ETS has always been international competition. Up to now, the answer has been massive reliefs for energy-intense industry; with the introduction of a Carbon Border Adjustment Mechanism (CBAM), this disadvantage might disappear.[54] In 2023 a new ETS (called ETS2) was created covering fuel combustion from buildings, road transport and small industry not yet covered by the existing ETS. It will be fully operational in 2027.

While the ETS is a market-based instrument, the EU relies on command-and-control regulation in other fields. The Industrial Emissions Directive (Directive 2010/75/EU) aims to lower emissions from industrial production (including e.g. energy industry) through an integrated approach prescribing the best available technology; but it leaves a lot of leeway to Member States especially regarding exemptions (most relevant for power plants). Much more powerful is the European regulation regarding transport emissions. Regulation (EU) 2019/631 sets CO_2 emission performance standards for new passenger cars and vans. In line with the EU's ambition to reach climate neutrality in 2050, this has been amended on 19 April 2023[55], introducing a 100 % CO_2 emission reduction target for all cars and vans registered from 2035 onwards.

In these fields of direct emission mitigation, the regulatory leeway of Member States is restricted.

54 For CBAM and its role as a green industrial policy instrument see Mehling, in this volume, 91 (111 ff.).

55 Regulation (EU) 2023/851 of the European Parliament and of the Council of 19 April 2023 amending Regulation (EU) 2019/631 as regards strengthening the CO2 emission performance standards for new passenger cars and new light commercial vehicles in line with the Union's increased climate ambition [2023] OJ L 110/5.

2. Renewable Energy Law

From the 2nd decade of climate policies, the EU started with renewable energy regulation (Directive 2001/77/EC).[56] The scope of this policy approach has meanwhile broadened, putting more emphasis on hydrogen and infrastructure.[57] The renewable energy law framework deals with definitions and structures for national policies, but leaves basic policy choices to Member States.

3. Energy Efficiency Law

Energy efficiency is an important approach towards decarbonization. Since 2018, this has been reflected in the Energy Efficiency First Principle (Article 3 of the Energy Efficiency Directive).[58] Actually, energy efficiency policies stem back to the oil crisis in the 70s and thus have a longer history than climate policies.[59]

The range of instrument mix that the EU applies in the field of energy efficiency is huge.[60] It starts with general financial instruments like the ETS. The main pillars of product energy efficiency policies are energy labeling, minimum energy performance standards and eco-design. Regarding buildings, the Energy Performance of Buildings Directive (EPBD) paves the way to all new buildings being zero-emission by 2030, and to a zero-emission building stock by 2050.[61]

---

56 Directive 2001/77/EC of the European Parliament and of the Council of 27 September 2001 on the promotion of electricity produced from renewable energy sources in the internal electricity market [2001] OJ L 283/33.

57 See in detail Saurer, in this volume, 51 (65 ff.).

58 See e.g. Tim Mandel/ Zsuzsanna Pató, 'Towards Effective Implementation of the Energy Efficiency First Principle: A theory-based classification and analysis of policy instruments' (2024) 115 Energy Research & Social Science 103613.

59 For the history of EU energy efficiency policies see Maria Gonzales-Torres et al., Review of EU Product Energy Efficiency Policies: What have we reached in 40 years?' (2023) 421 Journal of Cleaner Production.

60 For an overview categorized according to market-failure criteria see Mandel/Pató (n 58).

61 For a review of 50 years of EU energy efficiency policies in buildings see e.g. Marina Economidou et al., 'Review of 50 Years of EU Energy Efficiency Policies for Buildings' (2020) 225 Energy and Buildings 110322.

The EU energy efficiency framework is the weakest of the areas of law described. Member States have a great deal of leeway to design their energy efficiency instruments.

4. Further Net-Zero Technologies

There is, of course, a great variety of emerging technologies that can contribute to the net-zero goal. Promoting them is part of an emerging European green industry policy based on the European Green Deal Industrial Plan.[62] The Net-Zero Industry Act of June 2024 (NZIA)[63] strives to enhance manufacturing capacities and increase the competitiveness of the net-zero sector. It expressly mentions in Article 3 (1) (a), alongside renewables and other technologies, "carbon capture, utilization, and storage technologies" and "energy from nuclear processes with minimal waste from the fuel cycle".

This shows that nuclear power can play an important role on the way to decarbonization in the form of small modular reactors (SMRs). It is up to the Member States to include them in their Long-Term Strategies (LTS) or NECPs. It must be emphasized here that this does not mean that classical nuclear power plants may be included.

Industrial Carbon Management (ICM) will also play an important role in achieving the net-zero goal. The EU's ICM Strategy was published on 6 February 2024.[64] The Net Zero Industry Act (NZIA) sets an EU-wide CO_2 storage objective to make 50 million tons of annual CO_2 injection available by 2030. How it is to be stored is regulated by the CCS Directive of 2009.

H. Conclusions

This contribution is only able to give an overview of a very comprehensive and still growing European framework for climate and energy transition

---

62 See Mehling, in this volume, 91 (107 ff.).

63 Entered into force on 29 June 2024; European Commission, 'Proposal for a Regulation of the European Parliament and the Council on establishing a framework of measures for strengthening Europe's net-zero technology products manufacturing ecosystem (Net Zero Industry Act)' COM (2023) 161 final.

64 European Commission, 'Towards an ambitious Industrial Carbon Management for the EU' COM (2024) 62 final.

law. Also, while some important instruments - especially the ETS as the centerpiece of EU climate policy – are nearly fully regulated at the European level, the European legal framework is designed for being supplemented and implemented by Member States. As a result, in the European Union, national and European climate and energy law are closely intertwined. As far as Member States are the object of legal comparison, the corresponding EU law framework must also be considered.

Bibliography

Bellanca M, `What, how and where: an assessment of multi-level European climate mitigation policies´, npj climate action 3 (2024) 119, <https://doi.org/10.1038/s441168-024-00200-7> accessed 18 July 2025

Brosset E/Maljean-Dubois S, 'The Paris Agreement, EU Climate Law and the Energy Union' in **Eliantonio M/Peeters M** (eds), Research Handbook on EU Environmental Law (Edward Elgar 2020) 4 ff. for the history of EU international climate politics 412 – 427

Bruegel, 'The Long Journey of EU Energy and Climate Policy' <https://www.bruegel.org/policy-brief/new-governance-framework-safeguard-european-green-deal> accessed 21 August 2024

Dechezleprêtre A/ Nachtigall D/Venmans F, 'The Joint Impact of the European Union Emissions Trading System on Carbon Emissions and Economic Performance' (2023) 118 Journal of Environmental Economics and Management 102758

Dupont C/Moore B/Boasson E L/Gravey V/Jordan A/Kivimaa P/Kulovesi K/Kuzemko C/Oberthür S/Panchuk D/Rosamond J/Torney D/Tosun J/Von Homeyer I, 'Three Decades of EU Climate Policy: Racing towards climate neutrality?' (2024) WIREs Climate Change 2024:15:e863

Economidou M/Todeschi V/Bertoldi P/D'Agostino D/Zangheri P/Castellazzi L, 'Review of 50 Years of EU Energy Efficiency Policies for Buildings' (2020) 225 Energy and Buildings 110322

European Commission, Communication from the Commission to the European Parliament, the Council, the European Economic and Social Committee of the Regions, 'Securing our future. Europe's 2040 climate target and path to climate neutrality by 2050 building a sustainable, just and prosperous society' COM (2024) 63 final

European Commission, Communication 'EU-wide assessment of the final updated national energy and climate plans: Delivering the Union`s 2030 energy and climate objectives' COM (2025) 274 final 2

European Commission, 'Joint Communication on the European Preparedness Union Strategy' JOIN (2025) 130 final 7 f.

European Commission, 'A Competitiveness Compass for the EU' COM 2025) 30 final

European Commission, 'The Clean Industrial Deal' COM (2025) 85 final

European Commission, 'Report of the Commission to the European Parliament and the Council on the Review of the Regulation on the Governance of the Energy Union and Climate Action' COM (2024) 550 final

European Commission, 'Proposal for a Regulation of the European Parliament and the Council on establishing a framework of measures for strengthening Europe's net-zero technology products manufacturing ecosystem (Net Zero Industry Act)' COM (2023) 161 final

European Commission, Report to the European Parliament and Council, '2022 report on the achievement of the 2020 renewable energy targets' COM (2022) 639 final

European Commission, 'Towards an ambitious Industrial Carbon Management for the EU' COM (2024) 62 final

European Environmental Agency, 'Trends and projections in Europe 2022' (2022) 10 EEA Report 15

European Parliamentary Research Service (EPRS), 'Briefing: Roadmap to EU climate neutrality – Scrutiny of Member States', May 2025, 2 f., <https://www.europarl.europa.eu/RegData/etudes/BRIE/2025/772887/EPRS_BRI(2025)772887_EN.pdf> accessed 18 July 2025

Fehling M, 'Energy Transition in the European Union and its Member States: Interpreting Federal Competence Allocation in the Light of the Paris Agreement' (2021) 10 Transnational Environmental Law 339–363

Gonzeles-Torres M/Bertoldi P/Castellazzi L/Perez-Lombard L, 'Review of EU Product Energy Efficiency Policies: What have we reached in 40 years?' (2023) 421 Journal of Cleaner Production 138442

Hölscher K/Wittmayer J M/Loorbach D, Transition versus transformation: What`s the difference, Environmental Innovation and Societal Transitions 27 (2018), doi:10.1016/j.eist.201710.007, 1 – 3

Huhta K/Romppanen S, 'Comparing Legal Disciplines as an Approach to Understanding the Role of Law in Decarbonizing Societies' (2023) 12 Transnational Environmental Law 649–670

Järnnäs M, 'Governing through the Nationally Determined Contribution (NDC): Five functions to steer states' climate conduct' (2024) 33 Environmental Politics 530–551

Knodt M, 'Instruments and modes of governance in EU climate and energy policy: from energy union to the European Green Deal', in **Knodt M** (ed), Handbook on European Union Climate Change Policy and Politics (2023) 202–215

Knodt M/Ringel M/Müller R, '"Harder" soft governance in the European Energy Union' (2020) 22 Journal of Environmental Policy & Planning 787–800

Kulovesi K/Oberthür S/Van Asselt H/Savaresi A, 'The European Climate Law: Strenghening EU Procedural Climate Governance?' (2024) 20 Journal of Environmental Law 1, 7

Linnér B-O/Wibeck V, 'Conceptualising variations in societal transformations towards sustainability' Environmental Science & Policy (2020), 106:222

Mai L, Navigating transformations: Climate change and the international law, Leiden Journal of International Law 2024, doi:10.1017/S092215624000062, 1- 22

Mandel T/Pató Z, 'Towards Effective Implementation of the Energy Efficiency First Principle: A theory-based classification and analysis of policy instruments' (2024) 115 Energy Research & Social Science,103613

Patterson J/Schulz K/Vervoort J/van der Hel S/Widerberg O/Adler C/Hurlbert M/Anderton K/Sethi M/Barau A, 'Exploring the governance and politics of transformations towards sustainability' Environmental Innovation and Societal Transitions 24 (2017), doi:10.1016/j.eist.2016.09.001, 1–16

Peeters M/Oberthür S/Moore B/Söebech O, 'Towards an EU Climate Governance Framework to Deliver on the European Green Deal' (2023) 7 ff.

Raggone S, 'European Comparative Law: Reasons for "enhanced comparison" and the role of the CJZU' (2021) 112 Revista de Derecho Politico 297–325

Romppanen S/Huhta K, 'The Interface between EU Climate and Energy Law' (2023) 30 Maastricht Journal of European and Comparative Law 45–62

Rosas A, 'European Law and National Law: A common legal system?' in **Karjalainen K et al.** (eds), International Actors and the Formation of Laws (Luxembourg 2022) 11–26

Vignarelli M C, 'Making the Energy Charter Treaty Climate-Friendly: An (Almost) Impossible Leap' (2022) European Yearbook of International Economic Law, 267–293

Viñuales J E, The International Law of Energy (Cambridge University Press 2022)

Von Bogdandy A, 'European Law Beyond "Ever Closer Union" Repositioning the Concept, its Thrust and the EJC's Comparative methodology' (2016) 22 European Law Journal 519–538

Woerdman E, 'Emissions Trading: Design, diffusion, and drawbacks' in: **Richards K R/van Zerben J** (eds), Policy Instruments in Environmental Law (2020) 261–278

Zaman S T, 'Exploring the Legal Nature of Nationally Determined Contributions (NDCs) under International Law' (2015) 26 Yearbook of international Environmental Law 98–126

EU Law Framework for Expansion of Renewable Energies

Johannes Saurer

A. Introduction

The EU pursues increasingly ambitious targets for renewable energy expansion. The target for the share of renewable energy in EU energy consumption in 2030 was raised from 27 % in a Council Decision of October 2014[1] to at least 42.5 % and possibly 45 % in Directive 2018/2001/EU of European Parliament and Council as amended by Directive 2023/241/EU of European Parliament and Council (RED III)[2] in November 2023. The increasing ambition reflects that renewable energies play a "fundamental role"[3] in the EU's plan to become the first climate neutral continent by 2050,[4] which is at the core of the European Green Deal of December 2019[5] and the EU climate law of 2021[6]. In addition, as the RePowerEU-Plan in reaction to the Russian invasion of Ukraine in 2022 emphasized,[7] renewable energies are connected to goals of energy security including security of supply, diversification of energy supply and affordability of energy prices. Moreover, re-

1 European Council (23 and 24 October 2014) - Conclusions, EUCO 169/14, 5.

2 Directive 2018/2001/EU on the promotion of the use of energy from renewable sources, 2018/2001 of the European Parliament and of the Council of 11 December 2018 on the promotion of the use of energy from renewable sources [2018] OJ L 328/82 as amended by Directive (EU) 2023/2413 of the European Parliament and of the Council of 18 October 2023 amending Directive (EU) 2018/2001, Regulation (EU) 2018/1999 and Directive 98/70/EC as regards the promotion of energy from renewable sources, and repealing Council Directive (EU) 2015/652 [2023] OJ L 2023/2413 (RED III), Art. 3 (1).

3 RED III (n 2), Recital 2.

4 Sirja-Leena Penttinen, 'Governing for Net-Zero in the European Union' in: Giuseppe Bellantuono/Lee Godden/Hannah Wiseman/Hanri Mostert/Zhang Hao (eds), *Handbook of energy law in the low-carbon transition* (De Gruyter 2023) 309, 314, 319.

5 European Commission, Communication 'The European Green Deal' COM (2019) 640 final.

6 Regulation 2021/1119/EU of the European Parliament and of the Council of 30 June 2021 establishing the framework for achieving climate neutrality and amending Regulations (EC) No 401/2009 and (EU) 2018/1999 [2021] OJ L 243/1 (European Climate Law), Art. 2 (1).

7 European Commission, Communication 'REPowerEU Plan' COM (2022) 230 final.

newable energy expansion aims for "broad socioeconomic benefits, creating new jobs and fostering local industries while addressing growing domestic and global demand for renewable energy technology".[8] The EU pursues a leading role in world markets for renewable energy technologies, especially in wind energy, geothermal technologies and hydropower.[9] To achieve the ambitious expansion targets, EU law constitutes a multi-dimensional legal framework of obligations and mandates for the expansion of renewable energies in EU Member States. This chapter will provide an overview of the EU law framework for renewable energy expansion.

B. Definitions and Empirical Development

Directive 2001/77/EC of European Parliament and Council[10] defined renewable energy as "renewable non-fossil energy sources (wind, solar, geothermal, wave, tidal, hydropower, biomass, landfill gas, sewage treatment plant gas and biogases)". Directive 2009/28/EC of European Parliament and Council (RED I)[11] and Directive 2018/2001/EU of European Parliament and Council (RED II)[12] contained similar definitions. Over time, the EU energy directive adopted more nuanced definitions. RED III included new renewable energy sources such as osmotic energy and ambient energy.[13] In addition, the revision of the Renewable Energy Directive in 2023 introduced the new legal category of "innovative renewable energies",

8 RED III (n 2), Recital 2.

9 European Commission, 'EU's Global Leadership in Renewables – Final synthesis report July 2021' (2021) 8: for 2018 a global leadership for the EU in world market shares of wind energy (67 %), geothermal technologies (42 %) and hydro power (39 %), while in solar energy exports the Asia-Pacific region, especially China was leading.

10 Directive 2001/77/EC of the European Parliament and of the Council of 27 September 2001 on the promotion of electricity produced from renewable energy sources in the internal electricity market [2001] OJ L 283/33.

11 Directive 2009/28/EC of the European Parliament and of the Council of 23 April 2009 on the promotion of the use of energy from renewable sources and amending and subsequently repealing Directives 2001/77/EC and 2003/30/EC [2009] OJ L 140/16 (RED I), Art. 2 (a).

12 Directive 2018/2001/EU on the promotion of the use of energy from renewable sources, 2018/2001 of the European Parliament and of the Council of 11 December 2018 on the promotion of the use of energy from renewable sources [2018] OJ L 328/82 (RED II), Art. 2 (1).

13 RED III (n 2), Art. 2 (a) (1).

which covers "renewable energy generation technology that improves, in at least one way, comparable state-of-the-art renewable energy technology or that renders renewable energy technology that is not fully commercialized or that involves a clear degree of risk exploitable".[14] Practical examples of such innovative technologies may include renewable hydrogen, building-integrated photovoltaics, floating offshore wind, and ocean energy.[15] In addition, RED III took a new, differentiated approach on biomass and implemented specific sustainability goals and standards for biomass use in energy generation in Art. 3 to Art. 3d of the Directive.[16]

Empirically, the share of renewable energies in the EU energy system has been constantly growing since the 1990s. In 1997, renewable energies accounted for 5.8 % of total gross inland consumption of energy in the European Union.[17] The share of renewable energies in EU energy consumption reached 14.4 % in 2010 and 23.0 % in 2022.[18] Focusing specifically on the electricity sector, the share of renewable energy sources is significantly higher. In 2022, renewable energy sources accounted for 41.2 % of gross electricity consumption in the EU. Taking a closer look at the composition of electricity generation, the quantitatively most important renewable energy technology is wind energy, with a share of 37.5 %.[19] The fastest-growing source in recent years is solar energy, which increased quantitatively from 7.4 TWh in 2008 to 210.3 TWh in 2022 and accounts for 18.2 % in 2022. The renewable energy portfolio is completed by hydropower (29.9 %),[20] solid biofuels (6.9 %) and other sources (7.5 %).[21] A closer look at the share of renewable energy in specific sectors shows a still low share of renewable

---

14 RED III (n 2), Art. 2 (14b).

15 See European Commission, 'EU's Global Leadership in Renewables – Final synthesis report July 2021' (2021) 8.

16 See also European Commission, Communication ''Fit for 55': delivering the EU's 2030 Climate Target on the way to climate neutrality' COM (2021) 550 final 10.

17 European Commission, Communication 'On the implementation of the Community Strategy and Action Plan on Renewable Energy Sources (1998 – 2000)' COM (2001) 69 final 6, 30 (table 1).

18 EEA, 'Share of energy consumption from renewable sources in Europe' <https://www.eea.europa.eu/en/analysis/indicators/share-of-energy-consumption-from?trk=public_post_comment-text&activeAccordion=546a7c35-9188-4d23-94ee-005d97c26f2b> accessed 27 May 2024.

19 Eurostat, 'Renewable energy statistics' <https://ec.europa.eu/eurostat/statistics-explained/index.php?title=Renewable_energy_statistics#Share_of_renewable_energy_more_than_doubled_between_2004_and_2022> accessed 7 May 2024.

20 ibid.

21 ibid.

energy in the transport sector (8.7 % in the EU in 2022 up from just 2 % in 2005).[22] The share of renewable energy in heating and cooling in the EU was 24.8 % in 2022 (up from 23 % in 2021).[23]

C. EU Competences for Renewable Energy Policy

The Treaty on the Functioning of the European Union (TFEU) provides a bundle of competence norms for EU policy in the context of renewable energies.

From an environmental law perspective, the EU competence for the environment in Art. 191, 192 TFEU enables EU legislation aiming to promote renewable energies as substitutes for fossil fuels. In addition, the EU competence for energy in Art. 194 TFEU enables EU legislation on renewable energy from an energy market perspective. As a default rule, both Art. 192 TFEU and Art. 194 TFEU refer to the ordinary legislative procedure (Art. 294 TFEU) and allow for majority voting. However, both articles contain "sovereignty clauses" in favor of the Member States' choice of energy resources, see Art. 192 (2) (c) TFEU and Art. 194 (2) TFEU. While there are textual and structural differences between both "sovereignty clauses",[24] they have in common that they both limit the material scope of EU legislation.[25]

---

22 EEA, 'Use of renewable energy for transport in Europe' <https://www.eea.europa.eu/en/analysis/indicators/use-of-renewable-energy-for#:~:text=In%202021%2C%209.1%25%20of%20the,points%20below%20the%202030%20target> accessed 28 May 2024.

23 Eurostat, 'Renewable energy for heating & cooling up to 25 % in 2022' <https://ec.europa.eu/eurostat/de/web/products-eurostat-news/w/ddn-20240227-2> accessed 5 September 2024.

24 Kaisa Huhta, 'The Scope of State Sovereignty under Article 194(2) TFEU and the Evolution of EU Competences in the Energy Sector' (2021) 70 International & Comparative Law Quarterly 991, 998.

25 For further discussion see Michael Fehling, 'Energy Transition in the European Union and its Member States: Interpreting Federal Competence Allocation in the Light of the Paris Agreement' (2021) 10 Transnational Environmental Law 339, 342 ff.; Huhta (n 24), 991, 1000 ff.; Angus Johnston/Eva van Der Marel, 'Ad Lucem? interpreting the new EU energy provision, and in particular the meaning of article 194(2) TFEU' (2013) 22 European Energy and Environmental Law Review 181 ff.; Sacha Garben, 'Art. 194 TFEU, para. 3' in: Manuel Kellerbauer/Marcus Klamert/Jonathan Tomkin, *The EU treaties and the Charter of Fundamental Rights – Commentary* (Oxford University Press 2019); Kim Talus/Pami Aalto, 'Competences in EU energy policy' in: Rafael Leal-Arcas/Jan Wouters (eds), *Research Handbook on EU Energy Law and Policy* (Edward Elgar 2017) 15, 23 ff.

The EU competence for harmonization of the internal market in Art. 114 TFEU can become relevant for EU renewable energy measures that relate to the internal energy market and aim for approximation of laws in the Member States.[26]

A further competence title related to energy is Art. 122 (1) TFEU, which enables the European Council to enact "appropriate measures" in case of emergency situations. Art. 122 (1) TFEU explicitly refers to instances in which "severe difficulties arise in the supply of certain products, notably in the area of energy" and, thus, covers constellations of major problems of energy supply.[27] A specific competence title for infrastructure projects related to renewable energies is included in Art. 170, 171 and 172 TFEU. According to Art. 170 and 171 TFEU the EU shall contribute to the establishment of trans-European networks including trans-European networks in the energy sector through a combination of guidelines, measures on the interoperability of the networks and financial support. Art. 172 TFEU allows for EU legislation in accordance with the ordinary legislative procedure (Art. 294 TFEU), but requires the approval of the Member State that is concerned by the guidelines and projects of common interest at stake.[28]

In legislative practice, EU institutions draw on all competence norms mentioned above. While Directive 2001/77/EC of the European Parliament and of the Council of 27 September 2001 on the promotion of electricity produced from renewable energy sources in the internal electricity market was based on the competence title for environmental law (then Art. 175 Sec. 1 EC Treaty) only,[29] RED II was based on the EU energy competence (Art. 194 Sec. 2 TFEU) only.[30] In contrast, RED III was based on a bundle of three competence titles: Art. 114, Art. 192(1) and Art. 194(2) TFEU.[31]

---

26 See Christian Calliess, 'Art. 172 AEUV para 4' in: Christian Calliess/Matthias Ruffert (eds), *EUV/AEUV Kommentar* (6th ed., Beck 2022).

27 Bruno de Witte, 'EU Emergency Law and its Impact on the EU Legal Order' (2022) 59 Common Market Law Review 3, 8 on the example of a Council regulation concerning minimum stocks of crude oil and/or petroleum products in the EU Member States; see also Leo Flynn, 'Art. 122 TFEU, para. 2' in: Manuel Kellerbauer/Marcus Klamert/Jonathan Tomkin, *The EU treaties and the Charter of Fundamental Rights – Commentary* (Oxford University Press 2019).

28 See Christian Calliess, 'Art. 172 AEUV para 5' in Christian Calliess/Matthias Ruffert (eds), *EUV/AEUV Kommentar* (6th ed., Beck 2022).

29 Directive 2001/77/EC on the promotion of electricity produced from renewable energy sources in the internal electricity market (n 10), preamble.

30 RED II (n 12), preamble.

31 See RED III (n 2), preamble.

Art. 122 TFEU was invoked as competence title for Council Regulation 2022/2577/EU of 22 December 2022 (a so-called "emergency regulation").[32] Art. 172 TFEU serves as the legal basis of Regulation 2022/869/EU of European Parliament and Council of 30 May 2022 on guidelines for trans-European energy infrastructure (so-called TEN-E-Regulation).[33]

D. EU Renewable Energy Targets

Since the early days of EU renewable energy policy in the 1990s, the EU has set union-wide targets for renewable energy expansion. In 1997 the EU Commission set out the indicative objective of 12 % for the contribution by renewable sources of energy to the EU's gross inland energy consumption by 2010.[34] The European Council affirmed this goal in 1998[35]. In 2007, the European Council set a mandatory target of a 20 % share of energy from renewable sources in overall EU energy consumption by 2020.[36] The 2020 goal of 20 % energy from renewables in EU energy consumption[37] was also incorporated in Art. 3 Sec. 1 RED I. Moreover, Annex I to RED I contained specific renewable energy expansion targets for each Member State.[38] The national 2020 targets for share of energy from renewable sources in energy consumption in Annex I varied considerably, e.g., between Belgium (13 %), Poland (15 %), Germany (18 %), France (23 %) and Sweden (49 %).

---

32 Council Regulation (EU) 2022/2577 of 22 December 2022 laying down a framework to accelerate the deployment of renewable energy ST/14787/2022/INIT [2022] OJ L 335/36.

33 Regulation (EU) 2022/869 of the European Parliament and of the Council of 30 May 2022 on guidelines for trans-European energy infrastructure, amending Regulations (EC) No 715/2009, (EU) 2019/942 and (EU) 2019/943 and Directives 2009/73/EC and (EU) 2019/944, and repealing Regulation (EU) No 347/2013 [2022] OJ L 152/45, preamble.

34 European Commission, Communication 'Energy for the future: renewable sources of energy' COM (97) 599 final 9 f.

35 Council Resolution of 8 June 1998 on renewable sources of energy [1998] OJ C 198/1.

36 European Council, 'Presidency Conclusions' (8/9 March 2007) 7224/1/07 REV 1, 21; see also European Commission, Communication '20 20 by 2020, Europe's climate change opportunity' COM (2008) 30 final 2.

37 For a discussion of the "20–20–20" see Sirja-Leena Penttinen, 'Governing for Net-Zero in the European Union' in: Bellantuono/Godden/Mostert/Wiseman (eds), *Handbook of energy law in the low-carbon transition* (De Gruyter 2023) 309, 310.

38 Heiko Krüger, *European Energy Law and Policy* (Edward Elgar 2016) 153 ff.

In 2014 – in advance of the global climate agreement planned for COP 21 in Paris – the EU began to target the year 2030.[39] The European Council set a target of at least 27 % for the share of renewable energy consumed in the EU in 2030.[40] The Energy Union strategy of February 2015 perpetuated the 27 % goal for 2030. The European Commission emphasized the EU's goal of "becoming the world leader in renewable energy, the global hub for developing the next generation of technically advanced and competitive renewable energies."[41] The Communication "Clean Energy For All Europeans" of 2016 made the implementation of the Paris Agreement a political priority and committed to a revision of EU renewable targets in light of the EU's Paris commitments.[42] The decreasing costs of renewable energy technologies gave additional motivation to increase the expansion target.[43]

Accordingly, Art. 3 Sec. 1 RED II[44] raised the overall target for the share of renewable energy consumed in the EU in 2030 to 32 %. However, the Union target was no longer translated into nationally binding targets,[45] because the European Council had linked its consent to the overall increase of the Union expansion goal for 2030 to the drop of quantitative national expansion goals.[46] Other than the 2020 goals in RED I, Art. 3 Sec. 2 RED II obliged Member States to reach the Union target collectively[47] and set adequate national contributions in their integrated national energy and climate plans under the Regulation on Governance of the Energy Union and

39 European Council, 'Presidency Conclusions' (23/24 March 2014) EUCO 169/14 1.

40 ibid 5.

41 European Commission, Communication 'A Framework Strategy for a Resilient Energy Union with a Forward-Looking Climate Change Policy' COM (2015) 080 final 15.

42 European Commission, Communication 'Clean Energy For All Europeans' COM (2016) 860 final 3.

43 Kati Kulovesi/Sebastian Oberthür, 'Assessing the EU's 2030 Climate and Energy Policy Framework: Incremental change toward radical transformation?' (2020) 29 RECIEL 145, 160.

44 Directive (EU) 2018/2001 of the European Parliament and of the Council of 11 December 2018 on the promotion of the use of energy from renewable sources [2018] OJ L 328/82.

45 Kulovesi/Oberthür 145, 160 (n 43).

46 See with further references Sabine Schlacke/Michèle Knodt, 'Das Governance-System für die Europäische Energieunion und für den Klimaschutz' (2019) ZUR 404, 405.

47 Eike Albrecht/Annegret Mordhorst, 'Die Energiekompetenz des Art. 194 AEUV und die 32 %-Zielvorgabe für den Anteil erneuerbarer Energien am Bruttoendenergieverbrauch in 2030 in der EU' (2019) EnWZ 343, 348.

Climate Action (Regulation 2018/1999/EU, "Governance Regulation")[48], which was enacted in parallel to RED II as a new instrument of procedural transition governance. Under the Governance Regulation the national 2020 goals of RED I retained some significance as starting points for indicative trajectories of national renewable energy expansion with reference points for 2022, 2025, 2027 and 2030.[49]

The European Green Deal of 2019 – a key political priority of the European Commission in the term 2019–2024[50] – announced the goal of climate neutrality for the EU by 2050 and a related effort to strengthen the role of renewable energies across all sectors.[51] As part of the "Fit for 55" package of July 2021, the European Commission proposed an increase of the EU 2030 target of the renewable share in energy consumption to 40 %.[52] The political dynamic of the energy crisis following the Russian invasion of Ukraine in February 2022 led to an even further increase. In the RePowerEU-Plan of May 2022, the European Commission proposed a share of 45 % for renewables in overall energy consumption in 2030.[53] Eventually, Art. 3 Sec. 1 RED III raised the expansion target to a share of renewable energy in energy consumption in the EU to "at least 42.5 %" in 2030 and amended an additional commitment that Member States "shall collectively endeavour" to reach a share of 45 % by 2030.[54]

EU law does not set renewable energy targets for the period beyond 2030. However, the EU's goal of climate neutrality in 2050 suggests that there will still be significant need for additional renewable energy capacity in the 2030s and 2040s to complete decarbonization across all sectors of

48 Regulation 2018/1999/EU of the European Parliament and of the Council of 11 December 2018 on the Governance of the Energy Union and Climate Action, amending Regulations (EC) No 663/2009 and (EC) No 715/2009 of the European Parliament and of the Council, Directives 94/22/EC, 98/70/EC, 2009/31/EC, 2009/73/EC, 2010/31/EU, 2012/27/EU and 2013/30/EU of the European Parliament and of the Council, Council Directives 2009/119/EC and (EU) 2015/652 and repealing Regulation (EU) No 525/2013 of the European Parliament and of the Council [2018] OJ L 328/1 (Governance Regulation).

49 Governance Regulation (n 48), Art. 4 sec. (a) (2).

50 Edoardo Chiti, 'Managing the ecological transition of the EU: The European Green Deal as a regulatory process' (2022) 59 Common Market Law Review 19, 20; Ruven C. Fleming/Romain Mauger, 'Green and Just? An Update on the 'European Green Deal'' (2021) 18 Journal for European Environmental & Planning Law 164, 165 ff.

51 European Commission, 'Green Deal' (n 4) 6.

52 European Commission, 'Fit for 55' (n 15) 9.

53 European Commission, 'RePowerEU' (n 7).

54 RED III (n 2), Art. 3 sec. 1.

economy and society.[55] Overall electricity demand in the EU is expected to rise in the coming decades despite significant efforts to enhance energy efficiency due to sector coupling and accordingly growing electricity demand in the transportation and building sector.[56] In February 2024 the European Commission issued the communication "Securing our future" to initial political and legal discourse on a 2040 climate target for the EU and corresponding additional sectoral measures to further reduce greenhouse gas emissions.[57] The European Commission aims for a 2040 climate target of a 90 % reduction of greenhouse gas emissions relative to 1990.[58] Further decarbonization in the electricity sector is envisioned as a central "building block" for achieving the 2040 target and proposes that the "electricity sector should come close to full decarbonisation in the second half of the 2030s".[59] The European Commission hints to the impact assessment accompanying the communication that projects that "renewable energy in majority, complemented by nuclear energy, will generate over 90 % of the electricity consumption in the EU in 2040".[60]

E. Requirements of the Regulation on the Governance of the Energy Union and Climate

Although RED III does not break down the Union target for renewable energy expansion for 2030 into specific national targets (see above), the EU takes the member state level of renewable energy expansion more and more into focus. This focus reflects that the fulfilment of the ambitious Union targets ultimately depends upon massive renewables expansion on the national level.

The Regulation on the Governance of the Energy Union and Climate Action (Governance Regulation)[61] contains several planning and reporting

55 See Krüger, *European Energy Law and Policy* 152 (n 38).

56 European Commission, Communication 'Powering a climate-neutral economy: An EU Strategy for Energy System Integration' COM (2020) 299 final 2 f.

57 European Commission, Communication 'Securing our future Europe's 2040 climate target and path to climate neutrality by 2050 building a sustainable, just and prosperous society' COM (2024) 63 final.

58 ibid 3.

59 Ibid 27.

60 ibid 13 (with further references).

61 Governance Regulation (n 48).

obligations for EU Member States related to renewable energy expansion. Renewable energy expansion is a key element of the "iterative process"[62] at the core of the Governance Regulation that is intended to achieve the goals of EU climate and energy policy over an extended period of time.[63] The "iterative process" of the Governance Regulation connects multiple procedural steps, including the initial enactment of integrated national energy and climate plans (NECP), review of the initial plans by the EU Commission, periodic (biannual) progress reporting by the Member States, assessments of progress by the Commission and duties to respond to insufficient ambition of integrated national energy and climate plans.[64]

Art. 4 (a) Nr. 2 and Art. 5 of the Governance Regulation explicitly require EU Member States to address renewable energy expansion in their integrated national energy and climate plans. EU Member States have to pay attention to the union target of renewable energy expansion in 2030[65] and set up an indicative trajectory for the period to 2030 that builds upon each Member State's (mandatory) 2020 goal.[66] Art. 5 and Annex II of the Governance Regulation provide further criteria that each Member State has to take into account in its national renewable energy target for 2030. Although these rules on renewable energy expansion do not set out legally binding national targets, they have significant factual effects, as they provide "a clear benchmark by which to assess individual national failures, and to apportion blame and shame".[67]

Art. 20 of the Governance Regulation contains specific requirements for EU Member States' reporting on renewable energy as part of the integrated national energy and climate progress reports. Inter alia, Member States have to report on indicative national trajectories for the overall share and sector-specific shares of renewable energy in gross final energy consumption from 2021 to 2030 and on the implementation of policies and measures to achieve the national contribution to the 2030 binding union target for re-

---

62 See on iterative planning processes Johannes Saurer, 'Wandel der Handlungsformen im Umweltrecht der EU' (2023) 56 Die Verwaltung 159, 163 f.

63 Kulovesi/Oberthür 145, 160 (n 43).

64 Ludwig Krämer, 'Planning for Climate and the Environment: the EU Green Deal' (2020) 17 Journal for European Environmental & Planning Law 267 ff.; Schlacke/Knodt 404, 406 f. (n 46).

65 Art. 4 (a) Nr. 2 and Art. 5 (2) of the Governance Regulation.

66 Art. 5 (1) d) of the Governance Regulation.

67 Leigh Hancher, 'EU energy governance—moving targets and flexible ambitions between opacity and opportunism?' (2022) 41 Yearbook of European Law 162, 168.

newable energy.[68] The progress reports of EU Member States including the area of renewable energy are basis for the overarching biannual assessment of progress by the European Commission.[69]

Art. 32 (3) of the Governance Regulation concerns the case that the European Commission concludes that a Member State has "insufficiently" progressed in renewable energy expansion compared to specific "national reference points". In this scenario Member States "shall" ensure that "additional measures" are implemented to increase the general and sector-specific deployment of renewable energy. The provision enlists various examples for such "additional measures" including "voluntary financial payment to the Union renewable energy financing mechanism".[70] The Union renewable energy financing mechanism is addressed in Art. 33 of the Governance Regulation to enable financial support for new renewable energy projects in the EU.[71] Art. 33 Nr. 5 of the Governance Regulation provides an incentive for member state payments to the financing mechanism as the generated renewable energy "shall be statistically attributed to the participating Member States, reflecting their relative payments". Requirements and procedures of the Union renewable energy financing mechanism are detailed in an Implementing Regulation by the European Commission.[72]

F. EU Law Requirements for Planning and Permit-Granting Procedures for Renewable Energy Installations in EU Member States

In recent years, EU law has increasingly addressed planning and permit-granting procedures for renewable energy installations in its Member States. Thus, the EU reacted to concerns that procedural barriers within Member States were responsible for overly long durations of planning and

68 Schlacke/Knodt 404, 407 (n 46).

69 See Governance Regulation (n 48), Art. 29.

70 For details see Leigh Hancher (n 67).

71 See Sirja-Leena Penttinen, 'Governing for Net-Zero in the European Union' in: Bellantuono/Godden/Mostert/Wiseman (eds), *Handbook of energy law in the low-carbon transition* (De Gruyter 2023) 309, 319.

72 Commission Implementing Regulation 2020/1294/EU of 15 September 2020 on the Union renewable energy financing mechanism C/2020/6123 [2020] OJ L 303/1.

permit-granting procedures and potentially putting the 2030 renewable energy target at risk.[73]

In 2018, the acceleration of renewable energy expansion through EU rules on permit-granting procedures was a key motive for RED II. For example, RED II introduced a time limit on permit procedures, alongside the one-stop-shop principle, to EU renewable energy law. The one-stop-shop principle requires Member States to designate a single administrative authority that operates according to the "front office" principle in order to help the applicant in light of institutionally complex permit-granting procedures.[74]

In December 2022, the European Council enacted Regulation 2022/2577/EU, laying down a framework to accelerate the deployment of renewable energy.[75] This regulation was based on Art. 122 TFEU and intended to contribute short-term solutions in reaction to the energy-related challenges resulting from the invasion of Russia in Ukraine. The legal basis of Art. 122 TFEU allowed for time-limited legal acts only, which led to a limitation of the legal validity of Regulation 2022/2577/EU to 18 months, that is, until mid-2024. The emergency measures of Regulation 2022/2577/EU included the imposition of short terms of maximum duration for permit-granting for solar energy equipment on existing structures (Art. 4 Nr. 1 Regulation 2022/2577/EU) and repowering of renewable energy power plants (Art. 5 Regulation 2022/2577/EU). Regulation 2022/2577/EU also contained a far-reaching substantive provision that assigned an "overriding public interest" to renewable energy projects that could be invoked in balancing constellations against conflicting private and public interests (Art. 3 Regulation 2022/2577/EU).[76] In December 2023, Regulation 2024/223/EU of the European Council (again based on Art. 122

73 European Commission, 'Guidance to Member States on good practices to speed up permit-granting procedures for renewable energy and related infrastructure projects' (2024) SWD 124 final 3.

74 See Johannes Saurer, 'Die einheitliche Stelle im immissionsschutzrechtlichen Genehmigungsverfahren für Erneuerbare Energien-Anlagen' (2024) NuR 577, 577 f.

75 Council Regulation (EU) 2022/2577 of 22 December 2022 laying down a framework to accelerate the deployment of renewable energy ST/14787/2022/INIT [2022] OJ L 335/36.

76 Antonis Metaxas, 'New Approaches and the Challenges of Gas Regulation in the EU' (2024) 17 Journal of World Energy Law and Business 69, 79 f.; Julia Wulff, 'Die Umsetzung der Erneuerbare Energien-Richtlinie (RED III) in nationales Recht' (2024) NVwZ 368, 372.

TFEU) extended the legal force of several rules of Regulation 2022/2577/EU to 30 June 2025.[77]

RED III[78] focused on planning and permit-granting procedures in the Member States. The revision introduced new instruments of spatial planning for renewable energy installations. Art. 15b Nr. 1 RED III obliges Member States to map areas necessary for national contributions towards the overall union renewable energy target for 2030. The scope of mapped areas should be adequate to meet the renewable energy targets set out in national energy and climate plans under the Governance Regulation. Art. 15c Nr. 1 RED III introduces renewable acceleration areas as a subset of areas necessary for national contributions under Art. 15b Nr. 1 RED III.[79] The designation of a renewable acceleration area has the legal effect that permit-granting procedures in such an area follow a specific legal regime that is detailed in Art. 16a RED III. Most significantly, Art. 16a Nr. 3 RED III exempts new applications for renewable energy plants from the duty to carry out an environmental impact assessment (EIA) under Directive 2011/92/EU. This exemption is justified on the grounds that environmental conditions of the affected location have been assessed earlier in the strategic environmental assessment (SEA) of the plan that designated the renewable acceleration area. Moreover, Art. 16a Nr. 3 RED III excludes territories with specific ecologic protection status from eligibility as a renewable acceleration area.

G. EU Law Requirements for National Support Schemes

National renewable energy support schemes that promote renewable energy through financial incentives[80] have to adhere to various norms and principles of EU law. The legality of national support schemes under EU primary law has been subject to various landmark rulings of the European

77 Council Regulation (EU) 2024/223 of 22 December 2023 amending Regulation (EU) 2022/2577 laying down a framework to accelerate the deployment of renewable energy [2024] OJ L 2024/23.

78 RED III (n 2).

79 Julia Wulff 368, 369 f. (n 75).

80 For a comparative overview on various types of tariff and financial support structures see Frédéric G. Sourgens/Edward Baldwin/Catherine Banet, *The Transnational Law of Renewable Energy* (Oxford University Press 2024) 144 ff.

Court of Justice[81] and has been widely discussed in scholarly literature.[82] A particularly important set of requirements concerns the rules on competition regarding state aid, Art. 107–109 TFEU. The general prohibition of state aid in Art. 107 Sec. 1 TFEU applies to all national support schemes that qualify as "state aid" in the sense of the norm. Not all national support schemes do constitute state aid according to Art. 107 Sec. 1 TFEU. Acting as court of review in a case of appeal against a decision by the General Court[83], the European Court of Justice held in 2019 that national feed-in tariffs as applied under the Federal Renewable Energy Act (EEG) in Germany did not constitute state aid under Art. 107 TFEU because the financing system at stake did operate independently from state resources.[84] The judgment of the European Court of Justice reversed the challenged judgement of the General Court and rejected the legal standpoint of the European Commission that had issued its influential guidelines on state aid under the assumption of a wide notion of state aid in context of national renewable energy support schemes.[85] National support systems that qualify as "state aid" under Art. 107 Sec. 1 TFEU can be justified under the formal and material requirements of Art. 107 Sec. 2 and Sec. 3 and Art. 108 TFEU. The European Commission has detailed its criteria for assessing state aid in support of renewable energy in notification cases in the Guidelines on State aid for climate, environmental protection and energy of 2022.[86]

---

81 See European Court of Justice, Case C-379/98, 13 March 2001, *PreussenElektra AG v Schleswag AG*, ECLI:EU:C:2001:160; European Court of Justice, Case C-206/06, 17 July 2008, *Essent Netwerk Noord BV v Aluminium Delfzijl BV*, ECLI:EU:C:2008:413; European Court of Justice, Case C-262/12, 19 December 2013, *Association Vent De Colère! Fédération nationale and Others v Ministre de l'Écologie, du Développement durable, des Transports et du Logement*, ECLI:EU:C:2013:851; European Court of Justice, Case C-405/16, *Germany v Commission,* ECLI:EU:C:2019:268.

82 For an overview of the debate see Leigh Hancher/Francesco Salerno, 'EU energy and competition: analysis of current trends and a first assessment of the new package' in: Rafael Leal-Arcas/Jan Wouters, *Research Handbook on EU Energy Law and Policy* (Edward Elgar 2017) 48, 51 ff.; Heiko Krüger, *European Energy Law and Policy* 154 ff. (n 38); Kulovesi/Oberthür 145, 160 f. (n 43).

83 General Court, Case T-47/15, 10 May 2016, *Germany v Commission*, ECLI:EU:T:2016:281.

84 European Court of Justice, Case C-405/16, *Germany v Commission*, ECLI:EU:C:2019:268.

85 For a discussion of the case see Francesco Salerno, 'How is the energy sector faring at the courts?' in: Martha M. Roggenkamp/Catherine Banet (eds), *European Energy Law Report XIV* (2021) 79, 80 ff.

86 European Commission, Communication 'Guidelines on State aid for climate, environmental protection and energy 2022' COM (2022) 481 [2022] OJ C 80/1.

Moreover, national renewable support schemes are regulated by the renewable energy directive. Art. 4 RED III generally acknowledges member state support schemes for energy from renewable sources but sets specific conditions, e.g., for direct price support schemes (shall be granted in the form of a market premium) and for tendering procedures (Art. 4 Nr. 3–6 RED III).[87] Art. 5 RED III allows for national support schemes for electricity from renewable sources that extend to other EU Member States. Art. 6 RED III obliges Member States to provide reliable long-term financial support schemes and avoid sudden shifts that negatively affect reliability and economic viability of financial renewable energy support.[88] Art. 9 and Art. 10 RED III concern joint projects between Member States, Art. 11 and Art. 12 RED III joint projects between Member States and third countries.

H. Infrastructure Dimension

The ambitious renewable energy expansion in the EU presents significant challenges to energy infrastructure. Across Europe, the transmission capacity of old and new electricity grid structures needs to be stabilized and increased, because the growth of renewable energies coincides with a growing absolute demand of electricity due to sector coupling. The European Commission strives to "ensure that grids become an enabler, not a bottleneck for the EU's fast clean transition"[89]. The expansion of renewable energies changes the European geography of energy generation and consumption. The addition of significant numbers of onshore and offshore windmills, photovoltaic installations, and other renewable energy facilities at hundreds of thousands locations by hundreds of thousand public and private investors results in a far-reaching decentralization of energy installations that need to be connected to the grid.[90] Charging infrastructure for e-mobility creates new hot spots of energy consumption.[91] Thus, the EU electricity grid needs additional interconnectors between national grids and must be expanded significantly in length.

87 Kulovesi/Oberthür 145, 161 (n 43).

88 ibid.

89 European Commission, Communication 'Grids, the missing link – An EU Action Plan for Grids' COM (2023) 757 final 2.

90 European Commission, Communication 'Grids, the missing link – An EU Action Plan for Grids' COM (2023) 757 final 1.

91 ibid.

In addition, the volatile nature of renewable energies – resulting from the dependence on natural processes (such as changes in wind conditions and the limited share of sun hours within absolute hours of the year) –, specific industrial demands of power supply and transportation conditions necessitate a massive increase in infrastructure for electricity conversion (power to X-facilities including electrolysers) and energy storage.[92] Moreover, the goal of energy system integration requires digitalization.[93] The implementation of "smart grids" and digital networks of renewable energy installations, storage facilities, net operators, private and industrial energy consumers provides "real time" data and enables "real-time" communication on supply and demand for electricity.[94] Thus, digitalization of electricity grids is a key element of European energy system integration and an important tool to balance electricity flows in order to reduce the absolute amount of electricity that needs to be transmitted.

The significant infrastructural challenges of renewable energy expansion are increasingly addressed by European energy law. For example, according to Art. 15e RED III,[95] grid projects and storage facilities can in general be part of renewable acceleration areas and benefit from their legal status.[96] Under the competence title of Art. 170–172 TFEU,[97] European Parliament and the European Council enacted Regulation 2022/869/EU on guidelines for trans-European energy infrastructure (TEN-E-Regulation 2022/869/EU).[98] Annex II of TEN-E-Regulation 2022/869/EU, enlists key energy infrastructure categories related to renewable energy expansion including

92 European Commission, Communication 'Securing our future Europe's 2040 climate target and path to climate neutrality by 2050 building a sustainable, just and prosperous society' COM (2024) 63 final 27.

93 European Commission, Communication 'Powering a climate-neutral economy: An EU Strategy for Energy System Integration' COM (2020) 299 final 1, 19.

94 European Commission, Communication 'Securing our future Europe's 2040 climate target and path to climate neutrality by 2050 building a sustainable, just and prosperous society' COM (2024) 63 final, 11, 13.

95 RED III (n 2).

96 But note the exemptions in Art. 15e RED III.

97 See above section C. and Jens-Peter Schneider, 'Energy and Trans-European Networks' in: Herwig C. H. Hofmann/Gerard C. Rowe/Alexander H. Türk (eds), *Specialized Administrative Law of the European Union: A Sectoral Review* (Oxford University Press 2018) 378, 393.

98 Regulation (EU) 2022/869 of the European Parliament and of the Council of 30 May 2022 on guidelines for trans-European energy infrastructure, amending Regulations (EC) No 715/2009, (EU) 2019/942 and (EU) 2019/943 and Directives 2009/73/EC and (EU) 2019/944, and repealing Regulation (EU) No 347/2013, O.J. L 152/45.

high- and extra-high-voltage overhead transmission lines, energy storage facilities, smart electricity grids and electrolyser facilities.[99]

Art. 3 (4) TEN-E-Regulation 2022/869/EU empowers the European Commission to include individual projects of Annex II-energy infrastructure categories in the "Union list of projects of common interest and projects of mutual interest". The Union list is enacted as a delegated regulation following a specific procedure involving public and private stakeholders.[100] Projects included in the Union list are assigned priority status in the national permit granting process (Art. 7 TEN-E-Regulation 2022/869/EU). They can benefit from the designation of a single national competent authority with responsibility for facilitating and coordinating the permit-granting process (Art. 8 TEN-E-Regulation 2022/869/EU) and from acceleration effects of specific time limits for the application process (Art. 10 TEN-E-Regulation 2022/869/EU). Moreover, these projects qualify for financial assistance under the Connecting Europe Facility[101] (Art. 18 TEN-E-Regulation 2022/869/EU).

I. Conclusion

The EU aims to almost double the share of renewable energies in energy consumption from 23 % in 2022 to 42.5 % in 2030. The ambitious expansion target for 2030 is motivated by a plurality of factors, including the EU's commitment to climate neutrality in 2050, energy security, energy autonomy and the socio-economic value of renewable energy industries. However, the EU has not set specific renewable expansion goals for the period between 2030 and the target year of climate neutrality, 2050. This leaves room for national specifics in energy transition strategies, e.g., for the very different policy choices of EU Member States on the role of nuclear energy in a carbon-neutral energy mix. EU law also covers the

99 See Tobias Leidinger, 'Die neue TEN-E-Verordnung: Transeuropäischer Netzausbau und Auswirkungen auf die deutsche Genehmigungspraxis' (2022) DVBl 1353, 1354.

100 Commission Delegated Regulation (EU) 2024/1041 of 28 November 2023 amending Regulation (EU) 2022/869 of the European Parliament and of the Council as regards the Union list of projects of common interest and projects of mutual interest [2024] OJ L 2024/1041.

101 Regulation (EU) 2021/1153 of the European Parliament and of the Council of 7 July 2021 establishing the Connecting Europe Facility and repealing Regulations (EU) No 1316/2013 and (EU) No 283/2014 [2021] OJ L 249/38.

implementation of renewable energy targets at the national level. Under Regulation 2018/1999/EU (Governance Regulation) Member States have to set up and renew integrated NECPs that include national trajectories of renewable energy expansion. EU law also requires Member States to implement various rules intended to accelerate planning and permit-granting procedures into national law. Moreover, Member States have to adhere to EU law requirements for national support schemes including EU state aid law (Art. 107–109 TFEU, guidelines of the Commission) and relevant provisions of the Renewable Energy Directive. The successful fulfillment of the EU's renewable energy targets through the expansion of renewable energy generation facilities depends on the simultaneous stabilization and expansion of infrastructures for storage and transportation. Thus, EU law also addresses the infrastructure dimension of renewable energy expansion through legal requirements for planning and licensing of national and transnational storage facilities and electricity grids. To enhance the balance of supply and demand, increase energy efficiency and decrease the need for new infrastructure, the EU aims for far-reaching digitalization of renewable energy generation facilities, points of energy consumption and electricity grids.

Bibliography

Albrecht E/Mordhorst A, 'Die Energiekompetenz des Art. 194 AEUV und die 32 %-Zielvorgabe für den Anteil erneuerbarer Energien am Bruttoendenergieverbrauch in 2030 in der EU' (2019) EnWZ 343

Calliess C, 'Art. 172 AEUV' in: **Calliess C/Ruffert M** (eds), *EUV/AEUV Kommentar* (6th ed., Beck 2022)

Chiti E, 'Managing the ecological transition of the EU: The European Green Deal as a regulatory process' (2022) 59 Common Market Law Review 19

de Witte B, 'EU Emergency Law and its Impact on the EU Legal Order' (2022) 59 Common Market Law Review 3

European Commission, 'EU's Global Leadership in Renewables – Final synthesis report July 2021' (Publications Office of the European Union 2021)

European Commission, Communication ''Fit for 55': delivering the EU's 2030 Climate Target on the way to climate neutrality' COM (2021) 550 final

European Commission, Communication '20 20 by 2020, Europe's climate change opportunity' COM (2008) 30 final

European Commission, Communication 'A Framework Strategy for a Resilient Energy Union with a Forward-Looking Climate Change Policy' COM (2015) 80 final 15

European Commission, Communication 'Clean Energy For All Europeans' COM (2016) 860 final 3

European Commission, Communication 'Energy for the future: renewable sources of energy' COM (97) 599 final

European Commission, Communication 'On the implementation of the Community Strategy and Action Plan on Renewable Energy Sources (1998 – 2000)' COM (2001) 69 final

European Commission, Communication 'Powering a climate-neutral economy: An EU Strategy for Energy System Integration' COM (2020) 299 final

European Commission, Communication 'REPowerEU Plan' COM (2022) 230 final

European Commission, Communication 'The European Green Deal' COM (2019) 640 final

Fehling M, 'Energy Transition in the European Union and its Member States: Interpreting Federal Competence Allocation in the Light of the Paris Agreement' (2021) 10 Transnational Environmental Law 339

Fleming R C/Mauger R, 'Green and Just? An Update on the 'European Green Deal'' (2021) 18 Journal for European Environmental & Planning Law 164

Flynn L, 'Art. 122 TFEU' in: **Kellerbauer M/Klamert M/Tomkin J**, *The EU treaties and the Charter of Fundamental Rights – Commentary* (Oxford University Press 2019)

Garben, S, 'Art. 194 TFEU', in: **Kellerbauer M/Klamert M/Tomkin J** (eds), *The EU treaties and the Charter of Fundamental Rights – Commentary* (Oxford University Press 2019)

Hancher L/Salerno F, 'EU energy and competition: analysis of current trends and a first assessment of the new package' in: **Leal-Arcas R/Wouters J**, *Research Handbook on EU Energy Law and Policy* (Edward Elgar 2017) 48

Hancher L, 'EU energy governance—moving targets and flexible ambitions between opacity and opportunism?' (2022) 41 Yearbook of European Law 162

Huhta K, 'The Scope of State Sovereignty under Article 194(2) TFEU and the Evolution of EU Competences in the Energy Sector' (2021) 70 International & Comparative Law Quarterly 991

Johnston A/van Der Marel E, 'Ad Lucem? interpreting the new EU energy provision, and in particular the meaning of article 194(2) TFEU' (2013) 22 European Energy and Environmental Law Review 181

Krämer L, 'Planning for Climate and the Environment: the EU Green Deal' (2020) 17 Journal for European Environmental & Planning Law 267

Krüger H, *European Energy Law and Policy* (Edward Elgar 2016)

Kulovesi K/Oberthür S, 'Assessing the EU's 2030 Climate and Energy Policy Framework: Incremental change toward radical transformation?' (2020) 29 RECIEL 145

Leidinger T, 'Die neue TEN-E-Verordnung: Transeuropäischer Netzausbau und Auswirkungen auf die deutsche Genehmigungspraxis' (2022) DVBl 1353

Metaxas A, 'New Approaches and the Challenges of Gas Regulation in the EU' (2024) 17 Journal of World Energy Law and Business 69

Penttinen S-L, 'Governing for Net-Zero in the European Union' in: **Bellantuono G/ Godden L/Mostert H/Wiseman H/Zhang H** (eds), *Handbook of Energy Law in the Low-Carbon Transition* (De Gruyter 2023) 309

Salerno F, 'How is the energy sector faring at the courts?' in: **Roggenkamp M/Banet C** (eds), *European Energy Law Report XIV* (Intersentia 2021) 79

Saurer J, 'Wandel der Handlungsformen im Umweltrecht der EU' (2023) 56 Die Verwaltung 159

Saurer J, 'Die einheitliche Stelle im immissionsschutzrechtlichen Genehmigungsverfahren für Erneuerbare Energien-Anlagen' (2024) NuR 577

Schlacke S/Knodt M, 'Das Governance-System für die Europäische Energieunion und für den Klimaschutz' (2019) ZUR 404

Schneider J-P, 'Energy and Trans-European Networks' in: **Hofmann H C H/Rowe G C/Türk A H** (eds), *Specialized Administrative Law of the European Union: A Sectoral Review* (Oxford University Press 2018) 378

Sourgens F G/ Baldwin E/Banet C, *The Transnational Law of Renewable Energy* (Oxford University Press 2024)

Talus K/Aalto P, 'Competences in EU energy policy', in: **Leal-Arcas R/Wouters J**, *Research Handbook on EU Energy Law and Policy* (Edward Elgar 2017) 15

Wulff J, 'Die Umsetzung der Erneuerbare Energien-Richtlinie (RED III) in nationales Recht' (2024) NVwZ 368

Tomorrow's EU Framework for Sustainable Fuels: The Emerging Regulatory Framework for Hydrogen and Related Fuels

Kim Talus and Sirja-Leena Penttinen

A. Introduction: New Sustainable Fuel Targets

Similarly to many other countries, the EU has been experiencing a hydrogen boom. The EU published an ambitious Hydrogen Strategy in 2020, constituting the backbone of all EU hydrogen activities. With the Russian invasion of Ukraine and ensuing need to cut dependencies on fossil fuel sources, the EU revised its hydrogen-specific targets with the introduction of the REPowerEU plan[1], the specific focus of which is to promote the production of clean energy and diversify the energy supplies of the EU. The 'Hydrogen Accelerator' targets regarding hydrogen, published along with the REPowerEU plan, focus both on domestic production as well as hydrogen imports. According to the targets, the EU seeks to produce 10 million tonnes of domestic hydrogen and to import an equal amount by 2030.

Whilst the EU Hydrogen Strategy (i) outlined the overall vision of 'how the EU can turn clean hydrogen into a viable solution to decarbonise different sectors over time'; (ii) identified the challenges to overcome; and (iii) presented a roadmap of action for the years to come at the policy level, the legally binding sector-specific targets for hydrogen are set out in the Renewable Energy Directive.

At the time of the publication of the Hydrogen Strategy, the Renewable Energy Directive of 2018 ('RED II')[2] was in force, and did not include any hydrogen-specific provisions or targets. Instead, the recast Renewable

1 European Commission, Communication 'REPowerEU Plan' COM (2022) 230 final.
2 European Parliament and the Council Directive (EU) 2018/2001 of 11 December 2018 on the promotion of the use of energy from renewable sources (recast) [2018] OJ L 328/82 (Renewable Energy Directive II).

Energy Directive of 2023 ('RED III')[3] sets out specific hydrogen-related sector-specific targets.[4]

The agreement is to raise the share of renewable energy in the EU's overall energy consumption to 42.5 % by 2030 with an additional 2.5 % indicative top-up that would, in line with the REPowerEU Plan[5], allow the EU to reach 45 %.[6] Hydrogen produced by relying on electrolysis powered by renewable energy sources falls under the scope of the Renewable Fuels of Non-Biological Origin (RFNBO) under the EU law, for which the newly agreed framework will create specific demand side targets for a range of end-use forms. The Directive 2023 sets out sector-specific targets for RFNBO.

In the industrial sector, according to Article 22a(1) the 2023 Directive, RFNBO should provide 42 % of the hydrogen utilised in industrial processes by 2030 and that by 2035, that percentage should rise to 60 %.[7] However, as a significant relaxation of these binding targets, Member States may rely on a derogation to reduce their RFNBO share in industry by 20 % provided they are: (1) on track with their use of renewable energy (national contribution to the binding overall EU target meets their expected contribution); and (2) are using no more than 23 % fossil-based hydrogen by 2030 and 20 % fossil-based hydrogen by 2035.[8] This requirement is conjunctive so that both conditions must be fulfilled for the derogation to apply.

In the transport sector, according to Article 25 of 2023 Directive, a binding combined sub-target for advanced biofuels and RFNBO is 1 % of

3 Directive (EU) 2023/2413 of the European Parliament and of the Council of 18 October 2023 amending Directive (EU) 2018/2001, Regulation (EU) 2018/1999 and Directive 98/70/EC as regards the promotion of energy from renewable sources, and repealing Council Directive (EU) 2015/652 [2023] OJ L 2023/2413 (2023 Directive or RED III).

4 Council of the European Union formally adopted the directive on 9 October 2023. See Council of the European Union, 'Renewable energy: Council adopts new rules' <https://www.consilium.europa.eu/en/press/press-releases/2023/10/09/renewable-energy-council-adopts-new-rules/> accessed 26 August 2024.

5 European Commission, 'REPower EU' (n 1).

6 See Council of the European Union, press release, 'Council and Parliament reach provisional deal on renewable energy directive' <https://www.consilium.europa.eu/en/press/press-releases/2023/03/30/council-and-parliament-reach-provisional-deal-on-renewable-energy-directive/> accessed 26 August 2024.

7 RED III (n 3) Article 22a.

8 RED III (n 3) Article 22b.

fuels in transport by 2025, increased to 5.5 % by 2030. By 2030, the binding minimum target for RFNBO is set at 1 %.[9]

In the maritime sector, under the 2023 Directive, Member States with maritime ports should aim to ensure that by 2030, RFNBO shall occupy 1.2 % of the total amount of energy supplied to the maritime transport section.[10] The FuelEU Maritime Regulation[11] provides targets to reduce the GHG emissions that come specifically from maritime transport. In addition to specific targets for lowering GHG emissions, the legislation sets targets for RFNBO. According to the goal, if the percentage of RFNBO is still less than 1 % in 2031, a 2 % binding objective will be set for 2034.[12]

Lastly, in the aviation sector, fuel suppliers are required by the Regulation on ensuring a level playing field for sustainable air transport ('ReFuelEU Aviation Regulation')[13] to blend sustainable aviation fuels and, starting in 2030, synthetic fuels with the current jet fuel provided at EU airports. The obligation set for the aviation fuel suppliers to ensure that all fuel made available to aircraft operators at EU airports contains a minimum share of 2 % SAF from 2025 and, from 2030, a minimum share of 1.2%synthetic fuels, with both shares increasing progressively towards 2050 at which point the requirement is 70 % for SAF and 35 % for synthetic fuels.[14] 'Sustainable aviation fuels' and 'synthetic aviation fuels' include certified biofuels, RFNBOs and recycled carbon aviation fuels.

These targets, as set out now in the legislative tool, are important for the uptake of sustainable fuels and RFNBO. By creating regulatory demand for these fuels, the legislature creates a stable demand that producers can rely on when making investment decisions. Having said this, some caveats need to be considered.

9 RED III (n 3) Article 25.

10 ibid.

11 European Parliament and the Council Regulation (EU) 2023/1805 of 13 September 2023 on the use of renewable and low-carbon fuels in maritime transport, and amending Directive 2009/16/EC [2023] OJ L234/48 (ReFuelEU Maritime Regulation).

12 ReFuelEU Maritime Regulation (n 11) Article 5.

13 The Council formally adopted the new Regulation on 23 October 2023. See Council of the European Union, 'RefuelEU aviation initiative: Council adopts new law to decarbonise the aviation sector' <https://www.consilium.europa.eu/en/press/press-releases/2023/10/09/refueleu-aviation-initiative-council-adopts-new-law-to-decarbonise-the-aviation-sector/> accessed 26 August 2024.

14 ReFuelEU Aviation Regulation (n 13) Annex I.

First, how stable is the regulatory regime put in place? Does it create legal certainty that these targets will be there in the long term? On the other side, are these targets realistic? Does the EU have all the necessary components to meet these targets? This last question relates, in particular, to RFNBO and the need for significant amounts of additional renewable electricity production.

Second, and in relation to the first, the EU has now sought to promote the use of hydrogen in particular in the decarbonisation of the hard-to-abate sectors, i.e. in those sectors where other mitigation measures, such as direct electrification, would be difficult to implement. These targets focus specifically on those sectors, industry and transport, where the potential for hydrogen to reduce greenhouse gas ('GHG') emissions is considered the greatest.

In light of the concerns as to whether there is sufficient demand to stimulate investment to hydrogen production, these legally binding targets, which have been adopted *inter alia* to do just that, have been warmly welcomed. However, the target for the transport sector, in particular, has been criticised as being too modest, in addition to which it should be noted that the specific ReFuelEU targets count towards the 'general' transport sector targets. At the same time, it now seems difficult to reach even these modest targets, as prices for RFNBO remain too high and investments are being delayed.

Finally, it should be noted that the 2023 Directive does not provide any additional details as to how EU Member States should reach the targets set; instead, the Member States are free to choose the measures required to reach their national contribution, whether it is via a variety of direct or indirect measures. Significant differences in Member States approaches are clear, some setting binding national targets and others refraining from doing so.

B. Classification of Various Fuels Under the EU Framework

1. Hydrogen

(a) RFNBO under EU law

Whilst the Directives have previously focused on biogenic fuels for transport, the winds are changing. Today the 'renewable liquid and gaseous fuels of non-biological origin' or 'RFNBO' has emerged as the key concept for hydrogen and other fuels. The concept refers to a group of fuels defined under Article 2 (36) of the 2018 Directive, which provides that 'renewable liquid and gaseous transport fuels of non-biological origin means liquid or gaseous fuels which are used in the transport sector other than biofuels or biogas, the energy content of which is derived from renewable sources other than biomass.' In other words, these fuels are produced from renewable energy sources other than biomass. The more recent 2023 Directive amended the definition by eliminating the reference to "transport".

At the EU level, the key concept with regard to hydrogen is RFNBO. The relevant rules concerning the RFNBOs are provided for in several interlinked regulatory acts. While Renewable Energy Directive sets out the definition for the RFNBO, the more detailed rules, providing the methodology to determine that hydrogen is produced from renewable energy sources and achieves at least 70 % GHG emissions savings, are included in the Commission's delegated acts. The Commission's delegated acts, the Commission Delegated Regulation on methodology setting out detailed rules for the production of renewable fuels of non-biological origin ('RFNBO delegated act')[15] and Commission delegated regulation setting out the GHG calculation methodology for RFNBO and recycled carbon fuels ('GHG Methodology')[16], were adopted in the summer of 2023. The objective of these delegated acts is to ensure that hydrogen is produced from renewable energy sources and achieves at least 70 % GHG emissions savings.[17]

These delegated acts are key parts of the EU regulatory framework for hydrogen, which includes *inter alia* energy infrastructure investments and state aid rules, as well as legislative targets for renewable hydrogen for Member States, hydrogen market frameworks as well as rules around low-

15 Commission Delegated Regulation (EU) 2023/1184 of 10 February 2023 supplementing Directive (EU) 2018/2001 of the European Parliament and of the Council establishing a Union methodology setting out detailed rules for the production of renewable fuels of non-biological origin [2023] OJ L 157/11.

16 Commission Delegated Regulation (EU) 2023/1185 of 10 February 2023 supplementing Directive (EU) 2018/2001 of the European Parliament and of the Council by establishing a minimum threshold for greenhouse gas emissions savings of recycled carbon fuels and by specifying a methodology for assessing greenhouse gas emissions savings from renewable liquid and gaseous transport fuels of non-biological origin and from recycled carbon fuels [2023] OJ L 157/20.

17 European Commission, 'Renewable hydrogen' <https://energy.ec.europa.eu/topics/energy-systems-integration/hydrogen/hydrogen-delegated-acts_en> accessed 26 August 2024.

carbon hydrogen. The RFNBO delegated act provides the rules in terms of which hydrogen, hydrogen-based fuels and other synthetic fuels can be considered RFNBO, and applies to both fuels produced within the EU and imported fuels. The GHG Methodology provides the methodology for calculating life cycle GHG emissions for RFNBO, in order to determine whether they comply with the EU's GHG emissions thresholds applicable to these fuels.

Furthermore, the RFNBO delegated act provides different rules relating to the source of electricity used for hydrogen production. This is notable as when electricity is fed into the grid, it is impossible to distinguish the origin of the electrons. Thus, if renewable electricity is fed into the grid, it is not necessarily the same electrons produced by renewable energy sources that consequently make it 'green', that will be consumed. As the EU seeks to create a *renewable* or *clean* hydrogen market, it is a priority for the EU to create rules to ensure that the electricity that powers the electrolysers is produced from (non-biological) renewable energy sources. As hydrogen in itself only produces water when consumed, the emissions associated with hydrogen production depend solely on the production method. Therefore, it is critical to be able to ensure that the electricity is renewables based.

Electricity required to power the electrolyser can be either acquired via a direct connection between the renewable energy facility and the electrolyser or from the grid. The EU Commission delegated act that provides for the criteria under which the hydrogen produced is considered 'renewable' under EU law, distinguishing between electricity obtained through a direct connection and via the grid. These rules will be examined in more detail in the following paragraphs.

(b) Qualification of Electricity from a Direct Connection With an Installation Generating Renewable Electricity as Fully Renewable

Article 3 of the RFNBO delegated act, 'Rules for counting electricity obtained from direct connection to an installation generating renewable electricity as fully renewable', provides the rules for situations where the electricity to a hydrogen or hydrogen-based fuel production facility is obtained from direct connection with an installation generating renewable electricity. In this case, electricity delivered via a direct line is recognised as fully renewable if the installation generating renewable electricity has not come into operation earlier than 36 months before the installation producing the renewable fuel thus fulfilling the 'additionality' requirement, which is discussed in more detail below. In addition, the installation producing electricity should not be connected to the grid. If there is a connection to the grid, a smart metering system is required to measure electricity flows from the grid that proves no electricity was taken from the grid to produce the relevant RFNBO.

(c) Qualification of Electricity Taken from the Grid as Fully Renewable

Article 4 provides the general rules for counting electricity taken from the grid. Under this article, there are various scenarios where hydrogen or hydrogen-based fuel producers may count electricity taken from the grid as fully renewable. These are: (i) the bidding zone rule; (ii) the emission intensity rule; and (iii) the imbalance settlement rule. If none of these alternatives apply, the fuel producer may rely on the general rules of additionality and temporal and geographical correlation to prove that the electricity is renewable.

First, under the bidding zone rule, electricity is considered renewable if the installation producing hydrogen or hydrogen-based fuels is located in a bidding zone where the average proportion of renewable electricity exceeded 90 % in the previous calendar year, and the production of hydrogen or hydrogen-based fuels does not exceed a maximum number of hours set in relation to the proportion of renewable electricity in the bidding zone.

Second, under the emission intensity rule, electricity is considered renewable if the installation producing RFNBO is located in a bidding zone where the emission intensity of electricity is lower than 18 gCO2eq/MJ. However, in this scenario the fuel producer must have concluded directly, or via intermediaries, one or more renewable power purchase agreements with economic operators, producing renewable electricity in one or more installations generating renewable electricity for an amount that is at least equivalent to the amount of electricity that is claimed as fully renewable and the electricity claimed is effectively produced in this or these installations, provided that conditions of temporal and geographical correlation are met.

Third, the electricity used to produce hydrogen or hydrogen-based fuel is considered renewable if consumed during an imbalance settlement period which the fuel producer can demonstrate, based on evidence from the national transmission system operator.

Finally, if none of scenarios 1 – 3 are present, electricity taken from the grid can still be considered fully renewable where fuel producers: (i) produce an amount of renewable electricity in their own installations that is at least equivalent to the amount of electricity claimed as fully renewable; or (ii) have concluded directly, or via intermediaries, one or more renewables power purchase agreements, and the conditions on additionality, temporal correlation and geographic correlation are met. These criteria are discussed next.

(d) Additional Requirements of Additionality Temporal and Geographic Correlation

One of the key challenges with the concept of RFNBO is that it requires significant amounts of renewable electricity. From a practical perspective it appears that unless there are sufficient amounts of renewable electricity generation within the power system, the policy would target those applications where the efficiency is at its highest. This often means direct electrification. The conversion of electricity into hydrogen requires significant amounts of energy, and losses in this conversion are in the range of 30–35 %. Similarly, 13–25 % of energy is lost when hydrogen is converted into derivatives, such as ammonia, for transportation purposes and then cracked back into hydrogen.[18]

In terms of renewable electricity, the European Commission estimates that 500–550 TWh of renewable electricity is needed to produce 10 Mt of RFNBO by 2030.[19] In 2022, the EU produced 2641 TWh (terawatt-hours) of electricity.[20] Out of this, 15.9 % was wind power and 7.6 % was solar power.[21] This means that these renewable energies accounted for 23.5 % of all power produced in the EU. This translates into 620 TWh of renewable electricity from wind and solar. The EU hydrogen ambitions based on RFNBO would require almost doubling its electricity generation based on wind and solar, and much of this of new capacity would be consumed by RFNBO production.

---

18 See, for example, Irena, 'Green hydrogen – A guide to policy making' (2020) <https://www.irena.org/-/media/Files/IRENA/Agency/Publication/2020/Nov/IRENA_Green_hydrogen_policy_2020.pdf> accessed 26 August 2024.

19 European Commission, 'Questions and Answers on the EU Delegated Acts on Renewable Hydrogen' <https://ec.europa.eu/commission/presscorner/detail/en/qanda_23_595> accessed 26 August 2024.

20 European Council, 'How is EU electricity produced and sold?' <https://www.consilium.europa.eu/en/infographics/how-is-eu-electricity-produced-and-sold/> accessed 26 August 2024.

21 ibid.

Clearly, this is an enormous challenge. Significant new renewable energy production is required to meet the demand from hydrogen production. At the same time, the direct electrification of sectors like household heating and road vehicle fleets is progressing, creating additional demand for clean power. This requires tradeoffs between direct electrification and power-to-X conversion. As direct electrification does not entail the same energy losses as power-to-X, it is clear that until we can meet the entire demand for renewable electricity, preference should be given to the most efficient solutions. This means direct electrification. The EU simply cannot afford to waste renewable electricity on applications with lower efficiencies.

In order to avoid the cannibalisation effect on renewable electricity that is prone to happen should the renewable hydrogen production take off at the levels envisaged by the EU, the central criterion in determining whether the electricity used to produce RFNBO is renewable is the additionality requirement. The objective of the additionality requirement is that the renewable electricity used in RFNBO production is in addition to the renewable electricity used to meet the overall renewable energy targets and is not diverted from more efficient uses.

If RFNBO is produced by relying on grid-supplied electricity, and none of the scenarios outlined above, as enshrined in Article 4, can be applied, fuel producers may rely on the additionality requirement. The additionality requirement entails that hydrogen or hydrogen-based fuel producers conclude power purchase agreements ('PPAs') with new (i.e. which have come into operation not earlier than 36 months before the hydrogen or renewable fuel facility) and unsupported (no operating or investment aid) renewable electricity generation capacity.[22] To support the early scale-up of electrolysers, a grandfathering clause was included in Article 4 and hydrogen or hydrogen-based fuel production capacity that comes into operation before 2028 is exempted from these rules for 10 years, up until 1 January 2038.

In addition, the fuel produced must meet the requirement of temporal and geographic correlation. What this essentially means, is that the time and location of the RFNBO production must match those of the electricity production. Temporal correlation requires that the production of the hy-

22 These requirements, among others, are further elaborated in the Commission 'Q&A implementation of hydrogen delegated acts' document. See European Commission, 'Q&A implementation of hydrogen delegated acts' <https://energy.ec.europa.eu/document/download/21fb4725-7b32-4264-9f36-96cd54cff148_en?filename=2024%2003%2014%20Document%20on%20Certification.pdf> accessed 26 August 2024.

drogen or hydrogen-based fuel uses electricity taken from the grid during either the same one-month period (until 31 December 2029) or the same one-hour period (starting from 1 January 2030) as the renewable electricity production under the relevant PPA. The temporal correlation condition is always considered to be met where the hydrogen or hydrogen-based fuel is produced during a one-hour period where the clearing price of electricity is lower or equal to 20 euros per MWh or lower than 36 % of the EU carbon price during the relevant period.

In turn, the geographic correlation rule requires that at least one of the following criteria is met:

1. the installation generating renewable electricity under the PPA is located, or was located at the time when it came into operation, in the same bidding zone as the electrolyser; and/or
2. the installation generating renewable electricity under the renewables PPA is located in an offshore bidding zone that is interconnected with the bidding zone where the electrolyser is located; and/or
3. the installation generating renewable electricity is located in an interconnected bidding zone, including in another Member State, and electricity prices in the relevant time period on the day-ahead are equal to or higher than in the production facility's bidding zone.

Member States may introduce additional criteria concerning the location of electrolysers and the installation producing renewable electricity in order to ensure compatibility of capacity additions with the national planning of the hydrogen and electricity grid. These additional criteria cannot, however, impact negatively on the functioning of the internal electricity market.

Under the definition provided by the Renewable Energy Directive and the RFNBO delegated act, hydrogen produced via electrolysis from renewable electricity fulfilling the requirements as set out in the delegated acts is considered RFNBO. However, hydrogen is not the only RFNBO, but instead, fuels such as ammonia, methanol or e-fuels are similarly considered RFNBOs when produced from renewable hydrogen. In this case, the fuel is produced from RFNBO and CO2. This means that the regulation of CO2 capture and utilisation is relevant for these other fuels.

There are three fuels that rely on CCU technology under the Renewable Energy Directive: e-fuels, recycled carbon fuels and biofuels where CO2 can used as feedstock in the production.[23] These will be examined next.

C. Other Sustainable Fuels Under the New EU Framework

1. Electrofuels

If the main target of the EU strategy is to create the preconditions for the production of renewable hydrogen, the second related leg of this strategy is focused on CO2. Electrofuels, better known by their acronym e-fuels, are produced by combining renewable hydrogen with captured CO2. The production of e-fuels therefore relies on carbon capture and utilisation (CCU).

CCU, however, requires significant amounts of additional electricity, just like hydrogen production. When done, these e-fuels then work like conventional fossil fuels with the key difference that they are climate-neutral – as such, they reduce the emissions associated with combustion car engines, and therefore provide a greener alternative while keeping the traditional combustion car industry alive as the same infrastructure can be relied on. E-fuels can be produced in either power-to-gas or power-to-liquid processes depending on the e-fuel required. While the first step of the production is hydrogen production by electrolysis from renewable electricity, the required e-fuel dictates the rest CO2 is combined with hydrogen to produce e-crude and synthetic methane or methanol, whereas nitrogen is combined to produce synthetic ammonia. Similar to its fossil fuel-based counterpart, synthetic crude oil must be refined to produce synthetic kerosene or diesel.

The difference to many other CCU options is that the captured CO2 used in e-fuel production is intended to be released back into the atmosphere at the point of use of the fuel. The essential element in e-fuels is thus CO2, which can be either captured from the atmosphere or from the industrial facilities that use fossil fuels in their operations. Because of the variety of methods and sources to capture CO2, the e-fuel (production) costs as well as sustainability credentials depend on the source of CO2. This is critical as a key issue with e-fuels, recycled carbon fuels and advanced

23 See also, Kim Talus/Reza Maddahi, 'Carbon Capture and Utilization Under EU Law; Impermanent Storage of CO_2 in Products and Pre-combustion Carbon Capture' (2024) 00 Journal of World Energy Law and Business 1.

biofuels is whether they can be counted towards EU, national or company level quotas or targets and EU or Member State levels.

When meeting the requirements of the GHG Methodology, e-fuels produced from renewable hydrogen and CO2 fall under the scope of RFNBO and can therefore be counted towards the fuel obligations under the Renewable Energy Directive or other sectoral rules (for aviation or maritime for example). As will be seen in more detail in the next section, in the context of recycled carbon fuels, meeting these quotas in the future will require the use of biogenic CO2.

2. Recycled Carbon Fuels

In addition to e-fuels, recycled carbon fuels are emerging as a more sustainable fuel alternative in the EU framework. Under Article 2 (35) of the Renewable Energy Directive, 'recycled carbon fuels' means liquid and gaseous fuels that are produced from liquid or solid waste streams of non-renewable origin which are not suitable for material recovery in accordance with Article 4 of Directive 2008/98/EC, or from waste processing gas and exhaust gas of non-renewable origin which are produced as an unavoidable and unintentional consequence of the production process in industrial installations. This definition of 'recycled carbon fuels' connects to the EU waste hierarchy under the Waste Framework Directive[24] and ensures that the priority is for recycling over fuel application.

These recycled carbon fuels can replace petroleum-based fuels with more sustainable options, similarly to e-fuels, that can be used directly in the existing transport infrastructure for maritime shipping or aviation, for example.[25]

As already stated, under Article 25 of the Renewable Energy Directive, the combined share of advanced biofuels and biogas produced from a range of biogenic waste[26] and of RFNBO in the energy supplied to the transport sector must be at least 1 % in 2025 and 5.5 % in 2030, of which at least

24 Directive 2008/98/EC of the European parliament and of the Council of 19 November 2008 on waste and repealing certain Directives [2008] OJ L 312/3.

25 For an early discussion, see Christopher Graves/Sune D. Ebbesen/Mogens Mogensen/Klaus S. Lackner, 'Sustainable hydrocarbon fuels by recycling CO2 and H2O with renewable or nuclear energy' 15/1 (2011) Renewable and Sustainable Energy Reviews 1.

26 This refers to the biogenic feedstock listed in Part A of Annex IX of RED II (n 2).

1 % is RFNBO in 2030. Member States can count recycled carbon fuels towards their transport targets[27] as long as the recycled carbon fuels meet the minimum requirements, especially that of GHG emissions savings of at least 70 %.

Therefore, the central criteria in determining whether recycled carbon fuels fall under the scope of sustainable fuels is the GHG emissions savings. GHG Methodology sets a minimum GHG emissions saving threshold of 70 % for all types of recycled carbon fuels.[28] As such, it is necessary for any renewable fuel that has carbon content to comply with this 70 % emission savings requirement. Given that the combustion of these fuels produces the same GHG emissions as fossil fuels, they rely on avoided emissions to meet the 70 % threshold. This can be done through captured and reused CO2. Captured CO2 can be deducted from the carbon footprint of the recycled carbon fuel (as well as RFNBO).

Emissions from existing use or fate include all emissions in the existing use or fate of the input that are avoided when the input is used for fuel production. These emissions include the CO2 equivalent of the carbon incorporated in the chemical composition of the fuel that would have otherwise been emitted as CO2 into the atmosphere. This means that the GHG Methodology treats sustainable CO2 as carbon neutral as the release of CO2 during combustion is still taken into account (and reduction only takes place at the level of fuel production). This includes CO2 that was captured and incorporated into the fuel provided that at least one of the following conditions is fulfilled:

(a) Industrial CO2: The CO2 has been captured from an industrial activity, accounted for upstream in an effective carbon pricing system and incorporated in the chemical composition of the fuel before 2036 (or 2041 in other cases than CO2 stemming from the combustion of fuels for electricity generation).
(b) Direct air capture of CO2.
(c) Biogenic CO2: The captured CO2 stems from the production or the combustion of biofuels, bioliquids or biomass fuels complying with the sustainability and GHG saving criteria and the CO2 capture did not receive credits for emission savings from CO2 capture and replacement under the 2018 Directive. Biomass may not be combusted strictly as a carbon source.

---

27 RFNBO delegated act and Article 25 of RED III (n 3).
28 Article 2 of the GHG Methodology. Also incorporated in Article 29a of RED III (n 3).

(d) CO_2 from RFNBO or recycled carbon fuels: The captured CO_2 stems from the combustion of RFNBO or recycled carbon fuels complying with the GHG saving criteria.
(e) Geological CO_2: The captured CO_2 stems from a geological source of CO_2 and the CO_2 was previously released naturally.[29]

As illustrated, the GHG Methodology prohibits the use of CO_2 stemming from industrial sources for the production of RFNBO from 2041 onwards. Options remaining are largely restricted to direct air capture or biogenic CO_2. Given the costs associated with direct air capture, without significant cost reduction, the clear focus after 2041 is on biogenic CO_2. Biogenic CO_2 comprises CO_2 that stems from the production or the combustion of sustainable biomass. CO_2 from the treatment of biogenic waste is also eligible. In order to be eligible to count as emissions from existing use or fate ex-use[30], biogenic CO_2 must comply with the sustainability and GHG saving criteria and must not have received credits for emissions savings from CO_2 capture and replacement.[31]

3. Biofuels Under the Renewable Energy Directive of 2023

Whilst the previous sections have discussed the regulatory framework concerning emerging new fuels such as hydrogen and e-fuels, biofuels continue to play a role in the EU decarbonisation efforts. As these emerging new fuels are not yet available at scale, there is still a need for liquid fuels for heavy transport, maritime transport and aviation, for instance. Biofuels are therefore considered a tool for increasing the share of renewable energy and reducing GHG intensity in the transport sector.

Biofuels were a major source of renewable energy within the EU in 2021. Within this area, primary solid biofuels held the largest share at 70.3 %. Liquid biofuels accounted for 12.9 %, the share of biogas/biomethane was 10.1 %, and the renewable share of municipal waste held a 6.6 % share.[32] This share is set to increase and, for example, the current EU production

29 Commission Delegated Regulation, 'GHG Methodology' (n 20).
30 "Emissions from inputs' existing use or fate".
31 European Commission (n 22).
32 European Commission, 'Union Bioenergy Sustainability Report' COM (2023) 650 final.

target for 2030 is to increase biomethane production by 50 % (up to 35 bcm of biomethane).[33]

Biofuels are considered in the specific transport targets under Article 25 of the Renewable Energy Directive, with the limitation that at least 1 % of the supplier fuel obligation needs to consist of RFNBO. The current focus is on advanced biofuels from feedstock listed in Part A of Annex IX of the Directive. These are non-food resources, like biowaste[34], biomass fractions of waste and residues from forestry and forest-based industries, or certain biomass fractions of mixed municipal waste. Under Article 25 of the Directive, Member States are also encouraged to set differentiated targets for advanced biofuels and biogas and RFNBO.

Importantly for national incentivisation schemes, and the demand of biofuels, Article 27 of the Renewable Energy Directive, which provides for the calculation rules for the minimum share of sustainable fuels in the transport sector, provides that the share of biofuels and biogas are considered to be twice its energy content.

For biomass, the Directive introduces stricter criteria on the use of biomass to ensure that the EU does not subsidise unsustainable practices. It provides that:

In line with the cascading principle, woody biomass should be used according to its highest economic and environmental added value in the following order of priorities: 1) wood-based products; 2) extending their service life; 3) re-use; 4) recycling; 5) bio-energy; and 6) disposal.[35] Member States' support schemes for bioenergy should therefore be directed towards such feedstocks for which little market competition exists with the

33 European Commission, 'REPowerEU' (n 1) 8. RED III (n 3) refers, in recital 9, to the achievement of the Union's target of an annual production of sustainable biomethane of 35 billion cubic meters by 2030, as set out in the Commission staff working document of 18 May 2022 accompanying the REPowerEU Plan, entitled 'Implementing the Repower EU Action Plan: Investment needs, hydrogen accelerator and achieving the bio-methane targets'.

34 Under point (4) of Article 3 of Directive 2008/98/EC, biowaste means 'biodegradable garden and park waste, food and kitchen waste from households, restaurants, caterers and retail premises and comparable waste from food processing plants'. Such biowaste from private households can be used as feedstock for advanced biofuels where they are subject to separate collection prior to the transport to a waste treatment facility.

35 RED III (n 3), preamble 4 and Article 3(3).

material sectors, and whose sourcing is considered positive for both climate and biodiversity.[36]

Member States are allowed to derogate from the cascading principle in duly justified circumstances, for example where required for security of energy supply purposes, such as in the case of particularly severe cold conditions. Member States are also allowed to derogate from the cascading principle where there are no industries or processing facilities that could make a higher added value use of certain feedstocks within a geographical perimeter.[37] These feedstocks are:

(a) necessary forest management activities, aiming at ensuring precommercial thinning operations or in compliance with national legislation on wildfire prevention in high-risk areas;
(b) salvage logging following documented natural disturbances; or
(c) harvest of certain woods whose characteristics are not suitable for local processing facilities.[38]

For processes that result in biomass being processed with fossil fuels in a common process, Article 28(5) of the Renewable Energy Directive empowers the Commission to adopt delegated acts specifying the methodology to determine the share of biofuel, and biogas for transport in this connection.

D. Discussion – Future Uncertainties

The general trend with the 2023 Directive is increasingly ambitious targets covering more and more sectors, but the possibility of giving the Member States the option to reduce their RFNBO share in the industry by 20 % is of importance as this allows for incorporating other types of low-carbon hydrogen such as blue, pink as well as orange. With this change, it is possible that Member States taking the advantage of the target reduction for RFNBO, would provide support for other types of low-carbon hydrogen. The clear advantage of this would be that it would better consider national circumstances. It would also alleviate the issue with the amounts of renew-

36 RED III (n 3), preamble 4.
37 RED III (n 3), preamble 4.
38 RED III (n 3), Article 3(3).

able electricity discussed above. For these low-carbon hydrogen options, the 70 % GHG emissions saving applies.[39]

In addition, an adjustment mechanism for the methodology identifying when electricity used for producing RFNBO can be considered fully renewable has been introduced. In this respect, the 2023 Directive incorporates the RFNBO delegated act rules on additionality, temporal correlation, and geographic correlation for RFNBO production, but further includes a possibility to revisit the methodology for defining RFNBO. By 1 July 2028, the Commission should assess the impact of the methodology defining when electricity used for producing RFNBO can be considered fully renewable. This report would need to assess in particular their impact on the availability and affordability of RFNBO for industry and transport and on the ability of the EU to achieve its RFNBO targets taking into account the EU strategy for imported and domestic hydrogen while minimising the increase in GHG emissions in the electricity sector and the overall energy system. If these objectives are not met and the EU targets for RFNBO for 2030 are not going to be met, then the Commission should review the EU methodology and, where appropriate, adopt a delegated act to modify such methodology to provide the necessary adjustments to the criteria in order to facilitate the ramp-up of the hydrogen industry.[40] These changes, and potential future changes, can create scope for policy adjustments that could work to reduce the challenges in meeting renewable electricity demands in the future.

The Strategy was adopted in 2020 – not too many years ago – and legislative action has since been taken to further the objectives as set out in the Strategy. This policy framework is already being adapted.[41] While the scope of the Strategy was very wide, covering many sectors such as household heating and road transport, the current legislative tools signal more targeted action, focusing on the hard-to-abate sectors such as transport – aviation and maritime – as well as industry. Some sectors, that were perhaps initially envisaged to be powered or fueled by hydrogen under the

39 For a discussion on other types of hydrogen within the EU framework, see Kim Talus/Francisca Gallegos/Jaqueline Pinto, 'Realism at the end of the rainbow? An argument towards diversifying hydrogen in EU regulation' (2024)17/4 Journal of World Energy Law and Business 217.

40 RED III (n 3), preamble 34a and Article 27(6).

41 For example, Germany revised its national hydrogen strategy in 2023, French revised strategy is expected in 2023 and RED III creates the potential for further amendments over the next years.

Strategy, are moving away from hydrogen as direct electrification is (still) considered the priority mechanism for decarbonization for various reasons, the most important of which are cost and efficiency. Similarly, while the initial focus seemed to be only on RFNBO, the current developments at the legislative level indicate a more flexible approach towards low-carbon hydrogen, as its role as a transition fuel – at least – has been acknowledged.

This lack of coherence between the overarching policy level and legislative level, due to many uncertainties and open questions, is natural and to be expected, but at the same time unfortunate as it reduces certainty about the desired end result. As the objective is the rapid creation of a hydrogen market, rapid deployment of capital for investments is a key consideration. While there is still uncertainty at the policy level, legislative action has also commenced. Both Member States and the EU are already regulating the future hydrogen market. Because of the uncertainties at the level of policy, it is likely that this detailed regulatory framework will be amended in the future. While understandable from the viewpoint of the regulation of new technologies and markets, this uncertainty nevertheless will have implications for the speed of investments within the EU.

The 2023 Directive extends the RFNBO rules to new sectors and sets new demand-side targets. At the same time, an important change which it brings about, contrary to the 2018 Directive, is that while the RFNBO sub-targets contribute towards the overall renewable energy targets, the renewable electricity used to produce RFNBO will not be counted.

When calculating the share of renewable energy in a Member State, RFNBO should be counted in the sector where they are consumed (electricity, heating and cooling, or transport). To avoid double-counting, the renewable electricity used to produce those fuels should not be counted. This will have the benefit of allowing the real energy consumed to be counted, taking account of energy losses in the process to produce those fuels. It also allows RFNBO imported into and consumed in the EU to be counted.[42] At the same time, this change will have trade implications between Member States, as those states that plan to import hydrogen will have the energy in imported hydrogen counted (Germany for instance), whereas those states that plan to export hydrogen cannot count the renewable electricity used to produce hydrogen towards their national targets (Finland for instance).

42 RED III (n 3), preamble 12, Article 7. For RFNBO imports, see Talus/Gallegos/Pinto (n 39).

This aggravates the renewable electricity problem for hydrogen-exporting Member States.

Bibliography

Council of the European Union, 'Renewable energy: Council adopts new rules' <https://www.consilium.europa.eu/en/press/press-releases/2023/10/09/renewable-energy-council-adopts-new-rules/> accessed 26 August 2024

Council of the European Union, press release, 'Council and Parliament reach provisional deal on renewable energy directive' <https://www.consilium.europa.eu/en/press/press-releases/2023/03/30/council-and-parliament-reach-provisional-deal-on-renewable-energy-directive/> accessed 26 August 2024

Council of the European Union, 'RefuelEU aviation initiative: Council adopts new law to decarbonise the aviation sector' <https://www.consilium.europa.eu/en/press/press-releases/2023/10/09/refueleu-aviation-initiative-council-adopts-new-law-to-decarbonise-the-aviation-sector/> accessed 26 August 2024

European Commission, Communication 'REPowerEU Plan' COM (2022) 230 final

European Commission, 'Q&A implementation of hydrogen delegated acts' <https://energy.ec.europa.eu/document/download/21fb4725-7b32-4264-9f36-96cd54cff148_en?filename=2024%2003%2014%20Document%20on%20Certification.pdf> accessed 26 August 2024

European Commission, 'Questions and Answers on the EU Delegated Acts on Renewable Hydrogen' <https://ec.europa.eu/commission/presscorner/detail/en/qanda_23_595> accessed 26 August 2024

European Commission, 'Union Bioenergy Sustainability Report' COM (2023) 650 final

European Council, 'How is EU electricity produced and sold?' <https://www.consilium.europa.eu/en/infographics/how-is-eu-electricity-produced-and-sold/> accessed 26 August 2024

European Commission, 'Renewable hydrogen' <https://energy.ec.europa.eu/topics/energy-systems-integration/hydrogen/hydrogen-delegated-acts_en> accessed 26 August 2024

Graves C/Ebbesen S D/Mogensen M/Lackner K S, 'Sustainable hydrocarbon fuels by recycling CO2 and H2O with renewable or nuclear energy' 15/1 (2011) Renewable and Sustainable Energy Reviews 1

Irena, 'Green hydrogen – A guide to policy making' (2020) <https://www.irena.org/-/media/Files/IRENA/Agency/Publication/2020/Nov/IRENA_Green_hydrogen_policy_2020.pdf> accessed 26 August 2024

Talus K/Maddahi R, 'Carbon Capture and Utilization Under EU Law; Impermanent Storage of CO2 in Products and Pre-combustion Carbon Capture' (2024) 00 Journal of World Energy Law and Business 1

Talus K/Gallegos F/Pinto J, 'Realism at the end of the rainbow? An argument towards diversifying hydrogen in EU regulation' (2024)17/4 Journal of World Energy Law and Business 217

Advancing the Energy Transition through Industrial Policy: Lessons from a Transatlantic Comparison

Michael A. Mehling

A. Introduction

Following years of mostly incremental progress, the urgency of climate change has increased pressure for a more transformative approach to decarbonization of the economy. Recently, this challenge has given rise to a growing trend towards deployment of green industrial policy to accelerate the transition from a fossil-fuel-based economy to a sustainable, low-carbon alternative. This chapter traces efforts of the United States (U.S.) and the European Union (EU) to harness green industrial policies as a means of achieving committed climate targets alongside further social and economic objectives, and explores the merits and possible risks of their distinct approaches.

During the administration of President Joseph R. Biden, the U.S. took a series of bold legislative steps including the Infrastructure Investment and Jobs Act (IIJA) and the Inflation Reduction Act (IRA), marking a pronounced shift from past reliance on executive rulemaking to public support for the production and deployment of low-carbon technologies as well as infrastructural renewal.[1] Similarly, the EU, with its ambitious European Green Deal and its implementing legislation, has embraced a comprehensive industrial policy framework to drive the region towards climate neutrality by 2050.[2] Both jurisdictions have seen a recent pivot in their policy approaches following major elections, yet still offer insightful lessons for the role of industrial policy in the decarbonization of energy systems.

---

1 Daniel A Farber, 'Turning Point: Green Industrial Policy and the Future of U.S. Climate Action' (2024) 11 Texas A&M Law Review 303.

2 Reinhilde Veugelers/Simone Tagliapietra/Cecilia Trasi, 'Green Industrial Policy in Europe: Past, Present, and Prospects' (2024) 24 Journal of Industry, Competition and Trade 4.

Legislative efforts deployed in the U.S. and the EU offer alternative models of how green industrial policy can facilitate the energy transition. While both jurisdictions have deployed a portfolio of measures, the U.S. approach has been dominated by fiscal incentives,[3] whereas the EU has deployed a more balanced combination of support measures and constraints.[4] In its exploration of the role of green industrial policy in accelerating the energy transition on both sides of the Atlantic, this chapter begins by defining green industrial policy and tracing its historical evolution (Section B). It then outlines the green industrial policy strategies of the United States and the European Union (Section C), and offers a comparative analysis that summarizes findings of the chapter and highlights risks and merits of each approach (Section D).

B. The Rise of Green Industrial Policy

Industrial policy – defined as government interventions that alter the structure of an economy, encouraging resources to move into sectors that are seen as desirable for future development[5] – has historically elicited mixed reactions. From criticism of its potential to distort markets[6] to acknowledg-

3 John ET Bistline/Neil Mehrotra/Catherine Wolfram, 'Economic Implications of the Climate Provisions of the Inflation Reduction Act' (Brookings 2023) <https://www.brookings.edu/wp-content/uploads/2023/03/BPEA_Spring2023_Bistline-et-al_unembargoedUpdated.pdf> accessed 26 August 2024.

4 Simone Tagliapietra/Reinhilde Veugelers, 'Developing a Green Industrial Policy for the European Green Deal' in Fernando J Díaz López/Massimiliano Mazzanti/Roberto Zoboli (eds), Handbook on Innovation, Society and the Environment (Edward Elgar Publishing 2023) 36.

5 Tilman Altenburg/Claudia Assmann, 'Green Industrial Policy: Concept, Policies, Country Experiences' (UN Environment 2017) <https://wedocs.unep.org/bitstream/handle/20.500.11822/22277/Green_industrial_policy.pdf> accessed 26 August 2024.

6 Reda Cherif/Fuad Hasanov, 'The Return of the Policy That Shall Not Be Named: Principles of Industrial Policy' (International Monetary Fund 2019) Working Paper 2019/074 <https://www.imf.org/en/Publications/WP/Issues/2019/03/26/The-Return-of-the-Policy-That-Shall-Not-Be-Named-Principles-of-Industrial-Policy-46710> accessed 26 August 2024; Shantayanan Devarajan, 'Three Reasons Why Industrial Policy Fails' (Brookings, 2016) <https://www.brookings.edu/articles/three-reasons-why-industrial-policy-fails>; Michelle Clark Neely, 'The Pitfalls of Industrial Policy' (1993) 1 The Regional Economist 10.

ment – in some cases even by earlier skeptics[7] – of its role in fostering economic growth and technological advancement, industrial policy has traditionally stirred forceful opinions. An initial wave of public debate about its merits and shortcomings was occasioned by the success of Japanese efforts to accelerate the economic recovery after World War II, in the process turning the country into a dominant exporter of commodities and consumer products.[8]

While western nations had certainly been known to resort to market interventions in support of vulnerable or strategic industries, the prevailing sentiment at the time – overshadowed by the broader geopolitical conflict between capitalist free-market and centrally planned economies – held that the costs of industrial policy outweighed its benefits.[9] More recently, however, interest in industrial policy has been renewed by the global ascent of Chinese manufacturing, which has likewise benefited from substantial government intervention and prompted accusations of unfair trade practices that have contributed to competitive distortions and excess supplies in key markets.[10]

Recent efforts to take stock of Chinese industrial policy initiatives have affirmed a surge especially in direct government subsidies, finding these to be several times higher than those in Europe and North America.[11] Still, research published by the International Monetary Fund has shown that the

7 Paul Krugman, 'How to Think About Green Industrial Policy' (New York Times, 9 May 2023); compare to Paul Krugman, 'Targeted Industrial Policies: Theory and Evidence' (1983) Proceedings: Economic Policy Symposium – Jackson Hole 123.

8 James E Vestal, 'Japanese Industrial Policy, Past and Future' in James E Vestal (ed), Planning for Change: Industrial Policy and Japanese Economic Development, 1945–1990 (Oxford University Press 1995).

9 See, in particular, Lester C Thurow, Head to Head: The Economic Battle Among Japan, Europe, and America (William Morrow & Co 1992); and earlier Richard N Cooper, 'Industrial Policy and Trade Distortion: A Policy Perspective' in Ali M El-Agraa (ed), Protection, Cooperation, Integration and Development: Essays in Honour of Professor Hiroshi Kitamura (Palgrave Macmillan UK 1987) <https://doi.org/10.1007/978-1-349-09370-0_3> accessed 26 August 2024.

10 Ravi Agrawal, 'The White House's Case for Industrial Policy' (*Foreign Policy*, 2 March 2023) <https://foreignpolicy.com/2023/03/02/live-industrial-policy-katherine-tai-trade-economy-chips-inflation> accessed 26 August 2024; Gerard DiPippo/Ilaria Mazzocco/Scott Kennedy, 'Red Ink: Estimating Chinese Industrial Policy Spending in Comparative Perspective' (Center for Strategic and International Studies (CSIS) 2022) <https://www.csis.org/analysis/red-ink-estimating-chinese-industrial-policy-spending-comparative-perspective> accessed 12 August 2024.

11 Wan-Hsin Liu et al., 'Foul Play? On the Scale and Scope of Industrial Subsidies in China' (Kiel Institute for the World Economy 2024) Policy Brief 173 <https://www.if

current wave of industrial policy activity is primarily driven by advanced economies, with subsidies again the most employed instrument.[12] A further trend with consequential implications is the inclusion of restrictions – such as local content requirements (LCRs) – in a vast majority of such subsidies, distorting international trade and prompting retaliatory measures from trade partners that increasingly threaten to fragment the global economy.[13]

Unlike earlier rounds of public debate on industrial policy, however, the current discussion is also influenced by the simultaneous need to respond to climate change and deliver political responses that advance investment in low-carbon technology manufacturing and deployment. For instance, the probably most aggressive example of contemporary industrial policy, the Chinese 'Made in China 2025' strategy, is heavily oriented towards supporting low-carbon technologies identified as 'strategically important', such as electric vehicles and renewable energy.[14]

Whereas traditional industrial policy has focused on productivity enhancement as a lever to ensure growing returns to capital and labor, this current wave of industrial policies also pursues sustainability goals and seeks to advance the requisite structural transformation of the economy. Often described with the label 'green industrial policy', its stated goal is to align social and economic interests with environmental policy outcomes.[15] By fostering an ecosystem conducive to the development and scaling of clean energy technologies, green industrial policies promise to catalyze

---

w-kiel.de/publications/foul-play-on-the-scale-and-scope-of-industrial-subsidies-in-china-32738> accessed 26 August 2024.

12 Simon Evenett et al., 'The Return of Industrial Policy in Data' (International Monetary Fund (IMF) 2024) Working Paper 2024/001 <https://www.imf.org/en/Publications/WP/Issues/2023/12/23/The-Return-of-Industrial-Policy-in-Data-542828> accessed 26 August 2024.

13 Réka Juhász/Nathan J Lane, 'The Political Economy of Industrial Policy' (National Bureau of Economic Research 2024) Working Paper 32507 <http://www.nber.org/papers/w32507> accessed 26 August 2024.

14 State Council, 'Notice of the State Council on the Publication of "Made in China 2025" (Unofficial Translation)' <https://cset.georgetown.edu/wp-content/uploads/t0432_made_in_china_2025_EN.pdf>; Similarly, the 14th Five-Year Plan sets out a mandate to 'develop and expand strategic emerging industries', see National People's Congress, 'The 14th Five-Year Plan for National Economic and Social Development and the Long-Range Objectives Through the Year 2035' <http://www.gov.cn/xinwen/2021-03/13/content_5592657.htm> accessed 26 August 2024.

15 Dani Rodrik, 'Green Industrial Policy' (2014) 30 Oxford Review of Economic Policy 469.

new industries, spur employment opportunities, and stimulate economic diversification.[16]

Several factors have favored the emergence of green industrial policy as a key strategy to address several interrelated priorities: deep economic shocks, rising geopolitical tensions, and the growing urgency of climate action. It first garnered widespread attention in the wake of the economic and financial crisis of 2008, when a 'green recovery' was advocated as a dual engine of economic revival and environmental sustainability.[17] Later, China's assertive move to dominate low-carbon technology manufacturing spurred a broader shift towards green industrial policy, highlighting the competitive and strategic dimensions of leadership in the transition to clean energy.[18]

More recently, the adoption of green industrial policies by the U.S. and the EU has also been justified by a strategic need to enhance energy security and fortify low-carbon technology supply chains against the backdrop of global challenges such as the COVID-19 pandemic and escalating geopolitical tensions.[19] A steady acceleration of climate policy ambition, both in international agreements and through national commitments, has also contributed to a growing sense that state intervention is justified beyond mere correction of market failures, for instance to address the high initial costs and attendant risks of relevant climate solutions, while also managing the social impacts and evolving workforce needs of a just energy transition.[20]

Its astonishing rise notwithstanding, the embrace of green industrial policy has also evinced concerns. Critics highlight the risks of policy misalign-

---

16 Jonas Nahm, Collaborative Advantage: Forging Green Industries in the New Global Economy (Oxford University Press 2021).

17 Edward B Barbier, A Global Green New Deal: Rethinking the Economic Recovery (Cambridge University Press 2010).

18 Joanna I Lewis, 'The Climate Risk of Green Industrial Policy' (2024) 123 Current History 14.

19 Miranda A Schreurs, 'Jockeying for Climate Leadership Amidst Rising Global Tensions: China, USA and the European Union' in Sebastian Biba (ed), Europe in an Era of US-China Strategic Rivalry: Challenges and Opportunities from an Outside-in Perspective (Springer Nature Switzerland 2024) 243.

20 Francesco Lamperti et al., 'The Green Transition: Public Policy, Finance, and the Role of the State' (2019) 88 Vierteljahrshefte zur Wirtschaftsforschung 73; going back to Mariana Mazzucato, The Entrepreneurial State: Debunking Public vs. Private Sector Myths (Anthem Press 2013); for a review of the evolving literature on industrial policy, see Réka Juhász/Nathan Lane/Dani Rodrik, 'The New Economics of Industrial Policy' (2024) 16 Annual Review of Economics 213.

ment leading to market distortions, where poorly calibrated policies might inadvertently hinder innovation by funneling resources into less efficient or unproven technologies, crowding out private investment, and nurturing rent-seeking behavior and reliance on governmental support rather than genuine market competitiveness.[21] Likewise, the aforementioned specter of protectionism and its threat to the international economic order is also evident in green industrial policy.[22]

Despite such risks, green industrial policy can play a beneficial role in advancing the global energy transition. Targeted support for research and development in low-carbon technologies can hasten innovation breakthroughs,[23] thereby contributing to decarbonization efforts everywhere. In a climate policy landscape marked by asymmetric climate action under the decentralized architecture of the Paris Agreement, declining low-carbon technology costs may prove essential to overcoming freeriding incentives, competitiveness concerns, and negative spillover effects such as emissions leakage.[24] Additionally, deployment of green industrial policy can also contribute to more diversified and resilient supply chains for rare earth metals and other critical materials and components, reversing excessive reliance on individual countries such as China.[25]

---

21 See, for instance, Scott Lincicome/Huan Zhu, 'Questioning Industrial Policy: Why Government Manufacturing Plans Are Ineffective and Unnecessary' (Cato Institute 2021) White Paper <https://www.cato.org/sites/cato.org/files/2021-09/white-paper-questioning-industrial-policy-updated.pdf> accessed 26 August 2024.

22 Kimberly A Clausing/Catherine Wolfram, 'Putting Progress over Protectionism in Climate Policy' (RealTime Economics, 19 December 2023) <https://www.piie.com/blogs/realtime-economics/putting-progress-over-protectionism-climate-policy> accessed 30 March 2024; Joanna I Lewis, 'The Rise of Renewable Energy Protectionism: Emerging Trade Conflicts and Implications for Low Carbon Development' (2014) 14 Global Environmental Politics 10.

23 Mariana Mazzucato, 'Financing the Green New Deal' (2022) 5 Nature Sustainability 93; David C Popp, 'Innovation and Climate Policy' (2010) 2 Annual Review of Resource Economics 275.

24 See, for instance, the global spillover benefits from solar energy support policies adopted in selected jurisdictions, Todd D Gerarden, 'Demanding Innovation: The Impact of Consumer Subsidies on Solar Panel Production Costs' (2023) 69 Management Science 7799; John Paul Helveston/Gang He/Michael R Davidson, 'Quantifying the Cost Savings of Global Solar Photovoltaic Supply Chains' (2022) 612 Nature 83.

25 Andreas Goldthau/Llewelyn Hughes, 'Protect Global Supply Chains for Low-Carbon Technologies' (2020) 585 Nature 28; Andreas Goldthau/Llewelyn Hughes/Jonas Nahm, 'The Political Logic of Reshoring in Low Carbon Technologies: Economic Interdependence and Green Industrial Policy' (2022) <https://papers.ssrn.com/abstract=4066047> accessed 26 March 2024; Jan Mertens et al., 'From Emissions

While discourses on green industrial policy may continue to oscillate between advocacy of its prospective benefits and concern about its potential risks, policy makers grappling with the need to advance decarbonization are likely to continue drawing on this policy option, not least at a time when climate policy features prominently on electoral agendas worldwide.[26] In a world of increasingly fragmented markets and growing geopolitical competition, that is likely to remain the case even as priorities evolve and some jurisdictions withdraw – at least temporarily – from efforts to decarbonize their economies. Ongoing evaluation of green industrial policies is therefore of continued relevance, as is understanding lessons derived from their design and implementation. Accordingly, the next section describes specific green industrial policy initiatives deployed in recent years in the United States and the European Union, and assesses their potential impact on the prospects of the energy transition and industrial decarbonization.

C. Transatlantic Approaches to Green Industrial Policy

1. Green Industrial Policy in the United States

(a) Background and Context

Although a notoriously unsteady actor in domestic and international climate policy, the United States has nonetheless pioneered the use of industrial policy in ways that have influenced other actors, including the EU. Lessons learned in the process therefore bear careful study as other jurisdictions – and indeed future U.S. administrations – turn to industrial policy to advance climate policy objectives and the decarbonization of energy systems.

U.S. deployment of green industrial policy can be traced back to the environmental movement of the 1960s and 1970s, which catalyzed the enactment of landmark legislation such as the Clean Air Act and the Clean Water Act. While these early efforts lacked an explicit link to industrial policy, they set the stage for subsequent discussions on sustainable industrial

to Resources: Mitigating the Critical Raw Materials Supply Chain Vulnerability of Renewable Energy Technologies' (2024) Mineral Economics <https://doi.org/10.1007/s13563-024-00425-2> accessed 26 August 2024.

26 David M Driesen/Michael A Mehling/David C Popp, 'Industrial Policy, Populism, and the Political Economy of Climate Action' (2024) 14 Nature Climate Change 414.

practices.[27] Environmental discourses eventually shifted political focus to climate change and the need for a low-carbon energy transition, with growing recognition of the role of government policy in supporting relevant industries.[28]

The American Recovery and Reinvestment Act of 2009, for instance, represented a significant investment in clean energy and environmental projects, highlighting the role of federal policy in catalyzing the transition to a green economy.[29] A generational economic crisis and the urgent need for job creation and economic revitalization presented a compelling case for investment in clean technologies and sustainable industries as a pathway to economic recovery and long-term sustainability.[30]

More recently, the Green New Deal resolution, introduced in Congress in 2019, marked a watershed moment in the U.S. discourse on climate policy and decarbonization.[31] Though not a legislative act, it articulated a vision for a comprehensive transformation of the economy to address climate change, social inequality, and economic stagnation through massive investments in low-carbon energy, infrastructure, and green jobs. This resolution reflected political preferences articulated across the left spectrum of the political landscape, and strongly influenced subsequent policy proposals.[32]

Following introduction of the Green New Deal, legislative efforts, including the Inflation Reduction Act,[33] Infrastructure Investment and Jobs Act,[34] and executive orders focused on clean energy and environmental sustain-

27 Farber (n 1).

28 Schreurs (n 19).

29 American Recovery and Reinvestment Act of 2009 (ARRA) 115.

30 Joseph E Aldy, 'A Preliminary Assessment of the American Recovery and Reinvestment Act's Clean Energy Package' (2013) 7 Review of Environmental Economics and Policy 136; Sanya Carley/Sean Nicholson-Crotty/Eric J Fisher, 'Capacity, Guidance, and the Implementation of the American Recovery and Reinvestment Act' (2015) 75 Public Administration Review 113.

31 Alexandria Ocasio-Cortez, 'Recognizing the Duty of the Federal Government to Create a Green New Deal' H.R. Res. 109 2019 [109].

32 Jon Bloomfield and Fred Steward, 'The Politics of the Green New Deal' (2020) 91 The Political Quarterly 770; David G Victor/Emily K Carlton, 'Technology to Solve Global Problems: An Emerging Consensus for Green Industrial Policy?' (2023) 18 Environmental Research Letters 091006.

33 To provide for reconciliation pursuant to title II of S. Con. Res. 14 2022 1818.

34 An act to authorize funds for Federal-aid highways, highway safety programs, and transit programs, and for other purposes 2021 429.

ability,[35] further solidified the U.S. embrace of green industrial policy. These efforts emphasized the role of the federal government in fostering innovation, supporting sustainable industries, and ensuring U.S. competitiveness in the global transition to a green economy.

Importantly, however, the deployment of industrial policy to advance decarbonization and other environmental objectives has by no means been a linear process. Periodically, the highly polarized nature of climate policy discourses has prompted consequential policy reversals, as witnessed most recently during the second administration of President Donald J. Trump. Already during his first year in office, signature policy successes of his predecessor – including executive rulemaking and legislative breakthroughs such as the IRA – were significantly curtailed or altogether abandoned.

The historical evolution of green industrial policy in the United States thus illustrates a complex and not always linear trajectory of using government intervention to combine environmental policy objectives with economic growth. From early environmental regulations to more recent legislative and policy initiatives that focus on advancing clean technology manufacturing and renewable energy production, the rise of green industrial policy reflects a growing sense that policies have to simultaneously advance economic, social, and environmental objectives in order to remain viable in a polarized political context.

(b) Central Features of U.S. Green Industrial Policy

The evolution of green industrial policy in the U.S. has been shaped by both legislative and executive initiatives, which have propelled and shaped the direction of policy development and implementation. Notable legislative efforts, such as the American Recovery and Reinvestment Act of 2009,[36] marked early attempts to integrate green investments into broader economic recovery measures. However, the push towards a cohesive green industrial policy gained momentum with more recent initiatives that explicitly

35 See, e.g., Executive Office of the President, 'Executive Order 14057: Catalyzing Clean Energy Industries and Jobs Through Federal Sustainability' <https://www.federalregister.gov/documents/2021/12/13/2021-27114/catalyzing-clean-energy-industries-and-jobs-through-federal-sustainability> accessed 5 September 2023.

36 ARRA (n 29).

targeted climate change and environmental sustainability as central pillars of economic policy.[37]

Following the 2020 general election, the Biden Administration played a decisive role in accelerating the U.S. pivot to green industrial policy. It was, in turn, heavily influenced by the introduction of the Green New Deal resolution in Congress,[38] which, although not enacted into law, framed the conversation on climate action within the broader context of social and economic reform, highlighting the interconnections between environmental sustainability, economic inequality, and social justice.[39] Guided by the recommendations of a 'Unity Task Force' appointed by Senator Bernard Sanders and presidential candidate Joseph R. Biden Jr., key elements of this progressive agenda found their way into Biden's electoral campaign platform.[40]

Soon after the election, the green industrial policy dimension of this political platform evolved into the 'Build Back Better' agenda, which eventually culminated – albeit in a diminished form, due to multiple political compromises required for passage – in the Infrastructure Investment and Jobs Act and Inflation Reduction Act. These acts represented landmark investments in clean energy, climate resilience, and environmental justice, reflecting a holistic approach that encompassed economic revitalization, job creation, and addressing the disproportionate impact of climate change on vulnerable communities.[41]

Chronologically the first of these legislative measures to pass in November 2021, the bipartisan Infrastructure Investment and Jobs Act (IIJA), earmarked $1.2 trillion towards revamping U.S. infrastructure, with a significant focus on sustainable and resilient systems.[42] Approximately $550 billion of new spending was allocated to various projects, including im-

37 Bistline/Mehrotra/Wolfram (n 3); Farber (n 1).

38 Alexandria Ocasio-Cortez, 'Recognizing the Duty of the Federal Government to Create a Green New Deal', H.R. Res. 109.

39 Schreurs (n 19); Victor/Carlton (n 32).

40 John Kerry et al., 'Biden-Sanders Unity Task Force Recommendations: Combating the Climate Crisis and Pursuing Environmental Justice' (2020) <https://joebiden.com/wp-content/uploads/2020/08/UNITY-TASK-FORCE-RECOMMENDATIONS.pdf> accessed 26 August 2024.

41 White House, 'Building a Clean Energy Economy: A Guidebook to the Inflation Reduction Act's Investments in Clean Energy and Climate Action' <https://www.whitehouse.gov/wp-content/uploads/2022/12/Inflation-Reduction-Act-Guidebook.pdf> accessed 26 August 2024.

42 Infrastructure Investment and Jobs Act.

provements to public transit, water infrastructure, and broadband access, as well as initiatives specifically aimed at bolstering the country's climate resilience and reducing greenhouse gas emissions. A notable aspect of the Act was its investment in electric vehicle (EV) infrastructure, aiming to create a nationwide network of EV chargers to facilitate the transition to electric transportation. Additionally, the IIJA appropriated funds to upgrade the electrical grid, addressing one of the most serious bottlenecks currently holding back more rapid deployment of renewable energy sources.[43]

Adopted the following year on a purely partisan vote, the CHIPS and Science Act of 2022 focused on strengthening the United States' semiconductor industry and scientific research infrastructure, recognizing the critical role of technology and innovation in economic competitiveness and national security.[44] The Act authorized approximately $280 billion in federal investments for semiconductor research, development, and manufacturing incentives, alongside substantial funding for science and technology research initiatives. While it primarily aimed to bolster the U.S. position in the global technology race, it acknowledged the strategic importance of semiconductors in a range of industries, including clean energy technologies, where advanced materials and components are essential for innovation and efficiency improvements. Not only did it indirectly advance the broader goals of U.S. green industrial policy by investing in the semiconductor industry and scientific research, but it also appropriated up to $67 billion to fund research directly relevant to decarbonization, including research on advanced zero-emissions technologies such as improved energy storage, hydrogen, carbon capture and storage, and fusion, greenhouse gas management, climate science research, as well as disaster-resilience research.[45]

---

43 Richard G Smead, 'Infrastructure Permitting and Friction in the Energy Transition' (2024) 40 Climate and Energy 27.

44 Making appropriations for Legislative Branch for the fiscal year ending September 30, 2022, and for other purposes 2022 1366. CHIPS stands for 'Creating Helpful Incentives to Produce Semiconductors'.

45 Robinson Meyer, 'Congress Just Passed a Big Climate Bill. No, Not That One.' (The Atlantic, 10 August 2022) <https://www.theatlantic.com/science/archive/2022/08/chips-act-climate-bill-biden/671095> accessed 31 March 2024; John F Sargent Jr./Manpreet Singh/Karen M Sutter, 'Frequently Asked Questions: CHIPS Act of 2022 Provisions and Implementation' (Congressional Research Service 2023) CRS Report R47523 <https://crsreports.congress.gov/product/pdf/R/R47523> accessed 26 August 2024.

In August 2022, finally, Congress narrowly passed the Inflation Reduction Act (IRA) on a partisan vote through the reconciliation process to avoid a potential filibuster in the U.S. Senate.[46] Hailed as the "most important climate action in U.S. history",[47] this measure sought to enhance energy security and bolster green innovation through a range of public investments in the form of tax credits, grants, loans and other subsidies. Overall investment volumes in climate change mitigation and adaptation remained uncertain, but were substantial, with the initial estimate by the Congressional Budget Office of $369 billion over a decade representing the lower end of projections.[48] Other calculations anticipated greater uptake of the uncapped tax credits, which would have increased the budgetary costs of the Inflation Reduction Act to levels up to three times higher than the official estimate.[49] A large share of funds appropriated under the Inflation Reduction Act was earmarked for the direct promotion of manufacturing in low-carbon technologies, with many of the incentives conditional on local content or assembly requirements aimed at relocating advanced technology manufacturing to the United States.

Specifically, the Inflation Reduction Act introduced several mechanisms designed to incentivize private investment in clean technologies and manufacturing. It earmarked an estimated $30 billion in production tax credits to accelerate U.S. manufacturing of solar panels, wind turbines, batteries, and critical minerals processing, a $10 billion investment tax credit to build clean technology manufacturing facilities, $20 billion in loans to establish new clean vehicle manufacturing facilities across the country, various grants and tax credits to reduce emissions from industrial manufacturing processes, including almost $6 billion for a new Advanced Industrial Facilities Deployment Program to reduce emissions from the largest industrial emitters like chemical, steel and cement plants, and over $9 billion for

46 Inflation Reduction Act of 2022.

47 Silvio Marcacci, 'The Inflation Reduction Act Is The Most Important Climate Action In U.S. History' (Forbes, 2022) <https://www.forbes.com/sites/energyinnovation/2022/08/02/the-inflation-reduction-act-is-the-most-important-climate-action-in-us-history> accessed 31 March 2024.

48 Congressional Budget Office, 'Estimated Budgetary Effects of Public Law 117–169, to Provide for Reconciliation Pursuant to Title II of S. Con. Res. 14' (Congressional Budget Office 2022) <https://www.cbo.gov/ publication/58455suisse> accessed 1 April 2023.

49 Bistline/Mehrotra/Wolfram (n 3); Credit Suisse, 'US Inflation Reduction Act: A Tipping Point in Climate Action' (Credit Suisse 2022) ESG Report <https://www.credit-suisse.com/treeprintusinflationreductionact> accessed 26 August 2024.

public procurement of clean technologies to create a stable market for clean products.[50] Additionally, substantial incentives for low-carbon electricity and fuels were intended to accelerate the decarbonization of the energy system, lowering the indirect emissions of U.S. producers.

Uniquely, the Inflation Reduction Act also addressed the social dimensions of the energy transition, allocating funds to disadvantaged communities and workers affected by the shift away from fossil fuels. This approach reflected the political strategy of ensuring that the benefits of the green economy are widely shared, promoting equity and environmental justice as central tenets of U.S. climate action, to secure broad public acceptance and political support.[51]

Beyond the foregoing legislative measures of the U.S. Congress, the Biden administration issued a number of executive orders that were aimed at advancing the green industrial policy agenda, setting targets for greenhouse gas emission reductions, promoting the sustainability of federal land, buildings, and procurement practices, and enhancing the resilience of critical infrastructure to climate change. Notably, the Executive Order on Catalyzing Clean Energy Industries and Jobs Through Federal Sustainability outlined significant efforts by the U.S. government to bolster environmental and energy efficiency across federal operations.[52] It revoked previous orders, aiming for a more robust and comprehensive approach to sustainability within federal agencies by emphasizing the transition to carbon pollution-free electricity, sustainable acquisition and procurement, and adapting federal operations to climate change impacts. The order set out several climate policy objectives, such as achieving a substantial percentage of zero-emission vehicle acquisitions by 2035 and a net-zero emissions building portfolio by 2045, and committed the administration to reducing emissions and supporting resilient supply chains through prioritized purchasing decisions favoring sustainable products and services. These actions were set to leverage the considerable purchasing power of the federal government to advance domestic policy objectives.

---

50 Andrei Marcu/Michael A Mehling/Aaron J Cosbey, 'CBAM in a Portfolio of Measures for Industrial Decarbonization' (European Roundtable on Climate Change and Sustainable Transition (ERCST) 2023) <https://ercst.org/cbam-in-a-portfolio-of-measures-for-industrial-decarbonization> accessed 31 March 2024.

51 Farber (n 1).

52 Executive Office of the President (n 35).

Finally, federal agencies and their executive rulemaking have been key components of the U.S. green industrial policy framework. Specifically, the Environmental Protection Agency (EPA) and the Department of Energy (DoE) play critical roles in implementing and enforcing regulations that support the transition to clean energy and sustainable practices. During the Biden administration, for instance, the Department of Energy announced an investment of $6 billion to accelerate innovation in clean energy technologies and foster partnerships between the government, private sector, and research institutions designed to reduce barriers to innovation and market entry.[53]

Much of the industrial policy agenda of the Biden administration was put to question when Donald J. Trump won the 2024 presidential election. One of his first measures on Inauguration Day was the adoption of an Executive Order revoking virtually all Executive Orders of his predecessor, including those related to green industrial policy and decarbonization.[54] In July 2025, Republican majorities in the U.S. House of Representatives and Senate also curtailed most fiscal incentives set out in the IRA.[55] Although grants and loans under that legislation had largely been awarded under the previous administration, actual disbursement was in many cases suspended pending further review by the Trump administration. Likewise, the new administration quickly began reviewing any proposed or adopted agency rules seeking to address climate change, forestalling their expected judicial review and possible recission by the Supreme Court as a result of the 2024 decision in *Loper Bright v Raimondo*.[56] Recent progress achieved with green industrial policy in the U.S. thus stands to stall or reverse, although the market forces it unleashed continue to drive investment in decarbonization.

---

53 Department of Energy, 'Biden-Harris Administration Announces $6 Billion to Transform America's Industrial Sector, Strengthen Domestic Manufacturing, and Slash Planet-Warming Emissions' <https://www.energy.gov/articles/biden-harris-administration-announces-6-billion-transform-americas-industrial-sector> accessed 31 March 2024.

54 Executive Office of the President, 'Executive Order 14148: Initial Rescissions of Harmful Executive Orders and Actions' <https://www.federalregister.gov/documents/2025/01/28/2025-01901/initial-rescissions-of-harmful-executive-orders-and-actions> accessed 15 July 2025.

55 To provide for reconciliation pursuant to title II of H. Con. Res. 14 2025 (One Big Beautiful Bill Act).

56 Supreme Court of the United States, *Loper Bright Enterprises, et al. v. Gina Raimondo, Secretary of Commerce, et al. Relentless, Inc. et al. v. Department of Commerce, et al.*, 28 June 2024, 144 S. Ct. 2244.

(c) Assessment

U.S. green industrial policy under the Biden administration, as exemplified by the IRA, IIJA, and CHIPS and Science Act, marked a significant pivot towards sustainable economic development and climate resilience. The cumulative impact of these policies has been profound, and was aimed at facilitating a comprehensive transformation across various sectors of the economy. From bolstering clean energy technologies to modernizing infrastructure and enhancing the nation's scientific and technological capabilities, these legislative efforts embodied a multifaceted approach to addressing the pressing challenges of climate change while ensuring economic growth and competitiveness. At the same time, the emphasis on sustainability and resilience in procurement practices, as guided by executive orders and departmental strategies, underscored a commitment to embedding environmental considerations into the fabric of federal operations.

Estimates suggest that these legislative measures – if fully operationalized by federal agencies – would have helped substantially narrow the gap between projected emissions and the Nationally Determined Contribution (NDC) submitted in 2021 by the Biden administration,[57] which required emissions to decline by 50–52 % below 2005 levels in 2030.[58] Impacts of these green industrial policy efforts did not only manifest themselves in terms of anticipated emission reductions, however. Already in the first year after its adoption, the IRA and the generous incentives it set out were seen as critical enablers for a 37 % increase in new clean energy and technology investment across the U.S. economy, and a 125 % year-on-year increase in clean technology manufacturing, particularly within electric vehicle and solar manufacturing.[59] Investment in clean energy production and industrial decarbonization also rose 15 % year-on-year, and household and business

57 John ET Bistline et al., 'Emissions and Energy Impacts of the Inflation Reduction Act' (2023) 380 Science 1324; Jesse D Jenkins and others, 'Climate Progress and the 117th Congress: The Impacts of the Inflation Reduction Act and Infrastructure Investment and Jobs Act' (Princeton University 2023) <https://repeatproject.org/docs/REPEAT_Climate_Progress_and_the_117th_Congress.pdf> accessed 26 August 2024.

58 United States, 'The United States' Nationally Determined Contribution. Reducing Greenhouse Gases in the United States: A 2030 Emissions Target' <https://unfccc.int/sites/default/files/NDC/2022-06/United%20States%20NDC%20April%2021%202021%20Final.pdf> accessed 26 August 2024.

59 Lily Bermel and others, 'The Clean Investment Monitor' (MIT Center for Energy and Environmental Policy Research (CEEPR) 2013) <https://www.cleaninvestmentmonitor.org/reports/202309> accessed 26 March 2024 accessed 26 August 2024.

retail investment in purchasing and installing clean technologies such as heat pumps and zero-emission vehicles (ZEVs) rose 32 % year-on-year.[60]

Unlike more conventional climate policy approaches, U.S. green industrial policy during the Biden administration represented an integrated approach to climate change mitigation and adaptation, economic strategy, and national security. As a result, many observers expected that a change in U.S. leadership after the 2024 elections would see the incoming administration tacitly or overtly continue the focus on technological innovation, workforce development, and broad access to the economic benefits of these policies, not least since a majority of clean energy activities benefitting from investment under legislation such as the Inflation Reduction Act were said to be located in Republican congressional districts.[61]

For many, therefore, the intensity and speed with which the Trump administration began dismantling key elements of the previous administration's industrial policy agenda came as a surprise. Not only does that policy reversal offer lessons about the political economy of climate action in a polarized political context, but it has also dramatically undermined the ability of the U.S. to achieve meaningful progress on decarbonization. Early assessments of the impact of executive and legislative repeal measures during the Trump administration, for instance, estimated that U.S. deployment of renewable energy would be 72 % lower over a decade,[62] and greenhouse gas emissions would increase by roughly 190 million metric tons per year in 2030 and 470 million tons in 2035.[63] Likewise, uncertainty about the evolving policy context began impacting new investment in clean technology manufacturing as early as the first quarter of 2025, which showed a marked

60 ibid.

61 Jeffrey Kupfer, 'The Conservative Case for Keeping the Inflation Reduction Act' (*The Hill*, 18 March 2024) <https://thehill.com/opinion/energy-environment/4538435-the-conservative-case-for-keeping-the-inflation-reduction-act/> accessed 31 March 2024; Kelsey Tamborrino/Josh Siegel, 'Big Winners from Biden's Climate Law: Republicans Who Voted against It' (*POLITICO*, 23 January 2023) <https://www.politico.com/news/2023/01/23/red-states-are-winning-big-from-dems-climate-law-00078420> accessed 31 March 2024.

62 Ben King and others, 'Ways and Means Brings the Hammer Down on Energy Credits' (Rhodium Group 2025) <https://rhg.com/research/ways-and-means-brings-the-hammer-down-on-energy-credits> accessed 15 July 2025.

63 Jesse D. Jenkins and others, 'Impacts of the One Big Beautiful Bill on the US Energy Transition' (REPEAT Project 2025) <https://doi.org/10.5281/zenodo.15801701> accessed 15 July 2025.

decrease relative to the preceding quarter after several years of accelerated growth.[64]

Of course, critics of industrial policy had previously pointed out that the approach chosen by the Biden administration was both costly and fraught with risk.[65] Still, few would have anticipated the rapid policy reversal and associated impacts on industry and households, including stranded assets and abandoned projects, heightened investment risk, and increased energy costs, that the Trump administration and its allies in Congress have been willing to tolerate in order to advance their fiscal policy agenda. Even demonstrated environmental, social, and economic benefits – including a concentration of induced investments in Republican districts – were insufficient to insulate the Biden administration's industrial policy efforts from partisan politics and thereby improve their political durability, a key advantage ascribed to green industrial policy over traditional climate policies. As such, the fleeting industrial policy turn in the U.S. serves as a cautionary tale of both its potential and political vulnerability.

2. Green Industrial Policy in the European Union

(a) Background and Context

Europe's journey towards establishing a green industrial policy framework can be traced back to the early recognition of environmental protection as a foundational pillar of its collective policy agenda. Over the last three decades, EU climate policy has evidenced a consistent trend of international leadership and progressively rising ambition on climate change mitigation, with Brussels increasingly exercising its legislative powers and claiming an expanding institutional mandate, greater responsibilities, and new areas of integration.[66] European leadership in climate and energy policy is

64 Rhodium Group and others, 'Clean Investment Monitor: Q1 2025 Update' (MIT Center for Energy and Environmental Policy Research 2025) <https://www.cleaninvestmentmonitor.org/reports/q1-2025-update> accessed 15 July 2025.

65 Adam Posen, 'America's Zero-Sum Economics Doesn't Add Up' (Foreign Policy, 2 April 2024) <https://foreignpolicy.com/2023/03/24/economy-trade-united-states-china-industry-manufacturing-supply-chains-biden> accessed 30 March 2024.

66 Camilla Bausch/Benjamin Görlach/Michael Mehling, 'Ambitious Climate Policy through Centralization? Evidence from the European Union' (2017) 17 Climate Policy 32.

also an extension of broader trends in the process of European integration, with concerted action being perceived inside the EU as a unifying and urgent agenda, while simultaneously allowing it to enhance its international standing as a global actor. In response to its international commitments under the Kyoto Protocol to the United Nations Framework Convention on Climate Change (UNFCCC), the EU adopted a European Climate Change Programme (ECCP) in 2000,[67] which was followed by a series of legislative measures aimed at reducing greenhouse gas emissions pollution and promoting sustainable practices across the Member States.

A landmark measure in this evolving policy landscape was the establishment of the EU Emissions Trading System (EU ETS) in 2005, the world's first major carbon market designed to cap and reduce greenhouse gas emissions from significant industrial emitters.[68] The EU ETS has represented a pioneering use of market-based mechanisms to drive environmental policy objectives, marking a dramatic pivot from earlier policy preferences of the EU, which had previously expressed skepticism about the instrument of emissions trading.[69] It presently operates in 30 countries – all 27 EU Member States of the EU as well as Iceland, Liechtenstein and Norway – and covers around 10,000 emitters in the power, heavy industry and aviation sectors accounting for roughly 40 % of EU GHG emissions. This makes the EU ETS a centerpiece of EU climate policy.[70] Over a dozen directives, regulations and decisions set out the legal framework of the

67 European Commission, 'Communication from the Commission to the Council and the European Parliament: EU Policies and Measures to Reduce Greenhouse Gas Emissions – Towards a European Climate Change Programme (ECCP)' COM (2000) 88 final' <https://eur-lex.europa.eu/LexUriServ/LexUriServ.do?uri=COM:2000:0088:FIN:EN:PDF> accessed 26 August 2024.

68 European Parliament and Council Directive 2003/87/EC of 13 October 2003 Establishing a Scheme for Greenhouse Gas Emission Allowance Trading Within the Community and Amending Council Directive 96/61/EC [2003] OJ L275/32.

69 Harro van Asselt, 'Emissions Trading: The Enthusiastic Adoption of an "Alien" Instrument?' in Andrew Jordan et al. (eds), Climate Change Policy in the European Union: Confronting the Dilemmas of Mitigation and Adaptation? (Cambridge University Press 2010); Brettny Hardy, 'How Positive Environmental Policies Affected Europe's Decision to Oppose and Then Adopt Emissions Trading' (2006) 17 Duke Environmental Law & Policy Forum 297; Jørgen Wettestad, 'The Making of the 2003 EU Emissions Trading Directive: An Ultra-Quick Process Due to Entrepreneurial Proficiency?' (2005) 5 Global Environmental Politics 1.

70 Jos M Delbeke, 'The Emissions Trading Scheme (ETS): The Cornerstone of the EU's Implementation of the Kyoto Protocol' in Jos M Delbeke (ed), EU Energy Law, Vol. IV: The EU Greenhouse Gas Emissions Trading Scheme (Claeys & Casteels 2006).

EU ETS, extending the market to new sectors and gases, establishing a common registry, and providing technical guidance and procedural details on design features such as auctioning and emissions monitoring, reporting, and verification (MRV).[71]

The transition towards a more defined green industrial policy became more pronounced over the past decade, as the European public – and, in particular, a growing force of environmental activists, such as the 'Fridays for Future' movement – articulated increasing concern about the climate crisis and the urgency of an ambitious policy response.[72] The European response to this challenge has been characterized by a strategic pivot towards leveraging industrial policy as a key instrument for promoting environmental sustainability and economic resilience. This shift was initially articulated through various policy documents and communications that emphasized the importance of supporting industries and technologies critical to the transition to a low-carbon economy. Most notable among these is the European Green Deal (EGD) announced in July 2019 by the incoming European Commission President Ursula von der Leyen during her campaign to secure political confirmation by the European Parliament.[73] It set out a policy roadmap to "transform the EU into a fair and prosperous society, with a modern, resource-efficient and competitive economy where there are no net emissions of greenhouse gases in 2050."[74]

Subsequent implementation measures included the European Climate Law, adopted as a regulation in June 2021, which enshrined in legally binding terms the aspiration to ensure a climate neutral European Union by

71 Damien Meadows et al., 'EU ETS: Pricing Carbon to Drive Cost-Effective Reductions across Europe', in Jos M Delbeke and Peter Vis (ed), EU Climate Policy Explained (Routledge 2015) 26.

72 Viktoria Spaiser/Nicole Nisbett/Cristina G Stefan, '"How Dare You?"—The Normative Challenge Posed by Fridays for Future' (2022) 1 PLOS Climate e0000053; Felix Noth/Lena Tonzer, 'Understanding Climate Activism: Who Participates in Climate Marches Such as "Fridays for Future" and What Can We Learn from It?' (2022) 84 Energy Research & Social Science 102360.

73 Ursula von der Leyen, 'Political Guidelines for the Next European Commission 2019–2024' (Publications Office of the European Union 2020) <https://data.europa.eu/doi/10.2775/101756> accessed 26 August 2024.

74 European Commission, 'Communication from the Commission to the European Parliament, the European Council, the Council, the European Economic and Social Committee and the Committee of the Regions: The European Green Deal' COM (2019) 640 final' <https://eur-lex.europa.eu/legal-content/EN/TXT/?uri=COM%3A2019%3A640%3AFIN> accessed 26 August 2024.

2050, and set a near term objective of a 55 % emissions reduction by 2030.[75] Additionally, a package of more than a dozen legislative and regulatory measures – the 'Fit for 55' package – was released in July 2021, with the individual measures gradually progressing towards passage through the legislative process between the European Parliament and the Council of the European Union.[76]

This ambitious agenda laid the foundation for an expansive suite of policy initiatives aimed at integrating green industrial policy more explicitly into the broader European economic strategy. For instance, the EU has sought to expand its policy toolset to include mechanisms such as the Carbon Border Adjustment Mechanism (CBAM), the Net Zero Industry Act, and the Critical Raw Materials Act (see *infra*, Section B), aiming to mitigate carbon leakage, promote clean industrial development, and ensure secure and sustainable supply chains.[77] More recently, it has heeded calls to strengthen its industrial base and economic competitiveness[78] by setting out elements of a Clean Industrial Deal.[79] In part, these measures can be seen as an EU response to U.S. industrial policy advances with the IRA, IIJA, and other initiatives that threatened to undermine industrial competitiveness and green leadership in Europe. Unlike the U.S., however, Europe

75 Regulation (EU) 2021/1119 of the European Parliament and of the Council of 30 June 2021 establishing the framework for achieving climate neutrality and amending Regulations (EC) No 401/2009 and (EU) 2018/1999 [2021] ('European Climate Law') 1.

76 Sabine Schlacke et al., 'Implementing the EU Climate Law via the "Fit for 55" Package' (2022) 1 Oxford Open Energy 1.

77 Sebastian Oberthür/Ingmar von Homeyer, 'From Emissions Trading to the European Green Deal: The Evolution of the Climate Policy Mix and Climate Policy Integration in the EU' (2023) 30 Journal of European Public Policy 445.

78 Mario Draghi, 'The Future of European Competitiveness' (European Commission 2024) <https://commission.europa.eu/topics/strengthening-european-competitiveness/eu-competitiveness-looking-ahead_en> accessed 15 July 2025.

79 European Commission, 'Communication from the Commission to the European Parliament, the European Council, the Council, the European Economic and Social Committee and the Committee of the Regions: The European Green Deal' COM (2019) 640 final' <https://eur-lex.europa.eu/legal-content/EN/TXT/?uri=COM%3A2019%3A640%3AFIN> accessed 26 August 2024; European Commission, 'Communication from the Commission to the European Parliament, the Council, the European Economic and Social Committee and the Committee of the Regions: The Clean Industrial Deal – A Joint Roadmap for Competitiveness and Decarbonisation' COM (2025)85 <https://commission.europa.eu/document/download/9db1c5c8-9e82-467b-ab6a-905feeb4b6b0_en?filename=Communication%20-%20Clean%20Industrial%20Deal_en.pdf> last accessed 15 July 2025.

has been able to sustain its climate policy ambition, although only by deepening its reliance on industrial policy approaches that simultaneously pursue environmental, social, and economic objectives.

(b) Central Features of EU Green Industrial Policy

The EU's green industrial policy is framed within a complex political and regulatory context, characterized by ambitious policy initiatives aimed at addressing the dual challenges of climate change and economic competitiveness. Central to this context are the European Green Deal and Clean Industrial Deal, complemented by strategic legislative acts and regulations designed to promote a comprehensive and integrated approach to green industrial development. In terms of implementation, these two policy strategies are exceptionally broad and set out goals that extend across all major sectors, including energy, industry, transport, buildings, and agriculture, accompanied by a roadmap with a timetable for the introduction of specific policies and measures in each thematic area. Specifically, they identified a need for new policies to, inter alia: increase EU climate ambition for 2030 and 2050, through a review and revision of relevant climate policy instruments, including emissions trading and energy taxation, as well as adoption of a new European Climate Law; promote the supply of clean, affordable and secure energy, including prioritization of energy efficiency and development of a power sector based largely on renewable resources; mobilize industry for a clean and circular economy; accelerate the shift to sustainable and smart mobility through increased adoption of sustainable and alternative fuels in road, maritime and air transport, strengthened emission standards for combustion-engine vehicles, measures to encourage the adoption of low-emission vehicles; and, more recently, a plan to improve energy affordability, create lead markets for clean industrial products, and scale investment in clean manufacturing.[80]

Taken together, this detailed roadmap illustrates a scope that extends well beyond environmental objectives, targeting economic growth, social equity, and technological innovation as integral components of the European green transformation. In response to evolving global challenges, such as supply chain disruptions and geopolitical tensions, the EU has sought to ex-

80 European Commission, 'The European Green Deal' (n 74); European Commission, 'Clean Industrial Deal' (n 79.

pand its climate policy toolset to include elements of industrial policy.[81] EU green industrial policy is thus intricately linked to broader concerns regarding industrial competitiveness, supply chain resilience, and energy security. The COVID-19 pandemic and subsequent geopolitical tensions, notably the Russian invasion of Ukraine, have highlighted the vulnerabilities of global supply chains and the strategic importance of energy independence. In response, the EU has intensified its efforts to develop a robust and diversified supply base for critical raw materials and to accelerate the deployment of renewable energy sources, thereby enhancing its strategic autonomy and resilience in the face of global uncertainties.[82] This strategic expansion of EU climate policy to a more full-fledged green industrial policy is particularly evident in the introduction of the Carbon Border Adjustment Mechanism (CBAM), the Net Zero Industry Act, and the Critical Raw Materials Act. Each is described in greater detail below.

Proposed in July 2021 as part of the 'Fit for 55' package, the CBAM is a pioneering policy instrument designed to prevent carbon leakage by applying a carbon price on imports of certain carbon-intensive goods.[83] It will successively replace free allocation of allowances as the primary safeguard against emissions leakage under the EU ETS. To do so, it extends the carbon price applied under the EU ETS to the emissions associated with imports of six product categories – cement, iron and steel, aluminum, fertilizer, electricity, and hydrogen – based on verified emissions data from foreign producers or default assumptions about the carbon intensity of these goods. From October 2023, importers have been required to declare the emissions embedded in covered goods entering the customs territory of the EU.[84] From 2026, importers will additionally need to purchase and annually surrender certificates in an amount equal to the independently

81 Kathleen R McNamara, 'Transforming Europe? The EU's Industrial Policy and Geopolitical Turn' (2023) Journal of European Public Policy 1.

82 Susanna Paleari, 'The Role of Strategic Autonomy in the EU Green Transition' (2024) 16 Sustainability; Tagliapietra/Veugelers (n 4).

83 Regulation (EU) 2023/956 of the European Parliament and of the Council of 10 May 2023 Establishing a Carbon Border Adjustment Mechanism [2023] OJ L 130/52.

84 Such declaration entails calculating the emissions released during the production of imported goods and obtaining validation of the emissions declaration by an accredited verifier, which is an independent third party. For goods that are not listed in Annex II of the CBAM Regulation, this obligation also extends to indirect emissions from production of electricity consumed during the production process. European Commission, 'Commission Implementing Regulation (EU) 2023/1773 Laying down the Rules for the Application of Regulation (EU) 2023/956 of the European Parliament

verified and declared emissions from the preceding year, with certificates priced at the same level as EU ETS allowances.[85]

The Net Zero Industry Act, meanwhile, is a legislative initiative aimed at accelerating the EU transition to a net-zero economy by bolstering the development and deployment of clean technologies across key industrial sectors.[86] This Act is part of the broader European Green Deal broader strategy to achieve climate neutrality by 2050, and operationalizes an earlier European Green Deal Industrial Plan focused on enhancing the EU's industrial competitiveness and innovation capacity in the green technology market.[87] The Act outlines a framework for providing targeted support to industries critical to the green transition, including renewable energy, energy storage, and carbon capture and utilization technologies. It proposes a mix of financial incentives, regulatory reforms, and research and development initiatives designed to stimulate investment, reduce bureaucratic hurdles, and foster collaboration between the public and private sectors. The Act also emphasizes the importance of skills development and workforce transition programs to ensure that the workforce is equipped to thrive in the emerging green economy.[88] By focusing on the strategic development of clean industries, the Net Zero Industry Act aims to position the EU as a global leader in green technology, ensuring long-term economic growth and job creation while meeting its ambitious climate targets. As such, it represents a step in aligning the EU's industrial policy with its environmental objectives, and also contributes to a socially just and inclusive transition.

---

and of the Council as Regards Reporting Obligations for the Purposes of the Carbon Border Adjustment Mechanism during the Transitional Period' [2023] OJ L 228/94.

85 Initially, the payment obligation will be prorated to reflect the remaining share of allowances allocated for free to EU producers, and gradually increase as free allocation is phased out.

86 Regulation (EU) 2024/1735 of the European Parliament and of the Council of 13 June 2024 Establishing a Framework of Measures for Strengthening Europe's Net-Zero Technology Manufacturing Ecosystem and Amending Regulation (EU) 2018/1724 [2024] OJ L 1735/1.

87 European Commission, Communication from the Commission to the European Parliament, the European Council, the Council, the European Economic and Social Committee and the Committee of the Regions 'A Green Deal Industrial Plan for the Net-Zero Age' COM (2023) 62 final <https://commission.europa.eu/system/files/2023-02/COM_2023_62_2_EN_ACT_A%20Green%20Deal%20Industrial%20Plan%20for%20the%20Net-Zero%20Age.pdf> accessed 17 March 2023.

88 Veugelers/Tagliapietra/Trasi (n 2).

Finally, the Critical Raw Materials Act is a legislative initiative designed to secure the European Union's supply of essential materials crucial for the green transition and digital economy.[89] Recognizing the strategic importance of critical raw materials (CRMs) such as rare earth elements, lithium, and cobalt, the Act aims to reduce European dependency on external sources and mitigate the risks associated with supply chain disruptions.[90] The Act envisions a comprehensive approach to enhancing European resilience with regard to these critical supply chains, including measures to boost domestic production, promote recycling and circular economy practices, and diversify supply chains through strategic partnerships with like-minded countries. It also emphasizes the need for sustainability and responsible sourcing in the extraction and processing of CRMs, addressing environmental and social concerns associated with CRM production. By aiming to secure a sustainable supply of CRMs, the Critical Raw Materials Act supports the EU in its ambitions in clean energy, digitalization, and the defense sector, all of which rely heavily on these materials.[91]

The political and regulatory context of the European Union's green industrial policy evidences a comprehensive and strategic approach to weaving together environmental, economic, and industrial policy strands. Recent political pressures have seen a recalibration of priorities towards greater emphasis on competitiveness and supply security, yet the long term ambition of EU climate policy remains unchanged. This consistent, forward-looking policy framework has helped position the EU as a global leader in green industrial development, and also serves as an important model for other countries seeking to integrate sustainability and economic prosperity in the transition to a green economy.

(c) Assessment

The EU's green industrial policy agenda has begun to reshape the industrial landscape in Europe, although it has yet to drive the desired investment in clean technology manufacturing. Because central initiatives – such as the

89 Regulation (EU) 2024/1252 of the European Parliament and of the Council of 11 April 2024 Establishing a Framework for Ensuring a Secure and Sustainable Supply of Critical Raw Materials and Amending Regulations (EU) No 168/2013, (EU) 2018/858, (EU) 2018/1724 and (EU) 2019/1020 [2024] OJ L 2024/1252.

90 Schreurs (n 19).

91 Mertens et al. (n 25).

CBAM, Net Zero Industry Act, and Critical Raw Materials Act – have only recently entered into force, one can only speculate about their expected impacts. Still, the CBAM, for example, signals a bold move towards leveling the global playing field, encouraging producers both within and outside the EU to adopt cleaner production methods.[92] This not only aids in reducing global carbon emissions, but also protects EU industries from unfair competition, thereby supporting jobs and economic growth within the union. The Net Zero Industry Act and Critical Raw Materials Act, moreover, aspire to substantiate the EU commitment to securing its industrial base and supply chains for essential materials.[93] Initiatives envisioned with the more recent Clean Industrial Deal stand to further bolster European competitiveness and industrial decarbonization.

Looking ahead, it is already apparent that EU green industrial policy sets a strategic direction for sustainable growth and competitiveness on the global stage. The emphasis on clean technologies and the transition to a circular economy presents an opportunity for the EU to lead in the creation of new markets and industries. Moreover, by promoting high standards of environmental protection and labor rights, the EU is poised to define global norms and practices for sustainable development in a manifestation of the 'Brussels Effect',[94] a normative diffusion process that is already in evidence with the CBAM spurring adoption of carbon pricing in EU trade partners around the world.[95] The impact of these policies will likely extend far beyond the borders of the EU, setting standards and practices that could inspire similar ambitions worldwide. In doing so, the European Union not only stands to advance greater sustainability at home, but also has an opportunity to demonstrate that industrial decarbonization can occur

92 Kimberly A Clausing/Catherine Wolfram, 'Carbon Border Adjustments, Climate Clubs, and Subsidy Races When Climate Policies Vary' (2023) 37 Journal of Economic Perspectives 137.

93 Oberthür/von Homeyer (n 71); Schreurs (n 18).

94 Anu Bradford, *The Brussels Effect: How the European Union Rules the World* (Oxford University Press 2020) <https://academic.oup.com/book/36491> accessed 26 August 2024.

95 Jos M Delbeke/Peter Vis, 'How CBAM Can Become a Steppingstone towards Carbon Pricing Globally' (European University Institute 2023) <https://cadmus.eui.eu/handle/1814/75472> accessed 26 October 2023 accessed 26 August 2024; Michael A Mehling/Geoffroy Dolphin/Robert A Ritz, 'The European Union's CBAM: Averting Emissions Leakage or Promoting the Diffusion of Carbon Pricing?' (University of Cambridge 2024) <https://www.jbs.cam.ac.uk/wp-content/uploads/2024/10/eprg-wp2416.pdf> accessed 15 July 2025.

alongside economic prosperity and resilience – a message many observers around the world will draw on as a benchmark for the success or failure of green industrial policy.

However, the successful implementation of this ambitious policy framework will require navigating a rapidly evolving political landscape. As the EU emerges from pivotal elections that have shifted political majorities in line with evolving priorities of the electorate, it must navigate complex global dynamics, including trade tensions and the geopolitical implications of the energy transition as well as a widespread trend towards protectionism and fragmented markets. Collaborative approaches, both within the EU and with international partners, will be crucial for advancing shared climate goals and ensuring a just transition for all stakeholders.[96] By embracing a globally oriented perspective and continuously adapting its policy toolkit, the EU can navigate the complexities encountered on the way to a successful green industrial policy strategy. Building on its decade-long journey of increasingly ambitious climate policy, and the more recent thrust of the European Green Deal and Clean Industrial Deal, the EU is equipped like few others to balance the risks and benefits of an industrial policy strategy. Still, that journey will not be easy, and a successful transition is far from guaranteed.

D. Conclusions

The European Union and the United States have each adopted distinct yet impactful green industrial policies. Whereas the U.S. vigorously embraced a green industrial policy strategy during the Biden administration and subsequently abandoned it again, demonstrating the political vulnerability of an approach specifically designed to withstand partisan challenges, Europe has succeeded in sustaining long-term climate policy continuity, but only by reconciling decarbonization objectives with economic and social priorities. Both jurisdictions thus display fundamental differences that are deeply anchored in institutional structures and the political economy on each side of the Atlantic, with the U.S. frequently defining climate policy paradigms, but then unable to sustain implementation due to persistent gridlock and

96 Chad P Bown/Kimberly A Clausing, 'How Trade Cooperation by the United States, the European Union, and China Can Fight Climate Change' (Peterson Institute of International Economics (PIIE) 2023) WP 23–8 <https://www.piie.com/sites/default/files/2023-10/wp23-8.pdf> accessed 26 March 2024.

shifts in leadership; and Europe often a reluctant follower that ends up pursuing these paradigms with continuity and technocratic leadership.

During the Biden administration's deployment of industrial policy, the U.S. chose to focus on fiscal incentives and other public investments in innovation and deployment to spur the growth of a domestic clean energy sector and drive adoption of clean technologies. Through legislative measures such as the IRA, the IIJA and the CHIPS and Science Act, it succeeded in creating a favorable context for investment in renewable energy, infrastructure modernization, and technological advancement, prioritizing economic stimulus and energy security, and leveraging federal support to catalyze industry-wide shifts towards greater decarbonization. Still, a change in political leadership upended this policy approach and stymied the already unfolding transformation, threatening U.S. climate leadership and raising questions about its reliability as a partner in international climate cooperation.

By contrast, EU green industrial policy, spearheaded by the European Green Deal and Clean Industrial Deal, has adopted a systemic approach to sustainability, weaving climate objectives into economic, social, and industrial fabrics. Its many elements, such as the CBAM and the CRMA, demonstrate a commitment to protecting its industrial base, securing supply chains, and growing domestic clean technology manufacturing. In that regard, it is not so different from industrial policy initiatives taken in recent years across the Atlantic, but unlike U.S. approaches it relies heavily on carbon pricing, coupling support measures that lower the cost of abatement with measures that increase the cost of emissions. In other words, the European vision of a carbon-neutral future emphasizes a more balanced deployment of financial incentives and regulatory measures to support a just and inclusive transition.[97]

Despite such differences in approach and starting point, both the EU and the U.S. offer valuable lessons for other jurisdictions looking to rely on green industrial policy to advance a combined environmental, social, and economic policy agenda in a global context of regional fragmentation and increasingly protectionist reflexes. These lessons can be summarized with the following five takeaways:

- *Integrating Sustainability Across Sectors*: The EU approach of embedding climate goals across all policy areas with the European Green Deal and

97 Veugelers/Tagliapietra/Trasi (n 2).

Clean Industrial Deal offers an effective blueprint for systemic change. Jurisdictions can learn from this approach by ensuring that sustainability is not siloed within environmental policy making, but is a central tenet of economic, social, and industrial policies over the long term.
- *Leveraging Fiscal Incentives for Rapid Innovation*: The brief U.S. success in utilizing tax incentives to stimulate clean technology deployment illustrates the power of fiscal policy in accelerating innovation. While the EU cannot replicate this approach given a lack of fiscal powers, other jurisdictions might consider similar incentives to drive investment and adoption of sustainable technologies, particularly in nascent industries.
- *Building Resilient and Diverse Supply Chains*: Both the EU and the U.S. have at different times advanced policy initiatives that set production targets and local content requirements for domestically sourced materials and components, recognizing the importance of secure supply chains for the energy transition. This is a critical step to ensure the resilience of clean energy industries against geopolitical and economic disruptions, yet also has to be balanced against the risks of economic fragmentation and decoupling, as well as protectionist reflexes.
- *Fostering International Collaboration*: The global nature of climate change and the interconnectedness of economies necessitate a collaborative approach to green industrial policy. Learning from EU efforts to project its normative aspirations internationally as well as U.S. initiatives to create partnerships with like-minded nations – for instance through free trade agreements that focus on critical raw materials – other jurisdictions should seek partnerships that advance shared goals, methodologies and practices.
- *Ensuring Equity and Inclusivity*: An essential lesson from both regions is the importance of integrating social equity into green industrial policy. Ensuring that the benefits of the green transition are widely shared, particularly among disadvantaged communities, is crucial for building public support and the necessary workforce for the energy transition. This aspect will become even more crucial as the global economy becomes more competitive, and domestic politics are increasingly encumbered by populist and nationalist movements.

By balancing systemic reforms with targeted incentives, building resilient supply chains, fostering international collaboration, and ensuring equity and inclusivity, jurisdictions can navigate the complexities of the green transition more effectively. Green industrial policy can play a vital role in advancing these objectives. At the same time, it remains unclear to what extent the potential risks and costs of heavy reliance on industrial policy – such as market distortions and freeriding, but also heightened geopolitical and trade tensions with partners around the world – will manifest themselves and offset some of the beneficial outcomes observed to date. In the end, however, the path forward for global sustainability will require not only innovation and investment but also a shared commitment to an equitable and resilient future.

Bibliography

Agrawal R, 'The White House's Case for Industrial Policy' (Foreign Policy, 2 March 2023) <https://foreignpolicy.com/2023/03/02/live-industrial-policy-katherine-tai-trade-economy-chips-inflation> accessed 26 August 2024

Aldy J, 'A Preliminary Assessment of the American Recovery and Reinvestment Act's Clean Energy Package' (2013) 7 Review of Environmental Economics and Policy 136

Altenburg T/Assmann C, 'Green Industrial Policy: Concept, Policies, Country Experiences' (UN Environment 2017) <https://wedocs.unep.org/bitstream/handle/20.500.11822/22277/Green_industrial_policy.pdf> accessed 26 August 2024

Asselt H, 'Emissions Trading: The Enthusiastic Adoption of an "Alien" Instrument?' in **Jordan A et al.** (eds), *Climate Change Policy in the European Union: Confronting the Dilemmas of Mitigation and Adaptation?* (Cambridge University Press 2010)

Barbier E, *A Global Green New Deal: Rethinking the Economic Recovery* (Cambridge University Press 2010) <https://www.cambridge.org/core/books/global-green-new-deal/A46C5F39C7A8B8F87B7B4AC8E8855BC4#fndtn-contents> accessed 26 August 2024

Bausch C/Görlach B/Mehling M, 'Ambitious Climate Policy through Centralization? Evidence from the European Union' (2017) 17 Climate Policy 32

Bermel L, 'The Clean Investment Monitor' (MIT Center for Energy and Environmental Policy Research (CEEPR) 2013) <https://www.cleaninvestmentmonitor.org/reports/202309> accessed 26 March 2024 accessed 26 August 2024

Bistline J, 'Emissions and Energy Impacts of the Inflation Reduction Act' (2023) 380 Science 1324

Bistline J/Mehrotra N/Wolfram C, 'Economic Implications of the Climate Provisions of the Inflation Reduction Act' (Brookings 2023) <https://www.brookings.edu/wpcontent/uploads/2023/03/BPEA_Spring2023_Bistline-et-al_unembargoedUpdated.pdf> accessed 26 August 2024

Bloomfield J/Steward F, 'The Politics of the Green New Deal' (2020) 91 The Political Quarterly 770

Bown C/Clausing K, 'How Trade Cooperation by the United States, the European Union, and China Can Fight Climate Change' (Peterson Institute of International Economics (PIIE) 2023) WP 23–8 <https://www.piie.com/sites/default/files/2023-10/wp23-8.pdf> accessed 26 March 2024

Bradford A, *The Brussels Effect: How the European Union Rules the World* (Oxford University Press 2020)

Carley S/Nicholson-Crotty S/Fisher E, 'Capacity, Guidance, and the Implementation of the American Recovery and Reinvestment Act' (2015) 75 Public Administration Review 113

Cherif R/Hasanov F, 'The return of the Policy That Shall Not Be Named: Principles of Industrial Policy' (International Monetary Fund 2019) Working Paper 2019/074 <https://www.imf.org/en/Publications/WP/Issues/2019/03/26/The-Return-of-the-Policy-That-Shall-Not-Be-Named-Principles-of-Industrial-Policy-46710> accessed 26 August 2024

Clausing K/Wolfram C, 'Carbon Border Adjustments, Climate Clubs, and Subsidy Races When Climate Policies Vary' (2023) 37 Journal of Economic Perspectives 137

Clausing K/Wolfram C, 'Putting Progress over Protectionism in Climate Policy' (Real-Time Economics, 19 December 2023) <https://www.piie.com/blogs/realtime-economics/putting-progress-over-protectionism-climate-policy> accessed 30 March 2024

Congressional Budget Office, 'Estimated Budgetary Effects of Public Law 117–169, to Provide for Reconciliation Pursuant to Title II of S. Con. Res. 14' (Congressional Budget Office 2022) <https://www.cbo.gov/ publication/58455suisse> accessed 1 April 2023.

Cooper R, 'Industrial Policy and Trade Distortion: A Policy Perspective' in **El-Agraa** (ed), *Protection, Cooperation, Integration and Development: Essays in Honour of Professor Hiroshi Kitamura* (Palgrave Macmillan UK 1987) 37

Credit Suisse, 'US Inflation Reduction Act: A Tipping Point in Climate Action' (Credit Suisse 2022) ESG Report <https://www.credit-suisse.com/treeprintusinflationreductionact> accessed 26 August 2024

Deese D, 'The Case for a Clean Energy Marshall Plan: How the Fight Against Climate Change Can Renew American Leadership' (2024) 103 Foreign Affairs 106

Delbeke J, 'The Emissions Trading Scheme (ETS): The Cornerstone of the EU's Implementation of the Kyoto Protocol' in **Delbeke J** (ed), *EU Energy Law, Vol. IV: The EU Greenhouse Gas Emissions Trading Scheme* (Claeys & Casteels 2006)

Delbeke J/Vis P, 'How CBAM Can Become a Steppingstone towards Carbon Pricing Globally' (European University Institute 2023) <https://cadmus.eui.eu/handle/1814/75472> accessed 26 October 2023 accessed 26 August 2024

Department of Energy, 'Biden-Harris Administration Announces $6 Billion to Transform America's Industrial Sector, Strengthen Domestic Manufacturing, and Slash Planet-Warming Emissions' <https://www.energy.gov/articles/biden-harris-administration-announces-6-billion-transform-americas-industrial-sector> accessed 31 March 2024

Devarajan S, 'Three reasons Why Industrial Policy Fails' (Brookings, 2016) <https://www.brookings.edu/articles/three-reasons-why-industrial-policy-fails/> accessed 26 August 2024

DiPippo G/Mazzocco I/Kennedy S, 'Red Ink: Estimating Chinese Industrial Policy Spending in Comparative Perspective' (Center for Strategic and International Studies (CSIS) 2022) <https://www.csis.org/analysis/red-ink-estimating-chinese-industrial-policy-spending-comparative-perspective> accessed 12 August 2024

Driesen D/Mehling M/Popp D, 'Industrial Policy, Populism, and the Political Economy of Climate Action' (2024) Vol. 14 Nature Climate Change 414

European Commission, 'Communication from the Commission to the Council and the European Parliament: EU Policies and Measures to Reduce Greenhouse Gas Emissions – Towards a European Climate Change Programme (ECCP)' COM (2000) 88 final' <https://eur-lex.europa.eu/LexUriServ/LexUriServ.do?uri=COM:2000:0088:FIN:EN:PDF> accessed 26 August 2024

European Commission, 'Communication from the Commission to the European Parliament, the European Council, the Council, the European Economic and Social Committee and the Committee of the Regions: The European Green Deal' COM (2019) 640 final' <https://eur-lex.europa.eu/legal-content/EN/TXT/?uri=COM%3A2019%3A640%3AFIN> accessed 26 August 2024

European Commission, Communication from the Commission to the European Parliament, the European Council, the Council, the European Economic and Social Committee and the Committee of the Regions 'A Green Deal Industrial Plan for the Net-Zero Age' COM (2023) 62 final <https://commission.europa.eu/system/files/2023-02/COM_2023_62_2_EN_ACT_A%20Green%20Deal%20Industrial%20Plan%20for%20the%20Net-Zero%20Age.pdf> accessed 17 March 2023

European Commission, 'Commission Implementing Regulation (EU) 2023/1773 Laying down the Rules for the Application of Regulation (EU) 2023/956 of the European Parliament and of the Council as Regards Reporting Obligations for the Purposes of the Carbon Border Adjustment Mechanism during the Transitional Period' (2023) OJ L 228/94

European Commission, 'Proposal for a Regulation of the European Parliament and of the Council Establishing a Framework for Ensuring a Secure and Sustainable Supply of Critical Raw Materials (Critical Raw Materials Act)' COM (2023) 160 final <https://eur-lex.europa.eu/legal-content/EN/TXT/?uri=CELEX%3A52023PC0160> accessed 16 March 2023

Evenett S, 'The Return of Industrial Policy in Data' (International Monetary Fund (IMF) 2024) Working Paper 2024/001 <https://www.imf.org/en/Publications/WP/Issues/2023/12/23/The-Return-of-Industrial-Policy-in-Data-542828> accessed 26 August 2024

Executive Office of the President, 'Executive Order 14057: Catalyzing Clean Energy Industries and Jobs Through Federal Sustainability' <https://www.federalregister.gov/documents/2021/12/13/2021-27114/catalyzing-clean-energy-industries-and-jobs-through-federal-sustainability> accessed 5 September 2023

Farber D, 'Turning Point: Green Industrial Policy and the Future of U.S. Climate Action' (2024) 11 Texas A&M Law Review 303

Gerarden T, 'Demanding Innovation: The Impact of Consumer Subsidies on Solar Panel Production Costs' (2023) 69 Management Science 7799

Goldthau A/Hughes L, 'Protect Global Supply Chains for Low-Carbon Technologies' (2020) 585 Nature 28

Goldthau A/Hughes L/Nahm J, 'The Political Logic of Reshoring in Low Carbon Technologies: Economic Interdependence and Green Industrial Policy' (2022) <https://papers.ssrn.com/abstract=4066047> accessed 26 March 2024

Hardy B, 'How Positive Environmental Policies Affected Europe's Decision to Oppose and Then Adopt Emissions Trading' (2006) 17 Duke Environmental Law & Policy Forum 297

Helveston J/He G/Davidson M, 'Quantifying the Cost Savings of Global Solar Photovoltaic Supply Chains' (2022) 612 Nature 83

Jenkins J, 'Climate Progress and the 117th Congress: The Impacts of the Inflation Reduction Act and Infrastructure Investment and Jobs Act' (Princeton University 2023) <https://repeatproject.org/docs/REPEAT_Climate_Progress_and_the_117th_Congress.pdf> accessed 26 August 2024

Juhász R/Lane N, 'The Political Economy of Industrial Policy' (National Bureau of Economic Research 2024) Working Paper 32507 <http://www.nber.org/papers/w32507> accessed 26 August 2024

Juhász R/Lane N/Rodrik D, 'The New Economics of Industrial Policy' (2024) 16 Annual Review of Economics 213

Kerry J, 'Biden-Sanders Unity Task Force Recommendations: Combating the Climate Crisis and Pursuing Environmental Justice' (2020) <https://joebiden.com/wp-content/uploads/2020/08/UNITY-TASK-FORCE-RECOMMENDATIONS.pdf> accessed 26 August 2024

Krugman P, 'How to Think About Green Industrial Policy' *New York Times* (9 May 2023)

Krugman P, 'Targeted Industrial Policies: Theory and Evidence' (1983) Proceedings: Economic Policy Symposium – Jackson Hole 123

Kupfer J, 'The Conservative Case for Keeping the Inflation Reduction Act' (The Hill, 18 March 2024) <https://thehill.com/opinion/energy-environment/4538435-the-conservative-case-for-keeping-the-inflation-reduction-act/> accessed 31 March 2024

Lamperti F, 'The Green Transition: Public Policy, Finance, and the Role of the State' (2019) 88 Vierteljahrshefte zur Wirtschaftsforschung 73

Lewis J, 'The Climate Risk of Green Industrial Policy' (2024) 123 Current History 14

Lewis J, 'The Rise of Renewable Energy Protectionism: Emerging Trade Conflicts and Implications for Low Carbon Development' (2014) 14 Global Environmental Politics 10

Lincicome S/Zhu H, 'Questioning Industrial Policy: Why Government Manufacturing Plans Are Ineffective and Unnecessary' (Cato Institute 2021) White Paper <https://www.cato.org/sites/cato.org/files/2021-09/white-paper-questioning-industrial-policy-updated.pdf> accessed 26 August 2024

Liu W, 'Foul Play? On the Scale and Scope of Industrial Subsidies in China' (Kiel Institute for the World Economy 2024) Policy Brief 173 <https://www.ifw-kiel.de/publications/foul-play-on-the-scale-and-scope-of-industrial-subsidies-in-china-32738> accessed 26 August 2024

Marcacci S, 'The Inflation Reduction Act Is The Most Important Climate Action In U.S. History' (2022) Forbes <https://www.forbes.com/sites/energyinnovation/2022/08/02/the-inflation-reduction-act-is-the-most-important-climate-action-in-us-history> accessed 31 March 2024

Marcu A/Mehling A/Cosbey A, 'CBAM in a Portfolio of Measures for Industrial Decarbonization' (European Roundtable on Climate Change and Sustainable Transition (ERCST) 2023) <https://ercst.org/cbam-in-a-portfolio-of-measures-for-industrial-decarbonization> accessed 31 March 2024

Mazzucato M, 'Financing the Green New Deal' (2022) 5 Nature Sustainability 93

Mazzucato M, The Entrepreneurial State: Debunking Public vs. Private Sector Myths (Anthem Press 2013)

McNamara K, 'Transforming Europe? The EU's Industrial Policy and Geopolitical Turn' (2023) Journal of European Public Policy 1

Meadows D et al., 'EU ETS: Pricing Carbon to Drive Cost-Effective Reductions across Europe', in **Delbeke J/Vis P** (eds), EU Climate Policy Explained (Routledge 2015) 26

Mehling MA et al., 'The European Union's CBAM: Averting Emissions Leakage or Promoting the Diffusion of Carbon Pricing?' (University of Cambridge 2024) forthcoming 2024

Mertens J et al., 'From Emissions to Resources: Mitigating the Critical Raw Materials Supply Chain Vulnerability of Renewable Energy Technologies' (2024) 37 Mineral Economics 669

Meyer R, 'Congress Just Passed a Big Climate Bill. No, Not That One.' (The Atlantic, 10 August 2022) <https://www.theatlantic.com/science/archive/2022/08/chips-act-climate-bill-biden/671095> accessed 31 March 2024

National People's Congress, 'The 14th Five-Year Plan for National Economic and Social Development and the Long-Range Objectives Through the Year 2035' <http://www.gov.cn/xinwen/2021-03/13/content_5592657.htm> accessed 26 August 2024

Nahm J, Collaborative Advantage: Forging Green Industries in the New Global Economy (Oxford University Press 2021)

Neely M, 'The Pitfalls of Industrial Policy' (1933) 1 The Regional Economist 10

Noth F/Tonzer L, 'Understanding Climate Activism: Who Participates in Climate Marches Such as "Fridays for Future" and What Can We Learn from It?' (2022) 84 Energy Research & Social Science 102360

Oberthür S/Von Homeyer I, 'From Emissions Trading to the European Green Deal: The Evolution of the Climate Policy Mix and Climate Policy Integration in the EU' (2023) 30 Journal of European Public Policy 445

Ocasio-Cortez A, Recognizing the Duty of the Federal Government to Create a Green New Deal' H.R. Res. 109 2019 (109)

Paleari S, 'The Role of Strategic Autonomy in the EU Green Transition' (2024) 16 Sustainability

Popp D, 'Innovation and Climate Policy' (2010) 2 Annual Review of Resource Economics 275

Posen A, 'America's Zero-Sum Economics Doesn't Add Up' (Foreign Policy, 2 April 2024) <https://foreignpolicy.com/2023/03/24/economy-trade-united-states-china-industry-manufacturing-supply-chains-biden> accessed 30 March 2024

Rodrik D, 'Green Industrial Policy' (2014) 30 Oxford Review of Economic Policy 469

Sargent J/Singh M/Sutter K, 'Frequently Asked Questions: CHIPS Act of 2022 Provisions and Implementation' (Congressional Research Service 2023) CRS Report R47523 <https://crsreports.congress.gov/product/pdf/R/R47523> accessed 26 August 2024

Schlacke S, 'Implementing the EU Climate Law via the "Fit for 55" Package' (2022) 1 Oxford Open Energy 1

Schreurs M, 'Jockeying for Climate Leadership Amidst Rising Global Tensions: China, USA and the European Union' in **Biba S** (ed), Europe in an Era of US-China Strategic Rivalry: Challenges and Opportunities from an Outside-in Perspective (Springer Nature Switzerland 2024)

Smead R, 'Infrastructure Permitting and Friction in the Energy Transition' (2024) 40 Climate and Energy 27

Spaiser V/Nisbett N/Stefan C, '"How Dare You?"—The Normative Challenge Posed by Fridays for Future' (2022) 1 PLOS Climate e0000053

State Council, 'Notice of the State Council on the Publication of "Made in China 2025" (Unofficial Translation)' <https://cset.georgetown.edu/wp-content/uploads/t0432_made_in_china_2025_EN.pdf>

Tagliapietra S/Veugelers R, 'Developing a Green Industrial Policy for the European Green Deal' in **Díaz López F/Mazzanti M/Zoboli R** (eds), Handbook on Innovation, Society and the Environment (Edward Elgar Publishing 2023) 36

Thurow L, *Head to Head: The Economic Battle Among Japan, Europe, and America* (William Morrow & Co 1992)

Tamborrino K/Siegel J, 'Big Winners from Biden's Climate Law: Republicans Who Voted against It' (POLITICO, 23 January 2023) <https://www.politico.com/news/2023/01/23/red-states-are-winning-big-from-dems-climate-law-00078420> accessed 31 March 2024

United States, 'The United States' Nationally Determined Contribution. Reducing Greenhouse Gases in the United States: A 2030 Emissions Target' <https://unfccc.int/sites/default/files/NDC/2022-06/United%20States%20NDC%20April%2021%202021%20Final.pdf> accessed 26 August 2024

Von der Leyen U, 'Political Guidelines for the Next European Commission 2019–2024' (Publications Office of the European Union 2020) <https://data.europa.eu/doi/10.2775/101756> accessed 26 August 2024

Vestal J, 'Japanese Industrial Policy, Past and Future' in **Vestal J** (ed), Planning for Change: Industrial Policy and Japanese Economic Development, 1945–1990 (Oxford University Press 1995)

Victor D G/Carlton E K, 'Technology to Solve Global Problems: An Emerging Consensus for Green Industrial Policy?' (2023) 18 Environmental Research Letters 091006

Veugelers R/Tagliapietra S/Trasi C, 'Green Industrial Policy in Europe: Past, Present, and Prospects' (2024) 24 Journal of Industry, Competition and Trade 4

Wettestad J, 'The Making of the 2003 EU Emissions Trading Directive: An Ultra-Quick Process Due to Entrepreneurial Proficiency?' (2005) 5 Global Environmental Politics 1

White House, 'Building a Clean Energy Economy: A Guidebook to the Inflation Reduction Act's Investments in Clean Energy and Climate Action' <https://www.whitehouse.gov/wp-content/uploads/2022/12/Inflation-Reduction-Act-Guidebook.pdf> accessed 26 August 2024

Part B –
The Law of Energy transition in European Countries: General Perspectives

General Perspectives on the Law of Energy Transition in Germany

Till Markus

A. Introduction

Germany's *Energiewende* is being driven by a myriad of factors: some technical, some economic, some political and some legal.[1] Many of these factors are inextricably linked and most of them are *sine qua non* conditions for its current status and future development. This article aims to understand the characteristics of these factors and their interactions. To this end, it will investigate the basic structures and mechanics of German energy politics, the energy market, and the law governing energy production. In addition, it will take a close look at the conflicting interests that Germany's governments, legislators and courts have had to balance out over the years and that have shaped, and will continue to shape, the transformation of energy production.

As a first step, it provides an overview of the composition of the German energy mix since the beginning of the energy transition (B.). As a second step, it presents some basic information on the political and constitutional system that shapes German energy policy (C.). In this regard, it will outline the structure of the political system (federalism), and key constitutional obligations with respect to energy supply and climate protection, which will be followed by a profile of relevant actors and their interests. Thirdly, it will present specific legally binding targets to guide and implement the energy transition (D.). It will conclude with five sections, all of which introduce central legislation regarding the nuclear phase-out (E.), the coal phase-out (F.), the move away from oil and gas (G.), and the transition towards renewable energy (H.) and green hydrogen (I.).

---

1 For a general account see e.g. Katharina Hillebrandt et al., 'Pathways to deep decarbonisation in Germany' (SDSN – IDDR 2015). See also contributions in Olaf Kühne/Florian Weber (eds), *Bausteine der Energiewende* (Springer 2018); German Environment Agency (Umweltbundesamt), 'Treibhausneutrales Deutschland im Jahr 2050' (2014).

B. The Transformation of the German Energy Mix

This article aims to provide both a systematic overview and a deeper understanding of the laws governing the German Energy Transition (*Energiewende*). It outlines the evolution of Germany's energy mix, gives background information on the political and constitutional system that shapes the German energy policy, and presents key legislation and policies on phasing out energy production based on nuclear power and coal, reducing oil and gas use, and developing renewables and green hydrogen. In doing so, it hopes to contribute to the possibility of future comparative studies in this highly dynamic field.

Reducing primary energy consumption and switching energy production to renewable energy sources are the two fundamental strategies for transforming the energy sector. In total, Germany has reduced its consumption of primary energy from 1990 to 2024 by just under 30 %. In 2024, approximately 20.0 % of the country's energy was provided by renewable sources. The energy sources' individual share in energy consumption is outlined in the following table:

Table 1: Germany's energy mix: share of primary energy consumption by source in 2024[2]

Source Type	**Total Share 1990**	**Total Share 2024**	**Specific Source**	**Specific Share 1990**	**Specific Share 2024 (approx.)**
Fossil fuels	86 %	77.3 %	Oil Natural gas Hard coal Lignite	35 % 15 % 15 % 21 %	36.5 % 25.9 % 7.3 % 7.6 %
Nuclear	11 %	0 %		11 %	0 %
Renewables	1.3 %	20 %	Waste Hydro Wind Solar Biomass Geothermal	1.3 %	1.1 % 0.5 % 3.9 % 2.2 % 8.8 % 0.8 %
Others	1.7 %	2.8 %	Others	1.7 %	2.8 %

2 AG Energiebilanzen e.V., 'Verbrauchsrückgang hat sich verlangsamt' (18 March 2025) <https://ag-energiebilanzen.de/verbrauchsrueckgang-hat-sich-verlangsamt/> accessed 31 May 2025.

Shares of renewable energy sources differ quite substantially between the electricity, heating, and transportation sectors. Renewable energy is particularly important for producing electricity (54.4 %), less for heating and cooling (18.1 %), and even less for transportation (7.2 %).[3] Among the renewables, on- and offshore wind turbines currently provide half of the electricity, while solar energy makes up for 26.1 %, biomass for 18 %, and hydropower for 7.8 %.[4] These numbers show that much of the primary energy consumption is still based on fossil fuels and they also indicate the challenges ahead: In the future, renewable energies will have to compensate for the reduction of power generated through nuclear and basically all types of fossil fuels. While Germany had planned to rely strongly on natural gas as a transitory means to lower its CO_2-emissions and compensate for nuclear power, Germany's access to natural gas was interrupted and severely reduced following the Russian invasion of Ukraine. And while Germany has been quite successful in transforming electricity production, it has not produced similarly good outcomes in the transportation or heating and cooling sectors.

C. Political, Constitutional, and Socio-Economic Backgrounds

The special features of Germany's energy policies can best be understood by a look at key historical events, the constitutional framework that obligates both the federal and sub-federal governments (the *Bund* and the *Länder*) to provide energy and combat climate change, and the actors involved in energy production.

1. Historical Developments

Historically, Germany invested heavily in mining and using hard coal (especially in West Germany) and lignite (especially in East Germany) for

3 Federal Ministry for Economic Affairs and Climate Actions (BMWK), Working Group for Renewable Energy Statistics (AGEE-Stat), 'Erneuerbare Energien in Deutschland, Daten zur Entwicklung im Jahr 2024' (2025) 6. Available online at <https://www.umweltbundesamt.de/sites/default/files/medien/479/publikationen/hgp_erneuerbareenergien_2024.pdf> accessed 31 May 2025.

4 ibid. 8.

energy production.[5] Huge coal deposits as well as rising global oil and gas production and trade provided for plentiful and relatively cheap energy during the 1950s and 1960s. Two major price shocks – caused by the oil crises in the early and late 1970s – forced Germany, however, to redirect its overall energy strategy: Energy saving as well as diversifying energy sources became important policy objectives.[6]

This shift also affected the political debate on the use of nuclear energy during the 1970s and 1980s. During this period a strong anti-nuclear movement developed. This movement was particularly important in the founding of the Green Party (which at least partially explains why the nuclear phase-out remains a key focus of theirs to this day[7]), gained momentum after the Chernobyl disaster in 1986, and achieved the political decision to phase out nuclear power in 1998.[8] This phase-out has been highly controversial over the years ('exiting the exit'), but the Fukushima nuclear accident in 2011 strongly influenced public opinion and led to renewed government dedication to the issue.

Politics in the 1980s were also increasingly influenced by growing concerns about the negative effects of burning coal (namely air pollution and acid rain), leading to the adoption of anti-air pollution legislation.

Energy policy in the 1990s was again strongly influenced by the European Union's efforts to liberalise energy markets, particularly by unbundling utilities and network operators. Since the early 1990s, climate change has also increasingly shaped the political debate about energy production.

---

5 Historical overviews can be found in many sources. See e.g. Henning Türk, 'Kleine Geschichte der Energiepolitik' (2022) 46–47 APuZ 17; Barbara Praetorius, 'Grundlagen der Energiepolitik' in Jörg Radtke/Weert Canzler (eds), *Energiewende: Eine sozialwissenschaftliche Einführung* (Springer 2019); Jürgen Friedrich Hake et al., 'The German Energiewende – History and Status Quo' (2015) 3 Energy 532; Thomas Saretzki, 'Energiepolitik in der Bundesrepublik Deutschland 1949–1999. Ein Politikfeld zwischen Wirtschafts-, Technologie- und Umweltpolitik' in Ulrich Willems (ed), *Demokratie und Politik in der Bundesrepublik 1949–1999* (Springer 2001).

6 See German Federal Constitutional Court (*Bundesverfassungsgericht* – BVerfGE) 30, 292 – Erdölbevorratung.

7 In 1984, it introduced a 'Bill concerning the immediate decommissioning of all nuclear installations in the Federal Republic of Germany' (Atomsperrgesetz) in the German Parliament. It was, however, rejected by the parliamentary majority. See Bundestag Printed Documents (*Bundestag-Drucksachen,* BT-Drs.) 10/1013 of 29 August 1984.

8 See below in section E.

All of these various developments together have amalgamated to form a range of key political goals regarding energy production and supply. These goals have been concisely expressed in then Chancellor Merkel's speech in 2011, held immediately after the Fukushima incident: According to her, German energy policy aims to 'reduce CO_2 emissions, phase out nuclear power, increase renewable energy production, and to guarantee competitive energy prices, a functioning infrastructure, energy efficiency and energy supplies'.[9] These objectives are also enshrined in key energy-related legislation currently in force.[10]

Overall, there is a broad consensus in German politics that the *Energiewende* is particularly necessary to effectively combat climate change. The Green Party's coming to power in 2021 and their political agenda within the new government was indicative of this.[11] In addition, the consensus was strengthened by a German Federal Constitutional Court (*Bundesverfassungsgericht*) landmark decision in 2021, which spelled out the government's constitutional obligations to effectively combat climate change.[12] Finally, Russia's aggression against Ukraine ended Germany's energy cooperation with Russia and forced Germany to a) reduce its dependence on gas, b) diversify its supply chains and c) accelerate its energy transformation.[13] Recent legislative actions to promote the *Energiewende* in the heating sector, however, have met strong public and political protests and created severe conflicts within the coalition ruling Germany till May 2025.[14] It

9 Bundeskanzlerin Angela Merkel, 'Der Weg zur Energie der Zukunft' (Government policy statement 09 June 2011) BT-PlPr 17/114, 12960 (A) ff.; see also Bundeskanzlerin Angela Merkel, 'Zur aktuellen Lage in Japan', (Government policy statement 17 March 2011) BT-PlPr 17/96, 10882 (D) ff.

10 See e.g. § 1 German Energy Act (*Energiewirtschaftsgesetz*), 21 Juli 2014, BGBL I 1066.; § 1 Renewable Energy Sources Law (*Erneuerbare-Energien-Gesetz*), 21 Juli 2014, BGBL I 1066.

11 The Social Democratic Party, the Green Party and the Free Democratic Party, *Mehr Fortschritt Wagen: Koalitionsvertrag 2021–2025* (2021) 20–51.

12 BVerfG, Order of the First Senate of 24 March 2021 – 1 BvR 2656/18 -, paras 1–270.

13 Felix Ekardt/Theresa Rath, 'Energiekrise: Rechtsentwicklungen auf EU- und Bundesebene – ein Update' (2023) NVwZ 293; Thomas Mann/Lorenz Lang, 'Ein klimaneutrales Stromnetz für Deutschland' (2023) DVBl 897; Wilfried Erbguth, 'Beschleunigung in Zeiten von Klima- und Energiekrise' (2023) Natur und Recht 242; Markus Ludwigs, 'Gewährleistung der Energieversorgungssicherheit in Krisenzeiten' (2022) NVwZ 1086.

14 Gesetz zur Änderung des Gebäudeenergiegesetzes, zur Änderung des Bürgerlichen Gesetzbuches, zur Änderung der Verordnung über Heizkostenabrechnung, zur Änderung der Betriebskostenverordnung und zur Änderung der Kehr- und Überprüfungs-

remains to be seen how stable the overall consensus will remain in face of the many short and medium-term efforts to accelerate the implementation of the energy transition. The new German government, that took office in May 2025, acknowledged in its coalition agreement that it would rely on new gas power plants to address the challenges of shifting to renewable energy production and to ensure competitive energy prices.[15]

2. Constitutional Background

Germany's energy politics, policies, and legislation are strongly shaped by the legal framework laid down in its Federal Constitution (*Grundgesetz*). The Constitution requires the state to provide energy and also to combat climate change: the interplay of these often competing interests is foundational for understanding the *Energiewende*. It is also helpful to know that the Constitution divides legislative and administrative powers between the federal and the sub-federal governments.

(a) Constitutional Objectives and Obligations

Guaranteeing energy supply and combatting climate change constitute two fundamental interests addressed by Germany's Federal Constitution, both of which are particularly important in the context of the *Energiewende*. In general, the two interests are framed as constitutional objectives. In addition, the Federal Constitutional Court has made clear how important it deems these objectives for safeguarding fundamental rights. Accordingly, both interests are to be pursued by the legislature, the executive, and the courts,[16] but especially by the legislature. In this regard, the Constitution grants it a wide margin of discretion (*Einschätzungsprärogative*). In implementing these objectives and protecting fundamental rights, however, all three powers must balance different constitutional interests carefully and make sure that none of them is disproportionately neglected.

---

ordnung, G. v. 16.10.2023 BGBl. 2023 I Nr. 280; Walter Frenz, 'EU-"Heizungsgesetz": eigentumsrechtliche und soziale Grenzen des Klimaschutzes' (2023) EuR 417.

15 The Christian Democrats, the Christian Social Democrats, The Social Democrats, Verantwortung für Deutschland: Koalititionsvertrag 2025–2029 (2025) 33.

16 Art. 1 (3) Grundgesetz.

In its interpretation of Germany's Federal Constitution, the Federal Constitutional Court has characterised the continuous and safe supply of energy 'as fundamental as the interest in our daily bread'.[17] It considers energy safety as a 'public task' and has declared it to be a 'supreme public good' that 'exists regardless of and unaffected by day-to-day politics'.[18] The Court has repeatedly argued that the state is required to guarantee sufficient energy supplies in order to meet its constitutional obligations a) to safeguard the fundamental right to a 'humane existence'[19] and also b) to give effect to its mandate as a 'social federal state',[20] see Art. 1 (1) and Art. 20 (1) German Constitution.[21]

The German Constitution also obliges the state to take climate action. Its Art 20a reads as follows: 'Mindful also of its responsibility towards future generations, the state shall protect the natural foundations of life and animals by legislation and, in accordance with law and justice, by executive and judicial action (...).'[22] In 2021, the Federal Constitutional Court has spelled out in great detail what this means in regard to Germany's obligations to combat climate change.[23] The Court particularly explained that Art. 20a GG 'includes the aim of achieving climate neutrality'.[24] Notably, the Court has argued that fundamental rights laid down in the Constitution constitute 'intertemporal guarantees of freedom' and afford 'protection against the greenhouse gas reduction burdens imposed by Art. 20a (...)

17 Translated by the author, see BVerfGE 91, 186 (206).

18 Translated by the author. The Court uses the term 'absolutes Gemeinschaftsgut', see BVerfGE 25, 25, 1 (16) and BVerfGE 30, 292 (323–24).

19 'Human dignity shall be inviolable.' Art. 1 (1) German Constitution (official translation).

20 'The Federal Republic of Germany is a democratic and social federal state', Art. 20 (1) German Constitution.

21 See BVerfGE 66, 248 (258); BVerfGE 30, 292 (324); See also Annette Guckelberger, 'Energie als kritische Infrastruktur' (2015) DVBl 1213 f.; see also Reinhard Ruge, *Die Gewährleistungsverantwortung des Staates und der Regulatory State: Zur veränderten Rolle des Staates nach der Deregulierung der Stromwirtschaft in Deutschland, Großbritannien und der EU* (Dunker & Humblot 2004) 218–232; Johannes Saurer, 'Verfassungsrechtliche Konfliktlagen im Klimaschutzrecht' in: *Bitburger Gespräche, Jahrbuch 2021* (C.H. Beck 2022) 97.

22 Official translation available online at <www.gesetze-im-internet.de/englisch_gg/> accessed 30 January 2024.

23 BVerfG, Order of the First Senate of 24 March 2021 – 1 BvR 2656/18 -, paras 1–270. Explaining and commenting this decision, Gerd Winter, 'The Intergenerational Effect of Fundamental Rights: A Contribution of the German Federal Constitutional Court to Climate Protection' (2023) Journal of Environmental Law 1.

24 BVerfG, Order of the First Senate of 24 March 2021 – 1 BvR 2656/18 -, para 2.

being unilaterally offloaded onto the future.'[25] The Constitution 'imposes an obligation to safeguard fundamental freedom over time and to spread the opportunities associated with freedom proportionately across generations.'[26] Based on this idea, the Court decided that the emission reduction goals in the Federal Climate Law (*Klimagesetz*) at the time were insufficient, forcing the legislature to revise the law and change its goal to achieve net-zero-emissions from 2050 to 2045, thus tightening the legal time frame for the *Energiewende*.

Notably, obligations resulting from Art. 20a GG do not take absolute precedence over other constitutional interests. In cases of conflict, they must be balanced with other constitutional interests and principles.[27] In this regard, however, the Federal Constitutional Court has pointed out that 'the obligation to take climate action is accorded increasing weight as climate change intensifies.'[28]

(b) Division of Legislative Powers

Regarding the energy sector, Germany's Federal Constitution delegates broad legislative powers to the federal legislature.[29] It is responsible for choosing between different energy sources and structuring the sector (generation and supply). Accordingly, most legislative acts on renewable energy production are adopted at the federal level. Energy related legislation in general is mainly based on three Articles. In particular, Art. 74.1.11 of the Constitution entitles the federal legislature to adopt laws on 'matters of the energy industry' (*Energiewirtschaft*). Based on this title, Germany's central energy act – the Federal Energy Industry Act (*Energiewirtschaftsgesetz* – EnWG) – was adopted and subsequently modified over the years. Most importantly, the EnWG defines energy supply as a service of public interest and includes provisions regulating energy prices as well as the planning and development of the electricity grids. In addition, Art. 73.1.14 and Art. 74.1.24 of the Constitution authorise the federal legislature to act on the civil de-

25 ibid para 4.
26 ibid para 4.
27 ibid para 2.a.
28 ibid para 2.a.
29 For a comparative perspective on both Germany's the US's Energy Federalism see Johannes Saurer/ Jonas Monast, 'Renewable Energy Federalism in Germany and the United States' (2020) 10 Transnational Environmental Law 293.

ployment of nuclear energy as well as air pollution. Federal states, however, still hold some important legislative powers and – even more so – administrative competences which are highly relevant for the implementation of the *Energiewende*.[30] It is estimated, for example, that 55 % of all energy related legislative acts at the federal level have to be supported by the federal states in second legislative chamber, i.e. the *Bundesrat* (Federal Council).[31] In addition, federal states have adopted their own climate laws and their local communities hold the competence to designate specific areas for renewable energy projects.[32]

3. Actors and their Interests

The *Energiewende* requires ambitious actions by all parties involved. This includes both vertical and horizontal coordination and cooperation of actors, i.e. at different government levels (local communities, federal states, the federation, the EU, and also between states) as well as among different ministries and important private stakeholders. It has been pointed out that Germany's federal states pursue varying interests regarding the *Energiewende*, depending on, for example, their overall emissions, the structure of their respective economies (whether focusing on industrial production or having a strong renewable sector), and their spatial policies.[33] At the federal level, the Ministry for Economic Affairs and Climate Actions is the most powerful ministry, being responsible for both energy and climate policy. It is supported by the Ministry for the Environment, Climate Action, Nature Conservation, Nuclear Safety, the Ministry for the Interior (responsible for developing the building sector), and the Foreign Ministry (responsible for Germany's international climate policy). In many cases, coordination with or consent from the other ministries is required by law,

30 In principle, the German Constitution assigns the power to implement federal legislation to the federal states, see Art. 83 German Constitution.

31 Michèle Knodt/Jörg Kemmerzell, 'Alle für die Energiewende? Akteure und Institutionen in der deutschen Energiepolitik' (2022) 46–47 APuZ 25 f.

32 Matthias Knauff, 'Landesklimaschutzgesetze' in Michael Rodi (ed), *Handbuch Klimaschutzrecht* (C.H. Beck 2022); Cathrin Zengerling, 'Kommunale Klimaschutzplanung' in Michael Rodi (ed), *Handbuch Klimaschutzrecht* (C.H. Beck 2022).

33 Stefan Wurster/Christina Köhler, 'Die Energiepolitik der Bundesländer. Scheitert die Energiewende am deutschen Föderalismus?' in Achim Hildebrandt/Frieder Wolf (eds), *Die Politik der Bundesländer. Zwischen Föderalismusreform und Schuldenbremse* (2nd edn, Springer 2016) 283–314.

providing checks and balances and giving an opportunity to the various ministries involved to promote their own sectoral interests.[34]

Two more specific sets of actors are also highly influential in shaping the *Energiewende*. German energy politics strongly relies on purpose specific – often *ad hoc* – commissions, councils, and working groups to develop, negotiate, and monitor policies.[35] These bodies are either composed of experts or of actors representing different societal interests.[36] In addition, despite all efforts to liberalise the energy sector, four major energy providers still dominate the German energy market. Together they constitute a powerful voice in German energy politics. In the past, these enterprises have often lobbied to their own immediate interests, usually obstructing the *Energiewende*.[37]

D. (Moving) Targets for the Energy Transition and Key Implementation Challenges

Germany has adopted a broad set of quantifiable targets for its energy transition. Such targets have been subject to continuous revision and adapted several times over the years, mainly in service of accelerating and fine-tuning the energy transition. Acceleration, however, has created several challenges. It has become clear, for example, that in order to achieve the envisaged goals, the government has to substantially increase its financial support for both research and development, and to level out financial burdens which have been unequally distributed. Accordingly, it has begun to invest heavily in research on PtX, carbon capture and storage, carbon capture and use, electricity storage, and digitalisation[38], as well as increasing funding for building hydrogen transport infrastructures,[39] and

34 Knodt/Kemmerzell (n 31) 28.

35 ibid 28 f.

36 Two of these bodies will be introduced later in this chapter, i.e. The Ethical Commission – Safe Energy Supply and The Coal Commission. See below sections E., F.

37 Gregor Kungl, *Die großen Stromkonzerne und die Energiewende* (Campus Verlag 2018); Claudia Kemfert, *Das fossile Imperium schlägt zurück. Warum wir die Energiewende jetzt verteidigen müssen* (Murmann 2017).

38 Bundesregierung, 'Forschungs- und Innovationsförderung des Bundes im Bereich der Zukunftsvorsorge – Forschung für Grundlagen und nachhaltige Entwicklung (Antwort der Bundesregierung auf kleine Anfrage)' BT-Drucksache 20/5758, 21.2.2023.

39 Bundesregierung, 'Fortschreibung der nationalen Wasserstoffstrategie – NWS 2023'

providing support for those who cannot afford increasing energy prices.[40] In addition, non-financial measures promoting acceleration include the shortening of administrative and court procedures concerning renewable energy projects[41], developing strategies and legislation for carbon capture and use or storage and CO_2-removal[42], and boosting international cooperation with a view to building transboundary electricity grids, increasing gas, solar energy and hydrogen imports, and the export of CO_2 for storage.[43]

Another challenge for administrations and legislatures is the need to balance increasingly tense conflicts and overcome acceptance issues with concerns over nature protection (e.g. effects on birds created by wind turbines)[44], restrictions on the free use of privately or municipally owned or administered land (e.g. because of electricity grid development)[45], and structural changes in specific economic sectors and labour markets (e.g.

<www.bmbf.de/SharedDocs/Downloads/de/2023/230726-fortschreibung nws.pdf?__blob=publicationFile&v=1> accessed 30 January 2024.

40 Bundesregierung, 'Überblickpapier der Bundesregierung zur Gas- und Strompreisbremse, 15.12.2022' <www.bmwk.de/Redaktion/DE/Downloads/Energie/gas-strompreis-bremse-ubersicht.pdf?__blob=publicationFile&v=1> accessed 30 January 2024.

41 Regarding procedures see e.g.Peter Schütte/Sarah Langstädtler, 'Deutschlandtempo als "new normal"?' (2024) ZUR 3; Angela Schwerdtfeger, 'Beschleunigungsgebiete für Erneuerbaren Energien – Fragen des Rechtsschutzes' (2023) EurUP 365; Angela Schwerdtfeger, 'Beschleunigung durch Beschränkung des Rechtsschutzes?' (2023) ZUR 451; Sabine Schlacke/Helen Wentzien/Dominik Römling, 'Beschleunigung der Energiewende: Ein gesetzgeberischer Paradigmenwechsel durch das Osterpaket?' (2022) NVwZ 1577.

42 Till Markus/Danny Otto/Daniela Thrän, 'Die Carbon Management Strategie und CCS im Lichte klima- und energierechtlicher Weichenstellungen' (2024) ZUR 387; Claudio Franzius, 'CDR-Technologien auf dem Weg in die Klimaneutralität' (2024) EurUP 119.

43 Claudio Franzius 'Beschleunigung des Markthochlaufs von Wasserstoff: Fördermöglichkeiten und Beschleunigungsaspekte für Infrastrukturen und Erzeugungsanlagen' (2024) ZUR 72; Bundesregierung, *The Revised German Hydrogen Strategy* (2023); see also below in Section I.

44 Illustrative BverfG (1 BvR 2523/13) Rotmilan, BverfGE [2018] 149, 407 [23]. See Wolfgang Köck/Till Markus, 'German Courts on Scientific Uncertainties in Nature Conservation Law' in Mariolina Eliantonio/Emma Lees/Tiina Poliniitty (eds), *EU Environmental Principles and Scientific Uncertainty Before National Courts – the case of the Habitats-Directive* (Bloomsbury: Hart Books, 2023).

45 See e.g. Pascal Langenbach, 'Zur Rezeption empirischer Forschung und psychologischer Verfahrenstheorie in der verwaltungsrechtlichen Debatte zur Akzeptanz des Stromnetzausbaus' (2022) Die Verwaltung 191; Johanna Decher, *Die Rechte der Gemeinden beim Ausbau des Übertragungsnetzes* (Mohr Siebeck 2022); see also articles in Kurt Faßbender/Wolfgang Köck (eds), *Aktuelle Entwicklungen und Probleme beim*

the closure of nuclear plants[46], coal mines, and coal power plants).[47] The following table provides an overview of the most important political and legal targets that drive the energy transitions:

Table 2: Political and Legal Targets for Germany's Energy Transitions

Target Type	Content and Timeframe
Emission Reductions	• Net Zero: 2045 / Negative Emission 2050[48] • Energy Sector: 280 by 2020 / 108 by 2030 (CO_2-eq mio t)[49]
Nuclear Phase-Out	• April 2023[50]
Coal Phase-Out	• 2038 (aiming for 2035)[51]
Oil & Gas Phase-Out	• Specific measures but no deadlines and no quantitative targets
Renewable Energies[52]	• 80 % electricity from renewable sources by 2030 • 160 GW from onshore wind by 2040 • 2 % of the German territory must be made available for onshore wind farms • 70 GW from offshore wind by 2045 • 400 GW from solar power by 2040 • 8.4 GW from biomass by 2030

Netzausbau (Nomos 2021). See also Birgit Peter, *Legitimation durch Öffentlichkeitsbeteiligung* (JCB Mohr 2020).

46 See below section E.

47 See below section F.

48 § 3 (2) Bundes-Klimaschutzgesetz (Federal Climate Act) of 12 December 2019 (BGBl. I 2513), which was amended by Article 1 of the Act of 15 July 2024 (BGBl. I 235).

49 ibid, § 4, Annex 2.

50 See below section E.

51 § 2 (2), Nr. 3, § 4 (1) Kohleverstromungsbeendigungsgesetz (KVBG). Germany committed itself internationally to exit by 2035, see G7, 'Climate, Energy and Environment Ministers' Meeting Communiqué, Ministerial meeting on Climate, Energy and Environment – 28–29–30 April' (2024).

52 Goals regarding renewable energy from onshore wind farms, solar power, and biomass are laid down in § 1 (2) and § 4 of the Renewable Energy Sources Act, Erneuerbare-Energien-Gesetz of 21 July 2014 (BGBl. I 1066), which was last amended by Article 1 of the Act of 21 February 2025 (BGBl. 2025 I Nr. 52). Goals for renewable energy from offshore wind farms are laid down in § 1 (2) Windenergie-auf-See-Gesetz of 13 October 2016 (BGBl. I S. 2258, 2310), which was last amended by Article 44 of the Act of 23 October 2024 (BGBl. 2024 I Nr. 323). Regarding the 2 % goal see Gesetz zur Erhöhung und Beschleunigung des Ausbaus von Windenergieanlagen an Land, BGBl. I 2022 1353.

Target Type	Content and Timeframe
Hydrogen	• 10 GW electrolysis capacity by 2030[53]
Electricity Grid	• Approx. 14,000 km extension planned[54]

E. Nuclear Exit

Very few countries in the world have decided to leave nuclear energy production entirely behind.[55] This is particularly true in regard to countries that have many, relatively modern, and comparatively safe facilities in operation.[56] Over 27 years (i.e. 1962 to 1989), Germany built and put into operation 32 commercial nuclear power plants. Their share in electricity production peaked around the year 2000 at roughly one third.[57] Different German governments have made the Nuclear Exit a top priority of their respective energy policy, outranking even the coal phase-out. Both nuclear energy production in general and the Nuclear Exit in particular have been highly controversial and led to severe political and legal conflicts, many of which ended up in the Germany's highest courts.[58]

Strong opposition to nuclear energy production emerged in the early 1970s, leading to protests in front of power plant construction sites as well as to legal actions before courts. Most litigation revolved around the

53 Bundesregierung, Wasserstoffstrategie (n 39).

54 Federal Ministry for Economic Affairs and Energy, 'Aktueller Stand des Netzausbaus' (2025), < https://www.bmwk.de/Redaktion/DE/Downloads/M-O/netzausbau-schreitet-voran.pdf?__blob=publicationFile&v=5> accessed 10 June 2026.

55 For a current overview see World Nuclear Association, Plans for New Reactor Worldwide (2023) <https://world-nuclear.org/information-library/current-and-future-generation/plans-for-new-reactorsworldwide.aspx> accessed 30 January 2024.

56 Examples include Italy, Spain, and Taiwan, ibid.

57 See, e.g. International Energy Agency, 'Germany' <www.iea.org/countries/germany> accessed 30 January 2024.

58 Joachim Radkau, *Aufstieg und Krise der deutschen Atomwirtschaft 1945–1975: Verdrängte Alternativen in der Kerntechnik und der Ursprung der nuklearen Kontroverse* (Rowohlt 1983); Alexander Glaser, 'From Brokdorf to Fukushima: The Long Journey to Nuclear Phase-out' (2012) 6 Bulletin of the Atomic Scientists 10–21; Dolores L Augustine, *Taking on Technocracy. Nuclear Power in Germany, 1945 to the Present* (Berghahn Books 2018); Stephen Milder, *Greening Democracy. The Anti-Nuclear Movement and Political Environmentalism in West Germany and Beyond, 1968–1983* (Cambridge University Press 2017).

following three arguments[59]: First, the risk of major accidents could not be ruled out. Second, exhaust air and waste water from regular operations and minor accidents could threaten human health. Third, the safe disposal of nuclear waste was not ensured. Only very few courts, however, decided over the years to annul permissions or actually stop operations.[60]

During the 1980s and particularly in the aftermath of the Chernobyl disaster in 1986, political support for nuclear energy began to fade. Two legislative proposals for a phase out were initiated in the federal parliament.[61] It took, however, until 1998 for the then ruling coalition between the Green Party and the Social Democrats to commit itself to a 'comprehensive and irreversible' exit.[62]

As a first step towards implementing the exit, the government negotiated and agreed with the four major German energy providers operating nuclear power plants. The agreements were integrated into the Nuclear Energy Act (*Atomgesetz*) on 25 July 2002.[63] From then on, no further permission for new nuclear plants would be issued and the existing ones were only allowed to produce a limited quantity of electricity (equalling 32 years' operation in total for each plant). Early shutdowns of old plants would also be incentivised by allowing the transfer of permissions to newer facilities. The law also allowed producers to store nuclear waste temporarily on-site at the power plants.[64]

In 2009 a new government – a coalition between the Christian Democratic Union and the Free Democratic Party – decided to maintain the ban of new facilities, but to extend the plants' overall operation time and to use

59 Gerd Winter, 'The Rise and Fall of Nuclear Energy Use in Germany: Processes, Explanation, and the Role of Law' (2013) 25 Journal of Environmental Law 95.

60 ibid.

61 BT-Drs. 10/1013 of 29 August 1984; BT-Drs. 11/13 of February 1987.

62 Coalition Agreement between the Social Democrats and the Green Party, *Aufbruch und Erneuerung – Deutschlands Weg ins 21. Jahrhundert* (1998) 16 <www.spd.de/fileadmin/Dokumente/Beschluesse/Bundesparteitag/koalitionsvertrag_bundesparteitag_bonn_1998.pdf> accessed 30 January 2024.

63 Law on the Structural Phasing Out of Nuclear Energy Use for Peaceful Purposes (Gesetz zur geordneten Beendigung der Kernenergienutzung zu friedlichen Zwecken), BGBl. 2002, I 1357. Amending particularly § 7 (1a-b) with Annex 3 AtG.

64 For a comprehensive sociological study on the issue of storing radioactive waste in Germany see Jens Pape, *Politik und Recht der Endlagerung radioaktiver Abfälle* (Nomos 2016).

them as a 'bridge technology' in the energy transition.[65] A new agreement was negotiated between the federal government and the four major energy suppliers in 2010 and was again integrated into the Atomic Energy Act. Producers would receive quotas allowing them to continue production with their older plants for eight more years, and with newer ones for 14 more years. In exchange, producers were required to pay fees that would be channelled into the energy transition.[66]

In response to the Fukushima accident in March 2011, the ruling government reconsidered its position on the role of nuclear power. Recognising a fundamental shift in public opinion and strategically anticipating several imminent elections in different federal states, the Federal Government decreed a 'nuclear moratorium', requiring safety checks for all operational nuclear power plants and a three-month shutdown for the seven oldest ones (and for one that had been out of operation due to technical issues). In addition, the government appointed an independent group of experts to develop an exit strategy (The Ethical Commission – Safe Energy Supply). Based on this advice, the government once again amended the Nuclear Energy Act: The formerly introduced extensions were withdrawn and provisional shutdowns were turned into permanent ones. Already granted production quotas, however, could be transferred to those plants still in operation.[67]

The Nuclear Exit was supposed to come to an end on 31 December 2023. The shut-down of the last three nuclear power plants was postponed, however, once more to 15 April 2023, to level out rising energy prices induced by the severe reduction in gas supply due to complications caused by the Russian invasion of Ukraine.[68] Discussions about reviving some of the most modern plants have not fully died down due to the energy prices remaining at high levels.[69]

65 The Christian Democrats, the Christian Social Democrats, and the Free Democrats, 'Coalition Agreement' (2012) 29 <www.kas.de/c/document_library/get_file?uuid=83dbb842-b2f7-bf99-6180e65b2de7b4d4&groupId=252038> accessed 30 January 2024.

66 11th Amendment of the Atomic Energy Act of 8 December 2010, BGBl. 2010 I 1814; Nuclear Fuel Tax Acts of 8 December 2010, BGBl, 2010 I 1804.

67 § 7 I lit. a-b, Annex 3 AtG (version of 22 April 2002).

68 19th Amendment of the Atomic Energy Act (19. AtGÄndG) vom 4.12.2022, BGBl. 2022 I 2153.

69 See e.g. two recent articles in important German newpapers: Christian Geinitz, 'CDU-Wirtschaftsrat: Atomkraft fortsetzen, Stromsteuer senken' *Frankfurter Allgemeine Zeitung* (Frankfurt 1 September 2023); Eric Gujer, 'Die deutsche Verblen-

F. Coal Phase-Out

As in other European countries, German industrialisation was fuelled by coal. For over a century between the 1860s and 1960s, coal was by far Germany's most important energy source. Coal's descent began slowly in the late 1950s when oil and gas became more easily available on the world market, making coal less competitive.[70] In recent decades, growing environmental concerns in general and climate targets in particular were additional drivers.[71] Decline was slow, however, and coal still accounted for nearly 30 % of the domestic electricity production in 2019.[72]

The intentional, systematic policy-driven exit arguably began in June 2018 when the German government, run by a coalition of the Christian and Social Democrats, established the Commission for Growth, Structural Change, and Employment (Coal Commission). The Coal Commission was composed of a broad spectrum of stakeholders and experts and mandated to draw up a strategy for phasing out coal-based energy production and mitigating the effects on regional economies and workers' interests.[73] Its report was submitted in January 2019[74] and formed the base for parliamentary negotiations of two laws, i.e. the Act to Reduce and End Coal-Powered Energy and Amend Other Laws (Coal Phase-Out Act) and the Structural Support for Coal Regions Act (Structural Support Act), which were adopted on 3 July 2020 and entered into force on 14 August 2020[75].

---

dung – Der Atomausstieg ist nichts als Ideologie' *Neue Züricher Zeitung* (Zürich 14 April 2023).

70 Franz-Josef Brüggemeier, 'Das Zeitalter der Kohle in Europa, 1750 bis heute' in bpb (ed), *Abschied von der Kohle: Struktur- und Kulturwandel im Ruhrgebiet und in der Lausitz* (2021) 12–25.

71 Tessa Coggio/Thane Gustafson, 'When the Exit? The Difficult Politics of German Coal' (2019) 37 German Politics & Society 47, 56.

72 See above section B.

73 Kommission "Wachstum, Strukturwandel und Beschäftigung", 'Abschlussbericht' (26 January 2019) 6 f. <www.bmwk.de/Redaktion/DE/Publikationen/Wirtschaft/abschlussbericht-kommission-wachstum-strukturwandelund-beschaeftigung.html> accessed 30 January 2024. See also Olaf Däuper, 'Die Empfehlungen der Kohlekommission: Inhalte und juristische Fragestellungen' (2019) EnWZ 153.

74 Kommission "Wachstum, Strukturwandel und Beschäftigung" (n 73); see also Katharina Baudisch/Dörte Fouquet, 'Germany's Coal Exit Plan: A Legal and Political Outline on How Germany Plans to Phase out Coal Fired Power Stations by 2038' (2019) 9 Renewable Energy Law and Policy Review 45 f.

75 The Coal Phase Out Act is structured in several sections. Each section includes either a stand-alone act or amendments to other laws. Each section is headed by an Article.

In principle, the Coal Phase-Out Act gradually demands reducing the use of coal-powered energy in Germany, aiming to ultimately stop in 2038. In particular, it lays down a timeline for ending electricity generation from hard coal and lignite. By 2022, power generated from both coal types had to be reduced to around 15 gigawatts (GW) each.[76] By 2030, reduction to 8 GW for hard coal and 9 GW for lignite must be achieved.[77] Even by 2038 at the latest, the use of coal-fired plants must come to an end.[78] This schedule may be subject to revision to decide whether the exit can be achieved by 2035.[79]

Targets are to be reached by different means for hard coal and lignite. For hard coal, a two-step approach has been adopted. First, until 2027 hard coal plant operators are called upon to voluntarily shut-down their power plants.[80] To incentivise operators, the act sets up an (reverse) auction system in which operators are granted the opportunity to competitively offer production reduction and receive financial compensation in return.[81] The German Federal Network Agency has organised the auctions and determined a maximum tender volume for each auction.[82] To motivate operators to shut down earlier, compensation sums have decreased each year. Second, after 2027, no more compensations will be paid and operators will simply be required to end their operation according to a specific plan.[83] With regard to lignite power plants, the Coal Phase-Out Act determines specific dates and rules for determining compensation sums for individual

Section 1 (headed by Article 1) includes the Act on the Reduction and Termination of Coal-fired Power Generation (Coal-fired Power Generation Termination Act), i.e. the Gesetz zur Reduzierung und zur Beendigung der Kohleverstromung (Kohleverstromungsbeendigungsgesetz – KVBG), see Gesetz zur Reduzierung und zur Beendigung der Kohleverstromung und zur Änderung weiterer Gesetze (Kohleausstiegsgesetz) vom 8. August 2020 (BGBl I S. 1818); Strukturstärkungsgesetz Kohleregionen vom 8. August 2020 (BGBl. I S. 1795).

76 § 2 (2) Nr. 1 Coal-fired Power Generation Termination Act.

77 ibid § 2 (2) Nr. 2.

78 ibid § 2 (2) Nr. 3, § 4.

79 ibid §§ 47, 56.

80 ibid §§ 10 ff.

81 In a 'reverse auction' the seller bids for the price at which he/she is willing to offer his or her good or service. For an illustrative explanation of how the auction system works under the Coal Phase Out Act, see Agora Energiewende, *Coal Phase-Out in Germany: The Role of Coal Exit Auctions* (2022) 13–20.

82 § 18, § 19 Coal-fired Power Generation Termination Act (n 75).

83 ibid §§ 27–39.

facilities (beginning in 2020 and ending in 2038).[84] This system is supplemented by a general ban of new coal-fired plants after 14 August 2020 (i.e. the day the Act entered into force)[85] as well as a general ban on burning coal for energy production (entering into force in different cases under specific conditions at different points in time).[86]

In addition to phasing out the use of coal, the Structural Support Act offers financial support to affected plant operators, workers, and regions. The Structural Support Act allocates 14 billion Euros to lignite coal regions until 2038 and 1.09 billion Euros to hard coal regions. It also channels a further 26 billion Euros to infrastructure projects and new jobs in federal agencies within the affected areas till 2038.[87] In addition, coal-plant workers 58 years of age and older who lose their jobs due to the decommissioning of plants will be compensated for a maximum of five years until they are eligible to retire (and receive a pension).[88]

The phase-out has been criticised on various grounds. Energy providers have argued that phasing out coal and nuclear would threaten energy safety and investment security, and increase costs for industrial production, thus creating a competitive disadvantage for Germany industries and enterprises.[89] Overall, compensation sums were regarded as too low.[90] Economic experts have opined that the government's exit strategy was much too

84 Lignite coal mines and lignite coal power plants operators will receive compensation for ending operations. Compensations sums are individually negotiated with the government, approved by the parliament, and laid down in contracts (öffentlich-rechtliche Verträge). §§ 40–50, 44 (1–3), Annex 2, 49 Coal-fired Power Generation Termination Act (n 75).

85 ibid § 53. This general ban was subject to one exception: plants which had received a permit before January 29, 2020. The exception was inserted to allow the modern hard coal-fired Datteln IV plant to operate.

86 § 51 Coal Phase Out Act (n 75).

87 See § 1 and § 11, § 27 (2) Structural Support Act (n 75).

88 § 57 Coal-fired Power Generation Termination Act (n 75).

89 See, e.g. Deutscher Industrie- und Handelskammertag, 'Stellungnahme zum Kohleausstiegsgesetz –
Kabinettsfassung' (19 May 2020)
<www.dihk.de/resource/blob/24158/baf1397129bd90dc52ba5b94dd6b1dc4/dihk-stellungnahme-
kohleausstiegsgesetz-kabinettsfassung-data.pdf> accessed 30 January 2024.

90 Some plant operators had argued and sued for higher compensations. See e.g. BVerfG, Beschluss der 1. Kammer des Ersten Senats vom 18. August 2020- 1 BvQ 82/20 -, Rn. 1–32. The file was rendered inadmissible. The plant operator was denied legal standing because the plant was 85.9 % owned by municipalities and could therefore not invoke fundamental rights.

costly: Increasing carbon prices in the EU's emission trading system as well as the growing competition from other energy sources would have rendered coal use unprofitable anyway and most likely caused a market induced phase-out (possibly even earlier).[91] Furthermore, it was argued that alternative governance approaches might have achieved the phase-out earlier and less costly.[92] The Green Party (which was not in government at the time) and green non-governmental organisations basically argued that the phase-out was too slow and that it would make achieving Germany's obligations under the Paris Agreement difficult.[93]

G. Oil & Gas

Like coal, oil and gas are emission-intensive fossil fuels. Not all fossil fuels, however, are equally harmful, and natural gas in particular performs better in regard to greenhouse gas emission intensity. Many countries have encouraged switching from coal or oil to gas and using it as a 'bridge fuel' to a low(er) greenhouse gas emission economy.[94] To this day, Germany has not adopted any specific targets for a gradual or final phase-out for oil and gas. It has, however, adopted several measures which aim to reduce the use of oil and gas, particularly targeting the transport and heating sector. The two most recent and pertinent measures will be highlighted here.

First, to put a price on emissions not covered by the European Emission Trading System (ETS), Germany has adopted the Fuels Emission Trading Act (*Brennstoffemissionshandelsgesetz* – BEHG) in 2021.[95] The basic rationale behind the act is to establish a national emission trading scheme that complements the ETS by requiring those who place CO_2-intensive fuels

91 See e.g. German Council of Economic Experts, 'Setting Out for A New climate Policy' (2019) 37–44 <www.sachverstaendigenratwirtschaft.de/fileadmin/dateiablage/gutachten/sg2019/sg_2019_en.pdf> accessed 30 January 2024.

92 Johann-Christian Pielow, 'Rechtsfragen des Kohleausstiegs' in Michael Rodi (ed), *Handbuch Klimaschutzrecht* (C.H. Beck 2022) 600 f.

93 For an overview of the green criticism see e.g. Louisa Reitbaur, 'The New German Coal Laws: A Difficult Balancing Act' (2021) 11 Climate Law 176, 185–187.

94 See e.g. Justin Gundlach/Michael B Gerrard, 'Climate Change and energy Transition Policies' in Jorge E Viñuales/Emma Lees (eds), *The Oxford Handbook of Comparative Environmental Law* (Oxford University Press 2019) 531, 565–567.

95 Brennstoffemissionshandelsgesetz of 12 December 2019 (BGBl. I 2728), which was last amended by Article 7 of the Act of 22 December 2023 (BGBl. 2023 I Nr. 412).

on the market to obtain and submit (tradeable) emission certificates and to gradually limit the total number of certificates ('upstream emissions trading').[96] This system in effect makes using oil and gas increasingly expensive and using renewable energy more attractive. Fuels covered by the new scheme include, for example, petrol, diesel, heating oil, natural gas, coal and materials for waste incineration.[97] Rising costs ought to be passed on to fuel end-users, who are thus incentivised to reduce their consumption.[98] From 2027 on the amount of certificates in national emission trading scheme will be linked (and thus limited) to Germany's overall emission budget granted under EU law.[99] In addition, the BEHG ensures that those participating in the ETS are not charged twice under the two trading regimes.[100] In such cases participants will be compensated.[101]

Second, to lower fossil fuel dependency in the heating sector, Germany recently adopted legislation to substantially amend its Building Energy Act (*Gebäudeenergiegesetz* – GEG).[102] This amending act has often been termed the 'Heating Systems Act' (*Heizungsgesetz*)[103], because it primarily establish-

96 § 1 BEHG.

97 § 2 Annex I BEHG.

98 The law intends to pass costs on to end users. It is the users (not the providers) of fuels who ultimately decide the quantities used, see Miriam Vollmer, 'BEHG/Nationales Brennstoffemissionshandelssystem (nEHS)' in Michael Rodi (ed), *Handbuch Klimaschutzrecht* (C.H. Beck 2022) 325 f.

99 See § 4 (1), S. 2 BEHG. The law refers to the overall emissions laid down in § 4 (1) and Annex I of the Regulation
(EU) 2018/842 of the European Parliament and of the Council of 30 May 2018 on binding annual greenhouse gas emission reductions by member states from 2021 to 2030 contributing to climate action to meet commitments under the Paris Agreement and amending Regulation (EU) No 525/2013 [2018] OJ L 156/26. Before 2027, there was not an overall cap, turning the price mechanism into a fee or tax. It was heavily discussed whether the fee or tax approach was in compliance with the German constitution, see Vollmer (n 97) 315.

100 In principle, this should not happen, see § 7 (5) BEHG.

101 § 11 (2) BEHG.

102 Gebäudeenergiegesetz of 08 August 2020 (BGBl. I S. 1728), which was last amended by Article 1 of the Act of 16 October 2023 (BGBl. 2023 I Nr. 280). The Building Energy Act has existed since 2020. It aims to reduce greenhouse gas emissions from buildings by increasing the use of renewable energy and unavoidable waste heat for energy supply. The Act requires that these measures be economically viable, socially acceptable, and efficiency-enhancing. See § 1 GEG.

103 Gesetz zur Änderung des Gebäudeenergiegesetzes, zur Änderung des Bürgerlichen Gesetzbuches, zur Änderung der Verordnung über Heizkostenabrechnung, zur Änderung der Betriebskostenverordnung und zur Änderung der Kehr- und Überprüfungsordnung, G. v. 16.10.2023 BGBl. 2023 I Nr. 280. See Thomas Hei-

es a set of requirements regarding the phasing out of oil- and gas-based heating systems for most types of buildings.[104] The GEG entered into force on 1 January 2024. In principle, from now on any new heating system that is installed has to run on 65 per cent renewable energy (but existing heaters may continue to be operated and broken heaters may be repaired).[105] The law distinguishes between new and existing buildings: While newly built houses generally fall within the remit of the general requirement from 1 January 2024 onwards, different deadlines apply for existing buildings as well as new buildings which are being constructed in urbanised areas (i.e. placed into 'gaps between existing bulidings' or *Baulücken*). This last exception allows for a better integration of newly built buildings into existing long-distance heating systems. Depending on the size of the city, deadlines are 30 June 2026 (for cities with less than 100,000 inhabitants) or 1 June 2028 (for cities with more than 100,000 inhabitants).[106] The law also provides that the 65 per cent obligation is automatically met where specific types of more sustainable heating systems are installed (e.g. systems connected to the local or regional public heating systems, electrical heat pumps, solar-thermal systems, biomass- or hydrogen-based heating systems, etc.)[107] The newly introduced regime also provides the government the opportunity to grant massive financial support for installing new heating systems, in some cases covering up to 70 % of the arising costs.[108] Despite the significant public funding, the Heating Systems Act has remained unpopular. The new government, which took office in May 2025, has indicated that it will abolish many of the requirements introduced by the Act.[109]

In parallel to revising the GEG, another central measure has been developed and adopted. The Heat Planning and Decarbonisation of Heating Networks Act (*Gesetz für die Wärmeplanung und zur Dekarbonisierung der Wärmenetze – Wärmeplanungsgesetz*) was passed by the German legislature

---

nicke, 'Das "Heizungsgesetz" – Die Voelle des Gebäudeenergiegesetzes und dem Blickwinkel von Art. 14 GG' (2024) KlimRZ 3.

104 § 2 GEG determines the types of buildings that fall within the act's remit.

105 § 71 (1) GEG.

106 § 71 (8) GEG.

107 § 71 (3), § 71 lit. b-h GEG.

108 Federal Ministry for Economic Affairs and Climate Actions, 'Richtlinie für die Bundesförderung für effiziente Gebäude – Einzelmaßnahmen (BEG EM) vom 21. Dezember 2023' (BAnz AT 29.12.2023 B1) 1–32.

109 The Christian Democrats, the Christian Social Democrats, The Social Democrats, Verantwortung für Deutschland: Koalititionsvertrag 2025–2029 (2025) 24.

on 17 November 2023 and entered into force on 1 January 2024.[110] The Act's main goal is also to transition away from fossil fuels in heat supply.[111] To this end, it requires federal states to systematically establish 'heat plans' for their respective territories.[112] In addition to this obligation, the law aims to significantly expand and promote heat supply by long-distance heating systems which will deliver energy from renewable sources or waste heat.[113] To this end, it sets ambitious targets for grid operators. For example, grids must derive at least 30 % of their heat from renewable energy sources or waste energy by 2030, and at least 80 % by 2040.[114] Both enhancing planning in general and decarbonising energy supply through long distance grid systems may strengthen the overall role of centralised heating systems in the future. This development will probably also be stimulated by § 109 GEG which entitles local municipalities (or associated municipalities) to require their respective citizens to connect their buildings to long-distance heating or cooling systems.[115]

H. Promoting Renewable Energy

It has been aptly pointed out that integrating renewable energy into existing energy systems meets three basic challenges: 'price competitiveness of renewable with traditional generation, difficulties in siting renewable facilities and transmission lines (...), and integrating renewables' variable outputs and financial profiles (...) into existing grid operations and accounting'.[116] Germany has responded to these challenges by adopting different sets of legislation.[117] Since the early 1990s the German government's efforts to

110 BGBl. 2023 Teil I Nr. 394, 1–30.
111 § 1 Wärmeplanungsgesetz.
112 § 4 – § 25 Wärmeplanungsgesetz.
113 § 2 Wärmeplanungsgesetz.
114 § 29 (1) Wärmeplanungsgesetz.
115 Municipalities are entitled to require connection 'for the purpose of climate and resource protection.' The provision had been introduced earlier in § 16 of the Renewable Energy Heating System Act (Gesetz zur Förderung Erneuerbarer Energien im Wärmebereich), Gesetz vom 07.08.2008 (BGBl. I S. 1658). On the legal nature and constitutional legality of this requirement see, in particular, Federal Administrative Court, Judgment 08.09.2016 (BVerwG 10 CN 1.15).
116 See e.g. Gundlach/Gerard (n 94) 531, 561.
117 For a more comprehensive overview see Michael Fehling's chapter in this book. See also for a more general account of the financial instruments supporting the energy

advance renewable energy production, however, had a strong focus on promoting the transformation of the electricity sector, particularly by creating financial incentives for investing in renewable energy production.[118] Efforts to expand and improve management of transmission lines began significantly later but have been increased and accelerated in recent years.[119] The following subsection will provide an overview of the measures which have aimed to promote the price competitiveness of renewables.[120]

The Electricity Feed-in Act of 1990 (*Stromeinspeisungsgesetz* – StrEG) constituted an important early step in this regard, establishing a kind of prototype approach for subsequent legislation: It required energy providers (which at that time also owned the energy transmission lines) to purchase renewable energy from producers in accordance with technology-specific feed-in tariffs.[121] This basic obligation established a reliable support scheme for producers by substantially lowering their investment risks. While this scheme had no significant impact on expanding solar energy production, wind power generation increased from 70 MW in 1990 to 4,445 MW by 1999.[122]

In 2000 the German legislature developed this approach into a more comprehensive system and adopted the Renewable Energy Sources Act (*Erneuerbare Energien Gesetz* – EEG). To this day, the EEG has remained Germany's central regulatory instrument to promote investments in renewable energy production. In 2000 its overall goal was to promote climate protection by doubling renewable energy production by 2010. Producers of renewable energy received the right to require transmission line operators to provide certain information, expand their grids, connect production units, accept their renewable energy (even prioritise it over energy derived from fossil fuels), and reimburse them in accordance with technology-spe-

transition Michael Rodi, 'Das Instrumentarium zur staatlichen Finanzierung der Energietransformation' (2023) 11 KlimR 322.

118 For a more comprehensive account of German law on the expansion of renewables see Fehling, in this volume, 301 ff.

119 Phillip Fest, 'Der Netzausbau im Recht der Energiewende' (2013) NvWZ 824; Mann/Lang, 'Ein klimaneutrales Stromnetz für Deutschland' (n 13).

120 For a more comprehensive analysis see Fehling, in this volume, 301 ff.

121 The Act was based on Art. 74.1.11 and Art. 74.1.24 of the German Constitution, Gesetz über die Einspeisung von Strom aus erneuerbaren Energien in das öffentliche Netz (Stromeinspeisungsgesetz – StrEG), 7.12.1990, BGBl. I 2633.

122 Jan Resthöft, 'Klimaschutz durch das Erneuerbare-Energien-Gesetz' in Michael Rodi (ed), *Handbuch Klimaschutzrecht* (C.H. Beck 2022) 401 f.

cific feedin tariffs.[123] In effect, the EEG provided for long-term price guarantees that would compensate producers of renewable energy for their relatively high production costs. The EEG also provided for a surcharge mechanism to refinance payments guaranteed to investors in renewable energy production. This surcharge was passed on to energy consumers.[124] Over the years, the EEG has been subjected to many minor and major revisions and has become increasingly complex. The basic mechanisms, however, have remained in place.

The most important legislative revision should briefly be outlined here. Major amendments took place in 2004, 2009, 2012, 2014, 2017, 2021, and 2023[125]; the 2014 and 2017 reforms in particular brought about fundamental changes to the existing system. In general, the EEG's early version could be described as a simple legal framework that aimed to massively ramp-up renewable energy production. Later versions added a lot more fine-tuning, necessary for overcoming specific conflicts and challenges emerging as the sector grew. Reforms mainly responded to changes in the market or to political and legal actions taken at European Union level: While production and installation costs for renewable energy decreased over the years, the overall public costs for the energy transition rose. In addition, the EU Commission grew increasingly critical of the distorting effects of Member States' support schemes on the Common European Market and sought a more competition-oriented development of the sector.[126] Against this background, the system of long-term feed-in tariffs was slowly phased out. The 2009, 2012, and 2014 reforms introduced and developed the possibility for renewable energy producers to sell their electricity directly on the electricity market.[127] The 2017 reform substantially modified the support scheme by deciding the level of public payments through auctions: First, the competent authority would announce a premium for the production of a certain quantity of renewable energy. Second, producers would submit

---

123 § 3 (1) EEG. For a comprehensive overview of the development of the EEG see Reshöft (n 120); Thorsten Müller, 'Vom Kartell- zum Umwelt(energie)recht' in Thorsten Müller (ed), *20 Jahre Recht der Erneuerbaren Energien* (Nomos 2012). See also Saurer/Monast (n 29) 299–302.

124 Energy intensive industries were exempted from the surcharge to maintain their global competitiveness.

125 For more details see Resthöft (n 120) 487–504.

126 See e.g. Commission Guidelines on State Aid for Environmental Protection and Energy 2014–2020.

127 § 17 EEG (2009). See also Resthöft (n 122) 493–496.

their bids by declaring how much energy they would offer to deliver for the respective premium. Third, the bidder offering the lowest price would win the auction. Fixed feed-in tariffs would become the exception and only be granted for small-scale installation (e.g. roof-top solar panels). With a view to geographically matching production with grid capacities, the EEG 2017 also lowered funding for onshore wind farms in areas that had insufficient grid capacities.[128] Finally, the 2017, 2021, and 2023 reforms introduced and developed specific pathways for the key renewable energy production methods (on- and offshore wind, solar energy, and biomass).[129] The 2023 reform aimed at substantially accelerating the expansion of renewable energy production, qualifying renewable projects as an 'overriding public interest', thus prioritising them over other public interests in administrative and judicial decision making. In addition, local communities are entitled to greater financial benefit from providing space for onshore wind farms. Finally, financial support for innovative projects involving hydrogen production and storage has been substantially increased.[130]

Ramping up renewable energy production has met many different challenges. Over the years, spatial, environmental, and acceptance issues have become increasingly visible. For example, optimal spaces for siting wind farms are grown scarce.[131] Only 4 % of potential sites on German territory are deemed 'optimal' in regard to farms' operational effectiveness, their impacts on adjacent neighbours, their optic effects on landscapes, and their potential for damaging fauna (particularly birds).[132] Specific conflicts have arisen, for example, in the context of building and expanding transmission lines.[133]

Notably, building transmission lines from north to south has been slowed down due to political opposition by some federal states and citizens.[134] In addition, local communities have become increasingly reluctant

128 See § 1 (2), S. 2 and § 36 c EEG 2017.

129 See table 1 above.

130 See § 2, § 6, §§ 28 lit. f and § 28 lit. g EEG (2023).

131 For an animated overview of spatial distribution of all renewable energy production units in Germany over time see the UFZ, 'EE-Monitor' (Renewable Energy Monitor) <https://web.aufz.de/ee-monitor/> accessed 30 January 2024.

132 Philip Tafarte/Paul Lehmann, 'Quantifying trade-offs for the spatial allocation of onshore wind generation capacity – a case study for Germany' (2021) 2 UFZ Discussion Paper.

133 See e.g. Urteil vom 06.04.2017 – BVerwG 4 A 2.16.

134 See e.g. Federal Administrative Court, SüdLink, Beschluss vom 09.05.2019, Az.: 4 VR 1.19, BVerwG, SüdOstLink, Beschluss vom 24.03.2021, 4 VR 2.20.

to plan and permit wind farms on their territories, arguing that burdens and benefits are not equally shared between them and the energy producers.[135] Many citizens living in close proximity to wind farms also began to challenge the permission and operation of wind farms before courts, claiming that they are negatively affected by farms' visual impact and noise, as well as experiencing safety issues.[136] Finally, some federal states have been reluctant to support wind farm development by adopting prohibitive spatial requirements regarding farms' distance from houses or urban areas. In response, to provide the necessary space for onshore wind farming, the federal legislature adopted a law that requires federal states to allocate at least 2 % of their territories to wind-farming, forcing them to grant more importance to wind energy in their spatial planning.[137]

I. Sector-coupling: the example of hydrogen

In June 2020 the German federal government adopted and published the 'National Hydrogen Strategy'. According to the Strategy, hydrogen 'will play a key role in enhancing and completing the energy transition'.[138] In this regard, the government deems five functions of hydrogen most important: hydrogen as an energy source, as a storage medium, for sector coupling, as a base substance for various chemical products, and to eliminate process-related emissions in different industrial processes.[139] The Strategy focuses on 'green hydrogen' (produced by using renewable energy[140]) and aims to promote its 'rapid market rollout'.[141] To this end, the government

135 Sachverständigenrat für Umweltfragen, *Klimaschutz braucht Rückenwind: Für einen konsequenten Ausbau der Windenergie an Land* (2022) 55–62.

136 ibid.

137 Gesetz zur Erhöhung und Beschleunigung des Ausbaus von Windenergieanlagen an Land, BGBl. I 2022 1353. For an overview of the far-reaching implications of this law, see: Claudio Franzius, 'Das Recht der Energiewende – Bestandsaufnahme und Entwicklungsperspektive' (Teil 1) (2025) JURA, forthcoming.

138 Bundesregierung, *The German Hydrogen Strategy* (2020) 2. English version available online at <www.bmbf.de/bmbf/shareddocs/downloads/files/bmwi_nationalewasserstoffstrategie_eng_s01.pdf?__blob=publicationFile&v=2> accessed 30 January 2024.

139 ibid 2.

140 Green hydrogen is defined by the Strategy as follows: 'green hydrogen is produced via the electrolysis of water; the electricity used for the electrolysis must derive from renewable sources. (...).' ibid 28.

141 ibid 3.

announced its intention to provide substantial investments in research and development, achieve specific targets for creating generation capacity (5 GW till 2030 and additional 5 GW till 2035), build up international hydrogen partnerships, and substantially expand transport infrastructures. Two institutions were also installed to support the hydrogen ramp-up, i.e. the 'National Hydrogen Council' (made up of 26 high-level experts from science, business and civil society) and a 'State Secretaries Committee on Hydrogen' (composed of high-ranking officials from the relevant ministries). Both units aim to provide continuous knowledge and organisational support.[142] Finally, the Strategy lays down an action plan including 38 specific measures to support hydrogen's market ramp-up. Measures include specific actions in different fields of application (industry, heat, infrastructure, transport, research and education), as well as political actions at the EU and international level.

In 2023, the National Hydrogen Strategy was substantially revised. These revisions were necessary due to changes in energy markets and to quickly become independent from Russian energy supply. The Revised Strategy's overall objective is to substantially accelerate hydrogen's build-up. To this end, targets for creating generation capacity till 2030 were doubled from 5 GW to 10 GW. In addition, the Government committed itself to establish a working 1,800 km long hydrogen grid by 2027/2028. Legally, the Government announced that it will adopt legislation to accelerate planning and permission procedures for hydrogen related facilities and to establish sustainable production, transport, and use standards both at the national and the international level.[143] The Government also made more explicit estimations regarding hydrogen demands and hydrogen supply. In 2023 it assumed that by 2030 demand for hydrogen in Germany will lie at 95 to 130 TWh, 50 to 70 percent of which will have to be satisfied by imports.[144] Sufficient imports, however, will have to be systematically organised and guided through a 'Hydrogen Import Strategy'. The Strategy was published in July 2024 and addresses topics such as ensuring sustainable extraterritorial production, transboundary transport infrastructures, and reliable financing of imported hydrogen.[145]

142 ibid 14–15.

143 Bundesregierung, *The Revised German Hydrogen Strategy* (2023) 5, 14, 26–29.

144 ibid 9.

145 See Bundesregierung, Import Strategy for hydrogen and hydrogen derivatives (2024). English version available at <https://www.bmwk.de/Redaktion/EN/Publ

The federal government has taken several legislative steps after publishing its first version of the Hydrogen Strategy.[146] Such laws address different factors that will enable hydrogen's build up, particularly regarding its production, (including permission procedures), its transportation through grids, its use as a fuel in the transportation sector.[147] The above mentioned EEG was amended and further implemented in 2021 to provide for a clear cut legal definition of hydrogen and to financially incentivise production (by exemptions from certain tax and fee schemes, and the EEG surcharge mechanism).[148] In addition, legal framework provisions were laid down for testing and deploying offshore hydrogen production facilities.[149] Most importantly, however, the Federal Energy Industry Act (EnWG) was substantially developed to provide legal certainty with a view to investing into the development of hydrogen grids, inter alia by laying down definitions (from now on, hydrogen is deemed as a form of energy under the law), giving provisions regarding the unbundling of grids, and also by regulating access to and fees for their use.[150]

Developing the legal frame for the German hydrogen ramp-up at the federal level is shaped by some specific challenges.[151] First, climate targets and energy scarcity have put severe pressure on the German government to accelerate the energy transition. Hydrogen is a key element in this regard and needs to be ready for large-scale deployment in just a few years. Second, the whole process is somewhat complicated by the fact that the

---

ikationen/Energie/importstrategy-hydrogen.pdf?__blob=publicationFile&v=7> accessed 28 July 2025.

146 Overview in Bundesregierung, *Fortschrittsbericht zur Umsetzung der Nationalen Wasserstoffstrategie* (2022) 27–31.

147 See Gesetzentwurf der Bundesregierung zur Beschleunigung der Verfügbarkeit von Wasserstoff und zur Änderung weiterer rechtlicher Rahmenbedingungen für den Wasserstoffhochlauf sowie zur Änderung weiterer energierechtlicher Vorschriften v. 29.5.2024, BT-Drs 20/11899 v. 21.6.2024.

148 See § 12 lit. i of the Verordnung zur Umsetzung des EEG 2021 und zur Änderung weiterer energierechtlicher Vorschriften, BT-Drucks. 19/29793 vom 19.05.2021.

149 Verordnung zur Vergabe von sonstigen Energiegewinnungsbereichen in der ausschließlichen Wirtschaftszone (SoEnergieV).

150 See the current versions of § 1, § 3 Nr. 14, § 28 lit j. to § 28 lit. s., § 112 lit b. and § 113 lit. a to § 113 lit. c ENWG.
See also Verordnung über die Kosten und Entgelte für den Zugang zu Wasserstoffnetzen (Wasserstoffnetzentgeltverordnung). See Ulrich Büdenbender, 'Die Regulierung von Wasserstoffnetzen nach der EnWG-Novelle 2021' (2022) 3 RdE 101.

151 Claudio Franzius, 'Das Recht der Energiewende – Bestandsaufnahme und Entwicklungsperspektiven' (Teil 2), (2025), JURA, forthcoming.

federation is 'locked-in' between its federal states and the European Union. On both levels, political and legal actions have been adopted and require substantial coordination efforts in order to avoid inhibiting progress and creating contradictions. It has been observed, for example, that the EU is waiting to see what its member states do, while member states like Germany wait for what happens at the EU level.[152] In addition, most German federal states have also developed their own hydrogen strategies which require coordination with each other and with the federal government.[153] Third, green hydrogen production, transport, and use all depend on large quantities of renewable energy. Renewable energy, however, is already a scarce resource in Germany and demand is likely to increase in the coming years.[154] In particular, land for producing renewable energy is becoming increasingly hard to find, thus making (complex) international partnerships for a fast hydrogen ramp-up inevitable. Accordingly, there is a strong need to develop hydrogen policies at the EU and international levels.

J. Conclusions

The German Energy Transition bears some specific and some generic characteristics. While its comprehensiveness and its current speed seem to be somewhat special, its challenges and conflicts are likely to be more generic. Both dimensions are particularly interesting for developing comparative perspectives.[155]

---

152 Claudio Franzius, 'Beschleunigung des Markthochlaufs von Wasserstoff – Fördermöglichkeiten und Beschleunigungsaspekte für Infrastrukturen und Erzeugungsanlagen' (2024) 2 ZUR 72–81; Christian Schneller, 'Der neue Rechtsrahmen für Wasserstoff – Provisorium oder Perspektive' (2021) 4 ER 135–146.

153 See Michèle Knodt et al., 'Mehr Kooperation wagen: Wasserstoffgovernance im deutschen Föderalismus. Interterritoriale Koordination, Planung und Regulierung' (2022) Kopernikus-Projekt Ariadne 5–32.

154 For example, other means to combat climate change will require both large amounts of renewable energy or space, i.e. technology or nature based carbon dioxide removal operations. See Till Markus, 'Land-use Implications of Carbon Dioxide Removal: An Emerging Legal Issue?' (2022) International Yearbook of Soil Law and Policy 107; See also Freia Harzendorf et al., 'Multi-Factor Site Assessment for Effective Direct Air Capture and Storage Roll-out' (2024) Environmental Research Letters (forthcoming).

155 See e.g. Gundlach/Gerard, (n 94); Michael Mehling, 'The comparative law of climate change: a research agenda' (2015) 24 RECIEL 341; Till Markus, 'Zur Rechtsvergleichung im nationalen und internationalen Umweltrecht' (2022) ZaöRV 649.

To this day, Germany is the only industrialised country to have plans for exiting both coal and nuclear energy. In addition, ambitious steps have also been taken with a view to reducing the use of oil and gas to transform the transportation and heating sectors. Altogether, this makes Germany a pioneer in energy transition, both in the European Union and globally.[156]

In addition, few industrialised countries currently seem to be transforming their energy sectors at a similarly fast pace. The Green Party rising to power in 2021, the Federal Constitutional Court's decision on Germany's obligations to increase its effort to combat climate change, and the Russian-Ukrainian conflict created powerful impulses. The latter has particularly pressured Germany to reduce its gas consumption earlier than planned, as well as to (at least) try to rely less on gas as a 'bridge fuel' to a low-carbon economy. All three causes together compel Germany to aggressively roll out renewable energy production, including the fast ramp-up of alternative energy carriers (such as green hydrogen), support infrastructures, and new technologies.[157]

Acceleration, however, catalyses challenges and fuels conflicts that currently put severe pressure on the overall political consensus regarding further steps to implement the energy transition.

Rising energy prices, particularly after the cut-back of Russian gas in 2022, have reignited political claims to extend deadlines for both the Nuclear Exit and the Coal Phase-Out. Major concerns were voiced with a view to the effects of rising prices on the industry's competitiveness ('unequal global playing field') and their disproportionate effect on lower-income populations. Populist movements have made use of people's fears regarding rising energy prices in particular and structural change in general, putting additional political pressure on the government to slow down the transition's pace.

Furthermore, promoting and scaling up renewables has created structural, environmental, and acceptance issues, bringing to light the energy

---

156 The complementary emission trading system and the Heating legislation can be characterised as proactive national climate actions within the European Union legal framework. See Claudio Franzius, 'Rechtliche Möglichkeiten einzelner Staaten zum unilateralen Schutz globaler Umweltgüter' in Till Markus/Markus Reese/Wolfgang Köck (eds), *Zukunftsfähiges Umweltrecht III: Unilaterale Beiträge zur globalen Nachhaltigkeitsordnung – Pflichten, Möglichkeiten, Grenzen* (Nomos 2023).

157 Schneller has rightly pointed out that the German hydrogen sector has to be developed basically from scratch. Schneller, 'Der neue Rechtsrahmen für Wasserstoff' (n 152) 135.

transition's spatial, ecological, and justice dimensions. Conflicting use interests, opposing environmental objectives, and distributional matters have kept the legislature, administrations, and courts increasingly busy over the years, requiring them to both substantially expand and fine-tune the body of law governing the energy transition. The necessity to accelerate the transition has put pressure on the government to meet these issues more quickly.

Acceleration is being supported mainly by two strategies, i.e. increasing public expenditure and improving governance. First, huge amounts of public support have been granted and promised for phasing out old technologies (coal, nuclear, and also for reducing the use of oil in the heating sector) and for rolling out new technology (research, development, imports of and infrastructures for green hydrogen). Second, in regard to improving governance, powers have been centralised (e.g. transferring climate action to the Ministry of Economics in 2021, [the decision was, however reversed by the new government in 2025]; assigning powers regarding the allocation of spaces for renewables partly to the federal level[158]), coordination among actors has been institutionalised (by creating new coordinating units e.g. the *Klimakabinett* in 2019, the *Bund-Länder-Kooperationsausschuss* regarding renewables in 2021, and the 'Hydrogen Council'), and administrative and court procedures have been streamlined in order to accelerate permission and implementation of renewable energy production and related infrastructure projects.

This chapter has aimed to sketch out a rough map of the central regulations and policy measures that pursue and put into effect the German *Energiewende.* To this end, it provided a brief introduction to its historical and constitutional background and a first glimpse at the roles played by different actors at different levels. It has also included a discussion of general legal targets when it comes to energy transition, followed by laws pertaining to phasing out or reducing the use of specific energy sources (nuclear, coal, oil and gas). Finally, an overview was given of legislation promoting the transition to renewables and green hydrogen. Such a map necessarily offers only an entry point for further comparative research on specific political

158 To provide the necessary space for onshore wind farming, the federal legislature adopted a law that requires federal states to allocate at least 2 % of their territories to wind-farming, forcing them to grant more importance to wind energy in their spatial planning. See Gesetz zur Erhöhung und Beschleunigung des Ausbaus von Windenergieanlagen an Land, BGBl. I 2022 1353.

strategies and legal measures, all of which tend to be complex in their formulation but even more so in their implementation.

Bibliography

AG Energiebilanzen e.V., Verbrauchsrückgang hat sich verlangsamt (18 March 2025) <https://ag-energiebilanzen.de/verbrauchsrueckgang-hat-sich-verlangsamt/> accessed 31 May 2025

Agora Energiewende, *Coal Phase-Out in Germany: The Role of Coal Exit Auctions* (2022) 13–20

Augustine D L, *Taking on Technocracy. Nuclear Power in Germany, 1945 to the Present* (Berghahn Books 2018)

Baudisch K/Fouquet D, 'Germany's Coal Exit Plan: A Legal and Political Outline on How Germany Plans to Phase out Coal Fired Power Stations by 2038' (2019) 9 Renewable Energy Law and Policy Review 45 f.

Brüggemeier F J, 'Das Zeitalter der Kohle in Europa, 1750 bis heute' in bpb (ed), Abschied von der Kohle: Struktur- und Kulturwandel im Ruhrgebiet und in der Lausitz (2021) 12–25

Bundesregierung, 'Forschungs- und Innovationsförderung des Bundes im Bereich der Zukunftsvorsorge – Forschung für Grundlagen und nachhaltige Entwicklung (Antwort der Bundesregierung auf kleine Anfrage)' BT-Drucksache 20/5758, 21.2.2023

Bundesregierung, *The German Hydrogen Strategy* (2020) 2. English version available online at <www.bmbf.de/bmbf/shareddocs/downloads/files/bmwi_nationalewasserstoffstrategie_eng_s01.pdf?__blob=publicationFile&v=2> accessed 30 January 2024

Bundesregierung, *The Revised German Hydrogen Strategy* (2023)

Bundesregierung, 'Fortschreibung der nationalen Wasserstoffstrategie – NWS 2023'<www.bmbf.de/SharedDocs/Downloads/de/2023/230726-fortschreibungnws.pdf?__blob=publicationFile&v=1> accessed 30 January 2024

Bundesregierung, 'Überblickpapier der Bundesregierung zur Gas- und Strompreisbremse, 15.12.2022' <www.bmwk.de/Redaktion/DE/Downloads/Energie/gas-strompreis-bremse-ubersicht.pdf?__blob=publicationFile&v=1> accessed 30 January

Bundesregierung, *Fortschrittsbericht zur Umsetzung der Nationalen Wasserstoffstrategie* (2022) 27–31

Büdenbender U, 'Die Regulierung von Wasserstoffnetzen nach der EnWG-Novelle 2021' (2022) 3 RdE 101

Coggio T/Gustafson T, 'When the Exit? The Difficult Politics of German Coal' (2019) 37 German Politics & Society 47, 56

Däuper O, 'Die Empfehlungen der Kohlekommission: Inhalte und juristische Fragestellungen' (2019) EnWZ 153

Decher J, *Die Rechte der Gemeinden beim Ausbau des Übertragungsnetzes* (Mohr Siebeck 2022)

Deutscher Industrie- und Handelskammertag, 'Stellungnahme zum Kohleausstiegsgesetz -Kabinettsfassung' (19 May 2020) <www.dihk.de/resource/blob/24158/baf1397129bd90dc52ba5b94dd6b1dc4/dihk-stellungnahme-kohleausstiegsgesetz-kabinettsfassung-data.pdf> accessed 30 January 2024

Ekardt F/Rath T, 'Energiekrise: Rechtsentwicklungen auf EU- und Bundesebene – ein Update' (2023) NVwZ 293

Erbguth W, 'Beschleunigung in Zeiten von Klima- und Energiekrise' (2023) Natur und Recht 242

Faßbender K/Köck W (eds), *Aktuelle Entwicklungen und Probleme beim Netzausbau* (Nomos 2021)

Federal Ministry for Economic Affairs and Climate Actions (BMWK), Working Group for Renewable Energy Statistics (AGEE-Stat), 'Erneuerbare Energien in Deutschland, Daten zur Entwicklung im Jahr 2024' (2025)**Federal Ministry for Economic Affairs and Climate Actions**, 'The Energy of the Future' (2021) 49–57

Federal Ministry for Economic Affairs and Climate Actions, 'Aktueller Stand des Netzausbaus' (2023) 5 <www.bmwk.de/Redaktion/DE/Dossier/netze-und-netzausbau.html> accessed 30 January 2024

Federal Ministry for Economic Affairs and Climate Actions, 'Richtlinie für die Bundesförderung für effiziente Gebäude – Einzelmaßnahmen (BEG EM) vom 21. Dezember 2023' (BAnz AT 29.12.2023 B1) 1–32

Federal Ministry of Education and Research, 'Welche Projekte für die internationale Wasserstoff-Kooperation fördert das BMBF?' <www.bmbf.de/bmbf/shareddocs/kurzmeldungen/de/woher-soll-dergruenewasserstoff-kommen.html> accessed 30 January

Fest P, 'Der Netzausbau im Recht der Energiewende' (2013) NvWZ 824

Franzius C, 'Das Recht der Energiewende – Bestandsaufnahme und Entwicklungsperspektiven (Teil 1; Teil 2)' (2025) JURA, forthcoming

Franzius C, 'CDR-Technologien auf dem Weg in die Klimaneutralität' (2024) EurUP 119

Franzius C 'Beschleunigung des Markthochlaufs von Wasserstoff: Fördermöglichkeiten und Beschleunigungsaspekte für Infrastrukturen und Erzeugungsanlagen' (2024) ZUR 72

Franzius C, 'Beschleunigung des Markthochlaufs von Wasserstoff – Fördermöglichkeiten und Beschleunigungsaspekte für Infrastrukturen und Erzeugungsanlagen' (2024) 2 ZUR 72–81

Franzius C, 'Rechtliche Möglichkeiten einzelner Staaten zum unilateralen Schutz globaler Umweltgüter' in **Markus T/Reese M/Köck W** (eds), *Zukunftsfähiges Umweltrecht III: Unilaterale Beiträge zur globalen Nachhaltigkeitsordnung – Pflichten, Möglichkeiten, Grenzen* (Nomos 2023)

Frenz W, 'EU-"Heizungsgesetz": eigentumsrechtliche und soziale Grenzen des Klimaschutzes' (2023) EuR 417

Geinitz C, 'CDU-Wirtschaftsrat: Atomkraft fortsetzen, Stromsteuer senken' Frankfurter Allgemeine Zeitung (Frankfurt 1 September 2023)

German Council of Economic Experts, 'Setting Out for A New climate Policy' (2019) 37–44 <www.sachverstaendigenratwirtschaft.de/fileadmin/dateiablage/gutachten/sg 2019/sg_2019_en.pdf> accessed 30 January 2024

German Environment Agency (Umweltbundesamt), 'Treibhausneutrales Deutschland im Jahr 2050' (2014)

German Environment Agency, 'Erneuerbare Energien in Zahlen' (08 March 2024) <www.umweltbundesamt.de/themen/klima-energie/erneuerbare-energien/erneuerb are-energien-in-zahlen > accessed 30 January 2024

Glaser A, 'From Brokdorf to Fukushima: The Long Journey to Nuclear Phase-out' (2012) 6 Bulletin of the Atomic Scientists 10–21

Guckelberger A, 'Energie als kritische Infrastruktur' (2015) DVBl 1213 f.

Gujer E, 'Die deutsche Verblendung – Der Atomausstieg ist nichts als Ideologie' Neue Zürcher Zeitung (Zürich 14 April 2023)

Gundlach J/Gerrard M B, 'Climate Change and energy Transition Policies' in **Viñuales J E/Lees E** (eds), *The Oxford Handbook of Comparative Environmental Law* (Oxford University Press 2019) 531, 565–567

G7, 'Climate, Energy and Environment Ministers' Meeting Communiqué, Ministerial meeting on Climate, Energy and Environment – 28–29–30 April' (2024)

Hake J F et al., 'The German Energiewende – History and Status Quo' (2015) 3 Energy 532

Harzendorf F et al., 'Multi-Factor Site Assessment for Effective Direct Air Capture and Storage Roll-out' (2024) Environmental Research Letters (forthcoming)

Heinicke T, 'Das "Heizungsgesetz" – Die Voelle des Gebäudeenergiegesetzes und dem Blickwinkel von Art. 14 GG' (2024) KlimRZ 3

Hillebrandt K et al., 'Pathways to deep decarbonisation in Germany' (SDSN – IDDR 2015)

International Energy Agency, 'Germany' <www.iea.org/countries/germany> accessed 30 Janurary 2024

Knauff M, 'Landesklimaschutzgesetze' in **Rodi M** (ed), *Handbuch Klimaschutzrecht* (C.H.Beck 2022)

Knodt M/Kemmerzell J, 'Alle für die Energiewende? Akteure und Institutionen in der deutschen Energiepolitik' (2022) 46–47 APuZ 25 f.

Knodt M et al., 'Mehr Kooperation wagen: Wasserstoffgovernance im deutschen Föderalismus. Interterritoriale Koordination, Planung und Regulierung' (2022) Kopernikus-Projekt Ariadne 5–32

Kommission "Wachstum, Strukturwandel und Beschäftigung", 'Abschlussbericht' (26 January 2019) 6 f. <www.bmwk.de/Redaktion/DE/Publikationen/Wirtschaft /abschlussbericht-kommission-wachstumstrukturwandelund-beschaeftigung.html> accessed 30 January 2024

Köck W/Markus T, 'German Courts on Scientific Uncertainties in Nature Conservation Law' in **Eliantonio M/Lees E/Poliniitty T** (eds), *EU Environmental Principles and Scientific Uncertainty Before National Courts -the case of the Habitats-Directive* (Bloomsbury: Hart Books, 2023)

Kühne O/Weber F (eds), *Bausteine der Energiewende* (Springer 2018)

Kungl G, Die großen Stromkonzerne und die Energiewende (Campus Verlag 2018); Claudia Kemfert, Das fossile Imperium schlägt zurück. Warum wir die Energiewende jetzt verteidigen müssen (Murmann 2017)

Langenbach P, 'Zur Rezeption empirischer Forschung und psychologischer Verfahrenstheorie in der verwaltungsrechtlichen Debatte zur Akzeptanz des Stromnetzausbaus' (2022) Die Verwaltung 191

Ludwigs M, 'Gewährleistung der Energieversorgungssicherheit in Krisenzeiten' (2022) NVwZ 1086

Mann T/Lang L, 'Ein klimaneutrales Stromnetz für Deutschland' (2023) DVBL 897

Markus T/Otto D/Thrän D, 'Die Carbon Management Strategie und CCS im Lichte klima-und energierechtlicher Weichenstellungen' (2024) ZUR 387

Markus T, 'Land-use Implications of Carbon Dioxide Removal: An Emerging Legal Issue?' (2022) International Yearbook of Soil Law and Policy 107

Markus T, 'Zur Rechtsvergleichung im nationalen und internationalen Umweltrecht' (2022) ZaöRV 649

Mehling M, 'The comparative law of climate change: a research agenda' (2015) 24 RECIEL 341

Merkel A, 'Der Weg zur Energie der Zukunft', (Government policy statement 09 June 2011) BT-PlPr 17/114, 12960 (A) f.

Merkel A, 'Zur aktuellen Lage in Japan', (Government policy statement 17 March 2011) BT-PlPr 17/96, 10882 (D) ff.

Milder S, *Greening Democracy. The Anti-Nuclear Movement and Political Environmentalism in West Germany and Beyond, 1968–1983* (Cambridge University Press 2017)

Müller T, 'Vom Kartell- zum Umwelt(energie)recht' in **Müller T** (ed), *20 Jahre Recht der Erneuerbaren Energien* (Nomos 2012)

Peter B, Legitimation durch Öffentlichkeitsbeteiligung (JCB Mohr 2020)

Pielow J C, 'Rechtsfragen des Kohleausstiegs' in **Rodi M** (ed), *Handbuch Klimaschutzrecht* (C.H. Beck 2022) 600 f.

Praetorius B, 'Grundlagen der Energiepolitik' in **Radtke J/Canzler W** (eds), Energiewende: Eine sozialwissenschaftliche Einführung (Springer 2019)

Radkau J, *Aufstieg und Krise der deutschen Atomwirtschaft 1945–1975: Verdrängte Alternativen in der Kerntechnik und der Ursprung der nuklearen Kontroverse* (Rowohlt 1983)

Reitbaur L, 'The New German Coal Laws: A Difficult Balancing Act' (2021) 11 Climate Law 176, 185–187

Resthöft J, 'Klimaschutz durch das Erneuerbare-Energien-Gesetz' in **Rodi M** (ed), *Handbuch Klimaschutzrecht* (C.H. Beck 2022) 401 f.

Rodi M, 'Das Instrumentarium zur staatlichen Finanzierung der Energietransformation' (2023) 11 KlimR 322

Ruge R, 'Die Gewährleistungsverantwortung des Staates und der Regulatory State: Zur veränderten Rolle des Staates nach der Deregulierung der Stromwirtschaft in Deutschland, Großbritannien und der EU' (Dunker & Humblot 2004) 218–232

Sachverständigenrat für Umweltfragen, *Klimaschutz braucht Rückenwind: Für einen konsequenten Ausbau der Windenergie an Land* (2022) 55–62

Saretzki T, 'Energiepolitik in der Bundesrepublik Deutschland 1949–1999. Ein Politikfeld zwischen Wirtschafts-, Technologie- und Umweltpolitik' in **Willems U** (ed), *Demokratie und Politik in der Bundesrepublik 1949–1999* (Springer 2001)

Saurer J, 'Verfassungsrechtliche Konfliktlagen im Klimaschutzrecht' in: *Bitburger Gespräche, Jahrbuch 2021* (C.H. Beck 2022) 97

Saurer J/Monast J, 'Renewable Energy Federalism in Germany and the United States' (2020) 10 Transnational Environmental Law 293

Schlacke S/Wentzien H/Römling D, 'Beschleunigung der Energiewende: Ein gesetzgeberischer Paradigmenwechsel durch das Osterpaket?' (2022) NVwZ 1577

Schneller C, 'Der neue Rechtsrahmen für Wasserstoff – Provisorium oder Perspektive' (2021) 4 ER 135–146

Schütte P/Langstädtler S, 'Deutschlandtempo als "new normal"?' (2024) ZUR 3

Schwerdtfeger A, 'Beschleunigungsgebiete für Erneuerbaren Energien – Fragen des Rechtsschutzes' (2023) EurUP 365

Schwerdtfeger A, 'Beschleunigung durch Beschränkung des Rechtsschutzes?' (2023) ZUR 451

Tafarte P/Lehmann P, 'Quantifying trade-offs for the spatial allocation of onshore wind generation capacity – a case study for Germany' (2021) 2 UFZ Discussion Paper

The Christian Democrats, the Christian Social Democrats, and the Free Democrats, 'Coalition Agreement' (2012) 29 <www.kas.de/c/document_library/get_file?uuid=83dbb842-b2f7-bf99-6180e65b2de7b4d4&groupId=252038> accessed 30 January 2024

The Social Democratic Party, the Green Party and the Free Democratic Party, 'Mehr Fortschritt Wagen: Koalitionsvertrag 2021–2025' (2021) 20–51

Türk H, 'Kleine Geschichte der Energiepolitik' (2022) 46–47 APuZ 17

UFZ, 'EE-Monitor' (Renewable Energy Monitor) <https://web.aufz.de/ee-monitor/> accessed 30 January 2024

Vollmer M, 'BEHG/Nationales Brennstoffemissionshandelssystem (nEHS)' in **Rodi M** (ed), *Handbuch Klimaschutzrecht* (C.H. Beck 2022) 325 f.

Winter G, 'The Intergenerational Effect of Fundamental Rights: A Contribution of the German Federal Constitutional Court to Climate Protection' (2023) Journal of Environmental Law 1

Winter G, 'The Rise and Fall of Nuclear Energy Use in Germany: Processes, Explanation, and the Role of Law' (2013) 25 Journal of Environmental Law 95

World Nuclear Association, *Plans for New Reactor Worldwide* (2023) <https://world-nuclear.org/information-library/current-and-future-generation/plans-for-new-reactorsworldwide.aspx> accessed 30 January 2024

Wurster S/Köhler C, 'Die Energiepolitik der Bundesländer. Scheitert die Energiewende am deutschen Föderalismus?' in **Hildebrandt A/Wolf** F(eds) Die Politik der Bundesländer. Zwischen Föderalismusreform und Schuldenbremse (2nd edn, Springer 2016) 283–314

Zengerling C, 'Kommunale Klimaschutzplanung' in **Rodi M** (ed), *Handbuch Klimaschutzrecht* (C.H. Beck 2022)

General Perspectives on the Law of Energy Transition in France

Marie Lamoureux

A. Introduction

There is no legal definition of energy transition in France, not even in the law that is specifically dedicated to it, which is the "Energy Transition for Green Growth Act" adopted in 2015.[1] It only gives a definition of green growth, but not of the energy transition needed to achieve it.[2] Nevertheless, it is usually said in France that the energy transition is a transition from a society based on high energy consumption and especially high consumption of fossil fuels to a more energy and carbon efficient society, promoting energy savings and low-carbon energy, especially renewable energies. There are some well-accepted elements in this definition, such as the development of renewable energies, but one may say that there is still some ambiguity about the exact meaning of this transition in France. This ambiguity concerns the question of whether it is a question of promoting renewable energies, or low-carbon energies, including therefore nuclear energy. If there is perhaps a French particularity in what the energy transition means and implies, it is certainly about the place that nuclear energy must have in the process, and we will see in this study the hesitations that existed in France in this regard and recent developments that provide a clearer answer.

Before coming to that, it has to be said that France has long been involved in the energy transition process and in the fight against climate change. In some respects, France benefits from significant advantages. Especially, France benefits from largely carbon-free electricity production. As of 2021, only 7.8 % of electricity generation comes from fossil fuels (coal, oil

1 Loi n° 2015-992 du 17 août 2015 relative à la transition énergétique pour la croissance verte.

2 Green growth is defined "as a mode of economic development that respects the environment, is low-energy and resource and carbon-efficient, socially inclusive, supports the potential for innovation and guarantees the competitiveness of businesses" (article L. 100-1 of the French Energy Code, resulting from the Energy Transition Act of 17 August 2015).

and natural gas).[3] It should be added that a very small proportion comes from coal, less than 1 % of total electricity production. France has also one of the lowest per capita emissions of advanced economies, well below the European average, thanks mainly to the role of nuclear energy.

But at the same time, France remains very dependent on fossil fuels in certain sectors such as transport, and fossil fuels still account for a very large share of the French total energy supply (47 %).[4] Furthermore, it appears that France faces difficulties in reaching some of its energy transition targets. France has failed to meet its 2020 target for energy efficiency and, even more significantly, its target for the development of renewable energies. Therefore, the situation is not unequivocal in France.

For this reason, a number of important texts have recently been adopted, aimed at speeding up the process. Two laws are worth mentioning, both adopted in 2023, just a few months apart. The first is the Renewable Energy Acceleration Act, adopted in March 2023.[5] The second is the Nuclear Acceleration Act, adopted in June 2023.[6] In both cases, the aim is essentially to speed up the procedures for setting up new low-carbon energy production facilities, whether renewable or nuclear. Only time will tell whether these new measures will produce significant results, but their very existence reflects the need to remedy certain shortcomings in order to accelerate the achievement of France's decarbonization objectives.

Before looking at these recent developments in more detail, we will provide an overview of the legal framework for the energy transition in France and of the objectives that France has set itself for the coming years (B). We will continue this overview by distinguishing between the efforts made to reduce the production and consumption of fossil fuels (C), the efforts made to develop renewable energies and energy savings (D), and the central place still occupied by nuclear energy in the French energy transition (E).

---

3 RTE, 'Bilan électrique' <https://bilan-electrique-2021.rte-france.com> accessed 30 October 2023.

4 Total energy supply in France, as of 2020: Oil 28 %, Natural Gas 15 %, Coal 4 %, Nuclear 41 %, Biofuels/waste 8 %, Hydro 2 %, Wind/solar 2 % (see International Energy Agency, 'France 2021 Energy Policy Review' 19 <https://iea.blob.core.windows.net/assets/7b3b4b9d-6db3-4dcf-a0a5-a9993d7dd1d6/France2021.pdf> accessed 20.08.2024).

5 Loi n° 2023–175 du 10 mars 2023 relative à l'accélération de la production d'énergies renouvelables.

6 Loi n° 2023–491 du 22 juin 2023 relative à l'accélération des procédures liées à la construction de nouvelles installations nucléaires à proximité de sites nucléaires existants et au fonctionnement des installations existantes.

B. The French Legal Framework for the Energy Transition

The French legal framework is largely based on the Energy Transition for Green Growth Act, adopted in 2015.[7] Several previous texts had already laid some foundations, notably in promoting renewable energies and energy savings.[8] Some subsequent texts have also made some changes,[9] but it can be said that the Energy Transition Act is the cornerstone of the French energy transition.[10] This text, and to a certain extent the other laws mentioned before, have enabled France to set clear objectives and put in place a wide range of tools to achieve them (even if experience shows that they are not always sufficient).

The main objectives of French energy policy arising from these laws have been codified in the preliminary part of the Energy Code. Most of them date from the Energy Transition Act, but some have been modified since then. These objectives, as listed in article L. 100–1 of the Energy Code, are essentially to ensure security of energy supply, maintain competitive energy prices, protect human health and the environment, and ensure a right of access to energy for all people. In addition to these general objectives, article L. 100–4 of the Energy Code sets out a host of quantified targets for different timeframes.

7 Loi n° 2015- 992 du 17 août 2015 relative à la transition énergétique pour la croissance verte.

8 In particular the 2005 law on energy policy guidelines (Loi n° 2005–781 du 13 juillet 2005 de programme fixant les orientations de la politique énergétique) and the two "Grenelle Acts" of 2009–2010 (Loi n° 2009–967 du 3 août 2009 de programmation relative à la mise en œuvre du Grenelle de l'environnement; Loi n° 2010–788 du 12 juillet 2010 portant engagement national pour l'environnement).

9 In particular the 2019 Energy and Climate Law (Loi n°2019–1147 du 8 novembre 2019 relative à l'énergie et au climat) and the 2021 Climate and Resilience Law (Loi n°2021–1104 du 24 août 2021 portant lutte contre le dérèglement climatique et renforcement de la résilience face à ses effets).

10 The process leading to the Energy Transition Act initially started with the organization of a national energy transition debate, an intensive stakeholder consultation (which was not usual in France at the time), aiming to establish a comprehensive and pluralist analysis of long-term challenges for the energy transition in France. The objective was to prepare the subsequent legislative process through the identification of consensual objectives and measures. Next, an arduous parliamentary debate took place and extended over 12 months to reach a final text.

Article L. 100–4 of the Energy Code states that

"I.-To respond to the ecological and climatic emergency, the national energy policy aims:
1° To reduce greenhouse gas emissions by 40 % between 1990 and 2030 and to achieve carbon neutrality by 2050 by dividing greenhouse gas emissions by a factor of more than six between 1990 and 2050 (...);
2° To reduce final energy consumption by 50 % by 2050 compared to the 2012 baseline, with intermediate targets of around 7 % in 2023 and 20 % in 2030 (...);
3° To reduce the primary energy consumption of fossil fuels by 40 % by 2030 compared with the reference year 2012, modulating this target by fossil fuel according to the greenhouse gas emission factor of each (...);
4° To increase the share of renewable energies to 23 % of gross final energy consumption by 2020 and to at least 33 % of this consumption by 2030; by this date, to achieve this objective, renewable energies must account for at least 40 % of electricity production, 38 % of final heat consumption, 15 % of final fuel consumption and 10 % of gas consumption (...);
4° bis To encourage the production of hydroelectric power, in particular small-scale hydroelectric power, taking care to maintain energy sovereignty, guarantee the safety of hydroelectric installations and encourage the storage of electricity;
4° ter To encourage the production of electricity from installations using mechanical wind energy located at sea, with the aim of gradually increasing the rate at which installed production capacity is allocated following competitive tendering procedures;
4° quater To encourage the production of electricity from agrivoltaic installations, within the meaning of article L. 314–36, by reconciling this production with agricultural activity, giving priority to food production and ensuring that there are no negative effects on agricultural land and prices;
5° (Repealed)[11]
6° To contribute to achieving the objectives for reducing atmospheric pollution (...);
7° To have a housing stock in which all buildings are renovated to meet "low energy building" or similar standards by 2050, by implementing

11 Until the law of 22 June 2023 this provision provided for the objective "To reduce the share of nuclear power in electricity production to 50 % by 2035" (see *infra* Section D).

a policy of thermal renovation of housing mainly for low-income households;
8° To achieve energy autonomy and an electricity production mix composed of 100 % renewable energies in the local authorities governed by Article 73 of the Constitution by 2030;
9° To multiply by five the quantity of renewable and recovered heat and cooling delivered by heating and cooling networks by 2030.
10° To develop low-carbon and renewable hydrogen and its industrial, energy and mobility uses, with a view to achieving approximately 20 to 40 % of total hydrogen and industrial hydrogen consumption by 2030;
11° To promote the management of electricity production, with the aim of achieving a demand-side response capacity of at least 6.5 gigawatts by 2028.

The Energy Code requires Parliament to review these targets every five years. Other planning instruments complement and specify these legislative targets, especially the multiannual energy plan, which is adopted by the government, and which specifies the objectives in more detail and over shorter periods. For example, it contains detailed targets for reducing the consumption of each fossil fuel and development targets for each renewable energy source. The current plan was adopted in 2020[12] and is due to be amended in the coming months. The multiannual energy plan, together with the national low-carbon strategy,[13] form the basis for the national energy and climate plan.

In light of these objectives, we can now assess the efforts made by France on the most important aspects of its energy transition policy, concerning

12 Décret n° 2020–456 du 21 avril 2020 relatif à la programmation pluriannuelle de l'énergie. On French energy policy objectives and the multiannual energy plan, see Marie Lamoreux, *Droit de l'énergie* (2nd ed., LGDJ, 2022), n° 117 ff.

13 The national low-carbon strategy is France's roadmap for climate change mitigation. It specifies emissions reduction targets by sector and provides for five-year carbon budgets. France was not able to meet the targeted reductions of its first 2015–2018 carbon budget. Therefore, in July 2021, the Council of the State requested the government to adopt all measures necessary to meet its greenhouse gas emission reduction commitments for 2030 (Conseil d'État, 1er juillet 2021, n° 427301, *Commune de Grande-Synthe*). In a second decision, the Council of the State noted that important measures had been adopted, but that they were still insufficient to consider that the first decision had been implemented. Consequently, the Council of the State issued a ruling requiring the government to take additional measures before June 30, 2024 (Conseil d'État, 10 mai 2023, n° 467982, *Commune de Grande-Synthe*).

the reduction in the use of fossil fuels, the development of renewable energies and energy savings, and the role assigned to nuclear energy.

C. The Path Towards Decreasing the Production and Consumption of Fossil Fuels

The French energy code provides for an objective to reduce the consumption of fossil fuels by 40 % by 2030 compared to the reference year 2012. This is notable because many national legislations do not include such a target. They usually include a target for the development of renewable energies and a target for the reduction of greenhouse gas emissions, which can of course be understood as involving a reduction in the use of fossil fuels, but there is not necessarily a quantified target for fossil fuels as such.

Beyond this objective, measures have been adopted in recent years directly targeting fossil fuels. It is not necessary to list them all here, but a few are worth mentioning. One of the most symbolic ones is the decision taken in 2017 to ban all activities of exploration and production of hydrocarbons on the French soil, either on its mainland or overseas territories. Some activities were already prohibited in France for several years regarding the oil and gas sectors, especially since the adoption in 2011 of a statute law that prohibited the use of fracking techniques and, consequently, prohibited the exploration and production of unconventional oil and gas, especially shale gas[14]. But more recently, the French legislation made a step further and a law adopted in December 2017 provided for the phasing out of all hydrocarbon and coal exploration and exploitation activities[15]. The law stipulates that no more hydrocarbon exploration permits can be granted, so it is no longer possible to initiate such activity on French soil. Nevertheless,

14 Loi n° 2011–835 du 13 juillet 2011 visant à interdire l'exploration et l'exploitation des mines d'hydrocarbures liquides ou gazeux par fracturation hydraulique. The constitutionality of this law was challenged, in particular by companies that had previously obtained research permits, but the Constitutional Court rejected their appeals: Conseil constitutionnel, 11 oct. 2013, n° 2013–346 QPC, *Sté Schuepbach Energy LLC.*

15 Loi n°2017–1839 du 30 décembre 2017 mettant fin à la recherche ainsi qu'à l'exploitation des hydrocarbures. The constitutionality of this law, like that of 2011 concerning shale hydrocarbons, was challenged, but the appeal was unsuccessful: Conseil d'État, 27 juin 2018, n° 419316, *Stés EGFEP & TEPGF.* See also Conseil d'État, 18 décembre 2019, n° 421004, *Sté IPC Petroleum France SA.*

an operating licence can still be issued to companies holding an exploration licence, but production activities must cease in 2040.[16]

At the time the law was passed, it was said that France was the first big industrial country to dare to take this commitment. But it has to be admitted that it looks more like a symbolic gesture, since France produces very little fossil energy: it no longer produces coal, and oil and gas production is very limited (around 1 % of national consumption). However, this has led to certain projects being put on hold.[17]

In any case, it is above all efforts to reduce fossil fuel consumption, rather than production, that must now be focused on. Action must therefore be taken in the sectors that consume the most fossil fuels, for example in the field of mobility or in the field of power generation.

As far as electricity production is concerned, France's is already very low-carbon. France uses relatively little fossil fuel for its electricity generation, but it can still be noted that some decisions have been taken to go a little further. Especially, there has been a drastic decline in coal-fired electricity generation over the last 10 years,[18] which today represents less than 1 % of French electricity production, and France has decided in 2019 to close its last coal-fired power stations.[19] However, in 2022 and 2023 France had to temporarily reverse this decision in order to cope with the unforeseen unavailability of part of the nuclear fleet due to necessary maintenance operations, which led to a temporary shutdown of a larger number of reactors than expected. But this is just a temporary measure to deal with an exceptional situation.[20]

---

16 By exception to the general principle that the concessions granted and the renewal of existing concessions cannot exceed the deadline of January 1st 2040, the permit may exceed this deadline when the licensee demonstrates to the administrative authority that the deadline does not allow to cover its research and exploitation costs, in order to achieve the economic equilibrium. When the law was passed, 33 exploration licences and 63 operating licences were in force.

17 This was particularly the case overseas, where projects were abandoned, notably in French Guiana.

18 – 81 % in the period 2010–2020.

19 Energy Code, art. L. 311–5–3, II, created by the 2019 Energy and Climate Law (Loi n°2019–1147 du 8 novembre 2019 relative à l'énergie et au climat). The purpose of this text is to set a cap on greenhouse gas emissions applicable to the activity of fossil-fuelled power stations, with the result that coal-fired power stations, which emit the most, could only operate for a few hours a year, leading to their closure.

20 In 2022, for the first time in a very long time, France was a net importer of electricity, whereas for years it had been a net exporter, and even a major exporter of electricity. This was mainly due to the unavailability of a large proportion of the nuclear

On the other hand, much remains to be done in other sectors, such as the mobility sector. On this point, in France, the decarbonization of mobility will mainly involve the development of electromobility. A policy to support the development of electric vehicles and the deployment of charging infrastructure has been put in place and is beginning to produce results.

At present only about 13 % of new passenger car sales are of electric cars, but this rate is increasing rapidly.[21]

At the same time, and given that the primary actor in the reduction of fossil fuel consumption is the consumer himself, various measures have been adopted concerning practices likely to influence his behaviour, such as advertising. For example, the law provides for a ban on advertising related to fossil fuels.[22] It also provides for a ban on advertising for new cars that emit too much greenhouse gas,[23] which paves the way for the future ban on the sale of new fossil fuel cars that has been decided in France for 2040.[24]

France is also one of the countries that have decided to withdraw from the Energy Charter Treaty. The main reason for this was that the rules set

fleet, partly as a result of scheduled maintenance operations (the maintenance of certain nuclear power plants had fallen behind schedule in 2020–2021 because of the Covid-19 pandemic) and partly because of an unexpected corrosion problem detected in certain power plants, leading to the unavailability of a larger number of reactors than expected. To deal with this situation, France has increased the production of its thermal power stations and has increased its imports.

21 France has ambitious targets and incentives, such as a bonus-malus system, a conversion bonus to support the switch to electric cars, subsidies for the purchase of electric vehicles and for the installation of charging stations. The Law on the Orientation of Mobility adopted in 2019 (Loi n° 2019–1428 du 24 décembre 2019 d'orientation des mobilités) require all sales of new passenger cars to be zero emission in 2040, and it introduced a wide range of measures to boost the role of alternative fuels (electricity, hydrogen, biogas).

22 The law states that "advertising relating to the marketing or promoting fossil fuels is prohibited" : article L. 229–61 of the Environment Code, created by the 2021 Climate and Resilience Act (Loi n°2021–1104 du 24 août 2021 portant lutte contre le dérèglement climatique et renforcement de la résilience face à ses effets).

23 Article L. 229–62 of the Environment Code, created by the 2021 Climate and Resilience Act (this provision will enter into force in 2028).

24 The 2019 Law on the Orientation of Mobility provides for "the end of the sale of new passenger cars and light utility vehicles using fossil fuels by 2040" (Loi n° 2019–1428 du 24 décembre 2019 d'orientation des mobilités, art. 73).

out in the treaty were likely to hinder the energy transition, particularly because of the protection offered to investments in the fossil fuel sector.[25]

It should be noted, however, that the energy crisis we have been experiencing since the end of 2021, leading to a very sharp rise in prices, has in some respects made it more difficult to achieve the targets. Indeed, some consumer support measures have led to increased subsidies for fossil fuels, particularly for the purchase of motor fuels. This is not in line with the decarbonization policy, but it shows how difficult it can sometimes be to combine the energy transition with the need for access to energy and the fight against energy poverty. On the other hand, the same crisis has led to greater emphasis being placed on the importance of energy savings and has produced significant results in this area as we will see below.

D. Efforts To Improve the Development of Renewable Energies and Energy Savings

The share of renewable energies in the French energy mix has risen significantly in recent years. For example, over the past decade, wind and solar photovoltaic electricity generation have largely increased, driving the share of renewables in electricity generation from 14 % in 2010 up to 24 % in 2020. Hydropower generation had long been significant, accounting for around half of renewable electricity production in 2020.

But it cannot be denied that there is still a lot of progress to be made. This is even more apparent now that France has failed to reach its 2020 renewable energy development target. By 2020, the target was a 23 % share of renewables in gross final energy consumption, and France only achieved around 19 %. Obviously, there is a gap between ambition and implementation. Moreover, the distance to the 2030 targets is increasing. For 2030, the current target is to increase the share of renewable energies to at least 33 % of gross final energy consumption, whereas France is currently at around 20 %. The law specifies the targets to be achieved in different sectors (electricity production, gas consumption, heat consumption, etc.) in order to reach this overall target. For example, the law specifies that renewable

25 On 1 December 2022, the French Minister for Europe and Foreign Affairs officially notified Portugal of France's withdrawal from the Energy Charter Treaty. Portugal, as depositary of the Treaty, acknowledged receipt of this notification on 7 December 2022. In accordance with the Treaty, this withdrawal will take effect one year later.

energies must account for 40 % of electricity production by 2030, whereas at present they only account for 24 %.[26] In other words, this production must be almost doubled. What's more, this target is set to rise even further, as France will have to revise its ambitions upwards as a result of changes in EU law.[27] Major progress will have to be made in the coming years.

It is therefore important to ask why the 2020 objective was not achieved. We will not go into detail here, as this will be covered in the chapter specifically devoted to renewable energies, but we will simply point out that the difficulties are essentially due to the following reasons. In terms of energy policy, it may be thought that France did not feel as much pressure as others to develop renewable energies on a massive scale because it already benefited from largely decarbonized energy, at least in the field of electricity production, due to the major role of nuclear energy. But the problem is also one of implementation, and from that point of view the main difficulties identified concern:

- the local acceptability of certain projects, particularly in the field of wind power;
- the excessive duration of permitting procedures, since the average duration of these procedures in France is significantly longer than the average for European countries;[28]
- lengthy litigation;
- a certain legal uncertainty, due to some retroactive reforms of support mechanisms that have undermined investors' confidence.

The legislature is gradually trying to resolve these difficulties. It recently took action by adopting, in March 2023, the Renewable Energy Acceleration Act, one of whose aims is to halve the time taken to complete administrative procedures.[29] Time will tell whether this objective will be achieved.

---

26 And 38 % of final heat consumption, 15 % of final fuel consumption and 10 % of gas consumption: Energy Code, art. L. 100–4 (see supra Section A).

27 Particularly in view of the new target for the development of renewable energies at Union level, raised to a minimum of 42.5 % of final electricity consumption by 2030 by the "RED III" directive: Directive (EU) 2023/2413 of the European Parliament and of the Council of 18 October 2023 amending Directive (EU) 2018/2001, Regulation (EU) 2018/1999 and Directive 98/70/EC as regards the promotion of energy from renewable sources, and repealing Council Directive (EU) 2015/652 [2023] OJ L 2023/2413.

28 For example, an average of 8 years for the commissioning of a wind farm.

29 Loi n° 2023–175 du 10 mars 2023 relative à l'accélération de la production d'énergies renouvelables. Several of the measures contained in this law are in line with the Euro-

Regarding energy savings, French law sets a target of halving final energy consumption by 2050 and to reduce it by 20 % by 2030, which is very ambitious. Many measures have been adopted in this area, although the results are not sufficient for the moment. Total final consumption in France decreased by around 5 % over the past decade, mainly thanks to improvements in the building and industry sectors. Significantly better results were achieved in 2022. However, they can be explained by a context of crisis. In response to it, the French State drew up an "energy sobriety plan", encouraging individuals and companies to reduce their energy consumption in a context of risk to security of supply and very high energy prices.[30]

But there is no guarantee that these good results will continue over time. Therefore, strong measures are still needed. The field of the energy performance of existing buildings is a good example of the evolution of French law. Originally, the measures were primarily of an incentive and informative nature: for example, the energy performance diagnosis which must be drawn up at the time of the sale or rental of the building, and which allows the buyer or the tenant to be informed of the building's level of energy performance. Today, it is much stricter measures that must be implemented. For example, the rents of housing with poor energy performance are frozen and the worst-performing units are considered indecent housing, which prohibits them from being rented.[31] Therefore, if the owner wants to rent his property, he is obliged to carry out energy renovation work. Significant public subsidies have been introduced to promote the implementation of these energy renovation works.

---

pean Council Regulation 2022/2577 of 22 December 2022 laying down a framework to accelerate the deployment of renewable energy and Directive (EU) 2023/2413 of the European Parliament and of the Council of 18 October 2023 amending Directive (EU) 2018/2001 ("RED III"), particularly with regard to the presumption of overriding public interest applicable to certain plants and installations for the production of energy from renewable sources. Other measures include developing and supervising agrivoltaics, speeding up the development of offshore wind power, which is lagging far behind in France, promoting the development of "corporate power purchase agreements", extending the obligation to install photovoltaic panels on certain buildings, and so on.

30 French Government, 'Plan de sobriété énergétique' (2022) < https://www.ecologie.gouv.fr/sites/default/files/dp-plan-sobriete.pdf> accessed 30 October 2023.

31 The 2019 "Energy and Climate Law" has made it mandatory to renovate the most energy-intensive residential buildings from 2028. Even before this date, to encourage landlords to carry out the work without delay, the law provides for a freeze on rents, followed by a ban on renting out the most energy-intensive dwellings.

E. The Continuing Central Role of Nuclear Energy

France is in a rather specific position regarding nuclear energy, which is the focus of much of the debate on the future of French energy policy. Indeed, France is mainly known as a nuclear country. France made the choice during the 70s to massively develop the nuclear industry in order to become self-sufficient and to offer to citizens low-cost electricity. The result is that nuclear power still represents around two thirds of French power production.[32] Therefore, it could be said that in the French context the real dilemma is not between fossil fuels and renewable energies, but between nuclear energy and renewable energies.

Nevertheless, ten years ago, following the Fukushima accident, there were many discussions about the future of nuclear power. Doubts were raised about whether the French energy transition involved questioning the role of nuclear power in the French energy mix. A kind of response was given by the Energy Transition Act adopted in 2015, which transcribed a form of compromise by keeping the nuclear option open while providing for a reduction in the share of nuclear power in national electricity production. The aim in 2015 was, therefore, to diversify energy sources, with less nuclear power and more renewable energy. In its original version, the Energy Transition Act provided for a target to bring the proportion of nuclear energy in electricity generation down to 50 % by 2025.[33] At the time, the share of nuclear power was around 70 %. In addition, the Energy Transition Act introduced a cap on installed nuclear capacity, which represented the current installed capacity at the time the law was passed (63,2 GW). In other words, the law provided for a ban on the creation and operation of new reactors, unless old reactors were first shut down.

But it was not a death sentence for nuclear energy in France, and subsequent events have largely confirmed this, even if it can be said that the issue has lacked clarity for a few years due to political hesitations.

Firstly, the law was amended to postpone the deadline. The original target date was 2025, but this was later extended to 2035, because it became apparent that a significant and rapid reduction in the share of nuclear power would entail major risks, particularly in terms of security of supply

32 69 % in 2021, RTE, 'Bilan électrique' (n 3).

33 2015 Energy Transition for Green Growth Act, article 1 (Loi n° 2015- 992 du 17 août 2015 relative à la transition énergétique pour la croissance verte).

and in terms of greenhouse gas emission levels.[34] It was found that the pace of development of renewable energy was too slow to allow for the rapid closure of a significant number of nuclear reactors. This is why the law was also amended to specify that any decision to shut down a nuclear reactor must take into account the requirements of security of supply and reduction of greenhouse gas emissions.[35]

Secondly, and even more clearly, the law was recently amended to repeal the target for reducing the share of nuclear power in electricity generation. The Nuclear Acceleration Act, adopted in June 2023,[36] once again promotes nuclear energy, as was the case before the 2015 law on energy transition. More precisely, the Nuclear Acceleration Act has two objectives. The first is to extend the operating life of existing nuclear power plants, as long as safety requirements are met.[37] The second is to simplify and accelerate procedures for the creation of new nuclear reactors, provided they are built within the perimeter of existing nuclear sites or nearby, with a view to facilitating the implementation of the nuclear energy recovery plan. At present, the construction of 14 new reactors is planned for the next few years. The means provided for this mainly consist of simplifying the administrative procedures required for the creation of nuclear reactors, whether under town planning law, environmental law or energy law. But this also meant repealing the provisions relating to energy policy objectives that were likely to prevent such a revival of the nuclear industry. This is why the law repealed the target for reducing the share of nuclear power in electricity generation, as well as the cap on installed nuclear capacity that had been set in 2015.

---

34 2019 Energy and Climate Law, article 1 (Loi n°2019-1147 du 8 novembre 2019 relative à l'énergie et au climat).

35 Energy Code, article L. 100-4, I bis, created by the 2021 Climate and Resilience Act (Loi n°2021-1104 du 24 août 2021 portant lutte contre le dérèglement climatique et renforcement de la résilience face à ses effets).

36 Loi n° 2023-491 du 22 juin 2023 relative à l'accélération des procédures liées à la construction de nouvelles installations nucléaires à proximité de sites nucléaires existants et au fonctionnement des installations existantes.

37 The nuclear power fleet is ageing in France, since many nuclear power plants were commissioned in the 1980s and were originally designed to operate for 40 years. Therefore, it is now a question of extending their lifetime. *Electricité de France* (EDF), which operates all of France's nuclear power stations, is currently engaged in a vast programme of refurbishing its nuclear reactor fleet and preparing it for operation beyond 40 years. The French regulatory system does not set a plant lifetime but requires the licensee to perform an in-depth safety review every 10 years. The Nuclear Acceleration Act amended certain provisions governing safety reviews.

This recent development confirms, if confirmation were needed, that the energy transition is not seen in France as involving giving up nuclear power. This was also very clear in the debates on the EU taxonomy for sustainable activities, in which France argued strongly for nuclear energy to be recognized for its contribution to climate change mitigation.[38]

The French legal framework for hydrogen further confirms this. Most of the measures put in place in France aim to promote not just "green" hydrogen, but low-carbon hydrogen more generally. For example, in 2020 France adopted a "national strategy for the development of low-carbon hydrogen"[39], and the objectives of the national energy policy, as set out in the Energy Code, include the aim of "developing low-carbon and renewable hydrogen and its industrial, energy and mobility uses, with a view to achieving approximately 20 to 40 % of total hydrogen and industrial hydrogen consumption by 2030".[40] In 2021, France adopted a text laying the foundations for the legal regime applicable to renewable hydrogen and low-carbon hydrogen.[41]

The aim is to promote low-carbon hydrogen as well as renewable hydrogen, and therefore to include hydrogen produced from electrolyzers using nuclear energy.[42] As a result, public support schemes benefit both low-carbon and renewable hydrogen (in the form of operating aid or investment

38 Nuclear activities have finally been included in the taxonomy: Commission Delegated Regulation (EU) 2022/1214 of 9 March 2022 amending Delegated Regulation (EU) 2021/2139 as regards economic activities in certain energy sectors and Delegated Regulation (EU) 2021/2178 as regards specific public disclosures for those economic activities [2022] OJ L 188/1.

39 French Government, 'Stratégie nationale pour le développement de l'hydrogène décarboné en France' <https://www.entreprises.gouv.fr/files/files/secteurs-d-activite/industrie/decarbonation/dp_strategie_nationale_pour_le_developpement_de_l_hydrogene_decarbone_en_france.pdf> accessed 30 October 2023.

40 Energy code, article L. 100–4, 10°.

41 2021 Ordinance on Hydrogen (Ordonnance n° 2021–167 du 17 février 2021 relative à l'hydrogène). The main provisions of this text have been codified in the Energy Code: articles L. 811–1 et seq.

42 The legislative definitions are as follows: "Renewable hydrogen is hydrogen produced either by electrolysis using electricity from renewable energy sources as defined in article L. 211–2, or by any other technology that uses exclusively one or more of these same renewable energy sources and does not conflict with other uses allowing their direct recovery (...). In all cases, its production process emits, per kilogram of hydrogen produced, a quantity of carbon dioxide equivalents less than or equal to a threshold.
Low-carbon hydrogen is hydrogen whose production process generates emissions less than or equal to the threshold for the qualification of renewable hydrogen,

aid granted following a tendering procedure),[43] and the same applies to the "guarantees of origin" and "traceability guarantees" provided for in these texts.[44] Once again, we see that the objective in France is to develop the use of low-carbon energies, including nuclear energy, and not just renewable energies.

F. Conclusion

In France, the objective of the energy transition is above all to contribute to the decarbonization of the economy by promoting the use of renewable and low-carbon energies. As a result, France is promoting renewable energies and nuclear energy as well. Concerning nuclear energy, after a few years of hesitation, France has returned to a very clear position in favour of nuclear energy, as evidenced by the adoption of the Nuclear Acceleration Act in June 2023. As for renewable energies, while they are indeed progressing in France, the pace of development does not appear to be fast enough and significant efforts remain to be made to achieve the targets set for 2030. Although it may not be enough to solve all the difficulties, the Renewable Energy Acceleration Act, which was adopted in March 2023, shows that the French authorities are aware of this necessity.

Bibliography

French Government, 'Stratégie nationale pour le développement de l'hydrogène décarboné en France' (2020) <https://www.entreprises.gouv.fr/files/files/secteurs-d-activite/industrie/decarbonation/dp_strategie_nationale_pour_le_developpement_de_l_hydrogene_decarbone_en_france.pdf> accessed 30 October 2023

without being able, however, to receive the latter qualification, because it does not meet the other criteria" (article L. 811-1 of the Energy Code).

43 Energy Code, art. R. 812-1 et seq. (created by Décret n° 2023-854 du 1er septembre 2023 relatif au dispositif de soutien à la production de certaines catégories d'hydrogène).

44 According to article L. 821-2 of the energy code, "if the renewable or low-carbon hydrogen produced is not mixed with another type of hydrogen or another gas between the stage of its production and that of its consumption and the guarantee issued is sold at the same time as the hydrogen produced, this guarantee attests to its physical traceability. It is called a 'traceability guarantee'". According to article L. 821-3 of the energy code, "if the renewable or low-carbon hydrogen produced is likely to be mixed with another type of hydrogen or another gas between the same stages or if the guarantee issued during its production is likely to be sold independently of the hydrogen produced, this guarantee attests to its origin. It is called a 'guarantee of origin'".

French Government, 'Plan de sobriété énergétique' (2022) < https://www.ecologie.gouv.fr/sites/default/files/dp-plan-sobriete.pdf> accessed 30 October 2023

International Energy Agency, 'France 2021 Energy Policy Review' <https://iea.blob.core.windows.net/assets/7b3b4b9d-6db3-4dcf-a0a5-a9993d7dd1d6/France2021.pdf> accessed 20.08.2024

Lamoreux M, *Droit de l'énergie,* 2nd edition, LGDJ 2022

RTE, 'Bilan électrique' <https://bilan-electrique-2021.rte-france.com> accessed 30 October 2023

General Perspectives on the Law of Energy Transition in Italy

Fabrizio Fracchia

A. Some Data about the Current National Energy Mix

As specified by the national Institute for Environmental Protection and Research (ISPRA),[1] in Italy gross inland energy consumption increased from 1990 until 2005 when it peaked at 189.4 Mtoe (Million Tonnes of Oil Equivalent). After an initial reduction caused by the economic crisis (149.8 Mtoe reached in 2014) and a further contraction due to measures implemented to contain the Covid-19 pandemic (-8.9 % lower than 2019 level and -4.4 % lower than 1990 level), in 2021 there was a rebound of energy consumption (+8.5 % higher than 2020) to 153.7 Mtoe.

According to data provided by the Italian Ministry of Environment and Energy Security,[2] in 2022, the gross energy availability consisted of 37.6 % natural gas, 35.7 % oil and petroleum products, 18.5 % renewables and bioliquids, 5 % solid fuels, and 2.5 % electricity.

Renewable gross inland consumption has more than quadrupled from 6.5 Mtoe in 1990 to 29.9 Mtoe in 2021 (19.4 % of gross inland consumption).[3]

---

1 Istituto Superiore per la Protezione e la Ricerca Ambientale, 'Efficiency and decarbonization indicators in Italy and in the biggest European Countries. Edition 2023' <https://www.isprambiente.gov.it/files2023/pubblicazioni/rapporti/r386-2023.pdf> accessed 31 August 2023.

2 Ministero dell'Ambiente e della Sicurezza Energetica, 'La situazione energetica nazionale nel 2022' 10 and Appendice A <https://www.mase.gov.it/sites/default/files/Archivio_Energia/LA%20RELAZIONE%20SULLA%20SITUAZIONE%20ENERGETICA%20NAZIONALE%20NEL%202022_MASE%20Luglio%202023.pdf> accessed 31 August 2023.

3 Istituto Superiore per la Protezione e la Ricerca Ambientale, 'Efficiency and decarbonization indicators in Italy and in the biggest European Countries. Edition 2023' 6 (n 1), according to which "The renewable electricity on total electricity production went from 16 % in 2005 to the top of 43.1 % in 2014, in 2021 the share is 40.2 %, with a particularly significant 152 increase in wind and photovoltaic sources. The contribution of hydropower remains decisive also in relation to the intrinsic variability of this source. Preliminary estimate shows an abrupt contraction of renewable share in 2022 (35.5 %), mainly due to the sharp reduction of hydroelectric generation".

In 2022, renewables found wide diffusion in Italy in all sectors of energy use (electricity, thermal, transport), despite the occurrence of some climatic phenomena that affected their uses and availability (reduced rainfall, relatively high average temperatures).

In line with the previous year, the share of total energy consumption covered by renewables is estimated at around 19 %.[4]

Some important decarbonization targets have been set by various plans and programmes adopted by Italy. According to the Integrated National Energy and Climate Plan 2019[5] (INECP, adopted by the Italian Government in compliance with the European Union's Regulation 2018/1999/EU), for instance, by 2030 the percentage of energy from renewable sources in gross final energy consumption shall be 30 % (22 % in transport), the percentage of reduction in primary energy consumption compared to the PRIMES 2007 scenario shall be 43 %, and the reduction of greenhouse gases in all non-ETS sectors shall be 33 % compared to 2005.

Targets established by the Integrated National Energy and Climate Plan have been revised and made more ambitious with the National Recovery and Resilience Plan (NRRP – Piano Nazionale di Ripresa e Resilienza: this plan is part of the Next Generation EU programme)[6] (considering the "Fit for 55" EU package) and the National Ecological Transition Plan

4 Ministero dell'Ambiente e della Sicurezza Energetica, 'La situazione energetica nazionale nel 2022' (n 2).

5 Ministero dell'Ambiente e della Sicurezza Energetica, 'Piano Nazionale Integrato per l'Energia e il Clima' <https://www.mimit.gov.it/images/stories/documenti/PNIEC_finale_17012020.pdf> accessed 31 August 2023.

6 The Plan was definitively approved by EU Council of Ministers through the Council Implementing Decision on July 13th 2021 on the approval of the assessment of the recovery and resilience plan for Italy (ST 10160/21; ST 10160/21 ADD 1; ST 10160/21 ADD 1 REV 1; ST 10160/21 ADD 1 REV 2; ST 10160/21 ADD 1 REV 2 COR 1). The Plan was necessary to enable access to the funds of the Recovery and Resilience Facility, which is the main component of the NGEU programme: Regulation (EU) 2021/241 of 12 February 2021 of the European Parliament and of the Council establishing the Recovery and Resilience Facility [2021] OJ L 57/17. The NGEU funding programme is the tool introduced by the European Union for post-Covid-19 pandemic recovery with the goal of relaunching the Member States' economy: see Commission, 'Europe's Moment: repair and prepare for the Next Generation' (Communication) COM (2020) 456 final. The Italian National Recovery and Resilience Plan presented foresees important investments: 191.5 billion euros will be financed through the RRF and 30.6 billion euros through the Complementary Fund, bringing the total investment to 222.1 billion euros.

(ETP, approved on 8 March 2022)[7], where it has been established that the contribution of renewable energies shall be at least 72 % by 2030, while the phase-out of coal should be achieved by 2025. In addition, in line with international and European commitments, Italian decarbonization ("net zero" emissions) shall be reached by 2050 and a reduction of 55 % in CO2 emissions shall be obtained by 2030.[8]

On July 1, 2024, the Ministries of Environment and Energy Security and of Infrastructure and Transport submitted to the European Commission the finalized text of the annual update of the Integrated National Energy and Climate Plan (INECP).

Regarding renewable energies, the Plan states: "Renewable energies occupy a prominent position in national energy policy. ... The aim is to reach a share of nearly 40 % of gross final energy consumption by 2030, aligning with the expected contribution to achieving the EU target. Regarding the dissemination of renewable energies in the transportation sector, the EU framework presents a favorable outlook; in fact, the RED III Directive has raised the 2030 target related to the share of consumption in the transportation sector covered by renewable sources, currently set at 14 % by RED II, to 29 %. Consequently, the obligation for suppliers to integrate renewable products into consumption will be gradually increased, extending its application to all transportation sectors and coordinating its effects with FuelEU Maritime and ReFuelEU Aviation regulations. Simultaneously, the use of more energy vectors is intended to be promoted, for instance, setting the goal to include in consumption a quantity of renewable fuels of non-biological origin and ensuring the contribution from the use of pure biofuels. In the thermal sector, the vector biogas (primarily) and hydrogen (particularly in the industrial sector) will increasingly be integrated, with a vision towards the possibility of cogeneration from nuclear production.

7 Governo Italiano, 'Delibera 8 marzo 2022 del Comitato interministeriale per la transizione ecologica Approvazione del Piano per la transizione ecologica ai sensi dell'art 57-bis, comma e) e seguenti del decreto legislativo 3 aprile 2006 n 152 [2022] OJ 138/47' <https://www.mase.gov.it/sites/default/files/archivio/allegati/PTE/PTE-definitivo.pdf> accessed 22.08.2024; ETP is the national multi sectoral plan for the period 2022–2050 that coordinates national environmental policies, digitization and energy transition towards the goal of ecological transition. The main objective of the Ecological Transition Plan is to achieve climate neutrality by 2050.

8 In June 2023, the Ministry of the Environment and Energy Security sent the proposal for updating the National Integrated Energy and Climate Plan to Brussels, thus starting the updating process that will lead to the final approval of the new text by June 2024.

From a technological perspective, it will be important to continue creating a favorable framework to accelerate the decarbonization of civil consumption through the widespread adoption of heat pumps in the civil sector, leaving the market to determine the most efficient option for each application and also assessing their contribution in cooling mode. "[9]

Many other plans have been set in Italy, also in the light of the dramatic geopolitical and energy crisis of 2022: suffice to mention the National Gas Containment Plan aimed at reducing gas demand in 2022,[10] and achieving the national target for filling gas stocks to at least 90 % of their capacity.[11]

B. Policies and Strategies Envisaged by Italy

In the light of the ongoing geopolitical crisis, some political initiatives can be mentioned.

Firstly, in order to reduce dependence on Russian gas and diversify the supply, Italy has made agreements with many other countries, such as Algeria, Egypt, Angola, the Republic of the Congo, Nigeria and Qatar.

Secondly, one floating storage and regasification unit (FSRU) is expected to be operational by the end of 2025 in Ravenna, while another one has been operational in Piombino since 2023.

Thirdly, on the topic of hydrogen, thanks to funds from the above-mentioned National Recovery and Resilience Plan, the State pledged 3.6 billion euros of investment by 2026 in projects to promote the development of the hydrogen supply chain. A number of ministerial decrees have been adopted to set out the administrative procedures supporting the construction of plants. In sum, Italy aims at (1) the development of projects for the use of hydrogen in industrial sectors that are hard to abate, such as the steel industry; (2) the establishment of "hydrogen valleys" using brownfield sites in order to create ecosystems that include both production and consumption of hydrogen; (3) enabling the use of hydrogen in heavy transport and in non-electrified railway sections.

---

9 Governo Italiano, <https://www.mase.gov.it/portale/documents/d/guest/pniec_2024_revfin_01072024-pdf> accessed 15 May 2025.

10 Ministero della Transizione Ecologica, 'Piano nazionale di contenimento dei consumi di gas naturale' <https://www.mase.gov.it/sites/default/files/archivio/comunicati/Piano%20contenimento%20consumi%20gas_MITE_6set2022.pdf> accessed 31 August 2023.

11 Decreto legge 1 marzo 2022 n 17 convertito in legge 27 aprile 2022 n 34 [2022] OJ 50/1.

Obviously, another strategy is a strong boost in favour of renewable energies. In this regard, mention may be made of a piece of national legislation,[12] which focuses on the objective of accelerating the country's sustainable growth path, laying down provisions on energy from renewable sources, in line with the European objectives of decarbonization of the energy system by 2030 and complete decarbonization by 2050.[13]

With regard to mobility, different investments are planned within the National Recovery and Resilience Plan (where energy transition is considered along with sustainable mobility), such as the development of electric recharging infrastructures and the renewal of bus and green train fleets.

C. The Legal Tools (Command and Control, Market-Based Tools) and the Public Interests that are Involved in the Transition

All the targets and strategies mentioned above are pursued through a continuous series of legislative amendments and "refinements".

The most relevant public interests considered are the protection of the environment[14], the implementation of the NRRP,[15] and the fight against energy crises related to war.[16]

12 Decreto legislativo 8 novembre 2021 n 199 [2021] OJ 285/4.

13 This Decree transposed the European 'RED II'.

14 Art. 16-septies, Directive (EU) 2023/2413 of the European Parliament and of the Council of 18 October 2023 amending Directive (EU) 2018/2001, Regulation (EU) 2018/1999 and Directive 98/70/EC as regards the promotion of energy from renewable sources, and repealing Council Directive (EU) 2015/652 [2023] OJ L 2023/2413 (RED III), provides that "Until climate neutrality is achieved, Member States shall ensure that, in the permit-granting process, the planning, construction and operation of renewable energy production installations, their connection to the grid, the grid itself, and storage facilities are considered to be of overriding public interest and in the interest of public health and safety when balancing legal interests in each individual case".

15 See (n 6).

16 Consider, for instance, decreto legislativo 8 novembre 2021 n 199 [2021] OJ 285/4; decreto legge 16 luglio 2020 n 76 convertito in legge 11 settembre 2020 n 120 [2020] OJ 228/1; decreto legge 31 maggio 2021 n 77 convertito in legge 29 luglio 2021 n 108 [2021] OJ 129/1; decreto legge 1 marzo 2022 n 17 convertito in legge 27 aprile 2022 n 34 [2022] OJ 50/1; decreto legge 17 maggio 2022 n 50 convertito in legge 15 luglio 2022 n 91 [2022] OJ 114/1; decreto legge 30 aprile 2022 n 36 convertito in legge 29 giugno 2022 n 79 [2022] OJ 100/1; decreto legge 9 agosto 2022 n 115 convertito in legge 21 settembre 2022 n. 142 [2022] OJ 185/1; decreto legge 24 febbraio 2023 n 13 convertito in legge 21 aprile 2023 n 41 [2023] OJ 47/1.

The “answer” to a complex problem – such as energy generation and supply – is a multifaceted set of measures, all of which are relevant to public law and give rise to a plurality of intervention models spanning from command and control to market-based tools (specifically through incentive mechanisms).

As can be seen from the cited list of some of the main and most recent sources of law enacted in the renewable energy sector,[17] there is an incessant flow of legislation. For this reason, the “annual law for the market and competition 2021”[18] empowered the government to reorganize the existing legislation on renewable energy sources, in order to achieve a significant reduction and rationalization of legislative provisions and to ensure a greater degree of legal certainty and simplification of procedures.

Under the delegated legislation, a legislative decree 190/2024, titled “Regulation of Administrative Regimes for the Production of Energy from Renewable Sources in Implementation of Article 26, Paragraphs 4 and 5, Letters b) and d), of Law No. 118 of August 5, 2022," came into force at the end of 2024[19].

It is not new that in our system there is a constant concern about regulatory and bureaucratic simplification, pursued, in particular, through the design of streamlined administrative regimes for the construction and operation of renewable energy plants and providing for substitutive powers in the event of inaction by the relevant administrative bodies.[20]

Organizational simplification measures have also been taken. For instance, national government has set up a specific EIA (Environmental Impact Assessment) Technical Commission for the NRRP projects (among which there are also those relating to renewable energies) and it has established a special Superintendence for the protection of cultural and landscape assets in cases where such assets are affected by the interventions under the NRRP.[21] An Interministerial Committee for the Ecological Tran-

17 See (n 16).

18 Legge 5 agosto 2022 n 118 [2022] OJ 188/1.

19 Decreto legislativo 25 novembre 25 2024 n 190 [2024] OJ 291/4.

20 In this regard, the National Recovery and Resilience Plan calls for two key reforms on renewable energies: “simplification of permitting procedures for on-shore and offshore renewable facilities, new legal framework to support renewable generation and extension of the timing and eligibility of current support schemes” and “new legislation to promote renewable gas production and consumption”.

21 Decreto legge 31 maggio 2021 n 77 convertito in legge 29 luglio 2021 n 108 [2021] OJ 129/1.

sition was also established, with the task of ensuring the coordination of national policies for the ecological transition and related programmes.

According to a multilevel approach, it is also of interest to mention the experience (for which relevant incentives are provided) of Energy Communities and Collective Self Consumption,[22] which allows the sharing of renewable electric energy among various producers and consumers located within the same area.

The relationship and the legal relevance of these strategies, measures and legal tools can be better explained by using the theoretical concept of energy transition (see below), which is a crucial component of the green transition due to the evident fact that energy production from traditional sources significantly contributes to climate change.

D. Notion of Energy Transition; Political Conception and Legal Implication.

1. The First Part of the Definition: the Transition as a "Form of a Function"

In general, the word "transition" expresses a shift from a *before* to an *after*. The adjective "energy", on the other hand, explains and indicates the direction of this change.

What has just been provided, however, is not yet a specific definition and, above all, it is not a legally useful definition.

In this respect, it should be added that even national and European legal sources do not offer any particular definition.

It is therefore necessary to take a further step, making a theoretical effort towards abstraction and starting from the few elements existing in the legal context.[23] First, it is worth focusing on the broader concept of

22 As of 30 September 2022, Italy had 17 Energy Communities and 37 Collective Self Consumption: data from Osservatorio ENEA, 'Energia: da ENEA un Osservatorio per promuovere le Comunità Energetiche Rinnovabili' <https://www.media.enea.it/comunicati-e-news/archivio-anni/anno-2023/energia-da-enea-un-osservatorio-per-promuovere-le-comunita-energetiche-rinnovabili.html> accessed 31 August 2023; See Governo Italiano, 'Art. 8 decreto legislativo 8 novembre 2021 n 199 [2021] OJ 285/4 and decreto MASE 7 dicembre 2023 n 414' <www.mase.gov.it> accessed 30 June 2024.

23 About transition in Italy: Francesco de Leonardis, *La transizione ecologica come modello di sviluppo di sistema: spunti sul ruolo delle amministrazioni* (2021) Diritto amministrativo 779; Michela Petrachi, *La tutela dell'ambiente nel prisma della transizione ecologica* (Giappichelli 2023); Giuseppe Severini, 'La "transizione" come ordinamento giuridico' (2022) Giustizia insieme <www-giustiziainsieme.it> accessed 24

ecological/green transition and observing how the latter constitutes one of the pillars of the above-mentioned National Recovery and Resilience Plan.

More specifically, the National Recovery and Resilience Plan, to be implemented in the span of five years, is structured around three strategic axes (digitization and innovation, ecological transition) and six fields of intervention (called "missions"). One of those pillars (with the greatest endowment of funds: 68.6 billion euros) is precisely (green revolution and) ecological transition (mission 2), aiming for progressive decarbonization. This mission is expected to be achieved by different tools. Among these, reforms aiming at the modernization of the country should be cited.[24] Worth mentioning is simplification, which is a tool that also involves, as already stated, renewable energies, to the extent that it aims at removing the "bottlenecks" to the diffusion and implementation of renewable energy plants.

The National Recovery and Resilience Plan is integrated with the National Ecological Transition Plan (ETP), according to which "energy production is the sector most responsible for greenhouse gas emissions – three-quarters of the global total according to data from the International Energy Agency. For this reason, the progressive replacement of fossil fuels with renewable energies represents the main necessary condition of the ecological transition".[25]

This is an important element that leads to a more complete understanding of the phenomenon: the energy transition is a condition of the ecological transition, which is one of the pillars of the NRRP.

November 2022; Tamara Favaro, *Regolare la "transizione energetica". Stato, mercato, innovazione* (Cedam 2020); See also Fabrizio Fracchia, *Transizioni: il punto di vista del diritto amministrativo* (Editoriale Scientifica 2024).

24 More in detail, the Plan provides for a twofold order of interventions, namely, "reforms" to be prepared and "investments" to be made. The Plan is centered on milestones and targets (M&T): the milestones define, in general terms, the relevant administrative and procedural steps: they are qualitative targets to be met through a given NRRP measure (reform and/or investment); The targets are the expected results of actions, quantified by measurable indicators: they are quantitative targets to be met through a given NRRP measure (reform and/or investment).

25 See above (n 8). Alongside the primary goal (achieving climate neutrality by 2050 and reducing greenhouse gas emissions by 55 % by 2030), the Plan sets additional objectives and areas of intervention, including decarbonization. Referring to the NECP, the Plan "envisions a further effort in energy-saving policies, particularly in the transport and building sectors, and an electrification of the primary energy system which, in the perspective of total decarbonization by 2050, will need to exceed 50 %".

However, the conclusion just reached remains unsatisfactory, as it would be more appropriate to provide a definition specific to the field of law. Otherwise, the transition would be described in the same manner as in other social systems (e.g., economics, history, politics).

Moreover, the definition and the paradigm that we intend to outline should be able to explain and include three further aspects of the notion of energy transition.

First of all, the energy transition is also a political goal. In this regard, it must be recalled the Italy's plan to "become the energy and gas hub of Europe" (this is the goal repeatedly indicated by Italian Prime Minister Giorgia Meloni in 2022).[26]

Secondly, the transition is aimed at achieving many other different and long-term legally binding goals. Of course, it has a clear environmental relevance, being connected to the 2030 UN Agenda for Sustainable Development and to the Paris Agreement. Nevertheless, the transition (in particular, the one towards renewable energies) is being carried out also in order to manage the consequences of war (suffice to think of Repower EU package)[27] and, in particular, to replace declining Russian gas supplies and boost energy security.[28] As a matter of fact, in the EU context, at the very beginning, the 1995 Green paper[29] stressed the objective of the security and therefore a goal clearly different from decarbonization and environmental protection. Again, in the case of Italy, suffice to mention the change in the

26 Governo Italiano, 'President Meloni's press statement with Prime Minister Abela' <www.governo.it/en/articolo/president-meloni-s-press-statement-prime-minister-ab ela/22914> accessed 31 August 2023.

27 European Commission, Communication 'REPowerEU: A Plan to Rapidly Reduce Dependence on Russian Fossil Fuels and Fast forward the Green Transition' COM (2022) 230 final 2022 < https://ec.europa.eu/commission/presscorner/detail/en/IP_22_3131> accessed 22 August 2024. The REPowerEU aims at ensuring the full implementation of the Fit for 55 package. The package sets the goal of achieving at least -55 % net greenhouse gas emissions by 2030 and climate neutrality by 2050 in line with the European Green Deal.

28 In Italy, decreto legge 31 maggio 2021 n 77 convertito in legge 29 luglio 2021 n 108 [2021] OJ 181/1 stated that the "prompt and punctual implementation of the interventions" included in the NRRP "assumes paramount value for the national interest".

29 European Commission, 'Green paper: For a European Union Energy Policy' COM (94) 659 final 1995 of 23 February 1995: "the energy policy objectives for the Community are appraised in terms of the challenges identified. These objectives are readily apparent involving, as they do, the management of policy to ensure the satisfaction of all least cost while meeting the requirements of security of supply and users' needs at the environmental protection". "The foreign policy of the Community needs to have security of energy supply as an objective".

name of the Ministry: the current Ministry of Environment and Energy Security was formerly called the Ministry of Ecological Transition. In conclusion, many interests are involved within the transition, often in contrast with each other.

The third aspect that must be taken into account in order to offer a convincing legal definition of transition is related to the results of studies on the National Recovery and Resilience Plan. Some scholars have considered it as an act of planning with both national legislative and EU law coverage[30] and, above all, related to a series of activities and initiatives carried out in view of a result. That means that a theoretical paradigm able to express this "continuity" and the relevance of the outcome (constituted by the progressive replacement of fossil fuels with renewable energies) is needed. The result is a legal constraint that arises from the law and that binds not only the Government and the entire Administration, but also the interpreters.[31] This is important considering the Recovery Plan (NRRP), where

30 Fabio Cintioli, 'Risultato amministrativo, discrezionalità e PNRR: una proposta per il Giudice' (2021) Giustizia-amministrativa 18 <www.giustizia-amministrativa.it> accessed 12 November 2021: "the administrative result seems to receive a coverage by EU law. The actions of the Plan are defined in an agreement, which in turn lays the foundations in EU Regulation 2021/241, and they respond to objectives that the Republic, as we said, intended to assume as its own in the context of this commitment, so that the way in which to achieve them – and the related risk of disregarding them – is not only a question of procedural autonomy of the Member State". About the nature of the NRRP, see also Luisa Torchia, 'Il sistema amministrativo italiano e il fondo di ripresa e resilienza' (2020) Astrid Online <www.astrid-online.it> accessed 10 November 2020; Antonella Sciortino, 'PNRR e riflessi sulla forma di governo italiana. Un ritorno all'indirizzo politico "normativo?' (2021) Federalismi <www.federalismi.it> accessed 28 July 2021; Nicola Lupo, 'Il Piano Nazionale di Ripresa e Resilienza (PNRR) e alcune prospettive di ricerca per i costituzionalisti' (2022) Federalismi <www.federalismi.it> accessed 12 January 2022; Marcello Clarich, 'Il PNRR tra diritto europeo e nazionale: un tentativo di inquadramento giuridico' (2021) 341 Astrid Online <www.astrid-online.it> accessed 21 July 2021.

31 Cintioli, 'Risultato amministrativo, discrezionalità e PNRR: una proposta per il Giudice' 13 (n 30): "The result is therefore consolidated in an act based on the law and which makes use of its strength and we can say, from this point of view, that that result commits not only the administration called to execute the Plan, but also the other legal operators, interpreters all, including Courts of course, which will have to be interested in that result also because – let us not forget – its achievement 'assumes rewarding value for the national interest'. Any delay or failure in meeting this objective could lead to the suspension of resource disbursement, followed by revocation and the obligation to repay".

the achievement of the outcomes[32] (including transition) is a condition to obtain European funds. As a consequence, this achievement must also have a legal relevance.

To sum up the reasoning developed up to now, the energy transition might be defined as a condition of the ecological transition; at the same time, it appears as a set of tools, that, from the legal point of view, are relevant only when considered as a whole and from the perspective of a functionalized continuity aimed towards a result. This outcome – although intertwined with multiple political and legal reasons – is the progressive replacement of fossil fuels with renewable energies.[33]

> I therefore put forward a preliminary definition: transition is a "form of a function".

The term "function" expresses the activity (considered as a whole) towards a goal[34]; the term "form" is used to explain that transition is the legal form through which the function can be seen being unfolded. It is the external and legally relevant manifestation of a function: the form visible to the observing scholar and, in particular, to the researcher of Administrative and Public law.

This function involves different measure and legal tools (from laws to administrative acts, actions and activities, aiming at reforms and achievement of goals) and different subjects (at several institutional levels): it even

32 Cintioli, 'Risultato amministrativo, discrezionalità e PNRR: una proposta per il Giudice' 14 (n 30) "The rationale is precisely that of the result. What else represent the Milestones and Targets through which the verification of compliance with the commitments undertaken by the Italian Government passes and will pass?"

33 In Italy, nuclear power plants were banned after a 2011 referendum in which Italians voted against a law supporting a national nuclear program. Previously, in November 1987, Italy had held its first national referendum concerning the repeal of the regulations allowing the siting of nuclear power plants by the CIPE (the Interministerial Committee for Economic Planning is an Italian governmental body), which Italian voters approved. Recently, on September 21, 2023, the first meeting of the National Platform for Sustainable Nuclear Energy (PNNS) took place. Its objective is to establish a clear pathway towards potentially resuming the use of nuclear energy in Italy. Ministero dell'Ambiente e della Sicurezza Energetica, 'Al MASE la prima riunione della Piattaforma Nazionale per un Nucleare Sostenibile' <https://www.mase.gov.it/comunicati/al-mase-la-prima-riunione-della-piattaforma-nazionale-un-nucleare-sostenibile> accessed 23 September 2023. See below (n 35).

34 This legal concept was suggested by Feliciano Benvenuti, *Funzione amministrativa, procedimento, processo* (1952) 2 Rivista trimestrale di diritto pubblico 118 in order to describe administrative procedure as a form of the administrative function.

involves the Courts and – to some extent – requires the cooperation of private actors.

2. The Second Part of the Definition: Setting the Problem, Considering Energy Transition, Structural Change in Society, Stop and Go, Multilevel Approach, Intergenerational Relations, Connections with Other Problems of Modernity

The objective of providing a comprehensive legal definition of the energy transition has not yet been completely achieved.

Other important aspects, in fact, must be considered.

Firstly, what we are witnessing nowadays is not simply a sectoral strategy: NRRP aims at a change in the structure of society, since it outlines a new model of social, institutional, and economic development. This aspect is well expressed by the final goal of 2030 UN Agenda for Sustainable Development: "transforming our world"[35]. Consequently, the ecological and energy transition is also a tool for a structural change in society as a whole.

Secondly, although the tendency to privilege renewable energy is very clear, we are witnessing a kind of "stop and go" in the transition. As already mentioned, regarding Italy, with strong measures towards simplification (including establishing the appointment of commissioners to speed up the permitting process),[36] a floating storage and regasification unit (FSRU) started operating in 2023 and another is expected to be operational by the end of 2025; from another point of view, consider the debate on reopening coal-fired power plants or the re-evaluation of nuclear power.[37] The problem of considering and explaining these aspects cannot be sidestepped, as

35 UN, 'Transforming our world: the 2030 Agenda for Sustainable Development', Resolution adopted by the General Assembly on 25 September 2015.

36 Art 5 decreto legge 17 maggio 2022 n 50 convertito nella legge 15 luglio 2022 n 91 Decreto Aiuti [2022] OJ 164/17.

37 See (n 33). About Taxonomy regulation (which is part of the EU action plan on financing sustainable growth), the European Parliament on 6 July 2022 did not object to the Commission's Taxonomy Delegated Act (approved on 2 February 2022) to include, under certain conditions, specific nuclear activities in the list of environmentally sustainable economic activities covered by the so-called EU Taxonomy (enabling investors to label and market investments in them as green). See Commission Delegated Regulation (EU) 2022/1214 of 9 March 2022 amending Delegated Regulation (EU) 2021/2139 as regards economic activities in certain energy sectors and Delegated Regulation (EU) 2021/2178 as regards specific public disclosures for those economic activities [2022] OJ L 188/1.

the definition of transition must also emphasize this ongoing recalibration and revision of objectives.

Thirdly, the transition can be carried out only by using a multilevel approach: international, EU, and local levels.

Fourthly, there is a sort of "unacknowledged yet influential presence" in the reasoning that is here carried on: the next generations. What is the place of this new actor in the legal paradigm that is being outlined? The relevance of this new subject/object of law is confirmed by a series of legal elements. Suffice to consider the phrase "Next Generation" used in the title (NGEU) of the aforementioned recovery and resilience project of Europe, which clearly places emphasis on these generations; all this is in line with art. 9, Italian Constitution (recently amended),[38] according to which the Italian Republic must take into consideration also the interest of future generations. The importance of considering these generations is implicit in the fact that many measures are characterized by a long-term perspective (and this aspect is a recurring trait in the transition). For instance, the horizon of the National Ecological Transition Plan is 2050, the year in which Italy must achieve the clear and ambitious goal of operating "at zero carbon emissions".

Finally, a further *aspect must be underlined:* the interconnection with other problems of modernity. The energy transition has to do with environmental crises, the issue of public finances, population growth, and geopolitical scenarios. All these crises must be considered and studied in the long term; they have an impact on future generations.

3. The Third Part of the Definition: The Transition as a Form of Fulfilment of (Common but Differentiated) Intergenerational Duties

The reconstructive and theoretical effort to be conducted, therefore, must consider that the transition: a) is part of a structural change in society, b) is a long-term process, c) is a path in which stop and go moments are possible despite the final goal remaining very clear, d) has to do with future generations and e) with other overarching themes and problems of modernity.

As mentioned above, the objective of these last paragraphs is to identify a conceptual scheme and a definition that are typical of the legal system, so

38 Legge costituzionale 11 febbraio 2022 n 1 Modifiche agli articoli 9 e 41 della Costituzione in materia di tutela dell'ambiente [2022] OJ 44/1.

as to avoid a mere description of the transition or to offer an "observation" analogous to that of another system (economics, history, politics).

To these ends, it is possible to add a further piece to the theoretical reconstruction, aimed at clarifying how, from the legal point of view, the transition is also the object of a specific set of rules, that of intergenerational relations and responsibility.[39]

This step is essential to provide a definition that is specifically legal, capable of indicating[40] to other social systems (economics, politics, science) whether the transition itself is legal or illegal, whether it is compatible with legal principles, as well as providing a set of legal rules that the institutions must comply with in carrying out a transition and that a judge can apply to review their choices.

It is therefore time to analyze the features of this branch of law, the object of which is intergenerational relations.

These regulations apply where an intergenerational responsibility arises and therefore, for instance, in the context of environmental crises, economic-financial crises, health issues, immigration, the issue of public finances, corruption, food crises, population growth, and of course, to energy crises.[41] The plausibility of the proposal outlined above (that is to say: progressive emergence of an autonomous sector of law, having as its object the responsibilities and intergenerational relations, that might guide the action of the various actors) is supported by different sets of considerations.

Firstly, all these crises (consider climate change, immigration and energy crisis) have similar characters: globality or, in any case, non-reducibility of problems to the scale of a single State (which also means globality of

39 The research programme – the expression is here used according to the meaning provided by Imre Lakatos, *The methodology of scientific research programmes* (CUP 1978) – which, applying a well-defined paradigm and described above, in the text, focuses on the emergence of this area of law is fed and marked by various scientific works: Fabrizio Fracchia/Pasquale Pantalone, *Decider(ci) per la morte: crisi, sostenibilità, energie rinnovabili e semplificazioni procedimentali. Interpretare il presente con il paradigma delle relazioni intergenerazionali nutrite di solidarietà*, (Editoriale Scientifica 2022); Pasquale Pantalone, *La crisi pandemica dal punto di vista dei doveri. Diagnosi, prognosi e terapia dei problemi intergenerazionali secondo il diritto amministrativo* (Editoriale Scientifica 2023).

40 In line with a Luhmannian approach, the purpose of the theory is to allow the legal system to fulfill its function of structuring expectations: Niklas Luhmann, 'Law as a Social System' in Fatima Kastner/Richard Nobles/David Schiff/Rosamund Ziegert (eds), *Oxford Socio-Legal Studies* (Oxford University Press 2004) 498.

41 Fracchia/Pantalone, *Decider(ci) per la morte: crisi, sostenibilità, energie rinnovabili e semplificazioni procedimentali* 88 (n 39).

causes and local dimension of effects and vice versa), widespread nature of the damage incurred, plurality of causes, spatial and temporal disconnection between cause and effect, information asymmetries, intertwining with ethics, relevance of technological innovation, difficulty in identifying the most appropriate decision-making centres, the need to organize differentiated responses, impact on justice and equity, and significant impact on public debt, public budgets and public administrations. Due to the presence of common characteristics, we need a common theoretical "filter" from a scientific point of view.

Secondly, the tendency to broaden the concept of sustainable development (the cardinal principle mentioned above) is undeniable. Just think of the 2030 UN Agenda for Sustainable Development and its 17 goals: they do not only concern the environment but, showing a very clear expansive attitude, cover many different areas. In many Constitutions (as for Italy: art. 81) sustainability has been enlarged as far as including the public debt and budget: another form of intergenerational responsibility.[42] The broadening of the scope of this principle justifies the attempt to unify the perspective of the investigation, so as to encompass the full range of legal relationships involved in the principle.

Thirdly: intergenerational problems often arise simultaneously, and are linked (for example, the intertwining of climate change and energy transition is evident) or related to each other in terms of cause and effect: the war crisis leads to obvious environmental and energy consequences; attempts to overcome the energy crisis produce significant environmental tensions or food crises, taking away space from agriculture;[43] bad environmental habits have effects not only on health, but also on pollution (think of

42 "The State shall ensure the balance between revenue and expenditure in its budget, taking into account the adverse and favorable phases of the economic cycle". It is also worth underlining the fact that Constitutional Court 18 [2019] OJ Special Series 8 1, reviewing the constitutional legitimacy of a regulation concerning the reformulation or remodulation of the long-term financial rebalancing plans of local authorities thus decided: "the very long time delay ends up conflicting even with elementary principles of intergenerational equity, given that both dating back and important deficits and the repayments of authorized loans will be burdened by future administered entities". And again: "intergenerational equity also entails the need not to burden disproportionately the growth opportunities of future generations, guaranteeing them sufficient resources for a balanced development".

43 The comparison between Covid pandemic and Black Death of Fourteen century in Europe is impressive: both periods are characterized by a) pandemic, b) climate change, b) population growth, c) financial crisis, d) moral crisis; e) war: see Pasquale Pantalone, *La crisi pandemica* (n 39).

the consumption of out-of-season or non-zero kilometer products); energy independence could prevent certain military conflicts or allow for stronger diplomatic action; in all cases, these problems affect justice, equity, public finance and so on.

Fourthly, intergenerational problems or their effects often appear unpredictable (economic crisis, financial crisis, health crisis, energy crisis). In reality, we often realize ex post that more responsible choices in the past could have prefigured them.

Lastly, their management takes place (or so one should hope) also at the supranational level (in particular at the European level: a good and paradigmatic example is by the common debt assumed at the EU level in relation to the Next Generation EU package).

The cornerstone of this unitarian branch of law is the principle of sustainable development, which expresses a canon of intergenerational responsibility.

In all the cases mentioned above, in fact, the decisions to be taken are aimed at safeguarding the interests of future generations, enabled by virtue of the fulfillment of duties on the part of current generations, who must set aside the claim of untouchable and impregnable rights.

In the Italian context, the paradigm of intergenerational responsibilities can now easily be based on Article 9 of the Italian Constitution (amended in 2022) which obliges the Republic to consider "also" the interests of future generations.

The transition (form of a function), therefore, is also and above all a form of fulfilment of (common but differentiated: see *infra*) intergenerational duties, set by a specific set of rules to which all the actors, behaviour and initiatives mentioned in section D 1, considered together, are subject. Even the legislature, when faced with intergenerational issues, and also in the case of transitions, should therefore set regulations in line with the above framework.

This paradigm is helpful towards tackling the problems of modernity: its pillars are environmental principles, which play a central role to guide the above-mentioned activities, not to mention that they have the undoubted advantage of penetrating every legal system. Initially, they seem related only to the environment; nevertheless, at a deeper glance, they are principles of the whole branch of law discussed here, which are established by art. 191, TFEU (in particular, "the polluter pays", the principle of "common but differentiated responsibility", the principles of prevention and precaution). The reason why the environment (with its principles) remains the driving factor in the construction of a set of rules applicable to the remaining intergenerational issues is that it is a stark reminder of one of the more tragic tendencies of modernity: to take strategic decisions that can impact future generations. The "strength" of the environmental issue, so worrying in modernity, forges the characteristics of the law of intergenerational choices. In conclusion, environmental law is the tip of a much larger, richer, and more complex iceberg, the paradigmatic example of the bundle of intergenerational problems: for this reason, the law has begun to regulate precisely this area. A classic example of a conflict (and a classic difficulty of modernity) that can be solved by applying the rules and the principles mentioned here is the one involving renewable energy and the landscape. The conflict is in particular generated by the temporal disconnection between aggressor and victim: the production of renewable energy can affect parts of the landscape and some people who inhabit it *hic et nunc* (the current "victims" of an "aggressive" anthropic activity); however, when environmental problems are measured in the long-term perspective, looking at humanity as a whole (not therefore simply focusing on the people who currently appear to be the victims), it is hard to deny that that renewable energy production benefits the environment that future generations will be able to inherit. It is up to politics to make a responsible decision also on behalf of future generations; the legal paradigm above outlined can provide the juridical basis (although very limited and restricted) for judicial or constitutional review in the light of the intergenerational depth.

As is usual happened in scientific fields, the function of the theoretical models suggested by scholars is twofold: solving problems and providing operational consequences deriving from general legal principles of this new sector of law (and this aspect has just been dealt with by referring to a specific problem), and describing the "real world" and the characteristics of the object of the research.

From the second point of view, the theory gives due emphasis to the next generations, given that they are firmly at the centre of this branch of law. Moreover, it is in line with the idea of a structural change in society (this transformation is exactly the final outcome when dealing with intergenerational problems) and with the fact that, during the period of energy crisis, the dimensions of solidarity and duty stand out (we are all called to contribute with individual sacrifices – including fiscal sacrifices –

to the containment of consumption and the achievement of objectives).[44] It also explains the multi-level approach, as each level is involved according to its responsibility. Stop and go moments are also easy to understand: the policies that impact future generations are long journeys; responsibility and intergenerational solidarity, by their nature, must be adapted and recalibrated, and suffer moments of crisis and arrest, while maintaining their final goal.

E. Concluding Remarks

In 2022, Italy used many different types of energy sources: 37,6 % of natural gas, 35.7 % of oil and petroleum products, 18.5 % of renewables and bioliquids, 5 % of solid fuels, 2.5 % of electricity. As far as renewables are concerned, over the last few years they have found widespread use in all sectors (electrical, thermal, transport).

Many policy initiatives – taken inter alia to reduce dependence on Russian gas and diversify supply – have been developed in the field of energy, paving the way for a continuous series of legislative measures, the most important of which is the NRRP.

Moreover, since a complex problem – such as energy generation and supply – has to be tackled with a complex approach, Italy has made use of

44 The dimension of solidarity already emerged from Regulation (EU) 2017/1938 of 25 October 2017 of the European Parliament and of the Council concerning measures to safeguard the security of gas supply and repealing Regulation (EU) 994/2010 [2017] OJ L 280/1. In the sixth whereas clause it is said that "energy security constitutes one of the objectives of the Energy Union Strategy, as set out in the Commission Communication of 25 February 2015 on a Framework Strategy for a Resilient Energy Union with a Forward-Looking Climate Change Policy, which also emphasized the "energy efficiency first" principle and the need to fully implement existing Union energy legal acts. The communication highlighted the fact that the Energy Union rests on solidarity, enshrined in Article 194 of the Treaty on the Functioning of the European Union (TFEU), and trust, which are necessary features of energy security. This Regulation is intended to boost solidarity and trust between the Member States and put in place the measures needed to achieve those aims. When assessing the preventive action plans and the emergency plans established by the Member States, the Commission should also be able to draw the attention of the Member States to the objectives of the Energy Union"; according to the tenth whereas clause, "in a spirit of solidarity, regional cooperation, involving both public authorities and natural gas undertakings, should be the guiding principle of this Regulation, to mitigate the identified risks and optimize the benefits of coordinated measures and to implement the most cost-effective measures for Union consumers".

a large number of different measures and models, ranging from command and control to market-based tools.

In order to explain the combination and legal relevance of these strategies, measures and legal instruments the theoretical concept of energy transition has been proposed.

The effort to provide a legally useful definition of transition and to offer an "observation" different from those suggested by the different branches of social science (economics, history, politics) leads to the notion of "form of function" and of "form of fulfilment of intergenerational duties (common but differentiated)", subject to a specific and unitary branch of law, whose cornerstone is the principle of sustainable development, which expresses a canon of intergenerational responsibility.

Bibliography

Benvenuti F, 'Funzione amministrativa, procedimento, processo' [1952] 2 Rivista trimestrale di diritto pubblico 118

Cintioli F, 'Risultato amministrativo, discrezionalità e PNRR: una proposta per il Giudice' (2021) Giustizia-amministrativa 18 <www.giustizia-amministrativa.it> accessed 12 November 2021

Clarich M, 'Il PNRR tra diritto europeo e nazionale: un tentativo di inquadramento giuridico' [2021] 341 Astrid Online <www.astrid-online.it> accessed 21 July 2021

De Leonardis F, *La transizione ecologica come modello di sviluppo di sistema: spunti sul ruolo delle amministrazioni* (2021) Diritto amministrativo 779

European Commission, Communication 'REPowerEU: A Plan to Rapidly Reduce Dependence on Russian Fossil Fuels and Fast forward the Green Transition' COM (2022) 230 final 2022 <https://ec.europa.eu/commission/presscorner/detail/en/IP_22_3131> accessed 22 August 2024

European Commission, 'Green paper: For a European Union Energy Policy' COM (94) 659 final 1995 of 23 February 1995

Favaro T, *Regolare la "transizione energetica". Stato, mercato, innovazione* (Cedam 2020)

Fracchia F, *Transizioni: il punto di vista del diritto amministrativo* (Editoriale Scientifica 2024)

Fracchia F/Pantalone P, *Decider(ci) per la morte: crisi, sostenibilità, energie rinnovabili e semplificazioni procedimentali. Interpretare il presente con il paradigma delle relazioni intergenerazionali nutrite di solidarietà*, (Editoriale Scientifica 2022)

Governo Italiano, 'Delibera 8 marzo 2022 del Comitato interministeriale per la transizione ecologica Approvazione del Piano per la transizione ecologica ai sensi dell'art 57-bis, comma e) e seguenti del decreto legislativo 3 aprile 2006 n 152 [2022] OJ 138/47' <https://www.mase.gov.it/sites/default/files/archivio/allegati/PTE/PTE-definitivo.pdf> accessed 22.08.2024

Governo Italiano, 'Art. 8 decreto legislativo 8 novembre 2021 n 199 [2021] OJ 285/4 and decreto MASE 7 dicembre 2023 n 414' <www.mase.gov.it> accessed 30 June 2024

Governo Italiano, 'President Meloni's press statement with Prime Minister Abela' <www.governo.it/en/articolo/president-meloni-s-press-statement-prime-minister-abela/22914> accessed 31 August 2023

Istituto Superiore per la Protezione e la Ricerca Ambientale, 'Efficiency and decarbonization indicators in Italy and in the biggest European Countries. Edition 2023' <https://www.isprambiente.gov.it/files2023/pubblicazioni/rapporti/r386-2023.pdf> accessed 31 August 2023

Lakatos I, *The methodology of scientific research programmes* (CUP 1978)

Luhmann N, 'Law as a Social System' in **Kastner F/Nobles R/ Schiff D/Ziegert R**(eds), Oxford Socio-Legal Studies (Oxford University Press 2004) 498

Lupo N, 'Il Piano Nazionale di Ripresa e Resilienza (PNRR) e alcune prospettive di ricerca per i costituzionalisti' (2022) Federalismi <www.federalismi.it> accessed 12 January 2022

Ministero dell'Ambiente e della Sicurezza Energetica, 'Al MASE la prima riunione della Piattaforma Nazionale per un Nucleare Sostenibile' <https://www.mase.gov.it/comunicati/al-mase-la-primariunione-della-piattaforma-nazionale-un-nucleare-sostenibile> accessed 23 September 2023

Ministero dell'Ambiente e della Sicurezza Energetica, 'La situazione energetica nazionale nel 2022' 10 and Appendice A <https://www.mase.gov.it/sites/default/files/Archivio_Energia/LA%20RELAZIONE%20SULLA%20SITUAZIONE%20ENERGETICA%20NAZIONALE%20NEL%202022_MASE%20Luglio%202023.pdf> accessed 31 August 2023

Ministero dell'Ambiente e della Sicurezza Energetica, 'Piano Nazionale Integrato per l'Energia e il Clima' <https://www.mimit.gov.it/images/stories/documenti/PNIEC_finale_17012020.pdf> accessed 31 August 2023.

Ministero della Transizione Ecologica, 'Piano nazionale di contenimento dei consumi di gas naturale' <https://www.mase.gov.it/sites/default/files/archivio/comunicati/Piano%20contenimento%20consumi%20gas_MITE_6set2022.pdf> accessed 31 August 2023

Osservatorio ENEA, 'Energia: da ENEA un Osservatorio per promuovere le Comunità Energetiche Rinnovabili' <https://www.media.enea.it/comunicati-e-news/archivio-anni/anno-2023/energia-da-enea-un-osservatorio-per-promuovere-le-comunita-energetiche-rinnovabili.html> accessed 31 August 2023

Pantalone P, *La crisi pandemica dal punto di vista dei doveri. Diagnosi, prognosi e terapia dei problemi intergenerazionali secondo il diritto amministrativo* (Editoriale Scientifica 2023)

Petrachi M, *La tutela dell'ambiente nel prisma della transizione ecologica* (Giappichelli 2023)

Sciortino A, 'PNRR e riflessi sulla forma di governo italiana. Un ritorno all'indirizzo politico "normativo?' (2021) Federalismi <www.federalismi.it> accessed 28 July 2021

Severini G, 'La "transizione" come ordinamento giuridico' (2022) Giustizia insieme <www.giustiziainsieme.it> accessed 24 November 2022

Torchia L, 'Il sistema amministrativo italiano e il fondo di ripresa e resilienza' (2020) Astrid Online <www.astrid-online.it> accessed 10 November 2020

UN, 'Transforming our world: the 2030 Agenda for Sustainable Development', Resolution adopted by the General Assembly on 25 September 2015

General Perspectives on the Law of Energy Transition in the United Kingdom

Chitzi C. Ogbumgbada and Kate McKenzie

A. Introductory Comments

The energy transition in the UK is commonly conceived as a transition to net zero.[1] This conception is primarily based on the 2008 Climate Change Act, a significant piece of legislation enacted by the British Parliament that grounds climate action in the UK.[2] Transitioning to net zero mainly involves reducing greenhouse gas emissions in the atmosphere to an insignificant volume through measures like deploying renewable energy, reducing energy consumption across society, implementing energy efficiency measures, and utilising carbon sinks. The aim is to prevent the worst effects of climate change from manifesting in this century. Nevertheless, there are issues associated with the transition to net zero, even though the transition is urgent and relevant.[3] In the UK, there is a question about how the energy transition can accommodate energy security, a concept that is interpreted by policymakers in the country as mainly ensuring that British households and businesses obtain energy at affordable prices, eliminating impediments against energy supply to the country, protecting means of livelihood dependent on fossil fuels, and lessening the impact of climate policies on the vulnerable.[4] Amidst these questions is the continuing role of domestic and international law and policy in helping to deliver net zero in a timely and urgent manner.

Following this brief introduction, this chapter begins by examining the UK's decarbonisation strategy as enunciated in its Nationally Determined Contribution (NDC) under international law and further considers its relevance for domestic energy law. It will discuss the national energy mix,

1 HM Government, *Net Zero Strategy: Build Back Greener* (HH Associates Ltd 2021).

2 Thomas L. Muinzer, *Climate and Energy Governance for the UK Low Carbon Transition: The Climate Change Act 2008* (Palgrave Macmillan 2019) 2.

3 See Daniel Yergin, *The New Map: Energy, Climate, and the Clash of Nations* (Penguin Books 2021).

4 HM Government, *Powering up Britain: Energy Security Plan* (HH Global 2023).

highlighting and examining the energy sources that provide electricity in the UK and how these align with the decarbonisation strategy. The chapter will further discuss the trade-offs inherent in deploying climate-compliant policies and facilitating energy security. It will then conclude with remarks about possible future trends in the energy transition in the UK.

B. Decarbonisation Strategy and Implication for Energy Law

In line with Article 4 of the Paris Agreement, the UK communicated its NDC to the United Nations Framework Convention on Climate Change (UNFCCC) in December 2020. It undertook to reduce economy-wide greenhouse gas emissions by at least 68 % by 2030, compared to 1990 levels.[5] Following COP26, which the UK hosted in Glasgow, the UK subsequently communicated an updated NDC that took account of the urgency of strengthening climate change response measures up to 2030.[6] Each NDC is based on five-year carbon budget cycles that were first introduced in the Climate Change Act 2008,[7] making the UK the first major economy to create legally binding targets to reduce greenhouse gas emissions to net zero by 2050.[8] The 2008 Act originally committed the UK to reducing its emissions by 80 % over 1990 levels by mid-century. The UK updated this target in 2019, increasing its ambition to reduce all GHG emissions by 100 % (achieving net zero) by 2050.

The UK's NDC and its Net Zero Strategy discuss emissions on a UK-wide ('whole of UK') basis, but a complicating factor for the UK is that it is made up of several devolved governments (Scotland, Northern Ireland, and Wales), as well as multiple Crown Dependencies and Overseas Territories. Each of the devolved governments has its own statutory GHG emissions reduction targets and decarbonisation strategies, which are outlined in the UK's NDC.[9] Complicating matters further, under the UK's Climate Change Act, the scope of emissions covered is limited to those emitted

5 See HM Government, *United Kingdom of Great Britain and Northern Ireland's Nationally Determined Contribution* (HH Associates Ltd 2022) 1.

6 ibid.

7 HM Government, Expert Participation, 'Climate Change Act 2008' <https://www.legislation.gov.uk/ukpga/2008/27/contents> accessed 21 February 2024.

8 HM Government, *Net Zero Strategy: Build Back Greener* (n 1) 39.

9 HM Government, *United Kingdom of Great Britain and Northern Ireland's Nationally Determined Contribution* (n 5) s 3(c).

in the UK and UK coastal waters. Therefore, the 'whole of UK' approach does not include emissions from UK Crown Dependencies and Overseas Territories in UK carbon budgets.[10] Broadly, the UK's 2020 (updated 2022) NDC commits the UK to a 68 % reduction of greenhouse gas emissions over 1990 levels, clarification about how the UK's NDC aligns with the Paris Agreement's temperature goal, as well as information on levelling up, public engagement, just transition, and green skills.[11]

The UK's *Net Zero Strategy: Build Back Greener*[12] outlines the policies and proposals needed to decarbonise the UK economy across all sectors to meet net zero by 2050, and it was submitted to the UNFCCC as the UK's second Long-Term Low GHG Emissions Development Strategy under the Paris Agreement.[13] The Net Zero Strategy indicates an economy-wide approach to greenhouse gas emissions reductions and outlines the reductions needed in each sector between 2020 and 2037.[14] While the Net Zero Strategy is quite ambitious, it is highly dependent on the development, availability, and deployment of key technologies such as low-carbon electricity generation and storage technologies, hydrogen production, carbon capture usage and storage (CCUS), and biomass carbon removal.[15]

1. Scope of the UK's NDC

The overall scope and coverage of the UK's NDC include an overall net reduction in greenhouse gas emissions across all sectors of the economy, excepting international aviation and shipping emissions.[16] The territorial scope of the UK's NDC is limited to the emissions and removals from England, Scotland, Wales and Northern Ireland, as well as those Crown Dependencies and Overseas Territories to which the UK's ratification of the Paris Agreement has been extended.[17] While the UK's NDC includes a

---

10 ibid 6.

11 ibid 3.

12 HM Government, *Net Zero Strategy: Build Back Greener* (n 1).

13 UNFCCC 'Long-Term Strategies Portal' <https://unfccc.int/process/the-paris-agreement/long-term-strategies> accessed 14 March 2024.

14 HM Government, *Net Zero Strategy: Build Back Greener* (n 1) 18.

15 ibid 69.

16 HM Government, *United Kingdom of Great Britain and Northern Ireland's Nationally Determined Contribution* (n 5) s 3(c).

17 ibid.

'whole of UK' economy-wide greenhouse gas emissions reduction strategy, most aspects of climate change and decarbonisation are matters for the various devolved governments, each of which has a different approach to decarbonisation and net zero.[18] The overall UK approach is outlined in the Net Zero Strategy, which is based on the Climate Change Act 2008 (2050 Target Amendment) Order 2019[19] and includes the UK's legally binding target of 100 % emissions reduction by 2050.[20]

The overall Net Zero Strategy, first published in October of 2021, builds on wider UK government policies, including the ten-point plan for a green industrial revolution[21] and several sector-specific policies including the British Energy Security Strategy (applies to England, Wales, and Scotland),[22] the Transport Decarbonisation Plan (mostly applies to the whole of the UK),[23] the Industrial Decarbonisation Strategy[24] to reduce industrial emissions across the UK, the Hydrogen Strategy (applies to the UK), and the Heat and Buildings Strategy[25] to decarbonise homes, commercial, industrial, and public sector buildings (some policies are specific to England only).

---

18 HM Government and the Devolved Administrations of Scotland, Wales, and Northern Ireland, Collaboration 'Net Zero Government Initiative – UK Roadmap to Net Zero' 4.

19 HM Government, 'The Climate Change Act 2008 (2050 Target Amendment) Order 2019' <https://www.legislation.gov.uk/uksi/2019/1056/contents/made> accessed 14 March 2024.

20 The Scottish Government published its updated climate change plan in April 2023, the Welsh government published its updated net zero plan and target in April 2022, and Northern Ireland published its Path to Net Zero Energy in December 2021.

21 HM Government, 'The Ten Point Plan for a Green Industrial Revolution' (*GOV.UK*, 18 November 2020) <https://www.gov.uk/government/publications/the-ten-point-plan-for-a-green-industrial-revolution> accessed 14 March 2024.

22 HM Government, 'British Energy Security Strategy – Secure, Clean and Affordable British Energy for the Long Term' <https://www.gov.uk/government/publications/british-energy-security-strategy> accessed 26 February 2024.

23 HM Government, 'Transport Decarbonisation Plan' (*GOV.UK*, 12 January 2023) <https://www.gov.uk/government/publications/transport-decarbonisation-plan> accessed 14 March 2024.

24 HM Government, 'Industrial Decarbonisation Strategy' (*GOV.UK*, 7 April 2021) <https://www.gov.uk/government/publications/industrial-decarbonisation-strategy> accessed 14 March 2024.

25 HM Government, 'Heat and Buildings Strategy' (*GOV.UK*, 1 March 2023) <https://www.gov.uk/government/publications/heat-and-buildings-strategy> accessed 14 March 2024.

The decarbonisation pathways set out in the UK's NDC translate to important changes and updates to energy law. The policies and proposals outlined in the UK's Net Zero Strategy: Build Back Greener cover the UK government's approach to each sector, including power, fuel supply and hydrogen, industry, heat and buildings, transport, natural resources, water and fluorinated gases, greenhouse gas removals, and public sector decarbonisation. The impact of the UK's NDC on energy law is best demonstrated by considering the amendments to a broad set of other regulations and bills, which are captured in the Energy Act (2023), set out below.

2. The Energy Act (2023)

First and foremost, the Energy Act (October 2023) is aimed at delivering cleaner energy that is more affordable and leads to long-term energy security.[26] Not surprisingly, the energy system in the UK is governed by a range of legislation, and the Energy Act (2023) amends several of these, including the Nuclear Installations Act 1965, the Enterprise Act 2002, the Energy Act 2004, the Energy Act 2008, the Gas Act 1986, the Rights of Entry (Gas and Electricity Boards) Act 1945, the Electricity Act 1989, the Petroleum Act 1998, the Utilities Act 2000, the Energy Act 2013, the Energy Act 2016, and the Heat Networks (Scotland) Act 2021, as well as the Climate Change Act 2008, which the Act amends to broaden the scope of GHG removals and the type of removal methods beyond land use.[27]

While the Energy Act (2023) is UK-wide legislation, provisions have effect primarily in England, Scotland, and Wales (i.e. Great Britain), with some provisions extending also to Northern Ireland. However, according to convention Westminster, the seat of the UK government, will not typically legislate on matters that fall within the competence of the devolved governments and instead will seek legislative consent of the developed legislatures under the Sewel Convention.[28]

26 HM Government, 'Energy Act 2023' <https://www.legislation.gov.uk/ukpga/2023/52/enacted> accessed 14 March 2024.

27 Department for Energy Security and Net Zero, 'Energy Bill [HL] Explanatory Notes' 28 <https://publications.parliament.uk/pa/bills/cbill/58-03/0295/en/220295en.pdf> accessed 14 March 2024.

28 HM Parliament, 'Sewel Convention' <https://www.parliament.uk/site-information/glossary/sewel-convention/> accessed 14 March 2024. To illustrate this complexity, the Scottish Government retains devolved power for onshore oil and gas licensing

Parts 1 and 2 of the Energy Act cover carbon capture, transport, and storage, as well as hydrogen production. This includes a government commitment to develop four new Carbon Capture Usage and Storage (CCUS) clusters by 2030. The UK government sees this as an area of economic regulation because operators of carbon-related pipeline transport and storage networks (often regional monopolies responsible for a broad range of network users, emitters and providers) will be licensed by an economic regulator granting the right to charge customers for delivery and operation of their network.[29] The Office of Gas and Electricity Markets (Ofgem) is given duties and functions under Part 1 of the Act to act as the economic regulator of CO_2 transport and storage, along with an economic licensing framework for such activities.[30] Authority for regulating the secure geological storage of CO_2 will remain with the Oil and Gas Authority (OGA)[31] and the relevant ministers of the devolved nations, as set out in the Energy Act 2008.[32] The UK government recognises the challenges of decarbonising industrial and commercial activities without viable alternatives and has committed to providing financial assistance to support such industries.[33]

Part 2 of the Energy Act establishes new powers to provide financial assistance, to establish the necessary frameworks, and the duties and responsibilities needed to manage contracts with CCUS entities and low carbon hydrogen producers. Based on consultations undertaken in 2021 under the auspices of the British Energy Security Strategy,[34] Part 2 of the Energy Act includes powers to appoint a future administrative body that would oversee a competitive process, along with powers to raise levies to fund and support a range of pathways that will facilitate hydrogen usage in a range of sectors.[35]

---

but does not have the power to tax oil and gas, nuclear energy regulation is reserved for the UK Government, but nuclear waste management remains devolved. Paul Cairney et al., 'How to Conceptualise Energy Law and Policy for an Interdisciplinary Audience: The Case of Post-Brexit UK' (2019) 129 Energy Policy 459, 462.

29 Department for Energy Security and Net Zero (n 27) 11 f.

30 HM Government, 'Energy Act 2023' (n 26) pt 1.

31 The OGA is now known as the North Sea Transition Authority (NSTA), which regulates the UK petroleum industry. See NSTA, 'About' <About Us – The North Sea Transition Authority (nstauthority.co.uk)> accessed 14 March 2023.

32 Department for Energy Security and Net Zero (n 27) 12.

33 ibid 11.

34 HM Government, 'British Energy Security Strategy – Secure, Clean and Affordable British Energy for the Long Term' (n 22).

35 HM Government, 'Energy Act 2023' (n 26) pt 2.

The Energy Act therefore also addresses the necessary new technologies, including low-carbon heat schemes, hydrogen trials, and fusion energy. Part 3 of the Energy Act takes into account the 2021 Heat and Buildings Strategy,[36] the Hydrogen Strategy[37], and the Net Zero Strategy[38] in order to transition away from fossil fuel-based energy sources. The Energy Act, in Part 3, gives new powers to the Department for Energy Security and Net Zero's Secretary of State to create a scheme to increase the sale and installation of low-carbon heating technologies, such as heat pumps, which is also intended to grow the supply chain for such technologies via strengthened investment incentives.[39]

In order to determine the viability of large-scale hydrogen use in heat provision, the Energy Act includes measures that will allow a hydrogen trial to be safely and effectively operated in order to enable the UK Government to make strategic decisions around hydrogen use in decarbonising heat in buildings in 2026.[40] Part 3 also amends the Nuclear Installations Act 1965 to explicitly exclude fusion energy facilities, meaning these facilities will not require a nuclear site licence, enabling fusion energy facility regulation in a more appropriate and hazard-proportional manner.[41] It further extends the powers of the Secretary of State for Transport under the Energy Act 2004 to include a range of fuels that could support particularly the aviation industry in decarbonisation.[42]

Based on the UK Government's commitments in its Energy White Paper 2020[43] and the Future Systems Operator consultation response 2022,[44] Part 4 of the Energy Act establishes a public sector body, which will operate independently from the government and will take on many functions

36 HM Government, 'Heat and Buildings Strategy' (n 25).

37 HM Government, 'UK Hydrogen Strategy' (*GOV.UK*, 14 December 2023) <https://www.gov.uk/government/publications/uk-hydrogen-strategy> accessed 14 March 2024.

38 HM Government, *Net Zero Strategy: Build Back Greener* (n 1).

39 HM Government, 'Energy Act 2023' (n 26) paras 15–17.

40 Department for Energy Security and Net Zero (n 27) 13.

41 HM Government, 'Energy Act 2023' (n 26) para 21.

42 ibid 22.

43 HM Government, 'Energy White Paper: Powering Our Net Zero Future' (*GOV.UK*, 18 December 2020) <https://www.gov.uk/government/publications/energy-white-paper-powering-our-net-zero-future> accessed 14 March 2024.

44 HM Government, 'Proposals for a Future System Operator Role' (*GOV.UK*, 20 July 2021) <https://www.gov.uk/government/consultations/proposals-for-a-future-system-operator-role> accessed 14 March 2024.

currently carried out by operators licensed and owned by National Grid plc. This Independent System Operator and Planner (ISOP) is also given powers, duties and functions related to the development of an energy transition system for electricity and gas, as well as a range of additional net zero-related roles.[45] The findings of the Government's Energy White Paper 2020 further highlighted that the current system of energy code governance adversely impacts the transition away from fossil fuels because of insufficient incentives, conflicting interests, and an inability to adequately influence changes in the code. The Act, in Part 5, therefore establishes a new governance framework by giving Ofgem's decision-making board greater powers to influence necessary changes in gas and electricity industry codes.[46]

Part 6 of the Energy Act relates to market reform and consumer protection, including competitive tendering for electricity projects, electricity storage, energy company obligations, and smart meters. The UK Government's commitment to fully decarbonising the electricity system by 2035, while also meeting an expected significant increase in demand, requires substantial changes to the current system of privately owned electricity networks across Great Britain[47] which stifles innovation and creates information gaps. The Energy Act therefore extends the competitive process under the Electricity Act 1989 to allow for new investment opportunities, improved investment efficiency, and innovative flexible solutions that will increase network efficiency and reduce consumer costs.[48] The energy network in Great Britain is made up of network enterprises that are regional monopolies, meaning that price control is the primary method through which Ofgem, as the economic regulator, can control the cost of energy which is passed on to consumers. The Energy Act, in Part 6, further empowers the Competition and Markets Authority (CMA) to have greater oversight over mergers between energy network enterprises in order to ensure consumer protection within Great Britain.[49]

In a continued effort to protect consumers and decarbonise the electricity grid, the UK Government plans to double the current Multi-purpose

45 HM Government, 'Energy Act 2023' (n 26) pt 4.

46 Department for Energy Security and Net Zero (n 27) 14–15; HM Government, 'Energy Act 2023' (n 26) paras 27–29.

47 This Part of the Energy Act 2023 applies only to Great Britain (England, Scotland and Wales), and does not have an impact in Northern Ireland.

48 HM Government, 'Energy Act 2023' (n 26) paras 32–33.

49 ibid 6.

Interconnector (MPI) capacity of 7.4 gigawatts by working closely with developers, regulators, and European partners, and seeks to achieve 50 gigawatts of offshore wind generation by 2030.[50] Supporting interconnection is a core part of the UK Government's energy strategy and is intended to enhance system flexibility, reduce consumer price, and meet increased electricity demand while decarbonising the sector in a low cost manner.[51] Interconnectors, along with electricity storage technologies and demand side responsiveness, are expected to help build needed flexibility into an energy system that includes high volumes of low carbon heat and power. Since the current electricity regulatory framework is not equipped to deal with some of the new technologies, such as electricity storage, Part 6 of the Energy Act 2023 is also intended to provide increased clarity by formalising electricity storage as a distinct subset of electricity generation.[52] The Act also gives energy suppliers more flexibility in meeting their obligations under the Energy Company Obligation (ECO) scheme, including protections that meet the Government's commitment to creating a fair and competitive market that reduces market distortion and undue financial constraints on smaller suppliers.[53]

Part 7 of the Energy Act 2023 covers heat networks, which are crucial to the UK's decarbonisation plans and are the most cost-effective way to decarbonise heating.[54] Ofgem, as regulator, is given extended powers that cover heat networks to ensure fair pricing and reliable heating supply to consumers while increasing the proportion of UK heat and hot water provided to consumers through heat networks from 2 % to 18 % of the UK supply by 2050.[55] The Heat and Buildings Strategy,[56] along with the Net Zero Strategy[57] set out the Government's commitment to transform the heat network across the UK. The Energy Act 2023 enables this transformation via heat network zoning changes that will allow for increased

50 Department for Energy Security and Net Zero (n 27) 16–17.

51 HM Government, 'Energy White Paper: Powering Our Net Zero Future' (n 43).

52 HM Government, 'Energy Act 2023' (n 26) pt 6.

53 ibid; HM Government, 'Transitioning to a Net Zero Energy System: Smart Systems and Flexibility Plan 2021' (*GOV.UK*) <https://www.gov.uk/government/publications/transitioning-to-a-net-zero-energy-system-smart-systems-and-flexibility-plan-2021> accessed 14 March 2024.

54 Department for Energy Security and Net Zero (n 27) para 53.

55 HM Government, 'Energy Act 2023' (n 26) pt 7.

56 HM Government, 'Heat and Buildings Strategy' (n 25).

57 HM Government, *Net Zero Strategy: Build Back Greener* (n 1).

collaboration between local governments, industry, and local stakeholders to find lowest cost solutions for decarbonising the heating sector. The combined measures, including a government investment of £338 million in the Heat Network Transformation Programme, are expected to save 13.1 million tonnes of CO_2 emissions across the UK's carbon budgets covering 2023 to 2037.[58]

Further in line with the Government's commitments in the Smart Systems and Flexibility Plan (2021)[59] and the Energy White Paper 2020,[60] provisions in the Energy Act governing smart appliances and load control envision a reduction in costs of up to £10 billion a year by 2050.[61] Part 8 of the Act includes provisions that set regulatory requirement for energy smart appliances and smart functionality for EV charging points and demand side response activities.[62] The Act also includes new powers for the Secretary of State to make changes to the current Energy Performance of Buildings (EPR) regime as well as the Energy Savings Opportunity Scheme (ESOP). Parts 9 and 10 of the Act provide replacement powers to the Secretary of State which were previously derived from EU law, enabling the Government to amend, revoke or replace existing powers under the EPR and ESOP, respectively.[63]

Crude oil-based fuels currently provide heating to 1.5 million homes in the UK and provide over 90 % of the energy used in transport (i.e. the movement of people and goods), and the sector shows substantial risks to the resilience of these fuel supplies.[64] While the Government has shied away from full regulation of the sector, the Energy Act 2023 does include measures that are intended to improve the resilience of the sector as well as reducing the risk of disruption. These include powers to require maintenance or improvement, risk reduction, and information powers, all of which allow the Government to identify risks within the fuel supply market before the need to implement emergency powers.[65] To further offset the supply and use of crude oil-based energy, the Act provides

58 Department for Energy Security and Net Zero (n 27) 19–20.
59 HM Government, 'Transitioning to a Net Zero Energy System: Smart Systems and Flexibility Plan 2021' (n 53).
60 HM Government, 'Energy White Paper: Powering Our Net Zero Future' (n 43).
61 Department for Energy Security and Net Zero (n 27) para 56.
62 HM Government, 'Energy Act 2023' (n 26) pt 8.
63 Department for Energy Security and Net Zero (n 27) 20–22.
64 ibid 69 f.
65 HM Government, 'Energy Act 2023' (n 26) pt 11.

powers that are intended to increase the speed with which offshore wind electricity generation is enabled, including assessments of the impact on the marine environment and potential compensatory measures for damage.[66] The Department for Energy Security and Net Zero Secretary of State is also given powers to respond to policy changes necessary to achieve net zero, potential court judgments, and to implement learnings from possible future marine pollution incidents involving offshore oil and gas production.[67] The Act also makes amendments to the cost recovery connected to decommissioning activities in the offshore oil and gas sector in line with the polluter pays principle,[68] as well as the decommissioning of nuclear sites, geological disposal of nuclear waste beneath the seabed, and compensation for nuclear damage.[69]

While the Energy Act 2023 goes to great lengths to implement necessary changes and enable actions that will bring the UK closer to the targets outlined in its NDC, criticism remains. The primary criticism comes from the UK's Climate Change Committee (CCC), which publishes regular assessments of the UK's progress on its Net Zero Strategy. Most recently, the CCC has raised concerns that the UK Government's approach is neither timely nor sufficient. In its February 2024 assessment, the CCC indicates that the UK Government underestimates the increase in energy demand and the necessary related emissions reductions such an increase requires.[70] The CCC has made clear that the committee has lost confidence that the Government is on track to meet its commitments and targets, primarily due to its recently announced delay in its phase out of fossil fuel vehicles and in meeting its heat pump installation targets,, as well as insufficient deployment of renewable electricity production.[71]

The remaining criticism of the UK's decarbonisation strategy is an over-reliance on new technologies, the funding and enabling legislation

66 Department for Energy Security and Net Zero (n 27) para 74; HM Government, 'Energy Act 2023' (n 26) pt 12.

67 HM Government, 'Energy Act 2023' (n 26) pt 12; Department for Energy Security and Net Zero (n. 27) para 75.

68 Department for Energy Security and Net Zero (n 27) para 76; HM Government, 'Energy Act 2023' (n 26) pt 12.

69 HM Government, 'Energy Act 2023' (n 26) pt 13.

70 Tom Dooks, 'CCC Assessment of Recent Announcements and Developments on Net Zero' (Climate Change Committee, 12 October 2023) 1 <https://www.theccc.org.uk/2023/10/12/ccc-assessment-of-recent-announcements-and-developments-on-net-zero/> accessed 14 March 2024.

71 ibid 2–5.

for which is broadly included in the Energy Act 2023. The CCC asserts that nearly half of the UK Government's emissions reduction plans are insufficient or at risk of failing to meet the 2030 target,[72] while others have criticised the Government's approach as being too heavily reliant on yet unproven technologies that will enable continued reliance of fossil fuels instead of transitioning away from such sources of energy.[73]

C. The National Energy Mix

The energy mix is an integral part of the energy transition mainly because it is constituted by energy sources that could either hamper or accelerate the transition to net zero. In the UK, natural gas is crucial in providing electricity to households, businesses, and other users. However, its influence in recent years has been waning in favour of cleaner and less polluting energy sources.[74] In 2023, natural gas generated 32 % of the UK's electricity needs, establishing its dominance as the single largest energy source for the year.[75] Gas to the UK is mainly sourced from the UK Continental Shelf, located in the North Sea, and imports in the form of liquified natural gas. The dominance of natural gas is indicative of the current approach in the UK to utilise this form of fossil fuel as part of its long-term decarbonisation plan,[76] ostensibly because gas is often positioned as a transition fuel. Although natural gas remains prominent in the UK's energy matrix, nuclear energy usage is also significant. In 2023, it generated 14.2 % of electricity in the UK.[77] Despite these contributions from fossil fuels to electricity generation, the UK is increasingly generating electricity from zero-carbon energy sources, which has led to the rising prominence of renewable energy in the energy mix.

---

72 ibid 7.

73 Sam D. Stephenson and Julian M. Allwood, 'Technology to the Rescue? Techno-Scientific Practices in the United Kingdom Net Zero Strategy and Their Role in Locking in High Energy Decarbonisation Pathways' (2023) 106 Energy Research & Social Science 103314, 7.

74 Simon Evans and Verner Viisainen, 'Analysis: UK Emissions in 2023 Fell to Lowest Level Since 1879' (*Carbon Brief*, 11 March 2024) <https://www.carbonbrief.org/analysis-uk-emissions-in-2023-fell-to-lowest-level-since-1879/> accessed 14 March 2024.

75 National Grid ESO, 'Britain's Electricity Explained: 2023 Review' <https://www.nationalgrideso.com/news/britains-electricity-explained-2023-review> accessed 13 March 2024.

76 HM Government, *Powering up Britain: Energy Security Plan* 15 (n 4).

77 National Grid ESO (n 75).

In 2023, wind and solar generated 29.4 % and 4.9 % of Britain's electricity needs, respectively.[78] These figures represented an improvement over the previous year, when both sources generated 26.8 % and 4.4 % of electricity in the UK.[79] Although other renewable energy sources like hydro and biomass contributed to electricity generation in 2023, the attention on wind and solar is due to their nature as newer forms of renewable energy. The growth of these fuels in the energy mix has been mainly due to the UK's abundant reserves of the sources and the investments that have been made towards generating electricity from them. Their increasing importance now means fossil fuel usage in the UK is declining. Coal use, for example, has dropped considerably in the UK, generating only 1 % of electricity in 2023. While the use of renewable energy continues to grow, and fossil fuel usage continues to fall, it is difficult to predict whether this trend represents a long-term picture of the UK's energy transition or a short-term trend that could fade away. The trend can be better understood in the context of broader issues associated with the energy transition, in particular the conflict between ensuring that net zero leads to a more climate-compliant future and ensuring that the objective of energy justice is achieved.

D. Trade-offs and the Energy Transition in the UK

The scale of potential trade-offs to be made in the context of the energy transition arose in 2023 when the UK Government announced two key energy policies.[80] The first relates to the decision to grant over one hundred licences to petroleum companies to drill for oil and gas in the North Sea,[81]

78 ibid.

79 National Grid ESO, 'Britain's Electricity Explained: 2022 Review' <https://www.nationalgrideso.com/news/britains-electricity-explained-2022-review> accessed 14 March 2024.

80 Chitzi C. Ogbumgbada, 'The Tension Between Energy Security Objectives and Climate Change Obligations in Recent UK's Energy and Climate Policies: An Assessment' (2025) OGEL 1 <https://www.ogel.org/article.asp?key=4155> accessed 09 June 2025. The decisions were made by the Conservative government then in power.

81 HM Government, 'Hundreds of New North Sea Oil and Gas Licences to Boost British Energy Independence and Grow the Economy – Press Release' (*GOV.UK*, 31 July 2023) <https://www.gov.uk/government/news/hundreds-of-new-north-sea-oil-and-gas-licences-to-boost-british-energy-independence-and-grow-the-economy-31-july-2023> accessed 14 March 2024.

where domestic gas production in the country mainly occurs. According to the government, the policy will aid the UK to reduce its dependence on imported gas, ensure a sufficient supply of gas to British households, businesses, and other users at affordable prices and rates, and protect jobs in the hydrocarbons industry.[82] The Government thereafter introduced the Offshore Petroleum Licensing Bill before the British Parliament to boost the frequency of petroleum auction rounds in the UK.[83]

The second policy concerns adjusting key net zero targets, which the Government argues represents a pragmatic, proportionate, and realistic approach to the transition.[84] Part of the Government's rationale is that the UK, as a developed economy, has taken more onerous climate change mitigation burdens and significantly cut its GHG emissions compared to other developed countries. The new policy includes adjusting the ban on petrol and diesel cars from 2030 to 2035, allowing the installation of oil and liquified petroleum gas boilers and new coal heating in off-gas-grid homes; delaying the phase-out of gas boilers in place of heat pumps in British homes; scrapping the obligation on landlords to utilise energy efficiency measures in their rented property; and scrapping several other green initiatives like car sharing and flight reductions to reduce carbon footprints, among others.[85]

While these policies may be justified from an energy security perspective, they risk placing the UK in a difficult position, given its commitment to

---

82 ibid.

83 HM Government, 'New Annual Oil and Gas Licensing Rounds to Boost UK Economy, Energy Independence and Transition to Net Zero – Press Release' (*GOV.UK*, 8 November 2023) <https://www.gov.uk/government/news/new-annual-oil-and-gas-licensing-rounds-to-boost-uk-economy-energy-independence-and-transition-to-net-zero> accessed 14 March 2024. The bill is before the House of Lords after passing its Third Reading in the House of Commons on 20 February 2024. See Alan Walker, 'Offshore Petroleum Licensing Bill 2023–24: Second Reading' (House of Commons Library, 04 January 2024) <https://commonslibrary.parliament.uk/research-briefings/cbp-9924/> accessed 16 July 2024.

84 HM Government, 'PM Recommits UK to Net Zero by 2050 and pledges a "fairer" path to Achieving Target to Ease the Financial Burden on British Families – Press Release' (*GOV.UK*, 20 September 2023) <https://www.gov.uk/government/news/pm-recommits-uk-to-net-zero-by-2050-and-pledges-a-fairer-path-to-achieving-target-to-ease-the-financial-burden-on-british-families> accessed 14 March 2024.

85 ibid.

transition to net zero in 2050, an obligation that is rooted in both domestic and international law. It will take some time however before the full ramifications of these policies will unravel.

E. Concluding Remarks

The energy transition is underway in the UK, and the impact of several laws and policies is already apparent. The decarbonisation strategy and the rising prominence of clean sources of energy indicate that the transition to net zero has already begun. Nevertheless, questions remain, such as whether current policies are effective in delivering net zero in a timely and urgent manner. A further question relates to how the transition could accommodate energy security, an issue that will likely continue to dominate debates on the energy transition in the UK in the foreseeable future.

Bibliography

Department for Energy Security and Net Zero, 'Energy Bill [HL] Explanatory Notes' <https://publications.parliament.uk/pa/bills/cbill/58-03/0295/en/220295en.pdf> accessed 14 March 2024

Dooks T, 'CCC Assessment of Recent Announcements and Developments on Net Zero' (Climate Change Committee, 12 October 2023) <https://www.theccc.org.uk/2023/10/12/ccc-assessment-of-recent-announcements-and-developments-on-net-zero/> accessed 14 March 2024

Evans S and Verner V, 'Analysis: UK Emissions in 2023 Fell to Lowest Level Since 1879' (Carbon Brief, 11 March 2024) <https://www.carbonbrief.org/analysis-uk-emissions-in-2023-fell-to-lowest-level-since-1879/> accessed 14 March 2024

HM Government, Expert Participation, 'Climate Change Act 2008' <https://www.legislation.gov.uk/ukpga/2008/27/contents> accessed 21 February 2024

HM Government, *Net Zero Strategy: Build Back Greener* (HH Associates Ltd 2021)

HM Government, *United Kingdom of Great Britain and Northern Ireland's Nationally Determined Contribution* (HH Associates Ltd 2022)

HM Government, *Powering up Britain: Energy Security Plan* (HH Global 2023)

HM Government, 'The Climate Change Act 2008 (2050 Target Amendment) Order 2019' <https://www.legislation.gov.uk/uksi/2019/1056/contents/made> accessed 14 March 2024

HM Government, 'Industrial Decarbonisation Strategy' <https://www.gov.uk/government/publications/industrial-decarbonisation-strategy> (GOV.UK, 7 April 2021) accessed 14 March 2024

HM Government, 'Heat and Buildings Strategy' <https://www.gov.uk/government/publications/heat-and-buildings-strategy> (GOV.UK, 1 March 2023) accessed 14 March 2024

HM Government, 'Energy Act 2023' <https://www.legislation.gov.uk/ukpga/2023/52/enacted> accessed 14 March 2024

HM Government, 'UK Hydrogen Strategy' <https://www.gov.uk/government/publications/uk-hydrogen-strategy> (GOV.UK, 14 December 2023) accessed 14 March 2024

HM Government, 'New Annual Oil and Gas Licensing Rounds to Boost UK Economy, Energy Independence and Transition to Net Zero – Press Release' (*GOV.UK*, 8 November 2023) <https://www.gov.uk/government/news/new-annual-oil-and-gas-licensing-rounds-to-boost-uk-economy-energy-independence-and-transition-to-net-zero> accessed 14 March 2024

HM Government, 'Hundreds of New North Sea Oil and Gas Licences to Boost British Energy Independence and Grow the Economy – Press Release' (GOV.UK, 31 July 2023) <https://www.gov.uk/government/news/hundreds-of-new-north-sea-oil-and-gas-licences-to-boost-british-energy-independence-and-grow-the-economy-31-july-2023> accessed 14 March 2024

HM Government, 'Proposals for a Future System Operator Role' <https://www.gov.uk/government/consultations/proposals-for-a-future-system-operator-role> (GOV.UK, 20 July 2021) accessed 14 March 2024

HM Government, 'Transitioning to a Net Zero Energy System: Smart Systems and Flexibility Plan 2021' (GOV.UK) <https://www.gov.uk/government/publications/transitioning-to-a-net-zero-energy-system-smart-systems-and-flexibility-plan-2021> accessed 14 March 2024

HM Government, 'Energy White Paper: Powering Our Net Zero Future' <https://www.gov.uk/government/publications/energy-white-paper-powering-our-net-zero-future> (GOV.UK, 18 December 2020) accessed 14 March 2024

HM Government, 'The Ten Point Plan for a Green Industrial Revolution' <https://www.gov.uk/government/publications/the-ten-point-plan-for-a-green-industrial-revolution> (GOV.UK, 18 November 2020) accessed 14 March 2024

HM Government, 'British Energy Security Strategy – Secure, Clean and Affordable British Energy for the Long Term' <https://www.gov.uk/government/publications/british-energy-security-strategy> accessed 26 February 2024

HM Government, 'Transport Decarbonisation Plan' <https://www.gov.uk/government/publications/transport-decarbonisation-plan> (GOV.UK, 12 January 2023) accessed 14 March 2024

HM Government, 'PM Recommits UK to Net Zero by 2050 and pledges a "fairer" path to Achieving Target to Ease the Financial Burden on British Families – Press Release' (GOV.UK, 20 September 2023) <https://www.gov.uk/government/news/pm-recommits-uk-to-net-zero-by-2050-and-pledges-a-fairer-path-to-achieving-target-to-ease-the-financial-burden-on-british-families> accessed 14 March 2024

HM Government and the Devolved **Administrations of Scotland, Wales, and Northern Ireland**, Collaboration 'Net Zero Government Initiative – UK Roadmap to Net Zero'.

HM Parliament, 'Sewel Convention' <https://www.parliament.uk/site-information/glossary/sewel-convention/> accessed 14 March 2024

Muinzer T L, *Climate and Energy Governance for the UK Low Carbon Transition: The Climate Change Act 2008* (Palgrave Macmillan 2019)

National Grid ESO, 'Britain's Electricity Explained: 2022 Review' <https://www.nationalgrideso.com/news/britains-electricity-explained-2022-review> accessed 14 March 2024

National Grid ESO, 'Britain's Electricity Explained: 2023 Review' <https://www.nationalgrideso.com/news/britains-electricity-explained-2023-review> accessed 13 March 2024

NSTA, 'About' <About Us – The North Sea Transition Authority (nstauthority.co.uk)> accessed 14 March 2023

Ogbumgbada C C, 'The Tension Between Energy Security Objectives and Climate Change Obligations in Recent UK's Energy and Climate Policies: An Assessment' (2025) OGEL 1 <https://www.ogel.org/article.asp?key=4155> accessed 09 June 2025.

Paul Cairney et al., 'How to Conceptualise Energy Law and Policy for an Interdisciplinary Audience: The Case of Post-Brexit UK' (2019) 129 Energy Policy 459

Stephenson S D and Allwood J M, 'Technology to the Rescue? Techno-Scientific Practices in the United Kingdom Net Zero Strategy and Their Role in Locking in High Energy Decarbonisation Pathways' (2023) 106 Energy Research & Social Science 103314

UNFCCC, 'Long-Term Strategies Portal' <https://unfccc.int/process/the-paris-agreement/long-term-strategies> accessed 14 March 2024

Walker A, 'Offshore Petroleum Licensing Bill 2023–24: Second Reading' (House of Commons Library, 04 January 2024) <https://commonslibrary.parliament.uk/research-briefings/cbp-9924/> accessed 16 July 2024

Yergin D, *The New Map: Energy, Climate, and the Clash of Nations* (Penguin Books 2021)

General Perspectives on the Law of Energy Transition in Denmark

Bent Ole Gram Mortensen

The green transition is characterized as the development which the energy supply in many western countries is currently undergoing. Primarily, the transition includes a reduction in the use of fossil fuels. This chapter is about the transition in Denmark, a country with approximately 6.0 mill. citizens.[1]

A. More Recent Historical Overview

Denmark has gone through a number of energy transitions. Wood was originally the common Danish resource for energy as well as for other purposes such as buildings and ships.[2] In resent historical times in Denmark, the extent of the forest has until recently had a significant correlation with the size of the population. The ravages of the Black Death in the 14th century and several centuries later, wars and other misfortunes and the resulting population reduction in the next few centuries gave way to the forest. Around the year 1600, 20–25 % of Denmark was covered with forest. But

1 The Kingdom of Denmark includes Denmark, Greenland, and the Faroe Islands. This chapter only discusses the legislation in Denmark.

2 On the topic of wood see Bent Ole Gram Mortensen, 'Fredskov – mere skov end fredning [Protected Forest – More Forest Than Protected]' in Nis Jul Clausen/Annette Kronborg/Nina Dietz Legind/Bent Ole Gram Mortensen (eds), *Festskrift til Hans Viggo Godsk Pedersen* (Liber Amicorum to Hans Viggo Godsk Pedersen, DJØF Publishing 2017) 389–408. See in general M. Rüdiger/A. Åberg, 'Energy in the Nordic World' (Aarhus Universitetsforlag. The Nordic World, 2024); Kirsten Gram-Hanssen, 'Energy Consumption in Homes – An historical approach to understanding new routines' in Mogens Rüdiger (ed), *The culture of Energy*, (New Castle 2008); K. Hvidtfelt Nielsen, 'Danish Wind Power Policies from 1976 to 2000: A Survey of Policy Making and Techno-Economic Innovation' in Volkmar Lauber (ed): *Switching to Renewable Power: A Framework for the 21st* Century (London 2005); Birgitte Wistofte/Harriet M Hansen/Flemming Petersen (eds), *Elektricitetens Aarhundrede* [The Century of Electricity](vol. 1, Copenhagen 1991); Birgitte Wistofte/Jytte Thorndahl/Flemming Petersen (eds), *Elektricitetens Aarhundrede* (vol. 2, Copenhagen 1992).

the population increased again, and slowly the pressure on the forest grew. In the middle of the 18th century, the forest's share was reduced to 8–10 %, and around 1800 it was down to 2–3 %. It was widely feared that society would come to a standstill as a result of a lack of wood.[3]

Over time, wood was partially replaced by the import of English and Scottish coal. From the middle of the 18th century, coal was increasingly used as an energy source in industry. Denmark became more and more dependent on imported energy. This was the first energy transition – fossil fuel. However, it came under pressure when Denmark was on the losing side of the Napoleonic wars.

Local hydropower and peat played a role until oil replaced it as the primary energy source, both in power plants, domestic heating and in the transport sector. However, the Yom Kippur War in 1973 and the Iranian revolution in 1979 gave rise to oil import problems and a jump in prices. At that time, Danish power plants were primarily oil-based but were now rebuilt for coal, the extraction of hydrocarbons from the Danish part of the North Sea was started, and a series of other energy policy measures was initiated.

It was not until the aftermath of the oil crisis of the 1970s that Denmark got laws on energy supply, first regarding electricity supply[4], then regarding heat supply including gas.[5] In the same period, Denmark got its first overall energy policy[6] and a construction law on natural gas supply.[7]

Since then, a number of energy plans have shifted Denmark towards a more diversified energy supply.

Until around 1990, energy plans and political agreements were focussed on making Denmark independent from imported oil. Hereafter, following inspiration from the UN Brundtland report- *Our Common Future*[8], the emission of greenhouse gases was also put into focus.

---

3 Thorkild Kjærgaard, *Den danske Revolution 1500–1800. En økohistorisk tolkning [The Danish Revolution 1500–1800. An ecohistorical interpretation]* (Gyldendal 1991) 23.

4 Act no. 54 of 25 February 1976 on electricity supply.

5 Act no. 258 of 8 June 1979 on heat supply.

6 Handelsministeriet [Ministry of Commerce], *Dansk Energipolitik 1976 [Danish Energy Policy 1976]* (Copenhagen 1976), Expansion of district heating and natural gas for residential heating based on municipal heating planning. Tightened energy standards for buildings and subsidies for e.g. re-insulation of homes, energy inspection, etc.

7 Act no. 232 of 8 June 1979 regarding natural gas supply.

8 Available at https://sustainabledevelopment.un.org/content/documents/5987our-common-future.pdf accessed 17 June 2025.

Currently, Denmark's two largest energy resources are fossil and renewable energy. Biomass makes up the main part of renewable energy. A large part of this is imported.[9]

As elsewhere, the energy supply is being electrified. Solar and wind energy are growing steadily. Solar parks and wind turbines on land can now be built without government subsidies, though recently the lack in growth in demand for electricity in the hours where solar and wind power produces most drives the prices down and weakening the business case for new solar and wind power. The same might also apply for offshore wind, but rising cost has recently made this unrealistic. Please see chapter C5: The Law of Renewable Energies in Denmark.

B. The Current Energy Supply and Policy

The energy sector in Denmark is generally characterized by broad political agreements. Traditionally, a political agreement is concluded by a majority of the parties of the Danish Parliament, after which the settlement is implemented through one or more (amending) laws. This was the case with Act no. 1392 of 27 December 2008, the Law of Expansion of Renewable Energy, where existing provisions regarding renewable energy electricity were combined into one law. The purpose of the law was to make the rules on installation and production of renewable energy plants as clear as possible for the interested parties.

In 1985, Denmark decided not to use nuclear power for its production of electricity. This policy continues to be supported by a majority in the Danish parliament. Among the population, the press reports on increasing support for nuclear power, although there does not seem to be a majority for this. Two Danish companies are currently developing smaller modularized reactor solutions. For decades, Denmark has imported electricity from Sweden and Germany, which have/had nuclear power in their production portfolio. It is uncertain whether or not the political ban on nuclear power will be lifted. However, it is less likely that nuclear power plants will be established in Denmark, except maybe for smaller test plants.

Because of the country's topography, hydropower is of no importance in Denmark except as imported energy. Electricity is primarily produced

9 Energistyrelsen [Danish Energy Agency], 'Energistatistik 2021' [Energy Statistics 2021] <https://ens.dk/sites/ens.dk/files/Statistik/energistatistik2021.pdf> accessed 17 June 2025.

via renewable energy and natural gas. There will within a few years be no coal-fired power plants left. Combined heat and power (CHP) play a large role in the energy supply, which ties electricity production together with space heating. Around 69 % of Danish homes are heated by district heating, a number which is increasing. District heating uses biomass, waste, and natural gas. Electric heat pumps are becoming increasingly important. Waste incineration has made a certain contribution, while geothermal energy has so far had close to no effect on the energy supply. However, this may change, as new projects are in the pipeline. Also the utilization of waste heat from industry may in the future contribute more to the district heating systems.

The transport sector is still dependent on oil, but electric cars are gaining ground. Hydrogen is of little significance for the Danish transport sector, and there is no publicly available network of hydrogen filling stations.

Denmark extracts oil and especially natural gas from the North Sea. It has been politically decided that this production must cease in 2050. In the period from 1997 to 2012, Denmark was a net energy exporter, but traditionally, the country has been dependent on the import of energy. In 2023, the degree of self-sufficiency was 59 %. For a short time, Denmark must once again will be a net gas exporter from 2024 onwards. It is uncertain to what extent, in particular, plans for offshore wind turbines will increase the country's degree of self-sufficiency.

The power transmission grid is owned by the state company Energinet (the TSO- Transmission System operator), while the distribution is owned by various private companies with a particular consumer-owned background. The natural gas transmission grid in Denmark is also owned by Energinet. The natural gas distribution network is also owned by the state.[10] In 2019, all Danish distribution of natural gas was brought together in Energinet's subsidiary company, Evida. In 2021, this company was purchased by the Ministry of Finance. Natural gas is in the process to be phased out or at least reduced as a source of domestic heating.

At the time of writing, no hydrogen network has been established. Nevertheless, in May 2023, a political agreement has been made concerning who will, if necessary, own and operate a hydrogen infrastructure in Den-

10 Originally, the natural gas distribution network was operated by regional companies owned by the local municipalities.

mark.[11] Evida will be responsible for a possible domestic hydrogen network (connection of domestic hydrogen producers and consumers), while Energinet will be system operators and will partially own the cross-border piped hydrogen infrastructure to a Danish receiving point, including cross-border hydrogen pipes across the country to hydrogen storage facilities, and offshore hydrogen pipes. On 4 April 2024, a majority in the Danish Parliament entered into a political agreement on the economic framework conditions for establishing a hydrogen transmission network in the western part of Denmark (Jutland) and down to Germany.[12]

In October 2023, state aid of 1.25 billion DKK was distributed to a total of 6 electrolysis projects of between 9 and 150 MW. It is uncertain whether Denmark can manage to establish a larger hydrogen industry or create a further use for it, e.g., for the production of methanol. It will demand an expansion of the production of renewable electricity in Denmark. Other projects without state aid are being planned or established. At Kassø in the southwest of Denmark, a plant with an expected annual e-methanol production of 32.000 tons has been established.

C. Fossil Fuels

The Danish gross share of fossil fuels in 2023 was registered by Eurostat[13] at 55.40 %. Among the EU countries, a lower share of fossil fuels was only found among four other countries all with a large share of nuclear power and hydropower respectively: Finland with 35.67 %, France 47.89 %, Latvia 53.77 % and Sweden 30.37 % fossil fuels. In 2013, Denmark's share was 75.91 %. There has thus been a significant reduction in the share of fossil fuels over recent years.

---

11 See Klima-, Energi- og Forsyningsministeriet [Danish Ministry for Climate, Energy and Utilities], Political agreement of 22 May 2023, 'Mulighed for etablering af brintinfrastruktur' [Possibility of establishing hydrogen infrastructure] <https://www.kefm.dk/Media/638204311368810699/Aftaletekst%20-%20mulighed%20for%20etablering%20af%20brintinfrastruktur.pdf > accessed 17 June 2025.

12 See Klima-, Energi- og Forsyningsministeriet [Danish Ministry for Climate, Energy and Utilities], Political agreement of 4 April 2024, 'Økonomiske rammevilkår for brintinfrastruktur' [Economic framework conditions for hydrogen infrastructure] <https://www.kefm.dk/Media/638478420542283365/%C3%98konomiske%20rammevilk%C3%A5r%20for%20brintinfrastruktur%20-2.%20delaftale%20om%20r%C3%B8rbunden%20brintinfrastruktur_april%202024.pdf> accessed 15 July 2024.

13 See Eurostat, 'Share of fossil fuels in gross available energy' <https://ec.europa.eu/eurostat/databrowser/view/nrg_ind_ffgae/default/table?lang=en> accessed 14 June 2025.

Natural gas consumption in Denmark has been declining over a number of years. In Denmark, around 40 % of the gas supply comes from biogas (2023). Lately the figure has been increasing sharply. Around 380,000 households corresponding to about 800,000 people have a gas boiler. The numbers are declining, and the political aim is phasing out natural gas for space heating in favour of district heating and electrically powered heat pumps. Different kinds of support schemes have been introduced in order to promote district heating and heat pumps.

Biogas is seen by many as an opportunity to get rid of fossil fuels in industries involving high process temperatures. Denmark is characterized by relatively large biogas plants that mainly operate on market terms. Manure is the largest energy source for biogas in Denmark. A previous consumption of energy crops is to be phased out.

1. Production

Since 1972, oil and natural gas have been extracted in Denmark. Production takes place in the Danish exclusive economic zone (EEZ) in the North Sea. The Danish Energy Agency estimated in August 2023 that the total reserves at the beginning of 2023 amounted to 139 million m^3 of oil and 77 billion Nm^3 gas. Daily production for 2023 is expected to be 3.4 million m^3 (approx. 58,000 barrels) of oil and 0.9 billion Nm^3 of gas (approx. 16,000 barrels of oil equivalent). Production is expected to increase in the coming years as a result of the completion of the renovation of the important Tyra gas field, but by 2030 at the latest, production will fall again as a result of the Danish North Sea fields being 'mature' and therefore production-wise in natural decline.

There are currently 21 oil and gas fields in operation. French Total has been the operator of the majority of the fields (16) since the purchase of Danish Mærsk Oil in 2017. There are a total of 55 platforms located in the Danish part of the North Sea, as well as a number of oil and gas pipelines between different platforms. In addition, there are two gas pipelines and one oil pipeline to the Danish west coast of Jutland as well as a gas pipeline to the Dutch NOGAT pipe system.[14]

14 The Danish offshore natural gas pipeline system is connected to the NOGAT system through the Tyra West – F3 pipeline.

In a political agreement of 3 December 2020,[15] it has been agreed by a majority in the Danish Parliament that oil and gas shall not be extracted in the Danish part of the North Sea after 2050, and that no new tender rounds shall be launched. There was no change to the possibility of applying for new exploration and production permits on the basis of mini-tender rounds[16] and neighbouring block procedures[17] towards 2050.

The production of oil and natural gas in Denmark will thus continue for many years independently of the green transition.

2. Consumption

The total energy consumption in Denmark has been relatively constant over the past 10 years at between 1,100 and 1,300 petajoules.

In 2024, Denmark's actual oil consumption accounted for 37.5 % of the total energy consumption (252 PJ out of 672 PJ). For natural gas, the proportion is 8.3 % and for coal and coke 2.8 %. By comparison, renewable energy accounted for 46.7 %.[18]

The last 20 years have been characterized by a significant drop in the consumption of fossil fuels, while the consumption of renewable energy has increased. However, a large part of the renewable energy consisted of solid biomass, which includes, inter alia, wood pellets and wood chips (24.9 % in 2024 of the total energy consumption). A large part of this was imported. It remains to be seen whether such a large consumption of solid biomass for energy purposes is sustainable.

---

15 See Klima-, Energi- og Forsyningsministeriet [Danish Ministry for Climate, Energy and Utilities], 'Aftale mellem regeringen (Socialdemokratiet), Venstre, Dansk Folkeparti, Radikale Venstre, Socialistisk Folkeparti og Det Konservative Folkeparti om fremtiden for olie- og gasindvinding iNordsøen af 3. december 2020' [Political agreement of 3 December 2020 on the future of oil and gas extraction in the North Sea] <https://kefm.dk/Media/0/3/Nords%C3%B8aftale%20(2).pdf> accessed8 June 2025.

16 At a mini-tender round, interested companies can apply for permission for an area, without a prior tender notice. A notice of the application is then published in the Official Gazette and in the Official Gazette of the European Union, after which other interested parties have the opportunity, within a period of 90 days, to submit their application.

17 If there are geological or production reasons for this, the holder of an existing permit can apply for a permit for an adjacent area (a neighboring block).

18 Key Figures from the Energistyrelsen [Danish Energy Agency], 'Preliminary Energy Statistics 2024' <https://ens.dk/service/statistik-data-noegletal-og-kort/maanedlig-og-aarlig-energistatistik> accessed 14 June 2025.

D. Electrification

As in many other countries, Denmark's energy consumption is at present in a process of significant electrification.

Electrification in Denmark is most pronounced among passenger cars. Electric cars account for 51 % of new cars in 2024. Electric cars and plug-in hybrids make up a total of 16.5 % of today's stock of 2.86 million passenger cars.[19]

The AFI Act (Alternative Fuels Infrastructure)[20] supports the spread of public charging stations for electric vehicles. The law also includes filling stations and LNG filling stations[21] as well as facilities for power supply from shore to vessels. Municipalities, regions, and joint municipal companies are given the opportunity to pay for a private operator to ensure the spread of charging stations.

E. Heating of Buildings

Heating of buildings is a traditional obligation of landowners. But as a result of the energy crises in the 1970s, updated legislation was introduced,[22] the purpose of which was to reduce the energy supply's dependency on oil. The municipalities were given a planning obligation, and it was hereby determined whether areas were to be supplied with district heating or natural gas, or whether it should be left to the choice of individuals, which at the time would often be an oil burner.

When it comes to domestic space heating, district heating is currently the most widespread technology. Approximately 69 % of Danish homes are heated with district heating.

In Denmark, a home needs heating and supply with hot domestic water. Originally, this was solely the responsibility of the owner. In light of the

19 Statistics Denmark, < https://www.dst.dk/da/Statistik/nyheder-analyser-publ/nyt/NytHtml?cid=48639#:~:text=Nyregistrerede%20motork%C3%B8ret%C3%B8jer%20december%202024,af%20elbiler%20med%2072%20pct.> accessed 14 June 2025.

20 Consolidated Act no. 1043 of 17 September 2024on infrastructure for alternative fuels for transport. Original Law no. 1537 of 19 December 2017. Implements AFI Directive 2014/94/EU. In the 'Fit for 55' legal package, the AFI Directive is proposed to be replaced with a Regulation. The AFI directive is now replaced by Regulation (EU) 2023/1804 on the deployment of alternative fuels infrastructure.

21 However, filling stations and LNG filling stations seems not to have any role in the electrification.

22 Act no. 258 of 8 June 1979 regarding the Heat Supply Act.

1970s oil crisis, a political desire for increased control over the energy supply arose. This desire first led to the adoption of the Electricity Supply Act and later, in 1979, the Heat Supply Act, which regulated collective heat supply in the form of district heating supply and natural gas supply. The latter has later been separated in Gas Supply Act.

Individual heat supply is not regulated in a particular supply act. There are relevant provisions in various other pieces of legislation. This concerns a ban on the use of certain technologies. Thus, it has been prohibited to install oil burners in new buildings from 2013, and from 2016 in existing buildings in areas with district heating or individual natural gas supply.[23] The Wood-Burning Stove Executive Order,[24] which entered into force on 1 August 2021, mandates the scrapping of wood-burning stoves from before 2003 in connection with a change of ownership within 12 months after the sale. The motive is health-related, as the large-scale emission of particles from old wood-burning stoves is assumed to cause both respiratory ailment and deaths. The provision is assumed to cover approximately 260,000 of Denmark's approximately 700,000 wood-burning stoves. Many of these wood-burning stoves only function as a supplementary energy source. However, there are approximately 100,000 houses that are primarily heated by a wood pellet stove. In the winter of 2022–23, these homeowners experienced increasing prices and feared an impending supply crisis.

Government support is currently provided for homeowners to phase out natural gas boilers faster than normal market conditions dictate.

Many Danish district heating installations have a solar heating system among their production facilities. There are currently (2023) more than 1.1 GW (thermal effect) of solar heating associated with Danish district heating installations.[25]

Although a solar heating system visually looks a lot like a solar park, a solar heating system is not subject to the special schemes in the Expansion of Renewable Energy Act, including the value loss scheme. Only three minor geothermal plants are in operation in Denmark. Licences by the municipalities to drill wells of a depth of less than 250 metres. If wells for geothermal plants are to go deeper than 250 metres, the Danish Energy Agency must be contacted in advance.

23 Act No. 577 of 18 June 2012.

24 Executive Order no. 1449 of 17 June 2021.

25 An overview of solar heating systems can be found at Solvarmedata, <https://solvarmedata.dk/> accessed 8 June 2025.

F. Biomass

In 2022, renewable energy accounted for 45.6 % of the total energy consumption in Denmark. Biomass made up the majority of the renewable energy with a share of 68 %. The remaining part came from solar, wind, water, geothermal energy, and heat pumps.[26]

Around 30 % of Denmark's consumption of biomass is covered via imports. Wood pellets constituted a total of 68 % of Denmark's import of biomass in 2022, while whole-tree chips constituted 19 %. Furthermore, there were imports of biodegradable waste, firewood, biodiesel, bioethanol, and biooil.[27]

However, the Danish production of biomass, especially in the form of biogas, has increased sharply since 2018. Biogas is promoted through public subsidies.

A significant part of Danish gas production consists of biogas. There are currently around 150 biogas plants in operation in Denmark. A significant expansion of biogas production capacity is excepted, in the form of both new plants and the expansion of existing plants.

A significant part of Danish production of biogas is based on waste products from agricultural animal production. Manure represents more than threequarters of the total feedstock input on agricultural biogas plants. However, energy crops such as corn and beets can be used in biogas. If animal production is reduced, the Danish production of biogas will be dependent on new sources.

A part of the biogas is upgraded to the calorific value equivalent of the North Sea's natural gas. This happens by removing CO2 from the biogas at an upgrading plant. By upgrading the calorific value of biogas, it can be introduced to and distributed via the natural gas distribution network. Over 30 % of gas consumption in Denmark is based on biogas. The number is increasing. In August 2023, Evida stated that 57th biogas plant had been connected to the natural gas grid.[28] It is a political ambition that Danish gas

26 See Statistics Denmark, 'Danmarks forbrug af biomasse til energi holder historisk højt niveau' [Denmark's consumption of biomass for energy remains at a historically high level] <https://www.dst.dk/da/Statistik/nyheder-analyser-publ/bagtal/2023/2023-08-23-Danmarks-forbrug-af-biomasse> accessed 7 June 2025.

27 See Danmark Statistics (n 27).

28 See Energistyrelsen [Danish Energy Agency], 'Evida tilkobler biogasanlæg nr. 57' [Evida connects biogas plant no. 57] <https://evida.dk/nyheder/evida-tilkobler-biogasanlaeg-nr-57/> accessed 8 June 2025.

customers in 2030 can be supplied exclusively with biogas. The fulfilment of this ambition is eased through the falling consumption of natural gas.

So far, the CO_2 (carbon dioxide) released has mostly been emitted to the atmosphere, but in the future, it can be a source for CCS (Carbon Capture and Storage) or PtX (Power-to-X-covers processes for converting renewably sourced electricity (power) to a substance or energy carrier). Tenders for CCS have been issued.

G. Development of Solar and Wind

1. Offshore

In 1991, Denmark established the world's first offshore wind farm – Vindeby – close to the island Lolland with a capacity of 5 MW. With the climate agreement on green power and heat from 25 June 2022,[29] there was a political majority in favour of tendering at least four gigawatts of offshore wind for realization by 2030 at the latest. Political agreements had already been made on offshore wind farms of a little over 16 gigawatts, of which two are energy islands (in the North Sea and around Bornholm). These political commitments have even been confirmed by international agreements in the form of The Esbjerg Declaration[30] and The Marienborg Declaration.[31]

Production of energy offshore requires state approval, cf. the Renewable Energy Act art. 22–29a. The approval authority has been delegated to the Danish Energy Agency. The Danish municipalities do not have authority when it comes to offshore plants, regardless of whether they are energy plants or other plants (e.g., sea farming).

On 1 February 2023, the case administration of 33 open-door offshore wind turbine projects was put on hold. The reason was uncertainty regarding the compliance of the open-door procedure with EU law.

29 Klima-, Energi- og Forsyningsministeriet, [Danish Ministry of Climate, Energy and Utilities], Delaftale om mere grøn strøm 2022 [Partial Agreement on More Green Electricity 2022] dated 25 June 2022 <https://www.kefm.dk/Media/637920977082432693/Klimaaftale%20om%20gr%C3%B8n%20str%C3%B8m%20og%20varme%202022.pdf> accessed 20 June 2025.

30 'The Esbjerg Declaration' <https://www.regeringen.dk/aktuelt/tidligere-publikationer/the-esbjerg-declaration/> accessed 20 June 2025.

31 'The Marienborg Declaration' <https://www.regeringen.dk/aktuelt/tidligere-publikationer/the-marienborg-declaration/> accessed 20 June 2025.

However, in March 2023, the case administration of 4 projects could be resumed. Common to the projects was the fact that they had received preliminary research permits in the period of 2014–2019. The market situation in 2023 was so different compared to this earlier period that were no longer any conflicts with EU law.

Two additional projects, which received establishing permits in the autumn of 2022, were assessed not to be in conflict with EU law. The projects in question received preliminary research permits in 2019 and 2018, respectively. All the remaining open-door projects was refused, primarily on the grounds that they are not in accordance with the marine plan. Several of the refusals were brought before the Energy Board of Appeal, which has turned them back to the Danish Energy Agency due to deficiencies in the reasoning. When the manuscript was submitted in June 2025, the Danish Energy Agency had not yet made any new decisions.

At the same time, the establishment of energy islands is already delayed and there is a real possibility that especially the North Sea energy island will not be economically feasible to establish. The energy island Bornholm in the Baltic Sea seems to be more realistically to establish.

2. Onshore

Danish onshore wind turbines have a capacity of 2.7 GW. For some time, wind turbines have had the reputation of being the most 'fertile crop on the field'. While it has proven attractive to the owners, the neighbours of the up to 180-meter-tall wind turbines have often been less enthusiastic.

In recent years, the expansion with solar cell plants has mainly taken place as field installations. The currently largest field installation is 340 hectares (340,000,000 m^2). The disadvantage of field installations is precisely the use of land space, which competes with other uses, including use for nature and the production of food. Mark installations currently seem to be the commercially most attractive form of solar cell plants. This is presumably due to economies of scale in the possibility of large plants and lower installation costs in fields than on buildings.

Solar cells on buildings have the advantage that the electricity produced can often be consumed closer to the solar cell plant, which reduces network costs. Furthermore, the utilization of buildings has the advantage that no other areas (e.g., agricultural land or nature) is included in the production of energy. It is to be expected that going forward, the technology on solar cells will make it more commercially relevant to utilize existing buildings and spaces for the production of electricity. So far, only a limited amount of commercial solar cells have been constructed on Danish roofs. Solar cells on the roof of ordinary households have formerly been popular due to the possibility of saving electricity tax. When this possibility was degraded, this extension came to a standstill.

The localization of wind turbines and solar parks is typically done by an installer of wind turbines or solar cells (often referred to as a developer) who has entered into an agreement with one or more owners of land (typically farmers) regarding the installation of the plants in question. However, before this happens, the installation is dependent on whether or not the municipality will grant planning permission for this. An overall national plan has been lacking.

However, with the 'Partial Agreement on More Green Electricity 2022',[32] a number of political parties representing a majority in the Danish parliament have agreed to ensure framework conditions that can enable a quadrupling of total electricity production from solar energy and onshore wind towards 2030.

Further, in October 2023, the government (which has a majority in Parliament) came up with a plan based on 32 state-designated areas[33] with a total potential for 127,000 GWh of production. However, at the time of submission of the manuscript, none of the designated areas have transformed into concrete projects.

H. The Dilemma of Conflicting Interests

One of the challenges of switching to renewable energy production is the many other considerations that also must be taken care of in a society: nature protection, appropriate waste management, food production, and groundwater protection.

32 Delaftale om mere grøn strøm 2022 [Partial Agreement on More Green Electricity 2022] dated 25 June 2022 <https://www.kefm.dk/Media/637920977082432693/Klimaaftale%20om%20gr%C3%B8n%20str%C3%B8m%20og%20varme%202022.pdf> accessed 20 June 2025.

33 Klima-, Energi- og Forsyningsministeriet [Danish Ministry of Climate, Energy and Utilities], 'Climate Action Plan' (October 2023) <https://kefm.dk/Media/638324394100598678/Udspil%20-%20Mere%20gr%C3%B8n%20energi%20fra%20sol%20og%20vind%20p%C3%A5%20land.pdf> accessed 20 June 2025.

1. Nature Protection

Denmark is a country with a limited amount of nature. The Danish Biodiversity Council pointed out in November 2023 in its annual report that there is worryingly little protected nature in Denmark.[34] Despite this, there seems to be acceptance by the Danish government that facilities for the production of renewable energy can be established in a protected manner.

Nature protection considerations represent a common area of conflict in connection with the establishment of large plants, including renewable energy plants. E.g., in connection with offshore wind turbines, offshore wind turbines can conflict with forage areas of sea birds and migration routes of migratory birds and bats.

A special scenario is the establishment of offshore wind power in the Wadden Sea, which is on the UNESCO World Heritage List. The three Wadden Sea countries – Denmark, Holland and Germany – confirmed at the latest in 2023 with the so-called Wilhelmshaven declaration not to build e.g. wind turbines within the relevant world heritage area: 'Reconfirming the existing trilateral agreement that prohibits the construction of wind turbines, oil and gas exploration, and exploitation and construction of new installations for oil and gas within the boundaries of the Wadden Sea World Heritage Site'.[35]

2. CCU or CCS

With the political agreement[36] of 20 September 2023 between 10 of the Danish Parliament's parties, which represents the vast majority of the members of Parliament, the future framework for CCS was determined.

34 Biodiversity Council, 'Mod robuste økosystemer – Årsrapport 2023' [Towards resilient ecosystems – Annual Report 2023] <https://www.biodiversitetsraadet.dk/viden/aarsrapport-2023> accessed 20 June 2025.

35 See point 28 i of Common Wadden Sea Secretariat, 'Wilhelmshaven Declaration. Ministerial Council, Declaration of the 14th Trilateral Governmental Conference on the Protection of the Wadden Sea' *(2023)* <https://www.waddensea-worldheritage.org/sites/default/files/2023_Wilhelmshaven%20Declaration_signed.pdf> accessed 20 June 2025.

36 Klima-, Energi- og Forsyningsministeriet, [Danish Ministry of Climate, Energy and Utilities] 'Aftale om styrkede rammevilkår for CCS i Danmark. Klimahandling – Vejen til fuld fangst og lagring af CO_2 i 2030' [Agreement on Strengthened Framework Conditions for CCS in Denmark. Climate Action – The Path to Full Capture and Storage of CO_2 in 2030] <https://kefm.dk/Media/638307862071081909/Aftale%2

The agreement is based on the premise that Denmark's 70 % reduction target in 2023 only can be achieved if CCS is included as a means of action. At the same time, it is assumed by the Geological Survey of Denmark and Greenland (GEUS) that Denmark's underground has room for a total of 12–22 billion tons of CO_2, which corresponds to up to 500 years of emissions from Denmark.

The agreement builds on other agreements that since 2020 have allocated up to a total of 38 billion DKK to CCS. It is therefore also a premise that CCS needs public aid. Thus, it is explicitly stated in the agreement that CCS 'in the years to come is expected to continue to be dependent on public aid.' In the long term, it is the idea that CCS is to be operated on marked terms, e.g., via financial incentives such as taxes, quotas on CO_2 from fossil sources, and possibly certificate sales.

In February 2023, the Danish Energy Agency announced the first three permissions for full scale CO_2 storage projects in the Danish Part of the North Sea. In March 2023, the first CO_2 was stored in the North Sea. In May, the Danish semi-state energy company Ørsted won a tendered establishment of the first full scale CCS project in Denmark. It is unknown whether there will be as great a demand for domestic CO_2 for PtX as, for example, methanol, that future CCS in the Danish underground must rely on imported CO_2. The Danish Energy Agency has issued a tender for Contract on subsidy for carbon capture, transport and storage. In May 2025 the Danish Energy Agency has selected 10 companies from a pool of 16 applicants to compete for DKK 28.7 billion in funding for Carbon Capture and Storage projects.[37]

In 2022, Denmark signed an agreement on cross-border transport of CO_2 with Belgium concerning geological storage under the seabed.

Rules on the transport of CO_2 are gathered in a special law on transport of CO_2. It is the intention that both private and state companies should be able to own, establish and operate infrastructure for the transport of CO_2. However, third-party access to all pipelines must be ensured.

The State's owner share via Nordsøfonden in storage licenses is set at 20 % going forward. This corresponds to what has been agreed upon for the three licenses issued in February 2023.

0om%20styrkede%20rammevilk%C3%A5r%20for%20CCS%20i%20Danmark%20af%2020.%20september%202023.pdf> accessed 20 June 2025.

37 See <https://ens.dk/en/press/10-companies-selected-compete-denmarks-ccs-fund-dkk-287-billion-carbon-capture-and-storage> accessed 20 June 2025.

3. Local Communities

The majority of wind turbine capacity and solar cell capacity have been established as parks by commercial developers. Household installations have a very limited contribution to the production capacity.

In some cases, an energy park is established by a community of citizens. Ownership of local energy parks could otherwise be one of the ways to achieve greater local acceptance of these plants. The lack of enthusiasm about becoming a neighbour to a large energy plant has often been characterised as an expression of NIMBYism, and the law also prescribes compensation for loss of value of a property. However, this does not change the fact that an outside developer typically makes money from establishing the facility, while the local residents have to live with the disadvantages such as impaired views and noise.

I. Conclusion

Denmark has gone through a number of energy transitions which, in varying degrees, have concerned wood, coal, oil, natural gas and, most recently, wind and solar power.

Security of supply has previously been an important element in Danish energy supply policy. Most recently, it was most strongly expressed in the oil crises of the 1970s, when oil was phased out in electricity production. However, other major considerations now also apply. First environmental and then climate consideration was included from the 1970s onwards.

However, the short-term gas supply crisis in connection with the war between Ukraine and Russia has also led to an increased political focus on phasing out gas for domestic heating.

With increasing geopolitical challenges, security of supply has again become relevant. And the green transition implies increasing use of domestic energy sources – solar and wind – which contribute to reducing the need to import energy resources.

However, there seems to be a conflict between these three considerations. Nature conservation can stand in the way of rapid expansion with solar and wind. There have been several cases where environmental permits have been rejected in the appeals body. Projects have been delayed with heavy losses. In the worst case, the basis for the business case in question disappears as a result of changes in market conditions during the appeal process.

Characteristic of the current green transition is that the political visions also include expansion with a larger export in mind, whether it is electricity produced from offshore wind, hydrogen, or methanol via PtX.

Bibliography

Biodiversity Council, 'Mod robuste økosystemer – Årsrapport 2023'Aarsrapport-Biodiversitetsraadet-2023' [Towards resilient ecosystems – Annual Report 2023] < https://www.biodiversitetsraadet.dk/viden/aarsrapport-2023https://www.biodiversitetsraadet.dk/pdf/2023/11/Aarsrapport-Biodiversitetsraadet-2023.pdf> accessed 20 June 2025.

Energistyrelsen [Danish Energy Agency], 'Energistatistik 2021' [Energy Statistics 2021] <https://ens.dk/sites/ens.dk/files/Statistik/energistatistik2021.pdf> accessed 8 June 2025.**Energistyrelsen** [Danish Energy Agency], 'Preliminary Energy Statistics 2024' <https://ens.dk/service/statistik-data-noegletal-og-kort/maanedlig-og-aarlig-energistatistik> accessed 14 June 2025

Energistyrelsen [Danish Energy Agency], 'Biogas in Denmark'<https://ens.dk/en/energy-sources/biogas-denmark> accessed 17 June 2025

Energistyrelsen [Danish Energy Agency], 'Evida tilkobler biogasanlæg nr. 57' 57' [Evida connects biogas plant no. 57] <https://evida.dk/nyheder/evida-tilkobler-biogasanlaeg-nr-57/> accessed 8 June 2025

Energistyrelsen [Danish Energy agency], 'Klimastatus og -fremskrivning 2023 (KF23): Transport Sektornotat nr. 4A' (2023) 6 f.

Eurostat, 'Share of fossil fuels in gross available energy' <https://ec.europa.eu/eurostat/databrowser/view/nrg_ind_ffgae/default/table?lang=en> accessed 8 June 2025

Gram-Hanssen K, 'Energy Consumption in Homes – An historical approach to understanding new routines' in **Rüdiger M** (ed), *The culture of Energy* (New Castle 2008)

Gram Mortensen B O, 'Fredskov – mere skov end fredning [Protected Forest – More Forest Than Protected]' in **Clausen N J/Kronborg A/Dietz Legind N/Gram Mortensen B O** (eds), Festskrift til Hans Viggo Godsk Pedersen (Liber Amicorum to Hans Viggo Godsk Pedersen, DJØF Publishing 2017) 389–408

Handelsministeriet [Ministry of Commerce], *Dansk Energipolitik 1976* [Danish Energy Policy 1976] (Copenhagen 1976)

Hvidtfelt Nielsen K, 'Danish Wind Power Policies from 1976 to 2000: A Survey of Policy Making and Techno-Economic Innovation' in **Lauber V** (ed): *Switching to Renewable Power: A Framework for the 21st* Century (London 2005)

Kjærgaard T, *Den danske Revolution 1500–1800. En økohistorisk tolkning The Danish Revolution [An ecohistorical interpretation]* (Gyldendal 1991)

Klima-, Energi- og Forsyningsministeriet [Danish Ministry of Climate, Energy and Utilities], political agreement of 22 May 2023, 'Mulighed for etablering af brintinfrastruktur' <https://www.kefm.dk/Media/638204311368810699/Aftaletekst%20-%20mulighed%20for%20etablering%20af%20brintinfrastruktur.pdf > accessed 17 June 2025

Klima-, Energi- og Forsyningsministeriet [Danish Ministry of Climate, Energy and Utilities], political agreement of 4 April 2024, 'Økonomiske rammevilkår for brintinfrastruktur' <https://www.kefm.dk/Media/638478420542283365/%C3%98konomiske%20rammevilk%C3%A5r%20for%20brintinfrastruktur%20-2.%20delaftale%20om%20r%C3%B8rbunden%20brintinfrastruktur_april%202024.pdf> accessed 8 June 2025

Klima-, Energi- og Forsyningsministeriet [Danish Ministry of Climate, Energy and Utilities], <https://www.kefm.dk/Media/637920977082432693/Klimaaftale%20om%20gr%C3%B8n%20str%C3%B8m%20og%20varme%202022.pdf> accessed 20 June 2025

Klima-, Energi- og Forsyningsministeriet [Danish Ministry of Climate, Energy and Utilities], 'Climate Action Plan' (October 2023) <https://kefm.dk/Media/638324394100598678/Udspil%20-%20Mere%20gr%C3%B8n%20energi%20fra%20sol%20og%20vind%20p%C3%A5%20land.pdf> accessed 8 June 2025

Klima-, Energi- og Forsyningsministeriet [Danish Ministry of Climate, Energy and Utilities], 'Aftale mellem regeringen (Socialdemokratiet), Venstre, Dansk Folkeparti, Radikale Venstre, Socialistisk Folkeparti og Det Konservative Folkeparti om fremtiden for olie- og gasindvinding iNordsøen af 3. december 2020' [Political agreement of 3 December 2020 on the future of oil and gas extraction in the North Sea] <https://kefm.dk/Media/0/3/Nords%C3%B8aftale%20(2).pdf> accessed 8 June 2025

Ministerial Council, Declaration of the 14th Trilateral Governmental Conference on the Protection of the Wadden Sea' *(2023)* <https://www.waddensea-worldheritage.org/sites/default/files/2023_Wilhelmshaven%20Declaration_signed.pdf> accessed 8 June 2025

Klima-, Energi- og Forsyningsministeriet [Danish Ministry of Climate, Energy and Utilities], 'Aftale om styrkede rammevilkår for CCS i Danmark. Klimahandling – Vejen til fuld fangst og lagring af CO_2 i 2030' [Agreement on Strengthened Framework Conditions for CCS in Denmark. Climate Action – The Path to Full Capture and Storage of CO_2 in 2030] <https://kefm.dk/Media/638307862071081909/Aftale%20om%20styrkede%20rammevilk%C3%A5r%20for%20CCS%20i%20Danmark%20af%2020.%20september%202023.pdf> accessed 8 June 2025

Regeringen [Danish Government], 'The Esbjerg Declaration' <https://www.regeringen.dk/aktuelt/tidligere-publikationer/the-esbjerg-declaration/> accessed 8 June 2025

Regeringen, 'The Marienborg Declaration' <https://www.regeringen.dk/aktuelt/tidligere-publikationer/the-marienborg-declaration/> accessed 8 June 2025

Rüdiger M/Åberg A, 'Energy in the Nordic World' (Aarhus Universitetsforlag. The Nordic World, 2024)

Solvarmedata, <https://solvarmedata.dk/>_accessed 8 June 2025

Statistics Denmark, 'Danmarks forbrug af biomasse til energi holder historisk højt niveau' <https://www.dst.dk/da/Statistik/nyheder-analyser-publ/bagtal/2023/2023-08-23-Danmarks-forbrug-af-biomasse> accessed 7 June 2025

Wistofte B/Hansen H M/Petersen F (eds), *Elektricitetens Aarhundrede* [The Century of Electricity] (vol. 1, Copenhagen 1991)

Wistofte B/ Thorndahl J/Petersen F (eds), *Elektricitetens Aarhundrede* [The Century of Electricity] (vol. 2, Copenhagen 1992)

General Perspectives on the Law of Energy Transition in Sweden

Melina Malafry

A. Introduction

Sweden and its Nordic neighbors are recognized as leaders in the energy transition required to counter the threat of climate change.[1] However, there is no specific law for the energy transition in Sweden. Rather, there are a number of circumstances which have led to the energy transition in Sweden. Despite being a relatively geographically large country, Sweden has a rather small population and is much less densely populated than other European countries. Its plentiful natural resources, historical events and various economic incentive systems (codified in laws) have also contributed to the energy transition in Sweden.

Despite this favorable status, Sweden still derives roughly 26 % of all energy from fossil energy. Most of this share is used in the transport sector, but several industries are also still reliant on fossil fuels in their production. Some large industries, such as steel (a historically and strategically important industry for Sweden), want to phase out fossil energy and replace it with green hydrogen, which will require a substantial expansion in fossil-free electricity generation.[2] The Swedish Energy Agency estimates that the electricity needed annually by 2050, in a high-electrification scenario, will be triple that of 2020's level.[3] In any scenario, the fossil-free electricity production must increase in Sweden. This chapter provides a background on the laws related to Sweden's energy transition in general and specifically

1 According to the latest International Energy Agency (IEA) country review, Sweden is a leader in the energy transition, see: IEA, 2019 Country Review Sweden, 'Sweden is a leader in the energy transition, according to latest IEA country review' <https://www.iea.org/news/sweden-is-a-leader-in-the-energy-transition-according-to-latest-iea-country-review> accessed 29 February 2024.

2 The hydrogen would be used instead of fossil fuels to heat up the steel, see: Swedish Environmental Protection Agency, 'Resultat i olika branscher 2022' <https://www.naturvardsverket.se/amnesomraden/klimatomstallningen/klimatklivet/resultat-i-olika-branscher-2022/gron-vatgas-for-fossilfri-varmning-av-stal/> accessed 29 February 2024.

3 The Swedish Energy Agency, *Scenarier över Sveriges energisystem 2023: Med fokus på elektrifieringen 2050* (2023) ER 2023:07, 9.

with regards the current obstacles in the expansion of renewable energy production in Sweden.

B. Energy Mix and Current Energy Goals in Sweden

Sweden's climate and energy goals are interlinked and closely aligned with the EU goals. The overall goal of zero net GHG emissions is to be reached by 2045. The overarching directive for Swedish energy policy is that it should be based on the same three pillars as energy cooperation in the EU. The energy policy aims to combine security of supply, competitiveness and ecological sustainability. It is stated on the government's homepage that:

> "the energy policy must thus create the conditions for efficient and sustainable energy use and a cost-effective Swedish energy supply with low negative impact on health, the environment and the climate, as well as facilitate the transition to an ecologically sustainable society."[4]

In addition to the goal of a fossil-free electricity system, there are additional energy efficiency goals. In 2030, Sweden must have 50 % more efficient energy use compared to 2005. It is also expressed that the transport sector has to reduce its greenhouse gases by 70 % by 2030 compared to the levels in 2010. However, even though Sweden has rather ambitious national political goals, the measures to reach those goals are not necessarily aligned.

In general, Sweden's energy mix has long been composed of largely renewable energy sources. At the turn of the century, a lot of hydropower was installed, and biomass has long been an important part of the energy mix and is, in fact, still increasing. In the past 40 years, the energy supplied by biomass has tripled.[5] In recent years biomass has accounted for about 30 % of the total energy supply (about 150 TWh).[6] Biomass is primarily

4 Swedish Government, 'Mål för energipolitiken' <https://www.regeringen.se/regeringens-politik/energi/mal-och-visioner-for-energi/> accessed 18 June 2025.

5 The Swedish Energy Agency, *Energy in Sweden 2022: with energy balance for years 1970–2020* (2022) ET 2023:1, 9.

6 The Swedish Energy Agency, 'Energy in Sweden Facts and Figures' (2025) <https://www.energimyndigheten.se/energisystem-och-analys/nulaget-i-energisystemet/energilaget//> accessed 18 juni 2025. Even though biomass is the largest source of energy in Sweden this Chapter is not focusing on that type of fossil-free energy but rater on other sources of renewable energy, primarily for electricity production as that is where the current energy transition will take place – through electrification.

used in district heating and by the industrial sector.[7] The transport sector is also increasingly incorporating biofuel into its fuel mix.[8]

Since the 1970s, the supply of fossil energy has decreased by more than half.[9] In 2023 fossil sources accounted for about 26 % (130 TWh) of the total energy supply in Sweden.[10]

Nuclear power increased between the 1970s and 90s and thereafter held steady until 2019, when a few of the reactors were taken out of operation.[11] In 2023 about 27 % of the total energy supplied was from nuclear fuel (136 TWh).[12]

Hydropower has been stable since the 1980s. In 2023 it accounted for about 13 % (66 TWh) of the total energy supply in Sweden.[13] Wind power has steadily increased since 2010. In 2023 the supply from wind power was 34 TWh (compared to 3 TWh in 2010).[14] In total it contributed to about 7 % of the total energy supply in 2023.

Biomass (30 %) is the largest source of energy in Sweden, followed by nuclear power (27 %), fossil fuels (26 %), hydropower (13 %), and wind power (7 %). The rest comes from a variety of sources, including a small portion from solar (3 TWh).[15] However, about 30 TWh of electricity has been exported in recent years,[16] so the percentages do not add up. Even though the supply of energy was 507 TWh (including 29 TWh export of electricity), the total energy use in Sweden was 353 TWh in 2023. The difference in energy is transformation losses, etc.[17] In 2023, the residential and service sector used 140 TWh, industry 136 TWh and the transport sector 78 TWh.[18]

The transport sector still uses fossil fuels in Sweden to a large extent. Also, industry uses fossil fuels in its production, but not as intensively as in transport. The housing and service sector only account for about 6 %

---

7 The Swedish Energy Agency (n 5), 9.
8 In 2020 the transport sector used about 17 TWh (compared to one TWh in year 2000), see: ibid 9.
9 ibid 8.
10 The Swedish Energy Agency (n 6), 9.
11 The Swedish Energy Agency (n 5), 9.
12 The Swedish Energy Agency (n 6).
13 ibid.
14 ibid.
15 ibid.
16 ibid.
17 ibid.
18 ibid.

of the energy (9 TWh) deriving from fossil energy. However, the transport sector is still heavily reliant on fossil fuels, with 69 % (54 TWh). Industry accounts for about 17 % (23 TWh) of energy deriving from fossil fuels.[19] The national goal of reducing carbon emissions in the transport sector by 70 % by 2030 therefore seems an efficient way of reducing carbon emissions in Sweden.

C. Historical and Political Background

Sweden began building out its electricity system during a period of industrialization. When industry demand for electricity rose, the Swedish Government responded by changing the water law in order to enable a fast expansion of hydropower.[20] The 1918 Water Law was adopted and was valid until 1983. However, due to nature protection laws, the development of hydro in Sweden essentially ceased in 1970. At this point Sweden had exploited most of its rivers. Now, a few rivers are protected as "national interests" in Chapter 4 of the Environmental Code and, as a result, hydropower cannot be developed in those rivers.[21]

Earlier hydropower traces back to medieval times, used to run mills. At that time, environmental laws were in place, ensuring that one-third of the river must be free-flowing and that fish connectivity must be ensured.[22] However later, when hydropower was introduced at large scale in Sweden, there were no environmental requirements and permits for the installation had no expiration, and many of those permits remain valid today.[23] Today the hydropower in Sweden is facing a different reality including a strict provision on water quality deriving from the EU Water Framework Directive.[24]

19 ibid.

20 See Evert Vedung/Magnus Brandel, *Vattenkraften, staten och de politiska partierna* (2001) 43.

21 Nationalälvarna are considered of national interest according to Chapter 4 of the Environmental code.

22 See The law for mills (1228).

23 For a historical overview of the hydropower development and its permit regime, see Jan Darpö, 'Tradition och förnyelse på vattenrättens område. Om mötet mellan gamla tillståndsregimer och moderna miljökrav' (2014) 214:2 Nordic Environmental Law Journal 101, 102; See Chapter 4, section 6 of the Environmental Code.

24 See Directive 2000/60/EC of the European Parliament and of The Council of 23 October 2000 establishing a framework for Community action in the field of water policy [2000] OJ L 327/1 (hereafter referred to as Water Framework Directive).

Another important event that fueled the energy transition in Sweden was the oil crisis in 1970s. Prior to the oil crisis, it was common that oil was used to heat up houses among other things. 80 % of Sweden's energy supply was from oil in the 1970s.[25] However, the oil crisis resulted in a move away from oil towards district heating in communities and cities,[26] electric heating, installations of heat pumps and burning of biomass instead of oil. Sweden also introduced its nuclear power and continued its expansion of hydropower. Thus, electricity became a cheap option to heat houses in the following years. As a result, Sweden's greenhouse gas emissions from home heating have decreased by 92 percent from 1990 to 2023 according to the Swedish Environmental Protection Agency.[27] However, the green house gas (GHG) emissions, in general, have increased between 2023 and 2024 in Sweden with 5,8 %, from 44,4 million ton to 51, 5 million ton according to the official statistics.[28]

In summary, Sweden's relatively fossil-free energy system is due to its naturally watercourse-rich environment, suitable for hydropower; the introduction of nuclear power; and a natural shift away from oil after the crisis. The increase in solar and wind has come only in recent years.

D. *Laws Enabling the Transition from Fossil Fuels*

There is no law that specifically focuses on the energy transition, but Sweden does have a Climate Law. Specifically, the Swedish Climate Act (2017:720) regulates the government's climate policy work. For example, Section 3 of the Climate Act states that the government's climate policy must be based on the long-term timed emissions target established by the Riksdag (Sweden's national legislative body). According to the aforemen-

25 The Swedish Government, 'Regeringens klimathandlingsplan – hela vägen till netto-noll' (2023) Skr. 2023/24:59, 21.

26 See the Swedish Energy Agency (n 5), 28 for more specific numbers on district heating. Today the use is between 54 and 60 TWh compared to about 10 TWh in 1970.

27 The Swedish Environmental Protection Agency, 'Sveriges utsläpp och upptag av växthusgaser', see: <https://www.naturvardsverket.se/data-och-statistik/klimat/sveriges-utslapp-och-upptag-av-vaxthusgaser/> accessed 18 juni 2025.

28 Statistikmyndigheten, 'Utsläppen av växthusgaser från Sveriges ekonomi ökade 2024', see: <https://www.scb.se/hitta-statistik/statistik-efter-amne/miljo/miljoekonomi-och-hallbar-utveckling/miljorakenskaper/pong/statistiknyhet/utslapp-till-luft-4e-kvartalet-2024/> accessed 18 juni 2025.

tioned paragraph, the work must also be conducted in a way that provides for the conditions for climate policy and budget policy goals to cooperate with each other. In addition, according to Section 4 of the Climate Act, the government must present a climate report to the Riksdag in the budget bill every year. In the year following ordinary parliamentary elections, the government must, according to Section 5 of the Climate Act, present a climate policy action plan. In each action plan, the government presents its policy to achieve the climate goals during the current term of office. The climate policy action plan was most recently presented by our current government on December 21st 2023.[29] In the plan, electrification was one of the core areas identified as important to reduce emissions.[30] Also, the permit processes for energy infrastructure have been identified by the government to be too complex and long,[31] a notion which has also been suggested multiple times by industry and has been the topic of state commissions.[32] However, the existence of long and complicated permit procedures has been disputed by some academics in Sweden,[33] which now is also supported by official statistics.[34]

This electrification would take place in both the transport sector[35] and the industrial sector, and create significant demand for more fossil-free electricity.[36] In the plan, an increase in nuclear power is emphasized as essential for a robust electricity system, due to it being a more stable source of electricity than solar and wind. However, an increase in all sources is still essential, according to the plan.

In 1991, Sweden became one of the first countries to introduce a carbon tax. The primary intention of a carbon tax is to change behavior, by reducing the incentive to use fossil fuels. Currently, as of 2025, the carbon

29 ibid.

30 ibid 13, 85.

31 ibid 74.

32 See for example SOU 2022:33, *Om prövning och omprövning- en del av den gröna omställningen*, (2022). there is also a ongoing state comission on the topic as well, Sveriges Riksdag, *Miljötillståndsutredningen*, Dir. 2023:78 (KN 2023:2) that published an interim report in 2025, see SOU 2024:98, *En ny samordnad miljöbedömnings- och tillståndsprövningsprocess*.

33 See Jonas Ebbesson/Jan Darpö, 'Professorer: Lobbyister och företag sprider myter om svensk miljölagstiftning' <https://www.altinget.se/artikel/professorer-lobbyister-och-foretag-sprider-myter-om-svensk-miljolagstiftning> accessed 29 February 2024.

34 See for example SOU 2024:98 (n 32), 657.

35 Swedish Government (n 25) 141.

36 ibid 14.

tax is 1510 SEK/tonne carbon.[37] However, in order to not double regulate companies that are also part of the EU Emission Trading System (EU ETS), their carbon tax is reduced. In Sweden there are about 800 facilities included in the EU ETS.[38]

In order to reduce the GHG emissions from the fuels used for transport, Sweden adopted a law to require that biofuels are mixed with fossil fuel.[39] Among other things, the idea was that this steering tool would contribute to reaching the national goal of a 70 % reduction in greenhouse gas emissions from domestic transport by 2030. From January 2022, the reduction requirement was 7.8 % for petrol and 30.5 % for diesel. In 2023 the reduction requirement for jet kerosene was 2.6 %. However, due to a recent political shift, the reduction requirements were contested. From January 2024 the reduction requirement for petrol and diesel was reduced to 6 % and by 2027 the plan was that the system would cease to exist.[40] However, from July 2025 reduction requirement is increased to 10 % for both diesel and petrol and the system will continue to exist for the foreseeable future.[41] Some scholars argue that the system is not an efficient way of cutting GHGs.[42] The EU *reduction requirement* is instead, after the implementation of RED III in 2023,[43] to be met through electricity sold from public

37 Swedish Government, see: <https://www.government.se/government-policy/taxes-and-tariffs/swedens-carbon-tax/> accessed 18 June 2025.

38 The Swedish Energy Agency, see: <https://www.energimyndigheten.se/en/sustainability/emissions-trading/Participating-in-EU-ETS/the-union-registry/compliance/> accessed 18 June 2025.

39 Lag (2017:1201) om reduktion av växthusgaser från visa fossila drivmedel.

40 See more: Swedish Energy Agency, 'Reduktionsplikt' <https://www.energimyndigheten.se/fornybart/hallbarhetskriterier/reduktionsplikt/> accessed 29 February 2024.

41 See recent changes in Law (2017:1201) on the reduction of greenhouse gas emissions from petrol and diesel.

42 See for example: Pierre Kjellin, 'Forskare sågar reformen med höjd reduktionsplikt för bensin och diesel' <https://transportnytt.se/forskare-sagar-reformen-med-hojd-reduktionsplikt-for-bensin-och-diesel/> accessed 29 February 2024. However, Riksrevisionen consider it an efficient instrument, see: Swedish Government, 'Riksrevisionens rapport om reduktionsplikten för bensin och diesel' <https://www.regeringen.se/contentassets/227afea1d2a24478b15c5323784e3eba/riksrevisionens-rapport-om-reduktionsplikten-for-bensin-och-diesel-skr.-20232444.pdf> accessed 29 February 2024.

43 Directive 2018/2001/EU on the promotion of the use of energy from renewable sources, 2018/2001 of the European Parliament and of the Council of 11 December 2018 on the promotion of the use of energy from renewable sources [2018] OJ L 328/82 as amended by Directive (EU) 2023/2413 of the European Parliament and of the Council of 18 October 2023 amending Directive (EU) 2018/2001, Regulation

charging stations, as fuel companies receive a direct incentive to support electrification, e.g. through an expansion of public charging stations.[44]

Sweden also has an energy tax on fuels and electricity. Currently, for electricity, it is 43,9 öre per kWh (not including VAT).[45] This tax's purpose is not primarily to change people's behavior, although adding tax to people's energy consumption surely has such an effect. One feature of the tax code is that small-scale producers of renewable energy are exempted from paying energy tax on the excess electricity that is distributed and sold. When it comes to solar, which is the most common type of energy produced at a small scale, the installation can have a maximum power of 500 kW.[46] Hence, small-scale renewable energy production is indirectly subsidized.

In addition, and specifically focusing on the introduction of renewable energy, *the electricity certificate system* has incentivized a transition towards more renewable electricity in Sweden.[47] An electricity certificate is basically a confirmation issued by the state that one megawatt hour (MWh) of electricity has been generated from renewable sources in accordance with the Electricity Certificate Act.[48] An individual producer of renewable energy can receive certificates for 15 years.[49] In addition, electricity suppliers are required to purchase electricity certificates corresponding to a certain proportion of the electricity that they sell, known as their quota obligation.[50] Electricity certificates are therefore traded on the Swedish and Norwegian markets to fulfil those quotas. The price is later added to the consumer's electricity bill. This incentive system implies that the renewable electricity producers are receiving an extra income by selling the certificates, in addition to the electricity price.

The electricity certificate system was introduced in 2003. Since 2012, the electricity certificate market has been common between Norway and Sweden, with a joint goal of increasing the renewable electricity production

(EU) 2018/1999 and Directive 98/70/EC as regards the promotion of energy from renewable sources, and repealing Council Directive (EU) 2015/652 [2023] OJ L 2023/2413 (hereafter referred to as RED III).

44 Swedish Government (n 25) 66 f.

45 See law (1994:1776) on energy taxes on fuel and electricity, Chapter 11, section 3.

46 ibid, Chapter 11, Section 2, Second paragraph, 2.

47 See the Swedish Energy Agency, 'The Swedish–Norwegian Electricity Certificate Market, ANNUAL REPORT 2020' (2020).

48 Electricity Certificate Act (Lag (2011:1200) om elcertifikat).

49 See the Swedish Energy Agency (n 5).

50 ibid 7.

by 28.4 TWh before 2020. This was already achieved in May 2019.[51] The Swedish parliament decided in 2017 to increase the target for 2030 by another 18 TWh. However, that was reached in March 2021. In 2022, there were no longer any new plants that could be eligible for certificates and the system is currently being phased out.

In order to move towards a green transition at the household level there is a "green" tax reduction for installations of solar cells and electric chargers since 2021.[52] However, the installation of solar cells has been subsidized since 2009.[53] Since 2023, households were temporarily eligible for government support to renovate their homes to be more energy efficient, for example, insulation and investment in heat pumps.[54] The policy gave some subsidies for the material cost of insulating your house or the material investment cost of buying a heat pump, etc. Up to 30,000 SEK could have been granted (50 % of material cost). A general subsidy for households wanting to renovate their current homes is also available, but an energy efficiency motive is not necessary for the subsidy. A private person can use up to 50,000 SEK deductions per year (30 % of the labor cost).

Hence, there are a number of laws governing various incentive systems, both towards industry (mainly carbon tax) and household level subsidies. However, there is no longer any incentive system in place for new large-scale renewable energy production.

E. Renewables in the Electricity System – Political Goals and Predictions

The increase of renewable energy has been a common goal for Swedish politicians. However, the goal of 100 % renewable electricity by 2040 has been adjusted to 100 % fossil-free electricity by 2040, as a concession to including nuclear power in the mix.[55]

---

51 ibid 5.

52 See Ordinance on tax reduction for green technology: Förordning (2020:1080) om förfarandet vid skattereduktion för installation av grön teknik.

53 See Ordinance on state support for solar cells: Förordning (2009:689) om statligt stöd till solceller.

54 See Ordinance on grants for energy efficiency in single-family homes: Förordning (2023:402) om bidrag för energieffektivisering i småhus. However, the subsidy ceased to exists in June 2025.

55 See Swedish Government (n 4).

The push for more fossil-free electricity is essential as electricity production has to increase to meet the future demand from the industry and transport sectors. As it stands today, Sweden is a net exporter of electricity. In recent years, Sweden has exported about 30 % of the electricity it produced.[56] However, in an increasingly electrified future, the fossil-free production of electricity has to increase, along with accompanying infrastructure for storage and reliable sources for baseline power to balance the grid (e.g. pump storage (hydro) and nuclear).

In the scenarios from the Swedish Energy Agency about 97–187 TWh will be needed annually for industry in 2050 in a high-electrification scenario.[57] In the industrial sector it is mainly the production of hydrogen that contributes to the increase in electricity. The idea is that hydrogen should be used in industrial processes, such as steel manufacturing, in order to move away from traditionally fossil fuel-intensive activities.[58] The electricity needed for production of hydrogen is estimated to be about 22–100 TWh in 2050. Fossil fuel use by the industrial sector is expected to decrease 58–70 % by 2050. Common among all the electrification scenarios, is that the use of fossil fuels will decrease by 70–77 % from 2020–2050.[59]

In the transport sector, the total energy consumption will decrease mainly as the car fleet is estimated to be totally electrified by 2050. By 2050, it is estimated that the transport industry will only require around 50 TWh, a reduction of 29 TWh from today's level.[60] However, such a transformation requires significant expansion of charging infrastructure and availability of rare materials for batteries, among other things.[61]

The housing and service sector is predominately fossil-free and the focus there is on energy efficiency measures, like changing from inefficient electric heating to heat pumps, etc. The total demand is expected to slightly increase due to data centers and increased electrified work machines.[62]

56 The Swedish Energy Agency (n 6). In 2024 the export was record high with 33,4 Twh, see:<https://www.svk.se/om-kraftsystemet/kraftsystemdata/elstatistik/> accessed 18 June 2025.
57 The Swedish Energy Agency (n 3).
58 RISE Research Institutes of Sweden, *Prestudy H2ESIN: Hydrogen, energy system and infrastructure in Northern Scandinavia and Finland* (2022) 3.
59 The Swedish Energy Agency (n 3) 12.
60 ibid 13.
61 ibid.
62 ibid.

In 2022, the new government changed the landscape for incentives in the Swedish market and important subsidies for offshore wind power were withdrawn, as well as bonuses for buying electric cars. Previously, the grid connection fee had been waived for offshore wind power, in order to promote the development of this renewable, but this implicit subsidy is no longer in place. The share of electric cars has grown, from 18 % of the newly registered cars in 2021 to 32 % in 2022[63] and 38 % in 2023,[64] indicating that since the withdrawn bonus (in November 2022), the uptake of electric vehicles has slowed. In September 2024, newly registered electric vehicles had decreased by 8 % compared to 2023. However, newly registered electric busses and electric trucks had increased in Sweden.[65]

Due to Sweden's relatively clean electricity production, politicians are pushing towards pursuing a broad electrification of society as a path towards achieving their climate goals. Hence, the future will require more electricity. It is too early to say if these changes can be accomplished without the subsidization of new renewable energy production in Sweden.[66]

In addition, there has been some backlash related to the availability of rare materials needed for all the batteries required by this transition towards electrification.[67] According to the EU Regulation on Critical Raw

63 Statistikmyndigheten, 'Tredubbling av elbilar på två år' <https://www.scb.se/hitta-statistik/redaktionellt/tredubbling-av-elbilar-pa-tva-ar2/#:~:text=Man%20skulle%20kunna%20s%C3%A4ga%20att,bilar%20%E2%80%93%20en%20f%C3%B6rdubbling%20sedan%202020> accessed 29 February 2024.

64 Trafikanalys, 'Samma nivå för nyregistrerade personbilar 2023 som året innan' <https://www.mynewsdesk.com/se/trafikanalys/pressreleases/samma-nivaa-foer-nyregistrerade-personbilar-2023-som-aaret-innan-3295203?utm_source=rss&utm_medium=rss&utm_campaign=Alert&utm_content=pressrelease> accessed 29 February 2024.

65 Trafikanalys, 'Elektrifierade fordon i Sverige – en analys av laddbara fordon över tid och geografi', Rapport: 2024:10, 14–15, see:<https://www.trafa.se/globalassets/rapporter/2024/rapport-2024-10-elektrifierade-fordon-i-sverige---en-analys-av-laddbara-fordon-over-tid-och-geografi.pdf> accessed 18 June 2025.

66 The Swedish Government, 'Budgetsatsningar inom energiområdet för att säkra tillväxt och grön omställning ' <https://www.regeringen.se/artiklar/2023/10/budgetsatsningar-inom-energiomradet-for-att-sakra-tillvaxt-och-gron-omstallning/> accessed 29 February 2024.

67 See Anahita Jannesar Niri/Gregory A. Poelzer/Steven E. Zhang/Jan Rosenkranz/Maria Pettersson/Yousef Ghorbani, 'Sustainability challenges throughout the electric vehicle battery value chain' (2024) 191 Renewable and Sustainable Energy Reviews, 114176.

Materials (CRM),[68] 10 % of our consumption of these materials should be sourced in the EU by 2030. It seems like a small contribution, but an electrification of the EU will require a significant scaling up. Rare materials have been found in northern Sweden, but the Sami people operate reindeer herding land in the same areas. The Sami are the aboriginal people in Sweden, meaning the conflict is not only of *national interest* but also a question about a possible violation of human rights. Nevertheless, importing these materials from China, Russia and Africa also has a negative social dimension.[69] The ability to recycle batteries and reuse the raw materials are therefore becoming crucial in enabling this transition.

F. The Administrative Structure in Sweden Relevant for Renewable Energy Activities

1. Municipal Planning Monopoly in Sweden

Another important aspect of the Swedish system is that the municipalities have a lot of power. The constitution expressly states that municipalities have a *planning monopoly*[70] and right of self-determination. There are a number of different municipal plans.[71] With regards to energy-related activities (for example wind power) these developments often take place in overview plans, which are not legally binding plans.[72]

This means that municipalities are self-governed to a large extent, although there is legislation in place, adopted at the national level, which the municipalities have to follow. Income taxes are primarily municipal-level

68 Regulation (EU) 2024/1252 of the European Parliament and of the Council of 11 April 2024 establishing a framework for ensuring a secure and sustainable supply of critical raw materials and amending Regulations (EU) No 168/2013, (EU) 2018/858, (EU) 2018/1724 and (EU) 2019/1020 (Critical Raw Materials Act).

69 See for example: Reuters, 'DR Congo presses Apple over minerals supply chain, lawyers say' <https://www.reuters.com/markets/commodities/dr-congo-presses-apple-over-minerals-supply-chain-lawyers-say-2024-04-25/> accessed 29 July 2024.

70 However, the planning process includes public participation and the County Administrative Board can intervene and reassess certain plans (detailed plans), or inform the municipality that the national interests are not accounted for in its audit opinion,, see Chapter 11, Section 10 and 11 and Chapter 3, Section 16 of the Swedish Planning and Building Act.

71 For a general description of the various plans, see Gabriel Michanek/Charlotta Zetterberg, *Den Svenska miljörätten* (2021) 527.

72 See Chapter 3, Section 3 of the Planning and Building Act.

taxes. However, the national goals associated with the climate or energy transition are not transposed as requirements for municipalities. The system lacks vertical integration. If any of the 290 municipalities do not work towards a sustainable energy transition in their activities and planning, there is no punishment. There are some municipalities that take climate change seriously and want to contribute to the energy transition, but it is not a formal requirement that can be enforced today.

As mentioned above, there is no obligatory planning for onshore wind power, but some municipalities have planned for wind power in their overview plans. In the marine environment, wind power development is planned in Marine Spatial Plans.[73] These plans are currently under consultation and are to be revised to include more wind power capacity in the sea.[74] However, none of the plans that include wind power are legally binding and the areas identified are not necessarily suitable locations from an environmental point of view. Thus, they do not sufficiently guide developers to find suitable locations for wind power today.

There are no *national plans* for renewable energy development, but there is some guidance from the state level through the instrument of "national interests". These interests represent protection both for general types of land and water areas, and specific geographic areas that are of national interest.[75] In Chapter 4 of the Environmental Code the national parliament has specified which areas of Sweden are considered to be of national interest while Chapter 3 of the Environmental Code describes a number of interests that shall be protected "as far as possible". Higher protection is only granted when considered to be of national interest.[76] Energy production, reindeer husbandry and nature protection are some examples of specific interests mentioned under Chapter 3 of the Environmental Code. Some geographical areas often host more than one of these

73 For more info on the Swedish Marine Spatial Plans, see: Swedish Agency for Marine and Water Management, 'Marine Spatial Planning' <https://www.havochvatten.se/en/eu-and-international/marine-spatial-planning.html> accessed 18 June 2025.

74 Swedish Agency for Marine and Water Management, see proposal for new plans: <https://www.havochvatten.se/planering-forvaltning-och-samverkan/havsplanering/forslag-till-andrade-havsplaner-2025.html>accessed 18 June 2025.

75 See the Environmental Code, Chapter 3 regarding general provisions and Chapter 4 regarding specific geographical areas.

76 In practice the various national interests are pointed out by the relevant state authority. However, such an identified area of interest is not legally binding. It is the Court that, in each individual case, assesses whether the interest is of national interest. See Michanek/Zetterberg (n 71) 159 f.

types of interest. These interests can function simultaneously, but in some cases, they are considered to be in conflict with one another. Conflicts between these interests are, in fact, common.[77] If the interests cannot be ensured simultaneous protection, the interest that better promotes good management from the point of view of public interest shall be prioritized.[78] The conflict should also be assessed in light of the main purpose of the Environmental Code: to promote sustainable development.[79]

When a site is considered to be of national interest, it is not totally protected. It is only *significant damage and detriment* that can be guarded against. There is, however, no clear definition of what this means. In the preparatory works, it is mentioned that protection does not cover "trivial" impact and that the measure must have a consistent negative impact, or a temporary very large impact, on the interest.[80] Hence, the instrument of national interests do not have a significant impact on how land use is prioritized in general as it only becomes legally relevant in the specific permit process and does not necessarily guide developers to find suitable locations for energy production today.

These national interests should be accommodated in the municipal plans. However, there is no priority between these interests in the plans, and if conflicts exist, they are handled at the permit stage in the individual assessment. If wind power is planned in an overview plan, the plan can later influence the permit authorities when deciding whether a specific wind power park is placed in a suitable location in accordance with the Environmental Code, even though the plan is not formally legally binding.[81] Thus, it is not until the permit stage – when wind power developers have chosen a location – that the location will be fully assessed. However, even if the location is suitable from an environmental point of view, the

77 The national interests are appointed by separate interest groups, for example; Sametinget points out the areas that are of importance for reindeer husbandry and the Swedish Energy Agency points out areas that are of importance for energy production.

78 Chapter 3, Section 1 of the Environmental Code.

79 ibid Chapter 1.

80 See Swedish government, Prop. 1997/98:45, part II, 30. 591; See Swedish government, Prop. 1985/86:3, 172. The meaning of "significant damage" was also discussed in the Vedabron Case where the Government suggested that while the installation would indeed seriously affect parts of the area, the overall assessment indicated that the area as a whole would not be significantly damaged by the development, see RÅ 1993 not 550.

81 For example, see MÖD 2005:66; MÖD 2007:47; and MÖD 2009:4.

municipality can hinder any wind power development due to its veto right under Chapter 16, Section 4 of the Environmental Code.

There are also specific municipal energy plans, first adopted in the 1970s, which are plans addressing how the municipality shall promote energy conservation and strive towards a secure and sufficient energy supply.[82] These energy plans shall – in addition to providing information on supply, distribution and use of energy in the municipality -also include an analysis of the impact the proposed activity has on the environment, health and the conservation of land and water and other resources.[83] These plans have not yet shown to be of any significant importance towards implementing energy political goals, but in a new state commission, it has been proposed that these plans shall be used to a greater extent for such purpose.[84]

In order to better steer towards national goals a more holistic planning approach has been identified as a possible solution for enabling sustainable use of our land and water areas.[85] Today there is the possibility to adopt regional plans, even though they would not be legally binding. Such plans have the potential to span municipal borders and introduce a more comprehensive approach to energy system planning, but are not currently used as such an instrument.[86]

In summary, there are plans that have the potential to influence the development of the energy system, but these plans are not legally binding. Another aspect of the plans is that they do not have a larger geographical perspective, which is needed in order to be efficient from an energy and environmental perspective. However, these types of plans are currently lacking in Sweden.

---

82 Section 1 of Lag (1977:439) om kommunal energiplanering.

83 ibid Section 3.

84 SOU 2023:18, *Värdet av vinden: Kompensation, incitament och planering för en hållbar fortsatt utbyggnad av vindkraften*, 98.

85 See Maria Pettersson, *Renewable Energy development and the Functioning of Law – A Comparative Study of Legal Rules Related to the Planning, Installation and Operation of Windmills* (Doctoral thesis, Luleå University of Technology 2008); Anna Christiernsson, *Rättens förhållande till komplexa och dynamiska ecosystem* (Doctoral thesis, Luleå University of Technology 2011); Melina Malafry, *Biodiversity Protection in an Aspiring Carbon Neutral Society, the relationship between biodiversity and renewable energy in a European Union context* (Doctoral thesis, Uppsala University 2016).

86 See Chapter 7 of the Planning and Building Act.

2. Legal framework in the energy transition and the land and environmental courts

The Environmental Code is the central legislation in Sweden when it comes to the expansion of renewable energy. Thus, wind power and hydropower, for example, require a permit under the Environmental Code (including reassessment of old permits). Large-scale solar parks do not require a permit under the Environmental Code but is considered such measure that will "significantly change the natural environment" and therefore need to undergo certain consultation, where the requirements under the Environmental Code are applied.[87] Since the main aim of the Environmental Code is to enable a *sustainable development*[88], this implies that Sweden's energy transition has to be a sustainable one.

Even if the permit procedure is undertaken under different legislation, the Environmental Code is still relevant due to its very wide scope of application. In addition, many other pieces of legislation refer to some of the basic rules stated under the Environmental Code. This is the case, for example, if an offshore wind park is located in Sweden's exclusive economic zone,[89] when a concession is needed for grid infrastructure,[90] or when a building permit is required for the installation of solar cells on a roof.[91]

Energy activities – like all other activities and measures – have to be in line with the general rules of consideration presented in Chapter 2 of the Environmental Code, independent of whether or not a permit is required for the activity.[92] The operator of the activity is the one who must show that these rules are fulfilled[93] and is required to acquire the information needed to mitigate any environmental impacts from the activity.[94] The precautionary principle, including the requirement to use the "best available technology", is codified in this chapter.[95] The most discussed provision in relation to wind power installations is Section 6. It stipulates that a *suitable site* should be chosen that makes it possible to achieve the purpose

87 See Chapter 12, Section 6 of the Swedish Environmental Code.
88 ibid Chapter 1, Section 1.
89 See Lag (1992:1140) om Sveriges ekonomiska zon, Section 6.
90 See Ellagen (1997:857) Chapter 2, Section 17. In addition, a hearing under 12:6 of the Environmental Code is needed.
91 See Planning and Building Act (2010:900), Chapter 2, Section 2 and 10.
92 See Michanek/Zetterberg (n 65) 106.
93 Chapter 2, Section 1 of the Environmental Code.
94 ibid Section 2.
95 ibid Section 3.

of the activity with a minimum of damage or detriment to human health and the environment. This provision is often applied in conjunction with Section 3. For example, if no mitigation measures are possible to avoid impact on a protected species, then the location may not be seen as suitable. If the applicant has not shown that it is the most suitable location, the Court or authority assessing the activity can deny the applicant's permit. The limitation to this requirement can be found in Chapter 2, Section 7 which states that the application of the consideration rules still need to be *reasonable*:

"The rules of consideration laid down in Sections 2 to 5 and Section 6's first paragraph shall be applicable where compliance cannot be deemed unreasonable. Particular importance shall be attached in this regard to the benefits of protective measures and other precautions in relation to their cost."

Thus, the general rules of consideration are preventive in nature, and indicate that responsibility resides with the developer to gather the sufficient knowledge of the potential environmental impact from its activity and to prove that the activity aligns with the consideration rules. These rules are often the basis for decisions by the relevant authority or courts when assessing permit decisions for activities, but they are also used when the authorities undertake supervision of activities. Since Sweden is a rather large country geographically, in cases where conflicts exist, such as with species protection, it is often ruled by the court that the developer has not shown that it is the most suitable location in accordance with Section 6.

The provision in the chapter ensures that the most suitable location is chosen for the activity and that the "best available technology" is used. It is based on this chapter that most permit conditions are formulated. This is true especially for ones that limit the impact on the environment during the construction, operation and dismantling of the installation.

With the exception of offshore wind power in the exclusive economic zone (which requires a government decision), most permits/concessions, etc. are appealed to the land and environmental courts in Sweden and either start at one of the 21 county administrative boards or at one of the five land and environmental courts in Sweden. The decisions from the county administrative boards are appealed to the land and environmental courts and finally the Land and Environmental Court of Appeal. If decisions start at the land and environmental court the final stage is the Supreme Court in Sweden. Some decisions start at the municipal level (for example building permits). Those decisions are appealed to the county administrative boards and can, in some cases, be appealed all the way to the Supreme Court.[96]

G. Conflicts in Electrification and the Expansion of Renewable Energy

1. Introduction

There are sustainability conflicts that may be an issue when deciding where to locate the renewable energy production. Even if a suitable location, from an environmental point of view, is chosen, wind power development can still be hindered by the municipal veto or the lack of grid infrastructure. But even though these hindrances exist, the increase in renewable energy production is still advancing steadily. This suggests that these potential conflicts may not ultimately be such a significant issue, and that there are still places where the conflicts do not arise, or can be mitigated. However, as renewable energy continues to expand and available land diminishes, these conflicts may become more apparent. This is especially the case since electrification, including expansion of renewable energy, cannot come at the expense of preserving important habitats and species or other values that are crucial to ensuring a *sustainable* energy transition.

2. Wind Power Development

(a) The Permit Procedure of Wind Power – General Conflicts Over Land and Water Areas

Wind power is steadily growing in Sweden, and has grown especially quickly for the past few years. In 2024, it produced 41 TWh and it was almost at the same level as nuclear (49 Twh) in Sweden.[97] In 2026, the Swedish Energy Agency estimates that the production will be 52 TWh (based on the current permitted installations from 2013–2017).[98]

---

96 That is the case when the Land and Environmental Court of Appeal makes it possible to appeal its decision (for example if case is of a prejudicial nature, see Chapter 5, Section 5, lag (2010:921) om Mark- och miljödomstolar.

97 Energiföretagen, see: <https://www.energiforetagen.se/49761b/globalassets/energiforetagen/statistik/energiaret/2024/energiaret_2024_250415.pdf >accessed 18 June 2025.

98 Swedish Government (n 25), 88.

In Sweden, the development of wind power requires a permit under the Environmental Code if the installation is sufficiently large,[99] as wind power is considered an "environmentally hazardous activity" based on the environmental effects it has, such as noise pollution.[100]

Depending on how far offshore the wind power installation is to be located, different permit regimes are applicable.[101] If the installation is located in the territorial sea, the municipal planning and veto is applicable and a permit is required under the Environmental Code. The application is sent to the Land and Environmental Court at the first instance due to its location offshore, and thus its status as a water activity[102] in addition to being an environmentally hazardous activity.

However, if the installation is within the economic zone, a permit is required by the government by the Law (1992:1140) on Sweden's exclusive economic zone.[103] But as mentioned before, the basic rules in the Swedish Environmental Code is applicable, hence the legal assessment is similar. For example, in *Stora Middlegrund*, the Government did not grant a permit because the location was not suitable from an environmental point of view.[104]

During a permit procedure for wind power, the rules of consideration in Chapter 2 of the Environmental Code are applied.[105] As the environmental impact from wind power is rather dependent on the wind farm's *location*, it is crucial that the developer chooses a location that is suitable from an environmental point of view.[106] And if in close proximity to people or vulnerable species, the permit is accompanied with suitable requirements – permit conditions – on measures to limit its impact. Permits commonly

99 The Miljöprövningsförordningen (2013:251)), Chapter 21, Sections 13–15.

100 Chapter 9 § 1, p. 3 of the Swedish Environmental Code.

101 For more information on the legal preconditions for offshore wind power in Sweden, see Melina Malafry/Marcus Öhman, *Rättsliga förutsättningar för havsbaserad vindkraft* (Vindval Report 7028 2022).

102 See Chapter 11 of the Environmental Code.

103 Lag (1992:1140) om Sveriges ekonomiska zon, Section 5.

104 The location was offshore in the exclusive economic zone. The location was also within a Natura 2000 site. See the government's decision on the 27 July 2023, KN2023/01037. A Natura 2000 permit was also denied as the County Administrative Board considered that there were still alternative locations, hence the derogation rules were not applicable, see decision of the County Administrative Board in Halland on the 13 March 2023 (3406–2021).

105 See below Section 6.2.

106 See Chapter 2, Section 6 of the Environmental Code.

place time limits on the construction phase for offshore wind power due to harbor porpoises and mating periods for fish,[107] and on the operating phase due to bats. A specific example of this would be that wind power turbines must be in "bat mode" during the summer period (15 July-30 September).[108] After the EU Court decision on "Skydda skogen",[109] where the EU Court emphasized that listed species are protected independent of their conservation status, "bat mode" has still been considered to be a sufficient mitigation measure to avoid impact on the listed bat species in case law.[110] The effect on birds is more difficult to mitigate, and it is common that the location has to be changed if it would have too severe an impact on certain species.[111]

Even though Sweden has a low population density, the Swedish Nature Protection Agency estimates that 98 % of its land area has existing interests present as well.[112] Despite these potential hindrances to development, according to Darpö, only about 9 % of the applications for wind farms, between 2014–2018, were prevented due to species protection.[113] This indicates that species protection may not be a large obstacle in Sweden yet.

The military's national interest covers about 30 % of the land area while the core areas used for reindeer herding encompass about 18 %.[114] When a conflict arises with the national interest of energy production, as illustrated by the development of wind power, it is not always one interest that trumps the other. In MÖD 2010:38 the Environmental Court of Appeal found that the interest in establishing a wind farm could be reconciled with the inter-

107 See for example judgment by the Land and environmental Court of Appeals on the 8 December 2015 in case number M 6960–14.

108 Bat mode implies that the rotor blades of the wind turbines are stationary. This must be carried out when the wind at hub height is less than 6 m/s with a duration of at least 10 minutes, during the period one hour before sunset to one hour after sunrise. See for example judgment by the Land and Environmental Court of Appeals on the 6 November 2017 in case number M 3892–17 and judgment by the Land and Environmental Court of Appeals on the 21 January 2019 in case number M 2579–17.

109 See judgment by the EU Court of Justice on the 4 March 2021 in case number C-473/19 and C-474/19.

110 See judgment by the Land and Environmental Court of Appeals on the 26 April 2022 in case number M 610–21.

111 See for example judgment by the Land and Environmental Court of Appeals on the 3 April 2014 in case number M 2504–13.

112 See the Swedish Nature Protection Agency, *Nulägesbeskrivning – vindkraftens förutsättningar, Underlag till Nationell strategi för en hållbar vindkraftsutbyggnad* (2021) 22.

113 Jan Darpö/Jonas Sandström, *Artskydd och beslutsprocesser* (2010) 10.

114 ibid 23.

ests of reindeer husbandry, the interest of recreation and the preservation of the landscape. However, in later case law, more attention was given to the cumulative effects of the wind farm on the interest of reindeer herding. In MÖD 2019:5, some of the wind turbines were accepted while others were not permitted due to their impact on nature and reindeer herding.

If the wind farm negatively affects a Natura 2000 site, a permit is required. A dispensation from the Species Protection Act is also required if certain species are affected. However, it is very seldom that the potential effect on species actually hinders wind power development in Sweden. There is also no case law (at least from the higher courts) where the derogation rules, from the nature protection directives, have been used in order to obtain permission for wind power.

When it comes to offshore wind power, it is more common that the activity effects a Natura 2000 site, and thus requires a Natura 2000 permit. The reason for this may be that those areas are not excluded when the areas for national interest are appointed at sea. On land, however, Natura 2000 areas are excluded.[115]

Even though conflicts with humans are less common at sea, offshore wind power is often in conflict with Sweden's national defense interests, especially in the Baltic. The government decides the permit issue when the interests of total defense are at risk of being affected. According to Chapter 21, Section 7 of the Environmental Code, in these cases the court must submit the matter to the government with an opinion. The interest of defense can thus prevent wind power installations if the intended wind farm can affect its interests. This was the case when it came to the *Taggen* wind farm, where a permit was never granted due to the interests of total defense.[116] The construction of the wind farm was determined to be hindered by a shooting range located 25 km away. In another case, *Hanöbukten/Blekinge offshore*, the government rejected the permit application because it affected

115 The Swedish Energy Agency, *Riksintresse vindbruk 2013* (2013). See also: Swedish Energy Agency, 'Riksintressen energiproduktion-vindbruk' <https://energimyndigheten.se/fornybart/tillstand-och-provning/riksintressen-for-energiproduktion/riksintressen-for-vindbruk/kriterier-och-undantag/> accessed 29 February 2024.

116 See: Vattenfall, 'Vindprojekt i Sverige' https://group.vattenfall.com/se/var-verksamhet/vindprojekt/taggen accessed 29 February 2024. Was only re-referred when the amendment permit also included water activities, see the Land and Environment Court of Appeals decision on 17 November 2017 in case no M 8189-17.

the interests of total defense.[117] In that case, there were more aspects to take into account as it was an important airspace and water area for air and submarine training, and the wind farm was considered able to affect the technical systems and radar operations in the bay.[118] The military has investigated how the interest can coexist, after a request by the government.[119] However, in November 2024 the governemnt rejected 13 wind power parks in the Baltic due to the military interest, after the total defence suggested that most of the Baltic was not suitable for wind power from their perspective.[120]

Also, due to the shallow water in the Baltic Sea, there are many places that are technically suitable for wind power, but where nature protection is also a concern. Harbor porpoises, overwintering birds (for example long-tailed ducks) and fish mating grounds are especially affected by offshore wind parks. Wind power has frequently been planned in close vicinity to Natura 2000 sites in Sweden.[121] Three of the parks that were assessed in 2023 by the Government required a Natura 2000 permit. In *Stora Middlegrund* the Natura 2000 permit was denied.[122] The county administrative board here also assessed its permissibility under the derogation rules, but found them not to be applicable as the applicant failed to show that no *alternative locations* for the wind park were possible.[123] In the other two cases – *Kattegatt Syd* and *Galatea-Galene* – the county administrative board awarded the permit in the first instance. However, both decisions

---

117 The land and environmental court first handled the question, but because the application affected the interest of the military, it must hand over the case to the government in accordance with Chapter 21, Section 7 of the Environmental Code. This must be done for the entire permit, the land and environmental courts may not decide on the conditions in any part (see MÖD 2005:13). See also the government's decision of 20 December 2016, no. M2013/00540/MR.

118 The government's decision of 20 December 2016, no. M2013/00540/MR.

119 The Swedish Defence Research Agency, *Möjligheter till samexistens mellan Försvarsmaktens verksamhet och utbyggd vindkraft* (2022 FOI-R-5293–SE). See also Sveriges Riksdag, *Samexistens mellan vindkraftverk och Försvarsmaktens behov.* (2020/21:2611).

120 Swedish government, see: <https://www.regeringen.se/regeringens-politik/miljo-och-klimat/havsbaserad-vindkraft/> accessed 18 June 2025.

121 One reason for this is that the areas of *national interest* for off shore wind power has a criterium of depth in the sea (under 35 meters).

122 Decision of the County Administrative Board in Halland on the 13 March 2023, no. 3406–2021.

123 According to 6 (4) of the Habitats Directive one of the requirements is that no alternative solutions exist.

have been appealed and one case is still at the Land and Environmental Court of Appeal awaiting a decision.[124]

Another problem with the Swedish system is that there is no *exclusivity* in the water, other than internal waters (closest to land).[125] Different companies can thus plan and apply for permits in exactly the same area. This was the case with *Kattegatt Syd*[126] and *Galena-Galatea,*[127] which had part of the park in the same area. Both these parks were to be located in the Swedish exclusive economic zone, hence, the government is responsible for the decision.[128] Based on a very vague evaluation, the government considered that *Kattegatt Syd* was preferred to *Galatea-Galene* as it promotes "long-term stewardship of public resources", as it has come furthest in the permit procedure.[129] A state commission has been looking into the issue and an auction system for offshore wind power has been proposed.[130]

(b) NIMBY and the Municipal Veto

As renewable energy development increases on shore, local resistance is also increasing. "Not in my back yard" (NIMBY) is a prevalent sentiment in the Swedish setting. Even though locals are not resistant to wind power in general, they do not want it in their close vicinity, where they can see or hear it.[131] This includes opposition for locating in areas that they use for recreation. This opposition has been the subject of a state official report discussing how people living nearby should and could be compensated.[132] As it is today, people can be part of the public consultations prior to a

124 The Natura 2000 permit for Kattegatt Syd has been confirmed by the Land and Environmental Court of Appeal but the case regarding Galene is still awaiting decision by the court. See: Land and Environmental Court of Appeals decision on the 18 February 2025 in case number M 7648–23.

125 If internal waters you need "rådighet" prior to applying for a permit, see Lag (1998:812) med särskilda bestämmelser om vattenverksamhet, Chapter 2, Section 1.

126 The government's decision on the 15 May 2023, KN2023/0160 (*Kattegatt Syd*).

127 The government's decision on the 15 May 2023, KN2023/01077 (*Galatea-Galene*).

128 See Lag (1992:1140) om Sveriges ekonomiska zon, Section 5.

129 See the government's decision on the 15 May 2023, KN2023/01077 (*Galatea-Galene)* 23 (n 129).

130 See SOU 2024:89, *Vindkraft i havet.*

131 See Maarten Wolsink, 'Wind power and the NIMBY-myth: institutional capacity and the limited significance of public support' (2000) 21 (1) Renewable Energy 49, 51.

132 SOU 2023:18, *Värdet av vinden* (n 86).

development of a wind farm as almost all wind parks are considered to have "significant environmental impact" and therefore be required to compose an environmental impact assessment (EIA).[133] If the opinions by the people living nearby are not accommodated they could appeal the decision if they are considered "concerned" by the decision.[134] The individuals do not need to be the neighbor to the wind farm, only to be disturbed by it any way, from noise etc. What is important is that the individuals that are disturbed by the wind power can appeal the decision if the nuisances are not only *theoretical or insignificant*.[135] For example, if it is possible to be disturbed by noise or sun glare/shading, the person has a right to appeal (independent of how far away that person lives).[136] Therefore, it is not possible to decide a certain distance from the wind power as it depends on the local surroundings.[137]

The *municipal veto* is also hindering wind power development in Sweden. Municipalities are strong political entities in Sweden with a large scope for self-determination, including a monopoly on planning, that is derived from the Swedish Constitution.[138] Due to a change in the law, the municipality was bestowed veto power when it comes to wind power specifically (Chapter 16, § 4 EC). In the past, a dual permit/approval was required for wind power, an approval under the Planning and Building Act (municipal decision) and an environmental permit under the Environmental Code. Since 2009, the procedure has changed and building approval under the Planning and Building Act is no longer needed. The aim was to speed up the processes for developing wind power,[139] but instead the municipal veto was introduced, which has worked to hinder these developments.

This veto is used at any stage of the permit procedure and does not require any reasoning or motivation. This has been confirmed in 2023 by the Land and Environmental Court of Appeal, where the municipality

133 See Chapter 6 of the Swedish environmental Code.

134 ibid Chapter 16, Section 12.

135 See for example NJA 2004 sid 590.

136 See for example MÖD 2005:33, MÖD 2005:33, MÖD 2006:66 and 29 September 2015 in case number M 5746-15.

137 However, if the distance is more than 4 km it is common that the individual is not considered concerned, hence, has no right to appeal. See for example MÖD 2009:11 and NJA 2012 s 921 (regarding offshore wind power and the wind farm was located 10-11 km away from shore).

138 See for example Chapter 1, Sections 1 and 7 Regeringsformen (RF) (Kungörelse (1974:152) om beslutad ny regeringsform).

139 See Swedish government, Prop. 2008/09:146.

changed their mind in the appeal process.[140] Currently, the municipal veto is one of the largest hindrances for wind power development in Sweden. Between 2020 and 2024 about 64 % (83 of 130) wind power projects on land was stopped due to the municipal veto.[141]

According to the Swedish Environmental Code, Chapter 16, Section 4, a municipality's agreement is a prerequisite for granting licenses to wind power installations. More specifically, the provision states:

"A permit for a wind power installation may be issued only if the municipality where the installation is intended to be constructed has agreed to it".

That the municipal veto is problematic and hinders development of wind power in Sweden has long been acknowledged[142] and discussed in the literature.[143] Michanek suggests that this municipal veto rule, which is exclusive to the permitting of wind power installations,[144] can be questioned with regard to Article 13 of the Renewable Energy Directive. He considers it questionable whether the provision is necessary and proportionate.[145] One could argue that, due to the specific governing structure in Sweden, where municipalities have strong local self-governance, it may be considered *necessary* that the municipality can decide how the land and water should be used in its municipality. It may be more difficult to argue that the provision is proportionate. Less intrusive rules could serve the purpose that the municipality has a say on wind power developments. For example, the veto could require a motivation as a minimum. The veto rule could also give rise to discriminatory practices, as some developers may be accepted and others not. Hence, the way that the veto rule is formulated and interpreted today may be in conflict with EU law. However, the legality of the provision has not yet been challenged, either by a wind power developer or the EU

140 Judgment by the Land and Environmental Court of Appeals on the 11 August 2023 in case number M 5427–22.

141 See Henrik Westander/Jacob Risber, 'Kommunala vetot landbaserad vindkraft 2020–2024' <file:///C:/Users/melte722/Downloads/Kommunala-vetot-landbaserat-2020–2024–2025–04–07.pdf> accessed 18 June 2025.

142 See SOU 2021:53, *En rättssäker vindkraftsprövning.*

143 See Gabriel Michanek, 'One national wind power objective and 290 self-governing municipalities' in Marjan Peeters and Thomas Schomerus (eds), *Renewable Energy Law in the EU – Legal Perspectives on Bottom-up Approaches* (Edward Elgar Publishing 2014) 144, 160; Melina Malafry (n 85) 76.

144 Although, other large-scale projects may also need a municipal approval when the government assesses the permissibility, see Chapter 17, section 6 of the Swedish Environmental Code.

145 See Michanek (n 143).

Commission.[146] It is also questionable how the municipal veto will stand as the new provisions on planning of acceleration areas for renewable energy activities are implemented.[147] Such planning does not have any room for municipal veto rule as what is important is that it is a suitable place for renewable energy production from a nature protection perspective more so than in terms of municipal preferences. However, it is uncertain whether or not the planning for acceleration areas will be utilized to a large extent in Sweden.

In summary, hindrances to onshore wind power development can arise due to noise pollution disturbing neighbors, conflict with Sami rights and reindeer herding, or a question of species protection. However, in practice, the most common hindrance in Sweden is the municipal veto power.

3. Photovoltaics in Sweden

(a) Introduction

The development of solar cell installations in Sweden has taken off rapidly, but began from a very low level. In 2022, the number of installations increased by 60 %, leading to a total installed capacity of 2384 MW, an increase of 50 % in installed capacity from the year before.[148] The installations in Sweden make a small overall contribution to electricity production in Sweden and there are not yet many large installations, with most confined to installations on roofs of buildings.

(b) Photovoltaics on Buildings

Photovoltaics have largely increased in recent years due to the 2022 "energy crisis" arising from the Russia's invasion of Ukraine. Personal installations on homeowners' roofs became an attractive investment, due to the soaring cost of electricity and strong reliance on electric heating in homes. Even though energy prices in Sweden have since fallen, the installation of solar cells still has a value for households, acting as a buffer from such periods of extreme electricity prices.

146 See Article 263 and Article 267 TFEU.
147 See RED III (n 43).
148 Swedish government, 89 (n 25). See also: Swedish Energy Agency (n 6).

There are also green subsidies in Sweden for installation of photovoltaics where 20 % of the costs (installation and material) are being covered by the government. A household with a photovoltaic installation can sell excess electricity that it generates. Hence, households can make money/save on future energy purchases. In addition, home production is exempted from energy taxes, as mentioned before.[149] Prior to the recent energy crisis, the installations of photovoltaics on home roofs were not always primarily an economic decision, but rather seen as a "environmentally friendly" thing to do, especially for the climate.[150]

Installation of photovoltaics on buildings in Sweden requires neither a permit nor approval from the authorities, expect under certain circumstances.[151] For example, if the building is a valuable building in accordance with Chapter 8, Section 13 of the Planning and Building Act, then a building permit is required. As a photovoltaic installation may distort a building with cultural value, it is important that the installation is assessed prior to its installation.[152]

Certain protected buildings under the Culture Environmental Act require a permit from the county administrative board prior to its installation.[153] It is common that the Church of Sweden has an interest in becoming more "environmentally friendly" and by installing photovoltaics the Church considers that it does something for the environment. However, historic churches often have high cultural value and the court often find during their assessment that an installation would distort the building's cultural value, and hence not be permissible.[154]

In practice, the majority of buildings do not possess cultural value that a photovoltaic installation would harm and thus there are no real legal obstacles or permit procedures to pass before an installation is undertaken. Rather, our dark winters, with very little light, may be the largest hindrance to broad deployment on the built landscape.

---

149 See below Section 4.

150 As discussed in Melina Malafry, 'Skyddet av kulturvärden i omställningen till ett koldioxidneutralt samhälle – En studie av det rättsliga skyddet av kulturvärden mot installation av solceller i plan- och bygglagen respektive kulturmiljölagen' (2020) 2 Nordic Environmental Law Journal 77.

151 See Plan and building Act (2010:900), Chapter 9, Section 3 c.

152 See for example MÖD 2021:21.

153 For a discussion on relevant case law, see Melina Malafry (n 85).

154 See RÅ 2007:75 (Fläckebo) and the judgment of the Administrative Court in Karlstad judgment on the 22 February 2021 in case number 4859–19 (Säffle).

(c) Large-Scale Photovoltaic Parks

A rather new development in Sweden is the large-scale installation of photovoltaic parks on the ground. The Swedish Government Official Reports on the Swedish Planning and Building Act did not advise that large installations located on the ground should require a building permit.[155] Neither is there a permit requirement under the Environmental Code. Due to its impact on the *natural environment*, a hearing in accordance with 12:6 of the Environmental Code has been required.[156] Even though there is no permit requirement under either the Environmental Code or the Planning and Building Act, it is possible for the developer to apply for a voluntary permit in accordance with the Environmental Code.[157] However, in another Government Official Report about the environmental assessment and permit processes in Sweden, it was suggested that large photovoltaic parks should require a legal assessment prior to their operation.[158]

There are examples of solar parks being built on agricultural land, where both food production and electricity production is combined.[159] However, the legal development is rather difficult as agricultural land is protected land according to the Swedish Environmental Code and its land use cannot be changed if not for reasons of public interest, and even then only if no alternative locations could be used instead.[160] However, this may change as the provision protecting farmland has room for interpretation and the farmer's interest may be considered to be of more importance in the future.

4. Hydropower

The largest share of renewable energy in Sweden comes from hydropower. According to the Swedish Energy Agency, hydropower counts for

155 See SOU 2021:47, *Ett nytt regelverk för bygglov.*
156 See judgment by the Land and Environmental Court of Appeals on the 11November 2022 in case number M 1026–22.
157 See Chapter 9, Section 6 b of the Environmental Code.
158 See SOU 2024:98 (n 32), 1184.
159 Landbruksnytt, 'Solel och lantbruk i kombination' <https://lantbruksnytt.se/solel-och-lantbruk-i-kombination/> accessed 29 February 2024.
160 See Land and Environmental Court of Appeals judgement on the 11November 2022 in case number M 1026–22 and M 15064–21.

around 65–70 TWh of electricity a year, representing about 44 % of Sweden's net electricity production (on average in the last 20 years).[161]

However, the majority of hydropower installations in Sweden have old permits,[162] and hydropower is putting a lot of pressure on the Swedish lakes and rivers due to water regulation and lack of connectivity. In order to decrease the environmental impact, reassessments are needed of the hydropower permits in Sweden. This is also needed due to the requirements under the EU Water Framework Directive.[163] The idea is that *modern environmental requirements*[164] need to be adopted for the hydro in Sweden, including those that have old permits, in order to meet our obligations by the Directive.

How modern environmental requirements should be introduced in Sweden has been under investigation for many years, as the reassessment system that was in place was not fit for the purpose. In 2014, it was calculated that the reassessments needed would take over 800 years.[165] In 2022, Sweden adopted a National Action Plan (NAP) for reviewing hydropower plants with an aim to introduce modern environmental requirements.[166] However, due to the "energy crises" – the rise in electricity prices after Russia's invasion of Ukraine – the Swedish Government first decided to pause the plan for a year.[167]

---

161 It is depending on the year but on average the last 10 years. See: Swedish Energy Agency (n 6).

162 The other hydropower permits were assessed under older water laws; 3 266 of them under the 1918 water law, 127 of them by even older laws, and 261 of them by the Water Law from 1983. See Swedish Government, *Vattenverksamhet* (SOU 2009:42) table 3.6, 95. As referred to in SOU 2014:35, *I vått och torrt – förslag till ändrade vattenrättsliga regler,* 270.

163 Water Framework Directive (n 24).

164 See Chapter 11, Section 27 of the Environmental Code.

165 See Swedish Government, *I vått och torrt – förslag till ändrade vattenrättsliga regler* (SOU 2014:35) 271.

166 See Swedish Agency for Marine and Water Management, 'Regeringens beslut och prövningsgrupper' <https://www.havochvatten.se/arbete-i-vatten-och-energiproduktion/vattenkraftverk-och-dammar/nationella-planen-nap/regeringens-beslut-och-provningsgrupper.html#:~:text=Den%20nationella%20planen%20f%C3%B6r%20omst%C3%A4llning,L%C3%A4nsstyrelsen%20ska%20ansvara%20f%C3%B6r%20samverkansprocessen> accessed 29 February 2024.

167 The Swedish Government, 'Omprövning av vattenkraftverkens miljötillstånd pausas 12 månader' <https://www.regeringen.se/pressmeddelanden/2022/12/omprovning-av-vattenkraftverkens-miljotillstand-pausas--12-manader/> accessed 29 February 2024. The pause has now been extended to July 2025, see: <https://www.regeringen.

The national plan aims to balance the need for improved ecological status with the need for hydropower.[168] The plan is to be undertaken within 20 years, putting the responsibility for reassessment on the hydropower owner. In order to introduce environmental requirements, it would basically mean that minimum flow would be increased and fish passages may need to be built. Some plants may also be required to be dismantled. A fund – the Hydroelectric Environmental Fund – was also introduced to finance the measures needed.[169] Even though there is a plan for how the current hydro plants will be brought into alignment with EU law and biodiversity protection, there is still much to be done, with many plants to reassess and very scant resources to do so. It is too early to say if the reassessment will result in a significant reduction in electricity production, or if it enables expansion of some of the hydropower stations, through the application of the derogation rules in the Directive.[170]

There are also plans to introduce pumped storage in old hydropower plants in Sweden, in order to enable more flexibility in the grid. However, the environmental consequences of such facilities are still uncertain.[171]

---

se/pressmeddelanden/2024/05/regeringen-forlanger-pausen-av-vattenkraftens-omprovning-till-1-juli-2025/> accessed 18 June 2025.

168 The law is changing in 2025 to enable a more "acceptable" reassessment of hydro power plants from an energy system perspective, see: <https://www.regeringen.se/pressmeddelanden/2025/05/forbattrade-villkor-for-omprovning-av-vattenkraften/> accessed 18 June 2025.

169 See Swedish Agency for Marine and Water Management, 'Vattenkraftens miljöfond' <https://www.havochvatten.se/bidrag-utlysningar-och-anslag/andra-bidrag-for-battre-havs--och-vattenmiljo/bidrag/vattenkraftens-miljofond.html#:~:text=%C3%85tta%20svenska%20energibolag%20har%20g%C3%A5tt,kan%20f%C3%A5%20hj%C3%A4lp%20av%20oss> accessed 29 February 2024.

170 The Swedish Energy Agency is predicting that the production will increase a small amount 0,5 TWh because of increased precipitation due to climate change, see Swedish Energy Agency (n 3).

171 See Vattenfall, 'Vattenfall tar Juktans pumpkraftverk till nästa steg' <https://group.vattenfall.com/se/nyheter-och-press/pressmeddelanden/2023/vattenfall-tar-juktans-pumpkraftverk-till-nasta steg#:~:text=Investeringsbeslut%20%C3%A4r%20planerat%20till%202027,ett%20av%20fyra%20p%C3%A5g%C3%A5ende%20expansions-projekt> accessed 29 February 2024.

5. Access to Grid Infrastructure

In Sweden, hindrances associated with access to the grid for electricity production from wind or solar and other variable sources have long been acknowledged and have been the topic of numerous discussions and legal proposals.[172] However, the permit system in Sweden is still considered a problem. One of the problems is that a concession for a transmission line is something that is applied for after a permit for the production site is settled. Hence, the time lapse between these permits can be very long. In a recent proposal for legislative change in Sweden due to the implementation of RED III, the law was proposed to be changed in order to combine the environmental impacts assessments for various parts pf the "project".[173] However, this was a possibility prior to RED III but not utilized in Sweden, as it is difficult to assess the environmental impact from the grid infrastructure prior to its actual assessment under the Electricity Act. Therefore, these procedures require a better integration in the Swedish system in order to function.

And now, as electrification is crucial for the carbon-neutral future, fossil-free electricity production must increase rapidly and be supported by a stable distribution infrastructure. Based on the way things work today, it is a challenge to get necessary grid infrastructure in place as fast as needed. This also implies that renewable energy production is not necessarily built in the most suitable locations from an environmental point of view, but rather where there is already access to necessary grid infrastructure. The status quo is therefore that the development of the electricity system is not very efficient. Better planning may be a way forward to enable a more sustainable and efficient energy transition.[174]

However, even if production sites are located close to current transmission lines, it is not certain that there is capacity for more electricity to be

172 Svenska Kraftnät, *Tröskeleffekter och förnybar energi – En rapport till Regeringen* (2009); Swedish government, Prop. 2013/14:156; and Malafry, *Biodiversity Protection in an Aspiring Carbon Neutral Society,* 78 (n 85).

173 Klimat- och näringslivsdepartementet (2025), *Promemoria: Genomförande av bestämmelser i förnybartdirektivet om tillståndsförfaranden för förnybar energi*, Dnr KN2025/00895.

174 Malafry, *Biodiversity Protection in an Aspiring Carbon Neutral Society* 278 (n 85).

distributed. This has been identified as an obstacle by the Swedish Energy Market Inspectorate.[175]

At the level of the transmission state operator (TSO) Svenska Kraftnät's level, there is a huge infrastructure expansion needed to meet the future demand of electricity. It is identified that not only more stable transmission lines are needed in Sweden, but also connection to the rest of the Nordic countries, etc. In addition, the system must be more flexible in order to handle more variable sources like wind and solar, which are expected to grow in the near future.[176] The current hydropower, peak power plants and an extension of the grid is considered important to balance the grid in the Nordic countries. A few challenges are identified by the Nordic TSOs. There is a need for "flattening the curve", to balance out the consumption and production of electricity. The slowness in the legal system is also expressed as a challenge, as infrastructure development often takes a long time due to the many parallel processes involved.[177] However, the most urgent challenge is that of stability, to enable more flexibility in the current system.[178]

H. Conclusion and Way Forward

The energy transition in the Swedish context may be very different from the rest of Europe. Since the oil crisis in the 1970s, a move away from oil has been natural in the Swedish economy, and coal and natural gas have not been a significant part of our energy mix in recent years. However, the transport sector is still reliant on fossil fuels. The transition we are facing is therefore more about the *electrification* of our energy system and society. Hence, the industrial and transport sectors are estimated to be highly dependent on fossil-free electricity in the future. A large increase in fossil-free electricity production is therefore needed. As available land is diminishing, conflicts may be intensified over land use. Land allocated to Sami people in the North, protected areas for biodiversity and species protection may

175 The Swedish Energy Market Inspectorate, *Kapacitetsutmaningar i elnäten*, Ei R2020:06.

176 Svenska Kraftnät et al., 'Nordic Grid Development Perspective 2023' <https://www.svk.se/siteassets/om-oss/rapporter/2023/svk_ngpd2023.pdf> accessed 29 February 2024.

177 However, this has long been acknowledged to be a problem but no changes have been proposed, see SOU 2019:30, *Moderna tillståndsprocesser för elnät.*

178 Svenska Kraftnät et al. (n 176) 14.

be diminished. However, a sustainable energy transition requires that other sustainability goals are also fulfilled, making it more important how and where we produce fossil-free electricity. Given the current EU-level push for fast deployment of renewable energy activities, long permit procedures are identified as a problem at the national level. However, as it is a complex process by nature – as many sustainability aspects have to be assessed – it is difficult to speed up these processes in general, even though in some cases the delay is not motivated.

Looking forward, the new requirements in RED III regarding mapping and planning for *acceleration areas* of renewable energy may be an important aspect in finding the right locations for renewable energy installations in the future. However, Sweden do not seem to think that it is a suitable instrument in the Swedish context, even though better planning could be benefical, not only for the environment, but also for the developer. The order, as it is today, where the developer chooses a location, and potential conflicts are handled first at the permit stage, is a very inefficient way of enabling an expansion of renewable energy. As *location* is the key to the renewable energy installation's *sustainability,* it is a crucial development that the planning infrastructure will be given more guidance, especially regarding areas that are to be excluded due to nature protection interests. If the planning is undertaken with an attempt to avoid or mitigate potential conflicts, we may enable a more sustainable energy transition, however, such planning requires a more integrated and holistic planning than the one that is in place in Sweden today.

Bibliography

Christiernsson A, *Rättens förhållande till komplexa och dynamiska ecosystem* (Doctoral thesis, Luleå University of Technology 2011)

Darpö J, 'Tradition och förnyelse på vattenrättens område. Om mötet mellan gamla tillståndsregimer och moderna miljökrav' (2014) 214:2 Nordic Environmental Law Journal 101, 102

Darpö J/Sandström J, *Artskydd och beslutsprocesser* (2010) 10

Ebbesson J/Darpö J, 'Professorer: Lobbyister och företag sprider myter om svensk miljölagstiftning' <https://www.altinget.se/artikel/professorer-lobbyister-och-foretag-sprider-myter-om-svensk-miljolagstiftning> accessed 29 February 2024

Finansinspektionen, 'Internpris på koldioxid – vad och varför?' <https://www.fi.se/contentassets/a252e77c5bea47adbdb95156890c3374/fi-analys-30-internpris-pa-koldioxid.pdf> accessed 29 February 2024

IEA, 2019 Country Review Sweden, 'Sweden is a leader in the energy transition, according to latest IEA country review' <https://www.iea.org/news/sweden-is-a-leader-in-the-energy-transition-according-to-latest-iea-country-review> accessed 29 February 2024

Kjellin P, 'Forskare sågar reformen med höjd reduktionsplikt för bensin och diesel' <https://transportnytt.se/forskare-sagar-reformen-med-hojd-reduktionsplikt-for-bensin-och-diesel/> accessed 29 February 2024

Landbruksnytt, 'Solel och lantbruk i kombination' <https://lantbruksnytt.se/solel-och-lantbruk-i-kombination/> accessed 29 February 2024

Malafry M, *Biodiversity Protection in an Aspiring Carbon Neutral Society, the relationship between biodiversity and renewable energy in a European Union context* (Doctoral thesis, Uppsala University 2016)

Malafry M, 'Skyddet av kulturvärden i omställningen till ett koldioxidneutralt samhälle – En studie av det rättsliga skyddet av kulturvärden mot installation av solceller i plan- och bygglagen respektive kulturmiljölagen' (2020) 2 Nordic Environmental Law Journal 77

Malafry M/Öhman M, *Rättsliga förutsättningar för havsbaserad vindkraft* (Vindval Report 7028 2022)

Michanek G, 'One national wind power objective and 290 self-governing municipalities' in **Peeters M/Schomerus T** (eds), Renewable Energy Law in the EU – Legal Perspectives on Bottom-up Approaches (Edward Elgar Publishing 2014) 144, 1

Michanek G/Zetterberg C, Den Svenska miljörätten (2021) 527

Niri A J/Poelzer G A/Zhang S E/Rosenkranz J/Pettersson M/Ghorbani Y, 'Sustainability challenges throughout the electric vehicle battery value chain' (2024) 191 Renewable and Sustainable Energy Reviews 114176

Pettersson M, *Renewable Energy development and the Functioning of Law – A Comparative Study of Legal Rules Related to the Planning, Installation and Operation of Windmills* (Doctoral thesis, Luleå University of Technology 2008)

Reuters, 'DR Congo presses Apple over minerals supply chain, lawyers say' <https://www.reuters.com/markets/commodities/dr-congo-presses-apple-over-minerals-supply-chain-lawyers-say-2024-04-25/> accessed 29 July 2024

RISE Research Institutes of Sweden, *Prestudy H2ESIN: Hydrogen, energy system and infrastructure in Northern Scandinavia and Finland* (2022) 3

Statistikmyndigheten, 'Tredubbling av elbilar på två år' <https://www.scb.se/hittastatistik/redaktionellt/tredubbling-av-elbilar-pa-tva-ar2/#:~:text=Man%20skulle%20kunna%20s%C3%A4ga%20att,bilar%20%E2%80%93%20en%20f%C3%B6rdubbling%20sedan%202020> accessed 29 February 2024

Statistikmyndigheten, 'Utsläppen av växthusgaser från Sveriges ekonomi ökade 2024' <https://www.scb.se/hitta-statistik/statistik-efter-amne/miljo/miljoekonomi-och-hallbar-utveckling/miljorakenskaper/pong/statistiknyhet/utslapp-till-luft-4e-kvartalet-2024//> accessed 18 June 2025

Swedish Agency for Marine and Water Management, 'Marine Spatial Planning' <https://www.havochvatten.se/en/eu-and-international/marine-spatial-planning.html> accessed 29 February 2024

Swedish Agency for Marine and Water Management, 'Havsplanerna ändras för att möta ökat elbehov', <https://www.havochvatten.se/planering-forvaltning-och-samverkan/havsplanering/forslag-till-andrade-havsplaner-2025.html> accessed 18 June 2025

Swedish Agency for Marine and Water Management, 'Vattenkraftens miljöfond'<https://www.havochvatten.se/bidrag-utlysningar-och-anslag/andra-bidrag-for-battre-havs--och-vattenmiljo/bidrag/vattenkraftensmiljofond.html#:~:text=%C3%85tta%20svenska%20energibolag%20har%20g%C3%A5tt,kan%20f%C3%A5%20hj%C3%A4lp%20av%20oss> accessed 29 February 2024

Swedish Agency for Marine and Water Management, 'Regeringens beslut och prövningsgrupper' <https://www.havochvatten.se/arbete-i-vatten-och-energiproduktion/vattenkraftverk-ochdammar/nationella-planen-nap/regeringens-beslut-och-provningsgrupper.html#:~:text=Den%20nationella%20planen%20f%C3%B6r%20omst%C3%A4llning,L%C3%A4nsstyrelsen%20ska%20ansvara%20f%C3%B6r%20samverkansprocessen> accessed 29 February 2024

Swedish Defence Research Agency, *Möjligheter till samexistens mellan Försvarsmaktens verksamhet och utbyggd vindkraft* (2022 FOI-R-5293–SE)

Swedish Energy Agency, Scenarier över Sveriges energisystem 2023: Med fokus på elektrifieringen 2050 (2023) ER 2023:07, 9

Swedish Energy Agency, 'Reduktionsplikt ' <https://www.energimyndigheten.se/fornybart/hallbarhetskriterier/reduktionsplikt/> accessed 29 February 2024

Swedish Energy Agency, Energy in Sweden 2022: with energy balance for years 1970–2020 (2022) ET 2023:1, 9

Swedish Energy Agency, 'Energy in Sweden Facts and Figures' (2025)< https://www.energimyndigheten.se/energisystem-och-analys/nulaget-i-energisystemet/energilaget > accessed 18 June 2025

Swedish Energy Market Inspectorate, Kapacitetsutmaningar i elnäten, Ei R2020:06

Swedish Environmental Protection Agency, 'Resultat i olika branscher 2022' <https://www.naturvardsverket.se/amnesomraden/klimatomstallningen/klimatklivet/resultat-i-olika-branscher-2022/gron-vatgas-for-fossilfri-varmning-av-stal/> accessed 29 February 2024

Swedish Environmental Protection Agency, 'Sveriges utsläpp och upptag av växthusgaser' <https://www.naturvardsverket.se/data-och-statistik/klimat/sveriges-utslapp-och-upptag-av-vaxthusgaser/> accessed 18 juni 2025

Swedish Government, 'Mål för energipolitiken' <https://www.regeringen.se/regeringenspolitik/energi/mal-och-visioner-for-energi/> accessed 29 February 2024

Swedish Government, 'Omprövning av vattenkraftverkens miljötillstånd pausas 12 månader'<https://www.regeringen.se/pressmeddelanden/2022/12/omprovning-av-vattenkraftverkensmiljotillstand-pausas--12-manader/> accessed 29 February 2024

Swedish Government, 'Riksrevisionens rapport om reduktionsplikten för bensin och diesel' <https://www.regeringen.se/contentassets/227afea1d2a24478b15c5323784e3eba/riksrevisionens-rapport-om-reduktionsplikten-for-bensin-och-diesel-skr.-20232444.pdf> accessed 29 February 2024

Swedish Government, 'Regeringen förlänger pausen av vattenkraftens omprövning till 1 juli 2025' <https://www.regeringen.se/pressmeddelanden/2024/05/regeringen-forlanger-pausen-av-vattenkraftens-omprovning-till-1-juli-2025/> accessed 18 June 2025

Swedish Government, 'Havsbaserad vind' <https://www.regeringen.se/regeringens-politik/miljo-och-klimat/havsbaserad-vindkraft/> accessed 18 June 2025

Swedish Energy Agency, *Riksintresse vindbruk 2013* (2013)

Swedish Energy Agency, 'Riksintressen energiproduktion-vindbruk' <https://energimyndigheten.se/fornybart/tillstand-ochprovning/riksintressen-for-energiproduktion/riksintressen-for-vindbruk/kriterier-och-undantag/>accessed 29 February 2024

Swedish Government, 'Regeringens klimathandlingsplan – hela vägen till nettonoll' (2023) Skr. 2023/24:59, 21

Swedish Government, 'Budgetsatsningar inom energiområdet för att säkra tillväxt och grön omställning ' <https://www.regeringen.se/artiklar/2023/10/budgetsatsningar-inom-energiomradet-for-att-sakra-tillvaxt-och-gron-omstallning/> accessed 29 February 2024

Swedish Government (Klimat- och näringslivsdepartementet), *Promemoria: Genomförande av bestämmelser i förnybartdirektivet om tillståndsförfaranden för förnybar energi*, Dnr KN2025/00895 (2025)

SOU 2009:42, *Vattenverksamhet* (2009)

SOU 2014:35, *I vått och torrt – förslag till ändrade vattenrättsliga regler (2014)*

SOU 2019:30, *Moderna tillståndsprocesser för elnät* (2019)

SOU 2021:47, *Ett nytt regelverk för bygglov* (2021)

SOU 2021:53, *En rättssäker vindkraftsprövning* (2021)

SOU 2022:33, *Om prövning och omprövning- en del av den gröna omställningen* (2022)

SOU 2023:18, *Värdet av vinden: Kompensation, incitament och planering för en hållbar fortsatt utbyggnad av vindkraften* (2023)

SOU 2024:89, *Vindkraft i havet* (2024)

SOU 2024:98, *En ny samordnad miljöbedömnings- och tillståndsprövningsprocess* (2025)

Swedish Government, Prop. 1997/98:45

Swedish Government, Prop. 1985/86:3

Swedish Government, Prop. 2008/09:146

Swedish Government, Prop. 2013/14:156

Swedish Nature Protection Agency, *Nulägesbeskrivning – vindkraftens förutsättningar, Underlag till Nationell strategi för en hållbar vindkraftsutbyggnad* (2021) 22

Svenska Kraftnät, *Tröskeleffekter och förnybar energi – En rapport till Regeringen* (2009) Prop. 2013/14:156

Svenska Kraftnät et al., 'Nordic Grid Development Perspective 2023' <https://www.svk.se/siteassets/om-oss/rapporter/2023/svk_ngpd2023.pdf> accessed 29 February 2024

Sveriges Riksdag, *Miljötillståndsutredningen* Dir. 2023:78 (KN 2023:2)

Sveriges Riksdag, *Samexistens mellan vindkraftverk och Försvarsmaktens behov.* (2020/21:2611)

Sveriges Riksdag, *En ordnad prövning av havsbaserad vindkraft* (Dir 2023:61)

Trafikanalys, 'Samma nivå för nyregistrerade personbilar 2023 som året innan' <https://www.mynewsdesk.com/se/trafikanalys/pressreleases/samma-nivaa-foer-nyregistrerade-personbilar-2023-som-aaret-innan-3295203?utm_source=rss&utm_medium=rss&utm_campaign=Alert&utm_content=pressrelease> accessed 29 February 2024

Trafikanalys, 'Elektrifierade fordon i Sverige – en analys av laddbara fordon över tid och geografi' Rapport: 2024:10 <https://www.trafa.se/globalassets/rapporter/2024/rapport-2024-10-elektrifierade-fordon-i-sverige---en-analys-av-laddbara-fordon-over-tid-och-geografi.pdf> accessed 18 June 2025

Energiföretagen, 'Energiåret 2024' <https://www.energiforetagen.se/49761b/globalassets/energiforetagen/statistik/energiaret/2024/energiaret_2024_250415.pdf> accessed 18 June 2025

Vattenfall, 'Vattenfall tar Juktans pumpkraftverk till nästa steg' <https://group.vattenfall.com/se/nyheter-och-press/pressmeddelanden/2023/vattenfall-tar-juktanspumpkraftverk-till-nasta steg#:~:text=Investeringsbeslut%20%C3%A4r%20planerat%20-till%202027,ett%20av%20fyra%20p%C3%A5g%C3%A5ende%20expansionsprojekt> accessed 29 February 2024

Vattenfall, '*Vindprojekt i Sverige*' https://group.vattenfall.com/se/var-verksamhet/vindprojekt/taggen accessed 29 February 2024

Vedung E/Brandel M, Vattenkraften, staten och de politiska partierna (2001) 43

Westander H/Risber J, 'Kommunala vetot 2020–2021' <https://svenskvindenergi.org/wp-content/uploads/2022/03/Kommunala-vetot-2020-och-2021-2022-03-18-slutversion.pdf> accessed 29 February 2024

General Perspectives on the Law of Energy Transition in Poland

Bartłomiej Nowak and Aleksandra Knap

A. Introduction

Poland has experienced dynamic economic growth over the past decade. Poland's GDP growth in 2022 was 4.9 %,[1] which is above the European Union average of 3.5 %.[2] This development has contributed to a significant increase in energy demand in both the transportation and industrial sectors, as well as in households. As a result, total final consumption (TFC) increased from 70 Mtoe to 75 Mtoe between 2010 and 2019.[3] Meanwhile, the average annual power demand is now 23.7 GW, with peak demand at 27.6 GW.[4] Moreover, in Poland, households' electricity charges in 2022 were lower (€0.1464 per KWh) than the European average (€0.2525 per KWh).[5]

Despite the overall increase in energy consumption in Poland, public awareness of the need for energy transition, environmental care, and conservation is also growing year by year. Factors that played a key role in the development of environmental awareness included the development of science and technology, globalization and interdependence, social activism, and NGOs. In 2022, the Ministry of Climate and Environment surveyed the environmental awareness of Polish residents. According to 91 % of respondents, climate change is either an important or a very important issue. In addition, respondents identified large emissions of carbon dioxide, sulfur dioxide and nitrogen oxides, and other chemical compounds from industri-

1 Worldbank, 'GDP Growth Poland' <https://data.worldbank.org/indicator/NY.GDP.MKTP.KD.ZG?locations=PL> accessed 26 August 2023.

2 Worldbank, 'GDP Growth European Union' <https://data.worldbank.org/indicator/NY.GDP.MKTP.KD.ZG?locations=EU> accessed 26 August 2023.

3 International Energy Agency, 'Poland 2022 Energy Policy Review' <https://www.iea.org/reports/poland-2022/executive-summary> accessed 28 August 2023.

4 Energy Regulatory Office, '2021 Rynek Hurtowy' <https://www.ure.gov.pl/pl/energia-elektryczna/charakterystyka-rynku/10372,2021.html> accessed 31 August 2023.

5 Eurostat, 'Electricity prices (including taxes) for household consumers, first half 2022' <https://ec.europa.eu/eurostat/statistics-explained/index.php?title=Electricity_price_statistics> accessed 29 August 2023.

al activities as the most important cause of air pollution in Poland.[6] On the one hand, Polish society is aware that an energy transition is needed, while on the other hand, the country's energy mix is largely based on coal, which has long been used as the primary energy resource. Consequently, this has resulted in a strong link between the hard coal and lignite mining sector and the Polish economy, thereby highlighting the challenges Poland faces in terms of energy transition.

B. The National Notion of Energy Transition

The Polish legislature does not use a single, legal definition of energy transition. However, Poland's energy transition is a broad socio-economic concept that aims, over the long term, to transform the country's energy system toward more sustainable, low-carbon and renewable energy. Naturally, this requires political commitment on the part of all political parties in the country and, importantly, the preparation of the coherent legal instrumentation needed to implement the changes. Among other things, the first step in this regard was the National Energy and Climate Plan 2021–2030, which was adopted by the Committee for European Affairs at its meeting on December 18, 2019.[7]

The strategic document indicating the direction of the energy transition is the Energy Policy of Poland until 2040. This document is one of nine strategies stemming from a document called the Country Development Management System. It is based on the country's medium-term development strategy, which was adopted on 14 February 2017 under the name Strategy for Responsible Development. The most important assumptions and investment areas of the energy sector were defined in accordance with the four pillars of the country's energy policy: equitable transformation, building a zero-carbon energy system, improving air quality, and energy sovereignty. These elements defined the so called Polish energy transition framework for businesses and local government units for the coming decades which are in line with the energy union and the objectives set for Poland.

6 Ministerstwo Klimatu i Środowiska, 'Badania świadomości ekologicznej mieszkańców Polski' <https://www.gov.pl/web/edukacja-ekologiczna/badania-swiadomosci-ekologicznej> accessed 08 August 2023.

7 For more on the issue of the National Energy and Climate Plan for the years 2021–2030, see below Section C 'Decarbonization Strategy'.

In the case of Poland, energy transformation is not only aimed at reducing dependence on coal but is primarily a process of reducing energy consumption, reducing greenhouse gas emissions, and promoting renewable energy sources. Energy transformation not only allows a reduction in business costs by introducing innovative solutions in the energy sector but also leads to the achievement of emission reduction targets (e.g. Fit for 55) to which EU member states have committed themselves.

Poland faces challenges in restructuring the energy sector transforming the socio-economic realities of coal mining and utilization on the one hand and increasing environmental awareness on the other. Most of the Polish public believes that an acceleration of the energy transition process is needed. Only a third of those surveyed assessed that the pace of this process is currently sufficient.[8]

C. Decarbonization Strategy

Poland, being a member state of the European Union, joined the Paris Agreement, meaning it did not submit a stand-alone Climate Implementation Plan (NDC) to the United Nations Framework Convention on Climate Change (UNFCCC). Nevertheless, Poland is actively participating in the European Union's joint efforts to achieve targeted emission reductions. In accordance with European Union legislation, Poland initially committed to reduce emissions by 7 % by 2030 compared to 2005 levels in sectors not covered by the Emissions Trading Scheme (EU ETS). However, in the context of the increased aspirations of the EU's Common Strategy to 2030, according to a proposal to amend the Regulation (EU) 2023/857,[9] the Polish target was raised to -17.7 % compared to 2005 levels.[10]

---

8 Bankier, 'Ogromne koszty polskiej transformacji energetycznej i równie ogromna luka inwestycyjna' (27 August 2023) <https://www.bankier.pl/wiadomosc/Ogromne-koszty-polskiej-transformacji-energetycznej-i-rownie-ogromna-luka-inwestycyjna-8595823.html> accessed 29 August 2023.

9 Regulation (EU) 2018/842 of the European Parliament and of the Council of May 30, 2018, on binding annual greenhouse gas emission reductions by Member States from 2021 to 2030 contributing to climate action to meet their commitments under the Paris Agreement and amending Regulation (EU) No. 525/2013 [2018] OJ L 156/26.

10 Regulation (EU) 2023/857 of the European Parliament and of the Council of 19 April 2023 amending Regulation (EU) 2018/842 on binding annual greenhouse gas emission reductions by Member States from 2021 to 2030 contributing to climate action to

The National Energy and Climate Plan for the years 2021–2030[11] is to become the answer to the implementation of the decarbonization strategy. The document outlines assumptions and goals, as well as policies and actions to realize the 5 dimensions of the energy union, i.e. energy security, internal energy market, energy efficiency, decarbonization, and support for research, innovation, and competitiveness. As a result, the obligation imposed on Poland by the provisions of Regulation (EU) 2018/1999[12] of the European Parliament and of the Council has been fulfilled. This regulation provides the basis for managing the energy union and taking climate action that will meet the 2030 energy union goals and targets.

The National Energy and Climate Plan for the years 2021–2030 was adopted by the European Affairs Committee at its meeting on December 18, 2019. The National Plan was created based on national development strategies of various sectors (Strategy for Sustainable Development of Transport until 2030, National Environmental Policy 2030, Strategy for Sustainable Development of Rural Areas, Agriculture and Fisheries 2030) and considering the assumptions of the Energy Policy of Poland until 2040.

The National Energy and Climate Plan 2030 (draft update of 29 February 2024) includes the ESR – Effort Sharing Regulation.[13] Based on this regulation, for the other sectors (buildings, road and maritime transport, agriculture, waste, or small industry), so far called non-ETS reduction effort, so far referred to as non-ETS, has set an EU reduction target of 40 % in 2030 compared to 2005 levels. Until now this level has oscillated at 29 %. However, for Poland, a binding emission reduction target of -17.7 % was set for the non-ETS sectors compared to 2005. The existing contribution

---

meet commitments under the Paris Agreement, and Regulation (EU) 2018/199 [2023] OJ L 111/1.

11 Ministerstwo Klimatu i Środowiska, 'National Energy and Climate Plan for the years 2021–2030 – submitted in 2019' <https://www.gov.pl/web/klimat/national-energy-and-climate-plan-for-the-years-2021-2030> accessed 16 November 2023.

12 Regulation (EU) 2018/1999 of the European Parliament and of the Council of 11 December 2018 on the Governance of the Energy Union and Climate Action, amending Regulations (EC) No 663/2009 and (EC) No 715/2009 of the European Parliament and of the Council, Directives 94/22/EC, 98/70/EC, 2009/31/EC, 2009/73/EC, 2010/31/EU, 2012/27/EU and 2013/30/EU of the European Parliament and of the Council, Council Directives 2009/119/EC and (EU) 2015/652 and repealing Regulation (EU) No 525/2013 of the European Parliament and of the Council [2018] OJ L 328/1.

13 Regulation (EU) 2023/857 (n 10).

goal (-7 % under the previous ESR)[14] was already considered by Poland as an ambitious commitment. Therefore, the current commitment is assessed even more so, as exceeding national capabilities.[15]

Initially, one of the goals was a 7 % reduction in greenhouse gas emissions on the mentioned non-ETS sector. However, this target was amended by Regulation (EU) 2023/857 to 17.7 %. Poland, in the National Energy and Climate Plan for the years 2021 – 2030 (draft update of 29 February 2024), has indicated that a level of 14.1 % is achievable for Poland in 2030. A key element positively influencing the country's sustainable development is the generation of energy from renewable energy sources (RES), so another of the targets was to increase RES by 21–23 % in gross final energy consumption. This target was also changed to a level of 31 %. Poland, however, has indicated that it is capable of achieving 29.8 % by 2030. In the original version of The National Energy and Climate Plan for the years 2021–2030, calculations at least related to energy efficiency improvements were made on the PRIMES 2007[16] scenarios. According to the revised directive in the update to the Plan, targets are set in relation to the PRIMES 2020 scenario.[17] The target, which from Poland's perspective will be the most difficult to achieve, is a 50–60 % reduction of coal in electricity production.

The European Commission's recommendations on the draft version of the National Energy and Climate Plan for the years 2021 – 2030 were released on 26 April 2024. The Commission notes that the assumptions presented by Poland for emission reductions, carbon sequestration, energy

---

14 National Centre for Emissions Management (KOBiZE), 'Poland's Eighth National Communication and Fifth Biennial Report under the UNFCCC' (Warsaw 2022) <https://unfccc.int/sites/default/files/resource/Poland_Report-NC8_BR5_27dec2022%20%281%29.pdf> accessed 04 July 2024.

15 Ministerstwo Klimatu i Środowiska, 'Krajowy Plan w dziedzinie Energii i Klimatu do 2030 r.' <https://commission.europa.eu/document/download/5118b15e-d380-49ae-b8bb-41cc81a28e15_pl?filename=PL_NECPupdate_Projekt_aKPEiK_tekst_ostateczny.pdf> accessed 02 July 2024.

16 The PRIMES (Price-induced market equilibrium system) model is based on 5-year steps, is suitable for medium- and long-term forecasts (up to 2070) and covers all EU and EFTA member states (except Liechtenstein) and candidate countries.

17 The EU 2020 Reference Scenario is the baseline scenario from which the specific scenarios and policy options used to assess options informing policy initiatives have been developed. This is all done as part of the European Green Deal package adopted by the European Commission in July 2021.

efficiency and the share of renewables remain lower than the official targets set out in Regulation (EU) 2023/857.[18]

However, the green transition efforts will be possible when additional EU funds are received, which will be allocated for a fair transition. It is therefore important to mention Poland's National Recovery and Resilience Plan,[19] which aims to rebuild the economic development that was lost during the Covid-19 pandemic. Initially, Poland was to receive €35.36 billion, of which €15.1 billion was to be allocated to green transformation. This would amount to 42.7 % of the funds received.[20] However, the amount currently stands at €59.8 billion, including €25.3 billion in grants and €34.5 billion in loans. This amount is €24.5 billion higher (a 69 % increase) than the original amount mentioned above. Includes an update of the maximum financial contribution in 2022, as well as two additional loans requested by Poland. In addition, it includes a non-refundable allocation for REPowerEU made available in 2023. The allocation of Poland is 8 % of the total financial contribution[21].

D. The National Energy Mix in the Context of the Energy Transition

Coal has a basic function in the energy and economic structure of the country. In 2020, Poland had the largest share of coal in power generation, TFC,[22] TES,[23] and electricity production. Moreover, Poland had the second-highest share of coal in heat production among International Energy Agency (IEA) member countries. This high percentage of coal use places

18 European Commission, 'Recommendation of 26.4.2024 on the draft updated integrated national energy and climate plan of Poland covering the period 2021–2030' C (2024) 2900 final <https://commission.europa.eu/document/download/b40cb8bb-4eaf-434b-a298-6f282fb8ed4a_en?filename=Recommendation_draft_updated_NECP_Poland_2024.pdf.pdf> accessed 04 July 2024.

19 Pol. Krajowy Plan Odbudowy i Zwiększania Odporności (KPO).

20 European Parliament, 'Briefing, Next Generation EU (NGEU) delivery – How are the Member States doing? Poland's National Recovery and Resilience Plan' <https://www.europarl.europa.eu/RegData/etudes/BRIE/2022/733665/EPRS-Briefing-733665-NRRP-Poland-FINAL.pdf> accessed 04 July 2024.

21 ibid.

22 TFC – Total final consumption.

23 TES – Total energy supply.

Poland second among IEA member countries in terms of CO2 intensity per unit of energy supplied and fourth in terms of CO2 intensity to GDP.[24]

In terms of EU member states, hard coal consumption in 2022 reached 160 million tonnes, of which Poland was responsible for the consumption of nearly 38 %. Responsible therefore for almost two-fifths of the total coal consumption in the European Union in 2022.[25] As a result, Poland has become the infamous leader not only of hard coal and lignite consumption but also of coal mining in the entire EU.

The large use of coal in the Polish economy is related to historical and geopolitical aspects, as well as rich deposits of the resource. After World War II, when the Polish People's Republic appeared on the map of Europe, it was a country dependent on the Union of Soviet Socialist Republics (USSR). Poland's relations with the USSR influenced the shape of Polish energy and economic policy. The investments related to the energy sector carried out at the time were mainly aimed at expanding the coal sector and the energy infrastructure based on it. This happened because mining (domestic extraction) was aimed at ensuring the country's energy security against potential threats from external supplies of energy carriers. At the time, energy based on gas or renewable energy sources was not a priority in energy policy and investment plans, as the main focus was on the dynamic development of heavy industry, requiring high energy inputs. Coal became the key source of energy for steel mills, steel plants, and other industries that formed the backbone of the centrally planned economy. Providing citizens with access to cheap energy was important to the communist authorities, and coal was one of the cheapest sources of energy at the time. Coal mining was therefore part of the state's strategy to meet the needs of society. From the perspective of its geopolitical location, Poland has rich deposits of hard coal. These deposits are found in the Upper Silesian Coal Basin, the Lublin Coal Basin, and the Lower Silesian Coal Basin.[26]

From the perspective of the gas sector, it is apparent that Poland, based on its own natural resources, is unable to meet its domestic needs. Prior to Russia's invasion of Ukraine, the Russian Federation was, on average, Poland's main supplier of fossil fuels over the past 20 years. The country's share of imports was 87 % for oil, 72 % for natural gas, and 62 % for coal. In

24 International Energy Agency (n 3).

25 Eurostat, 'Coal production and consumption up in 2022' <https://ec.europa.eu/eurostat/web/products-eurostat-news/w/ddn-20230622-2> accessed 28 August 2023.

26 Muzeum Geologiczne, 'Węgiel kamienny ' <https://www.pgi.gov.pl/muzeum/kopalnia-wiedzy-1/12580-wegiel-kamienny.html> accessed 28 August 2023.

2021, most coal was imported from Russia: more than 8.25 million tonnes (66.2 % of all imported coal). This coal mainly went to households and local heating plants.

As a result of Russia's aggression against Ukraine, serious concerns have also grown about the availability of hydrocarbons, not only in Poland but across Europe, resulting in a significant increase in the price of these raw materials. As a result, the Polish government has taken steps to secure coal and gas supplies. Among other things, intervention coal imports were made from sources other than the Russian Federation, including South Africa, Australia, Kazakhstan, and Colombia.[27] In the case of gas, when Gazprom halted gas deliveries to Poland in April 2022, a series of diversification measures were taken, resulting in a move away from Russian gas entirely at the beginning of 2023. By the same token, gas supplies were increased from the northern direction (Norway), the western direction (Germany), and by sea through the LNG terminal (USA) and domestic production. Also noteworthy is the fact that in 2022 Poland reduced its gas consumption by 17 % compared to 2021, according to data from the Ministry of Climate and Environment.

Consequently, due to the turmoil in the raw materials market caused by the disruption of supply chains, several legislative solutions were introduced in Poland to curb the rise in prices of energy carriers. Among other things, a law-based system was introduced for the purchase of preferential solid fuel for households,[28] as well as the so-called "energy shield," a set of legislative solutions that help combat rising energy prices. Citizens, including vulnerable consumers (those in energy poverty or unable to pay utility bills), and selected companies benefit from a few allowances and compensations. An example is the Law on Special Solutions for the Protection of Electricity Consumers, which compensates for increases in electricity prices. The same solution is applied to the gas market, where prices for households consumers are frozen as of January 1, 2023. There is also a VAT refund for gas for the lowest-income households and limit on the increase in heat prices to a maximum of 40 % compared to the previous year. The statutory solutions also involve the introduction of compensation for energy supply companies.

27 Ministry of State Assets, 'Summary report on intervention coal import and distribution in the 2022/2023 heating season' (Warsaw 2023).

28 The Act of October 27, 2022, on the preferential purchase of solid fuel for households (Journal of Laws 2022, item 2236).

From the perspective of the energy mix by fuel type in 2022, by far most of the electricity generated in Poland came from coal-fired power plants, which account for 50 %, almost 27 % from lignite-fired power plants, and only 6 % from gas-fired units. Renewable energy sources, primarily wind farms and photovoltaics, accounted for 16 %, and hydroelectric power plants accounted for less than 2 % of the electricity generated. It is worth noting that there is a year-on-year decline in coal production.[29] Polish legislator has defined renewable energy sourcesas: "renewable, non-fossil energy sources including wind energy, solar energy, aerothermal energy, geothermal energy, hydrothermal energy, hydropower, wave, current and tidal energy, energy obtained from biomass, biogas, agricultural biogas and bioliquids".[30] Renewable electricity generation accounted for 30.7 % of the national generation mix in April 2024, according to Energy Forum calculations. Wind farms made up 16 % of the above result. Photovoltaics were responsible for 10.5 per cent. Meanwhile, 1.8 % came from hydropower and 2.4 % from biomass.[31] From a March 2024 perspective, coal still accounted for the largest share of electricity generation. Hard coal (42.95 %) and lignite (20.84 %) dominated. However, a significant increase in green energy became noticeable, with wind farms contributing 14.45 % to power generation and other renewables 8.86 %.[32]

In May 2025, coal remained the primary source of electricity generation in Poland, with hard coal accounting for 37.33 % and lignite for 18.64 % of total production. Among renewable energy sources, wind power generated 13.01 % of electricity, while other renewables - such as photovoltaics, biomass, and hydropower - contributed a combined 19.25 %; hydropower plants alone provided 1.81 %. The share of natural gas in the energy mix amounted to 9.96 %[33]. The data of May 2025 clearly indicate an increase in

---

29 Polskie Sieci Elektroenergetyczne, 'Raport 2022 KSE' <https://www.pse.pl/dane-systemowe/funkcjonowanie-kse/raporty-roczne-z-funkcjonowania-kse-za-rok/raporty-za-rok-2022#r6_2> accessed 26 August 2023.

30 The Act of February 20, 2015, on the renewable energy sources (Journal of Laws 2023, item 1762).

31 Nowa Energia, 'Miesięcznik Forum Energii' (10 May 2024) <https://nowa-energia.com.pl/2024/05/10/miesiecznik-forum-energii-4/> accessed 01 July 2024.

32 Rynek elektryczny, 'Produkcja energii elektrycznej w Polsce LIPIEC 2024 r.' <https://www.rynekelektryczny.pl/produkcja-energii-elektrycznej-w-polsce/> accessed 29 April 2024.

33 Rynek elektryczny, 'Produkcja energii elektrycznej w Polsce MAJ 2025 r.' <https://www.rynekelektryczny.pl/produkcja-energii-elektrycznej-w-polsce/> accessed 22 June 2025.

the share of renewable energy sources, accompanied by a decline in the role of coal in the structure of electricity generation.

There are challenges of key importance for the Polish economy related to the energy transition. and thus, to the projected decline in the share of coal in the energy mix, which, according to plans, will not exceed 56 % by 2030 (although with high increases in the price of CO2 emission allowances, it could fall even to 37.5 % according to Energy Policy of Poland until 2040 (EPP2040) data). In the following years, the demanding task is to ensure a dynamic yet safe growth of power from renewable energy sources (RES) to reach a level of no less than 32 % in the structure of net domestic electricity consumption by 2030 (according to EPP2040). And while coal's dominance in Poland's energy mix continues, Poland has achieved a significant breakthrough toward energy transition. Thanks to government support for photovoltaics, PV installation capacity[34] increased from a meager 0.2 GW to an impressive 7.7 GW between 2016 and 2021. This growth was made possible primarily by the deployment of small, distributed PV systems in the residential sector, which in total provided 5.9 GW of capacity.[35]

In addition, Poland has an offshore wind strategy. It has signed contracts for a total capacity of 5.9 GW, which are eventually expected to come online by 2027, with plans to reach at least 11 GW by 2040. Moreover, Poland is a signatory to the Baltic Declaration for Offshore Wind Energy.[36] And while the dominance of traditional energy sources has been maintained so far, Poland is trying to actively pursue a sustainable energy future. On the other hand, legislation is also emerging that is hindering the realization of the energy transition rather than accelerating it. An example is the Windmill Law.[37] Initially, there was the 10H rule,[38] which meant that the construction of a wind power plant was limited by the rule that the minimum distance

34 The Ministry of Energy, in cooperation with the Ministry of the Environment, introduced the "My Electricity" program. The main objective of this program was to increase energy production from micro photovoltaic sources. The program's budget was approx. 200 million euros and was aimed at households.

35 International Energy Agency (n 3).

36 European Commission, 'Baltic Ministers endorse commitment for closer cooperation on offshore energy' <https://commission.europa.eu/news/baltic-ministers-endorse-commitment-closer-cooperation-offshore-energy-2020-09-30_en> accessed 29 August 2023.

37 Law of May 20, 2016, on investments in wind power plants (Journal of Laws 2021, item 724, as amended).

38 It was introduced by the Law of May 20, 2016, on investments in wind power plants (Journal of Laws 2021, item 724).

between the power plant and residential buildings, nature conservation areas, and forest complexes must be ten times the height of the turbine including raised blades, which is 500 meters. In fact, the rule has reduced the pace of development of onshore wind power projects. What's more, on April 23, 2023, amended regulations came into force, which changed the distance from 500 meters to 700 meters,[39] making the existing regulations far less favorable for wind investments.

Nuclear power will also begin to play a significant role in Poland's energy mix from 2035 onward. The goal of the Polish Nuclear Power Programme is to build and commission nuclear power plants in Poland. These power plants are to have a total installed capacity of about 6 to 9 GWe. To be able to achieve this goal, 5 basic tasks have been established for the governmental administration. These are: human resources development, infrastructure development, support for domestic industry (e.g. support for national companies to obtain and implement costly quality certification, support for clusters or other initiatives to bring together interested companies), strengthening the nuclear supervision system and proper public communication and information. The above investment is expected to contribute to the diversification of electricity sources, as well as to the stabilisation of energy prices. In addition, emissions will be reduced, and a stable power source will be. All the above factors shall improve the competitiveness of the Polish economy. Poland has a target of putting in place its first reactor with a capacity of 1 to 1.6 GW by 2033 and commissioning six reactors with a total capacity of 6 to 9 GW by 2043. The target is for RES and nuclear to account for 50.8 and 22.6 percent of market share, respectively, by 2040. The new strategy EPP2040 will also reduce the role of coal. In 2040, it is to have an 8 % share in the Polish energy sector.[40]

At the end of May 2024, the National Centre for Research and Development (NCRD)[41] prepared an update of the 'National Energy and Climate Plan 2021–2030'. NCRD has taken the electrification of the district heating sector as the right way to decarbonise it NCRD's analysis assumes that the

---

39 Law of March 9, 2023, on amending the Law on investments in wind power plants and some other laws (Journal of Laws 2023 item 553).

40 Ministry of Funds and Regional Policy, 'The National Recovery and Resilience Plan' (Warsaw 2022) 187 <https://www.funduszeeuropejskie.gov.pl/media/109762/KPO.pdf> accessed 30 August 2023.

41 NCBR – Pol. Narodowe Centrum Badań i Rozwoju, Engl. NCRD – The National Centre for Research and Development. NCRD is an executive agency of the Polish Ministry of National Education.

Polish electricity system will ultimately rely mainly on offshore and onshore wind power and photovoltaic power plants. Those energy sources will be supplemented by nuclear power and gas-fired biomethane power plants.[42]

E. Power-to-X Technologies – Alternative Energy Sources – Hydrogen

Hydrogen is increasingly being identified in the public space as one of the elements of the energy transition. The Polish legislature has included hydrogen-related issues in the Law of January 11, 2018, Electromobility and Alternative Fuel[43], and in the Polish Hydrogen Strategy until 2030.[44]

The Law of Electromobility and Alternative Fuels includes, among other things, conditions for the operation of clean transport zones and information obligations regarding alternative fuels. Moreover, definitions related to different types of hydrogen are included, including low-emission, electrolytic, and renewable.

The Polish Hydrogen Strategy until 2030 (PHS) is a strategic document that defines the direction of development of the hydrogen market in Poland. The PHS assumes six objectives to be implemented as part of the hydrogen market development strategy. These objectives in terms of envisaged time horizons, which are set for 2025 and 2030. Moreover, the implementation of the objectives contained in the PHS is expected to contribute significantly to the decarbonization of the sectors with the highest energy consumption, as well as to help implement green hydrogen production on an industrial scale.

The first goal is to implement hydrogen technologies in the power and heating industries. Within this goal, it is assumed that hydrogen will reach viability most quickly using renewable energy sources, such as offshore wind and photovoltaics.

Another priority is the use of hydrogen as an alternative fuel in the transportation sector, which will introduce sustainable mobility in Poland. In the

42 NCBR, 'NCBR opracowało "Koncepcję dekarbonizacji ciepłownictwa systemowego"' <https://www.gov.pl/web/ncbr/ncbr-opracowal-koncepcje-dekarbonizacji-cieplownictwa-systemowego> accessed 02 June 2024.

43 Law of January 11, 2018, on electromobility and alternative fuels (Journal of Laws 2023, Item 875, 1394, 1506, 1681).

44 Ministerstwo Klimatu i Środowiska, 'Polska Strategia Wodorowa do roku 2030' <https://www.gov.pl/web/klimat/polska-strategia-wodorowa-do-roku-2030> accessed 30 August 2023.

context of road transport, hydrogen is planned as a source of propulsion, especially for vehicles used in public transport and heavy transport. As an aside, it can be mentioned that the world's first hydrogen locomotive was built in Poland.[45]

Implementation of the third goal focuses on supporting the decarbonization of the industry. This is to be facilitated by using only low-carbon hydrogen. According to the Polish Hydrogen Strategy (PHS),[46] only blue and green hydrogen is assigned to low-carbon hydrogen, rejecting gray hydrogen without CCUS technology. Considering the PHS, the application of hydrogen technologies is particularly important in fuel production, non-metallic mineral extraction, chemical production, and steel production. An important factor in increasing the role of hydrogen in industry is the idea of creating hydrogen regional ecosystems, also known as hydrogen valleys. Currently, there are eight hydrogen valley projects in Poland, which cover almost the entire area of the country: Pomeranian Hydrogen Valley, West Pomeranian Hydrogen Valley, Greater Poland Hydrogen Valley, Lower Silesia Hydrogen Valley, Silesia and Lesser Poland Hydrogen Valley, Subcarpathian Hydrogen Valley, Central Hydrogen Valley, and Masovian Hydrogen Valley.[47]

Another goal is to develop hydrogen production in new installations. According to PHS guidelines, hydrogen production is to be characterized by low or zero greenhouse gas emissions. In addition, it is assumed that hydrogen production installations should be placed optimally near renewable energy sources and in centers of demand centers of demand, forming energy clusters, which will significantly improve Poland's energy security.

The fifth goal of the PHS is the efficient and safe transmission, distribution, and storage of hydrogen. Initially, the envisioned hydrogen transportation would involve rail and road. Meanwhile, cooperation at the EU level would support the development of hydrogen transportation infrastructure under the European Hydrogen Backbone program.

The final goal is to create a stable regulatory environment. This is the most important step towards developing a regulatory structure to enable

45 Pesa, 'Kolejowa premiera roku – PESA zaprezentowała lokomotywę wodorową na TRAKO' <https://pesa.pl/kolejowa-premiera-roku-pesa-zaprezentowala-lokomotywe-wodorowa-na-trako/> accessed 30 August 2023.

46 The strategic document that defines the direction of development of the hydrogen market in Poland.

47 Agencja Rozwoju Przemysłu, 'Doliny wodorowe' <https://arp.pl/pl/jak-dzialamy/doliny-wodorowe/> accessed 24 August 2023.

the use of hydrogen in transport as an alternative fuel. The second step is the development of a hydrogen legislative package that considers market aspects. The final stage in legislative activities concerning the PHS is expected to be the precise definition of legal issues related to the operation of the hydrogen market, with the aim of implementing EU regulations in this regard. In the Government's legislative and programme work list of 27 May 2024,[48] information on the draft Energy Law[49] was published. In addition to the fact that the above legislative measures are one of the milestones of the National Reconstruction Plan, the draft amendment enables the implementation of Objective 6 'Creation of a stable regulatory environment' of the PSW. This is because the amendment is part of a legislative package called the 'Constitution for Hydrogen'. The aforementioned draft was sent to public consultation by the Ministry of Climate and Environment and subsequently submitted for opinion. The draft amendment provides for, among other things, the creation of rules for the certification and designation of hydrogen operators, regulation of the licensing of hydrogen storage activities.

F. Perspectives of Energy Transition in Poland

Combining sectors in Poland, particularly through the electrification of the mobility and heating sectors, is key to achieving greenhouse gas emission reduction targets and accelerating decarbonization. This approach allows the use of surplus renewable energy and increased energy efficiency in many sectors of the economy.

Also, improving the energy efficiency of buildings to make them less energy-intensive will be an important step. Therefore, all new buildings that will be constructed in Poland (a building that has received a building permit after 2021, a project created according to old guidelines, the formalities of which have not been finalized, as well as a modernized or expanded building) must meet the relevant conditions, which are defined by the

48 Ministerstwo Klimatu i Środowiska, 'Draft Act amending the Energy Law and certain other acts (UD36)' <https://www.gov.pl/web/klimat/konsultacje-publiczne-projektu-ustawy-o-zmianie-ustawy--prawo-energetyczne-raz-niektorych-innych-ustaw-ud36> accessed 14 July 2024.

49 The Act of April 10, 1997, Energy Law (Journal of Laws 2024, item 266).

decree of the Minister of Infrastructure.[50] These have been included in the new energy standard commonly referred to as WT 2021.[51]

This standard is largely concerned with reducing the heat transfer coefficient of building components: for example, walls, roofs, and windows. Therefore, good insulation is required, including thermally insulated windows and energy-efficient exterior doors. What's more, the WT 2021 standard is expected to popularize RES, as they are required to reduce the share of non-renewable energy.[52] Conventional coal-fired stoves, oil-fired boilers, and modern gas-fired boilers face difficulties in meeting the stringent requirements of the WT 2021 standard. Therefore, to meet them, it becomes necessary to include renewable energy sources in the energy balance of buildings.[53] The WT 2021 standard was created in response to the pro-environmental policy of the European Union and the adoption of three standard demands, which are called the 3 x 20 energy and climate package.[54]

As a result, this will help reduce carbon emissions associated with energy consumption in the construction sector.

In the context of Poland's energy transition, there are also significant tensions between three key aspects: greening energy generation, ensuring the security of the energy supply, and maintaining energy affordability. These aspects may come into conflict and require finding an appropriate compromise.

Regarding the issue of greening energy generation, the goal is to increase the share of renewable energy sources (RES) thanks to which greenhouse gas and pollution emissions will be reduced. However, to be able to put RES

---

50 Regulation of the Minister of Infrastructure of April 12, 2002, on the technical conditions to be fulfilled by buildings and their location (Journal of Laws 2022.0.1225, i.e.).

51 WT – Pol. warunki techniczne, Engl. Technical conditions.

52 Regulation of the Minister of Infrastructure of April 12, 2002, on the technical conditions to be fulfilled by buildings and their location (Journal of Laws 2022.0.1225, i.e.).

53 Corab, 'Standard energetyczny WT 2021. Jakie ma wymagania?' (02 December 2021) <https://corab.pl/aktualnosci/standard-energetyczny-wt-2021-jakie-ma-wymagania> accessed 31 August 2023.

54 Directive 2009/28/EC of the European Parliament and of the Council of April 23, 2009, on the promotion of the use of energy from renewable sources amending and subsequently repealing Directives 2001/77/EC and 2003/30/EC [2009] OJ L 140/16, but the directive was in force until June 30, 2021. It was repealed by Directive (EU) 2018/2001 of the European Parliament and of the Council of December 11, 2018, on the promotion of the use of energy from renewable sources (recast) [2018] OJ L 328/82.

energy into circulation, it is necessary to meet the challenges associated with the variability of weather conditions in Poland, as well as to carry out infrastructure modernization. The modernization of infrastructure as well as the entire energy transition will entail huge costs, which according to various estimates will amount to €135 billion by the end of 2030.[55] The investment costs will be spread over time, but at the same time passed on to consumers in the form of higher energy prices. In turn, this could have a negative impact on the competitiveness of the Polish economy and lead to deterioration in the financial situation of households. Therefore, the biggest challenge is to find a balance between carrying out an effective energy transition and maintaining affordable energy for citizens.

G. Summary

Poland faces the enormous challenge of meeting the demands of combating climate change and decarbonization, especially given the heavy reliance of the Polish energy sector, and consequently the economy, on coal. Efforts are being made to develop new projects and strategies, as well as legislative changes that lead to the energy transition. However, the pace of this work seems to be unsatisfactory in Poland. A good example is the RES sector including wind farms. Current plans are ambitious, especially in terms of increasing RES in the national energy mix, it will be very difficult to achieve a decisive reduction of coal in the energy supply chain without appropriate legislative changes. As a result, continuing to maintain dependence on coal not only slows down the energy transition process but most importantly generates unnecessary costs, given that the price of carbon allowances in the EU ETS system, according to all forecasts, will rise. Poland's energy sector thus now faces a difficult choice between the transformation of traditional power generation technologies and the need to remain competitive, in a low-emission future. Moreover, Poland's energy transition requires a huge financial outlay, according to the E&Y report,[56] in the order of €135

---

55 Bankier (n 8).

56 Polish Electricity Committee, 'Poland's Energy Transformation Path' (Warsaw 2022) 113, <https://pkee.pl/publications/raport-ey-i-pkee-polska-sciezka-transformacji-ener getycznej/> accessed 27 September 2023.

billion.[57] This implies the need to support the energy companies on which the main burden of Poland's energy transition rests with EU funds. With additional EU funds, it will be possible to fill the investment gap resulting from Poland's goal of achieving climate neutrality.

Bibliography

Agencja Rozwoju Przemysłu, 'Doliny wodorowe' <https://arp.pl/pl/jak-dzialamy/doliny-wodorowe/> accessed 24 August 2023

Bankier, 'Ogromne koszty polskiej transformacji energetycznej i równie ogromna luka inwestycyjna' (27 August 2023) <https://www.bankier.pl/wiadomosc/Ogromne-koszty-polskiej-transformacji-energetycznej-i-rownie-ogromna-luka-inwestycyjna-8595823.html> accessed 29 August 2023

Corab, 'Standard energetyczny WT 2021. Jakie ma wymagania?' (02 December 2021) <https://corab.pl/aktualnosci/standard-energetyczny-wt-2021-jakie-ma-wymagania> accessed 31 August 2023

Energy Regulatory Office, '2021 Rynek Hurtowy' <https://www.ure.gov.pl/pl/energia-elektryczna/charakterystyka-rynku/10372,2021.html> accessed 31 August 2023

European Commission, 'Recommendation of 26.4.2024 on the draft updated integrated national energy and climate plan of Poland covering the period 2021–2030' C (2024) 2900 final <https://commission.europa.eu/document/download/b40cb8bb-4eaf-434b-a298-6f282fb8ed4a_en?filename=Recommendation_draft_updated_NECP_Poland_2024.pdf.pdf> accessed 04 July 2024

European Commission, 'Baltic Ministers endorse commitment for closer cooperation on offshore energy' <https://commission.europa.eu/news/baltic-ministers-endorse-commitment-closer-cooperation-offshore-energy-2020-09-30_en> accessed 29 August 2023

European Parliament, 'Briefing, Next Generation EU (NGEU) delivery – How are the Member States doing? Poland's National Recovery and Resilience Plan' <https://www.europarl.europa.eu/RegData/etudes/BRIE/2022/733665/EPRS-Briefing-733665-NRRP-Poland-FINAL.pdf> accessed 04 July 2024

Eurostat, 'Electricity prices (including taxes) for household consumers, first half 2022' <https://ec.europa.eu/eurostat/statistics-explained/index.php?title=Electricity_price_statistics> accessed 29 August 2023

Eurostat, 'Coal production and consumption up in 2022' <https://ec.europa.eu/eurostat/web/products-eurostat-news/w/ddn-20230622-2> accessed 28 August 2023

International Energy Agency, 'Poland 2022 Energy Policy Review' <https://www.iea.org/reports/poland-2022/executive-summary> accessed 28 August 2023

Ministerstwo Klimatu i Środowiska, 'Badania świadomości ekologicznej mieszkańców Polski' <https://www.gov.pl/web/edukacja-ekologiczna/badania-swiadomosci-ekologicznej> accessed 08 August 2023

57 The issue is considered above in Section F. 'Perspectives of Energy Transition in Poland'.

Ministerstwo Klimatu i Środowiska, 'Draft Act amending the Energy Law and certain other acts (UD36)' <https://www.gov.pl/web/klimat/konsultacje-publiczne-projektu-ustawy-o-zmianie-ustawy--prawo-energetyczne-raz-niektorych-innych-ustaw-ud36> accessed 14 July 2024

Ministerstwo Klimatu i Środowiska, 'Krajowy Plan w dziedzinie Energii i Klimatu do 2030 r.' <https://commission.europa.eu/document/download/5118b15e-d380-49ae-b8bb-41cc81a28e15_pl?filename=PL_NECPupdate_Projekt_aKPEiK_tekst_ostateczny.pdf> accessed 02 July 2024

Ministerstwo Klimatu i Środowiska, 'Polska Strategia Wodorowa do roku 2030' <https://www.gov.pl/web/klimat/polska-strategia-wodorowa-do-roku-2030> accessed 30 August 2023

Ministerstwo Klimatu i Środowiska, 'National Energy and Climate Plan for the years 2021–2030 -submitted in 2019' <https://www.gov.pl/web/klimat/national-energy-and-climate-plan-for-the-years-2021-2030> accessed 16 November 2023

Ministry of Funds and Regional Policy, 'The National Recovery and Resilience Plan' (Warsaw 2022) 187 <https://www.funduszeeuropejskie.gov.pl/media/109762/KPO.pdf> accessed 30 August 2023

Ministry of State Assets, 'Summary report on intervention coal import and distribution in the 2022/2023 heating season' (Warsaw 2023)

Muzeum Geologiczne, 'Węgiel kamienny ' <https://www.pgi.gov.pl/muzeum/kopalnia-wiedzy-1/12580-wegiel-kamienny.html> accessed 28 August 2023

National Centre for Emissions Management (KOBiZE), 'Poland's Eighth National Communication and Fifth Biennial Report under the UNFCCC' (Warsaw 2022) <https://unfccc.int/sites/default/files/resource/Poland_Report-NC8_BR5_27dec2022%20%281%29.pdf> accessed 04 July 2024

NCBR, 'NCBR opracowało "Koncepcję dekarbonizacji ciepłownictwa systemowego"' <https://www.gov.pl/web/ncbr/ncbr-opracowal-koncepcje-dekarbonizacji-cieplownictwa-systemowego> accessed 02 June 2024

Nowa Energia, 'Miesięcznik Forum Energii' (10 May 2024) <https://nowa-energia.com.pl/2024/05/10/miesiecznik-forum-energii-4/> accessed 01 July 2024

Pesa, 'Kolejowa premiera roku – PESA zaprezentowała lokomotywę wodorową na TRAKO' <https://pesa.pl/kolejowa-premiera-roku-pesa-zaprezentowala-lokomotywe-wodorowa-na-trako/> accessed 30 August 2023

Polish Electricity Committee, 'Poland's Energy Transformation Path' (Warsaw 2022) 113 <https://pkee.pl/publications/raport-ey-i-pkee-polska-sciezka-transformacji-energetycznej/> accessed 27 September 2023

Polskie Sieci Elektroenergetyczne, 'Raport 2022 KSE' <https://www.pse.pl/dane-systemowe/funkcjonowanie-kse/raporty-roczne-z-funkcjonowania-kse-za-rok/raporty-za-rok-2022#r6_2> accessed 26 August 2023

Rynek elektryczny, 'Produkcja energii elektrycznej w Polsce LIPIEC 2024 r.' <https://www.rynekelektryczny.pl/produkcja-energii-elektrycznej-w-polsce/> accessed 29 April 2024

Rynek elektryczny, 'Produkcja energii elektrycznej w Polsce MAJ 2025 r.' <https://www.rynekelektryczny.pl/produkcja-energii-elektrycznej-w-polsce/> accessed 22 June 2025.

Worldbank, 'GDP Growth Poland' <https://data.worldbank.org/indicator/NY.GDP.MKTP.KD.ZG?locations=PL> accessed 26 August 2023

Worldbank, 'GDP Growth European Union' <https://data.worldbank.org/indicator/NY.GDP.MKTP.KD.ZG?locations=EU> accessed 26 August 2023

Part C –
The Law of Energy Transition in European Countries: Special Focus on the Law of Renewable Energies

The Law of Renewable Energies in Germany

Michael Fehling

A. Empiric development: growing gap between official policies (goals) and reality

In the 1990/2000s, Germany was a pioneer in Europe in promoting renewable energy in the form of (onshore) wind power and rooftop solar installations. The model of a feed-in priority into the electricity grid combined with a fixed, long-term guaranteed feed-in tariff led to an expansion dynamic that significantly exceeded expectations.[1]

From around 2012, however, the voices denouncing allegedly inefficient excessive subsidization gained political momentum. In doing so, they also questioned EU state aid law. However, with regard to the Electricity Feeding Act [*Stromeinspeisungsgesetz*][2], the predecessor of the Renewable Energy Sources Act 2000 [*Erneuerbare-Energien-Gesetz – EEG 2000*[3]], the European Court of Justice (ECJ) had found that the feed-in tariff to be paid by the electricity transmission system operators did not constitute state aid at all (Art. 107(1) TFEU[4]) because this did not involve any direct or indirect transfer of State resources.[5] Much later, the ECJ essentially confirmed

1 For a similar observation see Johannes Saurer/Jonas Monast, 'Renewable Energy Federalism in Germany and the United States' (2021) TEL 293 302 f.; for data on the development over time see Bundeskartellamt, 'Monitoringbericht 2022' *(Monitoring Report)* (2022) 96 <www.bundeskartellamt.de/SharedDocs/Publikation/DE/Berichte/Energie-Monitoring-2022.pdf?__blob=publicationFile&v=4> accessed 17 June 2025.

2 BGBl 1990 I 2633, expired by Article 4 of the Act of March 29, 2000 (BGBl 2000 I 305).

3 BGBl 2000 I 305, expired by Article 4 of the Act of July 21, 2004 (BGBl 2004 I 1918).

4 Consolidated version of the Treaty on the Functioning of the European Union [2012] OJ C 326/47.

5 Case C-379/98 *PreussenElektra AG v Schleswag AG* EU:C:2001:160 [2001] ECR I-02099, para 59.

this in 2019[6] for the Renewable Energy Sources Act 2012 [*Erneuerbare-Energien-Gesetz – EEG 2012*[7]].[8]

The practice of transmission system operators to pass on their costs for feed-in tariffs, which were rising steadily with the expansion, down the economic chain to the – mainly private – electricity customers led to concerns about excessively high electricity prices.[9] The expansion of renewable energies in electricity generation thus became a victim of its own success. The unabated momentum towards expansion with the help of the fixed feed-in tariff – which remained in place only for small-scale plants – was succeeded by a cap on expansion by means of fixed tendering quotas for a market premium from 2014 onwards. This model had already been preferred by the Commission in its state aid directives and later on was also enshrined in the then Renewable Energy Directive[10].

For offshore wind power plants, a somewhat different system of interdependence between planning approval and support was introduced in the Offshore Wind Energy Act [*Windenergie-auf-See-Gesetz – WindSeeG*[11]]. In other respects, too, the regulatory framework has become increasingly complicated. This especially applies to the interaction between location planning and plant approval (onshore) or plan approval (offshore) on the one hand and tender competition for the market premium on the other hand. In the meantime, the tendered quantities of renewably electricity generated by Onshore Wind Energy could no longer be fully awarded due to a lack of sufficient bids.[12] The procedure is widely regarded as too

---

6 Case C-405/16 *Federal Republic of Germany v European Commission* EU:C:2019:268 [2019].

7 BGBl 2008 I 2074, expired by Article 23 of the Act of July 21, 2014 (BGBl 2014 I 1066).

8 This has probably changed at least with the EEG 2023 because now state resources are used in the refinancing system, compare Section C. 2. (b) with (n 52).

9 Bundesministerium für Wirtschaft und Klimaschutz, 'Durchschnittlicher Strompreis für einen Haushalt in Cent/kWh (Jahresverbrauch: 3.500 kWh)' *(Average electricity price for a household in cents/kWh (annual consumption: 3,500 kWh))* <www.bmwk.de/Redaktion/DE/Downloads/I/Infografiken/durchschnittlicher-strompreis-haushalt.pdf?_blob=publicationFile&v=6> accessed 17 June 2025.

10 For the whole development until 2020 also compare Saurer/Monast (n 1) 300–302.

11 BGBl. 2016 I 2258, last amended by Article 44 of the Act of October 23, 2024 (BGBl. 2024 I Number 323).

12 Bundesnetzagentur, 'Ergebnisse der Ausschreibungsrunden für Windenergie-Anlagen an Land' *(Results of the bidding rounds for onshore wind turbines)* <www.bundesnetzagentur.de/DE/Fachthemen/ElektrizitaetundGas/Ausschreibungen/Wind_Onshore/BeendeteAusschreibungen/start.html> accessed 17 Junel 2025; Victoria Harsch/Johannes Antoni, 'Alternativen der Förderung erneuerbarer Energien abseits

time-consuming and the risk of ending up without funding and stranded investments may be too great.

Nevertheless, the Renewable Energy Sources Act 2023 [*Erneuerbare-Energien-Gesetz 2023 – EEG 2023*[13]) and the simultaneously amended Offshore Wind Energy Act [*WindSeeG*] have made the expansion targets even more ambitious: The share of electricity generated from renewable energies is to be increased to at least 80 % by 2030 (Sec. 1(1) Renewable Energy Sources Act 2023 – *EEG 2023*). This necessitates a doubling of the proportion of electricity generated from renewable energy sources in overall electricity consumption (with a projected electricity consumption of 780 terawatt-hours[14]).[15] In 2024, its share merely amounted to about 54,4 %.[16] With the completion of the coal phase-out scheduled for 2038 at the latest, the aim is to achieve a carbon-neutral electricity supply in Germany (Sec. 1a(1) Renewable Energy Sources Act 2023 – *EEG 2023*). This goes beyond the European requirements. The following section will take a closer look at the instruments – some of which are new or have been made more concise

des Ausschreibungsmodells im Lichte des EU-Rechts' *(Alternatives to the tendering model for supporting renewable energies)* (2023) EnWZ 3.

13 BGBl. 2014 I 1066, last amended by Article 1 of the Act of February 21, 2025 (BGBl. 2025 I Number 52).

14 Julian Brandes/Markus Hahn/Charlotte Senkspiel et al., 'Wege zu einem klimaneutralen Energiesystem. Die deutsche Energiewende im Kontext gesellschaftlicher Verhaltensweisen – Update für ein CO_2-Reduktionsziel von 65 % in 2030 und 100 % in 2050' *(Paths to a climate-neutral energy system. The German energy transition in the context of of societal behavior – Update for a CO_2 reduction target of 65 % in 2030 and 100 % in 2050)* (2010) ISE Fraunhofer, 10 <https://www.ise.fraunhofer.de/content/dam/ise/de/documents/publications/studies/Fraunhofer-ISE-Studie-Wege-zu-einem-klimaneutralen-Energiesystem-Update-Zielverschaerfung.pdf> accessed 17 June 2025; a recent Monitoring Report projects lower electricity consumption of 600 to 700 terawatt-hours in 2030, see Energiewirtschaftliches Institut an der Universität zu Köln, 'Energiewende. Effizient. Machen – Monitoring Bericht zum Start der 21. Legislaturperiode' *(Energy. Transition. Efficiency. – Monitoring Report at the start of the 21st legislative term)* (2025) <https://www.bundeswirtschaftsministerium.de/Redaktion/DE/Publikationen/Energie/energiewende-effizient-machen.pdf?__blob=publicationFile&v=20> accessed 23 September 2025.

15 Bundesregierung, 'Ausbau erneuerbarer Energien massiv beschleunigen' *(Rapidly accelerate the expansion of renewable energies)* (2023) <https://www.bundesregierung.de/breg-de/service/archiv-bundesregierung/novelle-eeg-gesetz-2023-2023972> accessed 17 June 2025.

16 Umweltbundesamt, Indikator: 'Anteil Erneuerbare am Bruttostromverbrauch' (Indicator: Share of Renewables in Electricity) (2025) <https://www.umweltbundesamt.de/indikator-anteil-erneuerbare-am#die-wichtigsten-fakten> accessed 17 June 2025.

– that are to be used to regalvanize the trend into a massively dynamic expansion.

B. Current challenges and obstacles for the expansion of renewables

The first challenge is to nearly double the share of renewable energies in electricity generation in just 13 years (until 2038) compared to the previous 25 years or so. At first glance, this seems manageable. However, electricity consumption is projected to increase considerably as a result of so-called sector coupling, i.e. the newly introduced use of electricity in the transport sector too (electromobility), partly in the heating sector (e.g. heat pumps) and finally – possibly after converting to hydrogen – even in industry applications.[17] This represents a major obstacle. Efforts in nature conservation and species protection render finding additional suitable sites on land and at sea increasingly difficult.

The share of renewable energy in the total energy consumption of all sectors merely amounted to about 22,4.% in 2024.[18] The target set by the EU was raised to 42.5 % for 2030 by the amended Renewable Energy Directive (RED III[19]).[20] In Germany, the overall goal is to achieve climate

17 Anna Brinkschmidt, 'Sektorkopplung im Energieregulierungsrecht' *(Sector coupling in energy regulation law)* (Mohr Siebeck 2024) 25.

18 Statista, 'Anteil Erneuerbarer Energien am Bruttoendenergieverbrauch in Deutschland in den Jahren 2005 bis 2024 ' *(Share of Renewable Energies in Germany on Total Energy Consumption in the Years 2005 to 2024.)*<https://de.statista.com/statistik/daten/studie/856326/umfrage/stromerzeugung-aus-erneuerbaren-energien-in-deutschland> accessed 17 June 2025.

19 Directive (EU) 2023/2314 of the European Parliament and the Council of 18 October 2023 amending Directive (EU) 2018/2001, Regulation (EU) 2018/1999 and Directive 98/70/EC as regards the promotion of energy from renewable sources, and repealing Council Directive (EU) 2015/65 [2023] OJ L 2023/2413 Art. 1 (2) (a); for the planned implementation in German law, which did not find a parlamentary majority, see Bundesministerium für Wirtschaft und Klimaschutz, 'Entwurf eines Gesetzes zur Umsetzung der Richtlinie (EU) 2023/2413 im Bereich Windenergie an Land und Solarenergie'*(Draft of a bill for the implementation of Directive (EU) 2023/2413 in the area of onshore wind energy and solar energy)* <https://www.bmwk.de/Redaktion/DE/Downloads/Gesetz/20240402-referentenentwurf-umsetzung-red-3-wind-an-land-und-solarenergie.pdf?__blob=publicationFile&v=4> accessed 17 June 2025.

20 For some Background see Alessandro Gemmo, 'European Renewable Energy Directive (RED III): updated ambitious targets to boost the renewable energy market' (2023) <https://sustainablefutures.linklaters.com/post/102ipy5/european-renewable-energy-directive-red-iii-updated-ambitious-targets-to-boost> accessed 17 June 2025;

neutrality by 2045 (Sec. 3(2) Federal Climate Protection Act [*Bundes-Klimaschutzgesetz – KSG*[21]]), that is, five years earlier than on European level (Art. 2(1) European Climate Law [*Europäisches Klimaschutzgesetz*[22]]). The gap between long-term aspirations and today's reality in this overall perspective on the energy transition is thus far greater than in the case of electricity generation. A rapid expansion of the hydrogen market is needed since certain sectors of (heavy) industry can only be decarbonized through the use of green hydrogen.[23]

As the share of volatile renewables in electricity generation continues to grow, securing the stability of the power grid will also become a problem. Prudently, Germany – in contrast to other European countries – terminated nuclear energy in 2023 (cf. Sec. 1 Number 1 Atomic Energy Act [*Atomgesetz – AtG*[24]]). The phase-out of coal-fired power generation, which is particularly detrimental to the climate, must by law be completed by 2038 at the latest, and if possible, by 2035 (see Sec. 2(2) Number 2, 47(1), 56 Coal-fired Power Generation Termination Act – [*Kohleverstromungsbeendigungsgesetz*] [25]). Thus, only natural gas currently remains to counter the volatility of the renewables and to stabilize the grid. As a result of the Russian war of aggression in Ukraine, Germany now heavily depends on LNG

Uta Stäsche, 'Reform des EU-Emissionshandelssystems, der Effort-Sharing-Verordnung, der Erneuerbare-Energien-Richtlinie und der Energieeffizienzrichtlinie – "Fit for 55"?' *(Reform of the EU Emissions Trading Scheme, the Effort Sharing Regulation, the Renewable Energies Directive and the Energy Efficiency Directive – "Fit for 55"?)* (2023) 6 KlimR 171 et seq.

21 BGBl. 2019 I 2513, last amended by Article 1 of the Act of July 15, 2024 (BGBl. 2024 I Number 235); compare also Bundesregierung, 'Intergenerational contract for the climate' (2021) <www.bundesregierung.de/breg-de/schwerpunkte/klimaschutz/climate-change-act-2021-1936846> accessed 17 June 2025.

22 Regulation (EU) 2021/1119 of the European Parliament and of the Council of 30 June 2023 establishing the framework for achieving climate neutrality and amending Regulations (EC) No 401/2009 and (EU) 2018/1999 [2023] OJ L 243/1.

23 Hana Mandová/Tiffany Vass/Araceli Fernandez Pales et al., 'The challenge of reaching zero emissions in heavy industry', (IEA, 2020) <www.iea.org/articles/the-challenge-of-reaching-zero-emissions-in-heavy-industry> accessed 17 June 2025.

24 BGBl. 1985 I 1565, last amended by Article 1 of the Act of December 4, 2022 (BGBl. 2022 I 2153). For an outdated unofficial version Bundesamt für Strahlenschutz, 'Act on the Peaceful Utilisation of Atomic Energy and the Protection against its Hazards (Atomic Energy Act)' <www.base.bund.de/SharedDocs/Downloads/BASE/EN/hns/a1-english/A1-07-16-AtG.pdf?__blob=publicationFile&v=2> accessed 29 April 2024.

25 BGBl. 2020 I 1818, last amended by Article 7 of the Act of February 21, 2025 (BGBl. 2025 I Number 51).

imports. In the medium term, natural gas will probably lose importance as a bridge technology.[26] Nevertheless, the new German Government is once again increasingly focussing on new gas-fired power plants with up to 20 GW generation capacity to bridge periods without sufficient wind and sun as a so-called power plant reserve [*Kraftwerksreserve*]. Unlike the previous one, the new government will probably even refrain from demanding that these new gas-fired power plants are already prepared for a later conversion to green hydrogen[27]. This harbours the risk of a lock-in effect. Therefore, the massive expansion of renewable alternatives alone is not sufficient to achieve the energy transition: We also badly need the rapid technical development of storage technology and, in the future, hydrogen storage facilities.

C. The legal framework resulting from several amendments

In the German Federal system, most of the relevant law is on the national level. Significant new regulations are contained in the "Act on Immediate Measures for the Accelerated Expansion of Renewable Energies and Further Measures in the Electricity Sector"[28], which amended many relevant specialized laws and came into force in large parts at the beginning of 2023. Further new laws are being added.

1. Preliminary remark on the distribution of competences between the federal government, the states and the municipalities

The central legislative competences for the energy transition are located on federal level (cf. Art. 74 Number 11 and 24 of the German Constitution,

26 Arguing in this direction: Der Informationsdienst des Instituts der deutschen Wirtschaft, 'Natural gas: The bridge is crumbling' (2023) <www.iwd.de/artikel/erdgas-die-bruecke-broeckelt-587736/> accessed 17 June 2025.

27 In favor of "technological openness" [*Technologieoffenheit*] CDU/CSU/SPD, 'Verantwortung für Deutschland – Koalitionsvertrag für die 21. Legislaturperiode' *(Responsibility for Germany – Coalition Agreement for the 21st legislative period)* (2025), para 1067–1072 <https://www.koalitionsvertrag2025.de/> accessed 17 June 2025.

28 Gesetz zu Sofortmaßnahmen für einen beschleunigten Ausbau der erneuerbaren Energien und weiteren Maßnahmen im Stromsektor, BGBl. 2022 I 1237.

the "Basic Law" [*Grundgesetz – GG*[29]]).[30] This also includes the financial support of renewable energies. Except for smaller photovoltaic installations (building permits under the building codes of the Federal States [*Länder*], based on Art. 70 Basic Law [*GG*], the Federation [*Bund*] has legislative power also regarding the approval for generation plants. Most important is the Federal Immission Control Act [*Bundes-Immissionsschutzgesetz – BImSchG*[31]], which regulates, inter alia, the approval of onshore wind energy plants and has been enacted due to Art. 74 Number 24 Basic Law [*GG*]. A difficult mixture of competences exists regarding location planning, especially for onshore wind turbines. Although the federal government is responsible for the legislation on urban land-use planning (Federal Building Code [*Baugesetzbuch – BauGB*[32]]) according to Art. 74 Number 18 Basic Law [*GG*], the state legislatures are responsible at an intermediate level of regional planning and for other supplementary regulations.

In contrast, according to Art. 83 Basic Law [*GG*] the Federal States [*Länder*] are mostly responsible for implementing the relevant federal laws. So concrete location planning for most generating installations (especially onshore wind and solar) is in the hands of the *Länder* and, at the most concrete level, the municipalities. On the basis of Art. 87(3) Basic Law [*GG*], only large-scale planning for electricity transmission grids is largely the responsibility of the Federal Network Agency [*Bundesnetzagentur – BNetzA*[33]], as well as, together with the Federal Maritime and Hydrographic Agency [*Bundesamt für Seeschifffahrt und Hydrograhie – BSH*[34]], planning approval and upstream planning for offshore wind power plants in the German exclusive economic zone.[35] Construction or immission control

29 BGBl. 1949 I 1, last amended by Article 1 of the Act of March 22, 2025 (BGBl. 2025 I Number 94); for an English version see: <www.gesetze-im-internet.de/englisch_gg/> accessed 17 June 2025.

30 For a short overview see Saurer/Monast (n 1) 299–301.

31 BGBl. 2013 I 1274, last amended by Article 11 of the Act of February 24, 2025 (BGBl. 2025 I Number 58).

32 BGBl. 2017 I 3634, last amended by Article 1 of the Act of December 20, 2023 (BGBl. 2023 I Number 394); for an outdated unofficial version ‚Federal Building Code' <www.lexadin.nl/wlg/legis/nofr/eur/arch/ger/Federal-Building-Code.pdf> accessed 17 June 2025.

33 Due to Sec. 1 Regulation on the Assignment of Approval Procedures for Interstate and Cross-Border Extra-High Voltage Power Lines to the Federal Network Agency [*PlfZV*].

34 Due to Sec. 66(2) Offshore Wind Energy Act [*WindSeeG*].

35 See also Saurer/Monast (n 1) 316–317.

permits for other generating installations are issued by the Federal States [*Länder*].

These interdependences reflect the complicated German federal system, whereby the legislative competencies are mainly associated with the federal level and the implementation competences are largely within the *Länder*. That is the so-called "administrative federalism" [*Vollzugsföderalismus*].[36] In recent years, it has significantly hampered the expansion of onshore wind energy because federal states such as Bavaria had set extremely large minimum distances from residential development (until recently 10 times the height of the turbine).[37]

2. Instruments for accelerating the decarbonization of power generation and accompanying change in the financing system

Above all, the amendments to the Renewable Energy Sources Act [*EEG 2023*], which came into force at the beginning of 2023, and in parallel also to the Offshore Wind Energy Act [*WindSeeG*] and to the Combined Heat and Power Act [*Kraft-Wärme-Kopplungsgesetz – KWKG 2023*[38]], are intended to lend new momentum to the energy transition. The Wind Energy Area Requirements Act [*Windenergieflächenbedarfsgesetz – WindBG*[39]]) and parallel amendments to the Federal Building Code [*BauGB*] are important for the identification of suitable sites. In the field of solar energy, the so called "Solar Package I" facilitates the expansion of photovoltaic systems (PV-Sys-

---

36 For this designation see e.g. Georg Hermes, 'Art. 83 para 16' in Horst Dreier (ed), *Grundgesetz Kommentar (Commentary on the Basic Law)* (3rd edn, Mohr Siebeck 2018); compare furthermore Saurer/Monast (n 1) 294; Arthur B. Gunlicks, *The Länder and German Federalism* (Manchester University Press 2003) 388.

37 More details by Saurer, Monast (n 1) 305–306, 314–315. Recently, this possibility has been mitigated, see Section C. 3.

38 BGBl. 2015 I 2498, last amended by Article 9 of the Act of December 20, 2022 (BGBl. 2022 I 2512).

39 BGBl. 2022 I 1353, last amended by Article 6 of the Act of July 26, 2023 (BGBl. 2023 I Number 202).

tems).[40] The amendment of several laws includes[41] increased support for the use of large-scale PV-Systems to expand solar energy in industry. For private individuals, this law makes it easier to use balcony power plants and to supply buildings with PV-Systems. In addition, area-efficient systems such as agricultural photovoltaics and parking photovoltaics are promoted. There might also be a "Solar Package II" in the near future.

(a) Decarbonization of electricity production

For the most part, the decarbonization of electricity generation still needs subsidization. Only the offshore wind power plants have become so profitable, that companies no longer request subsidies, instead paying a small fortune in recent auctions for the privilege to build their installations in certain offshore areas.[42]

For the generation of electricity from other renewables, the financial support through a market premium (in particular Sec. 20, 22–23a Renewable Energy Sources Act 2023 – *EEG 2023*) and for small-scale plants a fixed feed-in tariff (cf. Sec. 21 Renewable Energy Sources Act 2023 – *EEG 2023*)·remain in the foreground. However, it is to be examined whether the funding of renewable energies via the market premium will be supplemented by other regulatory approaches in the future, e.g. by so-called "contracts for difference". For this purpose, the draft for new law contained an authorization to issue a regulation for future adjustments to the support system. However, this authorization did not become part of the Renewable Energy Sources Act 2023.

40 Gesetz zur Änderung des Erneuerbare-Energie-Gesetzes und weiterer energiewirtschaftlicher Vorschriften zur Steigerung des Ausbaus photovoltaischer Energieerzeugung' (*Bill amending the Renewable Energy Sources Act and other provisions of energy industry law to increase the expansion of photovoltaic energy generation*)(BGBl. 2024 I Number 151).

41 See Felicitas Strauch/Bettina Hennig/Veronika Widmann, 'Das Solarpaket I – Überblick über Änderungen am EEG und EnWG' (*The Solar Package I – Overview and Changes in the EEG and EnWG*) (2024), ZNER 291.

42 Due to Sec. 16–22 or Sec. 50–55 Offshore Wind Energy Act [*WindSeeG*]; compare furthermore Bundesnetzagentur 'Verfahren der Beschlusskammer 6 zu Windenergieanlagen auf See und Offshore-Anbindungsleitungen' *(Proceedings of Decision Panel 6 on offshore wind turbines and offshore grid connection lines)* <https://www.bundesnetzagentur.de/DE/Beschlusskammern/BK06/BK6_72_Offshore/BK6_offshore.html> accessed 17 June 2025.

In order to achieve the new expansion target for 2030, the expansion paths (in particular Sec. 4–4a Renewable Energy Sources Act 2023 – *EEG 2023*) and tender volumes for the individual technologies (in particular Sec. 28–28g Renewable Energy Sources Act 2023 – *EEG 2023*) were significantly increased, both in the Renewable Energy Sources Act 2023 [EEG 2023] and in parallel in Sec. 1(2) Offshore Wind Energy Act [*WindSeeG*].

The tendering of the subsidized kilowatt hours continues to be carried out mainly separately according to the types of onshore wind power plants, solar plants on roofs and open-air plants, plants with biomass and biomethane plants as well as hydropower. The "Solar Package I" further strengthens differentiation by creating separate sub-segments in the tenders for area-efficient solar installations such as agricultural photovoltaics and parking lot photovoltaics.[43] Technology-neutral tenders remain the major exception due to the very different technical and financial framework conditions (cf. Sec. 28e, 39n Renewable Energy Act 2023 – *EEG 2023*). In addition, further innovative concepts are promoted in an additional tender segment. This relates above all to the reconversion of green hydrogen into electricity (Sec. 28g, 39p Renewable Energy Act 2023 – *EEG 2023*) and plant combinations of renewable energies with local hydrogen-based electricity storage (Sec. 28f, 39o Renewable Energy Act 2023 – *EEG 2023*), in order to stabilize renewable generation and test its storage in hydrogen and reconversion into electricity.[44] "Green" hydrogen is also being considered for the first time at another point in the support system for generated electricity: New biomethane (Sec. 39k(2) Renewable Energy Act 2023 – *EEG 2023*) and new combined heat and power plants (Sec. 6(1) S. 1 Nr. 6 Combined Heat and Power Act 2023 – *KWKG 2023*) must already be aligned with hydrogen ("H2-ready") as a precaution for a later conversion.

The need for a competitive tendering procedure was reduced to some extent, and fixed feed-in tariffs again granted to a somewhat greater extent, by raising the de minimis thresholds from the previous 750 kW to the

43 With an overview about agricultural photovoltaic Philipp Berg, Licht und Schatten – Vorgaben für Agri-PV-Anlagen und ihre Auswirkungen auf die Vertragsgestaltung *(Light and Shadow – Requirements for Agri-PV Systems and Their Impact on Contract Design)* (2024) EnWZ 55.

44 Bundesregierung, 'Entwurf eines Gesetzes zu Sofortmaßnahmen für einen beschleunigten Ausbau der erneuerbaren Energien und weiteren Maßnahmen im Stromsektor' *(Draft bill on immediate measures for accelerated expansion of renewable energies and further measures in the electricity sector)* (BT-Drs 20/1630, 2022) 4 <https://dserver.bundestag.de/btd/20/016/2001630.pdf> accessed 17 June 2025.

extent of 1 MW permitted by EU law[45] (Sec. 22(2) sentence 2 No. 1, (3) sentence 2 No. 1 Renewable Energy Sources Act 2023 – *EEG 2023*). In addition, wind and solar projects of so-called "Citizen Energy Companies" (*Bürgerenergiegesellschaften*)[46] are exempted from the tendering process, too (Sec. 22(2) sentence 2 No. 3, (3) sentence 2 No. 2, Sec. 22b(1) (2) Renewable Energy Sources Act 2023 – *EEG 2023*) and can thus be realized without bureaucracy. This is intended to strengthen the diversity of players and local acceptance.[47] A new support program for citizen energy was launched to accompany these measures.[48] The structure of the subsidy was adjusted in various places to make the expansion of renewable generation capacity more attractive again, for example by increasing tariffs or suspending previous degressions (cf. Sec. 36b, 39g(5) No. 3, Sec. 49 Renewable Energy Sources Act 2023 – *EEG 2023*).[49]

(b) New refinancing system

The expansion of subsidies costs a lot of money. To prevent a (further) massive increase in electricity prices, the previous refinancing system for market premiums and fixed feed-in tariffs was changed. In the past, the costs were passed down the economic chain from the transmission system operators to the electricity customers and increased the electricity price as the so-called EEG apportionment [*EEG-Umlage*]. Instead, the corresponding expenses of the transmission system operators now lead to a compensation claim against the Federal Republic of Germany (cf. Sec. 58(1) EEG 2023 in conjunction with Sec. 6(1) Energy Financing Act [*Energiefinanzierungs-*

45 European Commission, Communication 'Guidelines on State aid for climate, environmental protection and energy 2022' [2022] OJ C 80/01 para 107(b)(i).

46 This basically means a company which consists of at least 50 natural persons who are resident in an area within a radius of 50 kilometers around the planned installation and in which all voting rights that are not held by natural persons (no more than 25 per cent) are held exclusively by micro, small or medium size enterprises and in which no member or shareholder of the company holds more than 10 per cent of the voting rights (see Sec. 3 no. 15 Renewable Energy Sources Act 2023 – *EEG 2023*).

47 BT-Drs 20/1630, 2022 (n 44) 3, 140.

48 ibid 141.

49 ibid 2, 186, 191, 197–198.

gesetz – EnFG[50]].[51] These claims are compensated by grants from the special fund "Climate and Transformation Fund" of the federal government. Therefore, the restrictions of state aid law (Art. 107–109 AEUV) apply to the present German support regime, because at least now it involves state resources.[52] Revenues from national fuel emissions trading[53] and the (first) European Union Emissions Trading System (EU-ETS I) are used primarily to finance the fund (cf. Sec. 4(1) Climate and Transformations Fund Act [*Klima- und Transformationsfondsgesetz – KTFG*[54]]. In this way, revenues from CO_2 pricing might de facto be partially returned to companies and electricity consumers,[55] but this is not guaranteed. The fund could also be financed from tax revenues (cf. Sec. 4(3) Climate and Transformations Fund Act – *KTFG*), although this is not currently planned[56]. After the new former federal government formed in the winter of 2021, it shifted €60 billion in unused loans originally intended to address the COVID-19 pandemic to the Climate and Transformation Fund.[57] However, the Federal Constitutional Court [*Bundesverfassungsgericht*] has classified this proce-

50 BGBl. 2022 I 1234, 1272 (Number 28), last amended by Article 8 of the Act of February 21, 2025 (BGBl. 2025 I Number 51).

51 With more details Michael Fehling 'Energie' (*energy)* Sec. 6 para. 152 et seq in: Michael Fehling/Jens-Peter Schneider (eds), *Regulierungsrecht* (*regulatory law) (*2nd ed., forthcoming, Mohr Siebeck).

52 According to the European Commission, state aid law was already applicable to the Renewable Energy Source Act 2021 [*EEG 2021*], see European Commission, 'Decision of 29 April 2021' C (2021) 2960 final, State Aid SA.57779 (2020/N) – Germany EEG 2021; also compare Harsch/Antoni (n 12) 6.

53 According to Art. 30 (c) (d) and (k), in 2027 or at least 2028, the new EU-ETS II will replace the national Emission Trading in the Fuel Emission Trading Act (*Brennstoffemissionshandelsgesetz*, BGBl. 2019 I 2728 (Number 50).

54 BGBl. 2010 I 1807 (Number 62), last amended by Article 3 of the Act of December 22, 2023 (BGBl. 2023 I Number 412).

55 Discharging companies and other electricity consumers is in line with Art. 10(3)(ha) of the Consolidated Version of the Directive 2003/87/EC of the European Parliament and of the Council of 13 October 2003 establishing a scheme for greenhouse gas emission allowance trading within the Community and amending Council Directive 96/61/EC [2003] OJ L 275/32.

56 Bundesregierung, 'Milliardeninvestitionen in Energiewende, Klimaschutz und Transformation' *(Billions invested in energy transition, climate protection and transformation)* (2023) <www.bundesregierung.de/breg-de/aktuelles/ktf-sondervermoegen-2207614> accessed 17 June 2025.

57 Michael Nienaber, 'Germany boosts its climate fund with 60 bln euro injection' (Reuters 13 December 2021) <www.reuters.com/markets/europe/german-cabinet-passes-climate-fund-booster-with-60-bln-euro-extra-budget-2021-12-13/> accessed 17 June 2025.

dure as unconstitutional.[58] The financing of numerous projects was therefore in jeopardy. However, in 2025, an amendment to the Constitution (Art. 143h GG) established a special fund [*Sondervermögen*] with its own credit authorization for additional investments in infrastructure and for additional investments to achieve climate neutrality by 2045 with a volume up to 500 billion Euro (Sec. 1 Sentence 1). From this money, 100 billion will be transferred into the Climate and Transformation Funds (Sec. 1 Sentence 4).

There are still other apportionments that increase the price of electricity, e.g. the offshore network apportionment and the combined heat and power apportionment. In the Energy Financing Act [*EnFG*], they were standardized and reduced in scope (cf. Sec. 3, 10 et seq. *EnFG*). This is intended to make self-consumption of self-generated electricity from renewable energies and storage projects somewhat more economically attractive.[59]

(c) Complex interaction of subsidizing renewables and emission trading

The new financing system therefore means that the promotion of renewable energies described above is primarily financed with the funds that emitters have to spend on their CO_2 certificates in the EU-ETS I and, in the future, the EU-ETS II. The financial burden laid on fossil fuels by emission trading makes renewable energies relatively cheaper in addition to subsidizing them. Moreover, the revenue from emissions trading will also be used to drive forward the decarbonization of other sectors. In Germany, funding is primarily provided for the energy-efficient refurbishment of buildings. However, funds are also being used to promote rail infrastructure, electromobility, the development of a hydrogen economy and semiconductor manufacturing.[60]

Critics have argued that financial support for renewables does not effectively protect the climate. The reason for this is said to be the EU-ETS I, from which the subsidies are sourced. If emissions are cut early in Germany, more certificates will be available for other emitters. CO_2 emissions

58 Judgment of the German Federal Constitutional Court of November 15, 2023 – 2 BvF 1/22.

59 BT-Drs 20/1630, 2022 (n 44) 142.

60 Bundesregierung (n 56).

would only shift within the EU.[61] This problem can be solved by cancelling the saved certificates.[62] Such a cancellation is possible under Art. 12(4) of the Emission Trading Directive 2003/87/EC.[63] However, the German government has not successfully used this option with regard to the coal-fired power plants that have already been shut down. Previous applications were rejected by the EU-Commission due to formal errors. No more applications were submitted in 2022. The former German government appeared to be relying on the adjustment of the market stability reserve. However, this can only lead to certificates being cancelled to a certain extent. The coal phase-out in Germany will therefore not be able to achieve its full potential for CO_2 reduction.[64]

3. Securing sufficient area for onshore wind energy development

The expansion of onshore wind energy also faltered since individual federal states [*Länder*] did not provide enough land for it. To remedy this shortage, Sec. 3(1) Wind Energy Area Requirements Act [*WindBG*] provides for the distribution of so-called "area contribution values" among the federal states [*Länder*]. Accordingly, by the end of 2027, 1.4 percent and by the end of 2032 2 percent of the territory must be designated for wind power plants. These values are intended to reflect the area requirements resulting from the expansion targets of the Renewable Energy Sources Act 2023 [*EEG 2023*]. The federal states [*Länder*] may continue to decide on minimum distances but must ensure that they achieve their area targets and thus contribute significantly to the expansion of wind energy. If they fail to do so, the state-specific distance rules will cease to apply (Sec. 249(7) Federal Building Code [*BauGB*]). However, valuable time is again at risk of being

61 Charlotte Kreuter-Kirchhof, 'Emissionshandel und Erneuerbare Energien Richtlinie' *(Emissions trading and the Renewable Energies Directive)* (2019) ZUR 396.

62 ibid.

63 Consolidated Version of the Directive 2003/87/EC of the European Parliament and of the Council of 13 October 2003 establishing a scheme for greenhouse gas emission allowance trading within the Community and amending Council Directive 96/61/EC [2003] OJ L 275/32; Such a deletion is possible if electricity generation capacities are shut down due to national measures.

64 Hendrik Kafsack, 'Der deutsche Kohleausstieg verpufft' *(The German coal phase-out is fizzling out)* (FAZ 21 October 2023) <www.faz.net/aktuell/wirtschaft/klima-nachhaltigkeit/klimapolitik-der-deutsche-kohleausstieg-verpufft-19257560.html> accessed 17 June 2025.

lost by 2027.[65] According to indications in the coalition agreement, the new federal coalition could even be inclined to weaken the requirements[66].

The examination of bird protection is said to be a major obstacle to onshore wind energy development. In order to accelerate the approval procedures, in 2022 Sec. 45b Federal Nature Conservation Act [*BNatschG*] standardized the assessment of the risk of killing and injuring bird species at risk of collision.[67] All bird species relevant to the assessment are listed in an annex to the Act, which specifies the legal consequences that apply based on the distance of a breeding site of the respective species to a wind turbine. A distinction is made between the "close range", the "central assessment area" and the "extended assessment area". If a breeding site is located outside the extended assessment area, it is irrefutably assumed that the risk of injury is not significantly increased.[68] This standardization should speed up procedures and give project developers legal certainty thanks to its uniformity throughout Germany. However, it is questionable whether this standardization is compatible with EU law. The EU Birds Directive does not limit the scope of the assessment.[69]

Now Sec. 6 Wind Energy Area Requirements Act [*WindBG*] goes even further by stipulating that an environmental impact assessment no longer has to take place in wind energy areas and that the species protection assessment described above no longer has to take place. Similar exceptions apply to offshore wind power (Sec. 72a Offshore Wind Energy Act [*WindSeeG*]). However, this only applies if the project is not located in a Natura 2000 area, a nature reserve or a national park. The competent authority must take measures to ensure the protection of birds on the basis of existing

---

65 For a similar, but more detailed analysis see Martin Kment, 'Beschleunigung des Ausbaus von Windenergieanlagen an Land' *(Accelerating the expansion of onshore wind energy installations)* (2023) NVwZ 959–963, 965.

66 Compare Coalition Agreement (n 27), para 1034–1038.

67 Oliver Hendrischke, 'Bewältigung naturschutzrechtlicher Konflikte beim Ausbau erneuerbarer Energien' *(Overcoming nature conservation legal conflicts in the expansion of renewable energies)* (2023) NVwZ 965, 969; Mathias Jaenicke, 'Aktuelle Rechtsfragen der baurechtlichen Zulässigkeit von Windenergieanlagen an Land' *(Current legal questions of the requirements in building law for onshore wind energy)* (2023) ZUR 291, 293–296.

68 Ibid 969.

69 For more detailed information see Sabine Schlacke/Helen Wentzien/Dominik Römling, 'Beschleunigung der Energiewende: Ein gesetzgeberischer Paradigmenwechsel durch das Osterpaket?' *(Accelerating the energy transition: A legislative paradigm shift through the Easter package?)* (2022) NVwZ 1581.

data.[70] Neither the developer nor the authority is required to collect new data. If no suitable and proportionate measures are available or if the existing data is more than five years old or insufficiently accurate, the wind turbine can still be approved.[71] The system operator must then pay an annual amount to the federal government, depending on the installed capacity, which is earmarked for species protection programmes.[72] All together, these changes will certainly accelerate the procedures for the approval of wind turbines. However, this will be at the expense of species protection.

In addition, Sec. 2 Renewable Energy Sources Act 2023 [*EEG 2023*] now states that the expansion of renewable energies is considered "overriding public interest". This classification has an impact on the exercise of discretion and substantive legal considerations, for example balancing processes in nature conservation law and species protection law. It also affects ongoing administrative and court proceedings.[73]

A further acceleration for the expansion of onshore wind energy is intended to be achieved through the implementation of the RED III Directive.[74] The legislative proposal of the former Federal Government outlined the establishment of designated "acceleration zones" for onshore wind energy projects. Within these zones, regulatory approval processes were intended for significant streamlining. Anticipated measures encompassed (further) simplifications in the realm of environmental impact assessments, scrutiny related to species protection, and alignment of projects with the

70 Wolfgang Rieger, '§ 6 WindBG – die nächste Runde im Konflikt zwischen dem Ausbau der Windenergie und dem *Artenschutz' (Sec. 6 WindBG – the next round in the conflict between the expansion of wind energy and species protection)* (2023) NVwZ 1042.

71 ibid 1044.

72 ibid 1045 f.

73 For an overview of the effects of the standard in the judiciary to date see: Thomas Lingemann, 'Der neue § 2 EEG in der verwaltungsgerichtlichen Rechtsprechung' *(The new Sec. 2 EEG in the case law of the administrative courts)* (2023) NVwZ 1634; furthermore, compare Frank Sailer/Maria Deuitinger 'Klimaschutz, Gesundheitsschutz und Versorgungssicherheit beim Ausbau erneuerbarer Energien' *(Climate proception, health protection and security of supply in the development of renewable energies)* (2023) ZUR 604, 609–611.

74 Bundesregierung, 'Entwurf eines Gesetzes zur Umsetzung der EU-Erneuerbaren-Richtlinie in den Bereichen Windenergie auf See und Stromnetze und zur Änderung des Bundesbedarfsplangesetzes' *(Draft Bill for the Implementation of the EU Renewable Energy Directive in the Areas of Offshore Wind Energy and Power Grids and for the Amendment of the Federal Requirement Plan Act)* (BT-Drs 20/11226) <https://dserver.bundestag.de/btd/20/112/2011226.pdf> accessed 17 June 2025.

management objectives stipulated by the Water Management Act *(Wasserhaushaltsgesetz – WHG)*. However, this bill no longer found a parliamentary majority after the former coalition broke up. The new Federal Government intends to present a new – perhaps less ambitious – draft bill to implement the RED III Directive[75].

4. Consequences of the expansion of renewable energies for the (grid) infrastructure

Planning and construction of the major new power lines from north to south are progressing quite slowly. Planning and construction times have amounted to more than 15 years. The hopes placed in the multi-stage planning process under the Network Expansion Acceleration Act [*Netzausbaubeschleunigungsgesetz – NABEG*] have not been fulfilled.[76] The delays and cost increases are due in part, but by no means exclusively, to the fact that, under political pressure from Bavaria, there has been a widespread switch from overhead lines to underground cables. The new coalition agreement rightly places particular emphasis on the synchronisation of wind power and grid expansion[77]. There seems to be some hope that the future demand for electricity could perhaps be lower than previously forecast, so that the grid expansion, but also the areas for wind energy, could be reduced a little. In this respect, there are monitoring and evaluation mandates[78]. However, it would be particularly dangerous for the achievement of the climate targets if the failure to push through electromobility and electricity-based heat generation were to result in a lower demand for electricity in the future. Without a massive acceleration of sector coupling (including the production of green hydrogen) with an inevitable significant increase in electricity demand, the renewed failure to meet the sector-specific reduction targets of the Climate Protection Act [*Klimaschutzgesetz*] for transport and buildings would be pre-programmed.

---

75 Coalition Agreement (n 27), para 971–980

76 For this reason, the legislator recently undertook a comprehensive amendment of the NABEG. Among other changes, the possibilities for exceptions to the comprehensive approval procedure were expanded. Furthermore, the integration of digital processes is anticipated to further expedite the procedural timeline. For more information see Fehling (n 51) Sec. 6 para 185 ff.

77 Coalition Agreement (n 27), para 138 f.

78 Coalition Agreement (n 27), para 983–985, 1034.

The development of hydrogen networks, primarily via the gradual conversion of existing natural gas networks, is still in its infancy. Legislators have already transferred the multi-stage planning regime for natural gas networks to hydrogen networks in 2021. Here, attempts are being made to accelerate the planning procedures through two measures. Firstly, for a hydrogen core network [*Wasserstoffkernnetz*] the Energy Industry Act (*Energiewirtschaftsgesetz – EnWG*)[79] provided for a simplified two-stage planning procedure (Sec. 28q). In the first step, transmission system operators had to submit a joint application for the design of the core network to the Federal Network Agency [*Bundesnetzagentur*] for approval. In a second step, the agency had to check whether the statutory authorisation requirements were met. The authority essentially affirmed this and accordingly granted approval on 22 October 2024 with minor modifications to the layout of the network. Like the other energy grids, the hydrogen core grid is to be financed in principle by grid utilisation fees. However, the state is subsidising its construction through advances, using an amortisation account, and provides a kind of guarantee for any shortfall remaining in this amortisation account (Sec. 28r Energy Industry Act – *EnWG*). This solution has already been authorised by the EU Commission under state aid law. For further hydrogen lines at a later date, the Energy Industry Act *[EnWG]* stipulates that there is an overriding public interest in hydrogen pipelines (Sec. 43l(1) Energy Industry Act – *EnWG*); this has a favourable effect on the balancing of all the interests concerned, which is necessary during the planning approval process.[80] Mere conversions of pipelines from natural gas to hydrogen only require notification (Sec. 113c Energy Industry Act – *EnWG*); this eliminates any time-consuming planning approval procedure. However, should carbon capture and storage (CCS) or even carbon capture and usage (CCU) actually be realised on a larger scale, some of the existing natural gas pipelines would probably also have to be converted into carbon pipelines.

It is problematic that planning for electricity, gas and hydrogen networks essentially takes place separately. Legal scholars are considering upstream integrated system planning, for which only rudimentary approaches can

79 BGBl. 2005 I 1970, 3621, last amended by Article 1 of the Act of February 21, 2025 (BGBl. 2025 I Number 51); unofficial outdated version in English Bundesregierung, 'Energy Industry Act' <https://energyblawg.wordpress.com/enwg/> accessed 17 June 2025.

80 For the effect of this amendment compare Section C. 3. above.

be found so far in Sec. 112b Energy Industry Act [*EnWG*], which were inserted in 2021.[81] Such integrated system planning [*Systementwicklungsplanung*] could not only consider the various transmission grids in their interplay for the energy transition, but also take the generation level into account to some extent and thus serve the implementation of the climate protection CO_2 reduction targets in an overarching manner.[82] However, system development planning only offers an advantage if it lays down binding guidelines in advance. This would guarantee planning security.[83] Otherwise, an additional planning level threatens to further slow down the planning process.

D. Significant problems remaining

The reforms address only individual difficulties; some structural problems remain largely unsolved.

1. High investment risk for preparing participation in the tendering process for a market premium

Especially for wind power plants, there are high hurdles for submitting a bid in the tender competition for a market premium. In particular, onshore plants must already have an immission control permit (Sec. 6 Federal Immission Control Act- *BImSchG*) according to Sec. 36(1) Number 1 Renewable Energy Sources Act 2023 – *EEG 2023*). The financial and time expenditure for this is considerable and acts as a deterrent. It remains to be seen to what extent the situation will be improved by the partial elimination of nature and species protection law.[84]

---

81 Georg Hermes, 'Die Systementwicklungsplanung – Instrument zur klimagerechten Transformation des Energiesystems' *(System development planning – an instrument for the climate-friendly transformation of the energy system)* (2022) EnWZ 99–103.

82 ibid 99 f.

83 See ibid 101.

84 Describing and classifying the changes: Thorsten Attendorn, 'Umweltrechtliche Ausnahmeabwägungen über die Zulassung von Wasser- und Windkraftanlagen nach dem "Osterpaket"' *(Environmental law exception considerations on the approval of water and wind power plants according to the "Easter Package")* (2022) NVwZ 1586 et seq.

One possibility to shorten the long approval procedures might be a so-called fictitious approval [*Genehmigungsfiktion*]. For example, the Climate Neutrality Foundation has proposed that after a certain period of time, the project is deemed to have been approved if it has not been rejected. The respective deadline depends on the project. In the case of a wind farm for which an environmental impact assessment must be carried out, it might be 22 weeks after receipt of all the necessary documents. For small projects, it might be 10 weeks.[85] The proposal for a deemed approval makes sense in principle but can only be implemented for such small projects. If an environmental impact assessment is required, this must not be undermined by such a fiction. This would not be compatible with the primacy of EU-law. Furthermore, such a fiction would have a negative effect if the agency lacks the necessary staff to deal with the applications in time.

In theory, a similar problem of overly high barriers to participation in the auction[86] might also arise for offshore wind farms, if the auction takes place before the planning process (cf. Sec. 16, 24(1) Number 1 Offshore Wind Energy Act – *WindSeeG*). Such a procedure is used for not preliminary checked areas [*nicht zentral voruntersuchte Flächen*] according to part 2, chapter 2 of this Act. In addition, applicants must already incur expenses for the preparation of an application for planning approval and the documents required for this purpose. Nevertheless, in offshore areas the economic incentives now seem to be high enough to guarantee the participation of a sufficient number of companies.

These problems could not be solved by switching to contracts for difference. Companies would also have to make advance payments in order to participate in a bidding procedure for the amount of the award price. A bidding procedure is necessary because of state aid law which also applies to contracts for difference.[87]

---

85 Stiftung Klimaneutralität, 'Genehmigungsverfahren beschleunigen mit einem Windenergie-an-Land-Gesetz' *(Accelerate approval procedures with a wind energy on land law)* (2021) <www.stiftung-klima.de/app/uploads/2021/05/2021-05-07-Genehmigungverfahren-beschleunigen-mit-einem-Wind-an-Land-Gesetz.pdf> accessed 17 June 2025.

86 See Section C. 2 (a).

87 See Harsch/Antoni (n 12) 8 (pointing at Communication from the Commission (n 45) para 121).

2. Slow grid extension and modernization

As already stated above, the acceleration of power grid expansion has not succeeded in any way so far. Nevertheless, only minor changes have been made in the relevant law. Most important, all distribution networks below 110 kV are now of "overriding public interest"[88] (Sec. 14d(10) Energy Industry Act- *EnWG*). It remains to be seen whether these changes will be sufficient. Legislators have announced new initiatives to this end and to accelerate the connection of offshore wind turbines, but no one knows what will come of them.

A sufficient supply of "green" hydrogen is also necessary for the transformation of the economy. To this end, the German legislator has decided to amend the Energy Industry Act [*EnWG*] to enable the financing of a hydrogen core network (Sec. 28r Energy Industry Act – *EnWG*).[89] It is to be 9.700 kilometers long and will be financed by the private sector, with the state providing certain guarantees. The core network shall connect the most important entry and exit points in Germany.[90] In contrast to the electricity sector, the construction of a wholly new grid is not necessary here.[91] Around 60 % of the network is to consist of rededicated natural gas pipelines. This will certainly help to speed up the construction. Hopefully, the new 40 % to be built can be constructed sufficiently quickly[92] considering that the investment costs amount to 19.8 billion euros.[93] In order not to burden the first few users of a hydrogen grid with excessively high grid

88 For the effect of this amendment, see Section C. 3. above.

89 For the reasons behind the amendment see Bundesregierung 'Entwurf eines Dritten Gesetzes zur Änderung des Energiewirtschaftsgesetzes' *(German Federal Government (Draft of a third law to amend the Energy Industry Act)* (BT-Drs 20/10014) <https://dserver.bundestag.de/btd/20/100/2010014.pdf> accessed 17 June 2025; also Bundesregierung, 'Wasserstoffnetz für Deutschland – Ausbau und Finanzierung' *(Hydrogen network for Germany – expansion and financing)* (2023) <www.bundesregierung.de/breg-de/aktuelles/energiewirtschaftsgesetz-2240764> accessed 17 June 2025.

90 For all of this see Bundesministerium für Wirtschaft und Klimaschutz, 'Gesetz zur Wasserstoff-Netzplanung und Kernnetz-Finanzierung beschlossen' *(Act on hydrogen network planning and core network financing adopted)* (2023) <www.bmwk.de/Redaktion/DE/Pressemitteilungen/2023/11/20231115-gesetz-zur-wasserstoff-netzplanung-und-kernnetz-finanzierung-beschlossen.html> accessed 17 June 2025.

91 Fehling (n 51) Sec. 6 para 193.

92 For more detailed information on the hydrogen core network see Markus, in this volume, 129 ff.

93 Vereinigung der Fernleitungsnetzbetreiber Gas, 'Hydrogen core network' (*fnb-gas*) <https://fnb-gas.de/wasserstoffnetz-wasserstoff-kernnetz/> accessed 17 June 2025.

usage fees, a so-called 'amortization account' [*Amortisationskonto*] is to be set up, with the help of which the costs are distributed over time. The federal government is to provide a kind of deficiency guarantee in the event that the amortisation account cannot be balanced in 2055.

3. Unsolved storage problems in view of the volatility of wind power and solar energy

Under new legislation, the promotion of electricity storage is addressed only marginally, namely together with power to gas in innovative new tenders. An overarching support concept and location planning are still lacking. In addition, there is probably a need for further efficiency improvements.

Proactive planning is indispensable, in particular since the extent of the required network expansion depends to a large extent on storage capacities available in the future. The legislature at least appears to be aware of this problem and has determined that the construction and operation of electricity storage facilities is in the overriding public interest[94] (Sec. 11c Energy Industry Act – *EnWG*).

4. Insufficient amount of green power and hydrogen in light of increasing demand due to sector coupling

Overall, it must be doubted whether the required amount of electricity from renewable energies will be available in time to attain the necessary expansion and climate targets. As already mentioned, the demand for renewably generated electricity and hydrogen will rise sharply as a result of sector coupling, even if is not clear how high the demand will be due to many forecasting uncertainties.[95] Several key political decisions such as the switch to electromobility or the production of green steel with hydrogen have already been made.[96] The long-term conversion of gas-fired power plants to hydrogen was also planned in order to stabilize the electricity grid in volatile times.[97] The new coalition, however, is much more focussed

94 For the effect of this amendment, see Section C. 3. above.
95 Brinkschmidt (n 17) 25–29.
96 ibid 34, 36.
97 Bundesministerium für Wirtschaft und Klimaschutz (n 90).

on Carbon Capture and Storage (CCS)[98]. The production of renewable electricity and hydrogen must therefore be increased very quickly. The acceleration instruments remain too rudimentary to be successful in meeting the ambitious schedule.

Closing this gap through imports, especially of green hydrogen, is probably only partially possible in the medium term. Negotiations are being conducted with other countries and agreements are being concluded, especially with Canada.[99] However, Germany is competing with many other industrialized countries for import capacities of green hydrogen which even do not yet exist. In addition, the (pipeline) infrastructure required for this is rudimentary at best. New floating LNG-terminals have been planned and built in record time and can theoretically be converted to hydrogen later.[100] However, it remains unclear how long theses terminals are still needed for LNG and when the prerequisites for an economical conversion will actually be in place. Even blue hydrogen, i.e. hydrogen from natural gas whose CO_2 emissions have been captured and stored, is also unlikely to be procured in sufficient quantities in time. Furthermore, the electricity from renewable energies required for CCS could also be used directly for the production of green hydrogen.[101]

Because of European Law, the German System of state funding for the promotion of green electricity also needs some reform. According to Art. 19(1) EU-Electricity Market Regulation [*Strombinnenmarktverordnung*][102], "direct price support schemes for investment in new power generating facilities for the generation of electricity from [renewable] sources [...] shall take the form of two-way contracts for difference or equivalent schemes with the same effects". However, it is doubtful whether it makes sense to switch from the tried-and-tested German system (market premium) to contracts for difference. Art. 19(1) of the Regulation leaves a great

98 Coalition Agreement (n 27), para 143–145.

99 Deutsche Welle, 'Germany and Canada sign hydrogen deal' (2022) <www.dw.com/en/germany-and-canada-sign-hydrogen-deal/a-62899992> accessed 17 June 2025.

100 Matia Riemer/Florian Schreiner/Jakob Wachsmuth, 'Conversion of LNG Terminals for Liquid Hydrogen or Ammonia' (2022) ISI Fraunhofer 6 ff. <https://www.isi.fraunhofer.de/content/dam/isi/dokumente/cce/2022/Report_Conversion_of_LNG_Terminals_for_Liquid_Hydrogen_or_Ammonia.pdf> accessed 17 June 2025.

101 See Cäcilia Gätsch, 'Blauer Wasserstoff im Kontext der Energiewende – Aktuelle Entwicklungen und Governance-Fragen' *(Blue hydrogen in the context of the energy transition – current developments and governance issues)* (2023) 10 KlimR 293–294.

102 Regulation (EU) 2019/943 of the European Parliament and of the Council of 5 June 2019 on the Internal Market for Electricity (recast).

deal of room for manoeuvre when it comes to the specific design of an "equivalent" future support system. Supplementing the current market premium system with a cap on market revenues would probably also be permissible[103]. In the case of green or low carbon hydrogen, on the other hand, where no tried-and-tested subsidy system yet exists in Germany, such contracts for difference – also known as climate protection contracts [*Klimaschutzverträge*] – are a very serious option. They are already widely used for the direct financial promotion of the use of green or low-carbon hydrogen in industry[104]. Other possible fields of application are the promotion of the construction of electrolysers or even the production of green hydrogen itself.

Last but not least, all funding instruments to accelerate technological progress must be measured against EU state aid law. The USA does not have to take such things into account. With the Inflation Reduction Act, it has launched a very large-scale aid programme to decarbonize the US economy.[105] This might amount to a structural disadvantage of Europe in the competition to attract investments in new "green" technologies.

E. Conclusion

Although there are some useful approaches in the most recent reforms, they get lost in even more confusing detailed regulations. The growing complexity of the European and German legislation might to a certain extent reflect path dependencies,[106] but this development is not inevitable. What is needed is a simplification and restructuring of the relevant law that would promise a significant acceleration of the expansion of renewable energies. At least, the simplification of the species protection assessment appears to be promising, albeit at the expense of environmental protection. Perhaps similar simplifications can also be implemented in other areas of

103 Michael Fehling, 'Finanzierung der Umstellung auf Wasserstoff zwischen Markt und Staat: Förderungsbedarf, Probleme, Rechtsrahmen', in: Akademie der Wissenschaften in Hamburg, Wasserstoff (Financing the Transition to Hydrogen between the Market and the State: Funding Requirements, Problems, Legal Framework, in: Academy of Sciences in Hamburg, Hydrogen), III. 1.3. (forthcoming).

104 For more details see Fehling (n 103), III. 5.2.

105 For a detailed description of the Inflation Reduction Act see Joel B. Eisen, 'Hydrogen Law and Policy Initiatives in the United States' (2024) ZUR 81.

106 Compare Saurer/Monast (n 1) 316–317, however, with a different use of the highly debated theory of path dependency.

the relevant law. As the saying goes: After the reform is before the reform. Time is pressing. We can hardly hope for a timely solution to the problems through technical innovations and market forces alone.

The next step might be a new legal framework for enabling carbon capture and storage (CCS) (and in the future even direct air capture) in Germany. The German government recently published a draft bill for this purpose.[107] Considerable controversy surrounds it´s pros and cons. Even most environmental NGOs now believe that to some extent this technique is unavoidable for the success of the transformation process, but that there are also severe risks for the environment. Furthermore, unreasonable hopes in this not yet mature and extremely expensive technology may postpone the necessary mitigation process. Because there are environmental interests on both sides of the issue, even environmental organizations are divided on this. A similar controversy arose before concerning the acceleration of authorisation procedures for renewable energies at the expense of environmental impact assessments.

After the previous financing model outside of the annual budget for a large number of subsidies has been declared unconstitutional[108], the 500 billion special fund, recently established by a constitutional amendment[109], offers new opportunities for financing investments in renewable energies and combating climate change[110]. A recent monitoring report underlines that the key challenges of the German energy transition lie primarily in the accelerated expansion of renewables, the modernization of grids, the provision of flexibility options, and the efficient use of every additional kilowatt-hour.[111] But at least part of the money can also be used for investments in infrastructure without any reference to climate protection or even contradicting it. It remains to be seen what the new German coalition – according to the coalition agreement with a particular focus on reducing

---

107 Bundesregierung 'Entwurf eines Gesetzes zur Änderung des Kohlendioxid-Speicherungsgesetz' *(Draft Bill to amend the Carbon Dioxid Storage Act)* BT-Drs. 21/1494 <https://dserver.bundestag.de/btd/21/014/2101494.pdf> accessed 23 September 2025.

108 See (n 58).

109 See above C. 2. (b).

110 For a short overview see Benjamin Wehrmann. Clean Energy Wire, 'Q&A: Germany´s new €500bln fund – What´s in it for Climate and energy?' (2025) <https://www.cleanenergywire.org/factsheets/qa-germanys-eu500-bln-infrastructure-fund-whats-it-climate-and-energy>, accessed 17 June 2025.

111 See Monitoring Report (n 14).

bureaucracy, competitiveness and increasing cost efficiency in climate protection[112] – will make out of it.

Bibliography

Attendorn T, 'Umweltrechtliche Ausnahmeabwägungen über die Zulassung von Wasser- und Windkraftanlagen nach dem "Osterpaket" (Environmental law exception considerations on the approval of water and wind power plants according to the "Easter Package") (2022) 41 NVwZ 1586 .

Berg P, 'Licht und Schatten – Vorgaben für Agri-PV-Anlagen und ihre Auswirkungen auf die Vertragsgestaltung' (Light and Shadow – Requirements for Agri-PV Systems and Their Impact on Contract Design) (2024) 13 EnWZ 55

Brandes J/Hahn M/Senkspiel C et al., 'Wege zu einem klimaneutralen Energiesystem. Die deutsche Energiewende im Kontext gesellschaftlicher Verhaltensweisen – Update für ein CO2-Reduktionsziel von 65 % in 2030 und 100 % in 2050' (Paths to a climate-neutral energy system. The German energy transition in the context of of societal behavior – Update for a CO2 reduction target of 65 % in 2030 and 100 % in 2050) (2010) ISE Fraunhofer, <https://www.ise.fraunhofer.de/content/dam/ise/de/documents/publications/studies/Fraunhofer-ISEStudie-Wege-zu-einem-klimaneutralen-Energiesystem-Update-Zielverschaerfung.pdf> accessed 17 June 2025

Brinkschmidt A, 'Sektorkopplung im Energieregulierungsrecht' (Sector coupling in energy regulation law) (Mohr Siebeck 2024) 25

Bundesamt für Strahlenschutz, (Federal Office for Radiation Protection), 'Act on the Peaceful Utilisation of Atomic Energy and the Protection against its Hazards (Atomic Energy Act)' <www.base.bund.de/SharedDocs/Downloads/BASE/EN/hns/a1-english/A1-07-16-AtG.pdf?__blob=publicationFile&v=2> accessed 17 June 2025

Bundesministerium für Wirtschaft und Klimaschutz (German Federal Ministry for Economy and Climate Protection), 'Durchschnittlicher Strompreis für einen Haushalt in Cent/kWh (Jahresverbrauch: 3.500 kWh)' (Average electricity price for a household in cents/kWh (annual consumption: 3,500 kWh)) <www.bmwk.de/Redaktion/DE/Downloads/I/Infografiken/durchschnittlicher-strompreis-haushalt.pdf?_blob=publicationFile&v=6> accessed 17 June 2025

Bundesministerium für Wirtschaft und Klimaschutz (German Federal Ministry for Economy and Climate Protection), 'Entwurf eines Gesetzes zur Umsetzung der Richtlinie (EU) 2023/2413 im Bereich Windenergie an Land und Solarenergie' (Draft of a bill for the implementation of Directive (EU) 2023/2413 in the area of onshore wind energy and solar energy) <https://www.bmwk.de/Redaktion/DE/Downloads/Gesetz/20240402-referentenentwurf-umsetzung-red-3-wind-an-land-und-solarenergie.pdf?__blob=publicationFile&v=4> accessed 17 June 2025

Bundesministerium für Wirtschaft und Klimaschutz (German Federal Ministry for Economy and Climate Protection), 'Das Solarpaket I im Überblick' (Federal Ministry for Economic Affairs and Climate Action, Overview of Solar Package I) <solarpaket-im-ueberblick.pdf (bmwk.de)> accessed 17 June 2025

112 See Coalition Agreement (n 27), for example para 901, 936, 944.

Bundesministerium für Wirtschaft und Klimaschutz, (German Federal Ministry for Economy and Climate Protection), 'Gesetz zur Wasserstoff-Netzplanung und Kernnetz-Finanzierung beschlossen' (Act on hydrogen network planning and core network financing adopted) (2023) www.bmwk.de/Redaktion/DE/Pressemitteilungen/2023/11/20231115-gesetz-zur-wasserstoff-netzplanung-und-kernnetz-finanzierung-beschlossen.html> accessed 17 June 2025

Bundeskartellamt (German Federal Cartel Office), 'Monitoringbericht 2022' (2022) <www.bundeskartellamt.de/SharedDocs/Publikation/DE/Berichte/Energie-Monitoring-2022.pdf?__blob=publicationFile&v=4> acessed 17 June 2025

Bundesnetzagentur (German Federal Network Agency), 'Ergebnisse der Ausschreibungsrunden für Windenergie-Anlagen an Land' (Results of the bidding rounds for onshore wind turbines) <www.bundesnetzagentur.de/DE/Fachthemen/ElektrizitaetundGas/Ausschreibungen/Wind_Onshore/BeendeteAusschreibungen/start.html> accessed 17 June 2025

Bundesnetzagentur (German Federal Network Agency) 'Verfahren der Beschlusskammer 6 zu Windenergieanlagen auf See und Offshore-Anbindungsleitungen' (Proceedings of Decision Panel 6 on offshore wind turbines and offshore grid connection lines) <https://www.bundesnetzagentur.de/DE/Beschlusskammern/BK06/BK6_72_Offshore/BK6_offshore.html> accessed 17 June 2025

Bundesregierung (German Federal Government), 'Ausbau erneuerbarer Energien massiv beschleunigen' (Rapidly accelerate the expansion of renewable energies) (2023) <https://www.bundesregierung.de/breg-de/service/archiv-bundesregierung/novelle-eeg-gesetz-2023-2023972>accessed 17 June 2025

Bundesregierung (German Federal Government), 'Entwurf eines Gesetzes zur Änderung des Kohlendioxid-Speicherungsgesetz' (Draft Bill to amend the Carbon Dioxid Storage Act) BT-Drs. 21/1494 <https://dserver.bundestag.de/btd/21/014/2101494.pdf> accessed 29 Setpember 2025

Bundesregierung, (German Federal Government), 'Entwurf eines Gesetzes zu Sofortmaßnahmen für einen beschleunigten Ausbau der erneuerbaren Energien und weiteren Maßnahmen im Stromsektor' (Draft bill on immediate measures for accelerated expansion of renewable energies and further measures in the electricity sector) (BT-Drs 20/1630, 2022) <https://dserver.bundestag.de/btd/20/016/2001630.pdf> accessed 17 June 2025

Bundesregierung,(German Federal Government), 'Entwurf eines Gesetzes zur Änderung des Erneuerbare-Energie-Gesetzes und weiterer energiewirtschaftlicher Vorschriften zur Steigerung des Ausbaus photovoltaischer Energieerzeugung' (Draft bill amending the Renewable Energy Sources Act and other provisions of energy industry law to increase the expansion of photovoltaic energy generation) (BT-Drs 20/8657, 2023) <https://dserver.bundestag.de/btd/20/086/2008657.pdf> accessed 17 June 2025

Bundesregierung, (German Federal Government) 'Intergenerational contract for the climate' (2021) <www.bundesregierung.de/breg-de/schwerpunkte/klimaschutz/climate-change-act-2021-1936846>accessed 17 June 2025

Bundesregierung, (German Federal Government) 'Entwurf eines Gesetzes zur Umsetzung der EU-Erneuerbaren-Richtlinie in den Bereichen Windenergie auf See und Stromnetze und zur Änderung des Bundesbedarfsplangesetzes' (Draft Bill for the Implementation of the EU Renewable Energy Directive in the Areas of Offshore Wind Energy and Power Grids and for the Amendment of the Federal Requirement Plan Act) (BT-Drs 20/11226) <https://dserver.bundestag.de/btd/20/112/2011226.pdf> accessed 17 June 2025

Bundesregierung, (German Federal Government), 'Milliardeninvestitionen in Energiewende, Klimaschutz und Transformation' (Billions invested in energy transition, climate protection and transformation) (2023) <www.bundesregierung.de/breg-de/aktuelles/ktf-sondervermoegen-2207614> accessed 17 June 2025

Bundesregierung, (German Federal Government), Wasserstoffnetz für Deutschland – Ausbau und Finanzierung' (Hydrogen network for Germany – expansion and financing) (2023) <www.bundesregierung.de/breg-de/aktuelles/energiewirtschaftsgesetz-2240764> accessed 17 June 2025

Bundesregierung, (German Federal Government), 'Federal Building Code' <www.lexadin.nl/wlg/legis/nofr/eur/arch/ger/Federal-Building-Code.pdf> accessed 17 June 2025

Bundesregierung, (German Federal Government), 'Energy Industry Act' <https://energyblawg.wordpress.com/enwg/> accessed 17 June 2025

Bundesregierung (German Federal Government), 'Entwurf eines Dritten Gesetzes zur Änderung des Energiewirtschaftsgesetzes' (German Federal Government (Draft of a third law to amend the Energy Industry Act) (BT-Drs 20/10014) <https://dserver.bundestag.de/btd/20/100/2010014.pdf> accessed 17 June 2025

CDU/CSU/SPD, 'Verantwortung für Deutschland – Koalitionsvertrag für die 21. Legislaturperiode' (Responsibility for Germany – Coalition Agreement for the 21st legislative period) <https://www.koalitionsvertrag2025.de/> accessed 17 June 2025

Der Informationsdienst des Instituts der deutschen Wirtschaft, 'Natural gas: The bridge is crumbling' (2023) <www.iwd.de/artikel/erdgas-die-bruecke-broeckelt-587736/> accessed 17 June 2025

Deutsche Welle, 'Germany and Canada sign hydrogen deal' (2022) <www.dw.com/en/germany-and-canada-sign-hydrogen-deal/a-62899992> accessed 17 June 2025

Energiewirtschaftliches Institut an der Universität zu Köln, 'Energiewende. Effizient. Machen – Monitoring Bericht zum Start der 21. Legislaturperiode' *(Energy. Transition. Efficiency. – Monitoring report at the start of the 21st legislative term)* (2025) <https://www.bundeswirtschaftsministerium.de/Redaktion/DE/Publikationen/Energie/energiewende-effizient-machen.pdf?__blob=publicationFile&v=20> accessed 29 September 2025

Eisen J B, 'Hydrogen Law and Policy Initiatives in the United States' (2024) 35 ZUR 81

European Commission, Communication 'Guidelines on State aid for climate, environmental protection and energy 2022' [2022] OJ C 80/01

European Commission, 'Decision of 29 April 2021' C (2021) 2960 final, State Aid SA.57779 (2020/N) – Germany EEG 2021

Fehling M 'Energie' (energy) Sec. 6 in: **Fehling M/Schneider J P** (eds), Regulierungsrecht (regulatory law) (2nd ed., forthcoming, Mohr Siebeck)

Fehling M, 'Finanzierung der Umstellung auf Wasserstoff zwischen Markt und Staat: Förderungsbedarf, Probleme, Rechtsrahmen' (Financing the Transition to Hydrogen between the Market and the State: Funding Requirements, Problems, Legal Framework), in: Akademie der Wissenschaften in Hamburg (forthcoming) III.

Gätsch C, 'Blauer Wasserstoff im Kontext der Energiewende – Aktuelle Entwicklungen und Governance-Fragen' (Blue hydrogen in the context of the energy transition – current developments and governance issues) (2023) 10 KlimR 290

Gemmo A, 'European Renewable Energy Directive (RED III): updated ambitious targets to boost the renewable energy market' (2023) <https://sustainablefutures.linklaters.com/post/102ipy5/european-renewable-energy-directive-red-iii-updated-ambitious-targets-to-boost> accessed 17 June 2025

Gunlicks A B, The Länder and German Federalism (Manchester University Press 2003) 388

Harsch V/Antoni J, 'Alternativen der Förderung erneuerbarer Energien abseits des Ausschreibungsmodells im Lichte des EU-Rechts' (Alternatives to the tendering model for supporting renewable energies) (2023) 12 EnWZ 3

Hendrischke O, 'Bewältigung naturschutzrechtlicher Konflikte beim Ausbau erneuerbarer Energien' (Overcoming nature conservation legal conflicts in the expansion of renewable energies) (2023) NVwZ 965

Hermes G, 'Art. 83' in **Dreier H** (ed), Grundgesetz Kommentar (Commentary on the Basic Law) (3rd edn, Mohr Siebeck 2018)

Hermes G, 'Die Systementwicklungsplanung – Instrument zur klimagerechten Transformation des Energiesystems' (System development planning – an instrument for the climate-friendly transformation of the energy system) (2022) 41 EnWZ 99

Jaenicke M, 'Aktuelle Rechtsfragen der baurechtlichen Zulässigkeit von Windenergieanlagen an Land' (Current legal questions of the requirements in building law for onshore wind energy) (2023) 5 ZUR 291

Kafsack H, 'Der deutsche Kohleausstieg verpufft' (The German coal phase-out is fizzling out) (FAZ 2023) <www.faz.net/aktuell/wirtschaft/klima-nachhaltigkeit/klimapolitik-der-deutsche-kohleausstieg-verpufft-19257560.html> accessed 17 June 2025

Kment M, 'Beschleunigung des Ausbaus von Windenergieanlagen an Land' (Accelerating the expansion of onshore wind energy installations) (2023) 42 NVwZ 959

Kreuter-Kirchhof C, 'Emissionshandel und Erneuerbare Energien Richtlinie' (Emissions trading and the Renewable Energies Directive) (2019) 30 ZUR 396

Lingemann T, 'Der neue § 2 EEG in der verwaltungsgerichtlichen Rechtsprechung' (The new Sec. 2 EEG in the case law of the administrative courts) (2023) 42 NVwZ 1634

Mandová H/Vass T/Fernandez Pales A et al., 'The challenge of reaching zero emissions in heavy industry', (IEA, 2020) <www.iea.org/articles/the-challenge-of-reaching-zero-emissions-in-heavy-industry> accessed 17 June 2025

Nienaber M, 'Germany boosts its climate fund with 60 bln euro injection' (Reuters 2021) www.reuters.com/markets/europe/german-cabinet-passes-climate-fund-booster-with-60-bln-euro-extra-budget-2021-12-13/ accessed 17 June 2025

Rieger W, '§ 6 WindBG – die nächste Runde im Konflikt zwischen dem Ausbau der Windenergie und dem Artenschutz' (Sec. 6 WindBG – the next round in the conflict between the expansion of wind energy and species protection) (2023) 42 NVwZ 1042

Riemer M/Schreiner F/Wachsmuth J, 'Conversion of LNG Terminals for Liquid Hydrogen or Ammonia' (2022) ISI Fraunhofer <https://www.isi.fraunhofer.de/content/dam/isi/dokumente/cce/2022/Report_Conversion_of_LNG_Terminals_for_Liquid_Hydrogen_or_Ammonia.pdf> accessed 17 June 2025

Sailer F/Deuitinger M 'Klimaschutz, Gesundheitsschutz und Versorgungssicherheit beim Ausbau erneuerbarer Energien' (Climate proception, health protection and security of supply in the development of renewable energies)(2023) 11 ZUR 604

Saurer J/Monast J, 'Renewable Energy Federalism in Germany and the United States' (2021) TEL 293

Schlacke S/Wentzien H/Römling D, 'Beschleunigung der Energiewende: Ein gesetzgeberischer Paradigmenwechsel durch das Osterpaket?' (Accelerating the energy transition: A legislative paradigm shift through the Easter package?) (2022) 41 NVwZ 1581

Stäsche U, 'Reform des EU-Emissionshandelssystems, der Effort-Sharing-Verordnung, der Erneuerbare-Energien-Richtlinie und der Energieeffizienzrichtlinie – "Fit for 55"?' (Reform of the EU Emissions Trading Scheme, the Effort Sharing Regulation, the Renewable Energies Directive and the Energy Efficiency Directive – "Fit for 55"?) (2023) 6 KlimR 171

Statista, 'Anteil Erneuerbarer Energien am Bruttoendenergieverbrauch in Deutschland in den Jahren 2005 bis 2024' (Share of Renewable Energies in Germany on Total Energy Consumption in the Years 2005 to 2024.)<https://de.statista.com/statistik/daten/studie/856326/umfrage/stromerzeugung-aus-erneuerbaren-energien-in-deutschland> accessed 17 June 2025.

Statistisches Bundesamt, (German Federal Office of Statistics), 'Electricity production in 2021: markedly higher proportion of conventional energy sources' (2022) <www.destatis.de/EN/Press/2022/03/PE22_116_43312.html> accessed 17 June 2025

Stiftung Klimaneutralität, (Climate Neutrality Foundation),'Genehmigungsverfahren beschleunigen mit einem Windenergie-an-Land-Gesetz' (Accelerate approval procedures with a wind energy on land law) (2021) <www.stiftung-klima.de/app/uploads/2021/05/2021-05-07-Genehmigungverfahren-beschleunigen-mit-einem-Wind-an-Land-Gesetz.pdf> accessed 17 June 2025

Strauch F/Hennig B/Widmann V, 'Das Solarpaket I – Überblick über Änderungen am EEG und EnWG' (The Solar Package I – Overview and Changes in the EEG and EnWG) (2024) ZNER 291.

Umweltbundesamt (German Federal Environment Agency), 'Erneuerbare Energien in Deutschland -Daten zur Entwicklung im Jahr 2022' (Renewable Energies in Germany Data on development in 2021) (2022) 15 <www.umweltbundesamt.de/sites/default/files/medien/479/publikationen/hg_erneuerbareenergien_dt_0.pdf> accessed 17 June 2025

Umweltbundesamt (German Federal Environment Agency), 'Indikator: Anteil Erneuerbare am Bruttostromverbrauch' (Indicator: Share of Renewables in Electricity) (2025) https://www.umweltbundesamt.de/indikator-anteil-erneuerbare-am#die-wichtigsten-fakten> accessed 17 June 2025

Vereinigung der Fernleitungsnetzbetreiber Gas (Association of Transmission System Operators Gas), 'Hydrogen core network' (fnb-gas) <https://fnb-gas.de/wasserstoffnetz-wasserstoff-kernnetz/> accessed 17 June 2025

Wehrmann B, 'Q&A: Germany´s new €500bln fund – What´s in it for Climate and energy?' (2025) <https://www.cleanenergywire.org/factsheets/qa-germanys-eu500-bln-infrastructure-fund-whats-it-climate-and-energy#> accessed 17 June 2025

The Law of Renewable Energies in France

Louis de Fontenelle

A. Introduction

When it comes to renewable energies, France stands out from the other Member States of the European Union because of the central role played by nuclear power.[1] To fully understand the specific issues involved in accelerating the production of renewable energies, we need to situate them in relation to nuclear energy.

The time has come to revive the nuclear industry. In his Belfort speech on 10 February 2022, Emmanuel Macron said: "*ce que nous avons à bâtir aujourd'hui, parce que c'est le bon moment, parce que c'est ce qu'il faut pour notre nation et parce que les conditions sont maintenant réunies, c'est la renaissance du nucléaire français*" ("*what we have to build today, because it is the right time, because it is what is needed for our nation and because the conditions are now in place, is the renaissance of French nuclear power*"[2]).[3] This political ambition led to the adoption of Law 2023–491 of 22 June 2023 on the acceleration of procedures relating to the construction of new nuclear facilities near existing nuclear sites and the operation of existing facilities.[4] The major changes introduced by this law are the removal of the target of a 50 % reduction in the share of nuclear power in the electricity mix by 2035,[5] the removal of the 63.2 gigawatt (GW) cap on nuclear gener-

1 Xavier Arnauld de Sartre/Justin Missaghieh-Poncet/Lise Desvallées, 'En France, l'acceptabilité sociale des technologies de décarbonation de l'énergie à l'ombre de la dépendance au nucléaire' (2022) 4 EEI.

2 The speech-marked parts in this book chapter were translated by the authors.

3 Emmanuel Macron, 'Reprende en main notre destin énergétique!' (Élysée 10 February 2022) <https://www.gouvernement.fr/upload/media/default/0001/01/2022_02_nucleaire_belfort.pdf> accessed 27 August 2024.

4 Law no. 2023–491 of 22 June 2023 on the acceleration of procedures relating to the construction of new nuclear facilities near existing nuclear sites and the operation of existing facilities, *JORF* no. 0144 of 23 June 2023, Text no. 1

5 Article 1 of the law amending Article L. 100–4 of the Energy Code.

ation capacity[6] and the simplification of procedures for the construction of EPR2 reactor projects (temporary simplification rules for a period of 20 years).[7]

Within this framework, renewable energies must find their place. The challenge is therefore one of coexistence between the nuclear and renewable energy sectors. Guillaume Dezobry described the various stages in the coexistence of renewable energies and nuclear power in France: Act 1 involved taking account of the arrival of renewable energies, Act 2 involved competition between nuclear and renewable energies, and Act 3 involved complementarity between nuclear and renewable energies.[8] Today, we are clearly moving towards Act 4, with a reaffirmed place for nuclear power and an additional role for renewable energies in the decarbonisation objective.

B. Definition of Renewable Energies

In France, the Energy Code defines renewable energies in Article L. 211–2 as follows.

> "*Energy produced from renewable sources, or 'renewable energy', is energy produced from renewable non-fossil sources, namely wind energy, solar thermal or photovoltaic energy, geothermal energy, ambient energy, tidal, wave or osmotic energy and other marine energy, hydroelectric energy, biomass, landfill gas, sewage treatment plant gas and biogas*".

6 Article 1 of the Act, which deletes Article L. 311–1 of the Energy Code, states that authorisation to operate any new electricity generation facility "may not be granted if it would have the effect of increasing the total authorised nuclear electricity generation capacity beyond 63.2 gigawatts".

7 Article 7 of the Act, which states that the rules in the section entitled "Measures Designed to Accelerate Procedures Relating to the Construction of New Nuclear Facilities near Existing Nuclear Sites" apply "to the construction of nuclear power reactors, including small modular reactors, which are planned to be located in the immediate vicinity of or within the perimeter of an existing basic nuclear facility mentioned in 1° to 3° of Article L. 593–2 of the Environment Code and for which the application for authorisation to create the facility referred to in Article L. 593–7 of the same code is submitted within twenty years of the promulgation of the present law".

8 Guillaume Dezobry, 'Mesures structurelles – Les investissements – La relance du nucléaire' (2023) 1 RFDA 34.

Since an order was issued in 2021[9], this definition has been in line with the European definition contained in Directive 2018/2001 (known as RED II[10]). Prior to this date, French law did not define renewable energies as opposed to fossil fuels.[11]

C. Legal sources

1. Provisions Common to Renewable Energies Under French Law

The main legal provisions relating to renewable energies are contained in Book II of the Energy Code, entitled "Managing Energy Demand and Developing Renewable Energies" (Articles L. 211–1 to L. 294–1).

In addition to these common provisions, French renewable energy law contains specific provisions for each renewable energy source to take account of their technical and economic characteristics. The purpose of the following is not to describe all the sectoral regulations, rather to give a general overview of the legal framework for renewables.

2. Developments in the French Legal Framework

(a) The Development of the Law Prior to the APER Act

The legal framework for the development of renewable energy sources has been gradually established since 2005. In recent years, there has been a

9 Order no. 2021–236 of 3 March 2021 transposing various provisions of Directive (EU) 2018/2001 of the European Parliament and of the Council of 11 December 2018 on the promotion of the use of energy from renewable sources and Directive (EU) 2019/944 of the European Parliament and of the Council of 5 June 2019 concerning common rules for the internal market in electricity, *JORF* no. 0054 of 4 March 2021, Text no. 4.

10 Directive (EU) 2018/2001 of the European Parliament and of the Council of 11 December 2018 on the promotion of the use of energy from renewable source [2018] OJ L 328/82.

11 The first version of the codification, prior to this ordinance, stated: "renewable energy sources are wind, solar, geothermal, aerothermal, hydrothermal, marine and hydraulic energy, as well as energy from biomass, landfill gas, gas from wastewater treatment plants and biogas. Biomass is the biodegradable fraction of products, waste and residues from agriculture, including plant and animal substances from land and sea, forestry and related industries, as well as the biodegradable fraction of industrial and household waste".

significant production of legislation, which can be explained by the desire of the public authorities to put in place a legal framework conducive to accelerating the production of renewable energy. This acceleration has also been in response to changes in European Union legislation and the obligation to implement directives under the Clean Energy Package.

- Law of 13 July 2005 on energy policy guidelines[12] (Title III – Renewable energies)
- Law of 3 August 2009 on the implementation of the Grenelle Environment Forum[13]
- Law of 12 July 2010 on the national commitment to the environment[14] (Chapter II Renewable energies (Articles 84 to 93).
- Law of 17 August 2015 on energy transition for green growth[15] (Title V – Promoting renewable energies to diversify our energy sources and make the most of our regions' resources Articles 104 to 122)
- Energy and Climate Act of 8 November 2019[16]
- Act of 22 August 2021 to combat climate change and build resilience to its effects[17] (Chapter IV – Promoting renewable energies, Articles 82 to 102)
- Law of 10 March 2023 on accelerating the production of renewable energy[18]
- Law of 23 October 2023 on green industry[19] (introduces new provisions, but only marginally, to enable the development of renewable energies)

Of course, all the regulatory provisions (decrees and orders) designed to apply and clarify French legislation must be added to this legislative framework.

12 Law no. 2005–781 of 13 July 2005 on energy policy guidelines, *JORF* no. 163 of 14 July 2005, Text no. 2.

13 Law no. 2009–967 of 3 August 2009 on the implementation of the Grenelle Environment Round Table, *JORF* no. 0179 of 5 August 2009, Text no. 2.

14 Law no. 2010–788 of 12 July 2010 on the national commitment to the environment, *JORF* no. 0160 of 13 July 2010, Text no. 1.

15 Law no. 2015–992 of 17 August 2015 on the energy transition for green growth, *JORF* no. 0189 of 18 August 2015, Text no. 1.

16 Law no. 2019–1147 of 8 November 2019 on energy and climate, *JORF* no. 0261 of 9 November 2019, Text no. 1.

17 Act no. 2021–1104 of 22 August 2021 to combat climate change and strengthen resilience to its effects, *JORF* no. 0196 of 24 August 2021, Text no. 1.

18 Law no. 2023–175 of 10 March 2023 on accelerating the production of renewable energy, *JORF* no. 0060 of 11 March 2023, Text No. 1

19 Law no. 2023–973 of 23 October 2023 on green industry, *JORF* no. 0247 of 24 October 2023, Text no. 1, Article 11, Article 17, Article 23.

The result is a complex legal framework, but also evolving and, therefore unstable:[20] "*D'innombrables retouches textuelles sont régulièrement adoptées, lorsqu'il ne s'agit pas de réformes plus profondes, qui témoignent du tiraillement constant du législateur [...] entre la volonté de promouvoir les énergies renouvelables et celle d'imposer un juste encadrement* "[21] ("*Numerous amendments to the text are regularly adopted, if not more far-reaching reforms, reflecting the legislator's constant tug-of-war [...] between the desire to promote renewable energies and the need to establish an appropriate framework.*")

This standards strategy aligns with developments in the European Union's legal framework to promote the development of renewable energies. French regulations incorporate and transpose European legislation.

However, despite this complex and evolving nature, there has been a turning point since the 2020s due to the combination of crises posed by COVID-19 and the war in Ukraine. The major difficulties experienced by energy systems and the serious questions relating to the security of supply in France and within the EU have led the State to adopt a very proactive strategy for the development of renewable energy (in conjunction with the reaffirmation of the role of nuclear power).

In other words, after a period of delay in the legal development of renewable energies, today's legal strategy is to facilitate the massive development of renewable energies in France. From this point of view, the most central law in this strategy is the APER law of March 2023.

(b) The APER Act of 2023

On 10 March 2023, the French Parliament adopted the law on accelerating the production of renewable energies. The main objective pursued by the French legislature is to encourage the quantitative development of renewable energy projects in order to make up for the delay in achieving the renewable energy production targets[22] and the formation of low-carbon industrial sectors compared with other European Union countries.

---

20 Marie Lamoureux, *Droit de l'énergie* (ed. LGDJ, 2nd edition, 2022) 462.

21 ibid.

22 Cour des Comptes, *Les soutiens à l'éolien terrestre et maritime. Exercices 2017 et suivants* (March 2023) 18. The Cour des Comptes observed: "France has not achieved the target set by Directive 2009/28/EC: final consumption of renewable energies (electricity and heat) amounted to 307 TWh in 2020. At 19.1 % of the total, up 10 %

The explanatory memorandum to the law sets out the reasons for this delay, focusing in particular on the cumbersome administrative procedures: "On average, it takes 5 years of procedures to build a solar farm requiring just a few months of work, 7 years for a wind farm and 10 years for an offshore wind farm. Our European partners often go twice as fast as we do. There are many reasons for this: the complexity of our administrative and litigation procedures compared with those of our European partners, a shortage of land that can be easily mobilised and reconciled with environmental issues, a lack of visibility over the planning process for offshore wind farms, problems with the acceptability and attractiveness of renewable energy projects, and a lack of ownership at local level. So we need to move much faster, without compromising our environmental requirements. Given the urgency of the situation in terms of climate and security of supply, temporary adjustments to speed up the implementation of projects are necessary for the energy transition".

The APER Act is structured as follows:

- Title I Measures to Promote the Use of Renewable Energies and their Integration into the Landscape (Articles 1 to 3)
- Title II Simplification and Territorial Planning Measures Aimed at Accelerating and Coordinating the Siting of Renewable Energy Projects and the Industrial Projects Needed for the Energy Transition (Articles 4 to 33)
- Title III Measures to Accelerate the Development of Solar, Thermal, PV and Agrivoltaic Energy (Articles 34 to 55)
- Title IV Measures to Accelerate the Development of Offshore Renewable Energy Production Facilities (Articles 56 to 66)
- Title V Measures Relating to Other Categories of Renewable Energy (Articles 67 to 85)
- Title VI Cross-sectoral Measures for Financing Renewable and Recovered Energy and Sharing the Value (Articles 86 to 103)
- Title VII Miscellaneous Provisions (Articles 104 to 116)

---

on 2005, it falls short of the 23 % target. It should be noted that France had accepted more ambitious targets for the introduction of renewable energy than most other countries, even though its electricity mix is highly decarbonised and the delay in achieving its targets is not attributable to the electricity mix alone, and particularly not to the wind power sector alone, but also to the insufficient reduction in overall energy consumption, including heating and transport".

The main measures contained in the APER Act[23] are aimed at achieving the following objectives:

- Simplification of administrative procedures to enable the development of renewable energy projects
- An original planning approach (renewable energy acceleration zones) to identify areas suitable for the development of renewable energy projects and to encourage social and territorial appropriation.
- Economic and financial support mechanisms to structure dedicated renewable energy sectors (offshore wind, PV solar, etc.)
- The introduction of legal mechanisms to ensure the legal and financial security of investments (long-term electricity and biogas sales contracts, for example).
- The development of a legal framework for offshore wind power[24] includes the introduction of a planning system (priority zones for the development of offshore wind power),[25] the introduction of a legal regime for floating wind power[26] and measures to provide economic and legal security for projects (such as the creation of a guarantee fund to compensate the operator for financial losses in the event of a court annulling a project authorisation decision).[27]
- The development of a legal framework for agrivoltaics, by drawing up a definition and implementing rules to prevent the risk of conflicts of use between farming and the production and use of energy.[28]

23 Christine Le Bihan-Graf/Pierre Jérémie, 'Les principales mesures de la loi relative à l'accélération de la production d'énergies renouvelables' (2023) 5 EEI study 11.

24 Nicolas Boillet/Gaëlle Guéguen-Hallouët, 'Principaux apports de la loi APER pour le déploiement des éoliennes en mer' (2023) AJDA 1179.

25 Article 56 of the APER law.

26 Article 63 of the APER law.

27 Article 24 of the APER law.

28 Article L. 314–36, Energy Code. Benoit Grimonprez, 'L'agrivoltaisme à la lumière du droit' (2023) AJDA 1168; Victoire Martin, 'Agrivoltaïsme : entre incitation et régulation – Regards croisés sur un droit en construction. – Note à partir des travaux du colloque au Palais du Luxembourg du 7 avril 2023' (2023) 11 EEI study 25.

D. Planning

1. National Planning

France has put in place a planning framework based on incorporating national objectives into local planning documents, which is ultimately translated into the development of renewable energies on the ground. The strategy is set first and foremost at the national level as part of an energy and climate programming law provided for in L.100 – 1, A of the Energy Code: the text stipulates that before 1er July 2023, and every 5 years after that, a law must determine and set the objectives of the national energy policy to respond to the ecological and climate emergency. This law must specify, in particular, "3°The objectives for developing and storing renewable energies for electricity, heat, fuel, gas and renewable and low-carbon hydrogen, for two successive five-year periods. In the case of hydroelectricity, the development and storage targets relate to changes in the production capacity of hydraulic installations, authorised and licensed in application of Article L. 511–5, as well as pumped storage stations".

The objectives set out in this law must be incorporated into the multi-annual energy programme (hereinafter referred to as the PPE), the content of which must be compatible with these objectives.[29] The PPE, provided for in L. 141–1 of the Energy Code, is set by decree and defines the terms and conditions for the public authorities' action in managing all forms of energy in France. This planning document, created by the 2015 TECV law (Loi de Transition Énergétique pour la Croissance Verte), has replaced the previous planning documents (Pluriannual et al. for electricity production, Pluriannual Investment Programme for heat production, Pluriannual Indicative Investment Plan for the gas sector). There is one document for mainland France and one for each non-interconnected zone. The document consists of a decree adopting the PPE, which also defines the main objectives and priorities for action, a report, and an explanatory summary of these guidelines and actions, accessible to the public. This PPE must be compatible with the programming law provided for in L. 100–1, A, and the objectives defined in L. 100–1, L. 100–2 and L. 100–4 of the Energy Code.

- Article L. 100–1 defines the main objectives of energy policy (competitiveness of the economy, security of supply, competitive and attractive energy prices, protection of human health and the environment, social

29 Article L. 100–1 A, Energy Code.

and territorial cohesion, combating fuel poverty, participation in the European Energy Union).

- Article L. 100–2 concerns the involvement of local and regional authorities and their groupings in achieving energy policy objectives. In particular, they are required to diversify energy supply sources by reducing the proportion of fossil fuels, diversifying energy production sources in a balanced way and increasing the proportion of renewable energy sources in final energy consumption.

For the time being, the new national energy policy has still not been implemented, despite the July 2023 deadline mentioned in Article L. 100–1 A. Legislation – a bill and a decree publishing the new PPE – is under consideration.

Today, the objectives for developing renewable energy sources are therefore partly contained in the law at L. 100–4 and partly in the PPE (see above, 4° to 4°, bis, ter, quart and 8°, 9°, 10° and 11° L.100 – 4).

The sectoral objectives for the development of renewable energies are specified in Article 3 of the decree of 21 April 2020 relating to the PPE[30]:

Table 1:

Installed Capacity on 12/31 (in GW)	2023	2028	
		Low Option	High Option
Onshore Wind Energy	24,1	33,2	34,7
Solar Enegry	20,1	35,2	44,0
Hydroelectricity (including tidal energy)	25,7	26,4	26,7
Offshore Wind Energy	2,4	5,2	6,2
Methanation	0,27	0,34	0,41

Source: Decree no. 2020–456 of 21 April 2020 on multiannual energy programming

Therefore, there is a significant ambition for development from 2019 to 2028, with a doubling of renewable energy installation capacity in 2028 compared with 2017.

However, if we look at the reality of renewable energy development, France is definitely behind schedule in meeting its targets. In a report

30 Decree no. 2020–456 of 21 April 2020 on multiannual energy programming, *JORF* no. 0099 of 23 April 2020, Text no. 3.

for 2023, 20.7 % of gross final energy consumption will be accounted for by renewable energy sources, 3 % short of the target set for 2020 (23 %). We can also see that a considerable amount remains to be done achieve a target of 33 % of energy from renewable sources in gross final energy consumption by 2030.[31]

Figure 1: Renewable energies – Share of renewable energies in gross final energy consumption and 2030 target (calculated according to the Directive (EU) 2018/2001)

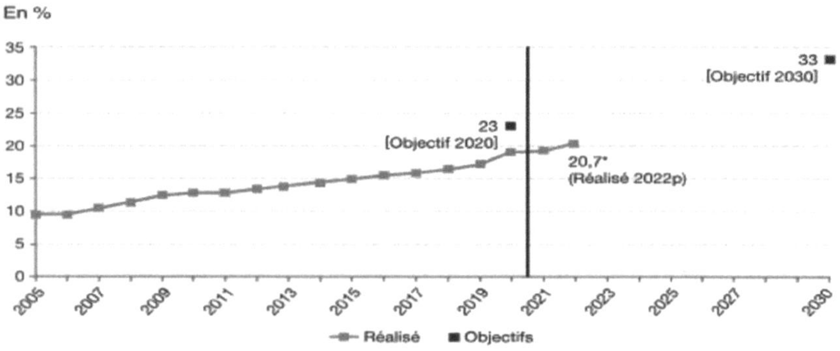

Source: Ministère de la transition écologique et de la cohésion des territoires, Chiffres clés de l'énergie – Édition 2023, Statistique publique, September 2023

2. Local Planning

National planning documents are then translated into local planning documents, with a multi-tiered organisation based on the following:

- The SRADDETs (L.4251 – 1 to L.4251 – 11 of the CGCT) set medium and long-term objectives for the use of renewable and recovered energy. These development objectives are compatible with the objectives mentioned for each sector in the PPE and with the regional renewable energy development objectives[32] as set out in L. 141–5–1 of the Energy Code. The regional renewable energy development targets are established by decree for mainland France after consultation with the regional councils

31 Ministère de la transition écologique et de la cohésion des territoires, *Chiffres clés de l'énergie* (Édition 2023, Statistique publique).

32 Article L. 4251–2, CGCT.

concerned. These targets are based on a common method and indicators that enable them to be monitored (L. 141–5–1, Energy Code).

- The PCAETs are specified in the French Environment Code at L.229 - 25 et seq. They are compulsory for the Lyon metropolitan area and the EPCIs à *fiscalité propre.*[33] These PCAETs define the action programme to be carried out in the EPCI or metropolitan area in order to increase the production of renewable energy and make the most of recovered energy potential, and to develop positive energy territories. This PCAET can also set targets for agrivoltaic installations (L.314 - 36 Energy Code).
- Renewable energies can also be covered by regional and urban planning documents, such as the SCOT, which can include guidelines in its orientation and objectives document that help to promote the energy transition, in particular through the development of renewable energies (Article L. 1141–10, 4°, Town Planning code). This is also the case for the regulations contained in PLUs, urban planning documents for groups of municipalities or communes, which can "delimit sectors in which the installation of renewable energy production facilities, including their connection works, is subject to conditions, provided that these installations are compatible with the inhabited neighbourhood or with the use of land located nearby, or that they are detrimental to the preservation of natural spaces and landscapes, architectural, urban and landscape quality, the enhancement of heritage and the integration of installations into the surrounding environment".[34]

In short, France aims to make its strategy coherent through a top-down approach based on setting national objectives, which are then translated into local planning documents, with a view to putting its energy policy into practice on the ground. However, obstacles to deploying this energy policy have been identified, which is why the APER law introduced a strategy based on identifying renewable energy acceleration zones (hereinafter ZAENR).

33 Article L. 229–26, Environment Code.
34 Article L. 151–42–1, Town Planning Code.

3. Renewable Energy Acceleration Zones

The Government seeks to regulate the siting of renewable energy projects on a national scale and is developing bottom-up spatial planning to this end.

The ZAENRs, set out in L. 141–5–3 of the Energy Code, are based on six principles: they must have the potential to accelerate the production of renewable energy in order to achieve the objectives of the national energy policy (set out in Article L. 100–4, Energy Code), those of the PPE and those that will be mentioned in the future programming law; they must contribute to solidarity between territories and to securing the supply, they must aim to prevent and control the dangers or inconveniences associated with their siting, they must take into account the diversification of renewable energy sources according to the territory, they must not, as a matter of principle, be included in national parks and nature reserves, nor, in the case of wind power, in special protection areas or special areas for the conservation of chiropterans in Natura 2000 areas; they must take into account the potential of areas of economic activity.

From a general point of view, the ZAENRs are based on consultation with all the players in the area and on the assumption of responsibility by the municipalities. The link between the State and the municipalities is established through a prefectural referent (*réferent prefectoral*) created for this purpose (Article L. 181–21–10). The duties of this prefectural contact are set out in Article L. 181–28–10 of the Environment Code and specified in a circular.[35] The prefectural referent is responsible for examining renewable energy development projects and industrial projects required for the energy transition. The prefectural referent is appointed by the State representative in the department, from among the sub-prefects. Without prejudice to the remit of the relevant departments, he is responsible for facilitating administrative procedures for applicants, coordinating the work of the departments responsible for examining authorisations and producing an annual report on the examination of projects in his area. They are also responsible for supporting local authorities in their energy transition planning. The circular states that "the role of the prefectural renewable energy referent is to

35 Ministère de la Transition Écologique et Solidaire/Ministère de la Cohésion des Territoires et des Relations avec les Collectivités Territoriales, *Circulaire du 28 novembre 2023 relative aux missions du référent préfectoral à l'instruction des projets d'énergies renouvelables et des projets industriels nécessaires à la transition énergétique et à la géothermie de minime importance* (ENER2331339J).

facilitate and provide support for regional renewable energy planning, particularly for local authorities, at a time when the development of renewable electrical and thermal energy production resources is essential to ensure our security of supply and combat global warming".

The ZAENRs are expected to contribute to the achievement of regional renewable energy development targets introduced by the Climate and Resilience Act, which will be formally adopted by decree.[36] This decree, which has not yet been adopted, should specify "a method and common indicators for monitoring the deployment and implementation of regional renewable energy development targets, in a way that is shared between the regions and the State, as well as between local authorities in the same region". These indicators are to be made public.

During the first phase,[37] the State and network operators will make available information "relating to the potential for the installation of renewable energy sources" to municipalities, EPCIs, energy distribution organising authorities, departments and regions. This information must be submitted within 2 months of the promulgation of the APER law, and will be updated each time the PPE is revised.

During the second phase, the municipalities have 6 months (this is not a deadline, however) to identify the acceleration zones. This identification follows a public consultation procedure, the details of which they are free to determine. The municipalities must then forward this initial zoning to the prefectural referent, to the EPCIs and, where applicable, to the SCoT.

During the third phase, the prefectural referent draws up the ZAENR map, after sending it to the regional energy committee for its opinion and organising a consultation within a territorial conference (including EPCIs and SCoT establishments).

36 Article L. 141-5-1, Energy Code: "Regional targets for the development of renewable energies are established by decree for the mainland metropolitan area, after consultation with the regional councils concerned, to contribute to the objectives mentioned in Article L. 100-4, in the law mentioned in I of Article L. 100-1 A and in the multiannual energy programming mentioned in Article L. 141-3. These objectives take into account the regional renewable and recovered energy potential that can be mobilised".

37 Article L. 141-5-3 II, Energy Code.

Figure 2: Identification of renewable energy acceleration zones

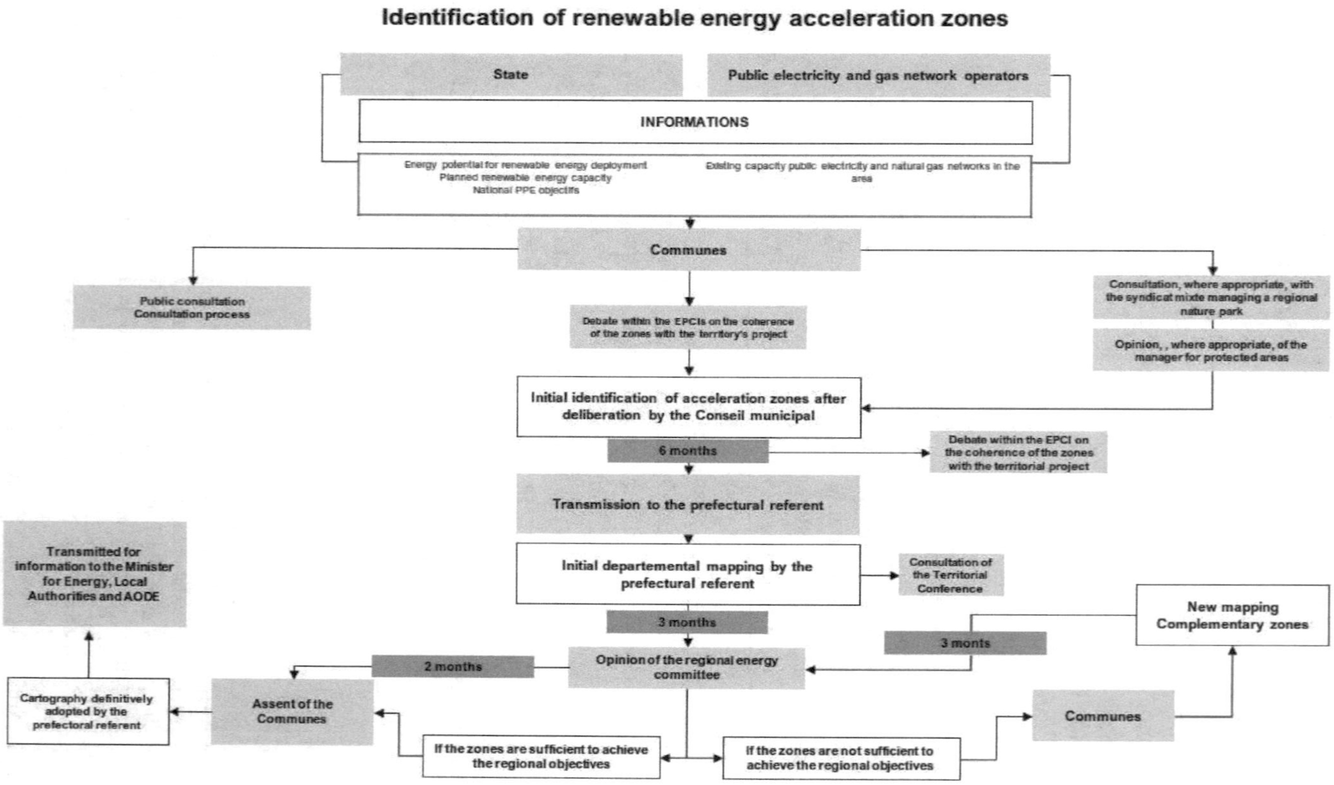

Source: created by Louis de Fontenelle (2024)

- If the ZAENRs are sufficient to achieve the regional objectives for the development of renewable energy – then the ZAENRs are definitively decided by the prefectural referent at the level of each department, after obtaining the assent of the communes in the department.
- If the ZAENRs are not sufficient to achieve the regional objectives for the development of renewable energy, then the municipalities will have to identify additional zones at the request of the prefectural referents. These new zones will be submitted to the regional energy committee within 3 months so that it can issue a new opinion. Then, within 2 months, the prefectural coordinator will have to draw up a department-wide map after obtaining the approval of the department's municipalities.
- The maps of these zones and the opinions are sent to the Minister for Energy and to local authorities and their groupings for information.

The identification of these ZAENRs must be renewed every five years, to coincide with the timeframe of the PPE. From 31 December 2027, they must contribute to achieving the objectives of the PPE.

In practical terms, these ZAENRs will serve a number of purposes, including simplifying administrative procedures and taking account of the location of renewable energy projects as part of the competitive procedures for obtaining public support (criteria for selecting beneficiaries).

Obviously, this zoning poses difficulties that were identified in the National Assembly's evaluation report: "The success of the scheme depends on local elected representatives taking ownership of it and on sufficient human and financial resources".[38]

E. Social acceptability

The issue of acceptability and even social appropriation is crucial. The public authorities are fully aware of this challenge. The explanatory memorandum to the APER 2023 law is very clear: "We need to move faster while creating the conditions for the acceptability and attractiveness of these projects, which are also decisive factors in their success and the development of future projects in other areas. Successfully meeting this

38 Henri Alfrandari/Eric Bothorel/Maxime Laisney/Nicolas Meizonnet, *Rapport d'information déposé en application de l'article 145-7 du Règlement par la Commission des affaires économiques sur l'application de la loi n° 2023-175 du 10 mars 2023 relative à l'accélération de la production d'énergies renouvelables* (2023).

dual challenge means removing all regulatory barriers once projects have been accepted locally by simplifying procedures and adopting a pragmatic local approach to project support. This bill aims to meet the dual challenge of local and regional acceptability on the one hand and speeding up and simplifying the process on the other. It is the cornerstone of our country's major energy transformation, which should enable France to become the first major country in the world to move away from dependence on fossil fuels while at the same time strengthening our energy independence and our exemplary climate credentials".

This question of social and territorial appropriation is based on three major issues: landscape integration, territorial sharing of value, and dispute management.

1. Landscape Integration of Renewable Energy Projects

The APER law introduces provisions relating to the proper integration of renewable energies into the landscape.[39] Article L. 141–4 of the Town Planning Code states that "the orientation and objectives document determines the conditions for implementing the strategic development project. It defines the general guidelines for organising the area, coordinating public policies and developing the area", and in particular incorporates "the preservation and development of biodiversity, natural resources, natural, agricultural and forest areas and landscapes, with the aim of integrating and enhancing the landscape quality of the various human activities, in particular renewable energy production and transmission facilities". Article L. 141–10 specifies that the guidance and objectives document defines the guidelines for " the preservation of landscapes and the integration and landscape quality of economic, agricultural, forestry and energy production and transport activities, and the natural, agricultural, forestry or urban areas to be protected, in particular because of their contribution to improving the quality of life. It specifies the way in which landscapes and their natural, historical and socio-cultural components are taken into account in development choices and ensures that the effects of visual saturation are limited. It transposes the relevant provisions of regional nature park charters to an appropriate scale".

39 Title I Measures to Promote the Use of Renewable Energies and their Integration into the Landscape (Articles 1 to 3).

In addition, with specific regard to wind turbines, the APER law introduces the "visual saturation" factor into the environmental authorisation regime for wind farm projects.[40] This means that environmental authorisation takes into account, where appropriate, the number of existing onshore wind power installations in the area concerned, in order to prevent visual saturation. The concept of "visual saturation" is not new. It was first found in administrative doctrine (concerning impact studies) and then in jurisprudence. However, this is the first time it has been incorporated into energy law[41] and has attracted criticism, particularly as it only applies to wind power (whereas large solar farms have an impact on the landscape).[42]

The question of landscape plays a central role in wind turbine litigation. From this point of view, the decision by the CE on 4 October 2023, n° 464855, Société Combray Energie, provided an interesting analysis. Before this decision,_the judge "classically assessed the damage to a monumental perspective or an architectural dimension, even if it meant making an incidental reference to historical elements to support the reasoning. Adding to this traditional assessment, but going beyond the spatial criterion alone, it now sees the landscape to be protected as having a specific cultural dimension. In this way, the Conseil d'État adds an intangible criterion to a previously tangible control".[43] In this instance, it also drew on a reference to Marcel Proust, "whose work is incorporated, as it were, into the site through the memorial force of literature".[44] Thus, "the innovative character of this decision consists in relating the control of the siting of a wind farm to the protection of cultural heritage, in this case literary".[45]

2. The Concept of Territorial Value-Sharing Introduced by APER Law

With a view to promoting social ownership and raising awareness among energy consumers, the APER Act introduces a new mechanism for territorial sharing of value. The Parliament even draws a parallel with the nuclear

40 Article L. 515–44, Environment Code.
41 Blanche Lormeteau/Rémi Radiguet, 'Le volet paysage dans la loi APER: panorama d'une approche pointilliste' (2023) AJDA 1156.
42 ibid.
43 Jean-Pierre Camby/Jean-Eric Schoettl, 'L'insertion des éoliennes dans un paysage : autant en emporte la subjectivité du juge' (2023) RFDA 1073.
44 ibid.
45 ibid.

industry: "In the same way that the nuclear fleet has enabled the French to benefit from electricity prices that reflect its competitiveness, we can, with renewable technologies, enable our territories and their inhabitants to benefit from their competitiveness".[46] The law thus introduces a mechanism for sharing the value of low-carbon energies, which is seen as "one of the keys to buy-in and ownership lies in demonstrating a concrete and direct benefit for local residents".[47]

The APER Act of 2023 devotes a chapter to measures promoting the territorial sharing of the value of renewable energies, with a view to improving the social acceptability of energy projects. However, an in-depth analysis of these mechanisms suggests that there will be difficulties in implementing them.[48] Similarly, decrees clarifying the legal provisions are still awaiting publication.[49]

The first mechanism, contained in Article L. 294–1 of the Energy Code, establishes an obligation for the members or shareholders of a REN production company to inform the mayor of the municipality or president of the EPCI where the REN project is located, so that they can make an offer to participate in the capital of this company (information no later than two months before the articles of association are signed). Similarly, in the event of the sale of all or part of the capital, the company must inform the mayor or president of the EPCI no later than 2 months before the sale so that they can make a purchase offer (if the municipality or EPCI remains silent, this will be deemed to be a refusal on expiry of the deadline). In principle, this mechanism should apply to all renewable energy sources. There are no penalties for failure to meet this obligation.

The second territorial value-sharing mechanism for financing the energy transition and biodiversity is based on the creation of a "territorial value-sharing contribution" for renewable energy electricity generation projects (Article L. 314–41 of the Energy Code) and biogas projects (Article L. 446–59, Energy Code). This scheme only concerns project developers who receive economic support (winners of the competitive tendering procedure

46 Explanatory memorandum on the APER law.

47 Explanatory memorandum on the APER law.

48 Louis de Fontenelle, 'Territorial value-sharing of renewable energies. Critical analysis of the French mechanism introduced by the 2023 Renewable Energy Acceleration Act', in Sébastien Bourdin (dir.), The Social Acceptability of Renewable Energy Projects, éd. Edward Elgar Publishing, (to be published 2025).

49 Chapter II: Measures to promote territorial sharing of the value of renewable energies (Articles 93 to 97).

under Article L. 311–10 of the Energy Code or of the call for projects under the experimental contract). These project sponsors are obliged to finance either energy transition projects (energy renovation, energy efficiency, mobility, combating fuel poverty) or projects to protect or safeguard biodiversity, supported by the municipality or EPCI. These contributions can be made either directly to a project, or by payment into a fund. The amount of the contributions is determined according to the installed capacity of the electricity generating facility, and may not be less than a threshold set by decree. There is a possibility that this contribution will take the form of an equity stake for energy transition projects. Biodiversity protection projects may be financed by payments to the French Biodiversity Agency, provided they are part of national operational action plans for the conservation or recovery of endangered species. The contribution is paid prior to the activation of the feed-in tariff and remuneration supplement contracts, with a reporting obligation for municipalities and EPCIs (annual report on the amount of the territorial contribution and its use).

The third provision is set out in Article 95 of the APER law. As part of the competitive tendering procedure, it may be specified that renewable energy production companies are required to offer a share of the capital to residents living near the project site or to the municipality or grouping of which it is a member, on whose territory the project is to be located, and to make their shares available to them, where appropriate. This provision is in line with the public authorities' desire to extend participatory investment to all renewable energy production projects.

The fourth and final provision is set out in Article 96 of the APER law. It provides for an exemption from payment of the occupancy fee by the REN production SA (*société anonyme*) or SAS (*société par actions simplifiées*) "if the proceeds of the fee thus collected are used to finance the acquisition of holdings in its capital".

3. Litigation

Renewable energy projects in France are the subject of litigation, sometimes systematically (in the case of developing renewable energy). The legislature has introduced measures to streamline litigation procedures. Litigation is a factor in slowing down the deployment of renewable energy projects. According to the impact study for the APER law: "Today, it is estimated that more than 75 % of authorisations issued for onshore wind farms are subject to appeal, and this figure rises to 100 % for offshore wind farms. Around 7 % of these appeals result in the authorisation being cancelled altogether".

The strategy to contain litigation is based on:

- The creation of a specialised institution to rationalise and simplify offshore wind energy litigation. The example of offshore wind power is topical. Before the 2020 law on the acceleration and simplification of public action,[50] offshore wind power litigation was assigned in the first and last instance to the Nantes Administrative Court of Appeal.[51] Since 2020, this litigation has been assigned to the Conseil d'Etat. The regulations list the decisions that may be appealed to the Conseil d'Etat at first and last instance.[52]
- The creation of a guarantee fund to compensate for part of the financial losses resulting from the annulment by an administrative judge of a decision authorising the deployment of renewable energy projects (lists of decisions specified in Article 24 of the APER law).
- Powers of regularisation attributed to the administrative judge.[53]

F. Support, Business Models and Contracts

The State has a multi-faceted strategy for supporting various types of projects (of varying sizes), carried out by different types of players. To achieve this, it has set up a number of mechanisms.

1. Feed-in Tariffs and Feed-in Premium

Under French law, there are two main support mechanisms that enable producers to make a profit from the energy they have produced, while obtaining a minimum guarantee to ensure a return in relation to the investment costs of renewable energy installations: the *tarif d'achat* (feed-in tariff) and the *complément de rémunération* (feed-in premium).

50 Law no. 2020–1525 of 7 December 2020 on accelerating and simplifying public action, JORF no. 0296 of 8 December 2020, Text no. 1.

51 François-Xavier Bréchot, 'Compétence nantaise en matière d'éolien en mer: autant en emporte le vent?' (2022) 1 AJDA 32.

52 Art. R. 311–1–1 CJA.

53 Article 60 of the APER law.

Despite the common rules, which relate in particular to the procedure for concluding these contracts and certain terms and conditions relating to their performance, they retain certain specific features that are unique to them.[54] The legal regime for the *tarif d'achat* is defined in Articles L. 314–1 to L. 314–13 of the Energy Code. The legal status of the *complément de rémunération* is defined in Articles L. 314–18 to L. 314–27 of the Energy Code.

The *tarif d'achat* seeks to ensure that the producer can sell all the energy produced. The *complément de rémuneration* aims to involve the producer directly in the market, while offering him economic support in the face of market fluctuations. These two support schemes have their own scope of application. The renewable energy installations eligible for each of the contracts differ according to certain technical and economic characteristics, in line with the degree of maturity of the renewable energy sector. The scope of these contracts varies, which explains why certain renewable energy sectors that have reached a sufficient degree of maturity and structuring are no longer eligible for the *tarif d'achat* contract, but only for the *complément de rémunération* contract (as in the case of "installations using mechanical wind energy located on land that do not have any wind turbine generator with a rated output of more than 3 MW and a maximum of six wind turbine generators").[55]

2. Long-Term Sales Contracts

Article 86 of law no. 2023–175 of 10 March 2023 on accelerating the production of renewable energy is dedicated to contracts for the direct sale of electricity and biogas, renewable gas and low-carbon gas ("contrats de vente directe d'électricité" and "contrat de vente directe à long terme de biogaz, de gaz renouvelable ou de gaz bas-carbone de gaz"). These contracts are better known as "*power purchase agreements*" (PPAs), over-the-counter contracts

54 Louis De Fontenelle/Stephane Andrieu, 'La valorisation de l'électricité produite par de l'énergie photovoltaique: analyse juridique des modèles de vente et d'autoconsommation' in David Bailleul/Helene Claret (eds), *Le développement de l'énergie photovoltaique* (Presses universitaires Savoie Mont Blanc 2023).

55 Order of December 29, 2022 amending the order of May 6, 2017 establishing the conditions for additional remuneration for electricity produced by electricity generation facilities using mechanical energy from wind, with a maximum of six wind turbines, JORF No. 0303 of December 31, 2022, Text No. 120.

for the sale of energy by a producer to an end consumer.[56] It is a model that breaks with the existing and traditional models of energy production and consumption, in other words a "new form of energy marketing".[57] The aim of the law is to develop the use of PPAs. In France, the use of PPAs is less widespread than in other EU countries.[58] "There are several reasons for this situation: the absence of a dedicated regulatory framework; the scale of public support (via feed-in tariffs or remuneration supplements), which was not compatible with the sale of guarantees of origin; the already highly decarbonised composition of the electricity mix due to nuclear power; and the cost of nuclear power".[59] In concrete terms, French law legally enshrines a certain model of PPA contracts: "For the purposes of Article L. 333–1(I)(2), the term 'direct electricity sales contract' means any contract for the sale of electricity by a producer connected to the mainland electricity grid to an end consumer for final consumption or to a network operator for its losses, without subsequent transfer" (Article R. 333–1, Energy Code[60]). It also opens up the possibility of mixed offers combining public support and direct sales as part of competitive tendering procedures. It now clearly states that contracting authorities and entities may enter into long-term direct sales contracts for electricity produced solely from renewable sources (Article L. 331–5 of the Energy Code), as well as long-term direct sales contracts for biogas, renewable gas or low-carbon gas (Article L. 441–6 of the Energy Code).

56 On these contracts, see in particular. Louis-Narata Harada/Marie Coussi, 'Les "Power Purchase Agreements" en France, un outil émergent au cœur de la transition énergétique' (2020) 87 BDEI 20; Mathias Dantin/Adil Kourtih, 'Corporate Power Purchase Agreements. Premiers retours d'expérience sur les points clefs de négociation' (2023) Cah. dr. entr dossier 14; Cecil Fontaine/Flavien Loustau, 'La commande publique à l'épreuve des nouvelles formes de commercialisation de l'énergie' (2023) 4 Contrats et Marchés publics study 2.

57 Louis de Fontenelle/Marie Lamoureux, 'Les contrats de vente directe d'électricité et de gaz' (2023) AJDA 1173.

58 E-CUBE, 'Analyse des dynamiques et des mécanismes publics de soutien aux énergies renouvelables favorables aux PPA en Europe' (10 February 2022) <www.cre.fr> accessed 27 August 2024.

59 De Fontenelle/Lamoureux (n 57) 1173.

60 Introduced by Decree No. 2024–613 of June 27, 2024 on the authorization to supply electricity and the reduction of the tariff for the use of public electricity networks, JORF n°0151 of June 28, 2024, Text No. 7.

3. Self-consumption and energy communities

The Clean Energy Package introduced the concept of self-consumption and energy communities. These concepts have been translated into French law. There are now several legal regimes:

- Individual and collective self-consumption as referred to in Articles L.315 – 1 to L.315 – 8 of the Energy Code
- Citizen energy communities and renewable energy communities as referred to in Articles L.291 – 1 to L.294 – 1 of the Energy Code. Recently, Decree 2023–287 of 26 December 2023 created the regulations applicable to energy communities.[61] It clarifies the distinction between renewable energy communities and citizen energy communities, and sets out the criteria for autonomy and geographical proximity, the procedures for withdrawing from these communities, and the conditions for compensating network operators.

These concepts aim to develop renewable energies through the direct involvement of citizens, local authorities and small and medium-sized enterprises in the local production and consumption of energy as part of local circuits.[62]

G. Administrative Simplification

The timeframe for developing renewable energy projects is conditioned by the procedural and formal stages to which they are subject. This is one of the main constraints for project developers.

The Government's instruction of 16 September 2022 on the organisation of the distribution and load shedding of natural gas and electricity consumption in the run-up to the winter of 2022–2023 and the acceleration of the development of renewable energy projects explained that "an unprecedented acceleration in the deployment of renewable energies (wind, photovoltaic, renewable gas, etc.) is essential if we are to meet our targets for reducing greenhouse gas emissions, break our dependence on imported

61 Decree no. 2023–1287 of 26 December 2023 on energy communities, JORF no. 0300 of 28 December 2023, Text no. 96.

62 François-Mathieu Poupeau/Blanche Lormeteau, *L'autoconsommation collective d'électricité en France: Émergence d'une innovation contrariée* (Presses des Mines 2024).

fossil fuels and ensure our security of supply, which is currently under threat in the short term. It is therefore up to the departmental prefects, who are responsible for enforcing the law, to ensure that the renewable energy development targets set out in the multiannual energy programme (PPE) are fully implemented. France can no longer be the only country in the European Union to fail to meet its binding national target for the development of renewable energies".[63] The aim of this original instruction is to facilitate and speed up the processing of applications for current and future renewable energy projects, and to ensure that no application will take longer than 24 months, except in very exceptional circumstances.

The procedures for authorising renewable energy projects are based on a succession of complex procedural stages[64] at the intersection of various provisions (urban planning law, environmental law, energy law). This means that it takes a long time to obtain permits and authorisations – "It takes an average of 5 years of procedures to build a solar farm requiring a few months of work, 7 years for a wind farm and 10 years for an offshore wind farm" (according to the explanatory memorandum to the APER law). The urban planning and environmental constraints are based on the idea of reconciling the interests likely to be affected by the project with the interests of the project itself. These constraints vary greatly depending on the nature of the project. There are specific rules depending on the sector concerned, and the characteristics and location of the project. For example, onshore wind power is subject to the ICPE and environmental authorisation regime (the aim of environmental authorisation is to bring together in a single authorisation several authorisations that a project developer must obtain), whereas photovoltaic power is essentially subject to town planning and energy law.

There is a desire to simplify and streamline the administrative authorisation process:

- The first manifestation is the presumption of major public interest in obtaining a "protected species" exemption (Article L.211 – 2–1 of the Energy Code).

63 Ministère de la transition énergétique, *Instruction du Gouvernement du 16 septembre 2022 relative à l'organisation de la répartition et du délestage de la consommation de gaz naturel et de l'électricité dans la perspective du passage de l'hiver 2022–2023 et à l'accélération du développement des projets d'énergie renouvelable* (ENER2226074C).

64 Pierre Delvolvé, 'Mesures structurelles – Les investissements – Les installations de production d'énergies renouvelables' (2023) RFDA 42.

- From a procedural point of view, the APER law also provides for a reduction in certain appraisal deadlines, 3 months in ZAENR, 4 on justification, (Article L. 123- 15 of the Environment Code), 15 days to deliver the public enquiry report, compared with 30 days today (Article L.223- 15 of the Environment Code (new version)).
- The APER law introduces rules to simplify repowering.
- In addition, Article L. 121–12–1 has been added to the Town Planning Code, stipulating that, as an exception to the principle of limiting the expansion of urban development (Article L. 121–8), photovoltaic and thermal production units may be set up, in exceptional circumstances, on brownfield sites "particularly industrial sites" listed by decree, after consultation with the Conservatoire de l'espace littoral et des rivages lacustres.

H. Conclusion: The Complexity of the Law and the Risk of a Deterioration in the Quality of Standards

Some authors have raised the issue of the deterioration in the quality of the standard,[65] both as regards the drafting of the standard and the content of the standard itself.[66] Today, the French Government is keen to control and steer the development of renewable energies in France, and to this end is putting in place a complex system of standards aimed at liberating

65 Philippe Terneyre, 'L'accélération de la dégradation de la norme législative' (2023) AJDA 1145.

66 The Conseil d'Etat has itself been critical of the impact study that preceded the APER law (CE, 15 and 22 September 2022, opinion on a draft law on the acceleration of renewable energies): "3. The impact study of the draft appears to be uneven, inadequate in several Articles, and even non-existent in certain important provisions. The shortcomings noted are due, firstly, to the absence of an inventory of the current situation, of precise data concerning the situations to which the measures relate, which, in some cases, corresponds to oversights that can be remedied, but, in other cases, seems to lend credence to the idea that the proposed changes to the texts are based on presuppositions rather than substantiated observations: this is the case, in particular, with the idea that litigation is a determining factor in the delays noted in the implementation of a project. Secondly, the impact study lacks justification for certain important choices, as well as legal analyses, even summary analyses, of the delicate points of the proposed provisions. Nor does it put into perspective the margins for progress that exist under constant law for speeding up projects. Finally, European Union law and international law have not always been sufficiently taken into account. The impact study should be completed on the various points mentioned above before the bill is submitted to Parliament".

renewable energies while at the same time protecting certain interests. The arsenal of planning and regulations makes this law very difficult to understand. It opens up possibilities for litigation, since the risk of litigation is increased by incorporating new concepts and notions. This overabundance of standards could have the opposite effect to that intended.

Bibliography

Alfrandari H/Bothorel E/Laisney M/Meizonnet N, *Rapport d'information déposé en application de l'article 145-7 du Règlement par la Commission des affaires économiques sur l'application de la loi n° 2023-175 du 10 mars 2023 relative à l'accélération de la production d'énergies renouvelables* (2023)

Boillet N/Guéguen-Hallouët G, 'Principaux apports de la loi APER pour le déploiement des éoliennes en mer' (2023) AJDA 1179

Bréchot F X, 'Compétence nantaise en matière d'éolien en mer: autant en emporte le vent?' (2022) 1 AJDA 32

Camby J P/Schoettl J E, 'L'insertion des éoliennes dans un paysage : autant en emporte la subjectivité du juge' (2023) RFDA 1073

Cour des Comptes, *Les soutiens à l'éolien terrestre et maritime. Exercices 2017 et suivants* (March 2023)

Delvolvé P, 'Mesures structurelles – Les investissements – Les installations de production d'énergies renouvelables' (2023) RFDA 42

De Sartre X A/Missaghieh-Poncet J/Desvallées L, 'En France, l'acceptabilité sociale des technologies de décarbonation de l'énergie à l'ombre de la dépendance au nucléaire' (2022) 4 EEI

Dezobry G, 'Mesures structurelles – Les investissements – La relance du nucléaire' (2023) 1 RFDA 34

Emmanuel Macron, 'Reprende en main notre destin énergétique!' (Élysée 10 February 2022) <https://www.gouvernement.fr/upload/media/default/0001/01/2022_02_nucleaire_belfort.pdf> accessed 27 August 2024

Dantin M/Kourtih A, 'Corporate Power Purchase Agreements. Premiers retours d'expérience sur les points clefs de négociation' (2023) Cah. dr. entr dossier 14

De Fontenelle L/Andrieu S, 'La valorisation de l'électricité produite par de l'énergie photovoltaique: analyse juridique des modèles de vente et d'autoconsommation' in **Bailleul D/Claret H** (eds), *Le développement de l'énergie photovoltaique* (Presses universitaires Savoie Mont Blanc 2023)

De Fontenelle L/Lamoureux M, 'Les contrats de vente directe d'électricité et de gaz' (2023) AJDA 1173

E-CUBE, 'Analyse des dynamiques et des mécanismes publics de soutien aux énergies renouvelables favorables aux PPA en Europe' (10 February 2022) <www.cre.fr> accessed 27 August 2024

Fontaine C/Loustau F, 'La commande publique à l'épreuve des nouvelles formes de commercialisation de l'énergie' (2023) 4 Contrats et Marchés publics study 2

Grimonprez B, 'L'agrivoltaisme à la lumière du droit' (2023) AJDA 1168

Harada L N/Coussi M, 'Les "Power Purchase Agreements" en France, un outil émergent au cœur de la transition énergétique' (2020) 87 BDEI 20

Lamoureux M, Droit de l'énergie (ed. LGDJ, 2nd edition, 2022) 462

Le Bihan-Graf C/Jérémie P, 'Les principales mesures de la loi relative à l'accélération de la production d'énergies renouvelables' (2023) 5 EEI study 11

Lormeteau B/Radiguet R, 'Le volet paysage dans la loi APER: panorama d'une approche pointilliste' (2023) AJDA 1156

Martin V, 'Agrivoltaïsme : entre incitation et régulation – Regards croisés sur un droit en construction. – Note à partir des travaux du colloque au Palais du Luxembourg du 7 avril 2023' (2023) 11 EEI study 25

Ministère de la transition écologique et de la cohésion des territoires, *Chiffres clés de l'énergie* (Édition 2023, Statistique publique)

Ministère de la transition énergétique, *Instruction du Gouvernement du 16 septembre 2022 relative à l'organisation de la répartition et du délestage de la consommation de gaz naturel et de l'électricité dans la perspective du passage de l'hiver 2022–2023 et à l'accélération du développement des projets d'énergie renouvelable* (ENER2226074C)

Ministère de la Transition Écologique et Solidaire/Ministère de la Cohésion des Territoires et des Relations avec les Collectivités Territoriales, *Circulaire du 28 novembre 2023 relative aux missions du référent préfectoral à l'instruction des projets d'énergies renouvelables et des projets industriels nécessaires à la transition énergétique et à la géothermie de minime importance* (ENER2331339J)

Poupeau F M/Lormeteau B, *L'autoconsommation collective d'électricité en France: Émergence d'une innovation contrariée* (Presses des Mines 2024)

Terneyre P, 'L'accélération de la dégradation de la norme législative' (2023) AJDA 1145

The Law of Renewable Energies in Italy

Chiara Mari

A. Energy transition in Italy: concept, objectives, tools and challenges

The expansion of renewable energy is a crucial component of environmental regulation in Italy,[1] relating to plans, programs, and simplified procedures. In particular, the National Recovery and Resilient Plan (NRRP)[2] and the Plan for the Ecological Transition (PET)[3] include measures for the gradual transition from the current state of energy production sources, mainly based on the use of fossil fuels, to a more efficient and less polluting combination of renewable energies.

The NRRP contains an ambitious reform project that the Italian government intends to implement as part of the European economic recovery programme (Next Generation EU) and which includes a "green revolution and ecological transition". The PET aims to implement the objectives of the UN 2030 Agenda for Sustainable Development[4] and European and national policies for the ecological transition. One of the objectives is related to the promotion of renewable energy.

According to the plans, the promotion of renewable energy sources requires collaboration between the public administration, businesses, and citizens, each with distinct but essential roles. Moreover, it can provide

1 The role of planning in the energy sector in Italy is investigated in Monica Cocconi, 'Planning and regulating the renewable electric energy' (2013) 1 Rivista quadrimestrale di Diritto dell'Ambiente 67.

2 National recovery and resilience plan, definitively approved with Council Implementing Decision on July 6, 2021 (OR. en) 10160/21, 44. The NRRP, which represents the most important and innovative of the tools contained in the Next Generation EU, is governed by EU Reg. 2021/241 of the European Parliament and of the Council of February 12, 2021 establishing the Recovery and Resilience Facility [2021] OJ L 57/17.

3 Governo Italiano, 'Plan for the Ecological Transition' (2022) approved by the Interministerial Committee for the Ecological Transition (CITE) according to art. 57 bis, paragraph 3, of legislative decree No.152/2006.

4 Transforming our world: the 2030 Agenda for Sustainable Development, Resolution adopted by the General Assembly on 25 September 2015, goal 7: "Ensure access to affordable, reliable, sustainable and modern energy for all".

economic development for private operators and benefits to the social community.[5]

In addition to the plans, recent legislative reforms have simplified authorization procedures for the expansion of renewable energies.[6] One need only consider the simplification and simplification *bis* decrees[7] that have taken place in the energy sector; the legislative decree No. 199/2021, which transposed Directive 2018/2001/EU on the promotion of the use of energy from renewable sources; the law decree No. 13/2023[8] for the implementation of the National Recovery and Resilience Plan; and lastly the legislative decree n. 190/2024 (Consolidated Law on Renewable Energy). These continual reforms have helped to improve the energy sector's efficiency.

To understand the relevance of plans and reforms, it is important to take into consideration some significant data related to the actual situation in Italy and future goals. In 2020, renewable energy plants generated 41.7 % of the country's gross production; renewable energy covered over 38 % of total electricity consumption. In particular, the renewable energy produced is divided into hydroelectric (40 %), solar (20 %), wind energy (16 %), and others.[9] The data shows that renewable sources represent a significant part of the energy produced and consumed, and, for this reason, ways to increase their use must be identified.

In this regard, it is interesting to evaluate future objectives for the expansion of renewable energies, based on national plans and regulations and identified by the Plan for the Ecological Transition referred to above. Regarding future goals, the contribution of renewable energies to electricity generation must reach at least 72 % by 2030 and by 2050, cover close to 100 % of the overall primary energy mix.[10] These are ambitious, but necessary goals for the Italian energy transition.

---

5 The Plan explains that the prerequisites for the ecological transition include “the public commitment, of individual citizens, of businesses” (10), and notes the need to “help (the) companies [...] by creating attractive financial and investment conditions” for energy transition, 25.

6 Federica Daniele/Stefano Clò/Enza Maltese/Alessandra Pasquini, ‘Unburdening Regulation: the impact of regulatory simplification on photovoltaic adoption in Italy‘ (University of Florence, working papers, 2022).

7 Law decree July 16, 2020, no. 76, converted into law September 11, 2020, n. 120; law decree May 31, 2021, n. 77, converted into law July 29, 2021, no. 108.

8 Converted into law April 21, 2023, no. 41.

9 Gestore dei Servizi Energetici, ‘Energy report from renewable sources‘ (2020), 16.

10 Plan for the Ecological Transition (n 3), 39.

In this context, this article aims to identify the critical issues in the application of Italian legislation on renewable energy and the legal instruments used to promote the energy transition according to the aforementioned national plans and programs. For this reason, it is essential to investigate three main aspects seen as "challenges" for the development of renewable energy in Italy: the simplification of procedures, the relevance of private activities, the social consensus on projects and its role in avoiding disputes.

B. *Authorization procedures: rules and problems in a public multilevel administration*

Italian legislation prescribes that energy activities must be authorized before they can start. To produce energy, different types of permits are required based on the power of the plants, including a single authorization and a simplified procedure. As a result, the analysis of the expansion of renewable energies in Italy must start with the "essential features" of the authorization procedures.[11]

In the first type of permission, the competent authority, through a single process that requires the involvement of all administrative authorities concerned, provides a single authorization for renewable energy projects. This meeting of all the authorities concerned (called "conferenza di servizi") allows the simultaneous representation of all public interests involved in the authorization process.

The regulation is specified in the legislative decree No190/2024[12]. According to Article -9, the construction, modification, and operation of electricity production plants that use renewable sources require a single authorization from the competent authority. The Region, the provinces delegated, or the Ministry of Environment and Energy Security (in the case of plants with installed thermal power equal to or greater than 300 MW) are responsible for granting this authorization. The authorization is issued

11 See Giovanna Pizzanelli, 'Buona amministrazione e regime delle energie rinnovabili' (Pisa University Press 2023).

12 Legislative Decree No. 190/2024 (Consolidated Law on Renewable Energy) has repealed the previous provisions contained in Legislative Decrees No. 287/2003 and No. 28/2011.

after a meeting of all the public administrations involved, in which the proposer can participate to provide information.[13]

The article specifies the terms of the conclusions of the procedures (120 days) and coordination with the environmental impact assessment that is considered "part" of the authorization. The purpose of this permit is to facilitate the advancement of renewable energy by unifying all essential authorizations for the installation, such as environmental, spatial, and building permits. With this unified permit, it is possible to obtain all the necessary authorizations for the plant's construction and operation.

For smaller plants, a more simplified procedure is applied (the so-called PAS). According to Article 8 of legislative decree No. 190/2024, the property owner must submit a declaration to the local municipality and provide a detailed report before beginning construction of the plant. This declaration is meant to confirm that the project is in compliance with approved urban planning guidelines and adheres to safety and sanitation standards. Once this declaration is submitted, the proposer can communicate with the public administration without the need for any additional authorizations.[14] Depending on the size of the plant, simplified procedures may be used which involve the exercise of the activity without the need for specific authorization procedures or the use of the legal instrument known as "conferenza di servizi"[15].

The brief analysis of the legislation shows that the authorization procedures are simplified – from a formal point of view – for several reasons: the ordinary authorization is a single or built-in permission; the legislation provides pre-established terms for the conclusion of the procedure; and the proceedings take place in the so-called "conferenza di servizi". In this regulatory framework, the simplification of procedures is the most important issue for the expansion of renewable energy. One need only consider that this energy permit legislation is subject to constant change due to the

13 Eugenio Picozza/Sergio Massimiliano Sambri (eds), *Il diritto dell'energia* (Padova, CEDAM, 2015) 574 ff.
Art. 9, legislative decree No. 190/2024.

14 In the absence of legal conditions, the municipality notifies the order not to carry out the intervention within 30 days. Furthermore, when the consent of other administrations is required, "conferenza di servizi" is applied.

15 Art. 7, legislative decree No. 190/2024 (the so-called "free" activity).

continuous adoption of different and new regulations to promote the best form of simplification.[16]

At this point, it is necessary to evaluate whether the establishment of a simplified procedure in Italian legislation is in itself a guarantee for the expansion of renewable energy production.

To answer this question, it is important to consider the critical issues in the concrete application of procedures. The initial problem is the identification by the proposer of which procedure to request (ordinary or simplified). Indeed, the assumptions of the procedures are not always clear, and for this reason, the choice is complex and delegated to the estimation of the proposer. One need only consider the tendency – not admitted in jurisprudence and law – to divide the plants into different parts to be able to request the PAS instead of the ordinary authorization.[17]

A different issue concerns the reduction of necessary steps in the procedure, like the participation of citizens, because the single authorization and the simplified permits do not provide for it in any case.[18] In effect, the participation of citizens is admitted only in the environmental assessment procedures that can be considered, according to the recent legislation, as a part of the single authorization, and does not always occur. Only specific projects indicated by legislation are subject to this assessment,[19] and, consequently, effective participation takes place only in those cases. This lack of a specific moment of general participation can lead to protests from citizens who show interest outside of the administrative procedures and after the authorization is granted. In other words, legislation does not always provide for a dialogue between the social community and the administration to obtain social consensus.

Furthermore, there are no significant consequences for not meeting deadlines because the public administration can decide after the expiration of the terms. Therefore, the specification of the term generally constitutes only an indication without actual consequences.[20] For this reason, proceed-

---

16 Marco Calabrò, 'Semplificazione procedimentale e esigenze di tutela dell'ambiente: l'autorizzazione integrata ambientale' (2010) 5 Rivista giuridica dell'edilizia 239.

17 Consiglio di Stato, sez. IV, June 12, 2020, No. 3433; Consiglio di Stato, sez. IV, September 1, 2016, No. 3783. See also art. 6, legislative decree No. 190/2024.

18 Unlike other authorizations that allow the intervention of interested parties in the initial phase of the procedure, such as the integrated environmental authorization.

19 Environmental Code, legislative decree No. 152/2006, art. 4 ff.

20 Chiara Mari, *Iniziativa privata e interessi pubblici nei procedimenti di autorizzazione per la transizione ecologica* (Editoriale scientifica 2023).

ings may also exceed the indicated deadlines and fail to comply with the simplification and acceleration requirements.

Finally, the continuous reforms of the discipline aimed at simplifying it can create uncertainty for operators and difficulties in application. Such consecutive reforms can, in effect, complicate the regulatory framework and make it fragmented.

These critical issues – related to the procedures – can frustrate the purposes of simplification of the legislation if they are not considered by the public decision-maker. To answer the previous question, it is also interesting to consider two more problems outside the procedures: multilevel governance and access to justice. Starting with the first problem, decision-making in the renewable energy sector is influenced at different levels: national, regional, and local. Indeed, the main rules are established at the national level, but renewable energy projects greatly impact local interests. For this reason, there is a need for more coordination between state, regional, and local authorities. In particular, the Region and municipality have different roles. The Region is responsible for planning and issuing authorizations, and it looks after the interests of a vast territory. Instead, the municipality is directly affected by the decision to build the plant and takes care of the interests of a limited territory.[21]

In this context, the difficulties in coordination are based on two aspects. First, the lack of decision-making power of the municipalities is evident because during the procedures, at the "conferenza di servizi", the negative opinion of the municipality can be overruled.[22] Secondly, there is the problem of political conditioning, because Regions and municipalities do not always share the same political ideas on the construction of renewable energy plants. Considering these issues, simplification requires the harmonization of the different levels of government.[23]

To further answer the previous question, we must also consider the problem of access to justice. Indeed, it is insufficient to focus merely on the

21 Marta De Giorgi, 'La semplificazione amministrativa tra esigenze di uniformità ed effettività delle politiche. Alla ricerca di un coordinamento stabile tra Stato e Regioni' (2011) 3 Istituzioni del federalismo 501; Francesco de Leonardis, 'Politiche e poteri dei governi locali nella tutela dell'ambiente' (2012) 4 Diritto amministrativo 779.

22 Consiglio di Stato, sez. IV, June 28, 2022, No. 5376. The municipality may eventually use the "remedy in opposition" according to art. 9 of Legislative Decree no. 190/2024.

23 Barbara Pozzo/Stefano Fanetti, 'Subnational resistance against renewable energy: the case of Italy' in: Marjan Peeters/Thomas Schomerus (eds), *Renewable Energy Law in the EU, Legal Perspectives on Bottom-Up Approaches* (Edward Elgar 2014) 165–186.

administrative decision-making process without considering the efficiency of court procedures. If the administrative procedures are simplified, but the court procedures are not efficient, the aim of promoting renewable energy can be hindered. Consequently, we can deduce that the expansion of renewable energy requires easy access to simple procedures for the settlement of disputes concerning the permit-granting process and the operation of renewable energy plants, as well as, where applicable, alternative dispute resolution mechanisms.[24] The primary issue in Italy is the absence of clear and simplified procedures for conflict resolution, leading to excessive delays in judicial proceedings that can take up to multiple years to conclude. In fact, the Code of Administrative Court Procedures does not establish a specific and simplified procedure for disputes relating to authorizations for renewable energies.[25] Therefore, it would be useful to introduce tools to speed up the adoption of the judge's decision.

Furthermore, alternative dispute resolution mechanisms are not always utilized because environmental interests require an effective balance by public authorities and cannot be the subject of agreements between administrations and private operators, especially in the case of larger plants. In other words, renewable energy permit disputes are too complex to be resolved with alternative dispute resolution mechanisms in every case.

In this context, we can conclude this part by saying that simplification in the field of renewable energy means not only faster procedures or fewer procedural phases, but also the application of adequate measures to achieve effective environmental conservation, like the exact identification of the conditions for applying the various authorizations, coordination between different levels of government, and efficient court procedures.[26]

C. The relevance of private activity

After examining the role of public administration, we can investigate the involvement of private actors, starting with economic operators. In effect, the

24 Luigi Maria Pepe, 'Exploring the Possibility of Energy Justice in Italy' (2022) 1 The Italian Law Journal 187.

25 Legislative decree July 2, 2010, No. 104. An accelerated procedure is envisaged only for energy infrastructures.

26 Marjan Peeters/Thomas Schomerus, 'Modifying Our Society with Law: The Case of EU Renewable Energy Law' (2014) 4 Climate Law 131.

plants are mostly managed by private entities because there is significant private investment.

Despite this, the participation of the private individual in the procedures and the "conferenza di servizi" is for the sole purpose of providing information. The private individual has no power to influence the decision. This can lead to a limitation of private initiative relating to projects since the private proposer cannot actively intervene and deal with the public decision-maker. Indeed, a dialogue between the private proposer and the administration appears relevant since the projects serve private interests but benefit the social community. From another point of view, the private can play a significant role outside of the procedures. In particular, the private individual can also act in conditions of "monopoly" if only one operator occupies the plants in the same territory. An example is the case in which the same operator manages most of the plants in a specific Region.[27] This allows it to influence the energy needs of the social community. For this reason, the manager must be assessed and monitored for compliance with environmental and service standards.

Italian legislation identifies forms of control over authorized activities that are based on cooperation between the private operator and the public administration.[28] After the assessment, the administration can caution the private operator and require the adoption of measures focused on environmental standards.[29] In this context, the public-private collaborative perspective is important for the expansion of renewable energy because it allows private individuals to collaborate in the adoption of the public authorization decision.

The role of the private individual does not end once authorization has been obtained. The authorization may be subject to subjective (transfer) or objective (remodulation of projects; renewals) modifications. However, the Italian regulation in this regard is generic. In particular, the legislature does not provide clear procedures for transferring authorization, although jurisprudence allows it. This causes uncertainty and difficulties for operators in subjective modifications of the authorization.

27 An example is given by the numerous wind parks realized in Puglia, a southern Italian Region.

28 Chiara Mari, 'Il ruolo del privato nei procedimenti per le energie rinnovabili: uno strumento per lo sviluppo sostenibile?' (2019) 16 Federalismi.it.

29 This is particularly evident for environmental authorizations governed by the Environmental Code, legislative decree No. 152/2006.

In terms of modifications, the variations considered substantial, and which require a new authorization, are not indicated in detail in Italian legislation. The regulations indicate only cases of no substantial variation,[30] without giving a complete and general definition of "relevant modification".[31] This lack of legislation can lead to uncertainty for plant managers because it is not clear when a new authorization is needed after the changes. Considering the analysis carried out, it is possible to indicate the solutions for the expansion of renewable energy in Italy through the role of the private operator. First, guidelines and soft law instruments can be used to guide project implementation and address regulatory uncertainty. Soft law provides a flexible tool that can adapt to the needs of economic operators and interested parties in a specific territory, without requiring changes to legislation.

It is also important to reduce the information asymmetries between the public administration and private individuals; the exchange of information allows for public-private collaboration. These instruments will be analyzed in the following section.

D. The use of guidelines, soft law, and the reduction of information asymmetries

The previous analysis emphasizes the use of soft law and the reduction of information asymmetries to promote renewable energies.

Starting with the soft law, guidelines, and operating manuals can be useful for effective cooperation between the public and private sectors in the energy area. These tools have many advantages. First, they can guide and help the proposer when the discipline is not clear, e.g., in the case of choosing the correct authorization or in the subjective modifications and transfer of the permit. Before requesting permission, they can assist the proposer in selecting the appropriate procedures from those established in the legislation. During the procedures, they can guide the proposer regarding their obligations towards the public administration. After the authorization has been granted, they can provide information on the transfer and any subsequent modifications.

30 See legislative decree No. 190/2024.

31 Alberto Muratori, La "modifica sostanziale" di impianti e progetti tra definizioni normative, giurisprudenza e ricadute pratiche' (2012) 2 Ambiente e sviluppo 147.

Secondly, the guidelines are written in a discursive form that is easy to understand for non- technical operators. This facilitates its application by economic operators, even if they do not have specific technical skills in the energy sector. The discursive form can guarantee greater clarity and comprehensibility of the rules to be followed within the ambit of the specific procedures.

Thirdly, the soft law is flexible and can be adapted to the specific situation according to the type and size of the plant and the impact on the area involved. Indeed, strict regulation makes applying to all renewable energy projects of different sizes, complexity, and territories difficult.

Lastly, the guidelines are an expression of best practices. Therefore, they guarantee the private operator to act in the quickest and most simplified way in the procedure and in the event of modifications to the authorization.[32]

In Italy, there are specific guidelines for renewable energy that are considered binding and adopted by ministerial decree.[33] Even if they are binding, they constitute a flexible tool because they explain the rules to be followed in a detailed and discursive way. This decree can be applied in connection with different kinds of manuals or operating guides that express a soft law that can be useful to accompany the proposer in the administrative procedure. In effect, the Directive on Renewable Energy 2018/2001/EU states that it is important to use manuals and guides to help private proposers and economic operators in the authorization request procedure and the following phases.[34] Manuals and guides can also be made available online to facilitate consultation by economic operators.

Furthermore, the Regions have adopted specific guidelines to encourage the expansion of renewable energies in their territories. The regional guidelines specify the procedures for obtaining authorization and dealing with the location of the plants. The regional guidelines are adopted to implement the rules established by the national guidelines and, therefore, cannot deviate from the provisions of the ministerial decree.[35] The presence

32 Fabrizio Fracchia/Pasquale Pantalone, 'La fisionomia delle linee guida: abbozzo di una traiettoria evolutiva con specifico riferimento al settore dei contratti pubblici' (2021) 1 Il diritto dell'economia 11.

33 Governo Italiano, Ministerial decree, 'Guidelines for the authorization of plants by renewable energy' (2010), compliant with legislative decree No. 190/2024 according to art. 14.

34 Art. 16, Directive 2018/2001/EU.

35 Consiglio di Stato Sez. IV, November 6, 2017, No. 5122.

of guidelines drawn up at a neighboring level of government can constitute adequate support for economic operators who are "guided" in the procedure according to the reference territory.

Moving to the reduction of information asymmetries, the effective exchange of data between the public administration and private operators to promote renewable energy is crucial. From a private point of view, the information helps citizens understand the relevance of the project and brings them to social acceptance; moreover, the same information can help proposers in the realization of the project because they can afford investments knowing the relative risks and benefits. From a public point of view, the information is useful for the administration, promoting decisions which take into consideration the interests of different parties, with particular attention to the needs of private operators and the social community. The exchange of information is based on the principle of transparency governed by legislative decree No. 33/2013 and can be carried out by implementing the publication of information on institutional websites. To this end, the information must be clear and understandable for the private individuals concerned. Otherwise, the simplification objectives are completely frustrated.[36]

Moreover, the exchange of information is relevant even if it takes place between private operators. Even horizontal cooperation between different operators contributes to the correct application of procedural steps, especially if the discipline is complex. In the case of subjective modifications, an exchange of information between the subjects involved makes it possible to transfer the authorization efficiently, immediately identifying the effective moment in which the authorization is transferred. Even when several applications for authorization are presented for plants in the same territory, a collaboration between proposers, in compliance with the competition rules, can avoid conflicts that stop the proceedings and the realization of the projects.

In this context, soft law instruments and the exchange of information can be jointly used for the expansion of renewable energy in Italy. The joint use of these tools can contribute to solving the critical issues analyzed above relating to the lack of clarity in the legislation and the difficulties of coordination between the public and private subjects involved.

36 Stefano Grassi, 'Tutela dell'Ambiente' (Dir. amm.), *Enciclopedia del diritto* (Annali I, Giuffrè Milano 2007) 1135 f.

E. The social consensus on projects and the deflation of litigation

Moving to the last point, it is crucial to consider the role of citizens in the transition to renewable energy and the relevance of participation. The reason is that the participation of local citizens and stakeholders can provide feedback on renewable energy projects, leading to the adoption of an appropriate public decision and promoting social acceptance. If the social community takes part in the decision, it is less inclined to oppose it with protests or appeals to the judge.

Participation may not always be guaranteed due to potential negative effects on simplification such as lengthening procedures and making decisions difficult to adopt. In other words, there is a problem of simplification versus participation. To solve the problem, it is necessary to analyze the reasons for the disagreement and the possible solutions. First, disagreements may derive from *NIMBY* (not in my backyard) *syndrome*, prejudicial resistance to projects.[37] Indeed, the social community believes that the plants have an excessive impact on their territory. The wind turbines that affect the landscape are an example. Disagreements also derive from a lack of knowledge of the projects by the citizens. The lack of clear and adequate information leads the social community not to approve projects deemed to be prejudicial. Finally, disagreements can be based on genuine criticism of projects. In some cases, projects affect territory already burdened by other systems or are "sensitive" from an environmental and landscape point of view.[38]

In this context, a possible solution for the social acceptance of projects consists of strengthening participation, allowing the social community to take an active part in realizing projects.

Participation can be promoted through tools such as inquiry or public debate. In Italy, a public debate is expected for major projects with an impact on the environment. Only a committee or association can participate in the debate, which is based on written observations and must be carried out within a predefined period.[39] The first applications demonstrate

37 David Foster/Joseph Warren, 'The nimby problem' (2021) 34/1 Journal of Theoretical Politics 145.

38 Rolf Wustenhagen/Maarten Wolsink/Mary Jean Burer, 'Social acceptance of renewable energy innovation: an introduction to the concept' (2007) 35 Energy Policy 2683.

39 Public debate is governed by the Public Procurement Code, legislative decree March 31, 2023, No. 36, art. 40.

that the debate must be carried out with small groups of well-informed citizens. Indeed, the participation of large numbers of citizens divided into several associations or committees makes it difficult for the real needs of the population to emerge. To encourage participation, the administration must provide clear and comprehensible information about the projects.[40]

Another instrument is "financial participation"; a developing tool that allows citizens to participate financially in projects (for example, with crowdfunding, bonds, and shares).[41] This approach ensures that the social community is actively involved in the project, even if not all citizens have the necessary financial resources. This could potentially exclude a portion of the population. However, this form of participation can be useful if combined with other methods as a complementary means of facilitating the intervention of private individuals. The economic aspect can also be considered through a possible reduction in taxes for citizens who live in territories affected by the plants. In this case, it is not the citizens who invest in the projects but the public sector that reduces the economic burden. These tools are not usually applied in the Italian legal system but, according to the regulatory framework, could be used in addition to the ordinary forms of procedural participation. Additionally, modern digital technologies can be useful in promoting participation by allowing interested parties to intervene remotely in the debate. In Italy, not all individuals possess the capability to utilize contemporary digital technologies and consequently, the public administration must facilitate their utilization through appropriate education and information. Even the plans referred to in the first section pay attention to the relevance of the digital transition, which is also useful for environmental sustainability.[42]

A final means of promoting participation consists of anticipating the moment of social community intervention. Individuals must be able to intervene "upstream" before applying for authorization. This will allow the social community to express its opinion on whether to carry out the project. Anticipated participation, which is found above all in the Aarhus

40 Emiliano Frediani, 'Le garanzie partecipative nella valutazione di impatto ambientale: strumenti tradizionali e dibattito pubblico in Istituzioni del Federalismo' (2020) 3, 657.

41 "There is, moreover, a need to find complementary approaches that would reduce citizen resistance against renewable energy, for instance by means of financial-participation arrangements". Marjan Peeters/Thomas Schomerus, 'Modifying Our Society with Law' (n 26) 139.

42 Luisa Torchia, *Lo Stato digitale. Una introduzione* (Il Mulino, Bologna 2023).

Convention,[43] does not find full application in Italian legislation because the intervention of the interested parties is only allowed in most cases after the submission of the authorization request. The anticipation of participation, even if not expressly provided for by national legislation, is usually used informally by proposers to get to know the opinions of the population before requesting authorization for projects.

In conclusion, such tools are useful because participation is aimed at avoiding disputes. If citizens participate in the procedure, they do not protest after the authorization has been issued, and they do not turn to the judge. Participation also increases social consensus and avoids dissent through protests or appeals to the judge. This is especially true when disagreements derive from prejudices or from scarce information that can be provided in the participatory forum. In other words, participation is essential to promoting social consensus and must be promoted with tools such as those outlined, keeping in mind the acceleration and simplification of procedures.

F. Concluding remarks

The efficient management of authorization procedures for the expansion of renewable energy in Italy requires the effective action of the public and private entities involved;[44] furthermore, a different practical and theoretical approach is needed.[45]

For public administration, it is crucial to organize adequate forms of control over the managers. Such a control ensures that the economic operator acts in compliance with environmental standards. In the event of a violation of the environmental rules, the administration communicates with the manager to modify the incorrect behavior.

---

43 Art. 6 of the Aarhus Convention states: "Each party shall provide for early public participation, when all options are open and effective public participation can take place".

44 In fact, "the inclusion of a plurality of stakeholders in program design and implementation as global cooperation between state and non-state, public and private, political and financial actors is essential to make (energy) projects effective". Laura Ammannati, 'Governing the Energy market between universal access to Energy and sustainable development' (2016) 14 Federalismi.it.

45 Giulio Napolitano, *Pubblico e privato nel diritto amministrativo* (Giuffré, Milano 2003); V. Cerulli Irelli, *Amministrazione pubblica e diritto privato* (Giappichelli, Torino 2011); Franco Mastragostino (ed), *La collaborazione pubblico e privato e l'ordinamento amministrativo* (Giappichelli, Torino 2011).

Moreover, the public administration must favor forms of active participation by citizens aimed at overcoming social disagreements on renewable energy projects. To this end, both participation in the process and alternative tools, such as public debate, "financial participation", and digital participation, can be used. In other words, the public administration has a fundamental role as a link between public purposes and the actions of economic operators and citizens. To this end, public officials must also be organized to manage the involvement of citizens through adequate preparation. The Italian Plan for the Ecological Transition expressly refers to the importance of preparing or educating public employees in the management of new forms of participation.[46]

From the side of the private operator, the attribution of a significant role to the private sector in the production of renewable energy cannot ignore its responsibility in carrying out the activity; this responsibility can also be achieved through adequate controls, in which the assumptions, objects, parameters, and consequent measures are clear. In other words, the private operator must be made responsible for acting in a sector that affects collective interests. Furthermore, effective dialogue between the private operator and the public administration, as well as between different private operators, is important to facilitate the carrying out of procedures and the realization of projects. The exchange of information is especially useful in the phases following the issuance of authorization, where the rules are not always clear.[47] Finally, citizens also play a decisive role because they can support or oppose projects. For this reason, it is important to create incisive forms of participation, which must necessarily be flexible and adapted to the realities of the individual territories involved in the construction of the plants. Participation is, in fact, fundamental to achieving social consensus on renewable energy projects, and, for this reason, it is important to jointly use different forms of participation to involve as many citizens as possible.

---

46 Maarten Wolsink, 'Wind power implementation: The nature of public attitudes: Equity and fairness instead of 'backyard motives'' (2007) 11 Renewable and Sustainable Energy Reviews 1188.

47 Friedemann Polzin, 'Mobilizing private finance for low-carbon innovation – A systematic review of barriers and solutions' (2017) 77 Renewable and Sustainable Energy Reviews 525–535.

In other words, the participatory tool used must be adapted to individual local realities and the needs of the social community.[48]

In this context, the expansion of renewable energy in Italy is based on cooperation between the public administration, the private sector, and citizens. This cooperation is founded on Art. 1 Paragraph 2 bis of law No. 241/90, which provides for the possibility of collaboration between the public and private sectors.[49] The cooperation can be based on different instruments. The first one is the use of soft law, like guidelines, which can help the operators in the presentation of the authorization application and the subjective and objective modification of the plants. Another essential element is the reduction of information asymmetries between public administrations and private managers or between different private operators. The exchange of information helps the private sector manage the complexity of the authorization, which is not crystallized but is subject to continual change. Lastly, it is essential to modify the cultural approach through the education of citizens and public servants. For this reason, the Ecological Transition Plan stresses the importance of the "collective education" of private and public actors for the promotion of green energy.

Ultimately, cultural change allows for the active involvement of private entities, i.e. economic operators and citizens, and the presence of a public administration attentive to the energy transition.

The expansion of renewable energy is also strictly related to the simplification of procedures. Simplification is useful if it is based not only on the acceleration of processes and the reduction of phases but also on the management of the complexity of the energy sector.[50] Indeed, the development of renewable energies is characterized by an intrinsic complexity that cannot be eliminated and must therefore be managed with adequate measures.[51] Simplification is, therefore, necessarily related to the need for coordination between public administrations, the use of soft law instru-

48 Veronica De Crescenzo/Francesca Simeoni, 'The role of citizen-based support and finance mechanisms for strengthening and managing energy transition' (Excellence in Services, 21st International Conference, Le Cnam Paris, 2018).

49 Art. 1 Paragraph 2 bis of law No. 241/90 states that: "Relations between the citizen and the public administration are based on the principles of collaboration and good faith".

50 Maddalena Ippolito, 'Environmental simplifications in digital transition' (2021) 2 Rivista giuridica Ambientediritto.it 12–23.

51 Bernardo Giorgio Mattarella, 'La semplificazione amministrativa come strumento di sviluppo economico' (2019) 11 Astrid on line, Rassegna 7.

ments, the overcoming of information asymmetries, and the involvement of citizens to avoid protests.

In conclusion, the expansion of renewable energy in Italy requires a collaborative effort between the public administration, citizens, and private operators for an effective promotion of environmental sustainability, favored by the innovative legislative and administrative framework illustrated above.

Bibliography

Ammannati L, 'Governing the Energy market between universal access to Energy and sustainable development' (2016) 14 Federalismi.it

Calabrò M, 'Semplificazione procedimentale e esigenze di tutela dell'ambiente: l'autorizzazione integrata ambientale' (2010) 5 Rivista giuridica dell'edilizia, 239

Cerulli Irelli V, *Amministrazione pubblica e diritto privato* (Giappichelli, Torino 2011)

Cocconi M, 'Planning and regulating the renewable electric energy' (2013) 1 Rivista quadrimestrale di Diritto dell'Ambiente, 67

Daniele F/Clò S/Maltese E/Pasquini A, 'Unburdening Regulation: the impact of regulatory simplification on photovoltaic adoption in Italy' (University of Florence, working papers, 2022)

De Crescenzo V/Simeoni F, 'The role of citizen-based support and finance mechanisms for strengthening and managing energy transition' (Excellence in Services, 21st International Conference, Le Cnam Paris, 2018)

De Giorgi M, 'La semplificazione amministrativa tra esigenze di uniformità ed effettività delle politiche. Alla ricerca di un coordinamento stabile tra Stato e Regioni' (2011) 3 Istituzioni del federalismo 501

De Leonardis F, 'Politiche e poteri dei governi locali nella tutela dell'ambiente' (2012) 4 Diritto amministrativo 779

Foster D/Warren J, 'The nimby problem' (2021) 34/1 Journal of Theoretical Politics 145

Fracchia F/Pantalone P, 'La fisionomia delle linee guida: abbozzo di una traiettoria evolutiva con specifico riferimento al settore dei contratti pubblici' (2021) 1 Il diritto dell'economia 11

Frediani E, 'Le garanzie partecipative nella valutazione di impatto ambientale: strumenti tradizionali e dibattito pubblico' in *Istituzioni del Federalismo* (2020) 3, 657

Gestore dei Servizi Energetici, 'Energy report from renewable sources' (2021)

Grassi S, 'Tutela dell'Ambiente' (Dir. amm.), *Enciclopedia del diritto* (Annali I, Giuffrè Milano 2007) 1135 f.

Governo Italiano, 'Plan for the Ecological Transition' (2022) approved by the Interministerial Committee for the Ecological Transition (CITE) according to art. 57 bis, paragraph 3, of legislative decree No.152/2006

Governo Italiano, Ministerial decree, 'Guidelines for the authorization of plants by renewable energy' (2010)

Ippolito M, 'Environmental simplification in digital transition' (2021) 2 Rivista giuridica Ambientediritto.it 12–23

Mastragostino F (ed), *La collaborazione pubblico e privato e l'ordinamento amministrativo* (Giappichelli, Torino 2011)

Mari C, *Iniziativa privata e interessi pubblici nei procedimenti di autorizzazione per la transizione ecologica* (Editoriale scientifica 2023)

Mari C, 'Il ruolo del privato nei procedimenti per le energie rinnovabili: uno strumento per lo sviluppo sostenibile?' (2019) 16 Federalismi.it

Mattarella B G, 'La semplificazione amministrativa come strumento di sviluppo economico' (2019) 11 Astrid on line, Rassegna 7

Muratori A, 'La "modifica sostanziale" di impianti e progetti tra definizioni normative, giurisprudenza e ricadute pratiche' (2012) 2 Ambiente e sviluppo 147

Napolitano G, *Pubblico e privato nel diritto amministrativo* (Giuffré, Milano 2003)

Peeters M/Schomerus T, 'Modifying Our Society with Law: The Case of EU Renewable Energy Law' (2014) 4 Climate Law 131

Pepe L M, 'Exploring the Possibility of Energy Justice in Italy' (2022) 1 The Italian Law Journal 187

Picozza E/Sambri S M (eds), *Il diritto dell'energia* (Padova, CEDAM, 2015) 574 ff.

Pizzanelli G, 'Buona amministrazione e regime delle energie rinnovabili' (Pisa University Press 2023)

Polzin F, 'Mobilizing private finance for low-carbon innovation – A systematic review of barriers and solutions' (2017) 77 Renewable and Sustainable Energy Reviews 525–535

Pozzo B/Fanetti S, 'Subnational resistance against renewable energy: the case of Italy' in **Peeters M/Schomerus T** (eds), *Renewable Energy Law in the EU, Legal Perspectives on Bottom-Up Approaches* (Edward Elgar 2014) 165–186

Torchia L, *Lo Stato digitale. Una introduzione* (Il Mulino, Bologna 2023)

Wolsink M, 'Wind power implementation: The nature of public attitudes: Equity and fairness instead of 'backyard motives'' (2007) 11 Renewable and Sustainable Energy Reviews 1188

Wustenhagen R/Wolsink M/Burer J M, 'Social acceptance of renewable energy innovation: an introduction to the concept' (2007) 35 Energy Policy 2683

The Law of Renewable Energies in the United Kingdom: Focus on Contracts for Difference

Agnieszka Ason

A. Introduction: the UK's Path to Net Zero

As noted in the UK General Chapter of this volume, the energy transition in the UK is a transition to net zero. The 2008 Climate Act committed the UK to reducing its greenhouse gas emissions by 80 % by 2050 compared to the 1990 baseline. In 2019, the 2050 Target Amendment Order amended the Climate Change Act 2008 by incorporating the following even more ambitious target:

> The target for 2050
>
> (1) It is the duty of the Secretary of State to ensure that *the net UK carbon account for the year 2050 is at least 100 % lower than the 1990 baseline.*
>
> (2) "The 1990 baseline" means the aggregate amount of—
>
> (a) net UK emissions of carbon dioxide for that year, and
>
> (b) net UK emissions of each of the other targeted greenhouse gases for the year that is the base year for that gas.[1]

As a result of this amendment, the UK government has set a legally binding target to reduce the UK's greenhouse gas emissions by 100 % by 2050 (compared with 1990 levels). This is typically referred to as the UK net zero target. To meet the net zero target, the UK has enacted robust legislation aimed at maintaining momentum and growth in renewable energies.

The Energy Act 2023 establishes both new and modified rules for "energy production and security and the regulation of the energy market"[2] and it reflects the UK's firm commitment to developing clean energy. Having grown exponentially from negligible levels (accounting for just 2 % of elec-

1 HM Government, 'Climate Change Act 2008' Section 1 <https://www.legislation.gov.uk/ukpga/2008/27/section/1> accessed 26 June 2025, emphasis added.

2 HM Government, 'Energy Act 2023' <https://www.legislation.gov.uk/ukpga/2023/52/contents> accessed 26 June 2025.

tricity generation in the UK in 1991[3]), renewable energy sources (wind, solar, biomass and hydro) now make up a significant proportion of the UK's electricity mix, as shown in the chart below.

Figure 1: 2023 electricity generation mix (by source) in the UK

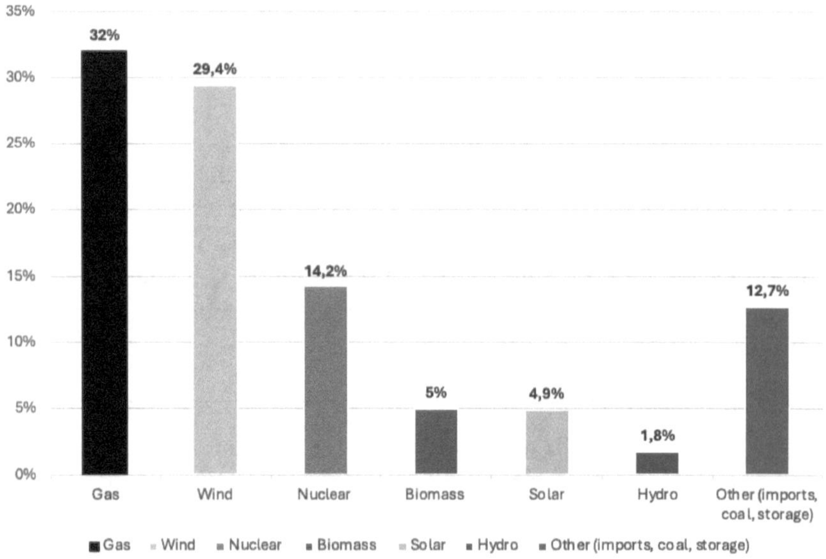

Source: Author based on Electricity System Operator's data[4]

In 2023, wind power contributed nearly one third of the UK's total electricity generation. The UK remains particularly committed to developing offshore wind and has "a world-leading ambition to deploy up to 50 GW by 2030, with up to 5 GW coming from floating offshore wind."[5] This target is accompanied by a commitment to shorten development timescales for future projects and is part of a wider aim to develop "fully decarbonised,

3 National Grid, 'How much of the UK's energy is renewable?' (2024) <https://www.nationalgrid.com/stories/energy-explained/how-much-uks-energy-renewable> accessed 26 June 2025.

4 Electricity System Operator, 'Britain's Electricity Explained: 2023 Review' (2024) <https://www.nationalgrideso.com/news/britains-electricity-explained-2023-review> accessed 26 June 2025.

5 Department for Energy Security and Net Zero, 'Offshore Wind Net Zero Investment Roadmap' (2023) <https://www.gov.uk/government/publications/offshore-wind-net-zero-investment-roadmap> accessed 26 June 2025.

reliable and low-cost power system by 2030", which "is most likely to be composed predominantly of wind and solar power generation".[6] For solar energy, the UK government aims to achieve 70 GW of solar power by 2035 (up from almost 16 GW in March 2024 and just 0.02 GW in January 2010[7]).

The expansion of renewable energy is widely recognised as key to achieving the UK net zero target. In practice, however, the development of renewable electricity generation has proved to be a difficult task, largely due to weak project fundamentals. This was the case for the first renewable power plants (solar and wind), which were more expensive per unit of electricity produced than fossil fuel power plants. To incentivise the deployment of a renewable technology that was still too costly to compete on its own with prevailing market alternatives, the UK government (like other governments around the world) has introduced various support schemes over the past few decades.

In principle, the aim of using incentive mechanisms for new technologies – either through direct subsidies or price stabilisation mechanisms – is to accelerate the deployment of these technologies and make them competitive over time, when the support mechanisms may become redundant once the new technologies are able to compete on their own merits in the open market. As more of a desired technology is deployed, its cost will fall through economies of scale and learning curve effects, making it more competitive with legacy technologies.

There are several government support mechanisms that can facilitate the deployment of clean energy. Over the past decade, Contracts for Difference (CfDs) have become the UK government's main mechanism for supporting renewable electricity generation. The UK, several EU Member States and other countries have recently announced (or reaffirmed) their intention to prioritise CfDs to support investment in renewable energy projects. Following the successful experience with CfDs in renewables, it has been recognised that the CfD concept may be suitable for other applications. Work is currently underway to develop CfD-based business models, initially for clean hydrogen and Carbon Capture and Storage (CCS), and there

6 Department for Energy Security and Net Zero, 'Net Zero Strategy: Build Back Greener' (2021) <https://www.gov.uk/government/publications/net-zero-strategy> accessed 26 June 2025.

7 House of Commons Library, 'Planning for Solar Farms – Research Briefing' (2024) <https://researchbriefings.files.parliament.uk/documents/CBP-7434/CBP-7434.pdf> accessed 26 June 2025.

is scope for a wider use of CfDs for low-carbon solutions as the energy transition progresses.

The key objective of this chapter is to examine the role of CfDs as enablers of renewable energy projects in the UK and to discuss their emerging applications to other clean energy solutions. The chapter also provides some comparative perspectives on the current and potential use of CfDs in other jurisdictions.

B. Contracts for Difference in the UK

CfDs were conceptualised in a 2011 White Paper by the (then) Department of Energy & Climate Change as "a new system of long-term contracts providing clear, stable and predictable revenue streams for investors in low-carbon electricity generation" and "a cheaper, more robust mechanism than the alternative support options available", providing "greater certainty" that the UK will meet its carbon emissions targets.[8] CfDs were formally introduced as part of the 2013 Electricity Market Reform[9] and they play a key role in the pending Review of Electricity Market Arrangements (REMA).[10]

1. The Mechanism

CfDs are risk management tools to provide price support for emerging technologies and to encourage desired behaviours, such as investment by private actors in more sustainable production methods. By providing stability and predictability of future revenue streams, CfDs encourage investment in new projects that might otherwise take many years to develop or not come to market at all if they were solely dependent on volatile market prices.

8 Department of Energy and Climate Change, 'Planning our electric future: a White Paper for secure, affordable and low-carbon electricity' (2011) <https://assets.publishing.service.gov.uk/media/5a78b0dce5274a2acd1890be/2176-emr-white-paper.pdf> accessed 26 June 2025.

9 Department for Energy Security and Net Zero, 'Electricity Market Reform Delivery Plan' (2013) <https://assets.publishing.service.gov.uk/media/5a7b9fe0e5274a7318b8fdfa/181213_2013_EMR_Delivery_Plan_FINAL.pdf> accessed 26 June 2025.

10 Department for Energy Security and Net Zero, 'Review of Electricity Market Arrangements (REMA): Second Consultation Document' (2024) <https://assets.publishing.service.gov.uk/media/65ef6694133c220011cd37cd/review-electricity-market-arrangements-second-consultation-document.pdf> accessed 26 June 2025.

There is no single definition of a CfD but the defining feature of CfDs is arguably the difference between the "market price" and the "strike price" agreed in advance by an electricity generator with the CfD counterparty. In the UK, CfDs are private law agreements between generators and the Low Carbon Contracts Company (LCCC), a government-owned entity.

If the market price for electricity generated by a generator is below the strike price specified in the contract, the LCCC makes payments to the generator to make up the difference. However, if the market price is above the strike price, the generator pays the LCCC the difference. This is illustrated by the chart below.

Figure 2: The Contract for Difference payment mechanism in the UK

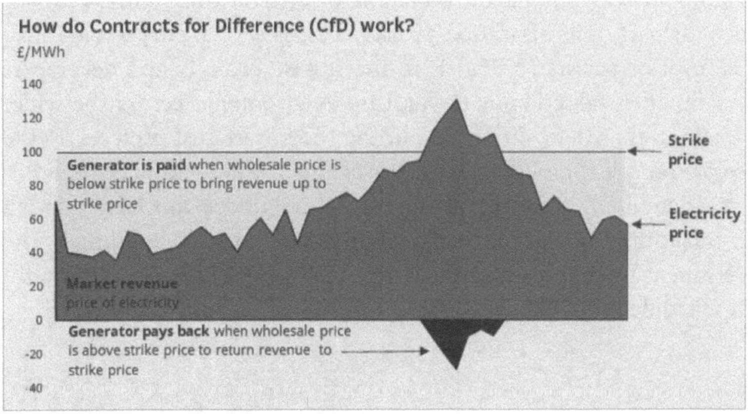

Source: House of Commons Library[11]

The LCCC is responsible for settling the contracts. The payments, and repayments, paid and received by the LCCC for the CfD scheme are passed on to consumers' electricity bills.

CfDs enable new renewable generation projects to avoid the volatility of wholesale electricity markets and to achieve a stable long-term revenue profile over the term of the CfD contract. A stable and predictable long-term revenue profile can be desirable for a number of reasons. In the case of renewable energy projects in particular, this stable revenue profile makes it

11 House of Commons Library, 'Contracts for Difference – Research Briefing' (2023) <https://researchbriefings.files.parliament.uk/documents/CBP-9871/CBP-9871.pdf> accessed 26 June 2025.

easier for these projects to be developed using a project finance structure that is attractive to institutional investors with a long-term investment profile. The long-term nature of these investments allows lenders to offer lower interest rate premiums and longer debt tenures, thereby reducing the cost of capital for projects and

creating a virtuous circle that reduces the cost of energy over time as more projects are developed.[12]

CfDs are awarded in the UK for 15 years through auctions to allow competition between technologies and help keep prices low. The government sets a budget in advance, then sealed bids of strike prices submitted by developers are accepted sequentially from the lowest to the highest until the budget is exceeded. In April 2023, the government launched a consultation process on the introduction of criteria other than cost for assessment as part of its allocation process for CfDs. The purpose of introducing non-price factors (NPFs) is to incentivise projects and developers to deliver broader value to society and the environment across the wider supply chain, rather than simply rewarding the lowest-cost projects. In the response to the call for evidence, the government has identified the NPFs which are potentially appropriate for valuation under the CfD auction process, including innovation, sustainability, and capacity building.[13] The UK government intends to introduce these NPFs from Allocation Round 7, which is scheduled for 2025, onwards.

---

12 For a discussion, see Agnieszka Ason/Julio Dal Poz, 'Contracts for Difference as the Instrument of Choice for the Energy Transition' (2024) Oxford Institute for Energy Studies <https://www.oxfordenergy.org/publications/contracts-for-difference-the-instrument-of-choice-for-the-energy-transition/> and Rahmat Poudineh, 'Can UK green hydrogen contract for difference (CfD) match the cost-saving success of renewable electricity?' (2025) <https://www.oxfordenergy.org/publications/can-uk-green-hydrogen-contract-for-difference-cfd-match-the-cost-saving-success-of-renewable-electricity/> accessed 26 June 2025. accessed 26 June 2025.

13 Department for Energy Security and Net Zero, 'Introducing a Contracts for Difference (CfD) Sustainable Industry Reward' (2024) <https://www.gov.uk/government/consultations/introducing-a-contracts-for-difference-cfd-sustainable-industry-reward> accessed 26 June 2025.

2. Renewable Power Generation

CfDs have been instrumental in accelerating the deployment of renewable generation and the pace of decarbonisation in the UK over the past decade. CfD generation accounted for 15.1 % of UK renewable generation in 2022.[14]

To date, there have been six competitive auctions (Allocation Rounds) for CfD capacity. The outcome of the first round (AR1) was announced in February 2015 and the sixth round (AR6) in September 2025. Most of the capacity (including 95–96 % of the capacity awarded in AR2 and AR3) was offshore wind.[15] Strikingly, in 2023, the fifth Allocation Round received no bids from the offshore wind sector. While some considered the auction a failure, given the pressing need to accelerate the development of offshore wind capacity was not fulfilled, AR5 still managed to tender contracts to almost 2 GW of solar projects and to almost 1.5 GW of onshore wind projects. The lack of bidders in the offshore wind sector provided much-needed information about the mismatch between expected cost reductions assumed by the UK government, and the reality of an industry that was navigating a changed context with increased interest rates and higher supply chain costs. The results served to illustrate the shortcomings of the CfD allocation process and triggered a review of the process and of the budget required to accelerate new offshore wind projects in the changed cost context.

With the results published in September 2024, AR6 awarded contracts for 5GW of offshore wind, 1GW of onshore wind, and 3GW of solar, alongside 400MW of floating offshore wind and 28MW of tidal stream (marking a significant recovery from AR5 in relation to offshore wind).

---

14 House of Commons Library, 'Contracts for Difference – Research Briefing' (2023) <https://researchbriefings.files.parliament.uk/documents/CBP-9871/CBP-9871.pdf> accessed 26 June 2025.

15 See Marijke Welisch/Rahmat Poudineh, 'Auctions for allocation of offshore wind contracts in the UK' (2019) Oxford Institute for Energy Studies < https://www.oxfordenergy.org/publications/auctions-allocation-offshore-wind-contracts-difference-uk/> accessed 10 July 2024; House of Commons Library, 'Contracts for Difference – Research Briefing' (2023) <https://researchbriefings.files.parliament.uk/documents/CBP-9871/CBP-9871.pdf> accessed 26 June 2025.

Figure 3: The results of six allocation rounds in the UK to date

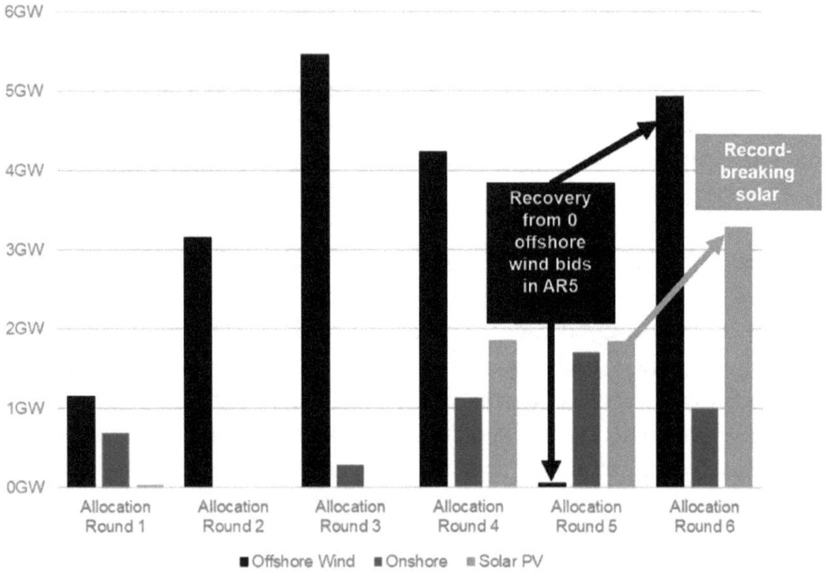

Source: Energy UK[16]

3. Other Clean Energy Projects

Following the successful experience with renewable CfDs, it has been recognised that the CfD concept may be suitable for applications beyond power generation. Work is underway in the UK on CfD-based business models, initially for clean hydrogen and CCS, but potentially evolving into multi-technology schemes.

(a) Hydrogen

The UK government's ambition is to deliver 5 GW of low-carbon hydrogen production capacity by 2030. Like in most other countries, the business

16 Energy UK, 'Energy UK Explains: Allocation Round 6' (2025) <https://www.energy-uk.org.uk/publications/energy-uk-explains-allocation-round-six/> accessed 26 June 2025

case for clean hydrogen in the UK relies on government policy.[17] The consultation on the design of a low-carbon hydrogen business model started in 2021 and resulted in the development of the UK Hydrogen Production Business Model (HPBM).

The HPBM is designed to incentivise the production and use of low-carbon hydrogen by providing producers with revenue support to overcome the operating cost gap between low-carbon hydrogen and fossil fuels to unlock private investment in hydrogen projects. Modelled after the CfD for renewable power, the HPBM is implemented through the Low Carbon Hydrogen Agreement (LCHA), a private law contract signed between a hydrogen producer and the LCCC. Following the earlier CfD precedent, the LCHA runs for a term of 15 years.

Revenue support under the HPBM is only provided for hydrogen volumes which: (i) comply with the Low Carbon Hydrogen Standard (LCHS), (ii) are sold to Qualifying Offtakers (volumes sold for export, blended into the natural gas grid, or sold to a Risk-Taking Intermediary are not qualifying) and (iii) are not sold and subsequently claimed under the Renewable Transport Fuel Obligation (RTFO) scheme. These conditions should ensure that only low-carbon hydrogen is supported, and that the value of this decarbonisation accrues to the UK and not to traders taking speculative positions in the emerging hydrogen market. It also ensures that volumes of hydrogen claimed under the RTFO are not supported under the HPBM in order to avoid overcompensation and market distortions.

LCHA effectively guarantees that even if producers cannot sell their hydrogen at a price high enough to recoup their cost of production and make an agreed return on investment then the counterparty will top them up to that level. The difference amount is calculated as the difference between the strike price (which is agreed by DESNZ at pre-contractual negotiations) and the reference price (which represents the market value of the hydrogen sold). The strike price is indexed to protect producers from cost changes beyond their control – for electrolytic producers, the strike price is indexed to Consumer Price Index (CPI), for CCS-enabled projects, the natural gas costs in the strike price are indexed to a natural gas benchmark and the non-gas costs to CPI.

---

17 See Martin Lambert, 'Clean Hydrogen Roadmap: Is greater realism leading to more credible paths forward' (2023) Oxford Institute for Energy Studies <https://www.oxfordenergy.org/wpcms/wp-content/uploads/2023/09/Clean-Hydrogen-Roadmap-ET25.pdf> accessed 26 June 2025.

The LCHA will not allow the producer to fully recoup its costs where hydrogen is sold below the prevailing natural gas price – i.e. at a discount relative to the closest fossil fuel alternative. If producers do sell below the prevailing natural gas price, then any revenue support payable will be paid up from that prevailing natural gas price.

The work on implementing the HPBM is in progress. In December 2023, the UK government awarded CfDs to 11 green hydrogen projects with a total capacity of 125 MW, as a result of the first Hydrogen Allocation Round (HAR1). HAR2 followed quickly in early 2024, reflecting the UK government's aim to achieve up to 1 GW of electrolytic hydrogen production in operation or under construction by 2025.[18] HAR2, launched in early 2024, aims to allocate up to 875 MW of electrolytic hydrogen capacity – a significant scale-up in comparison with 27 shortlisted projects announced in April 2025.[19]

(b) Carbon Capture and Storage

Carbon Capture and Storage (CCS) is a key mitigation technology for the global energy system to reach its net zero target, but several characteristics and risks make financing CCS projects challenging. In response to those challenges, governments have adopted different approaches as they attempt to establish a sustainable CCS market through contributing capital and sharing costs and risks (that range from "minimal" to "full" government control options[20]).

In the UK, CCS plays a key role in the Net Zero Strategy and there has been significant government involvement in establishing the CCS market, including the ongoing work on developing CfD-based business models for CCS projects.

---

18 Department for Energy Security and Net Zero, 'Second Hydrogen Allocation Round (HAR2) Application Guidance Document' (2023) <https://assets.publishing.service.gov.uk/media/657b07c30467eb001355f853/hydrogen-allocation-round-2-application-guidance.pdf> accessed 26 June 2025.

19 Department for Energy Security and Net Zero, Notice: Second Hydrogen Allocation Round (HAR2) Application Guidance Document <https://www.gov.uk/government/publications/hydrogen-allocation-round-2-har2-projects> accessed 26 June 2025.

20 Bassam Fattouh/Hasan Muslemani/Raeid Jewad, 'Capture Carbon, Capture Value: An Overview of CCS Business Models' (2024) Oxford Institute for Energy Studies <https://www.oxfordenergy.org/publications/capture-carbon-capture-value-an-overview-of-ccs-business-models/> accessed 26 June 2025.

The Dispatchable Power Agreement (DPA), the planned contractual framework for power generation with CCS is a private law contract between a carbon-emitting power generator and the LCCC, based on the standard terms and conditions of the CfD for the fourth allocation round (AR4) and adapted to enable natural gas-fired CCS power plants to play a mid-merit role in meeting electricity demand, displacing unabated thermal power plants. The indicative Heads of Terms (HoTs) for the DPA were published in 2020. Departing from the usual 15-year contract term for renewables CfDs, generators have flexibility to choose an appropriate term length for the DPA that is between 10 and 15 years (regardless of whether developing a new build, repowered or retrofitted project).

The Industrial Carbon and Capture Contract (ICC Contract), which is another relevant contractual framework for CCS projects, has been drafted to offer consistency with the AR4 CfD and the DPA. The indicative HoTs for the ICC Contract were published in 2021. Many provisions of the earlier CfD contracts have been included in the HoTs, subject to minor alterations (e.g. references to 'generator' have been changed to 'emitter'), with other areas requiring substantial amendments to cater for the bespoke elements of the ICC business model. In essence, the ICC Contract is a private law contract between the emitter and the LCCC, which is for a 10-year contractual payment term with the option for a 5-year extension (subject to certain conditions). Like for the DPA, several updates on the proposed contract design for the ICC Contract have been published to date.

(c) Multi-technology Schemes

The examples of support schemes discussed above apply to either hydrogen, or CCS. This approach can be explained through the difference in business models for the relevant technologies but, at a later stage, it is feasible that CfD schemes for low-carbon solutions, like is common for renewable CfD schemes, will be applicable to two or more technologies (potentially grouped into different categories or "pots" in the allocation process).

Notably, a multi-technology approach is common feature of Carbon Contracts for Difference (CCfDs), similarly named support schemes. An example is the Dutch SDE++ scheme, which applies to five technology categories: renewable electricity, renewable heat, renewable gas, low-carbon heat, and low-carbon production. In the most recent and widely publicised development, in March 2024, German government launched the first bidding round of its estimated €50 billion scheme for so-called "Climate Protection Contracts" (*Klimaschutzverträge*), which work as CCfDs. The German CCfDs will offer payments for 15 years to industrial players (such as steel and chemicals producers) to switch to using green hydrogen, CCS, or other low-emissions methods of production. The scheme will also indirectly incentivise investment in production of green hydrogen infrastructure, such as hydrogen production plants and pipelines.

The German CCfDs include an early termination option after three years in the event that low-carbon production becomes cheaper than the alternative. The early termination feature is important as governments experiment with CfD-type instruments in different markets. One of the biggest challenges in creating a functioning market for clean hydrogen is exactly how to incentivise demand, given that early movers may be wary of committing to long-term contracts, knowing that the cost of low-carbon products (e.g. low-carbon hydrogen) will fall over time. The early termination feature attempts to address this delicate balance by offering long-term support contracts that are in place when prices are too high, but can be terminated when the competitive market starts to drive prices down. The UK HPBM model attempts to address the same challenge in a slightly different way by providing incentives in the CfDs for hydrogen producers to work with their offtakers (and customers) to bring prices down over time.

C. Contracts for Difference in Other Jurisdictions: Comparative Perspectives

Outside the UK, CfDs have been used to support renewable power projects mainly within the EU. A recent study found that CfDs have so far been used in nine EU Member States: France, Spain, Denmark, Greece, Hungary, Ireland, Italy, Poland, and Portugal.[21] In October 2023, the European Commission approved a CfD scheme for offshore wind projects notified by Lithuania and, in March 2024, a Romanian CfD scheme for solar and onshore wind projects. A CfD scheme is currently under development in Belgium and reportedly considered for clean energy projects in other EU Member States (including Estonia and Slovenia). Outside the EU, CfDs

21 Lena Kitzing et al., 'Contracts-for-Difference to support renewable energy technologies: Considerations for design and implementation' (2024) Florence School of Regulation <https://fsr.eui.eu/publications/?handle=1814/76700> accessed 26 June 2025.

have been used to support clean energy projects in other European jurisdictions (for example, in Albania, Serbia, and Norway). Outside Europe, CfDs have been applied sparingly. In Australia, for example, CfDs were initially introduced at state level (in Victoria) and are currently being considered for national rollout. In New Zealand, CfDs also feature prominently in consultation documents submitted as part of the process of developing a regulatory framework for offshore renewable energy and are seen as a compelling option for the local market.

For low-carbon solutions, CfDs are fast emerging as a mechanism to unlock the hydrogen economy. France, for example, plans to facilitate the deployment of 1 GW of electrolysis capacity through CfDs by 2026. At the EU level, CfDs have been considered among the potential design options for the European Hydrogen Bank. The pilot auction for the European Hydrogen Bank that opened in November 2023 was for a fixed premium subsidy.[22] However, CfDs can be considered for a competitive bidding process at the EU level at a later stage, especially when a reference clean hydrogen price is determined.

In Japan, a CfD scheme for the supply of low-carbon hydrogen was launched in 2024. The Japanese CfD scheme is for 15 years and is intended to subsidize the difference between the "Strike Price", which is the price required to establish a low-carbon hydrogen supply project, and the "Reference Price", which is the market price for fuels for which low-carbon hydrogen is a substitute. While the UK HPB requires identifying only one offtaker, Japan's Contract for Difference mandates that suppliers and offtakers jointly develop a Low Carbon Hydrogen Plan and that offtakers make new capital investments, ensuring greater demand certainty and coordinated growth of the market. As of May 2025, the CfD scheme was reportedly "oversubscribed, with applications significantly exceeding the ¥3trn ($21bn) budget."[23]

22 European Commission, 'European Hydrogen Bank pilot auction: 132 bids received from 17 European countries' (2024) <https://climate.ec.europa.eu/news-your-voice/news/european-hydrogen-bank-pilot-auction-132-bids-received-17-european-countries-2024-02-19_en> accessed 10 July 2024.

23 Hydrogen Insight, 'Significantly oversubscribed' $21bn Japanese clean hydrogen tender will be awarded on rolling basis: ministry' (2025) <https://www.hydrogeninsight.com/production/significantly-oversubscribed-21bn-japanese-clean-hydrogen-tender-will-be-awarded-on-rolling-basis-ministry/2-1-1822221> accessed 26 June 2025.

The discussion on using CfDs to support hydrogen projects is currently starting in other parts of the world and there is certainly scope for considering CfDs to incentivise hydrogen economy in other jurisdictions.[24]

D. Conclusions and Outlook

After a decade of market experience, the UK government continues to see the CfD scheme as fundamental to its net zero objectives. New CfD schemes are currently either planned or under development in several jurisdictions. Recent work on CfDs outside Europe will increasingly change the role (and common perception) of CfDs as a Europe-centric support scheme. In a parallel development, CfDs are no longer exclusively focused on renewable and nuclear power generation and are increasingly applicable to low-carbon solutions.

For any new CfD scheme, a detailed legal, regulatory and contractual framework needs to put in place. The whole process spanning from legislative proposals to the actual contracts typically takes several years and involves multiple stakeholders, including through public consultations of the scheme. When considering CfDs as a revenue support mechanism for clean energy projects, governments need to address a number of questions about how to finance, structure and manage the scheme. In the long term, one of the key considerations for a successful CfD scheme will be how to manage the instrument in a changing market environment. CfDs need to provide legal certainty to the market, but as such need to be continually refined to fully reflect prevailing market conditions and the state of development of the relevant technologies. The challenge will therefore be how to maintain CfDs and, if necessary, how to modify them in a way that does not infringe on the rights of their beneficiaries.

Eventually, CfDs in their current form will be phased out – as is usual with support schemes for any new technology, most likely when the fundamentals of clean energy projects improve to the point where they can be fully market driven, including through long-term market procurement mechanisms such as PPAs.

However, given the pressing need to accelerate investment in energy transition solutions, in the short-term the opposite will be true, with the

24 For a more comprehensive comparative discussion, see: Agnieszka Ason/Julio Dal Poz (n 12).

demand for more (and more effective) revenue support having to be offered not only to renewable power projects but to other clean energy solutions such as hydrogen and CCS. Over the past decade, the growing demand for support schemes for clean energy has created a favourable environment for the introduction of CfDs. Applying the CfD approach to low-carbon solutions and other emerging uses will bring new challenges (e.g. in terms of the design of new CfDs and their interaction with CCfDs and other support schemes), but will also offer the benefit of building on the experience and lessons learned – mainly in the UK – from the successful use of CfDs to date.

Bibliography

Ason A/Dal Poz J, 'Contracts for Difference as the Instrument of Choice for the Energy Transition', Oxford Institute for Energy Studies <https://www.oxfordenergy.org/publications/contracts-for-difference-the-instrument-of-choice-for-the-energy-transition/> accessed 26 June 2025

Department for Energy Security and Net Zero, *Electricity Market Reform Delivery Plan* (2013) <https://assets.publishing.service.gov.uk/media/5a7b9fe0e5274a7318b8fdfa/181213_2013_EMR_Delivery_Plan_FINAL.pdf> accessed 26 June 2025

Department for Energy Security and Net Zero, *Net Zero Strategy: Build Back Greener* (2021) <https://www.gov.uk/government/publications/net-zero-strategy> accessed 26 June 2025

Department for Energy Security and Net Zero, *Second Hydrogen Allocation Round (HAR2) Application Guidance Document* (2023) <https://assets.publishing.service.gov.uk/media/657b07c30467eb001355f853/hydrogen-allocation-round-2-application-guidance.pdf> accessed 26 June 2025

Department for Energy Security and Net Zero, *Offshore Wind Net Zero Investment Roadmap* (2023) <https://www.gov.uk/government/publications/offshore-wind-net-zero-investment-roadmap> accessed 26 June 2025

Department for Energy Security and Net Zero, *Review of Electricity Market Arrangements (REMA): Second Consultation Document* (2024) <https://assets.publishing.service.gov.uk/media/65ef6694133c220011cd37cd/review-electricity-market-arrangements-second-consultation-document.pdf> accessed 26 June 2025

Department for Energy Security and Net Zero, *Introducing a Contracts for Difference (CfD) Sustainable Industry Reward* (2024) <https://www.gov.uk/government/consultations/introducing-a-contracts-for-difference-cfd-sustainable-industry-reward> accessed 26 June 2025

Department for Energy Security and Net Zero, *Notice: Second Hydrogen Allocation Round (HAR2) Application Guidance Document* (2023)

Department of Energy and Climate Change, *Planning our electric future: a White Paper for secure, affordable and low-carbon electricity* (2011) <https://assets.publishing.service.gov.uk/media/5a78b0dce5274a2acd1890be/2176-emr-white-paper.pdf> accessed 26 June 2025

Electricity System Operator, *Britain's Electricity Explained: 2023 Review* (2024) <https://www.nationalgrideso.com/news/britains-electricity-explained-2023-review> accessed 26 June 2025

Energy UK, 'Energy UK Explains: Allocation Round 6' (2025) <https://www.energy-uk.org.uk/publications/energy-uk-explains-allocation-round-six/> accessed 26 June 2025

European Commission, *European Hydrogen Bank pilot auction: 132 bids received from 17 European countries* (2024) <https://climate.ec.europa.eu/news-your-voice/news/european-hydrogen-bank-pilot-auction-132-bids-received-17-european-countries-2024-02-19_en> accessed 26 June 2025

European Commission, *European Hydrogen Bank pilot auction: 132 bids received from 17 European countries* (2024) <https://climate.ec.europa.eu/news-your-voice/news/european-hydrogen-bank-pilot-auction-132-bids-received-17-european-countries-2024-02-19_en> accessed 26 June 2025

Fattouh B/Muslemani H/Jewad R, 'Capture Carbon, Capture Value: An Overview of CCS Business Models' (2024) Oxford Institute for Energy Studies <https://www.oxfordenergy.org/publications/capture-carbon-capture-value-an-overview-of-ccs-business-models/> assessed 26 June 2025

House of Commons Library, *Contracts for Difference – Research Briefing* (2023) <https://researchbriefings.files.parliament.uk/documents/CBP-9871/CBP-9871.pdf> accessed 26 June 2025

House of Commons Library, *Planning for Solar Farms – Research Briefing* (2024) <https://researchbriefings.files.parliament.uk/documents/CBP-7434/CBP-7434.pdf> accessed 26 June 2025

Hydrogen Insight, *Significantly oversubscribed' $21bn Japanese clean hydrogen tender will be awarded on rolling basis: ministry* (2025) <https://www.hydrogeninsight.com/production/significantly-oversubscribed-21bn-japanese-clean-hydrogen-tender-will-be-awarded-on-rolling-basis-ministry/2-1-1822221> accessed 26 June 2025

Kitzing L et al., 'Contracts-for-Difference to support renewable energy technologies: Considerations for design and implementation' (2024) Florence School of Regulation <https://fsr.eui.eu/publications/?handle=1814/76700> accessed 26 June 2025

Lambert M, 'Clean Hydrogen Roadmap: Is greater realism leading to more credible paths forward' (2023) Oxford Institute for Energy Studies <https://www.oxfordenergy.org/wpcms/wp-content/uploads/2023/09/Clean-Hydrogen-Roadmap-ET25.pdf> accessed 26 June 2025

National Grid, *How much of the UK's energy is renewable?* (2024) <https://www.nationalgrid.com/stories/energy-explained/how-much-uks-energy-renewable> accessed 26 June 2025

Poudineh R, 'Can UK green hydrogen contract for difference (CfD) match the cost-saving success of renewable electricity?' (2025) <https://www.oxfordenergy.org/publications/can-uk-green-hydrogen-contract-for-difference-cfd-match-the-cost-saving-success-of-renewable-electricity/> accessed 26 June 2025

Welisch M/Poudineh R, 'Auctions for allocation of offshore wind contracts in the UK' (2019) Oxford Institute for Energy Studies <https://www.oxfordenergy.org/publications/auctions-allocation-offshore-wind-contracts-difference-uk/> accessed 26 June 2025

The Law of Renewable Energies in Denmark

Helle Tegner Anker and Bent Ole Gram Mortensen

A. Introduction – Targets and Results

Renewable energy (RE), and in particular wind energy, has been, and still is, a strong element in the fulfilment of climate-related policy targets in Denmark. The Danish 2020 Climate Act[1] stipulates an overall target of climate neutrality in 2050, as well as a 70 % reduction of greenhouse gas emissions by 2030, and 50–54 % by 2025, compared to 1990 levels.

More specifically, a broad political agreement was reached in June 2022 to quadruple onshore wind and solar power by 2030, and to significantly expand offshore wind from 2.3 to 12.9 GW in 2030, and potentially 35 GW in 2050.[2]

The 2022 agreement was a follow-up to several comprehensive energy agreements and initiatives adopted since 2008.[3] The 2008 agreement[4] set a target of 20 % renewable energy for total energy consumption in 2011, including also the establishment of 400 MW[5] offshore capacity by 2012. The 2008 agreement also led to the adoption of the Renewable Energy Act.[6] In

1 Act no 965 of 26 June 2020 on Climate. Latest consolidated version: Consolidated Act no 2580 of 13 December 2021 as changed by Act no 2387 of 14 December 2021.

2 Klima-, Energi og Forsyningsministeriet [Danish Ministry of Climate, Energy and Utilities], 'Klimaaftale om grøn strøm og varme 2022' (Climate Agreement regarding Green Power and Heat 2022) (25 June 2022). <https://kefm.dk/Media/637920977082432693/Klimaaftale%20om%20gr%C3%B8n%20str%C3%B8m%20og%20varme%202022.pdf> accessed 26 May 2025.

3 For a general overview *see* e.g. Jon B Skjærseth et al., *Wind Power Policies and Diffusion in the Nordic Countries. Comparative Patterns* (Palgrave Macmillan 2023) 27–34.

4 Klima-, Energi- og Forsyningsministeriet [Danish Ministry of Climate, Energy and Utilities], 'Aftale mellem regeringen (Venstre og Det Konservative Folkeparti), Socialdemokraterne, Dansk Folkeparti, Socialistisk Folkeparti, Det Radikale Venstre og Ny Alliance om den danske energipolitik i årene 2008–2011' (Political Agreement on Danish energy policy in the years 2008–2011) < https://skm.dk/aktuelt/publikationer/ovrige-publikationer/aftale-om-den-danske-energipolitik-i-2008-2011> accessed 26 May 2025.

5 Later reduced to 350 MW.

2012, a new political energy agreement[7] set a target of increasing onshore capacity by 1800 MW (net 500 MW), offshore by 1000 MW and nearshore by 500 MW by 2020. The objective was to reach a 50 % wind energy share of electricity consumption by 2020. A 2018 agreement[8] established a target of 55 % renewables in total energy consumption by 2030, and targets for increasing offshore wind to a total capacity of 2400 MW. However, at the same time, the 2018 agreement aimed to reduce the number of onshore turbines by more than 50 % in 2030, setting a ceiling of 1850 onshore turbines. The deployment of new onshore wind turbines should thus be dependent upon the removal of older turbines. In the 2020 agreement, the ceiling for onshore turbines was postponed until 2040, but it has not been completely abolished yet, despite the 2022 targets to quadruple onshore wind. The 2020 energy agreement[9] also included the objective of establishing two offshore energy islands (5 GW) by 2030. Whether the ceiling in fact limits the development of onshore wind is doubtful, as there is no ceiling on the size of wind turbines. Thus, repowering can take place with fewer and larger wind turbines. Likewise, the agreement does not contain a restriction on field-based solar installations.

Apart from setting specific targets for wind (and solar) energy, the energy agreements have also laid out initiatives regarding the economic conditions for the deployment of RE. After the liberalization of the electricity market in the late 1990s, the State offered different types of subsidies such as price supplements to the market price to ensure the desired expansion. Operating aid was used rather than establishment aid. As the efficiency of wind turbines increased, the State reduced the value of the price supplements several times. Over time, a cap on the subsidies was introduced as well.

6 Act no 1392 of 27 December 2008 on Expansion of Renewable Energy. Latest consolidated version: Consolidated Act no 1031 of 6 September 2024.

7 Klima-, Energi- og Forsyningsministeriet [Danish Ministry of Climate, Energy and Utilities], 'Aftale af 22. marts 2022 mellem regeringen (Socialdemokraterne, Det Radikale Venstre, Socialistisk Folkeparti) og Venstre, Dansk Folkeparti, Enhedslisten og Det Konservative Folkeparti om den danske energipolitik 2012–2020' (Political Agreement of 22 March 2012 regarding the Danish Energy Policy 2012–2020).

8 *See* also Birgitte E Olsen/Bent OG Mortensen, 'Offshore wind licensing in Denmark' in Ignacio H Anchustegui/Tina S Hunter (eds), *Offshore Wind Licensing* (Edward Elgar Publishing 2024) 87–88.

9 Klima-, Energi- og Forsyningsministeriet, [Danish Ministry of Climate, Energy and Utilities], 'Klimaaftale for energi og industri mv. 2020' (Climate Agreement regarding Energy and Industry etc. 2020) (22 June 2020) <https://www.kefm.dk/Media/4/2/aftaletekst-klimaaftale-energi-og-industri.22.06.2020pdf.pdf> accessed 26 May 2025.

However, the State only changed the system of subsidies for future wind turbines. Existing wind turbines were granted permission to remain regulated by the level of subsidies from when they were established. Currently, it is no longer necessary for the state to grant subsidies for the establishment of onshore wind turbines or solar parks. Subsidies are still provided for a number of older wind turbines onshore. However, these support schemes have been phased out, so support does not apply to new wind turbines.

In contrast to onshore wind turbines, offshore wind turbines have been promoted through tenders where there has been competition for the lowest subsidy. With a tender with a deadline of 2021 (offshore wind farm Thor), it turned out that there was no need for subsidies. Instead, the State could collect a 'concession fee'. The German energy developer RWE was awarded the rights to develop the farm based on a contract for differences (CfD) of 0.01 ore/kWh (€0.0013). It entails that all revenue which RWE generates from energy production will have to be passed on to the Danish state until a ceiling of 2.8 billion DKK (€375,646) is reached. This amount corresponds to a payment of an average of just over 2 ore/kWh (€0.0027) over the park's 30-year lifespan. It was until recently uncertain whether this could be seen as an expression of a general shift from subsidies to concession fees in the case of offshore wind. Increasing establishment costs, including interest rates, may stand in the way of this.

On 22 April 2024, the Danish Energy Agency published a tender for 6 GW of offshore wind, to be completed in 2030, half of which in the Danish part of the North Sea. However, no bids had been received by the bidding deadline of 5 December 2024 for the North Sea capacity. The market situation for offshore wind both internationally and nationally had changed, and the starting point that the state could receive concession fees instead of having to provide state aid was no longer present. On 19 May 2025, a new political agreement was reached on a re-tender in the autumn and bidding deadlines in 2026 and 2027. This opens up the possibility of state aid, and other burdensome conditions have been changed as well.

Energy agreements have also focused on reducing obstacles to the RE transition. This is particularly the case as regards local opposition to RE installations. The 2008 Energy Agreement and the subsequent Renewable Energy Act introduced different compensation schemes. The schemes have been subject to amendments and adjustments over the years, see further below. Furthermore, the 2022 agreement also addresses perceived obstacles that are linked to planning and permit procedures. Initiatives include state involvement in the designation of sites for 'energy parks' and the potential easing of restrictions regarding nature, landscape, and cultural heritage, as well as additional guidance for the local authorities.

In general, the RE targets and the specific targets for wind energy have gradually been met. It must be kept in mind that other energy sources than wind and solar, including in particular biomass and biogas, have an important position as regards the share of the total energy consumption. RE is partly domestic energy and thus contributes to reducing dependence on imported energy. This applies in particular to wind and solar, while some biomass for energy purposes is imported. Renewable energy accounted for 47.6 % of total energy consumption in Denmark in 2024 (334 PJ).[10] Biomass made up the majority of renewable energy with 68 %. The remaining part came from solar, wind, water, geothermal energy, and heat pumps. Wind energy covered 53.2 % of electricity consumption in 2022. Solar power has increased from 3.6 % in 2021 to 6.2 % in 2022.[11] Further production increases appeared in 2023 and 2024. This higher production may, however, also be due to weather conditions and not necessarily increased installed capacity. The capacity of solar power has grown in the last few years, whereas the rate of new onshore wind energy projects has dropped to a very low level. There may be different reasons for this development, but some obstacles have been identified, including delays in decision-making procedures and appeals, biodiversity concerns, grid connection, etc. Thus, the 2022 targets of quadrupling onshore wind and solar capacity before 2030 appear very ambitious. Yet, in December 2023 a political agreement between 8 political parties representing the majority of the members of the Danish Parliament was reached on new framework conditions for onshore expansion of RE, including designation of energy parks (solar and wind), relaxing the rules for nature protection, and increasing compensation for municipalities and neighbours.[12]

---

10 Energystyrelsen [Danish Energy Agency] Foreløbig energistatistik 2024 [Preliminary energy statistics 2024] < https://ens.dk/analyser-og-statistik/maanedlig-og-aarlig-energistatistik > accessed7 June2025.

11 Energinet, '2022 sætter dansk rekord i vind og sol' (Press announcement, 29 December 2022) <https://via.ritzau.dk/pressemeddelelse/13667585/2022-saetter-dansk-rekord-i-vind-og-sol?publisherId=10304728&lang=da> accessed 26 May 2025.

12 Klima-, Energi- og Forsyningsministeriet [Danish Ministry of Climate, Energy and Utilities], 'Klimaaftale om mere grøn energi fra sol og vind på land 2023' (Climate agreement on more green energy from solar and wind on land 2023) <https://kefm.dk/Media/638379734168312589/Klimaaftale%20om%20mere%20gr%C3%B8n%20energi%20fra%20sol%20og%20vind%20p%C3%A5%20land%202023.pdf> accessed 26 May 2025.

In the following, we will introduce the legal framework for wind and solar power in Denmark, focusing on planning and permit procedures for the siting and establishment of wind and solar farms as well as tender procedures and grid connection. Furthermore, we will briefly explain the specific compensation schemes that have been adopted in Denmark with the aim of increasing local acceptance of wind and solar farms. Lastly, we will discuss some of the main obstacles to the further deployment of renewables. The chapter focuses on commercial wind and solar farms, whereas the special arrangements for household installations are not included. These do no longer contribute significantly to electricity production in Denmark.

B. Legal Framework – Onshore vs Offshore

1. Introduction

The legal framework for RE, and in particular wind and solar power, can be divided into different sets of rules. One set of rules governs the siting of wind and solar power installations, including in particular planning, permit, and (environmental) assessment requirements. Another set of rules governs the economic aspects of the establishment of wind and solar power, namely the use of tariffs and tender procedures. The rules on grid access etc. are also relevant in this respect. Lastly, a third set of rules establishes different compensation schemes that are aimed at promoting local acceptance of wind and solar power installations.

2. Siting and Establishment – Planning and Permits

In Denmark, the siting of onshore and offshore RE installations such as wind and solar power are subject to different procedures. While planning and permit procedures for onshore wind and solar power in general rest with the local authorities, planning, and permit procedures for offshore wind rest with the state authorities in accordance with the Renewable Energy Act, in particular the Energy Agency. Offshore wind turbines are not defined in the Renewable Energy Act, even though the term is used in several of its provisions. However, offshore wind turbines (in Danish "havvindmølle") were defined in section 1(3)(2) of the former Wind Turbine Executive Order[13] as 'a wind turbine that is established in the territorial waters or the exclusive economic zone, and where the wind turbine's foundation is not visible at regular sea level'. Installations established on land, for example on a dyke made for that purpose, are not considered to be offshore wind turbines. The current Wind Turbine Executive Order[14] contains no such definition.

(a) Onshore

Onshore wind and solar power are subject to planning and permit procedures, including environmental assessment requirements. Onshore wind installations have been subject to specific planning rules since 1994 in the form of a so-called national planning directive.[15] The national planning directive establishes certain requirements that the municipalities must comply with when they adopt municipal or local plans for wind energy projects. This includes requirements that wind turbines can only be established in areas designated as wind energy sites in the municipal plan, and that they cannot be established closer than four times the total height to neighbouring dwellings. There are also specific requirements that turbines should be established in an easily comprehensible geometric pattern, and that it must be ensured that the cumulative landscape effects with other turbines within 28 times the total height are insignificant. In May 2024, a national planning directive for solar power installations was issued.[16] The planning directive establishes that municipal planning guidelines should observe a 150 m distance to urban areas, summer cottage areas, and villages, and a requirement of 150 to 750 m to dwellings depending upon whether the solar power installation will be on one, two, or three sides of the dwelling. Due consideration should also be taken as regards agricultural, nature, and landscape interests.

For wind turbines, the municipal plans should designate potential wind turbine areas and include provisions as regards the expected number and maximum height of the turbines. For solar power, it is not clear whether there is an option only to lay down principles for the establishment of solar power in the municipal plan. Most wind and solar energy projects will also

13 Executive Order no 1296 of 14 June 2021 on grid connection of wind turbines.
14 Executive Order no 1343 of 29 November 2024 on grid connection of wind turbines.
15 Now Executive Order no 923/2019 on planning for and permits to wind turbines.
16 Executive Order no 440 of 3 May 2024 on planning for solar power installations.

require the adoption of a local plan that must include detailed provisions, e.g., regarding the exact position and number of turbines, as well as the minimum and maximum height. A building permit may also be required.

Furthermore, an EIA permit is needed in most cases if the project may have a significant effect on the environment, cf. the Environmental Assessment Act.[17] A strategic environmental assessment (SEA) will normally also be required both as regards municipal plans and local plans. Furthermore, the assessment of potential effects on Natura 2000 sites and Annex IV species must be complied in accordance with the rules laid down in two executive orders.[18] The general protection of birds is governed by separate rules.[19]

The municipalities are the competent authorities both as regards municipal and local plans, and the EIA permit. A former limitation of the municipal planning powers to turbines up to 150 m was abolished in 2019. However, as part of the 2022 energy agreement and the 2023 follow-up, state agencies (the Energy Agency, the Plan and Rural District Agency, and the Environmental Protection Agency) initiated a national designation of potential 'energy parks'. This has also led to the adoption of new legislation in June 2024 for 'energy parks'[20] which means electricity production from renewable energy sources on land (wind turbines and solar panels) as well as any associated PtX plants.[21] The new Act sets a procedure for state designation of energy parks with an annual production of min. 100 GWh/year based upon an open call for proposals. The relevant municipality must as a main rule accept the designation. The minister will in specific cases, or upon request from the municipality, have the power to call in the subsequent planning powers of the municipality. Furthermore, it might be an option that a project could be adopted by an Act of Parliament. Within the energy parks, the municipalities or other relevant authorities will have the option

---

17 Consolidated Act no 4 of 3 January 2023 on environmental assessment of plans and programs and of concrete projects (EIA).

18 Executive Order no 1383 of 26 November 2016 on the administration of the Planning Act in relation to international nature protection areas and protection of certain species, and Executive Order no 1098 of 21 August 2023 on the designation and administration of international nature protection areas and protection of certain species.

19 *See* further Helle T Anker/Birgitte E Olsen, 'EU species protection law and wind energy: Current challenges and Danish experiences' (2023) 32(1) European Energy and Environmental Law Review 36–46.

20 Act no 614/2024 on state designated energy parks.

21 Act no 614 of 11 June 2024 on state designated energy parks.

to grant derogations from national nature protection rules. Nevertheless, at least an EIA, including relevant assessments regarding Natura 2000 sites, Annex IV species and birds, will be necessary for the individual projects. The designation of energy parks is not coordinated with the implementation of the revised EU RE Directive[22] or the Emergency Regulation.[23] In this respect, a separate set of rules is being developed under the Renewable Energy Act headed by the Energy Agency.[24]

(b) Offshore

Offshore wind turbines have so far not been subject to ordinary planning and construction legislation. The interests protected by such legislation on land have instead been provided for in the licensing arrangements of the Renewable Energy Act, seeking also to incorporate environmental assessment requirements. Nevertheless, a certain element of state planning is linked to offshore turbines established according to tender procedures as the tender is made for one (or more) specific sites. These tenders have in general been based on political plans regarding the siting of offshore wind farms. The first specific plan for offshore wind turbines was published in 1997. The plan identified a number of marine areas where there was potential for establishing offshore wind turbines. Subsequently, other potential offshore sites have been identified by the Energy Agency. However, the designation of potential offshore sites must now be part of the maritime spatial plan.[25] This also applies to offshore projects under the so-called open-door procedure. The open-door procedure has been aimed at facilitating small-scale 'local' offshore projects without prior designation of potential sites. However, the open-door procedure was put on hold in 2022/2023 following

22 European Parliament and Council Directive 2023/2413 amending Directive 2018/2001, Regulation 2018/1999 and Directive 98/70/EC as regards the promotion of energy from renewable sources, and repealing Council Directive (EU) 2015/652 [2023] OJ L 2023/2413.

23 Council Regulation (EU) 2022/2577 of 22 December 2022 laying down a framework to accelerate the deployment of renewable energy, OJ L 335/36, as amended by Council Regulation (EU) 2024/223 [2022] OJ L 2024/223.

24 Act no 673/2024 on amendment of the Renewable Energy Act.

25 Danish Maritime Authority, 'Denmark's maritime spatial plan' <https://havplan.dk/en/page/info> accessed 26 May 2025.

a significant increase in the number of applications.[26] In December 2023 the Government decided to close the open-door procedure. Most of the remaining open-door projects have been refused by the Energy Agency primarily on the grounds that they are not in accordance with the maritime spatial plan. Several of the refusals were brought before the Energy Board of Appeal, which has returned them to the Energy Agency due to deficiencies in the reasoning. Subsequently, the Danish Energy Agency has indicated in a consultation letter to the rejected open door projects that the Danish Energy Agency finds the allocation of a sea area following the open door procedure to be in breach of EU state aid rules. However, this is a dubious argument, especially after no bids were received for 3 GW of offshore wind, where the precondition was precisely the payment of concession fees.

A licence is granted by either a procurement procedure (tender)[27] or the open-door procedure;[28] see section 22(2) of the Renewable Energy Act. Tendering takes place in accordance with the Procurement Directive's provisions on concession contracts, see further below.

The licensing arrangements of the Renewable Energy Act for offshore wind turbines are strongly influenced by the regulations in the area of hydrocarbons (oil and natural gas). In general, under the Renewable Energy Act, the establishment of an offshore wind farm requires permits at three stages: (1) a preliminary investigation licence, (2) an establishment licence, and (3) an exploitation licence; see Chapter 3 of the Renewable Energy Act. Licences are issued by the Energy Agency, to which the Minister has delegated this task.[29] The Renewable Energy Act does not prevent the licences being granted simultaneously. For offshore wind turbines, the provisions of the Renewable Energy Act replace the general requirements for permits

26 *See* about the open door and the hold in Birgitte E Olsen/Bent OG Mortensen, 'Offshore wind licensing in Denmark' 92–94 (n 8).

27 *See* sec. 23(1) of the Renewables Act, which provides that the research permit is to be given to the successful party in a procurement procedure. The Act does not give details about what criteria should be considered important in connection with tenders. It is thus up to the Minister to lay down the criteria, as long as they are lawful. It is explicitly assumed in the *travaux préparatoires* to Bill L 108/2008 that the procurement shall otherwise be in accordance with the EU procurement rules.

28 The Minister has wide discretion to refuse an investigation licence under the open-door procedure, and sec 23(4) of the Renewables Act provides for a relevance requirement.

29 Executive Order no 259 of 6 March 2025 on the tasks and powers of the Danish Energy Agency.

in the Electricity Supply Act (Elforsyningsloven)[30] for establishing new electricity-generating plants or making significant alterations to existing plants.[31] Under sec. 22(7) of the Renewable Energy Act, a preliminary investigation licence gives an exclusive right to a specified area for a specified period. The assignment of a licence requires the approval of the Minister. But it appears from the special comments on Bill L 108/2008 (paragraph 15) that such approval is intended to ensure that preliminary licences are only assigned to projects that will be able to obtain establishment and exploitation licences. The starting point is that the licence-holder must pay for the preliminary investigation. However, sec. 23(3) of the Renewable Energy Act provides for the possibility of a preliminary investigation, or part of it, being carried out by the state Transmission System Operator (TSO), Energinet.[32]

3. Tender Procedures and Grid Connection

(a) Onshore

Tenders have so far not been used onshore. In principle, the state could use tenders for land that the state already owned or acquired for the purpose of establishing renewable energy plants. However, it is normal for a developer to contact landowners in order to buy or rent land for setting up either wind turbines and/or solar cells. It is then up to the developer to obtain the necessary permits, including planning permits.

Furthermore, the renewable energy plant must be connected to the collective electricity grid either at distribution level or transmission level. Following the grid connection order,[33] the developer must pay for grid connection up to the relevant voltage level of at least 50–60 kV. Any necessary network reinforcement must be financed by the network company.

30 Consolidated Act no 1248 of 24 October 2023 on Electricity Supply.
31 *See* sec 1(2)(2) of Executive Order no 548 of 29 May 2024 on permits to establish or alter an electricity-generating Installation (the *Power Station Executive Order*).
32 Energinet is a state-owned undertaking responsible for the electricity transmission and distribution system in Denmark.
33 Executive Order no 1343 of 29 November on grid connection of power plants.

(b) Offshore

The offshore tender procedure has historically been initiated on the basis of a political agreement. Thus, the tenders have not come continuously but have been dependent on a political majority deciding upon one or more offshore wind farms.

Prior to the tender process, the Danish Energy Agency carries out preparatory work, including planning and feasibility studies of the site(s). Initially, the tender is announced to the market via an 'advance notice'. This notice sets out the overall framework for the upcoming tender. Next, a pre-qualification round is carried out with a view to appointing suitable candidates. The pre-qualified companies will then be invited to submit offers in accordance with the established tender conditions. Typically, there will also be individual negotiations prior to submitting a final offer. Based on the final offers, the award decision is made.

Tendering of areas for offshore wind will in the future take place within areas designated as development zones for renewable energy in the maritime spatial plan. However, it is possible to implement an offshore wind project outside a designated renewable energy development zone. Simply, a change to the maritime spatial plan is required with consultation of other governmental and possibly municipal authorities, preparation of planning supplements, impact assessments, and public consultation.

Whoever wins the tender will according to the Renewable Energy Act be granted a preliminary investigation permit. The concessionaire must prepare an environmental impact assessment that describes the specific project's impact on the environment, including, for example, the project's visual impact on the area and its impact on the population, flora, fauna, seabed, marine mammals, fish, etc.

The actual establishment of the offshore wind farm requires an establishment permit according to the Renewable Energy Act. The permit is issued on the basis of the environmental impact report and consultation responses received in connection with the 2nd publicity phase. The permit gives the concessionaire the right to start construction work.

In order for the offshore wind farm to be allowed to produce electricity, the concessionaire must obtain an electricity production permit according to the Renewable Energy Act.

If the wind farm has a capacity of more than 25 MW, an electricity production permit is also required according to the Electricity Supply Act. An application for an electricity production permit must contain documentation that the conditions of the establishment permit have been or will be met, and that the concessionaire has the technical and financial capacity to operate the park. Electricity production permits for tender parks are granted for 30 years, while electricity production permits are granted for at least 20 years.

After the end of use, the developer is obliged to re-establish the previous condition in the area, including carrying out cleaning as well as decommissioning and disposing of the facility. The Danish Energy Agency must approve the decommissioning plan. A detailed assessment of the plan's possible environmental impacts must be submitted together with the plan. By 2025, only one offshore wind farm had been decommissioned. An extension of the electricity production permit for one farm has been granted, subject to a positive outcome of a technical investigation of the safety of the turbines. Several older offshore wind farms are expected to apply for an extension of the electricity production permit. Actual repowering (including technical changes to the offshore wind turbine installation) is possible, but a permit has not yet been granted.

4. Compensation Schemes

The Renewable Energy Act since 2008 contains a number of schemes with the specific aim to promote the local population's acceptance of the expansion of wind turbines and solar cells.[34] The schemes are administered by the Danish Energy Agency.

The loss of value scheme was established by the 2008 Renewable Energy Act. According to the scheme, the developer must compensate for any loss of value above 1 % that owners of residential properties may suffer as a re-

34 For a general introduction to the original schemes, *see* Birgitte E Olsen/Helle T Anker, 'Local acceptance and the legal framework: the Danish wind energy case' in L Squintani/H Vedder/M Reese/B Vanheusden (eds), *Sustainable energy united in diversity: challenges and approaches in energy transition in the EU* (European Environmental Law Forum Book Series 2014) 137–156. *See* also Frederik Waage, 'Compensating neighbors to windmills, solar energy panels and other sources of renewable energy in Denmark' in Carina R Hamer/Hans VG Pedersen/Nis J Clausen (eds), *Festskrift til Bent Ole Gram Mortensen [Liber Amicorum to Bent Ole Gram Mortensen]* (DJØF Publishing 2022); Marie L Jørgensen/Helle T Anker/Jesper Lassen, 'Distributive fairness and local acceptance of wind turbines: The role of compensation schemes' (2020) 138 Energy Policy 11294; Marie L Jørgensen, 'Low-carbon but corrupt? Bribery, inappropriateness and unfairness concerns in Danish energy policy' (2020) 71 Energy Research & Social Science 101663.

sult of the establishment of a nearby wind or solar farm. The scheme is lex specialis to the ordinary, unwritten nuisance law. The scheme is based on losses in the sale value of the property and only covers the residence itself and nearby living areas. The loss in value is based both on the dominant character of the facilities (e.g. wind turbines of 180 meters or a solar park of 340 hectares as new examples), noise, and shadow cast. The loss in value is determined by a special valuation authority after an inspection of the property.

The sales option scheme was introduced in 2020 as an integral part of the loss of value scheme. If a property within six times the total height of a wind farm or 200 m from a solar farm is affected by a loss of value, the valuation authority sets a price for which the developer is obliged to buy the property. However, the obligation to purchase only covers the area within the same cadastral number on which the residential property is located. It can be problematic, as it is often somewhat random how a property is divided into cadastral numbers.

As an alternative, the developer and the property owner can also enter into a voluntary agreement for either compensation or the purchase of the nearby property. If the developer buys the property, he can choose to either resell or rent the property after the wind or solar park is established. If necessary, the developer can choose to demolish the property and install solar cells on it. In certain places, the developer buys up large parts of smaller villages and then leaves the remaining inhabitants of the village with a somewhat smaller village.

The renewable energy bonus scheme in 2020 replaced the former right to buy shares scheme. The bonus scheme entitles the residents within 8 times the total height of wind turbines and 200 m from solar farms to receive an annual bonus based on the plant's production. The bonus is paid by the renewable energy plant owner. The scheme aims to give the neighbours a gain in addition to any value loss. The size of the bonus will vary over the lifetime of the plant, as it depends on the plant's production and the electricity price. The estimated bonus is currently around 6500 DKK (€872) for wind farms and 2500 DKK (€335) for solar farms. A 2023 Government initiative aims to increase the bonus by 50 %.[35] It is now implemented in the Renewable Energy Act.[36]

A so-called green pool in 2020 replaced the former green scheme that was state financed via consumer charges. The new scheme requires the developer to pay an amount per installed MW to the municipality, in which renewable energy installations are installed, or the municipality or municipalities that have the right to object to open-door offshore wind turbines. The municipality administers the green pool funds, and the funds can be used widely for municipal initiatives. However, it is intended that the funds should primarily support projects applied for by close neighbours for the renewable energy plant as well as green measures in the municipality. A purpose of the scheme is to motivate municipalities to grant the necessary permits for the project. Following a 2023 Government initiative increasing green pool funds by 150 %, the payment obligation is 313,000 DKK/MW (€42,013) wind and 125,000 (€16,769) DKK/MW solar energy.

In addition, the Guarantee Fund offers the possibility of a guarantee for the financing of local cooperatives' feasibility studies, etc., in connection with the installation of wind turbines or solar cells. The scheme aims to help smaller local initiatives to be able to complete a project. The vast majority of the installed wind and solar parks are, however, established by large commercial companies.

C. Main Obstacles and Policy Initiatives

Despite a high share of renewables in Denmark, in particular wind energy, several obstacles to further deployment of wind and solar power have been identified and to some extent also addressed in different policy initiatives. Local opposition has since 2008 mainly been addressed through the compensation schemes referred to above. However, the compensation schemes may not necessarily have succeeded in promoting local acceptance. In particular, the value loss scheme has been criticized for increasing rather

35 Regeringen, Klimahandling [Climate Action] (Danish Government, 2023) <https://kefm.dk/Media/638324394100598678/Udspil%20-%20Mere%20gr%C3%B8n%20energi%20fra%20sol%20og%20vind%20p%C3%A5%20land.pdf> accessed 26 May 2025.

36 See Act no 670 of 11 June 2024.

than reducing conflicts.[37] On the other hand, the new bonus scheme and also the green pool scheme may have more positive effects. However, the schemes may also increase costs -particularly those of wind farms – significantly.[38] Consequently, there is a delicate balance and a need for thorough considerations in the use of such schemes. Furthermore, other perceived obstacles have been addressed more recently, including decision-making procedures and appeals, nature protection and biodiversity concerns as well as grid connection and capacity.

In accordance with the 2023 political agreement, new legislation has been adopted aimed to address such obstacles. Apart from the new Act on Energy Parks relaxing certain (national) nature protection rules, an amendment of the rules regarding appeals of RE-decisions to the Planning Appeals Board, the Environment and Food Appeals Board, and the Energy Appeals Board has also been adopted in June 2024.[39]

1. Decision-Making Procedures and Appeals

(a) Onshore

The planning and permit procedures for onshore wind and solar projects are, on the face of it, relatively simple. Nevertheless, municipal and local planning may be fraught with difficulties. It can be questioned whether the planning system works as intended. Often the local authorities have been reluctant to designate potential wind (or solar) sites in the municipal plan, i.e. at the strategic planning level.[40] In such cases, it may be the developers rather than the municipalities that steer the development, doing so by ad-hoc planning for individual project applications rather than strategic planning based on considerations of the variety of different land use inter-

---

37 Marie L Jørgensen/Helle T Anker/Jesper Lassen, 'Distributive fairness and local acceptance of wind turbines: The role of compensation schemes' (2020) 138 Energy Policy 11294.

38 Helle T Anker/Lars B Andersen/Birgitte E Olsen, Sol og vind – det samme sind? [Sun and wind – the same mind?] in Carina R Hamer/Hans VG Pedersen/Nis J Clausen (eds), *Festskrift til Bent Ole Gram Mortensen [Liber Amicorum to Bent Ole Gram Mortensen]* (DJØF Forlag, 2022) 31–61.

39 Act no 640 of 11 June 2024.

40 Helle Anker, 'Notat om kommunal planlægning for vindmøller' (IFRO Report No 2016/26, 2016) < https://researchprofiles.ku.dk/en/publications/notat-om-kommunal-planl%C3%A6gning-for-vindm%C3%B8ller > accessed 26 May 2025.

ests. Furthermore, the physical or spatial planning character of municipal planning may not always be capable of also taking infrastructure/grid and consumption patterns into consideration. As regards the new national designation of energy parks an initial screening in 2023 of potential sites was based on site proposals from municipalities and developers. The proposed sites were screened based on different criteria, in particular neighbouring dwellings, nature and environmental concerns, and cultural heritage. It does not appear that there was any reference to e.g. agricultural interests or any attempts to locate energy parks close to other technical installations, e.g. highways. Nonetheless, access to the grid and critical infrastructure was taken into account. In general, however, there appears to be a lack of strategic planning and identification of relevant principles for the siting of wind and solar farms. Particularly, there are no principles or incentives to plan for wind and solar power close to other technical installations, or even to use existing structures such as roofs. The 2022 energy plan, however, suggests a new subsidy scheme for such projects.

Public participation procedures are fairly basic in the Danish Planning Act. There is a simple requirement of public consultation for a period of 8 weeks in most cases. There are no requirements for public hearings or meetings in the Planning Act. However, there is wide access to appealing a planning decision (and strategic environmental assessment) to the Planning Appeals Board (PKN). Similarly, an EIA permit can be appealed to the Environment and Food Appeals Board (MFKN). The two appeals boards share the same secretariat. Following a period of relatively long delays, since 2021, a deadline of 6 months has been set for a decision in the appeals boards for wind and solar projects. Nevertheless, in some cases, the appeals boards have declared the plans null and void primarily due to inadequate information regarding the potential effects on Natura 2000 sites, Annex IV species, birds, or other environmental concerns. In such cases, the local authorities must make new assessments and also adopt new plans, which may cause significant delays. It is possible to challenge an appeals board decision in court, although this happens very rarely.[41]

41 Four RE court cases have been concluded since 2012 (publish in the Danish journal 'Miljøretlige Afgørelser og Domme' [Environmental Legal Decisions and Judgments] often abbreviated as MAD. See MAD2012.394Ø, MAD2012.1947H, MAD2017.250B, MAD2019.244V).

The Government has established an 'energy crisis group'[42] with the task of removing obstacles and reducing time for decision-making procedures. No specific time-limits have been set, though, apart from those that may apply according to the EU Emergency Regulation. New rules adopted in June 2024, however, aim to facilitate a more expeditious appeal process, to some extent also limiting the scope of review of the Appeals Boards.[43] The Government has also indicated that the State may offer to designate and potentially adopt Acts of Parliament for energy park sites. In particular, the use of Acts of Parliament may have the consequence that there will be no access to administrative appeals and thus reduce administrative procedures and delays. This option has been applied regarding the energy island in the North Sea.[44] However, this may contradict the Aarhus Convention as the administrative appeals system provides an easily accessible and affordable option for appeals as opposed to the general courts.

(b) Offshore

The offshore decision-making processes are quite complex. The combination of a three-layered licence system with the tender procedure has caused significant obstacles and delays for some offshore projects, e.g. the Vesterhav Syd project (see below). Furthermore, the apparent lack of a formal planning procedure for the designation of offshore sites has also created some uncertainties in relation to environmental assessment procedures and public participation. It has even been possible to establish projects under the so-called open-door procedure characterized by no prior planning or designation of sites. Following the adoption of the Danish maritime spatial plan in 2023, offshore RE projects now need to be within designated development zones for renewables.

The traditional decision-making procedures at the national level for offshore activities have faced some difficulties in accommodating requirements for environmental assessment, at both strategic and project levels, as well as public participation and access to justice requirements.[45] Despite a lack of formal planning procedures for offshore activities prior to the

42 Please see <https://www.en.kefm.dk/> accessed 2 June 2025.

43 Act no 640 of 11 June 2024.

44 Act no 2379 of 14 December 2021 on design and construction of an energy island in the North Sea.

45 Helle T Anker/Birgitte E Olsen, 'Blæst på havet: om beslutningsprocesser for havvindmøller i Danmark' in Jan Darpö, Maria Forsberg, Maria Pettersson/Charlotta

maritime spatial plan, procedures for strategic environmental assessment and the associated public participation were applied according to the Environmental Assessment Act. Even though there is now a formal maritime spatial plan where potential offshore sites for wind (or solar) farms should be designated, it must be kept in mind that amendments to the maritime spatial plan, including new offshore sites, must still be subject to strategic environmental assessment. Issues regarding strategic environmental assessment can be appealed to the Environment and Food Appeals Board as there is no administrative appeal option for the maritime spatial plan as such.

Furthermore, the environmental impact assessment procedure has in practice been linked to the preliminary investigations, and it has previously been carried out by the state authorities (Energinet) prior to the tender procedure. Nevertheless, access to justice on environmental matters in the form of administrative appeals to the Energy Appeals Board is linked to the licence for establishment granted to the developer after the tender procedure. These complexities were illustrated in the Vesterhav Syd case.

The Vesterhav Syd project was originally envisaged as one of six potential coastal-near offshore projects in 2012. In 2013–14, preliminary investigations and an EIA were carried out by the Danish TSO, Energinet, while a tender procedure was initiated, and in 2016, Vattenfall won the tender and was granted a permit for establishment. The permit for establishment was appealed to the Energy Appeals Board by local landowner associations, primarily on the grounds that the EIA procedure had not been adequate. The Energy Appeals Board[46] decided to repeal the licence for establishment as the EIA was inadequate since the details of the project would only be determined after the granting of the licence for the establishment. Thus, a supplementary EIA would be required.

The case illustrates the complex interplay between the EIA and permit procedures on the one side, and the tender procedure on the other, as the details of a project could only be elaborated after the identification of the developer in the tender procedure.[47] In the current system the responsibili-

Zetterberg (eds), *Miljörätten och den förhandlingsovilliga naturen: Vänbok till Gabriel Michanek* (Iustus Förlag 2019) 13–34.

46 Vesterhav Syd, Energy Appeals Board decision of 20 December 2018, no 18/00219, 18/00222, 18/00225 (MAD2018.419).

47 Helle T Anker/Birgitte E Olsen, 'Blæst på havet: om beslutningsprocesser for havvindmøller i Danmark' in Jan Darpö, Maria Forsberg, Maria Pettersson/Charlotta Zetterberg (eds), *Miljörätten och den förhandlingsovilliga naturen: Vänbok till Gabriel Michanek* (Iustus Förlag 2019) 13–34.

ty of carrying out an EIA is more clearly placed on the developer being granted a preliminary investigation permit *after* winning the tender. However, Energinet still conducts site-investigations, including a wide range of geophysical, geotechnical and environmental surveys, prior to the tender with the purpose to reduce bid risk and minimize the need for additional site-investigations and environmental surveys later in the project development process and during EIA of the individual projects.[48]

2. Nature Protection and Biodiversity

As mentioned above, a major perceived obstacle to wind energy projects in particular is conflicting nature protection interests. It is mainly EU-protected habitats and species under the Habitats and Birds Directives that set the strictest requirements.[49] However, Danish nature protection legislation may also create obstacles.

There are several examples that failure to provide adequate assessment regarding the potential effects on Natura 2000 sites has led to decisions in the appeals boards – both the Planning Appeals Board, the Environment and Food Appeals Board, and the Energy Appeals Board – to declare plans and EIA permits null and void. This reflects the strict interpretation by the CJEU and the requirement for a high degree of certainty in an appropriate assessment demonstrating that there must be 'no reasonable scientific doubt remaining as to the absence of adverse effects on the integrity of the area in question.'[50] Furthermore, the assessment 'may not have lacunae and must contain complete, precise and definitive findings and conclusions

48 Danish Energy Agency, Notes on environmental assessment for offshore wind farm tenders, <https://ens.dk/en/energy-sources/offshore-procedures-permits> accessed 11 June 2025.

49 For a more detailed analysis in the Danish context, *see* Helle T Anker/Birgitte E Olsen, 'EU species protection law and wind energy: Current challenges and Danish experiences' (2023) 32(1) European Energy and Environmental Law Review 36–46. *See* also Sanne Akerboomand et al., 'Wind Energy Projects and Species Protection Law: A Comparative Analysis of the Application of EU Law in Five Member States' (2019) 28 European Energy and Environmental Law Review 144–158 and more generally Hendrik Schoukens/Kees Bastmeijer, 'Species protection in the European Union. How strict is strict?' in CH Born et al. (eds), *The Habitats Directive in its EU Environmental Law Context* (Routledge 2014) 121–142.

50 E.g. C-164/17 *Grace and Sweetman v An Bord Pleanala*, ECLI:EU:C:2018:593 para 41, and C-441/17 Commission v Poland, para 113, ECLI:EU:C:2018:255.

capable of removing all reasonable scientific doubt as to the effects of the proposed works on the protected area concerned'.[51] In one case (Thorup Sletten) concerning 18 new wind turbines (150 m) replacing 10 existing, smaller turbines next to a Natura 2000 site designated for the protection of several bird species, the appeals boards found that for two designated bird species (marsh harrier and hen harrier), the assessment of the effects, especially regarding collision risks, was insufficient.[52] In addition, displacement effects had not been examined with regards to species-specific displacement zones. The appeals boards found that the appropriate assessment was not sufficiently detailed and substantiated to demonstrate the absence of adverse effects, and the plans and permits were declared null and void. The municipality made a new assessment and adopted plans and permits in 2023. Following new appeals the Planning Appeals Board and the Environment and Food Appeals Board in February 2024 confirmed the municipal plans and permit.[53] In another case (Bogø Inddæmningen)[54] concerning eight wind turbines on farmland 80 m from a Natura 2000 site designated for the protection of i.a. sea eagles and barnacle geese, the appeals boards did not accept a general presumption that collision risks in the order of 1–2 % would not affect any bird species at the population level. The plans and EIA permit were also declared null and void in this case. There are, however, also examples that wind energy projects close to Natura 2000 sites have been accepted. This includes a project for two new wind turbines (80 m) replacing two existing turbines (Tåsinge II) in a coastal area 150–200 m from a Natura 2000 site designated for the protection of several birds, including sea eagles.[55] The appeals boards accepted the conclusions in the appropriate assessment that the project would not have adverse effects on the local population of sea eagles. There are so far no examples in Denmark of the derogation clause in Art. 6(4) of the Habitats Directive being used for wind energy projects.

---

51 E.g. C-164/17 para 39.

52 Thorup Sletten, MAD2021.172 PKN and Cases no NMK-18-09916, NMK-19-00745 & NMK-19-00746 MFKN. NMK is an abbreviation for 'Natur- og Miljøklagenævnet' [Nature and Environment Appeals Board].

53 Thorup Sletten II, Planning Appeals Board Case No 23/12886 and Environment and Food Appeals Board Case no 23/10651.

54 Bogø Inddæmningen, Cases no 21/11970PKN, 21/13196, 21/11976, and 21/11973MFKN.

55 Tåsinge II, Cases no 21/00253, 20/12346, 21/02402 & 21/02411 PKN and Case no 20/12345 & 21/00280 MFKN.

Annex IV species such as bats may be particularly vulnerable to wind turbines, especially at low wind speeds where insects and consequently bats are attracted to the turbine towers. While certain (rare) bat species may also be subject to the Natura 2000 protection, the decisive criterion for Natura 2000 species is the population status. Yet for Annex IV species, the CJEU has indicated that the direct protection against deliberate killing or disturbance in Article 12 is at individual specimen level, and that 'deliberate' includes not only intentional capture or killing of a specimen but also, at the very least, the possibility of such capture or killing being accepted.[56] Such strict protection can be difficult to comply with which has also been reflected in the amendment of the Renewable Energy Directive[57] as well as in the so-called Emergency Regulation.[58] According to these rules, killing or disturbance will not be considered deliberate if appropriate mitigation measures have been taken (RED III) or if species conservation measures at the population level are a prerequisite for the presumption of and priority for RE as an overriding public interest (Emergency Regulation). In Denmark, the protection of bats has led to the adoption of project-specific measures in the form of periodic shutdowns from dusk to dawn during the summer and early fall at low wind speeds.[59]

The protection of birds that are not subject to protection through the designation of Natura 2000 sites must also be considered. Again, the CJEU has interpreted Art. 5 on deliberate killing or disturbance strictly to include not only intentional killing but also unintentional killing or disturbance where the mere possibility of killing or disturbance has been accepted. Furthermore, the CJEU has clearly rejected that the prohibition can be made dependent upon whether the species is at some level of risk or suffering a long-term decline in population.[60] So far, the Danish appeals boards have mainly examined whether an EIA/SEA provides an adequate assessment of such effects, e.g., by local observations and registrations of bird species.

56 Joined cases C-473/19 and C-474/19, para 51.

57 European Parliament and Council Directive (EU) 2023/2413 amending Directive (EU) 2018/2001, Regulation (EU) 2018/1999 and Directive 98/70/EC as regards the promotion of energy from renewable sources, and repealing Council Directive (EU) 2015/652 [2023] OJ L 2023/2413.

58 Council Regulation (EU) 2022/2577 of 22 December 2022 laying down a framework to accelerate the deployment of renewable energy [2022] OJ L 335/36.

59 E.g. Marsvinslund, MAD2021.244 PKN.

60 Joined cases C-473/19 and C-474/19 *Skydda Skogen* para 82, ECLI:EU:C:2021:166 para 36.

For relevant species, it may be necessary to estimate specific collision risks or mortality rates considering the local conditions. In an onshore case (Rendbæk Øst), the Environment and Food Appeals Board emphasized that the EIA included information on collision risk and minimum distances between wind turbines and golden eagles from various scientific studies.[61] In this case, the EIA permit and plans were upheld by the appeals boards. However, the appeals board decisions were appealed to the courts but have been discontinued due to a settlement. In another recent decision by the Energy Appeals Board regarding an offshore project (Aflandshage), the permits granted by the Energy Agency were declared null and void primarily due to inadequate assessment of the potential effects on affected bird populations and on bats.[62]

Other environmental issues may also create obstacles to wind energy projects in particular, e.g. potential effects on the aquatic environment due to the lowering of groundwater tables. More generally, the EIA requirements have caused particular obstacles in relation to the decision-making procedure for offshore turbines which led to the repeal of a permit for one offshore installation, Vesterhav Syd, see above.

3. Grid connection and capacity

Grid connection of especially large projects on agricultural land has been a challenge for the distribution and transmission network as discussed above. Delays in being able to connect the RE plant to the electricity grid are a common obstacle. This is because solar parks and wind turbines are often located in sparsely populated areas where the electricity grid has not been designed to be able to transport electricity from a local electricity production plant. As the capacity of wind turbines and solar farms has grown, the need for reinforcements of the power grid's capacity arises more frequently. Expansion of the transmission network often takes 5 years or more, while new RE plants can be established within 1–2 years. The Danish TSO (Energinet) has drawn up capacity maps to guide developers in where they can find the shortest connection times. Nevertheless, the consulting firm Rambøll expects the Danish electricity grid to be expanded

61 Environment and Food Appeals Board decision of 10 December 2021 in Case no 21/06969 and 21/06968 (Rendbæk Øst).

62 Aflandshage, Energy Appeals Board decision of 4 July 2023 in Case no 22/16705.

at a cost of 110 billion DKK. Furthermore, developers are also dependent on finding places with available land, good space, and a suitable distance from neighbours.[63]

A major expansion of the Danish electricity grid will be required in order to be able to handle an increased amount of electricity production. The speed of expansion may become a temporary barrier to the growth of RE capacity. Often, however, it will be an advantage to combine wind turbines and solar cells in an area, as the two different production technologies rarely produce at maximum capacity at the same time.

The planned expansion of renewable energy capacity will also mean that Denmark cannot itself consume the electricity produced in the traditional way. It is possible that a direct export can take place from the future Danish energy islands planned for. However, many developers plan to use the electricity produced to form electrofuels (in Denmark often referred to as Power-to-X or simply PtX). An example is the 340-hectare solar park at Kassø in South Jutland. A methanol factory has been there and went operative in 2025.

With the Government foundation Responsibility for Denmark from December 2022, the Government established the National Energy Crisis Staff (NEKST), which is to ensure faster action on acute green challenges. Based on recommendations from this, an agreement was concluded on 20 December 2024 on faster and more efficient expansion of the electricity grid,[64] and a number of so-called acceleration areas were identified with a view to expanding the electricity transmission grid. The agreement includes, among other things, faster options for expropriation, including expropriation with the purpose to enable compensatory nature.

D. Conclusion

While Denmark has been a frontrunner, especially regarding wind energy, there is an increasing number of perceived obstacles to further deployment of renewables. Still, ambitious climate and RE targets have been set, and national initiatives to 'clear the way' for more wind and solar energy are

63 See ArcGIS, 'Capacity map' <https://storymaps.arcgis.com/stories/eb5b387e376f49b8996d5e7c47fbdd37> accessed 7 June 2025.

64 Klima-, Energi og Forsyningsministeriet, <https://www.kefm.dk/Media/638745300510439819/Aftale%20om%20hurtigere%20og%20mere%20effektiv%20udbygning%20af%20elnettet.pdf> accessed 7 June 2025.

put in place. Furthermore, PtX is seen as an important component in the Danish energy transition, although it creates huge energy demands in itself.

Nevertheless, there appears to be a lack of proper strategic planning for new RE projects, both onshore and offshore. Onshore, the designation of new sites – including the national energy parks – is to a large extent based on proposals from the developers, and it can be questioned to what extent the authorities are actually steering the development through proper planning processes. Offshore, there has been a lack of formal planning procedures, but the designation of potential RE sites are now part of the maritime spatial plan. Furthermore, decision-making procedures, including administrative appeals, are regarded as an obstacle to the deployment of wind and solar power and new legislation aims to limit the scope of review. More specifically, environmental assessment requirements and EU protection of Natura 2000 sites, Annex IV species, and birds are highly complex and have been identified as a major obstacle both as regards offshore and onshore wind projects. In most cases, however, it is inadequate assessments of the potential effects on e.g. birds or bats that lead to plans and permits being declared null and void. It is not necessarily so that nature protection law prevents the projects from being adopted, and so far, there have been no examples of using the derogation options for renewables. Nevertheless, legislation that will make it possible to relax Danish nature protection legislation has been adopted, while the implementation of the EU legislation to accelerate RE runs on a separate track.

It is uncertain whether such legislation will actually promote renewable energy projects, or perhaps rather lead to more opposition. Local opposition has since 2008 mainly been addressed through the compensation schemes referred to above. Nevertheless, the compensation schemes may not necessarily have succeeded in promoting local acceptance. Furthermore, the schemes may also increase costs significantly, particularly in the case of wind farms. Thus, there is a delicate balance and a need for thorough considerations in the use of such schemes.

Finally, it must be noted that grid connection and capacity is- at least temporarily – an obstacle to the growth of RE. A major expansion of the Danish electricity grid is required in order to be able to handle an increased amount of electricity production. At the same time, today, the deployment of renewables is to a large extent market driven as subsidies and price supplements have gradually been abolished. This also means that the energy transition is sensitive to economic conditions and financial markets.

Bibliography

ArcGIS, 'Capacity map' <https://storymaps.arcgis.com/stories/eb5b387e376f49b8996d5e7c47fbdd37> accessed 7 June 2025

Akerboom S et al., 'Wind Energy Projects and Species Protection Law: A Comparative Analysis of the Application of EU Law in Five Member States' (2019) 28 (4) European Energy and Environmental Law Review 144

Anker H T, 'Notat om kommunal planlægning for vindmøller' (IFRO Report No. 2016/26 2016) < https://researchprofiles.ku.dk/en/publications/notat-om-kommunal-planl%C3%A6gning-for-vindm%C3%B8ller > accessed 26 May 2025

Anker H T/Olsen B E, 'EU species protection law and wind energy: Current challenges and Danish experiences' (2023) 32 (1) European Energy and Environmental Law Review 36

Anker H T/Andersen L B/Olsen B E, 'Sol og vind – det samme sind? [Sun and wind – the same mind?]' in: **Hamer C R/Pedersen H V G/Clausen N J** (eds), *Festskrift til Bent Ole Gram Mortensen [Liber Amicorum to Bent Ole Gram Mortensen* (DJØF Forlag 2022)

Anker H T/Olsen B E, 'Blæst på havet: om beslutningsprocesser for havvindmøller i Danmark [It blows on the sea: on decision-making processes for offshore wind turbines in Denmark]' in: **Darpö J/Forsberg M/Pettersson M/Zetterberg C** (eds), *Miljörätten och den förhandlingsovilliga naturen: Vänbok till Gabriel Michanek [Liber Amicorum to Gabriel Michanek]* (Iustus Förlag 2019)

Energinet, 'Capacity map' <https://storymaps.arcgis.com/stories/eb5b387e376f49b8996d5e7c47fbdd37> accessed 7 June 2025

Energinet, '2022 sætter dansk rekord i vind og sol' (Press announcement, 29 December 2022) <https://via.ritzau.dk/pressemeddelelse/13667585/2022-saetter-dansk-rekord-i-vind-og-sol?publisherId=10304728&lang=da> accessed 26 May 2025

Jørgensen M L/Anker H T/Lassen J, 'Distributive fairness and local acceptance of wind turbines: The role of compensation schemes' (2020) 138 Energy Policy 11294

Jørgensen M L, 'Low-carbon but corrupt? Bribery, inappropriate-ness and unfairness concerns in Danish energy policy' (2020) 70 Energy Research & Social Science 101663

Klima-, Energi og Forsyningsministeriet, [Danish Ministry of Climate, Energy and Utilities], 'Klimaaftale om grøn strøm og varme 2022' (Climate Agreement regarding Green Power and Heat 2022)(25 June 2022) <https://kefm.dk/Media/637920977082432693/Klimaaftale%20om%20gr%C3%B8n%20str%C3%B8m%20og%20varme%202022.pdf> accessed 26 May 2025

Klima-, Energi og Forsyningsministeriet, [Danish Ministry of Climate, Energy and Utilities], 'Aftale mellem regeringen (Venstre og Det Konservative Folkeparti), Socialdemokraterne, Dansk Folkeparti, Socialistisk Folkeparti, Det Radikale Venstre og Ny Alliance om den danske energipolitik i årene 2008–2011' (Political Agreement on Danish energy policy in the years 2008–2011) accessed 22 October 2023

Klima-, Energi og Forsyningsministeriet, [Danish Ministry of Climate, Energy and Utilities], 'Klimaaftale om mere grøn energi fra sol og vind på land 2023' (Climate agreement on more green energy from solar and wind on land2023)<https://kefm.dk/Media/638379734168312589/Klimaaftale%20om%20mere%20gr%C3%B8n%20energi%20fra%20sol%20og%20vind%20p%C3%A5%20land%202023.pdf> accessed 12 December 2023

Klima-, Energi og Forsyningsministeriet, [Danish Ministry of Climate, Energy and Utilities], 'Klimaaftale for energi og industri mv. 2020' (Climate Agreement regarding Energy and Industry etc. 2020)(22 June 2020) <https://www.kefm.dk/Media/4/2/aftaletekst-klimaaftale-energi-og-industri

Olsen B E/Anker H T, 'Local acceptance and the legal framework: the Danish wind energy case' in **Squintani L/Vedder H/Reese M/Vanheusden B** (eds), *Sustainable energy united in diversity: challenges and approaches in energy transition in the EU* (European Environmental Law Forum Book Series 2014)

Olsen B E/Mortensen B O G, 'Offshore wind licensing in Denmark' in IH Anchustegui and TS Hunter (eds), *Offshore Wind Licensing* (Edward Elgar Publishing 2024)

Schoukens H/Bastmeijer K, 'Species protection in the European Union. How strict is strict?' in: **Born C H** et al. (eds), *The Habitats Directive in its EU Environmental Law Context* (Routledge 2014) 121–142

Skjærseth J B et al., *Wind Power Policies and Diffusion in the Nordic Countries. Comparative Patterns* (Palgrave Macmillan 2023) 27–34

Waage F, 'Compensating neighbors to windmills, solar energy panels and other sources of renewable energy in Denmark' in: **Hamer C R/Pedersen H V G/Clausen N J** (eds) *Festskrift til Bent Ole Gram Mortensen [Liber Amicorum to Bent Ole Gram Mortensen]* (DJØF Forlag 2022)

Comparing the Law of Energy Transition in Europe – Concluding Essay

Johann-Christian Pielow and Kate McKenzie

A. Introduction

The energy transition presents significant challenges for all states involved. To "transition" implies moving away from traditional system structures in response to new objectives, and replacing them with fundamentally innovative, even "disruptive," management concepts. This process of change is complicated by the inherent complexity of the energy transition itself, as well as by the variability of its technical, economic, political, and legal frameworks. Legally, the situation is particularly complex due to the involvement of numerous old and new stakeholders in the energy sector. The interplay between power plant operators, grid operators, storage and other facility managers, energy traders, consumers, aggregators, efficiency consultants, service providers, as well as actors from the IT industry[1] and many others, multiplies the legal relationships that must be addressed. At the same time, sufficient planning and investment security is required for market participants, which can be facilitated through expedited administrative procedures and the reduction of bureaucratic barriers. Additionally, it is crucial to ensure broad societal support over decades, while avoiding the risks of "energy poverty," whether in households or industries. Since none of this can be achieved overnight, the energy transition is also fraught with prognostic uncertainties regarding all of its accompanying factors. The Russian invasion of Ukraine underscored the sector's vulnerability to geopolitical influences, and with the increasing tensions in global trade, particularly in relation to China and the USA, more dark clouds loom on the horizon.

1 See for example Markus, in this volume, 129 (137 ff.).

1. The Benefits of Comparative Legal Analysis

In addressing the complexity and uncertainty inherent in the energy transition, a useful approach is to look at foreign legal systems. This is particularly relevant in the context of the energy transition, following the commitment of nearly 200 signatory states to the Paris Agreement, in which they agreed to shared goals while maintaining autonomy in their implementation. An analysis from a comparative law perspective can reveal different strategies for pursuing these objectives, and once effective practices are identified, they can encourage adoption and replication.[2]

Comparative legal analysis remains valuable even when broad areas of energy and climate law, as thoroughly discussed in Part A of this volume, are already deeply integrated into European law. The legal framework governing the "Energy and Climate Union,"[3] established in 2015, has expanded through initiatives such as the European Green Deal, the "Fit for 55" legislative package, and the REPowerEU Plan, resulting in an increasingly rigorous and detailed set of requirements—often in the form of directly applicable regulations under Article 288(2) TFEU. Despite the increasing rigidity and specificity of these regulations, the legal framework remains largely "final" in nature. In principle, the EU legislature, as exemplified by legal acts on the promotion of renewable energy and energy efficiency, essentially limits itself to the setting of common goals, within which member states must then define their own national objectives, while maintaining the discretion to decide on the "form and means" of implementation, in accordance with the definition of "directives" in Article 288(3) TFEU. The relative degree of flexibility granted to member states — despite numerous often excessive (and sometimes "overregulated") detailed procedural requirements, such as obligations regarding organization, information, and cooperation — inevitably leads to different implementation strategies. A comparative analysis of these strategies is therefore indispensable when considering the common goals to be achieved at EU level.[4]

2 For detailed discussion, see Till Markus, 'Zur Rechtsvergleichung im nationalen und internationalen Umweltrecht' 80 (2020) ZaöRV, 650, particularly 666 ff.

3 See European Commission, Communication 'Framework Strategy for a Resilient Energy Union with a Forward-Looking Climate Change Policy' (25 February 2015) COM (2015) 80 final.

4 Successful examples of comparative legal analysis, especially in energy law, can be found in Markus (n 2) and Johannes Saurer/Jonas Monast, 'Symposium Foreword: The Law of Energy Transition in Federal Systems' (2021) 10 Transnational Environmental

Moreover, legislative implementation of European directives at the national level is not sufficient on its own. The effectiveness of EU legal acts ultimately depends on their efficient incorporation into the administrative practices of member states. Comparative studies of cooperation and coordination mechanisms, as well as the administrative realities that differ from one country to another, can provide valuable insights.[5] Finally, a comparison of national regulatory structures, which are both directed by and interlinked with EU law, can generate impulses for the further development of supranational law, fostering a "reciprocal development process" that benefits both national and EU-level legal frameworks.[6]

2. "Proper" Comparative Legal Analysis

Comparative legal analysis, however, cannot merely consist of a sequence of descriptive and more or less disorganized country reports on specific legal questions.[7] This is particularly true in the field of public law concerning energy supply, which has traditionally been regarded as a core element of state sovereignty.[8] This domain is embedded within the specific traditions of national (economic) administrative law, constitutional law, and the respective state organizations. Furthermore, seemingly comparable legal concepts and institutions (such as "public service") may carry entirely

Law, pp. 205 ff.; see also Martha Roggenkamp/Catherine Redgwell/Anita Ronne/Inigo del Guayo (eds), *Energy Law in Europe* (OUP), 3d ed. 2016, with detailed conclusions of the editors to the national reports in Part IV (Chapter 16).

5 The European Commission also takes this into account by continuously commissioning in-depth studies on the implementation of EU law, particularly regarding its practical effectiveness in the administrative realities of member states. For example, the primary author of this chapter, along with colleagues from other EU countries, is involved in a detailed study (including stakeholder surveys) on the implementation of Regulation (EU) 2022/869, which provides guidelines for trans-European energy infrastructure.

6 Eberhard Schmidt-Aßmann, *Das Allgemeine Verwaltungsrecht als Ordnungsidee*, Springer, Heidelberg 1998, 37; see also Johann-Christian Pielow, Grundstrukturen öffentlicher Versorgung, Jus Publicum 58, Mohr-Siebeck, Tübingen 2001, 106 f.

7 For examples from environmental law, see 'Beispiele' by Markus (n 2) 658.

8 This is also reflected in the reservation in favour of national energy policy expressed in Article 192 para. 2 (c) and Article 194 para. 2 second subpara., TFEU.

different meanings from one country to another.[9] There is always the risk, therefore, of merely comparing apples and oranges, a phenomenon often referred to as the *false friends syndrome*.[10] Legal systems are, of course, also shaped by "soft" factors, such as social norms, ideologies, or even the mentalities of the country in question. For example, attitudes toward climate-related impacts in Mediterranean countries is markedly different from those in the windswept, rain-laden regions of northern Europe.

A truly "holistic" approach to comparative legal analysis must consider these particular contextual factors[11] — reflecting national "legal cultures" — yet this naturally makes the process especially time-consuming and demanding.[12] According to prevailing opinion, comparative law methodology should always be "functional" in nature.[13] At the heart of comparative law is the need to precisely define the legal and factual issues (*tertium comparationis*) to be addressed, independent of system categories or concepts derived from the analyst's own legal system. The objective is to identify functional equivalents for solutions in the legal systems being compared.

3. Further Approach

A more in-depth analysis of the law governing the energy transition in Europe, particularly within the framework of "functional" comparative legal analysis as described above, cannot be fully accomplished based on

9 See, for example, the comparison between the French "service public" and the German concept of "Daseinsvorsorge" with regard to energy supply, as discussed by Pielow (n 6) 111 ff., 288 ff.

10 Johannes Veigel, 'Die funktionale Methode bei der Rechtsvergleichung' 30 (2021) Juridica International, 71 ff., 72 <https://doi.org/10.12697/JI.2021.30.09> accessed 18 February 2025, also considering, Jaakko Husa, *A new Introduction to Comparative Law*, Bloomsbury 2015, 119.

11 See Markus (n 2) 74 in accordance with Konrad Zweigert/Hein Kötz, *Einführung in die Rechtsvergleichung*, Mohr-Siebeck, 3. ed. 1996 Tübingen 33 ff.; for in-depth detail on the necessarily context-dependent comparative law *Kischel*, Rechtsvergleichung, 2019, particularly 269 ff.

12 In the context of the energy transition, various reports and "factsheets" from the European Commission on the implementation status in member states, as well as the country reports (Country Insights) on the energy transition in IEA member countries, available under "Countries & Regions" on the IEA website, provide useful guidance. See http://iea.org/countries.

13 For an in-depth discussion of the method of functional comparative law and the controversy surrounding it, see Uwe Kischel, *Rechtsvergleichung*, 2019, 93 ff.; also Veigel (n 10).

the contributions to this volume. For one, the contributions reports only cover a selection of European countries including several EU member states and the UK. Furthermore, the country-specific studies vary in content and thematic emphases. However, the informational value of the provided insights in national systems of energy law is considerable. Based on these, it is possible to identify some notable similarities, as well as significant differences and certain shortcomings in the energy transition laws of the countries studied. These will be outlined in the following sections, with the understanding that, due to space constraints, the selection of issues to be discussed is necessarily subjective on the part of the authors.

B. General & systemic perspectives

1. Understanding of "energy transition"

It is commonly agreed that the 'energy transition' is about turning away from the use of fossil fuels, now with the goal of comprehensive 'decarbonisation' or 'net zero'. In legal terms, this understanding stems less from energy law than from various countries' cross-sector climate protection legislation, for example in the UK and Germany. A legally binding or generally accepted definition, however, exists neither at the European, nor, as far as can be seen from the contributions to this book, at the national level. The term 'energy transition' notably appears as a legal term in the title of the French "Loi relative à la transition énergétique pour la croissance verte" of 2015.[14] However, it is not described in any more detail within the law itself. Instead, reference is made to the definition of 'green growth' in the French Energy Code. This definition, however, marks the generally recognised cornerstones of what is generally understood by energy transition, namely: the economical use of natural resources (particularly of fossil fuels), increasing energy efficiency and decarbonisation, as well as the expansion of renewable energies. At the same time, the French law calls for a socially acceptable energy policy that promotes innovation and supports the competitiveness of businesses, in addition to 'combating energy poverty'.[15] Similarly, the German Federal Energy Industry Act (Energiewirtschaftsgesetz), without using the term 'Energiewende', states in its article 1 para 1 that the purpose

14 Act no. 2015–992 of 17 August 2015, J.O.R.F. no. 189 of 18 August 2015.
15 Cf. article 100–1 Code de l'Énergie.

of the Act is "to provide the general public with a secure, low-priced, consumer-friendly, efficient, environmentally friendly and greenhouse gas-neutral grid-based supply of electricity, gas and hydrogen, which is increasingly based on renewable energies." In the end, the term 'energy transition' proves to be more of a topos of political programme than a binding legal or statutory term. As part of the 'ecological' transition, the term energy transition is also being used in the names of ministries, for example in France and also in Spain. Interestingly, the energy crisis in the EU resulting from the war in Ukraine led to the renaming of the Italian Ministry of Ecological Transition as the Ministry of Environment and Energy Security.

2. Target hierarchies and conflicts / trade-offs

National climate and energy policies are converging along the EU's long-term decarbonisation targets; only a few countries go beyond the targets set by the EU (net zero by 2050). However, the way in which interim goals are weighted and related to each other varies substantially from one country to another. In this context, reference is often made to the tension within the energy trilemma encompassing security, affordability and the maximization of environment- and climate-friendliness. In legal terms, addressing this tension always requires a balancing of competing interests. Ideally, each individual concern is taken into account as comprehensively as possible (as is known in German law as the 'optimization rule').

Nevertheless, differences in the importance attached to a 'secure' and 'affordable' energy supply can be observed across the EU: In the UK in particular, the energy transition prioritises security of supply and affordability and builds incentives for increased competition within the domestic energy industry. The above mentioned Section 1, para 1 of the German Federal Energy Industry Act (Energiewirtschaftsgesetz) lays down similar priorities. This stance contrasts in particular with the perspective presented in the chapter on the law of energy transition in Italy in general perspective by *Fabrizio Fracchia* in this book, who sees the ultimate purpose of the energy transition as being in service to "intergenerational responsibility".[16] This position is possibly influenced by the 'climate decision' (*Klimabeschluss*) of the German Federal Constitutional Court and the 'intertemporal freedom safeguard' developed there in favour of future generations. However, the

16 See Fracchia, in this volume, 183 (196).

German court by no means recognised 'intergenerational justice' as an 'absolute' value, but explicitly required that this objective must always be weighed against other conflicting constitutional values (including the requirement of a secure and affordable energy supply). This holds true across EU countries, as none of the existing court decisions on climate-related sate obligations, suggest a one-sided focus on 'intergenerational responsibilities'.

Meanwhile the Russian-Ukraine war has further accelerated efforts towards decarbonisation, for example causing the European Commission to devise and implement its RePowerEU-strategy. Under this strategy, the expansion of renewable energies – also referred to in Germany as *Freiheitsenergien* or "freedom energy"[17] – and energy efficiency will play a central role in reducing dependence on energy imports from outside the EU.

At the same time, however, the energy crisis triggered by the Russian attack also led to the reactivation of fossil energies, with the extension – quantitatively and/or over time – of domestic oil and gas production in Denmark and Great Britain, and to the renaissance of nuclear power, especially in France. As is well known, nuclear energy was previously integrated into the EU's approach to the energy transition, largely in response to diplomatic pressure from France. Specifically, it was recognised as a low-carbon technology in the EU's taxonomy legislation, and later as a net-zero technology in the Net Zero Industry Act. This, along with its high base load capacity, is encouraging other countries to also expand their use of nuclear power. This is the case notably in Sweden, where nuclear power already accounts for 28 % of electricity generation, and in Poland, which plans to build six new reactors by 2033. In the UK, nuclear power accounts for a good 14 % of the electricity mix (2023) and new plants, for which the EU already approved state aid, are under construction. In Italy,[18] an (open-ended) 're-evaluation' of nuclear power is pending and in Denmark, public opinion is turning against the 'nuclear ban' of early 1985.[19] Notwithstanding the ongoing expansion of renewable energies, existing climate protection measures have been relativised, especially in the UK, in view of the progress already made in reducing CO_2 emissions in this country, and

17 This is how the Federal Minister of Finance, Christian Lindner, spoke about them at the special session of the German Bundestag on the war in Ukraine on 27 February 2022, cf. Bundesregierung, 'Bulletin no. 25–4 of 27 February 2022' < https://www.bundesregierung.de/resource/blob/992814/2008588/627752e2e498a2a857553f6c91bde8f6/25-4-bmf-ukraine-data.pdf?download=1> accessed 17 March 2025.

18 See Fracchia, in this volume, 183 (194 f.).

19 See Mortensen, in this volume, 223 (225).

in order to create a "pragmatic, appropriate and realistic approach" for the continued transition process.[20] One example of this relativised shift is the delay of the ban on internal combustion engines in the transport sector from 2030 to 2035. In the meantime, new dependencies on energy imports from non-EU countries are already on the rise thanks to the procurement of "climate-friendly", in particular "green" hydrogen.

3. Highly diverse transformation paths

Overall, the highly varied natural settings (e.g. large potential for water-based energy in the north, particularly in Sweden), regulatory contexts (e.g. degrees of centralization, illustrated by the different legal approaches of Germany and France), as well as the national energy mix of a given country, continue to drive regulatorily divergent strategies regarding their "transformation pathways"[21].

(a) Timelines of energy transition

This heterogeneity is already reflected in the historic beginnings of different countries' energy transitions: Denmark made a particularly early start, with the oil crises of the 1970s providing a powerful impetus and including a massive expansion of biomass-fired district heating systems,[22] as did, albeit to a lesser extent, Sweden.[23] In other countries, however, the energy transition did not become an earnest policy issue before the turn of the millennium. In Germany, for example, it has only been rapidly accelerating since the reactor accident at Fukushima;[24] the situation is similar in France.[25] The phase-out of coal-fired power generation has also progressed more rapidly and with less political noise in, for example, France and Spain than in other countries. Meanwhile, the UK also just took its last coal-fired power plant off the grid in September 2024 – far ahead of the controversial and hesitant phase-out processes in Germany and particularly in Poland.

---

20 See Ogbumgbada/McKenzie, in this volume, 205 (218).
21 Inspired by Johannes Saurer, 'Transformationspfade in Energiesystemen' (2019) 2, Der moderne Staat (dms) 282 (283 ff.).
22 See Mortensen, in this volume, 223 (230 f.).
23 See Malafry, in this volume, 241 (245).
24 See Markus, in this volume, 129 (132 f., 141 ff.).
25 See Lamoureux, in this volume, 167 (178).

(b) (Path) Dependencies of multiple preconditions

Transformation paths are impacted by these historical developments, and this is particularly the case in countries that have a very traditional energy mix. There is a stark contrast in the speed and possible approaches to transitioning away from fossil fuel toward renewable energy sources between countries that continue to rely on coal, particularly Poland and to a lesser extent Germany, and those, like France, where nuclear power plays a dominant role. Other countries have long had a high proportion of wind, solar and/or hydro power (the latter accounts for 40 % of the electricity mix in Sweden) and/or biomass, as in Denmark. The German 'double phase-out' of nuclear energy (by April 2023) and of coal-fired power generation (by 2038 at the latest) will lead to correspondingly greater challenges in the procurement and distribution of renewable energies (including hydrogen) and accompanying measures (electricity storage, grid expansion and management, gas-fired base load power plants as a 'bridge technology').

Other framework conditions for the transition process include the density of settlement and of industrialisation in each country. Sweden's population, for example, is predominantly rural,[26] whereas in highly urban Germany the transport of wind power, which is mainly generated on the coasts, to the centre and south of the country adds additional complexity.[27] Additionally, there are geographical and climatic characteristics that impact transition plans, particularly where there is greater potential for wind and solar energy production.

(c) Heterogeneity in the expansion of renewable energies and energy efficiency

In line with the requirements of EU law, all countries surveyed in this book (including the UK, even after Brexit) focus their approach to the energy transition on expanding renewable energies and increasing energy efficiency. Beyond this overarching approach, countries demonstrate vastly different ambitions and interests in how to achieve their goals.

26 See Malafry, in this volume, 241 (241, 261).
27 See Fehling, in this volume, 301 (316).

(aa) Expansion paths for RE

The lowest ambition to expand renewable energy sources are seen in Poland, given the continued dominance of coal-fired power generation (for the time being until 2049). The situation is similar in France due to the country's decades-long reliance on nuclear energy or rather due to the revitalization thereof in the wake of the energy crisis triggered by the war in Ukraine.

(bb) Energy efficiency

The objective of massive energy savings, the primary concern under EU law ('energy efficiency first'), is also viewed differently in the countries studied in this book: In some chapters, energy efficiency is not identified as a stand-alone objective or it is merely a secondary consideration, while in the Polish contribution, for instance, the dominant use of domestic coal means that a drastic reduction in energy use, especially in the building sector, is seen as something of a 'silver bullet' for energy system transformation.[28] The efforts toward energy efficiency in Denmark[29] and Sweden[30] starting in the 1970s should be highlighted here, where plans to further increase energy efficiency in these countries focus primarily on the transport and the industry sector.

One should bear in mind that economists criticise ever more rigid legal constraints on energy usage and warn of significant economic risks.[31] Reference is made to the enormous future increase in demand for electricity, resulting from sector coupling and power-to-x technologies (e-mobility, heat pumps, etc.). In any case, rising energy prices, rising emissions trading system (ETS) costs, as well as carbon taxes could prompt industrial and private consumers to increase their energy efficiency on their own initiative.

28 See Nowak/Knap, in this volume, 279 (284 ff.).

29 See Mortensen, in this volume, 223 (224 ff.).

30 See Malafry, in this volume, 241 (244 ff.).

31 See for example and among many others Clemens Fuest (IFO Institute, Munich), 'Das Energieeffizienzgesetz bedroht das Wirtschaftswachstum' in: Handelsblatt (11 May 2023) < https://www.handelsblatt.com/meinung/gastbeitraege/gastkommentar-das-energieeffizienzgesetz-bedroht-das-wirtschaftswachstum-/29142748.html> accessed 18 February 2025.

(d) (Other) Innovative technologies

The promotion of renewable forms of propulsion in the transport sector also varies depending on the energy mix of the respective country. As already mentioned, the UK postponed its ban on internal combustion engine vehicles by five years to 2035. France plans to complete this phase-out even later, by 2040. Nevertheless, in all countries analysed in this book, the electrification of the transport sector is a top priority. Therefore, and for reasons of energy efficiency, hydrogen and e-fuel concepts tend to play only a subordinate role. The situation is similar for energy in buildings, especially if, as in Denmark, Sweden and the UK, widespread district heating networks, which are already subject of special network regulation, can be used.

Meanwhile, a transnational consensus seems to be emerging regarding the role of hydrogen in the energy transition. It is to be used primarily for decarbonisation in energy-intensive industries and also in heavy-duty and non-electrified rail transport. It is not (yet) considered to have a significant future in the domestic heating sector or private transport, due to, among other things, the lack of a supply infrastructure. Still, some more ambitious plans exist, particularly in Poland (including for electricity generation, heating and the entire transport sector),[32] while in Denmark the production of e-methanol supported by hydrogen (e.g. for shipping, but also for export purposes) is already being tested in a large-scale plant in Kassø.[33] Germany is also very ambitious when it comes to hydrogen: As a result of the Ukraine crisis, targets to build up electrolyser capacities by 2030 have been doubled and the development of a nationwide 'hydrogen core [transport] network' is on the way.[34] A legal framework for hydrogen production as well as pipeline infrastructure and their regulation (network access!) reportedly exists in Germany, France and the UK as well as, to some extent, in Poland.

Overall, from the rainbow of hydrogen, the initial focus on 'green' hydrogen ('no carbon' hydrogen, produced using excess renewable energy) is being relativised, partly as a result of the French push in favour of 'low carbon' hydrogen, especially from nuclear energy (pink hydrogen).[35] The use of

32 See Nowak/Knap, in this volume, 279 (280 ff.).
33 See Mortensen, in this volume, 223 (227).
34 See Markus, in this volume, 129 (154 f.)
35 See Lamoureux, in this volume, 167 (180 f.).

'blue' hydrogen from fossil sources also increasingly appears as an option. 'Blue' hydrogen will primarily be used in combination with carbon capture and storage (CCS) technology, which in turn has long been recognised by the Intergovernmental Panel on Climate Change as an unavoidable tool and is actively being pursued by the EU Commission. CCS as well as carbon capture and utilization (CCU) are considered particularly suitable for those industrial production processes (e.g. cement production) in which the use of other 'green' technologies (e.g. hydrogen) is unprofitable. Broad legal regulations already exist in the UK and in Denmark, driven by the availability of considerable potential storage sites in the North Sea. Denmark is already emerging as an important storage location for the removal of CO_2 from Belgium and, in the future, from Germany.[36] Contrary to the previously more restrictive legal situation, the German federal government recently initiated a draft bill to expand CCS technology.[37] In Denmark, where biogas is already widely used and partially processed using carbon separation to feed into the natural gas grid, bioenergy with carbon capture and storage (BECCS) is to take on a larger role. Indeed, the country plans to deploy BECCS also for power to x-purposes in the future.

There is growing recognition that de-fossilisation alone will not lead to climate neutrality. Thus, ecosystem and geochemical negative emission technologies (NETs) are attracting more attention, and lawmakers are taking initial steps to adapt to this reality. CCS and CCU as already mentioned above are the target of regulation but need to be considered more broadly as part of holistic carbon management approaches, since the net-negative accounting of emissions is a complex topic linked to questions of product life cycle analysis, monitoring, reporting and accounting. One example of a strategic approach to NETs is Germany, which is currently working on its long-term strategy for negative emissions and recently announced the cornerstones for its carbon management strategy. Countries across Europe are slowly implementing terms and measures according to their individual approaches, but the process has only just begun, both at the national and the European level.

36 See Mortensen, in this volume, 223 (236 f.).

37 See draft law to amend the Carbon Dioxide Storage Act of 21 June 2024 (BT-Drs. 20/11900); on similar initiatives in other EU states, i.a. France, see European Commission, Communication 'Towards an ambitious Industrial Carbon Management for the EU' COM (2024) 62 final 4 ff.

3. Interim conclusion

There are relevant differences between EU-countries' approaches to the energy transition when it comes to their sectoral strategies, their pace and their use of decarbonisation options other than renewables (nuclear power, NETs, CCS etc.). Countries have significantly different perspectives on phase-out policies and binding decisions. As a result, the energy mix across Europe remains diverse.

C. Steering instruments and legal barriers

From a comparative law perspective, the legal instruments that serve the implementation of national decarbonisation strategies are of particular interest. Do they provide legal certainty, and with it the planning and investment security, that all stakeholders in the energy sector have repeatedly demanded? What legal obstacles do these instruments encounter? And do they really advance the energy transition?

1. Regulatory frameworks – between hard and soft law

(a) Transition "planning"

In compliance with the Paris Agreement, which calls on the parties to make nationally determined contributions (NDC), and the Governance Regulation (EU) 2018/1999, which serves to implement it uniformly throughout the EU, all Member States surveyed here have Integrated National Energy and Climate Plans (NECP). These NECPs describe the guiding principles for the five dimensions of the European Energy and Climate Union, and also the policies, measures and programmes planned for their implementation. Whether or not this can already be considered a pan-European concordance may be drawn into question when one considers the sometimes quite detailed supplementary recommendations of the EU Commission for the revision of the NECP's.[38] These plans were to be updated by 30 June

38 See, for example, European Commission, '8th Report from the EU Commission on the State of the Energy Union' (24 October 2023) COM (2023) 650 final.

2024 and this deadline was met by all countries observed in this book, with the exception of Poland.[39]

National energy and climate plans are indeed binding under international and EU law. Nevertheless, plans' are a largely undefined legal category. The same applies to accompanying and purely political (net zero) strategies,[40] programmes and the like. Their binding effect ultimately depends on how they are normatively embedded in national legal systems, which would require more in-depth investigation.

(b) Statutory law

There are also striking differences in the way the energy transition is being accompanied by formal legislation / statutory law. Germany, Denmark, Sweden and the UK have their own climate protection laws with emission reduction targets for individual sectors, including the energy industry. However, the sub-targets and measures of the 'energy transition' are often regulated in a barely manageable multitude of individual laws and supplementary regulations such as ordinances and decrees. In Italy, for example, there is an 'incessant flow of legislation' that is addressed by initiatives for regulatory, bureaucratic or organizational simplification;[41] the same applies in Germany. The practical benefit of a separate and cross-sectoral climate protection law depends, in turn, on the position such a law occupies in the national hierarchy of norms – does it have normative priority, or does it operate (solely) at the same level as other (energy) laws?

France offers a good example of how energy and climate policy objectives can be combined at (only) one normative level: The targets set out in the French 'Energy Transition for Green Growth Act' (2015) were incorporated into the extensive Code de l'énergie, which covers all stages of the energy related value-chain.[42] The situation is similar with the British Energy Act of 2023, which takes up the goals of the Climate Change Act of 2008

39 Cf. European Commission, 'National energy and climate plans' <https://commission.europa.eu/energy-climate-change-environment/implementation-eu-countries/energy-and-climate-governance-and-reporting/national-energy-and-climate-plans_en> accessed 06 November 2024.

40 For example in the UK, see Ogbumgbada/McKenzie, in this volume 205 (208 ff.); for Italy, see Fracchia, in this volume, 183 (186 ff.).

41 See Fracchia, in this volume 183 (188).

42 See Lamoureux, in this volume 167 (169 ff.).

and the Net Zero Strategy of 2021, along with sectoral energy strategies, and comes along as a fairly modern and comprehensive set of rules, with detailed sections on CCS, hydrogen (infrastructures) and even fusion energy.[43] In contrast to the French model, the UK's Energy Act mainly amends and supplements already existing laws such as the Electricity or Nuclear Acts,[44] so that the UK continues to show a plethora of multi-branched individual laws. Nevertheless, the Energy Act seems to be approaching a consolidation and simplification of the entire energy-related legislation – also needed in other countries[45] – which is primarily geared to climate targets. It may also serve as a best practice model for other countries where the system of standards remains rather fragmented.[46] Possible and, due e.g. to technical developments, increasingly necessary amendments and modifications to such 'umbrella laws' must, of course, be designed in such a way that maintains a generally clear and consistent set of rules.

Ultimately, the fundamental and directional decisions taken on the design of the energy transition should ideally extend beyond the narrow time frame of individual legislative periods and thus be designed to be 'timeless' to a certain extent. In this regard, the Danish practice of consensus politics is worthy of mention. Consensus agreements, while often time consuming, are used in Denmark to safeguard energy policy decisions in the long term. They are agreed across party lines in parliament and specific (implementing) legislation is only enacted on this basis. This practice can contribute to legal and planning certainty as well as to broad social acceptance – even if one has to admit that the 'consensus democracy' is a typically Danish phenomenon and may be impossible in the legislative cultures of other countries.

2. Diversity of instruments

Similarities, but also significant differences, exist with regard to the nature and manner of state control instruments.

---

43 Cf. insofar section 156 of the Energy Act.

44 For more details see Ogbumgbada/McKenzie, in this volume, 205 (207 ff.).

45 For Germany, see Fehling, in this volume 301 (319 ff.); for Sweden, see Malafry in this volume, 241 (273 f.).

46 In Italy, the government has recently been tasked with reorganising the existing legislation on renewable energy sources in order to significantly reduce and rationalise the legal provisions, and to ensure a higher degree of legal certainty and a simplification of procedures (see Fracchia, in this volume, 183 (187 ff.).

(a) Set of measures between the state and the market

In all countries included in this volume, a mix of command and control instruments on the one hand, and market-based or incentive instruments on the other, can be discerned. The range of methods used in the former extends from legal prohibitions, such as those used in the German coal and nuclear phase-out, or advertising and traffic bans for emission-intensive vehicles, to behavioural mandates like the required use of non-fossil fuels or innovative heating types, including compulsory connection to district heating systems.[47] At the other end of the spectrum, there are incentive instruments, namely in the form of direct or indirect state funded subsidies. In between these two extremes, we find hybrid systems with market-based elements, most notably the obligation to participate in public tenders for certain types of (RE or baseload) power plants, as well as purely levy-based steering by means of energy and/or CO_2 taxes, the latter being in place in Sweden since 1991.[48]

As mentioned, combinations of the different types of instruments are possible and even common. The more diverse the steering mix becomes, the more coordination is necessary in order to avoid counter-productivity. This applies e.g. to the legal support of certain technical development paths under the aspect of new (desirable) energy technologies: If the aim is to promote the growth of e-mobility, the question arises as to whether and to what extent this should be at the expense of other technologies, such as e-fuels. A similar situation applies to the balancing of highly volatile feed-ins of electricity from wind and solar power into traditional electricity grids: here, it is important to coordinate grid requirements with those for flexible balancing mechanisms and the use of electricity storage. Furthermore, regulations on the operation of electricity storage systems and hydrogen infrastructures (electrolyser, H2 pipelines, etc.) must be seamlessly integrated into the existing competition and unbundling regime of the EU energy market.

47 See Markus, in this volume, 129 (138 ff.).
48 See Malafry, in this volume, 241 (247).

(b) In particular: promoting renewable energies

Meanwhile, the legal requirements for an increased expansion of renewable energies in electricity generation seem to be moving closer together – likely as a result of increasing competition in the sector, but also due to increasingly stringent and standardising EU requirements (RED III, among others). In the past, funding regimes with purchase obligations for grid operators at legally fixed feed-in tariffs or even pure subsidy regimes dominated. Only in exceptional cases did 'competitively' designed models exist, such as the Swedish electricity certificate system introduced as early as 2003, which has been operated jointly with Norway since 2012 and is now to be phased out.[49]

(aa) Increasing competition

Meanwhile, the mix of instruments is becoming more 'colourful' everywhere. Pure feed-in tariffs, market premiums and other subsidy systems are increasingly being replaced by public tenders (especially for offshore wind power), direct marketing with bilateral Power Purchase Agreements (PPAs) and the like. Furthermore, Contracts for Difference (CfDs), which have been the method of choice in the UK for years, are increasingly being discussed as an effective means of public-private hybrid financing of RE projects, both within and outside the EU.[50] They protect investors from the volatilities of wholesale energy markets through agreements with government agencies to mutually offset price differences on the electricity exchange over a period of about 10 to 15 years, based on a fixed price. This is intended to ensure a reliable amortisation of the RE project and also contribute to the stability of electricity prices. In addition to electricity generation from renewables, CfDs are also recommended for hydrogen and CCS projects and for (large-scale) projects to decarbonise energy-intensive industries (e.g. steel production), in the form of Carbon Contracts for Difference (CCfDs). However, the high cost of developing the necessary

49 See Malafry, in this volume, 241 (248 f.).

50 For a detailed account of developments in the UK, see Ason, in this volume, 379 (379 ff.).

legal framework[51] and the inherent problems with state aid legislation[52] remain as challenges to their effectiveness.

(bb) Planning and social acceptance

Furthermore, the contributions in this volume unanimously emphasise the need for (further) acceleration and simplification of planning and approval procedures for RE projects, i.e. with binding requirements from national legislatures for the designation of priority areas for wind and for (large) solar power plants.[53] What is called for is a noticeable reduction in bureaucracy (cutting red tape), a streamlining of subsequent court proceedings as well as the expansion of the early participation of civil society in those proceedings.[54] In order to increase social acceptance of changes in energy infrastructure, legal requirements for operators to offer residents and municipalities the opportunity to co-invest in new projects, especially in wind park projects[55], and also the promotion of local energy communities,[56] are on the rise as well.[57]

In view of increasingly complex and interdependent energy systems, there are also calls for more holistic and integrated planning of electricity, gas and hydrogen plants, along with pipelines, storage facilities and

51 Ason, in this volume 379 (382), with references also to CfD practice in other countries on 379 (390 ff.). The introduction of CfDs was also considered in the draft of the German Renewable Energy Sources Act (EEG 2023), but they were not (yet) included in the final law, see Fehling, in this volume, 301 (309) with references to further high investment risks at 301 (319 f.). However, a comparable mechanism for financially supporting the development of a hydrogen core network was introduced in May 2024 in § 28r of the German Federal Energy Industry Act (Energiewirtschaftsgesetz).

52 See Fehling, in this volume, 301 (311 f.).

53 As to the recent "Solar (accelerating) package" in Germany see Fehling, in this volume, 301 (308 ff.).

54 See in particular for Italy, Mari, in this volume, 361 (372).

55 See for example the "Citizen's Energy Act" in some German States, like in North Rhine-Westphalia 19 Dec. 2023. The Federal Constitutional Court justified this encroachment on the entrepreneurial freedom of the plant operators – under certain conditions – with the improvement of social acceptance for new onshore wind turbines to promote the further expansion of this RE, cf. decision of 23 March 2022, BVerfGE 161, 63 ff.

56 See for Denmark, Mortensen, in this volume, 223 (238).

57 So e.g., as a result of another political agreement from 2023, in Denmark, see Anker/Mortensen, in this volume, 397 (400).

large-scale industrial consumption systems.[58] To this end, in the UK, a state-owned but independent National Energy System Operator (NESO) was created in 2024 from parts of the former transmission system operator National Grid.[59] NESO is responsible for integrated planning and coordination among all electricity, gas and hydrogen networks "with a whole system perspective across energy sectors and by balancing the guiding principles net zero, ensuring security of supply, and ensuring efficiency and economy".[60]

(cc) Interim conclusion

Regarding the extension of renewable energies, all countries analysed are facing a new phase of regulatory challenges, while new technologies (like hydrogen and negative emission technologies) are now facing similar early challenges. Phase one consisted of setting up effective financial support schemes, but this is no longer the most important lever. Instead, new instruments are needed to:

(1) secure acceptance for an accelerated expansion
(2) reduce bureaucratic hurdles to speed up planning and installation of new plants
(3) solve conflicts between different objectives (especially climate and nature conservation)
(4) enable sector coupling (mainly driven by a hydrogen economy). In this regard we observe differences regarding choice of technology – some countries choose specific technologies at an early stage, others try to keep technology choice open.

(c) Role of public companies

The corporate structures in the energy sector also play an important role in the instrument mix. Energy transition targets are sometimes easier to

58 See e.g. Fehling, in this volume, 301 (322), and into the same direction the recently amended articles 14d (1) and 112b of the German Federal Energy Industry Act (Energiewirtschaftsgesetz).
59 According to Part 5 of the Energy Act 2023.
60 For further information see the new NESO website at NESO, <www.neso.energy> accessed 06 November 2024.

implement through public companies like the state-owned transmission system operators in France (*RTE* for electricity), Denmark (*Energinet* for electricity, gas and gas distribution networks) and Sweden (*Svenska Kraftnät*). By contrast, in Germany the sell-off of electricity and gas transmission grids to mostly foreign investors, including the Dutch state-owned *TenneT*, began in the early 2000s. Recent attempts in Germany to establish a national (transmission) grid company with state participation, not least with a view to the cost-intensive expansion of the electricity transmission grid, including lines connecting to offshore wind farms, failed, largely due to budget deficits.[61] On the German electricity and gas distribution level, on the other hand, around 900 municipal energy suppliers are working to facilitate the energy transition at the local level. They are also involved at the municipal level through Germany's new *Wärmeplanungsgesetz* (Heat Planning and Decarbonisation of Heating Networks Act), which aims, among other things, to expand the district heating supply by means of renewable energies. In Denmark, by contrast, electricity distribution networks are operated by private companies, albeit with significant participation of electricity consumers.[62]

3. Legal barriers and areas of tension

In addition to the trade-offs already mentioned in section B. 2., it is also interesting to look at specific legal tensions that have been identified as obstacles to a rapid and effective energy transition.

(a) Energy infrastructure between climate and (other) environmental law

The widespread demand, also in view of increasing NIMBYism, for acceleration and simplification of the relevant planning and approval procedures for the expansion of wind power and large-scale solar installations has al-

61 After the state-owned KfW Bank took a stake in the 50Hertz electricity TSO in 2018, the Dutch TenneT TSO GmbH recently wanted to sell its high-voltage grid to this bank. After years of negotiations, the plan failed due to the German government's current budgetary problems, see TenneT, 'TenneT und KfW beenden die Verhandlungen über einen Komplettverkauf von TenneT Deutschland ergebnislos.' (21 June 2024) <https://tennet-drupal.s3.eu-central-1.amazonaws.com/default/2024-06/200624_Pressemitteilung%20TenneT_DE.pdf> accessed 06 November 2024.

62 See Mortensen, in this volume, 223 (226).

ready been mentioned. This ultimately applies to all energy infrastructures and, with increasing and cross-sectoral 'electrification', in particular to the expansion of power transport and distribution lines. A reason given for protracted approval procedures in all countries is also the fact that plant constructions are subject to conflicting other – and often overly complex – (EU) environmental law, namely in the form of strict requirements for the protection of nature, land and biodiversity, as well as the marine environment in the case of offshore plants.[63] Sometimes national environmental law goes even further than EU law. For example, Sweden's extremely rigid environmental code is often criticised for creating challenges and, in addition to strict nature and biodiversity protection,[64] national defence concerns. The interests of Indigenous People (*Sámis*), including reindeer herding and subsistence hunting, have repeatedly been named as obstacles to acceleration and simplification of energy-related approvals.[65]

Possibly, those obstacles can be counteracted using the privileged regulations for the development of renewable energies of the EU Emergency Regulation 2022/2577,[66] which have now been largely incorporated into RED III.[67] National legislators must appropriately designate priority areas or renewable energy plants, grids and storage assets as being "in the overriding public interest and serving the public health and safety." As already demonstrated in some countries, and demanded in others,[68] whether this obligation sustainably supports the acceleration of procedures remains to be seen. In this context, reference is also made to the shortage of skilled personnel in public authorities. This is why, for example, legal requirements

63 For Germany: see Markus, in this volume, 129 (150 ff.); for Denmark: see Mortensen, in this volume, 223 (236). also with reference to international law agreements for the protection of the Wadden Sea; for Poland: see Nowak/Knap, in this volume, 279 (288 ff.).

64 In this respect, the ECJ has already had to intervene in favour of the approval of wind farms and against the protection of bats, cf. Malafry, in this volume, 241 (260).

65 For details, see Malafry, in this volume, 241 (252 ff.).

66 Council Regulation of 22 December 2022 laying down a framework to accelerate the deployment of renewable energy, OJ EU L 335/36 (it was only valid for 18 months).

67 See in particular Article 15a et seq. of Directive (EU) 2018/2001, as amended by Directive (EU) 2023/2413 of 18 October 2023.

68 For Germany see Fehling, in this volume, 301 (320 f.); for Denmark see Anker/Mortensen, in this volume, 397 (417); for Sweden see Malafry, in this volume, 241 (252 ff.).

for (shortened) procedural deadlines or the legal fiction of authorisation after procedural deadlines have expired may prove ineffective.[69]

Contradictions with regard to the EU emissions trading system have been identified as another challenge to the coordination of climate protection instruments. In particular, the cancellation of emission certificates, that are no longer used due to the expansion of renewable energies or the decommissioning of coal-fired power plants, is proving complicated. This results in a waterbed effect, in that the certificates that become 'free' in one country are used for emissions in other parts of the EU.[70] Furthermore, it remains to be seen what impact the implementation of a separate emissions trading system ('EU ETS II')[12] for sectors not covered by ETS I will have, in particular in the building and transport sectors.[71] Will it contradict the measures taken by states so far, for example on building renovation and the conversion of heating systems, or do the instruments complement each other in a meaningful way and also take social aspects into account (keyword 'energy poverty')?

(b) Confusion and conflicts over responsibilities

In countries that have a decentralised or federalised system of government, further challenges present themselves. Common criticism includes the unclear, conflicting or insufficiently coordinated legislative powers for energy system transformation and climate protection at the federal/national and regional level.[72] In the UK, a somewhat unique example of devolved powers, many relevant "UK-wide" laws are only applicable in England and Wales; while the devolved legislatures in Scotland and Northern Ireland (and sometimes Wales) determine the laws applicable to them.[73] Sweden has similar challenges with its tradition of strong municipal self-govern-

69 See Fehling, in this volume, 301 (301 ff.).

70 For more details, see Fehling, in this volume, 301 (313).

71 According in particular to Directive (EU) 2023/959 of the European Parliament and of the Council of 10 May 2023 amending Directive 2003/87/EC establishing a system for greenhouse gas emission allowance trading within the Union and Decision (EU) 2015/1814 concerning the establishment and operation of a market stability reserve for the Union greenhouse gas emission trading system, OJ EU L 130, 134. See now and in particular Articles 30a et seq. of the consolidated ETS Directive 2003/87/EC.

72 For Germany: see Markus, in this volume, 129 (136 f.); for Italy: see Mari, in this volume, 361 (366 ff.).

73 See Ogbumgbada/McKenzie, in this volume, 205 (206 ff.).

ment: Swedish municipalities can thwart practically any planning decision impacting the location of energy infrastructures due to their planning monopoly.[74] Again and in general, more effective and standardised requirements are being demanded, in order to accelerate planning and approval, particularly from national and federal legislators.

Conflicts of responsibilities can also be identified in the area of executive power, depending on the number of authorities involved. In the UK, for example, the administrative landscape is quite diverse. By contrast, the planning and approval of offshore wind farms in Denmark is in the hands of the national energy regulatory authority.[75] The same applies in Germany to the Federal Maritime and Hydrographic Agency, although there are exceptions for installations in the territorial sea.[76] Furthermore, the planning of extra-high voltage lines that cross federal or state borders is carried out centrally by the (German) Federal Network Agency. In the interest of efficient law enforcement, it may be advisable to accelerate the establishment of such "bundling authorities", in line with the tendency towards the formation of so-called 'one-stop agencies' that already exist in EU law (including in the RED III).

(c) Energy transition and the money

Finally, the many challenges of the energy transition are increasingly posing serious financing problems. Immense investment is required and these investments often include (unattractive) very long-term amortisation, including investment in energy-intensive industries. Securing the required funding is again a question between the market and the state. In this respect, the hybrid instrument of contracts for difference (CfDs, particularly in the UK) was already mentioned above as a useful vehicle. Nevertheless, states are facing problems in raising the necessary funds, often due to already tight budgets. It is revealing in this respect that the Italian decarbonisation strategy appears quite prominently as part of the National Recovery & Resilience Plan, the implementation of which has the benefit of considerable available European funding (Next Generation EU).[77] In Poland, too, especially the expansion of renewable energies is being made contingent on

74 For details, see Malafry, in this volume, 241 (252 f.).
75 See Anker/Mortensen, in this volume, 397 (401 f.).
76 See Fehling, in this volume, 301 (307).
77 See Fracchia, in this volume, 183 (184 ff.).

(further) EU funding.[78] In Germany, the provision of additional funds for the energy transition failed due to the 'debt brake' in the constitution and the serious reservations expressed by the Federal Constitutional Court.[79] Budgetary issues present challenges between national and sub-national governments: for example, the (German) federal and state governments increasingly transfer mandatory actions to local authorities, such as complex planning obligations relevant for local heating networks, but do not provide for sufficient counter-financing at the local level, causing significant budget shortfalls and financial constraints.

Finally, the aforementioned question of intergenerational justice arises again: The Italian Constitutional Court grappled with the problem from the point of view of state-owned debt and unequal financial burdens on young and old. In its judgement of 2019 the Court stated that "intergenerational equity also entails the need not to burden disproportionately the growth opportunities of future generations, guaranteeing them sufficient [financial] resources for a balanced development".[80] The dilemma that arises is obvious: on the one hand, energy system transformation and climate protection serve intergenerational justice; on the other hand, the latter is jeopardised to the extent that disproportionately high state funds are used or debts, to be paid by those same future generations, are incurred for this purpose.

Against this backdrop, the (further) development of alternative and innovative financing facilities is all the more important. More than ever, this also requires cooperation with the (private) financial services sector. At the same time, costs must be continuously reduced at all levels of the energy transition. This, in turn, requires, once again, better coordination of individual steering instruments and the most integrated development of the entire energy system possible.

D. Outlook / lessons to be learnt

The chapters presented in this book cover only a portion of EU states and the UK. The individual contributions also have different focuses and may not be free of subjective judgements. Nevertheless, some central conclusions can be formulated from the aggregate:

78 See Nowak/Knap, in this volume, 279 (284).
79 Cf. judgment of the Federal Constitutional Court of 15 November 2023 (2 BvF 1/22).
80 Quoted from Fracchia, in this volume, 183 (197) footnote 42.

- Implementation of both the international and European requirements for decarbonisation of the energy sector is progressing quite rapidly throughout Europe. The expansion of renewable energies, which are increasingly able to hold their own in the competitive arena, is proving particularly successful.
- Nevertheless, national decarbonisation strategies differ quite significantly from one another. This is mainly due to different preconditions and traditions in terms of energy and social policy, as well as geographical/geological, economic and legal factors. In this sense, the energy transition in each country also proves to be an important part of the economic and legal culture of each country.
- The energy transition is susceptible to economic cycles and crises, including as a result of budget deficits and the war in Ukraine. In a pronounced 'discovery process', the course of the energy transition in each country is ultimately similar to the Echternach hopping procession – with some progress and repeated setbacks.
- States must balance their mix of instruments for the energy transition within the tension between (unilateral) sovereign/regulatory and (cooperative) market and incentive mechanisms. Despite all the differences in the details, they are converging, not least thanks to the unifying force of EU law. There are also striking similarities in the key legal obstacles to the energy transition, such as ongoing conflicts of responsibilities, lengthy and bureaucratic planning processes and pressing financing constraints.
- Despite all the differences, comparative law provides a number of noteworthy best practices. In view of the ever-changing challenges of the energy transition, for example in the ramp-up of a hydrogen energy economy, there is every reason to cultivate the dialogue among and between EU states more than ever.
- Also, and for a long time already, the European Commission has been making use of comparative law methodology, in particular when monitoring the status of implementation in the states. Hence, an intensified comparative exchange, also with this institution, must be recommended. This may serve the further necessary fine-tuning and coordination of European and national energy transitions, not least by identifying regulatory breaches (inconsistencies and incoherencies), as well as by avoiding unnecessary transaction costs, e.g. as a result of excessive bureaucratic requirements – all of this in the spirit of a 'just (energy) transition'.

- Overall, comparative law may also contribute to the rationalisation of energy transition law. It is not without reason that a 'growing gap between official policies and reality' is emerging.[81] Best practice examples from other countries, based on tangible issues, can support the (desirable) return to more pragmatism.

Eventually, the practical success of energy transition depends upon pragmatic solutions. May the contributions in this volume help to consolidate dos and don'ts by strengthening the comparative law dialogue among us.

Bibliography

Bundesregierung, 'Bulletin no. 25–4 of 27 February 2022' < https://www.bundesregierung.de/resource/blob/992814/2008588/627752e2e498a2a857553f6c91bde8f6/25-4-bmf-ukraine-data.pdf?download=1> accessed 17 March 2025

European Commission, Communication 'Towards an ambitious Industrial Carbon Management for the EU' COM (2024) 62 final 4 ff.

European Commission, '8th Report from the EU Commission on the State of the Energy Union' (24 October 2023) COM (2023) 650 final

European Commission, 'National energy and climate plans' <https://commission.europa.eu/energy-climate-change-environment/implementation-eu-countries/energy-and-climate-governance-and-reporting/national-energy-and-climate-plans_en> accessed 06 November 2024

European Commission, Communication 'Framework Strategy for a Resilient Energy Union with a Forward-Looking Climate Change Policy' (25 February 2015) COM (2015) 80 final

Fuest C (IFO Institute, Munich), 'Das Energieeffizienzgesetz bedroht das Wirtschaftswachstum' in: Handelsblatt (11 May 2023) < https://www.handelsblatt.com/meinung/gastbeitraege/gastkommentar-das-energieeffizienzgesetz-bedroht-das-wirtschaftswachstum-/29142748.html> accessed 18 February 2025

Husa J, *A new Introduction to Comparative Law*, Bloomsbury 2015, 119

Kischel U, *Rechtsvergleichung*, 2019, 93 ff.

Markus T, 'Zur Rechtsvergleichung im nationalen und internationalen Umweltrecht' 80 (2020) ZaöRV, 650

NESO, <www.neso.energy> accessed 06 November 2024

Roggenkamp M/Redgwell C/Rønne A/Del Guayo I (eds), *Energy Law in Europe* (OUP), 3d ed. 2016

Saurer J, 'Transformationspfade in Energiesystemen' (2019) 2, Der moderne Staat (dms) 282 (283 ff.)

Saurer J/Monast J, 'Symposium Foreword: The Law of Energy Transition in Federal Systems' (2021) 10 Transnational Environmental Law 205–210

81 See Fehling, in this volume, 301 ff..

Schmidt-Aßmann E, *Das Allgemeine Verwaltungsrecht als Ordnungsidee*, Springer, Heidelberg 1998, 37

Pielow J-C, *Grundstrukturen öffentlicher Versorgung*, Jus Publicum 58, Mohr-Siebeck, Tübingen 2001, 106 f.

TenneT, 'TenneT und KfW beenden die Verhandlungen über einen Komplettverkauf von TenneT Deutschland ergebnislos. TenneT bereitet strukturelle Finanzierungsalternativen für das Deutschlandgeschäft vor' (21 June 2024) <https://tennet-drupal.s3.eu-central-1.amazonaws.com/default/2024-06/200624_Pressemitteilung%20TenneT_DE.pdf> accessed 06 November 2024

Veigel J, 'Die funktionale Methode bei der Rechtsvergleichung' 30 (2021) Juridica International, 71 ff., 72 <https://doi.org/10.12697/JI.2021.30.09> accessed 18 February 2025

Zweigert K/Kötz H, *Einführung in die Rechtsvergleichung*, Mohr-Siebeck, 3. ed. 1996 Tübingen